All in One®

Recommended by **Teachers,** Trusted by **Toppers**

ACCOUNTANCY

Class 11

EVERYTHING YOU NEED TO SCORE

- Simplified Theory
- Topicwise Illustrations & Practice Questions
- All Types of Exam Pattern Questions
- CBQs; MCQs, A-R, Case Based
- Sample Question Papers

CBSE Exams 2026

AF889363

Authors

Swati Gupta
Sarvesh Kumar Mittal

arihant
SUCCESS AND NOTHING LESS

arihant
SUCCESS AND NOTHING LESS

ARIHANT PRAKASHAN
(School Division Series)

ADMINISTRATIVE & PRODUCTION OFFICES
Regd. Office
'Ramchhaya' 4577/15, Agarwal Road, Darya Ganj, New Delhi -110002
Tele: 011- 47630600, 43518550; Fax: 011- 23280316
Head Office
Kalindi, TP Nagar, Meerut (UP) - 250002, Tel: 0121-7156203, 7156204

SALES & SUPPORT OFFICES
Agra, Ahmedabad, Bengaluru, Bareilly, Chennai, Delhi, Guwahati, Hyderabad, Jaipur, Jhansi, Kolkata, Lucknow, Nagpur & Pune.

PO No : TXT-XX-XXXXXXX-X-XX

Published By Arihant Publications (India) Ltd.

For further information about the books published by Arihant, log on to www.arihantbooks.com or e-mail at info@arihantbooks.com
Follow us on

PRICE ₹515.00

PRODUCTION TEAM

Publishing Managers	*Cover Designer*	*Inner Designer*
Mahendra Singh Rawat & Keshav Mohan	Salman Shaikh	Ankit Tyagi
Project Head	*Page Layouting*	*Proof Reader*
Saurabh Gupta	Amit Bansal, Vikas Kumar	Apoorvi

Index *cum* Study Planner

One Book- Endless Features

to Help you Succeed

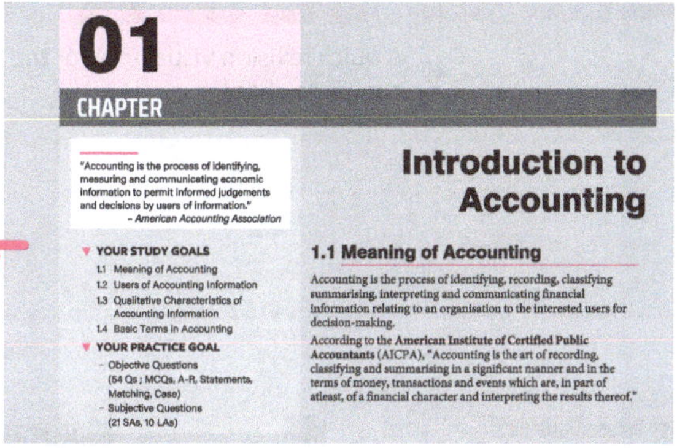

In this Chapter

At the start of each chapter, all the topics of the chapter have been listed, so that students may know what they are going to study.

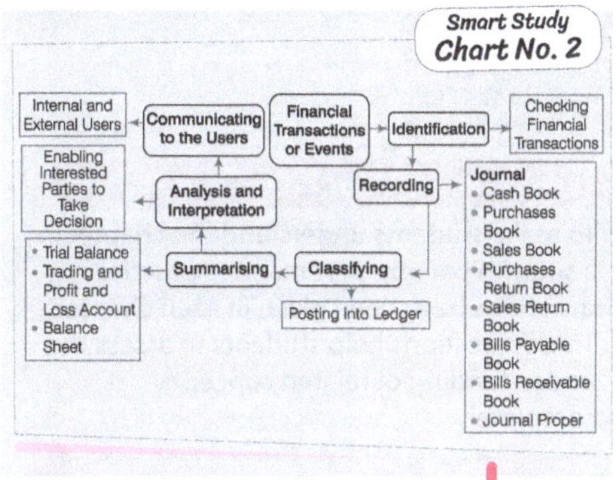

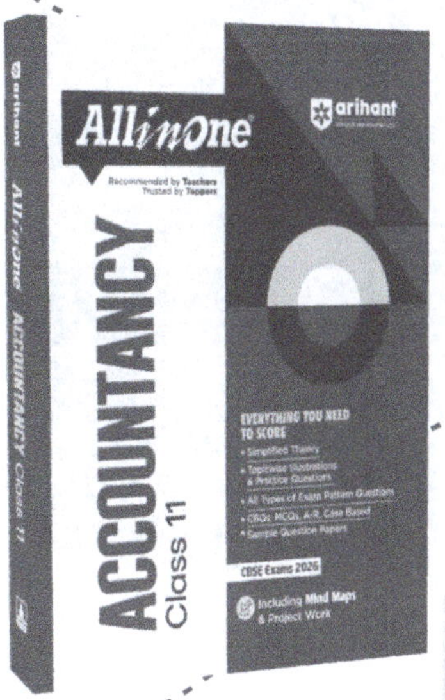

Complete Theory in Each Chapter

Each chapter has Complete, Easy to Understand and Simplified theory covering latest syllabus and latest NCERT Textbook. Theory is developed in such a way that it is Suitable for all typer of learners.

Smart Study Chart

To quickly recall the Concepts, Smart Study Charts are given at many places.

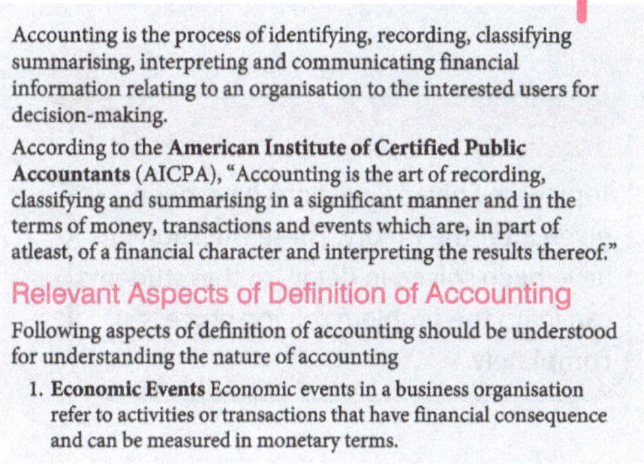
Accounting is the process of identifying, recording, classifying summarising, interpreting and communicating financial information relating to an organisation to the interested users for decision-making.

According to the **American Institute of Certified Public Accountants** (AICPA), "Accounting is the art of recording, classifying and summarising in a significant manner and in the terms of money, transactions and events which are, in part of atleast, of a financial character and interpreting the results thereof."

Relevant Aspects of Definition of Accounting

Following aspects of definition of accounting should be understood for understanding the nature of accounting

1. **Economic Events** Economic events in a business organisation refer to activities or transactions that have financial consequence and can be measured in monetary terms.

One Book- Endless Features

to Help you Succeed

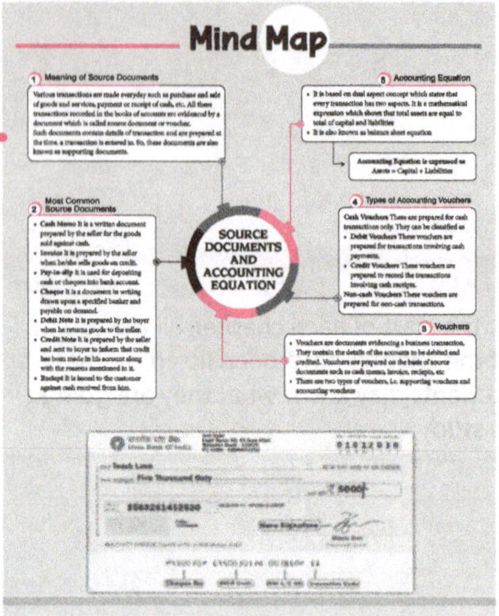

Mind Map

A quick revision visual tool for the complete chapter.

Topicwise Solved Questions

Journal

Solved Question 1 Write journal entries for the following transactions.

2024

Jan 1	Amit commenced business with cash ₹ 50,000 and furniture ₹ 25,000.
Jan 3	He purchased goods worth ₹ 30,000 from Rahul. Out of it half was purchased on credit.
Jan 5	Sold goods to Priya ₹ 20,000.
Jan 10	Goods returned by Priya ₹ 3,000 (Sale value ₹ 4,000).
Jan 12	Goods purchased from Vishal ₹ 40,000.
Jan 15	Goods returned to Karan ₹ 8,000.
Jan 20	Bought goods for cash ₹ 10,000.
Jan 25	Paid cartage ₹ 500.
Jan 30	Paid interest on loan ₹ 2,000.

Sol. JOURNAL

Date	Particulars		LF	Amt (Dr)	Amt (Cr)
2024					
Jan 1	Cash A/c	Dr		50,000	
	Furniture A/c	Dr		25,000	
	To Capital A/c				75,000
	(Being capital introduced in cash and furniture)				
Jan 3	Purchase A/c	Dr		30,000	
	To Cash A/c				15,000
	To Rahul				15,000
	(Being purchased goods, half on credit)				
Jan 5	Priya	Dr		20,000	
	To Sales A/c				20,000
	(Being goods sold to Priya)				
Jan 10	Sales Return A/c	Dr		4,000	
	To Priya				4,000
	(Being goods returned to Priya)				
Jan 12	Purchase A/c	Dr		40,000	
	To Vishal				40,000
	(Being goods purchased on credit)				
Jan 15	Karan A/c	Dr		8,000	
	To Purchase Return A/c				8,000
	(Being goods returned to Karan)				
Jan 20	Purchase A/c	Dr		10,000	
	To Cash A/c				10,000
	(Being goods purchased for cash)				
Jan 25	Cartage A/c	Dr		500	
	To Cash A/c				500
	(Being paid cartage)				
Jan 30	Interest on Loan A/c	Dr		2,000	
	To Cash A/c				2,000
	(Being paid interest on loan)				
	Total			1,89,500	1,89,500

Solved Question 2 Write journal entries for the following transactions.

2024		Amt (₹)
(i)	Deposited into bank account	20,000
(ii)	Amount withdrawn from bank account	5,000
(iii)	Withdrawn from bank account for personal expenses	2,000
(iv)	Transferred from bank account to fixed deposit account	3,000
(v)	Goods bought from Arnav. Paid by cheque	2,000
(vi)	Paid salary ₹ 2,000, rent ₹ 1,000 and for a fan purchased ₹ 1,500	—
(vii)	Charged by bank for its services	200
(viii)	Interest allowed by bank	500

Sol. JOURNAL

Date	Particulars		LF	Amt (Dr)	Amt (Cr)
(i)	Bank A/c	Dr		20,000	
	To Cash A/c				20,000
	(Being deposited in bank account)				
(ii)	Cash A/c	Dr		5,000	
	To Bank A/c				5,000
	(Being withdrawn from bank account)				
(iii)	Drawings A/c	Dr		2,000	
	To Bank A/c				2,000
	(Being withdrawn for personal expenses)				
(iv)	Fixed Deposit A/c	Dr		3,000	
	To Bank A/c				3,000
	(Being transfer from bank account)				
(v)	Purchase A/c	Dr		2,000	
	To Bank A/c				2,000
	(Being purchased goods and paid by cheque)				
(vi)	Salary A/c	Dr		2,000	
	Rent A/c	Dr		1,000	
	Fan A/c	Dr		1,500	
	To Cash A/c				4,500
	(Being paid salary, rent and for fan)				

Topicwise Practice Questions

To make students understand the chapter in a smooth part-by-part manner, practice questions have been given in each chapter. These questions help students to assess the understanding of related concepts completely.

Topicwise Solved Questions

Topicwise Solved Questions have been given after the theory. These Questions have been solved in detail, so that students can learn the problem solving process completely.

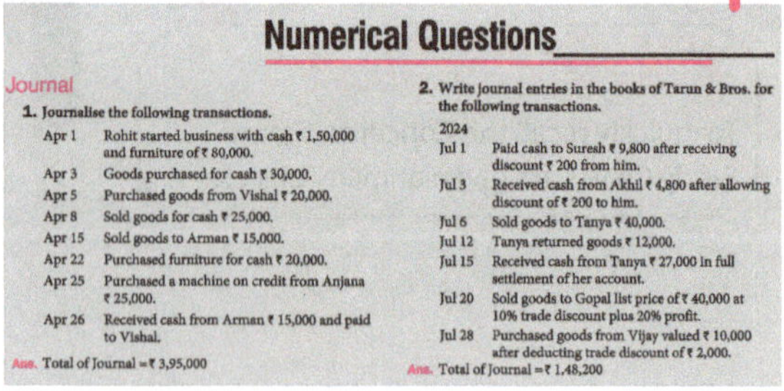

Numerical Questions

Journal

1. Journalise the following transactions.

Apr 1	Rohit started business with cash ₹ 1,50,000 and furniture of ₹ 80,000.
Apr 3	Goods purchased for cash ₹ 30,000.
Apr 5	Purchased goods from Vishal ₹ 20,000.
Apr 8	Sold goods for cash ₹ 25,000.
Apr 15	Sold goods to Arman ₹ 15,000.
Apr 22	Purchased furniture for cash ₹ 20,000.
Apr 25	Purchased a machine on credit from Anjana ₹ 25,000.
Apr 26	Received cash from Arman ₹ 15,000 and paid to Vishal.

Ans. Total of Journal = ₹ 3,95,000

2. Write journal entries in the books of Tarun & Bros. for the following transactions.

2024

Jul 1	Paid cash to Suresh ₹ 9,800 after receiving discount ₹ 200 from him.
Jul 3	Received cash from Akhil ₹ 4,800 after allowing discount of ₹ 200 to him.
Jul 6	Sold goods to Tanya ₹ 40,000.
Jul 12	Tanya returned goods ₹ 12,000.
Jul 15	Received cash from Tanya ₹ 27,000 in full settlement of her account.
Jul 20	Sold goods to Gopal list price of ₹ 40,000 at 10% trade discount plus 20% profit.
Jul 28	Purchased goods from Vijay valued ₹ 10,000 after deducting trade discount of ₹ 2,000.

Ans. Total of Journal = ₹ 1,48,200

One Book- Endless Features

to Help you Succeed

Theoretical and Objective Questions

To make students completely prepared for examination, these questions contain Exam Pattern Questions. They cover all types of questions, like; MCQs, Case Based Questions, Assertion-Reason & SA Type Questions. All the questions are fully explained helping students to understand, how to write the answers to get full marks in the exam.

Theoretical Questions

Short Answer Type Questions

1. When an account is said to have a debit balance and credit balance?

Ans. An account shows a debit balance when the debit side exceeds the credit side. It shows a credit balance when the credit side exceeds the debit side. e.g. If cash account's total of debit side is ₹ 50,000 and total of credit side is ₹ 30,000 then it will show debit balance of ₹ 20,000.

2. Describe the features of a journal.

Ans. The main features of a journal are

(i) It records day-to-day business transactions in the order in which they happen.
(ii) It provides a complete record of each transaction in a single entry.
(iii) It follows the double entry system, recording both debit and credit aspects of each transaction.
(ii) It does not provide instant information about a transaction.
(iii) Since a journal is often handled by only one person, it limits the implementation of an internal control system.
(iv) Cash transactions are usually recorded in a separate cash book, not in the journal itself.

6. Imagine you're starting a small business and need to keep track of every financial transaction, from purchase to sale and you want to record these transactions in an organised manner. Describe the process involved in documenting transactions in a journal. Additionally, explore how journal differ from ledger? **Competency Based Que**

Ans. The process of recording in a journal begins by documenting transactions in chronological order.

Objective Questions

Multiple Choice Questions (MCQs)

1. Journal is called a book of
   (a) original entry (b) prime entry
   (c) Both (a) and (b) (d) None of these
2. From the following, which account is a nominal account?
   (a) Drawings account (b) Capital account
   (c) Purchase account (d) Bank account
4. Rule of 'debit the receiver and credit the giver' applies to
   (a) personal account (b) real account
   (c) nominal account (d) None of these
5. 'Debit all expenses and losses and credit the incomes and gains' applies to
   (a) cash account (b) purchase account
   (c) machine account (d) None of these

Project Report

A project report is a written statement of what the analyser analyses in his/her evaluation. The project report needs to be prepared with great care and consideration.

A project report should

- be handwritten
- be concise
- be clear
- have diagrammatic presentation
- have topics with suitable headings
- end up with conclusion

Elements

Try to ensure that your report contains the following elements

Title Page

This should include the project title, name of the company on which you are conducting your research and name of the student. You can also list the name of your school, class and subject teacher.

Acknowledgement

It is usual to thank those individuals, who have particularly provided useful assistance, technical or otherwise, during your project. In this, you praise your supervisor as he/she will have invested quite a lot of time in overseeing your progress. You can also give a note of thank to the department of the company, which provides you a relevant data.

Content Page

This should list the main sections and sub-sections of your report. Choose self-explanatory titles with their respective pages and use double spacing for clarity. Content should be impressive and explanatory so that the reader would clearly understand the motto of the project.

Try to avoid too many levels of sub-heading.

Project Work

Sample Question Papers

To make students practice of examination in real sense, there are 3 Sample Question Papers at the end. All these Sample Questions Papers are exactly prepared on the latest syllabus & pattern of examination.

Project Work

As per the latest syllabus, 20 marks have been kept for the project work. To make the students ready for this portion of the syllabus, a supplement of project work (covering 3 projects) is provided.

SAMPLE QUESTION PAPER 1

A Highly Simulated Sample Question Paper for CBSE Class XI Examination

ACCOUNTANCY

Time : 3 Hours **Max. Marks : 80**

General Instructions

1. This question paper contains 34 questions divided in two parts A and B.
2. Alll questions in both the parts are compulsory.
3. All parts of questions should be attempted at one place.
4. Marks for questions are indicated against each questions.
5. There is no overall choice. However, an integral choice has been provided in 7 questions of **one** mark, 2 questions of **three** marks, 1 question of **four** marks and 2 questions of **six** marks.

Part-A

1. The last step of accounting process is (1)
   (a) communicating (b) indentifying
   (c) summarising (d) interpreting result
2. Which of these is not a business transaction? (1)
   (a) Bought furniture of ₹ 10,000 for business
   (b) Paid for salaries of employees ₹ 5,000
   (c) Paid son's fees from her personal bank account ₹ 20,000
   (d) Paid son's fees from business ₹ 2,000

Or Which of the following must be a characteristic of a standard voucher?
   (a) It should be printed on good quality paper
   (b) Debit or credit amount should be written in figures against the amount
   (c) Description of transaction should be given account wise
   (d) All of the above

3. Identify the incorrect statement. (1)
   (a) India has followed dual GST model, i.e. Central (GST) and State (GST)
   (b) Goods and services tax is a value added tax
   (c) An integrated tax (GST) would be levied and collected by the centre on interstate supply of goods and services
   (d) The list of exempted goods and services are different for the Centre and the State

Or According to ...., the entire life of business should be divided into time intervals for the measurement of the profits of business.
   (a) going concern concept (b) accounting period principle
   (c) consistency concept (d) principle of prudence

4. Which source document is prepared by the seller for goods sold against cash? (1)
   (a) Pay-in-slip (b) Receipt (c) Cash memo (d) Invoice

Latest Course Structure

One Paper

Time: 3 Hours

Total Marks : 80

Units		Marks
PART A: Financial Accounting-I		
Unit 1	Theoretical Framework	12
Unit 2	Accounting Process	44
		56
Part B: Financial Accounting-II		
Unit 3	Financial Statements of Sole Proprietorship	24
		24
Part C: Project Work		**20**

PART A FINANCIAL ACCOUNTING-I

UNIT 1 Theoretical Frame Work

Units/Topics	Learning Outcomes
Introduction to Accounting • Accounting- concept, meaning, as a source of information, objectives, advantages and limitations, types of accounting information; users of accounting information and their needs. Qualitative characteristics of accounting information. Role of accounting in business. • Basic accounting terms: entity, business transaction, capital, drawings, liabilities (non - current and current); assets (non-current and current), expenditure (capital and revenue), expense, revevne, income, profits, gains, losses, purchases, sales, goods, stock, debtors, creditors, vouchers, discount (trade discount and cash discount) • **Theory Base of Accounting** • Fundamental accounting assumptions: GAAP concept. • Basic accounting concept : Business entity, money measurement, going concern, accounting period, cost concept, dual aspect, revenue recognition, matching, full disclosure, consistency, conservatism, materiality and objectivity. • System of accounting. Basis of accounting : cash basis and accrual basis. • Accounting Standards : Applicability of Accounting Standards (AS) and Indian Accounting Standards (IndAS). • Goods and Services Tax (GST) : Characteristics and advantages.	After going through this unit, the students will be able to: • describe the meaning, significance, objectives, advantages and limitations of accounting in the modem economic environment with varied types of business and non-business economic entities. • identify / recognise the individual(s) and entities that use accounting information for serving their needs of decision making. • explain the various terms used in accounting and differentiate between different related terms like current and non-current, capital and revenue. • give examples of terms like business transaction, liabilities, assets, expenditure and purchases. • explain that sales/purchases include both cash and credit sales/purchases relating to the accounting year. • differentiate among income, profits and gains. • state the meaning of fundamental accounting assumptions and their relevance in accounting. • describe the meaning of accounting assumptions and the situation in which an assumption is applied during the accounting process. • explain the meaning, applicability, objectives, advantages and limitations of accounting standards. • appreciate that various accounting standards developed nationally and globally are in practice for bringing parity in the accounting treatment of different items. • acknowledge the fact that recording of accounting transactions follows double entry system. • explain the bases of recording accounting transaction and to appreciate that accrual basis is a better basis for depicting the correct financial position of an enterprise. • Explain the meaning, advantages, and characteristics of GST.

UNIT 2 Accounting Process

Units/Topics	Learning Outcomes

Recording of Business Transactions

- Voucher and Transactions: Source documents and vouchers, preparation of vouchers, accounting equation approach: meaning and analysis, rules of debit and credit.
- Recording of Transactions: Books of Original Entry- Journal, Special Purpose books, Cash Book: Simple, cash book with bank column and petty cashbook, Purchases book, Sales book, Purchases return book, Sales return book, journal proper.

Note: Including trade discount, freight and cartage expenses for simple GST calculations

- Ledger: Format, posting from journal and subsidiary books, balancing of accounts

Bank Reconciliation Statement

- Need and preparation, Bank Reconciliation Statement

Depreciation, Provisions and Reserves

- Depreciation: Meaning, features, need, causes, factors
- Other similar terms: Depletion and Amortisation
- Methods of Depreciation: Straight Line Method (SLM), Written Down Value Method (WDV)

Note: Excluding change of method

- Difference between SLM and WDV; Advantages of SLM and WDV
- Method of recording depreciation
  Charging to asset account, Creating provision for depreciation/accumulated depreciation account.
- Treatment of disposal of asset
- Provisions and Reserves: Difference
- Types of Reserves:
  Revenue reserve, Capital reserve, General reserve, Specific reserve, Secret reserve
- Difference between capital and revenue reserve

After going through this unit, the students will be able to:

- explain the concept of accounting equation and appreciate that every transaction affects either both the sides of the equation or a positive effect on one item and a negative effect on another item on the same side of accounting equation.
- explain the effect of a transaction (increase or decrease) on the assets, liabilities, capital, revenue and expenses.
- appreciate that on the basis of source documents, accounting vouchers are prepared for recording transaction in the books of accounts.
- develop the understanding of recording of transactions in journal and the skill of calculating GST.
- explain the purpose of maintaining a Cash Book and develop the skill of preparing the format of different types of cash books and the method of recording cash transactions in Cash book.
- describe the method of recording transactions other than cash transactions as per their nature in different subsidiary books.
- appreciate that at times bank balance as indicated by cash book is different from the bank balance as shown by the pass book / bank statement and to reconcile both the balances, bank reconciliation statement is prepared.
- develop understanding of preparing bank reconciliation statement.
- appreciate that for ascertaining the position of individual accounts, transactions are posted from subsidiary books and journal proper into the concerned accounts in the ledger and develop the skill of ledger posting.
- explain the necessity of providing depreciation and develop the skill of using different methods for computing depreciation.
- understand the accounting treatment of providing depreciation directly to the concerned asset account or by creating provision for depreciation account.
- appreciate the method of asset disposal through the concerned asset account or by preparing asset disposal account.

Trial balance and Rectification of Errors

- Trial balance: objectives, meaning and preparation
  (**Scope:** Trial balance with balance method only)
- Errors: classification-errors of omission, commission, principles, and compensating; their effect on Trial Balance.
- Detection and rectification of errors.
  (i) Errors which do not affect trial balance
  (ii) Errors which affect trial balance
- preparation of suspense account.

- appreciate the need for creating reserves and also making provisions for events which may belong to the current year but may happen in next year.
- appreciate the difference between reserve and reserve fund.
- state the need and objectives of preparing trial balance and develop the skill of preparing trial balance.
- appreciate that errors may be committed during the process of accounting.
- understand the meaning of different types of errors and their effect on trial balance.
- develop the skill of identification and location of errors and their rectification and preparation of suspense account.

PART B FINANCIAL ACCOUNTING-II

UNIT 3 Financial Statements of Sole Proprietorship

Units/Topics	Learning Outcomes
Financial statements • Meaning, Objectives and Importance : revenue receipts and capital receipts. Capital expenditure, revenue expenditure and deferred revenue expenditure. Opening journal entry. • Trading and profit and loss account: gross profit, operating profit and net profit. Preparation. Balance sheet: need, grouping, marshalling of assets and liabilities. Preparation. • Adjustments in preparation of financial statements with respect to closing stock, outstanding expenses, prepaid expenses, accrued income, income received in advance, depreciation, bad debts, provision for doubtful debts, provision for discount on debtors, abnormal loss, goods taken for personal use/staff welfare, interest on capital and managers commission. • Preparation of Trading and Profit and Loss account and Balance Sheet of sole proprietorship with adjustments. **Incomplete Records** • Features, reasons and limitations. Ascertainment of Profit/Loss by Statement of Affairs Method (excluding conversion method)	After going through this unit, the students will be able to: • State the meaning of financial statements and the purpose of preparing them. • state the meaning of gross profit, operating profit and net profit and develop the skill of preparing trading and profit and loss account. • explain the need for preparing balance sheet. • understand the technique of grouping and marshalling of assets and liabilities. • appreciate that there may be certain items other than those shown in trial balance which may need adjustments while preparing financial statements. • develop the understanding and skill to do adjustments for items and their presentation in financial statements like depreciation, closing stock, provisions, abnormal loss etc. • develop the skill of preparation of trading and profit and loss account and balance sheet.

PART C PROJECT WORK (ANY ONE)

1. Collection of source documents, preparation of vouchers, recording of transactions with the help of vouchers.
2. Preparation of Bank Reconciliation Statement with the given cash book and the pass book with twenty to twenty-five transactions.
3. Comprehensive project of any sole proprietorship business. This may state with journal entries and their ledgering, preparation of Trial balance, Trading and Profit and Loss Account and Balance Sheet. Expenses, incomes and profit (loss), assets and liabilities are to be depicted using pie chart / bar diagram.

PART A
FINANCIAL ACCOUNTING-I

01
CHAPTER

Introduction to Accounting

"Accounting is the process of identifying, measuring and communicating economic information to permit informed judgements and decisions by users of information."
– *American Accounting Association*

YOUR STUDY GOALS

1.1 Meaning of Accounting
1.2 Users of Accounting Information
1.3 Qualitative Characteristics of Accounting Information
1.4 Basic Terms in Accounting

YOUR PRACTICE GOAL

- Objective Questions (54 Qs ; MCQs, A-R, Statements, Matching, Case)
- Subjective Questions (21 SAs, 10 LAs)

1.1 Meaning of Accounting

Accounting is the process of identifying, recording, classifying summarising, interpreting and communicating financial information relating to an organisation to the interested users for decision-making.

According to the **American Institute of Certified Public Accountants** (AICPA), "Accounting is the art of recording, classifying and summarising in a significant manner and in the terms of money, transactions and events which are, in part of atleast, of a financial character and interpreting the results thereof."

Relevant Aspects of Definition of Accounting

Following aspects of definition of accounting should be understood for understanding the nature of accounting

1. **Economic Events** Economic events in a business organisation refer to activities or transactions that have financial consequence and can be measured in monetary terms.

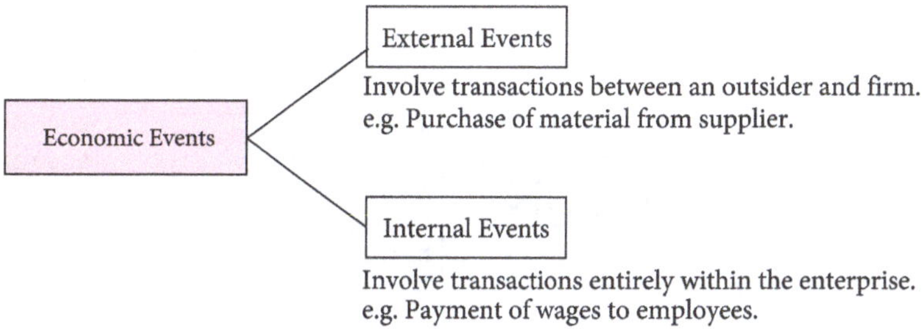

2. **Identification, Measurement, Recording and Communication**

Process	Description
Identification	Involves identifying transactions that are of financial nature and relate to the enterprise.
Measurement	Only those transactions are considered that can be measured in monetary terms.
Recording	It is the process of entering business transaction in the books of original entry in terms of money.
Communication	It involves communicating financial statements to various users, i.e. management, internal and external users.

3. **Organisation**
   - It refers to a businesss enterprise, whether for profit or not for profit motive.
   - It can be a sole proprietary, partnership firm, cooperative society, company, local authority or any other associations of persons.
4. **Interested Users of Information**
   These users can be divided into two broad categories
   (i) **Internal Users** They include CEO, Vice-president, managers, etc.
   (ii) **External Users** They include creditors, investors, labour unions, etc.

Characteristics of Accounting

Alongwith identification, measurement, recording and communication, following are some additional characters of accounting

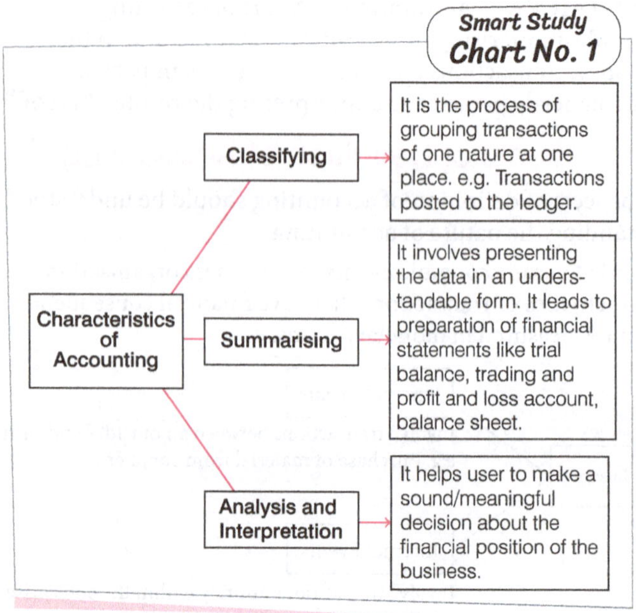

> **Accounting as an Art or a Science**
> - Accounting is both an art as well as a science.
> - Accounting is an **art** of recording, classifying and summarising financial information.
> - Accounting is also a **science** as it is an organised knowledge based on certain principles.

Accounting Process

Accounting process starts with identifying financial transactions, involves recording, classifying and summarising and ends with interpreting accounting information to various concerned parties.

Accounting process can be explained with the help of the diagram given below

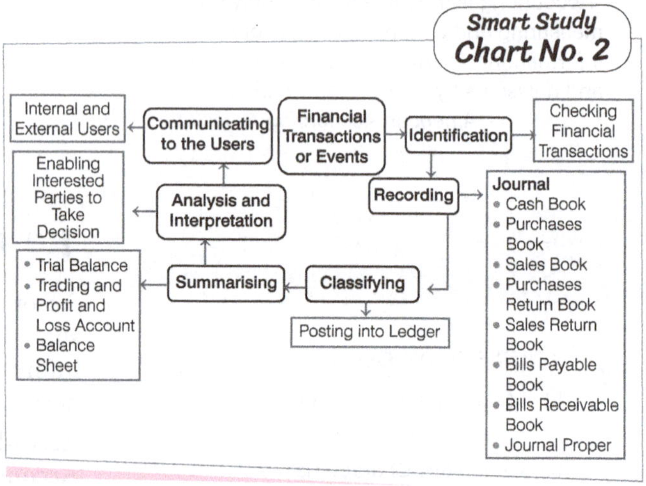

Bookkeeping, Accounting and Accountancy

Bookkeeping It is an art of recording transactions in the books of accounts.
It is the part of accounting. It is concerned with identifying, measuring recording and classifying economic transactions.

Accounting It is a wider concept than bookkeeping. It is concerned with summarising, analysing, interpreting and communicating the information to final users.

Accountancy It is a theoretical body of knowledge of accounting. It is theory part of accounting whereas accounting relates to applying knowledge of accountancy.

> **Fact**
> Bookkeeping is a part of accounting and accounting is the part of accountancy.

Objectives of Accounting

Objectives	Explanation
Systematic recording of business transactions	Records all financial transactions or events of the enterprises and enables verefiability and acts as an exidence.
Calculation of profit and loss	Determines the profit earned or loss sustained by a business.
To ascertain financial position	To provide a snapshot of financial position by recording various assets and liabilities.
To provide accounting information to its users	It provide accounting information to users for making judgements. It can be in the form of reports, graphs, etc.
To assist the management and protecting assets	It assist management by providing information for decision-making, control, budgeting and protect assets by keeping a proper record.

Advantages of Accounting

- It provides financial information of the business and financial position.
- It replaces memory by removing necessity to remember the transactions.
- It makes possible to compare current performance with the past year's performance.
- It makes possible to settle tax liabilities.
- If facilitates raising loan by providing accounting information to banks and financial statements.
- It acts as an evidence in court by keeping systematic record, when required.

Branches of Accounting
(Types of Accounting Information)

Branch	Purpose
Financial accounting	It keeps a record of all financial transactions to determine profit and loss, ascertain financial position and provide information to users.
Cost accounting	It focuses on determining the total cost and per unit cost of goods and services provided.
Management accounting	It presents accounting information to aid management in planning and controlling the business operations.
Tax accounting	It is used for preparing tax returns. Income Tax and GST are computed on the basis of this accounting.
Social responsibilities accounting	It is the process of identifying, measuring and communicating the contribution of a business to the society. The contributions consists of providing employment, environmental contribution, product safety, etc. This accounting measures the cost of these contributions and benefit to the society.

Functions of Accounting

The main functions of accounting are as follows

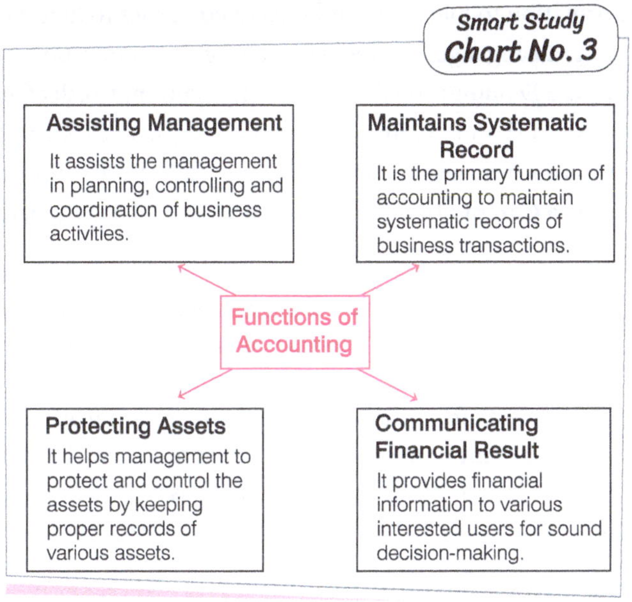

Limitations of Accounting

Limitations

Ignore Qualitative Elements

As accounting is confined to monetary transactions only, it ignores qualitative elements because these cannot be measured in money but business is also benifitted due to these elements. e.g. Quality of employee, etc.

Ignore Price Level Changes

Price level changes are ignored while preparing financial statements as accounting statements are prepared at historical cost. Unless price level changes are considered, accounting information will not show true financial results.

Includes Personal Judgement

Accounting is affected by personal bias and judgement in various situations such as choice of method of depreciation, inventory valuation, etc. Due to this fact, accounting information may not show true results.

Affected By Window Dressing

The terms window dressing means manipulating accounts so as to present financial statements in a way to show better position than the actual. e.g. Closing stock may be over valued, charging expenses excessively, etc.

Different Roles of Accounting

Earlier the role of accounting was limited to recording of transactions. But, now the role has shifted to providing information to managers and interested parties to help them take appropriate decisions. It includes role of accounting

1. **As a Language** It serves as a means of communication.
2. **As a Economic Reality** It determine current worth of an enterprise.
3. **As an Historical Record** It records only hat has happened i.e. part transactions.
4. **As an Information System** It communicates accounting information to its users.
5. **As a Commodity** It provides specialised information, required by the society.

Accounting as a Source of Information

Accounting acts as a source of information among various users in following ways

- It provides information to take economic decisions.
- Act as principal source of information to end users of accounting service.
- It provides information to judge the managerial efficiency.
- It provides input to analyse and interprete financial statements.
- It provides information for inter-firm as well as intra-firm comparison.
- It provides information about Corporate Social Responsibility (CSR) of the company.

1.2 Users of Accounting Information

Users of accounting information may be categorised as follows

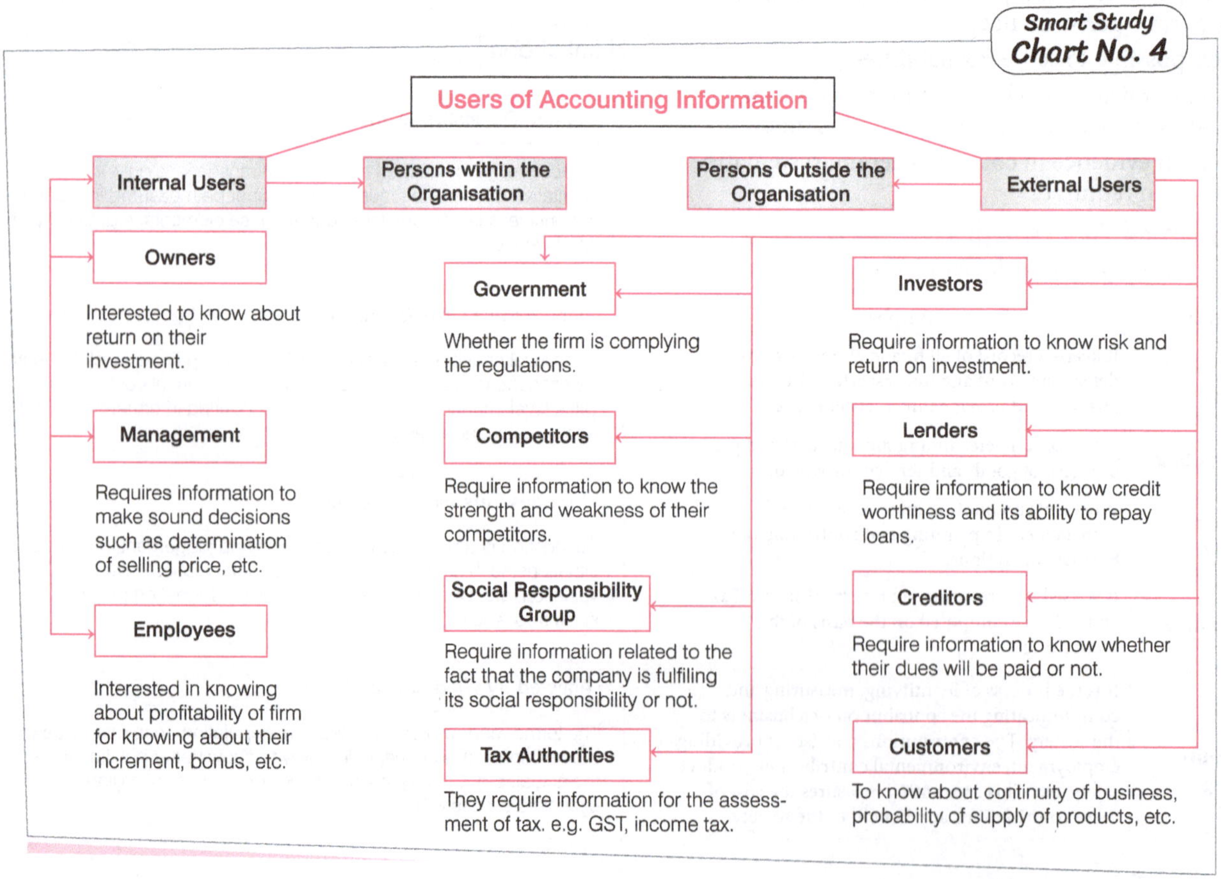

1.3 Qualitative Characteristics of Accounting Information

1. **Reliability** Accounting information must be factual and verifiable. It should be free from errors and bias.
2. **Relevance** Accounting information must be relevant to the decision-making needs of the users. Irrelevant information should not be included.

   To be relevant, information
   - must be available in time.
   - must help in prediction and feedback.
   - must influence the decision of the user.
3. **Understandability** Accounting information provided to decision-makers must be able to be interpreted in same sense as it was prepared and conveyed to them.
4. **Comparability** Users should be able to compare the accounting information.

   Accounting reports must belong to a common period and use common unit of measurement and format of reporting.
   - **Inter-firm Comparison** Comparison with that of other firm.
   - **Intra-firm Comparison** Comparison of information of a same firm with past performance.

Basic Terms in Accounting

1. **Entity** It can be defined as a distinct unit which performs business activity. e.g. Infosys Ltd, Reliance (Company) Kundan Jewellers (Sole proprietorship) Batra and Sons (Partnership), etc. are all different forms of business organisations which are treated as a distinct entity from accounting point of view.
2. **Business Transaction** It means a financial transaction entered into by various parties and recorded in the books of accounts. It can be a cash transaction or a credit transaction. e.g. Purchase of goods, receipt of money from debtors, payment to a creditor, incurring expenses, etc.
3. **Assets** Assets are property (movable or immovable) or legal rights owned by an individual or business. These are used by a business to generate cash or income.

   Assets can be classified into two types

   (i) **Current Assets** Current assets are those assets which are held primarily for the purpose of sale or these assets are expected to be converted into cash within a period of one year or within the operating cycle of the business. e.g. Cash in hand, cash at bank, debtors, stock, etc are examples of current assets.

   Key Point
   Operating cycle is the time calculated from the point when raw material is purchased, converted into finished goods, sold and cash is realised from the customer.

   (ii) **Non-current Assets** These are the assets held by the business not with the purpose to resell but are held either as investment or to facilitate business operations i.e. for the purpose of producing goods and services.

   Non-current assets are of following types
   - **Tangible Assets** These assets can be touched and seen. Such as machinery, furniture, etc.
   - **Intangible Assets** These assets cannot be touched or seen. Such as goodwill, patents, etc.
4. **Liabilities** These are the obligations or debts that an enterprise has to pay at some time in future. It means the amount owed (payable) by the business to outsiders and to owners.

   Liabilities towards the outsiders are called **external** or **outside liabilities** like creditors, loans, outstanding expenses, etc. Liabilities towards the owners are called **internal liabilities** such as capital, accumulated profit, etc.

   Liabilities can be classified as

   (i) **Current Liabilities** These are payable during the course of a year or within the operating cycle of a business. e.g. Bank overdraft, creditors, bills payable, etc.

(ii) **Non-current Liabilities** These are payable after one year or beyond the operating cycle of a business. e.g. Debentures, long-term loans, bank loan, etc.

Point to Remember
Generally, the term liabilities refers to external liabilities.

5. **Capital** Capital is the amount invested by the owner in the business. It may be in the form of cash or in the form of assets. The following relationship should be kept in mind relating to assets, liabilities and capital

$$\text{Capital} = \text{Assets} - \text{Liabilities}$$

6. **Drawings** It is the amount withdrawn by the owner in cash or assets from the business for personal use. Drawings reduce the capital of the owner in the business.
7. **Goods** Goods are the articles in which a business deals. It is a term that applies to all the items which are purchased for resale or which are used for producing the finished products which are also meant to be sold. e.g. For a furniture dealer, furniture is goods, while for others it is treated as an asset. Similarly, for a vehicle dealer, vehicle is goods.
8. **Sales** Sales are total revenues from goods or services sold or provided to customers. Sales includes both cash and credit sales. e.g. In case, 100 units are sold @ ₹ 10 per unit for cash, ₹ 1,000 is called as the amount of cash sales. In case, 200 units are sold @ ₹ 10 per unit to Bharat on credit, ₹ 2,000 is called as the amount of credit sales.
9. **Sales Return** Goods sold when returned by the purchaser are termed as sales return or return inwards.
10. **Purchases** The term 'purchases' is used for purchase of goods in which the business deals and not fixed assets. The term 'purchases' includes both cash and credit purchases of goods. e.g. If 100 units are purchased @ ₹ 10 per unit of cash, ₹ 1,000 is called as the amount of cash purchase.

    In case, 100 units are purchased @ ₹ 20 per unit from Vishal on credit, ₹ 2,000 is called as the amount of credit purchase.
11. **Purchases Return** Goods returned are known as purchases return or return outwards. Goods purchased may be returned when they are not as per specification or are defective or due to any other reason.
12. **Stock/Inventory** It is the articles which are held by an enterprise for the purpose of sale in the ordinary course of business or for the purpose of using it in the production of goods meant for sale.

    Stock in the beginning of the year is referred to as **opening stock** and stock at the end of the year is referred to as **closing stock**. Also stock can be of finished goods, of work-in-progress or of raw material.
13. **Expenses** The costs incurred by a business in the process of selling goods or services is known as expenses. It may be in the form of cash payment (salaries, wages, rent), reduction in the value of asset, cost of goods sold, etc.
14. **Expenditure** It is the amount spent or liability incurred for some benefit or acquiring assets, goods and services. Types of expenditures are

    (i) **Capital Expenditure** It is the expenditure incurred to acquire assets or for improving the quality of existing assets. e.g. Amount spent on purchase/erection of machinery, building, purchase of furniture for office.

    (ii) **Revenue Expenditure** It is the expenditure on the routine activities of the business. e.g. Purchase of goods, rent paid, salaries paid, etc.
15. **Cost** Cost is the amount of expenditure incurred on, or attributable to a specified article, product or activity. Cost can be classified as

    (i) **Direct Cost** This cost is identifiable with the product/service being produced. e.g. For a table, cost of wood is a direct cost.

    (ii) **Indirect Cost** This cost is not identifiable with the product/service being produced. e.g. For a table, the rent of the factory where the table is being manufactured, is indirect cost.

16. **Revenue** It means the money received or receivable in a business. Sources of revenue are sale of goods, rent received, commission received, interest received, dividend received, etc.
17. **Receipts** The amount received or receivable by selling assets, goods or services is known as receipts. The receipts are categorised into two parts
    (i) **Capital Receipts** The amount received or receivable by selling assets is known as capital receipts. e.g. Capital contribution from owners, amount received from sale of fixed assets/investments, amount received by way of loans.
    (ii) **Revenue Receipts** The amount which is received or receivable against the sale of goods or services is known as revenue receipts. e.g. Interest and dividend received on investments, money obtained from sale of goods, commission and fees received for services rendered.
18. **Profit** The income earned by the business from its operating activities, is referred to as profit. It is the excess of revenue of a business over its cost during an accounting year.

    It can take the following two forms
    (i) **Gross Profit** It is the excess of revenues over direct cost of the product/service.
    (ii) **Net Profit** It is the excess of revenues over direct as well as indirect costs of a product/service.

> **Key Point**
> Operating activity refers to the normal business activity of the firm. e.g. For a footwear shop, sale of footwear is operating activity.

19. **Gain** It is a profit of irregular or non-recurring nature. It is a profit that arises from events or transactions which are incidental to business such as sale of fixed assets, winning a court case, etc.
20. **Income** The profit earned during an accounting period is referred to as income. It is referred to as the difference between revenue and expense.

    e.g. Goods costing ₹ 1,00,000 are sold for ₹ 2,00,000. Here cost is ₹ 1,00,000 and revenue is ₹ 2,00,000. Difference between the two is income (i.e. 2,00,000 – 1,00,000 = ₹ 1,00,000).
21. **Loss** The excess of expenses of a period over its revenues and other income is termed as loss. e.g. If revenue is ₹ 1,00,000 and expenses are ₹ 1,20,000, then loss will amount to ₹ 20,000 (1,20,000 – 1,00,000).
22. **Discount** It is any type of reduction in the selling price of the goods. Discount is generally of two types
    (i) **Trade Discount** When the discount is allowed by a seller to its customers at a fixed percentage on the list price of the goods on account of trade practice, then it is called trade discount.
    (ii) **Cash Discount** When discount is allowed to customers for making prompt payment, it is called cash discount.
23. **Trade Receivables** The term 'trade receivables' includes the outstanding amount due from the goods sold and services rendered on credit. It includes debtors and bills receivable.
    (i) **Debtors** These are persons and/or other entities who owe to the business an amount for buying goods and services on credit.
    (ii) **Bills Receivable** It is a legal document received from a debtor in which he agrees to pay the amount due on a specified future date.
24. **Trade Payables** The term 'trade payables' is the amount payable against goods purchased and services availed on credit in the normal course of business. It includes creditors and bills payables.
    (i) **Creditors** These are persons and/or other entities who have to be paid by the business an amount for providing goods and services on credit.
    (ii) **Bills Payable** It is a legal document given by the firm to a creditor in which the firm agrees to pay the amount due on a specified future date.
25. **Vouchers** Vouchers are documents evidencing a business transaction. A voucher details the accounts that are debited and credited. It is prepared on the basis of source documents such as cash memo, invoice or bill, receipt, etc.

Mind Map

INTRODUCTION TO ACCOUNTING

1 Meaning of Accounting

Accounting is the process of identifying, recording, classifying, summarising, interpreting and communicating financial information to the interested users for decision-making.

2 Economic Events

Economic events refers to activities that have financial consequences. They can be classified as

- **External Events** Involve transactions between an outsider and firm.
- **Internal Events** Involve transactions within the enterprise.

3 Characteristics of Accounting

- **Identification** Identifying transactions which are related to the business.
- **Recording** Only those transactions are recorded which are of financial character.
- **Measurement** Only those transactions are considered which can be measured in money.
- **Classifying** Transactions of one nature are grouped at one place.
- **Summarising** It involves presenting the data in understandable form. It involves preparation of trial balance, trading and profit and loss account and balance sheet.
- **Interpretation** It helps users to make a sound decision about the financial position of the business.
- **Communicating** It includes the communication of data to the users who analyse them as per their requirements.

4 Accounting as an Art or a Science

- Accounting is both an art as well as science
- Accounting is an art of recording financial information
- Accounting is also a science as it is an organised knowledge based on certain principles

5 Bookkeeping, Accounting and Accountancy

- Bookkeeping is an art of recording transactions in the books of accounts
- Accounting starts from summarising and ends with communicating financial results
- Accountancy is a theoritical body of knowledge of accounting
- Bookkeeping is that part of accounting and accounting is the part of accountancy

6 Objectives of Accounting

- To keep systematic records of business transactions
- To determine profit or loss
- To ascertain financial position
- To provide accounting information to its users
- To assist the management and protecting assets

7 Advantages of Accounting

- Provides financial information and financial position
- Replaces memory by removing necessity to remember transactions
- Makes possible comparison of past performance with current performance
- Makes possible to settle tax liabilities

8 Branches of Accounting

- Financial accounting
- Management accounting
- Social responsibilities accounting
- Cost accounting
- Tax accounting

9 Limitations of Accounting

- Ignore qualitative elements
- Ignore price level changes
- Includes personal judgements
- Affected by window dressing

10 Interested Users of Information

Internal Users Include owners, management, employees

External Users Include creditors, investors, lenders, tax authorities, customers, government, competitors, social responsibility group, etc

11 Qualititative Characters

- Accounting information must be reliable
- Accounting information must be relevant to the decision-making needs of the users
- Accounting information must be understandable
- Accounting information must be able to compare the past performance with current performance

12 Basic Terms in Accounting

Entity, business transactions, assets (current assets and non-current assets), liabilities (current and non-current liabilities), capital, drawings, goods, sales, sales return, purchases, purchases return, stock, expenses, expenditure (revenue and capital), cost, revenue, reciepts (revenue and capital), profit (gross and net), gain, income, loss, discount (trade and cash), trade recievables (debtors and bills recievables), trade payables (creditors and bills payables), vouchers.

Objective Questions

Multiple Choice Questions (MCQs)

1. The process of grouping transactions of one nature at one place is called

(a) summarising (b) classifying
(c) recording (d) reporting

2. Accounting process starts with

(a) measuring (b) identifying
(c) recording (d) communication

3. .... refers to a systematic knowledge of accounting concerned with the principles and techniques.

(a) Bookkeeping (b) Accountancy
(c) Accounting (d) All of these

4. Which of the following statements is/are incorrect in relation to a business transaction? **Competency Based Que**

I. Bought furniture of ₹ 10,000 for business.
II. Paid for salaries of employees ₹ 5,000.
III. Paid sons' fees from her personal bank account ₹ 20,000.
IV. Paid sons' fees from business ₹ 2,000.

Codes

(a) I and II (b) II and III
(c) Only III (d) Only IV

5. Which of the following is wider than bookkeeping?

(a) Accounting (b) Accountancy
(c) Both (a) and (b) (d) None of these

6. Which of the following is correct with respect to objectives of accounting?

(a) To ascertain profit or loss
(b) To communicate accounting information to its users
(c) To protect business assets
(d) All of the above

7. Financial accounting is concerned with

(a) determining profit or loss
(b) ascertaining financial position
(c) Both (a) and (b) (d) None of the above

8. Which of the following is referred to as management accounting? **Competency Based Que**

(a) Focuses on estimating future revenues, costs and other measures to forecast activities and their results
(b) Provides information about the company as a whole
(c) Reports information that has occurred in the past that is verifiable and reliable
(d) Provides information that is generally available only on a quarterly or annual basis

9. Which of the following statements is/are correct?

I. Cost accounting provides information for management accounting and financial accounting.
II. Cost accounting provides pricing information from marketing studies.
III. Cost accounting provides financial information regarding the cost of acquiring resources.
IV. Cost accounting provides non-financial information regarding the cost of operational efficiencies. **Competency Based Que**

Codes

(a) I, II and IV (b) II, III and IV
(c) I, II and III (d) II and IV

10. .... is concerned with the ascertainment of total cost and per unit cost of goods/services produced/ provided by a business firm.

(a) Financial accounting (b) Management accounting
(c) Cost accounting
(d) Human resource accounting

11. Which of the following statement is correct with respect to limitation of accounting? **Competency Based Que**

(a) The primary objective is to maintain systematic record of business transactions
(b) Closing stock may be overvalued due to the manipulation of accounts
(c) The management is expected to act as the trustee of the companies
(d) All of the above

12. Identify the correct sequence of accounting as a source of information. **Competency Based Que**

(i) Recording of data in books of accounts.
(ii) Preparation of summaries in form of financial statements.
(iii) Communication of information.
(iv) Analysis and interpretation of information.

Codes

(a) (i), (ii), (iii), (iv) (b) (i), (ii), (iv), (iii)
(c) (ii), (i), (iii), (iv) (d) (iii), (ii), (iv), (i)

13. Which statement is correct from the following? **Competency Based Que**

(a) Accounting provides information to take economic decisions
(b) Accounting provides information about corporate social responsibility
(c) Accounting provides information to judge the managerial efficiency
(d) All of the above

14. **"Unnecessary and irrelevant information should not be included." Which quality of accounting information is reflected by this statement?** Competency Based Que

(a) Comparability (b) Reliability
(c) Relevance (d) Understandability

15. **Which qualitative characteristic of accounting information is reflected when accounting information is clearly presented?** NCERT

(a) Understandability (b) Relevance
(c) Comparability (d) Reliability

16. **Deepti wants to buy a building for her business on August, 2005. Which of the following is relevant data for her decision?** NCERT; Competency Based Que

(a) Similar business acquired the required building in 2000 for ₹ 10,00,000
(b) Building cost details of 2003
(c) Building cost details of 1998
(d) Similar building cost in August, 2005 for ₹ 25,00,000

17. **Use of common unit of measurement and common format of reporting promotes** NCERT

(a) comparability (b) understandability
(c) relevance (d) reliability

18. **......... is/are internal user(s) of accounting information.**

(a) Managing director (b) Supervisor
(c) Chief executive (d) All of these

19. **Which of the following statement is correct?** Competency Based Que

(a) Competitors require information to know strength and weakness of their competitor
(b) Government require information for allocating resources and compliance to regulations
(c) Management requires accounting information to know about their invested capital
(d) Both (a) and (b)

20. **Who would most likely use an entities' financial report to determine whether or not the business entity is eligible for a loan?** Competency Based Que

(a) Lenders and financial institutions
(b) Debtors
(c) Government (d) Customer

21. **Which of the following is incorrect?** Competency Based Que

(a) Gain is a profit of non-recurring nature
(b) Vouchers are documents evidencing a business transaction
(c) Bills receivable is a legal document received from a debtor in which he agrees to pay the amount on a specified date
(d) Sales are cash revenues from goods and services sold or provided

22. **The amount received or receivable by selling assets, goods or services is known as**

(a) receipts (b) profit (c) income (d) gain

23. **ABC Ltd. deals in selling and purchasing of furniture. Furniture is**

(a) goods for ABC Ltd. (b) asset for ABC Ltd.
(c) intangible assets for ABC Ltd.
(d) None of the above

24. **Mr. A an electronic goods dealer, gifted a TV of value of ₹ 25,000 to his friend Mr. B. It will be recorded in books as** Competency Based Que

(a) drawings (b) expenses
(c) capital (d) sales

25. **A firm earns a revenue of ₹ 20,000 and the expenses to earn this revenue are ₹ 12,000. Calculate its income.** Competency Based Que

(a) ₹ 20,000 (b) ₹ 12,000
(c) ₹ 8,000 (d) Zero

26. **Assets which are expected to be converted into cash within one year are ....**

(a) current assets (b) tangible assets
(c) intangible assets (d) non-current assets

Assertion-Reason

Direction (Q.No. 27 to 37) *Read the following Assertion (A) and Reason (R) and choose the correct alternative from the following*

Alternatives

(a) Both Assertion (A) and Reason (R) are true and Reason (R) is the correct explanation of Assertion (A)
(b) Both Assertion (A) and Reason (R) are true, but Reason (R) is not the correct explanation of Assertion (A)
(c) Assertion (A) is false, but Reason (R) is true
(d) Assertion (A) is true, but Reason (R) is false

27. **Assertion** (A) If revenue is ₹ 50,000 and expenses are ₹ 60,000 then loss will amount to ₹ 10,000.

Reason (R) The excess of expenses of a period over its revenues is termed as loss.

28. **Assertion** (A) Amount spent on purchase of a machinery is a capital expenditure.

Reason (R) Capital expenditure is related with routine activitiy of the business.

29. **Assertion** (A) For medicines dealer, medicines are goods.

Reason (R) Goods are the articles in which a firm deals.

30. **Assertion** (A) Union and social responsibility groups requires accounting information to know the stability and profitability of a firm. They are called internal users.

Reason (R) Internal users are the persons inside the organisation.

31. **Assertion** (A) Bank overdraft is a liability.

Reason (R) Liability means the amount owed by the business to the outsiders and to the owners.

32. **Assertion** (A) Bookkeeping is the part of accounting.

Reasons (R) It starts with identifying and ends with classifying.

33. **Assertion** (A) Accounting assists the management for taking sound decisions for the smooth operation of a business.

Reason (R) Without accounting information, a manager is not able to make decisions about budgeting, forecasting, etc.

34. **Assertion** (A) "A firm received a large order to supply the goods" will not be recorded in the books of accounts.

Reason (R) Only those transactions which can be measured in monetary terms are recorded.

35. **Assertion** (A) Environmental protection groups are one of the multiple external users of accounting information.

Reason (R) Social responsibility groups can only use the information available to general public to know the impact of business on environment and steps taken by an enterprise for the protection of environment.

36. **Assertion** (A) Bookkeeping involves summarising the classified transactions in the form of profit and loss account and balance sheet.

Reason (R) Bookkeeping is an art of recording in books of accounts, the monetary aspect of commerical or financial transactions. It is concerned with record keeping maintenance of books of accounts.

37. **Assertion** (A) Prepaid expenses are a part of current assets.

Reason (R) Current assets involves assets which can be converted into cash within one year as well as assets for which service or benefit will be available against these assets without further repayment.

Two Statements Based MCQs

Direction (Q. No. 38 to 43) *Read the following statements carefully and choose the correct alternatives*

Alternatives

(a) Both the statements are correct
(b) Both the statements are incorrect
(c) Statement I is correct and Statements II is incorrect
(d) Statement I is incorrect and Statement II is correct

38. **Statement I** Trade receivables means debtors and bills receivables.

Statement II Assets which are expected to be converted into cash within one year are called current assets.

39. **Statement I** In accounting, there is no need to rely on memory as all transactions are systematically recorded.

Statement II Accounting records does not help in the settlement of various tax liabilities.

40. **Statement I** Cost of goods manufactured is determined by cost accounting.

Statement II Budgeting, sales forecasting is the part of management accounting.

41. **Statement I** To be comparable, accounting reports must belong to a common period and use common unit of measurement.

Statement II Reliability means that users must be able to depend on the information.

42. **Statement I** Stock in the beginning of the year is referred to as opening stock.

Statement II Articles which are held by an enterprise for the purpose of sale in the ordinary course of busines are called goods.

43. **Statement I** Bookkeeping starts where accounting ends.

Statement II Accounting is historical in nature as it does not reflect the current worth of a business.

Matching

44. Match the following

Column I	Column II
A. Amount invested by the owner in the business	(i) Drawings
B. Amount withdrawn by the owner	(ii) External users
C. Tax authorities	(iii) Internal users
D. Employees	(iv) Capital

Codes

	A	B	C	D		A	B	C	D
(a)	(i)	(ii)	(iii)	(iv)	(b)	(ii)	(iii)	(i)	(iv)
(c)	(iv)	(i)	(ii)	(iii)	(d)	(iii)	(iv)	(i)	(ii)

45. Match the following

Column I	Column II
A. Limitation of accounting	(i) Goods
B. Articles in which a business deals	(ii) Closing stock
C. Advantage of accounting	(iii) Ignores qualitative elements
D. Unsold goods left at the end of year	(iv) Evidence in legal matter

Codes

	A	B	C	D		A	B	C	D
(a)	(iv)	(i)	(ii)	(iii)	(b)	(i)	(ii)	(iii)	(iv)
(c)	(iv)	(ii)	(iii)	(i)	(d)	(iii)	(i)	(iv)	(ii)

46. Match the following

Column I	Column II
A. Payable during the course of a year	(i) Purchase
B. Distinct unit performs business activity	(ii) Entity
C. Payable after one year or beyond operating cycle	(iii) Current liability
D. Used for the goods in which a business deals	(iv) Non-current liability

Codes

	A	B	C	D		A	B	C	D
(a)	(i)	(ii)	(iii)	(iv)	(b)	(iii)	(ii)	(iv)	(i)
(c)	(iii)	(i)	(iv)	(ii)	(d)	(i)	(ii)	(iv)	(iii)

47. Match the following

Column I	Column II
A. Removes necessity to remember the transaction	(i) Limitation of accounting
B. Window dressing	(ii) Advantage of accounting
C. Accounting starts with identifying and ends with interpreting accounting information	(iii) Internal user
D. Chief executive of a company	(iv) Accounting process

Codes

	A	B	C	D		A	B	C	D
(a)	(ii)	(iii)	(i)	(iv)	(b)	(ii)	(i)	(iv)	(iii)
(c)	(i)	(ii)	(iii)	(iv)	(d)	(i)	(ii)	(iv)	(iii)

48. Match the following

Column I	Column II
A. Bills receivable	(i) Current liability
B. Bank overdraft	(ii) Current asset
C. Debentures	(iii) Non-current asset
D. Machinery	(iv) Non-current liabilities

Codes

	A	B	C	D		A	B	C	D
(a)	(ii)	(i)	(iv)	(iii)	(b)	(ii)	(i)	(iii)	(iv)
(c)	(iii)	(ii)	(i)	(iv)	(d)	(iii)	(i)	(ii)	(iv)

Case Based MCQs

Direction *Read the following case study and answer the questions 49 to 51 on the basis of the same*

Sen and Shetty are two friends who have just attended their first class of accountancy. The friends were intrigued by the different branches of accounting and their widespread application. Sen personally liked the branch of accounting in which fund flow statement and budgetary control is used and that branch helps in planning and controlling of operations.

As the concept of accounting was further explored, they began discussing the different users of accounting. Sen said that he finds it interesting that even the employees demand information relating to business.

Shetty said he finds more interesting the fact that even competitors want information on the relative strengths and weaknesses of the enterprise and for making comparisons. Shetty further said that even accounting helps owners to compare one year's costs, expenses and sales with those of other years. However, they were quite shocked by the fact that the management worker relations was not taken into consideration in the accounting.

Meanwhile, Sen and Shetty had an argument at the end of the discussion. Sen was saying that accounting is an art whereas Shetty was saying that accounting is a science. Their teacher came in and said something to them which made them stop the argument.

49. Which branch of accounting is liked by Sen?

(a) Financial accounting (b) Cost accounting
(c) Management accounting (d) Tax accounting

50. Which advantage of accounting is being talked by Shetty in last part of first para?

(a) Provides information regarding profit and loss
(b) Provides completes and systematic record
(c) Enables comparative study
(d) Evidence in legal matters

51. Which limitation of accounting is being talked by them?

(a) Influenced by personal judgement
(b) Omission of qualitative information
(c) Incomplete information (d) Based on historical costs

Direction *Read the following case study and answer the questions 52 to 54 on the basis of the same*

Ben and Jones started with cash ₹ 10,000 and machinery ₹ 1,00,000. They decided to set-up a production line for PPE kits for the protection from Covid-19 virus. As their demand expanded, they decided to purchase one more machinery. For the same, they took bank overdraft and purchased the machinery. The quality of the company's product was very high and therefore, it could develop a reputation for itself in the market and business was flourishing.

After 1.5 years, their old machinery turned obsolete so they decided to sell the same. They sold it and got some cash proceeds. To further increase the brand presence among the concerned stakeholders, they decided to run advertisements from the cash proceeds of machinery sold. As more and more customers demanded their product, they decided to launch a discount for bulk purchases. The discount was not to be recorded in the books of accounts. This campaign was successful and they earned lot of profits from the same.

52. **Which type of liability is discussed in the passage?**
(a) Non-current (b) Current
(c) Both (a) and (b) (d) Can't be determined

53. **Which asset is discussed in the line, "The quality of the company's product was very high and therefore, it could develop a reputation for itself in the market and business was flourishing"?**
(a) Tangible (b) Intangible
(c) Current (d) Both (a) and (c)

54. **Which type of discount is being discussed in the last part of passage?**
(a) Trade discount (b) Cash discount
(c) Both (a) and (b)
(d) Can't be determined

Answers

1. (b) classifying **2.** (b) identifying
3. (b) Accountancy **4.** (c) Only III
5. (c) Both (a) and (b)
6. (d) All of the above **7.** (c) Both (a) and (b)
8. (a) In management accounting, the managers plans for future of the entity, these plans are prepared on the basis of previous track record and also after making adjustment for the future possible causes.
9. (c) I, II and III **10.** (c) Cost accounting
11. (b) Closing stock may be overvalued due to the manipulation of accounts
12. (b) (i), (ii), (iv), (iii) **13.** (d) All of the above
14. (c) Relevance **15.** (a) Understandability
16. (d) Similar building cost in August, 2005 for ₹ 25,00,000
17. (a) comparability **18.** (d) All of these
19. (d) Both (a) and (b)
20. (a) Lenders and financial institutions
21. (d) Sales are cash revenues from goods and services sold or provided
22. (a) receipts
23. (a) Goods are the articles in which a business deals. Here, ABC Ltd. deals in furniture, hence furniture is goods for ABC Ltd.
24. (a) Mr. A gifted goods to his friend. Thus, this transaction is of personal nature and will be treated as drawings.
25. (c) Income = Revenue – Expenses
= 20,000 – 12,000 = ₹ 8,000
26. (a) current assets
27. (a) Both Assertion (A) and Reason (R) are true and Reason (R) is the correct explanation of Assertion (A)
28. (d) Amount spent on acquisition of fixed assets (machine in this case) is a capital expenditure as it will yield benefits over a long period of time.
Expenditure which is incurred for routine activities is called revenue expenditure not the capital expenditure.
29. (a) Both Assertion (A) and Reason (R) are true and Reason (R) is the correct explanation of Assertion (A)
30. (c) Assertion (A) is false, but Reason (R) is true
31. (a) Both Assertion (A) and Reason (R) are true and Reason (R) is the correct explanation of Assertion (A)
32. (b) Both Assertion (A) and Reason (R) are true, but Reason (R) is not the correct explanation of Assertion (A)
33. (a) Both Assertion (A) and Reason (R) are true and Reason (R) is the correct explanation of Assertion (A)
34. (a) Both Assertion (A) and Reason (R) are true and Reason (R) is the correct explanation of Assertion (A)
35. (a) Both Assertion (A) and Reason (R) are true and Reason (R) is the correct explanation of Assertion (A)
36. (c) Accounting involves summarising the classified transactions in the form of profit and loss account and balance sheet.
37. (a) Both Assertion (A) and Reason (R) are true and Reason (R) is the correct explanation of Assertion (A)
38. (a) Both the statements are correct
39. (c) Systematic accounting records help in settlement of various tax liabilities.
40. (a) Both the statements are correct
41. (a) Both the statements are correct
42. (a) Both the statements are correct
43. (d) Bookkeeping starts with recording of transactions.
44. (c) (iv) (i) (ii) (iii) **45.** (d) (iii) (i) (iv) (ii)
46. (b) (iii) (ii) (iv) (i)
47. (b) (ii) (i) (iv) (iii)
48. (a) (ii) (i) (iv) (iii)
49. (c) Management accounting
50. (c) Enables comparative study
51. (b) Line "......... the management-worker relations was not taken into consideration in the accounting."
52. (b) The passage talks about bank overdraft.
53. (b) The given line point towards goodwill which is an intangible (non-current) asset.
54. (a) The passage says, "The discount was not to be recorded in the books of accounts." This is an characteristic of trade discount.

Subjective Questions

Short Answer Type Questions

1. "Economic events are known as a happening of consequence to a business organisation." Discuss.
Competency Based Que

Ans. A business organisation involves economic events. These are known as a happening of consequence to a business organisation.

Economic events consist of transactions which are measurable in monetory terms. e.g. Sold goods for cash or on credit, purchase of machine, etc.

Economic events are of two types

(i) **External Events**
The transactions between an outsider and organisation are called external events.

(ii) **Internal Events**
The transactions which occur entirely within organisation are called internal events.

2. State the steps involved in the process of accounting.

Ans. The steps involved in the process of accounting are

(i) Identifying financial transactions
(ii) Recording in the books of accounts
(iii) Classifying the recorded entries
(iv) Summarising
(v) Analysis and interpretation of financial statements
(vi) Communicating to the users

3. Explain the accounting process with the help of a diagram.

Ans. Accounting process starts with identifying financial transactions, involves recording, classifying and summarising and ends with interpreting accounting information to various concerned parties.

Accounting process can be explained with the help of the diagram given below

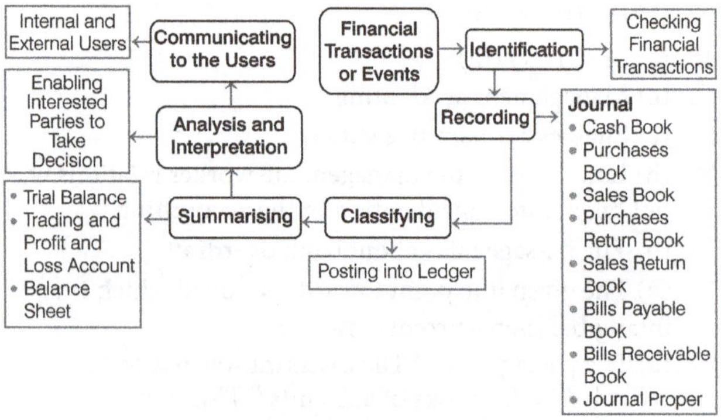

Accounting Process at a Glance

4. "The CEO of Zeminee Ltd. awarded one of his employees as employee of the year. This recognition, while valuable, does not affect the company's financial position." Which limitation of accounting is discussed above? Explain.
Competency Based Que

Ans. The limitation of 'omission of qualitative information' is discussed above.

Accounting records only those transactions and events which can be expressed is terms of money such as sale or purchase of goods, salary paid, etc. Non-monetary transactions i.e. those transactions which cannot be expressed in terms of money are not recorded in the books of accounts.

Example of such transactions are value of human resources, appointment of a new managing director, etc. These transactions may be important for the business but these are not recorded in the books of accounts because these cannot be measured in monetary terms.

5. Define bookkeeping, accounting and accountancy. With the help of diagram, explain the relationship between bookkeeping, accounting and accountancy.
Competency Based Que

Ans. Bookkeeping
Bookkeeping is an art of recording in the books of accounts, the monetary aspect of commercial and financial transactions. It is a part of accounting. It is concerned with identifying, recording and classifying economic transactions and events.

Accounting
Accounting is a wider concept than bookkeeping. It starts where bookkeeping ends. It is concerned with summarising the economic transactions, analysis and interpretation of economic transactions and events and communicating the results to final users.

Accountancy
Accountancy refers to the entire body of the theoretical knowledge of accounting. It is the theory part of accounting, whereas accounting relates to applying the knowledge of accountancy.

Diagrammatically, the relationship can be viewed as

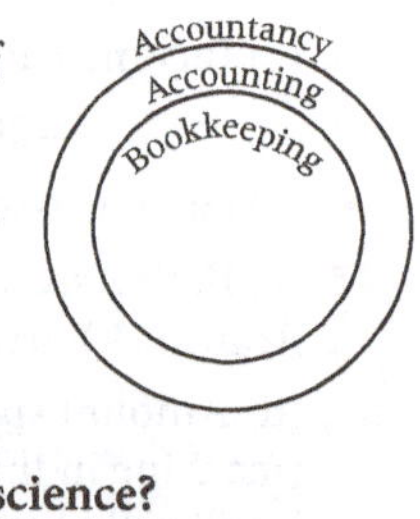

6. Why is accounting considered as a science?

Ans. (i) As the science is an organised body of knowledge based on certain principles, accounting also relies on universally accepted concepts (like GAAP or IFRS).

(ii) Accounting helps in forecasting future trends by analysing past financial data and it identifies cause and effect relationships such as increased sales lead to higher profits.

Based on above facts, it can be concluded that accounting is a science. One thing should be noted that accounting is an inexact science because it outcomes can differ as it includes personal judgements.

7. Accounting provides information about the profitability and financial soundness of a concern. In addition, it provides other valuable information also. However, accounting has certain limitations. Explain any three such limitations. **Competency Based Que**

Ans. The drawbacks or limitations of accounting are as follows

(i) It is historical in nature. It does not reflect the current worth of a business.

(ii) The figures given in financial statements ignore the effects of changes in price level.

(iii) It is not free from the personal bias and personal judgement of the people dealing with it.

8. "The role of accounting has changed over the period of time." Do you agree? Explain. **NCERT; Competency Based Que**

Ans. Yes, I agree. Earlier the role of accounting was limited to recording of transactions. Now, it has shifted to providing information to managers and interested parties, to help them take appropriate decision. It is now regarded as an information system.

9. Why is accounting called an art?

Ans. Art is technique of achieving some pre-determined objective. It is related with application of knowledge. Accounting is also called an art because it records, classify and summarise financial transactions and applies all the knowledge provided in accountancy.

10. What is the primary reason for business students and others to familiarise themselves with the accounting discipline? **NCERT**

Ans. The primary reason for business students and others to study accounting discipline is to acquire knowledge, which is helpful in understanding accounting information. It is so because accounting information is presented and communicated to various interested parties in the form of financial statements, reports, graphs, charts, etc, which is difficult to understand unless the user has the desired knowledge.

11. "Accounting infromation provided to the users must be interpreted by them in the same sense as it was prepared and conveyed to them." Which quality of accounting information is reflected in above statement? Discuss briefly. **Competency Based Que**

Ans. The quality of accounting reflected in this statement is 'understandability'. The information provided in financial statements must be understandable by the users.The accounting inforamtion must be interpreted by them in the same sense as it was prepared and conveyed to them. It means that the data should be easy to comprehend and free from ambiguity.

12. "Accounting information should be comparable." Do you agree with this statement? Give two reasons. **NCERT; Competency Based Que**

Ans. Yes, accounting information should be comparable because

(i) it helps to make inter-firm comparisons, i.e. to find out how a firm has performed as compared to the other firms.

(ii) it helps to make inter-period comparisons, i.e., to find out how it has performed as compared to the previous years.

13. If the accounting information is not clearly presented, which of the qualitative characteristic of the accounting information is violated? **NCERT; Competency Based Que**

Ans. If the accounting information is not clearly presented, it will violate the qualitative characteristic of understandability. Unclear presentation of information makes it difficult for the user to understand it.

14. What are the informational needs of internal users?

Ans. (i) **Owners**

These are interested in knowing about the profit earned or loss suffered by the business, besides the safety of their capital.

(ii) **Management**

The management requires accounting information for making various decisions such as determination of selling price, cost controls and reduction, investments, etc.

(iii) **Employees and Workers**

The employees and workers are interested in knowing about the profit earned by an enterprise so that they can demand for bonus or wage hike. Also, whether the firm has deposited its share into the provident fund and employees state insurance, etc.

15. What do you mean by 'capital' and 'drawings'?

Ans. When an owner invests his personal assets or any amount in the business, then such investment is called capital. On the other hand, cash or any other asset withdrawn by the owner for his personal use is called drawings.

16. Giving examples, explain each of the following accounting terms

(i) Fixed assets **(ii) Gain** **(iii) Profit**
(iv) Revenue **(v) Expenses**
(vi) Short-term liability **(vii) Capital**

Or Define revenue and expenses. **NCERT**

Ans. (i) **Fixed Assets**
It refers to those assets which are held for continued use in the business for the purpose of producing goods and services and not meant for resale.
e.g. Plant and machinery, land and building, etc.

(ii) **Gain**
It is a profit of irregular or non-recurring nature. It is a profit that arises from events or transactions which are incidental to business. e.g. The value of land increased from ₹ 2,00,000 to ₹ 2,50,000.

(iii) **Profit**
The income earned by the business from its operating activities, is referred to as profit. Excess of revenue of a business over its cost is termed as profit.
e.g. A shirt manufacturer had to incur a cost of ₹ 1,00,000 to produce 10,000 shirts. These shirts were sold for ₹ 1,50,000. So, ₹ 50,000 is the profit earned.

(iv) **Revenue**
It means the amount received from sale of goods or services. e.g. A shirt manufacturer sold 10,000 shirts for ₹ 1,50,000. So, ₹ 1,50,000 is the revenue.

(v) **Expenses**
The cost incurred by a business in the process of earning revenue are known as expenses. It can be in the form of cash payment. e.g. ABC company paid ₹ 20,000 as salaries, reduction in the value of asset, etc.

(vi) **Short-term Liability**
Those liabilities which are to be paid within one year are referred to as short-term liability. e.g. PQ Ltd. has to pay ₹ 1,00,000 against loan taken from a bank by next month. So, ₹ 1,00,000 is short-term liability for PQ Ltd.

(vii) **Capital**
It is the amount invested by the owner in the business. It may be in the form of cash or in the form of asset.

17. Name the term associated with the following. Competency Based Que

(i) **The articles in which a business deals.**
(ii) **The amount invested by the owner in the business.**
(iii) **The person who owes amount to the business on account of credit sales of goods or services.**
(iv) **The person to whom amount is owed on account of credit purchases of goods or services.**

Ans. (i) **Goods**
If a firm deals in furniture then for such a firm, furniture is considered as goods.

(ii) **Capital**
X invested ₹ 2,00,000 and furniture worth ₹ 50,000 then capital would be ₹ 2,50,000.

(iii) **Debtors**
Ram sold goods to Shyam on credit then Shyam will be considered as a debtor.

(iv) **Creditors**
Vijay purchased goods from Mohan on credit than Mohan will be called as creditor.

18. Define inventory or stock. Explain briefly the different kinds of inventory.

Ans. It is the articles which are held by an enterprise for the purpose of sale in the ordinary course of business or for the purpose of using it in the production of goods meant for sale.

Inventory are of following kinds

(i) **Inventory of Raw Material**
It includes raw material used for manufacturing of goods. e.g. Stock of cloth to be used for shirts.

(ii) **Inventory of Work-in-progress**
It comprises of goods which are in the process of being finished i.e. they are partly finished goods.

(iii) **Inventory of Finished Goods**
It includes finished goods in saleable condition.

19. Distinguish between debtors and creditors. NCERT

Ans. The differences between debtors and creditors are

Debtors	Creditors
Debtors are parties who owes debt towards the company.	Creditors are the parties to whom the company owes a debt.
Payments are received from them.	Payments are made to them.
They are shown as assets in the balance sheet under current assets.	They are shown as liabilities in the balance sheet under current liabilities.

20. Differentiate between capital expenditure and revenue expenditure.

Ans. Differences between capital expenditure and revenue expenditure

Basis	Capital Expenditure	Revenue Expenditure
Nature	It is incurred for the acquisition/erection of a fixed asset.	It is incurred for the day-to-day running of the business.
Purpose	It is also incurred for the purpose of increasing the earning capacity of the business.	It is incurred for the maintenance of earning capacity.
Benefit	It yields benefit over a long period.	It yields benefits for a maximum period of one year.
Treatment in Accounts	It is shown in the balance sheet.	It is shown in trading and profit and loss account.

21. **Explain the factors which necessitated systematic accounting.** NCERT

Ans. The factors which necessitated systematic accounting are

(i) **To Assess Return on Investment**
The owners/shareholders use accounting to see if they are getting a satisfactory return on their investment and to assess the financial health of their company/business.

(ii) **For Making Comparison**
The directors/managers use accounting for making both internal and external comparisons in their attempts to evaluate the performance. They may compare the financial analysis of their company with the industry figures in order to ascertain the company's strengths and weaknesses.

(iii) **To Know the Paying Ability**
The creditors (lenders) want to know if they are likely to get paid and look particularly at liquidity, which is the ability of the company/organisation to pay its debts as they become due.

(iv) **To Make Investment**
The prospective investors use accounting to assess whether or not to invest their money in the company/organisation.

(v) **For Assessing Tax Liability**
The government and regulatory agencies such as Registrar of Companies, departments require information for the payment of various taxes such as Value Added Tax (VAT), Income Tax (IT), etc. This necessitated the need for systematic accounting.

Long Answer Type Questions

22. **"Accounting is the art of recording, classifying and summarising in a significant manner and in terms of money, transactions and events, which are, in part at least, of a financial character and interpreting the results thereof."**
—American Institute of Certified Public Accountants
The above definition brings out some characteristics of accounting. Explain briefly. Competency Based Que

Ans. Following are the characteristics of accounting

(i) **Accounting is an Art as well as Science**
Accounting is an art because it requires creativity, judgement and experience to effectively communicate financial information. Accounting is also a science because it is also an organised body of knowledge based on certain principles and accounting standards.

(ii) **Recording of Transactions of Financial Character Only**
Only those transactions are recorded which are of financial character.
There may be transactions which cannot be measured in monetary terms, although such transactions are important for the business but these are not recorded. e.g. Quality of a manager, strike by employees, etc.

(iii) **Classifying**
After recording transactions in journal or subsidiary books, the transactions are classified. Classification is a process in which transactions of one nature are grouped and posted in a separate account. The book in which various accounts are opened is called 'ledger'.

(iv) **Summarising**
It is the art of presenting the classified data in a manner which can be understood and interpreted easily. It involves preparation of final accounts i.e. trading and profit and loss account and balance sheet.

(v) **Interpretation**
In accounting, the result of the business are interpreted to know about the profitability and financial position of the business by various interested parties such as proprietor, manager, creditors, employee, etc.

(vi) **Communicating**
Accounting also includes the communication of financial data to the users who can analyse them as per their needs.

23. **Explain briefly the advantages of accounting.**

Ans. The various advantages of accounting are as follows

(i) **Provides Financial Information about the Business** Accounting provides financial information i.e. profit earned or loss incurred during the period. It helps various users to make sound decisions.

(ii) **Replaces Memory**
It is not necessary to remember the transactions because in accounting, transactions are record systematically. Every transaction is recorded reducing the risk of forgetting important details.

(iii) **Facilitates Comparative Study**
It enables users of accounting information to compare current years's result with those of past years.

(iv) **Helps in Settlement of Tax Liabilities**
Proper accounting records helps in settlement of various tax liabilities such as income tax, GST, etc.

(v) **Helps in Raising Loans**
Accounting provides information in a true and fair view with respect to performance of the business. Banks and financial institutions grants loans on the basis of information easily.

(vi) **Evidence in Court**

Accounting provides systematic record of financial transactions which acts as a valid evidence in the court when required.

24. A business regularly tracks its incomes, expenses and assets to ensure accurate financial reporting and informed decision-making. What are the primary functions that accounting serves in facilitating such activities and managing financial information effectively? Competency Based Que

Ans. Accounting performs the following main functions

(i) **Maintaining Systematic Records**

It is a main function of accounting to maintain complete and systematic records of all business transactions.

(ii) **Preparation of Financial Statements**

Accounting aims to prepare financial statements which include profit and loss account and balance sheet.

(iii) **Protecting Assets of Business**

Accounting keeps proper records of all assets and management can control over them easily.

(iv) **Communicating the Financial Results**

Another main function of accounting is to communicate financial information to the interested users.

(v) **Providing Help to Management**

By providing information on the right time, accounting helps management in planning, controlling and decision-making.

(vi) **Compliance of Legal Needs**

Accounting, to comply with various laws, provides various statements hence, it protects the business against penalties.

(vii) **Fixing Responsibility**

Accounting determines the profitability of each department of a firm hence, it fixes the responsibility of each department.

25. "The purpose of this branch of accounting is the assist management for taking sound decisions for smooth operations of the business." Competency Based Que

(i) Discuss the branch of accounting reflected in above statement.

(ii) Discuss any two other branches of accounting.

Ans. (i) The branch of accounting related in the given statement is 'management accounting'.

Management Accounting

It is the use of accounting techniques for providing information to help all levels of management in planning and controlling the activities of business to enable decision-making.

The purpose of management accounting is to assist the management in taking rational policy decisions and to evaluate the impact of its decisions and actions.

(ii) Other two branches of accounting are as follows

(a) **Financial Accounting**

The process of identifying, measuring, recording, classifying, summarising, analysing, interpreting and communicating the financial transactions and events is known as financial accounting.

The purpose of this branch of accounting is to keep a record of all financial transactions, so that

- The profit earned or loss sustained by the business during an accounting period can be worked out.
- The financial position of the business as at the end of the accounting period can be ascertained.
- The financial information required by the management and other interested parties can be provided.

(b) **Cost Accounting**

It is the process of ascertaining and controlling the cost of a product, operation or function. The purpose of cost accounting is to analyse the expenditure, so as to ascertain the cost of various products manufactured by the firm and fix the prices. It also helps in controlling the costs and providing necessary costing information to management for decision-making.

26. Explain main objectives or utility of accounting.

Ans. The following are the main objectives or utility of accounting

(i) **To Keep Systematic Record of Business Transactions**

It is the main objective of accounting to keep complete and systematic record of business transactions according to specified rules. It helps to avoid omissions and fraud.

(ii) **To Calculate Profit or Loss**

The second main objective is to ascertain the net profit earned or loss incurred during a particular period. To determine the profit or loss, trading and profit and loss account are prepared at the end of each accounting period.

(iii) **To Find out the Reasons Leading to Net Profit or Net Loss**

It is also a key objective of accounting to find out the factors leading to net profit or net loss, providing valuable insight to improve financial performance.

(iv) **To Ascertain the Financial Position**

For this, after preparing the profit and loss account, a statement called 'balance sheet' is prepared which shows the values of assets and liabilities. With the help of balance sheet, one can ascertain financial position of the business.

(v) **To Provide Information**

The objectives of accounting also includes communicating financial information to the interested parties which helps them to take meaningful decisions about the business.

27. Explain the qualitative characteristics of accounting information. NCERT

Ans. Qualitative characteristics are the attributes of accounting information which tend to enhance its understandability and usefulness. In order to assess whether accounting information is useful, it must possess the characteristics of reliability, relevance, understandability and comparability. The qualitative characteristics of accounting information are

(i) **Reliability**

It means the users must be able to depend on the information. It must be factual and verifiable. A reliable information should be free from error and bias. To ensure reliability, the information disclosed must be credible, verifiable by independent parties, must use the same method of measuring and be neutral and faithful.

(ii) **Relevance**

Accounting information presented by financial statements must be relevant to the decision-making needs of the users. Unnecessary and irrelevant information should not be included. To be relevant, information must be available in time, must help in prediction and feedback and must influence the decisions of users.

(iii) **Understandability**

The information provided in financial statements must be understandable by the users. Understandability implies that the accounting information provided to the decision makers must be interpreted by them in the same sense as it was prepared and conveyed to them.

(iv) **Comparability**

It means that the users should be able to compare the accounting information. To be comparable, accounting reports must belong to a common period and use common unit of measurement and format of reporting. When accounting information of a period is compared with that of other period, it is known as **intra-firm comparison.** When accounting information of an enterprise is compared with that of other enterprises, it is known as **inter-firm comparison.**

28. "There are multiple external users of a business entity. Different users require different information according to their need." Describe the information required by the various external users. Competency Based Que

Or **Describe the informational needs of external users.** NCERT

Ans. The various external users and their informational needs are as follows

(i) **Investors and Potential Investors**

They require information on the risks and return on investment.

(ii) **Unions and Employee Groups**

They require information on the stability, profitability and distribution of wealth within the business.

(iii) **Lenders and Financial Institutions**

They require information on the creditworthiness of the company and its ability to repay loans and pay interest.

(iv) **Suppliers and Creditors**

They require information on whether amount owed will be repaid when due and on the continued existence of the business.

(v) **Customers**

They require information on the continued existence of the business and thus, the probability of a continued supply of products, parts and after sales service.

(vi) **Government and Other Regulators**

They require information on the allocation of resources and the compliance to regulations.

(vii) **Social Responsibility Groups**

These groups require information related to the fact that the company is fulfilling its social responsibility or not. e.g. Environmental groups require information on the impact of business activities on environment and its protection.

(viii) **Competitors**

They require information on the relative strengths and weaknesses of their competitors and for comparative and benchmarking purposes.

29. Explain the meaning of gain and profit. Distinguish between these two terms. NCERT

Ans. **Gain**

When a firm earns profit from its activities which are non-recurring or irregular nature, such profit is called gain. e.g. Profit on sale of fixed assets.

Profit

The income earned by a business firm from its main operating activities is called profit. It is the difference of revenue (sales) and expenses.

The differences between gain and profit are

Gain	Profit
It is of irregular or non-recurring nature.	It is of regular or recurring nature.
It arises from non-operating activities, i.e. those activities which are incidental to the main activity of the business.	It arises from operating activity of the business.
e.g. Appreciation in value of land by ₹ 1,00,000. So, ₹ 1,00,000 is the gain.	e.g. A shirt is sold for ₹ 250. The cost of shirt is 200. So, ₹ 50 is the profit.

30. Distinguish between financial accounting, cost accounting and management accounting.

Ans. The differences between financial accounting, cost accounting and management accounting are

Basis	Financial Accounting	Cost Accounting	Management Accounting
Meaning	The process of identifying, measuring, recording, classifying, summarising, analysing, interpreting and communicating the financial transactions and events is known as financial accounting.	The process of ascertaining and controlling the cost of a product, operation or function is known as cost accounting.	The use of accounting techniques for providing information to help all levels of management in planning and controlling the activities of business to enable decision-making is known as management accounting.
Purpose	To keep record of all financial transactions.	To analyse the expenditure so as to ascertain the cost of various products manufactured by the firm and fix the prices.	To assist the management in taking rational policy decision and to evaluate the impact of its decision and actions.
Data Used	Qualitative aspects are not recorded.	Only qualitative aspect is recorded.	Uses both qualitative and quantitative concepts.

31. Distinguish between bookkeeping, accounting and accountancy.

Ans. The differences between bookkeeping, accounting and accountancy are

Bookkeeping	Accounting	Accountancy
Bookkeeping is maintained by junior staff.	Accounting is maintained by senior staff.	Accountancy is maintained by the professionals.
It is the primary stage.	It is the secondary stage.	It is the complete process which includes both, bookkeeping and accounting.
It is concerned with recording of day-to-day transactions.	It is based on bookkeeping.	It is helpful in decision-making.
It is concerned with identification, recording and classification of financial transactions.	It is concerned with summarising, interpretation and communication of financial results.	It refers to the entire body of the theory and practice of accounting.

02

CHAPTER

To bring uniformity and consistency to the process of accounting in order to enhance its utility, theory base of accounting, consisting principles, concepts, rules and guidelines, is developed.

YOUR STUDY GOALS

2.1 Accounting Principles
2.2 System of Accounting
2.3 Basis of Accounting
2.4 Accounting Standards (AS)
2.5 Goods and Services Tax (GST)

YOUR PRACTICE GOAL

- Objective Questions (51 Qs ; MCQs, A-R, Statements, Matching, Case)
- Subjective Questions (22 SAs, 13 LAs)

Theory Base of Accounting

Theory base of accounting includes principles, concepts, conventions, rules and guidelines developed over a period of time. Apart from these, Accounting Standards issued by ICAI also constitute the theory base of accounting, which are expected to be followed, in order to bring consistency in the accounting practices.

2.1 Accounting Principles

Accounting principles are a uniform set of rules or guidelines which are developed to ensure uniformity and easy understanding of the accounting information.

Smart Study Chart No. 1

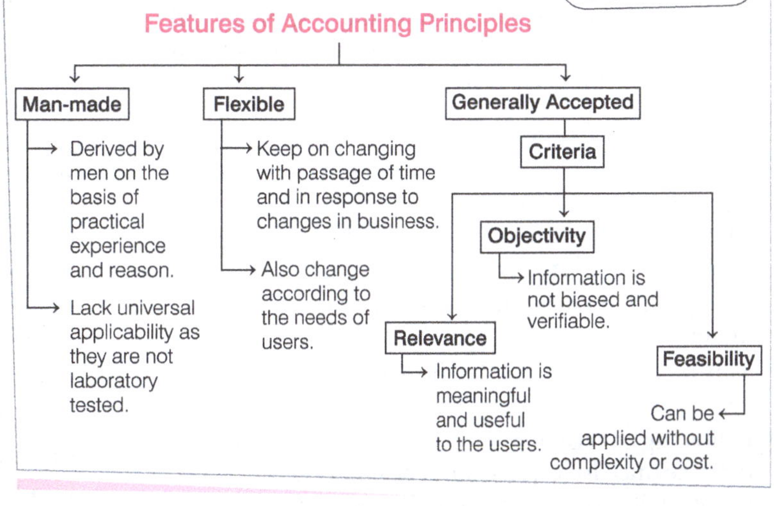

Generally Accepted Accounting Principles (GAAP)

- GAAP refers to the rules or guidelines adopted for recording and reporting of business transactions, in order to bring uniformity in the preparation and presentation of financial statements.
- These principles are also referred as concepts and conventions.
- Principles are generally accepted if they are relevant, objective and feasible.

Fundamental Accounting Assumptions/Concepts

It refers to the basic assumptions, rules and principles which works as the basis of recordings business transactions and preparing accounts. These are as follows

1. Going Concern Assumption

- It is assumed that the business firm would continue its operations for a fairly long period of time and would not be liquidated in the near future.
- **Practical Implications**
  - Facilitates recording fixed assets on the basis of their cost value and maximum life.
  - A distinction is made between capital and revenue expenditure.
  - Profits are computed every year, so that the performance of the business can be adjudged.
  - Total cost of the machinery is not to be treated as an expense in the year of purchase itself.
  - Outside parties enter into long-term contacts with the enterprise.
- e.g. If a machinery is purchased which would last for the next 10 years then, the cost of the machinery will be spread over the next 10 years for calculating the net profit or loss for each year.

2. Consistency Assumption

- Accounting policies and practices once chosen and followed, should be applied uniformily and consistently over the years i.e. they should not be changed year after year.
- It helps the financial statements to be more understandable and comparable.
- This method helps in inter-firm and inter-period comparisons.
- Following consistency should not mean that, the practice once followed cannot be changed. It can be changed, if it is required by law or accounting standards.

3. Accrual Assumption

- A transaction is recorded at the time, it takes place and not at the time when settlement is done.
- In other words, revenue is recorded when sales are made or services are rendered and if is irrelevant as to when cash is received against such sales.
- Similarly, expenses are recorded at the time they are incurred and it is irrelevant as to when payment is made in cash for such expenses.
- e.g. Goods are sold to Raju on 1st January, 2022 on a credit of 3 months. In this instance, sale will be recorded on 1st January, 2022 although the amount will be received on 1st April, 2022.

Point to Remember

In the course of accounting process, it is assumed that a business is following these concepts. If this is not the case, then the business should disclose this fact in the financial statements alongwith the reasons for not following the concept.

Accounting Principles : Concepts and Conventions

- Concept refers to the necessary assumptions and items which are fundamental to accounting practice.
- Convention denotes customs or traditions as a guide to the preparation of accounting statements.

Various concepts and conventions are

1. Business Entity or Accounting Entity Principle

- Business is treated as a separate entity distinct from its owners.
- All transactions are recorded from the point of view of business and not from the point of view of owner.
- The capital introduced by the owner is treated as liability from the point of view of business.
- Due to this principle, owner's personal property, investment and expenditures are kept seperate from the recording of business transactions in the books.
- e.g. Ram started his business with cash. He purchased stock, machinery and furniture and deposited money into the bank account and also kept some cash in hand. From accounting point of view, cash introduced by Ram is a liability for the business and is referred to as capital. The assets purchased are of the business and not of the owner.

2. Money Measurement Principle

- Only those transactions are recorded which can be expressed in monetary terms.
- In other words, non-financial transactions do not find place in accounting records.

- e.g. Sale of goods or payment of expenses or receipt of income, etc. will be recorded as these can be expressed in monetary terms.
  However, dispute among the owners or managers, appointment of a manager, efficiency of management, quality of product, etc. will not be recorded in the books of accounts because it cannot be converted or recorded in terms of money.
- Although this concept is not free from limitations
  - Due to change in price value of money does not remain the same over a period of time.
  - Thus accounting does not reflect a true and fair view of affairs of the business, as change in the value of money is not reflected in the books.

3. Accounting Period Principle

- It refers to the span of time at the end of which the financial statements are prepared.
- According to it, life of a business is divided into smaller periods (usually one year).
- According to the amended income tax law, a business has to compulsorily adopt financial year beginning on 1st April and ending on 31st March in the next calendar year as its accounting period.
- Apart from this, companies whose shares are listed on stock exchange, are required to publish quarterly results to ascertain profitability and financial position at the end of every three months period.

4. Full Disclosure Principle

- There should be reporting of all significant information relating to the economic affairs of the business and it should be complete and understandable.
- Whether information should be disclosed or not depends upon whether such information will affect decision-making of the users or not.
- To ensure proper disclosure of accounting information, Companies Act has provided a format for the preperation of financial statements.
- e.g. If a company is involved in a legal dispute that might result in a large financial liability, the details must be disclosed in the financial statements.

5. Prudence or Conservatism Principle

- It states that 'do not anticipate profits but provide for all probable losses'.
- In other words, this principle suggests that we should make provisions for probable future expenses but ignore any future probable gain, unitil it actually happens.
- It provides guidance for recording transactions in the books of accounts and is based on the policy of playing safe.
- It ensures that the financial statements present a realistic picture of the working affairs of the business.
- e.g. Closing stock is valued at lower of cost or net realisable value, as per this concept only.

6. Materiality Principle

- It states that only those transactions should be recorded in detail which are material or relevant for the preparation of financial statements.
- It is a matter of judgement to decide whether a particular information is material for a business or not. Also, it depends on the nature and/or amount of that item.
- According to American Accounting American Association (AAA), an item should be recorded as material, if there is a reasons to believe that knowledge of it would influence the decision of an informed investor.
- e.g. ₹ 1,00,000 spent on advertising is material for a business having turnover of ₹ 3,00,000 whereas, it is immaterial for a business having turnover of ₹ 30,00,00,000.

7. Cost Concept or Historical Cost Principle

- Fixed assets are recorded in the books of accounts at their cost price including acquisition cost, transportation cost, installation and cost for making the asset ready for use.
- Adoption of historical cost brings objectivity in recording as the cost of acquisition is easily verifiable from the purchase documents.
- Book value of the asset is decided on the basis of cost less depreciation without giving consideration to its market price.
- Depreciation to be charged on assets is calculated on the basis of cost of asset.
- e.g. Machinery is purchased for ₹ 10,00,000. At the end of the accounting period, it is found that the market value of machinery is ₹ 15,00,000. However, it will be recorded in the books at ₹ 10,00,000 only.

8. Matching Cost or Matching Principle

- Expenses incurred in an accounting period should be matched with revenues of that period.
- All revenues earned during that year, whether received during that year or not, and all cost incurred, whether paid during the year or not should be taken into account while ascertaining profit or loss for that year.

- Adjustments are made for expenses not paid or for those paid in advance.
- e.g. If there is unsold stock at the end of the accounting period, then its cost needs to be carried over to next year, so that such cost can be recognised or adjusted with the revenue earned with the sale of such stock.

9. Dual Aspect or Duality Principle

- It is the foundation or the basic principle of accounting.
- It states that every transaction has a dual (two- fold) effect and should therefore be recorded at two places.
- According to this principle, we get accounting equation

Assets = Capital + Liabilities or Assets = Owner's Equity + Outsider's Liabilities

- When a firm purchases a machine of ₹ 1,00,000 by taking a loan.
  - Assets (Machine) will be increased by ₹ 1,00,000
  - Liability (Loan) will be increased by ₹ 1,00,000

10. Revenue Recognition Principle (Realisation Principle)

- It requires that revenue for a business transaction should be recorded only when it is realised.
- Revenue is assumed to be realised when a legal right to receive it arises. e.g. A sale of goods on 31st March, 2024 by Ajay will be considered revenue of 2023-24.
- If actual cash is received on a later date then it is not considered for recognising the revenue.
- e.g. If a business sells goods in January, 2022 and receives the amount from such sale in April, 2022 then revenue will be considered as recognised in January, 2022 when sale is made and not when payments is received from such sale.

11. Verifiable Objective Concept/ Objectivity Concept

- Accounting information should be verifiable and should be free from personal bias.
- Every transaction should be based on source documents.
- e.g. A building purchased for ₹ 20,00,000 must be recorded/supported by an evidence such as purchase agreement.

Note Of the above principles, principle of full disclosure, conservatism and materiality are conventions and the rest are concepts.

2.2 System of Accounting

The system of recording transactions in the books of accounts are generally classified into two types *viz.* double entry system and single entry system.

Smart Study Chart No. 2

System of Accounting

Double Entry System

- Developed by Luca Pacioli in Italy in 15th century.
- Based on the principal of dual aspect.
- It is a complete system as both aspects of a transaction are recorded in the books of accounts.

Single Entry System

- It is not a complete system of maintaing records of financial transactions.
- It does not record two fold effect of every transaction.
- Only cash transactions are recorded.
- It is also known as 'accounts from incomplete records'.
- Accounts maintained under this system are incomplete and unsystematic and thus, not reliable.

Features

- Maintains complete record of each transaction.
- Recognises atleast two aspects of each transaction.
- One aspect is debited and other is credited.
- Total of all debits is equal to total of all credits.
- Helps in establishing arithmetical accuracy.

Advantages

- There are less chances of errors due to recording on the basis of scientific and logical rules.
- Present correct income or loss, assets and liabilities.
- Accuracy is established by preparing trial balance.
- Profit and loss during a period can be determined by preparing profit and loss account.
- Financial position can be ascertained by preparing balance sheet at the end of accounting period.

Disadvantages

- It is complex and hard to understand.
- It requires expert knowledge.
- As it is complex, there is greater possibility of committing errors.

2.3 Basis of Accounting

The most significant function of accounting is to determine profits or losses of a business in an accounting period. They can be determined either on cash basis or on accrual basis.

Smart Study Chart No. 3

Basis of Accounting

Cash Basis

- Entries in the books of accounts are made, when cash is recieved or paid.
- Revenue and expenses are recognised at the time when cash is received or paid and not at the time of sale or purchase.

Advantages

- It is very simple.
- It is an objective approach.
- Suits organisations which mostly have cash transactions.

Disadvantages

- It does not provide true or fair view of financial position.
- It ignores matching principle.
- It does not differentiate between revenue and capital items.

Accrual Basis

- Revenue is recognised when sale takes place.
- It is irrelevant, whether payment for such sale is received or not.
- It is based on realisation and matching principle.
- Adjustments are made for outstanding and prepaid expenses.

Advantages

- More scientific.
- Shows true and fair view of financial position.
- Show correct profit or loss.
- Recognied by Companies Act, 2013.

Disadvanages

- It is complicated as compared to cash basis.
- It is a time consuming process.

2.4 Accounting Standards (AS)

They are the written statements consisting of formal accounting rules and guidelines issued by the accounting body of the country (such as Institute of Chartered Accountants of India) that are to be followed while preparation and presentation of financial statements.

Aspect Related to Accounting Standards

Topic	Description
Need	• They facilitate transparent and meaningful reporting of financial information. • They reduce accounting alternatives to reasonable and practical level. • They enhance comparability of financial statements. • They encourage consistency in accounting practices.
Nature	• Framework of practices and guidelines which facilitate reliability and comparability to financial statements. • Bring uniformity in accounting practices. • Design and mould the business by prescribing and recommending accounting practices. • Cannot violate the prevailing law of the country. • Are flexible as they provide alternative practices.
Objectives	• To promote better understanding of financial statements. • To minimise the diverse accounting policies and practices with the aim to eliminate them to the possible extent. • To enhance reliability of financial statements. • To facilitate meaningful comparison of financial statements of two or more entities.

Topic	Description
Utility/ Benefits	• Provides the norms and guidelines on the basis of which financial statements should be prepared. • Uniformity in the preparation and presentation of financial statements. • Create a sense of confidence amongst various users. • Helps auditors in auditing the accounts. • Simplify the accounting information in financial statements. • Render reliability to financial statements.
Limitations	• Rigid in nature, thus fails to offer flexibility in applying accounting statndards. • Cannot over ride the statue. • Mandatory in nature thus they restrict initiative for better presentation and disclosure. • Obstruct the judgement of the auditors.

Applicability of AS

- Applicable to all types of organisations, engaged in any industrial and business activity except for purely charitable organisations.
- Applicable to sole proprietorship firm, partnership firm, societies, trust, hindu undivided families, cooperatives and companies.
- Required to maintain certain level of uniformity at international level.
- It is important that the financial statements must be prepared in accordance with certain standards.
- Thus, accounting standards are being converged with International Financing Reporting Standards (IFRS).
- In India, Ministry of Corporate Affairs in collaboration with Institute of Chartered Accountants of India established Indian Accounting Standards (Ind-AS).
- These are applicable to the certain class of companies under the Companies (Indian Accounting Standards) Rules, 2015 as adopted as 16th February, 2015.

Indian Accounting Standards (Ind-AS)

- These are a set of accounting standards notified under Section 133 of the Companies Act, 2013.
- They are formulated keeping in view the Indian economic and legal environment with a view to converge with International Financing Reporting Standards (IFRS).
- They are based on clearly stated principles.

Applicability of Ind-AS

- These Ind-AS are firstly approved by ICAI (Institute of Chartered Accountants of India) and then sent for approval of NACAS (National Advisory Committee on Accounting Standards).
- Then, once the Ministry of Corporate Affairs give approval for these standards, they are notified in official gazette.
- The Government of India has issued notification regarding 41 Ind-AS so far.
- The government has clarified that unlisted companies with net worth of under ₹ 500 crore and urban cooperative banks with net worth of under ₹ 200 crore won't be required to adopt Ind-AS.

2.5 Goods and Services Tax (GST)

- It is a value added tax levied on most goods and services, sold for domestic consumption. In other words, it is a destination based tax on consumption of goods and services.
- This Act was passed in Parliament on 24th March, 2017. It came into effect from 1st July, 2017.
- It is paid by the consumers. However, it is remitted to government by businesses selling goods and services.
- It has replaced many indirect taxes levied by centre and state government.
- Central level taxes that have merged into GST are excise duty, service tax, central sales tax.
- State level taxes that have merged into GST are octroi and entry tax, purchase tax, entertainment tax, VAT, luxury tax, tax on lottery.

Classification/Categories of GST

1. **Central GST** It is levied by central government on intra-state sales i.e. sales within the state.
2. **State GST** It is levied by state government in the course of intra-state sales.

3. **Union Territory GST** Union territories such as Chandigarh, Puducherry, etc. levey Union Territory GST on sales made within the Union Territory.
4. **Integrated GST** It is levied on inter-state sales of goods and services.

Note CGST, SGST and Union GST are charged at half the prescribed rate of GST. e.g. If rate is 18% then CGST will be levied by the centre 9% and SGST/Union GST will be levied by 9%.

Characteristics of GST

- GST is a comprehensive indirect tax which has replaced all indirect taxes levied by centre and state government except few taxes levied by local bodies.
- Components of GST are Central GST, State GST and Integrated GST (IGST).
- There are uniform GST rates on goods and services across all States and union territories.
- GST can be collected/charged if the seller is registered under GST.
- GST is a value added tax because GST paid is set-off against GST collected.
- There is no multiple levy of tax on goods and services, such as sales tax, entry tax, octroi, entertainment tax or luxury tax, etc.

Advantages of GST

- With the introduction of GST, multiple types of taxes levied on goods and services has been abolished.
- GST has reduced the administrative cost for the government as it has widened the tax base and increased revenue to Centre and State Government.
- GST has reduced compliance cost and increases voluntary compliance.
- GST has affected rates of tax to the maximum of two floor rates.
- GST has removed the cascading effect on taxation.
- GST will promote economic efficiency and sustainable long-term economic growth.
- As GST is neutral to business processes, business models, organisational structure and geographical location, it will eventually promote economic efficiency and sustainable long-term economic growth.
- GST help in increasing export by extending competitive edge in international market.
- GST results in enhancing manufacturing and distribution system.

GST Rate Structure

For collection of GST, goods and services are divided into 5 slabs

Essential items including food	0%
Common use items	5%
Standard rate	12%
Maximum goods and all services standard rate	18%
Luxury items and tobacco	28%

Input GST GST paid on purchase of goods and services is termed as Input GST. Input GST is not a cost for the purchaser but is an asset because it can be set off against GST collected (i.e. Output GST). However, in certain cases it cannot be set off against GST collected.

Output GST GST collected from customers on sale of goods and services is termed as Output GST.

Important Points Related to GST

1. **Transactions on which GST is Not Levied**
   - Amount introduced into the business as capital
   - Depreciation/Amortisation
   - Supply of goods and/or services or both to embassies of other countries
   - Educational services
   - Amount withdrawn by proprietor for personal use
   - Amount deposited into bank/withdrawn from bank
   - Health services (consulting only)
   - Interest paid/payable or interest received/receivable
   - Advance received against sale/purchase
   - Payment of travelling expenses
   - Supply of services to government
   - Bad debts written-off and bad debts recovered
   - Payment of wages and salary
   - Amount paid to creditors and discount received
   - Cheque issued for purchase
   - Payment of electricity and water bills
   - Amount received from debtors and discount allowed
2. **Cases where GST Paid cannot be Set-off against GST Collected**
   - Payment for health insurance
   - Donations
   - Samples
   - Free gift to staff
   - Drawings
   - Repairs and maintenance of building
   - Payment of membership fee of a club, health and fitness centre
   - Food and beverages expenses (restaurant bills)
   - Purchase of vehicles

3. **Cases where GST Paid** (i.e. Input GST) **is Reversed**
   - Purchase return
   - Goods lost or stolen
   - Cash discount received
   - Goods given as donation
   - Goods destroyed or written-off
   - Drawings by the proprietor
   - Goods given away as gift or charity
   - Goods distributed as free samples
   - Goods distributed among staff
4. **Cases where GST Collected** (i.e. Output GST) **is Reversed**
   - Sales return
   - Cash discount allowed
5. **Reverse Charge** Reverse charge means that GST is not charged by the seller but is paid by the purchaser of goods and/or services or both in the government account.
   It is claimed by the purchaser as 'input GST'. Goods and services that are subject to GST under reverse charge are
   - Purchase of goods and/or services from an unregistered taxpayer
   - Payment of fee to lawyers
   - Payment of fee outside India
   - Payment for use of copyright

List of Accounting Standards (Ind-AS)

AS No.	Title
AS-1	Disclosure of Accounting Policies
AS-2	Valuation of Inventories
AS-3	Cash Flow Statement
AS-4	Contingencies and Events Occurring after the Balance Sheet Date
AS-5	Net Profit or Loss for the Period, Prior Period Items and Changes in Accounting Policies
*AS-6	Depreciation Accounting
AS-7	Construction Contracts
*AS-8	Accounting for Research and Development
AS-9	Revenue Recognition
AS-10	Property, Plant and Equipment
AS-11	The Effect of Changes in Foreign Exchange Rates
AS-12	Accounting for Government Grants
AS-13	Accounting for Investments
AS-14	Accounting for Amalgamations
AS-15	Employee Benefits
AS-16	Borrowing Costs
AS-17	Segment Reporting
AS-18	Related Parties Disclosures
AS-19	Leases
AS-20	Earnings Per Share
AS-21	Consolidated Financial Statements
AS-22	Accounting for Taxes on Income
AS-23	Accounting for Investments in Associates in Consolidated Financial Statements
AS-24	Discontinuing Operations
AS-25	Interim Financial Reporting
AS-26	Intangible Assets
AS-27	Financial Reporting of Interests in Joint Venture
AS-28	Impairment of Assets
AS-29	Provisions, Contingent Liabilities and Contingent Assets
*AS-30	Financial Instruments: Recognition and Measurement
*AS-31	Financial Instruments: Presentation
*AS-32	Financial Instruments: Disclosures

* *These standards have been withdrawn by ICAI*

List of Indian Accounting Standards (Ind-AS)

AS No.	Title
Ind-AS 101	First-time Adoption of Indian Accounting Standards
Ind-AS 102	Share-based Payment
Ind-AS 103	Business Combinations
Ind-AS 104	Insurance Contracts
Ind-AS 105	Non-current Assets Held for Sale and Discontinued Operations
Ind-AS 106	Exploration for and Evaluation of Mineral Resources
Ind-AS 107	Financial Instruments: Disclosures
Ind-AS 108	Operating Segments
Ind-AS 109	Financial Instruments
Ind-AS 110	Consolidated Financial Statements
Ind-AS 111	Joint Arrangements
Ind-AS 112	Disclosure of Interests in Other Entities
Ind-AS 113	Fair Value Measurement
Ind-AS 114	Regulatory Deferral Accounts
Ind-AS 115	Revenue from Contracts with Customers
Ind-AS 1	Presentation of Financial Statements
Ind-AS 2	Inventories
Ind-AS 7	Statement of Cash Flows
Ind-AS 8	Accounting Policies, Changes in Accounting Estimates and Errors
Ind-AS 10	Events after the Reporting Period
Ind-AS 11	Construction Contracts
Ind-AS 12	Income Taxes
Ind-AS 16	Property, Plant and Equipment
Ind-AS 17	Leases
Ind-AS 18	Revenue
Ind-AS 19	Employee Benefits
Ind-AS 20	Accounting for Government Grants and Disclosure of Government Assistance
Ind-AS 21	The Effects of Changes in Foreign Exchange Rates
Ind-AS 23	Borrowing Costs
Ind-AS 24	Related Party Disclosures
Ind-AS 27	Separate Financial Statements
Ind-AS 28	Investments in Associates and Joint Ventures
Ind-AS 29	Financial Reporting in Hyper Inflationary Economies
Ind-AS 32	Financial Instruments : Presentation
Ind-AS 33	Earnings per Share
Ind-AS 34	Interim Financial Reporting
Ind-AS 36	Impairment of Assets
Ind-AS 37	Provisions, Contingent Liablilities and Contingent Assets
Ind-AS 38	Intangible Assets
Ind- AS 40	Investment Property
Ind-AS 41	Agriculture

Mind Map

THEORY BASE OF ACCOUNTING

1 Meaning of Accounting Principles

Accounting principles are a uniform set of rules or guidelines which are developed to ensure uniformity and easy understanding of the accounting information.

2 Generally Accepted Accounting Principles (GAAP)

GAAP refers to rules or guidelines adopted for recording and reporting of business transactions, in order to bring uniformity in the preparation and presentation of financial statements.

3 Fundamental Accounting Assumptions

- **Going Concern** It is assumed that the business firm would continue its operations for a fearly long period and would not be liquidated in the near future.
- **Consistency** Accounting policies and practices once chosen and followed should be applied uniformly and consistently over the years.
- **Accrual** A transaction is recorded at the time it takes place and not at the time when settlement is done.

4 Accounting Principles: Concepts and Conventions

Concept refers to the necessary assumptions and items which are fundamental to accounting practice. Convention denotes customs or traditions as a guide to the preparation of accounting statements. Various concepts and conventions are

- Business entity principle
- Money measurement principle
- Accounting period principle
- Full disclosure principle
- Prudence or conservatism principle
- Materiality principle
- Historical cost concept
- Matching principle
- Dual aspect principle
- Revenue recognition principle
- Verifiable objective concept

5 System of Accounting

- **Double Entry System** It is based on the principal of dual aspect. It is a complete system as both aspects of a transaction are recorded in the books of accounts.
- **Single Entry System** It is an incomplete system of mantaining accounts. It does not record two fold effect of every transaction. Only cash transactions are recorded.

6 Basis of Accounting

- **Cash Basis** Entries in the books of accounts are made, when cash recieved or paid.
- **Accrual Basis** Revenue is recognised when sale takes place. It is irrelevant, whether payment for such sale is recieved or not.

7 Accounting Standards (AS)

These are the written statements consisting of formal accounting rules and guidelines issued by the accounting body of country such as ICAI of India.

Objectives
- To promote better understanding of financial statements
- To minimise the diverse accounting policies and practices
- To enhance reliability of financial statements
- To facilitate meaningful comparison of financial statements

Utility
- Provides the norms and guidelines on the basis of which financial statements should be prepared
- Uniformity in the preparation and presentation of financial statements
- Create a sense of confidence amongst various users
- Helps auditors in auditing the accounts
- Simplify the accounting information in financial statements
- Render reliability to financial statements

8 Applicability of Accounting Standards

- Applicable to all types of organisations engaged in any industrial and business activity except for purely charitable organisations
- Required to maintain certain level of uniformity at international level
- It is important that the financial statements must be prepared in accordance with certain standards
- These are applicable to the certain class of companies under the Companies Rules, 2015 as adopted on 16th February, 2015

Indian Accounting Standards (Ind-AS)
- These are a set of accounting standards notified under Section 133 of the Companies Act, 2013
- They are formulated keeping in view the Indian economic and legal environment with a view to converge with International Financing Reporting Standards (IFRS)

Applicability of Indian Accounting Standards
- The Government of India has issued notification regarding 41 Ind-AS so far
- The government has clarified that unlisted companies with net worth of under ₹ 500 crore and urban cooperative banks with net worth of under ₹ 200 crore would not be required to adopt Ind-AS

9 Goods and Services Tax (GST)

It is a value added tax levied on most goods and services sold for domestic consumption.

Characteristics
- It has replaced all indirect taxes except few taxes levied by local bodies
- Components of GST are Central GST, State GST and Integrated GST (IGST)
- There are uniform GST rates on goods and services across all States and union territories
- GST can be collected/charged if the seller is registered under GST

Advantages
- With the introduction of GST, multiple types of taxes levied on goods and services has been abolished
- It has reduced compliance cost and increases voluntarily compliance
- It has removed the cascading effect on taxation
- It will promote economic efficiency and sustainable long-term economic growth

Objective Questions

Multiple Choice Questions (MCQs)

1. According to the consistency concept, accounting policies and practices once choosen should be applied uniformly over the years. This concept is important when .... accounting practices are equally acceptable.

(a) alternative (b) same
(c) different (d) Both (a) and (c)

2. "A transaction is recorded at the time, it takes place and not at the time when settlement is done." To which accounting a concept, the statement relates? Competency Based Que

(a) Accrual concept (b) Verifiable concept
(c) Consistency assumption (d) None of these

3. "All transactions are recorded from the point of view of firm and not from the point of view of owner/ proprietor." To which accounting principle does the above statement relate? Competency Based Que

(a) Prudence principle
(b) Materiality principle
(c) Accounting entity principle
(d) None of the above

4. 'Outstanding salary' of the current year, though not paid, is shown in the profit and loss account as per which accounting concept?

(a) Historical cost concept
(b) Matching concept
(c) Prudence or conservatism concept
(d) None of the above

5. "A claim of a very big amount pending in a court against a firm should be informed to the users in financial statements."
The above statement is related with which accounting convention? Competency Based Que

(a) Materiality convention (b) Convention of conservatism
(c) Full disclosure convention (d) None of these

6. Among the following, a convention is an exception of full disclosure convention.

(a) Prudence convention (b) Materiality convention
(c) Both (a) and (b) (d) None of these

7. Stock-in-trade are to be recorded at cost price or market price whichever is less, it is based on .... principle.

(a) prudence (b) historical cost
(c) cost benefit (d) business entity

8. A trader has made a sale of ₹ 65,500 out of which cash sales amounted to ₹ 25,000. He showed trade receivables on 31st March, 2023 at ₹ 40,500. Which concept is followed by him? Competency Based Que

(a) Going concern (b) Cost
(c) Accrual (d) Money measurement

9. In income measurement and recognisation of assets and liabilities, which of the following concepts goes together?

(a) Periodicity, accrual, matching
(b) Cost, accrual, matching
(c) Going concern, cost, realisation
(d) Going concern, periodicity, reliability

10. During the life time of an entity, accounting produce financial statements in accordance with which basic accounting concept? NCERT

(a) Conservatism (b) Matching
(c) Accounting period (d) None of these

11. If a firm believes that some of its debtors may default, it should act on this by making sure that all possible losses are recorded in the books. This is an example of the .... concept. Competency Based Que

(a) prudence (b) consistency
(c) materiality (d) duality

12. An enterprise change method of depreciation from straight line to written down value method. This information should be disclosed through the financial statements and the accompanying notes. This concept is Competency Based Que

(a) objectivity concept (b) full disclosure
(c) matching concept (d) accounting period concept

13. Manya, a proprietor of a firm earned revenue of ₹ 5,00,000 during the financial year 2024-25. She received cash ₹ 4,50,000 during the year and paid ₹ 1,30,000 for expenses including outstanding expenses of ₹ 20,000 of the previous year. Ascertain the amount of profit as per cash basis of accounting.

(a) ₹ 2,20,000 (b) ₹ 2,70,000
(c) ₹ 4,50,000 (d) ₹ 3,20,000

14. Which of the following is a disadvantage of double entry system?

(a) The financial position of business can be ascertained
(b) It requires expert knowledge to keep account under this system
(c) It is a scientific system of recording business transaction
(d) None of the above

15. **"This system is incomplete and unsystematic hence, not reliable. It is followed by small business firms as it is very simple and flexible."**

The above statement is indicating to which accounting system? **Competency Based Que**

(a) Double entry system
(b) Single entry system
(c) Accounts for incomplete records
(d) Either (b) or (c)

16. **"Revenue is recognised at the time when cash is received not at the time of sale." To which basis of accounting, statement is indicating?** **Competency Based Que**

(a) Cash basis (b) Accrual basis
(c) Double entry (d) None of these

17. **What will be the net profit or loss of Mr. Rehman if he adopts cash basis of accounting and cash sales are ₹ 5,00,000, credit sales are ₹ 4,00,000, expenses paid ₹ 3,60,000, ₹ 60,000 is still to be paid?** **Competency Based Que**

(a) ₹ 1,40,000 (b) ₹ 80,000
(c) ₹ 5,40,000 (d) None of these

18. **Calculate net profit as per accrual basis of accounting.**

Cash sale ₹ 6,00,000, credit sale ₹ 3,60,000, expenses paid ₹ 1,20,000, outstanding expense for the year ₹ 80,000.

(a) ₹ 8,80,000 (b) ₹ 8,40,000
(c) ₹ 7,60,000 (d) ₹ 10,40,000

19. **"Accounting Standards provide norms or guidelines." Which among the following is right option as benefit of Accounting Standards?** **Competency Based Que**

(a) Provide uniformity
(b) Provide basis of preparing financial statements
(c) Help to auditors
(d) Simplifying accounting information

20. **Which tax from the following have been merged into GST?**

(a) Wealth tax (b) Income tax
(c) Service tax (d) None of these

21. **Choose the corrrect option in respect of objectives of GST.**

(a) Eliminate classification dispute between goods
(b) Bring uniformity in tax rates
(c) Ensure free movement of goods across the country without any additional tax
(d) All of the above

22. **Identify the incorrect statement.** **Competency Based Que**

(a) India has followed dual GST model i.e. centre (GST) and state (GST)
(b) Goods and services tax is a value added tax
(c) An integrated tax (GST) would be levied and collected by the center on inter-state supply of goods and services
(d) The list of exempted goods and services are different or the centre and the state

23. **Which of the following statement is incorrect?** **Competency Based Que**

(a) A transaction is recorded at the time it takes place
(b) Accounting policies and practices should not be changed year after year
(c) All the transactions are recorded in the books on the assumption that it is a non-continuing enterprise
(d) All are correct

24. **Which of the following is correct with respect to feature of accounting principles?** **Competency Based Que**

(a) Accounting principles are man-made
(b) Accounting principles keep changing with the passage of time
(c) Accounting principles are generally accepted
(d) All are correct

25. **Which of the following is incorrect?** **Competency Based Que**

(a) In accrual basis of accounting, both cash and credit transactions are recorded
(b) In accrual basis of accounting, advance/outstanding income and expenses are adjusted
(c) Cash basis of accounting is recognised by the Companies Act, 2013
(d) Cash basis of accounting is acceptable as it reveals the required information

26. **Choose the correct statement.** **Competency Based Que**

(a) Closing stock is valued at lower of cost or net realisable value
(b) Sale of goods or payment of expenses will be recorded as these can be expressed in monetary terms
(c) If a business sells goods on 31st March, 2024 and received the amount on 1st April, 2024 then revenue will be recognised in 2023-24
(d) All are correct

Assertion-Reason

Direction (Q.No. 27 to 36) *Read the following Assertion (A) and Reason (R) and choose the correct alternative from the following*

Alternatives

(a) Both Assertion (A) and Reason (R) are true and Reason (R) is the correct explanation of Assertion (A)
(b) Both Assertion (A) and Reason (R) are true, but Reason (R) is not the correct explanation of Assertion (A)
(c) Assertion (A) is correct, but Reason (R) is incorrect
(d) Assertion (A) is incorrect, but Reason (R) is correct

27. **Assertion** (A) All transactions are recorded from the point of view of owner, not the firm.

Reason (R) Business is treated as separate entity distinct from its owner.

28. **Assertion** (A) An accountant of a firm anticipated a profit of ₹ 2,00,000 for the year ended 2024-25 and recorded the same in books of accounts.

Reason (R) As per prudence or conservation principle, we can not anticipate profits.

29. **Assertion** (A) Adjustments are made for expenses not paid or for those paid in advance.

Reason (R) According to matching principle, expenses incurred in an accounting period should be matched with revenues of that period.

30. **Assertion** (A) NOP Ltd. purchased a machinery of ₹ 20,000 which is supposed to last for 20 years. The accountant decides to spread the cost of machinery for next 20 years for calculation of profit and loss.

Reason (R) According to consistency concept, accounting principles and methods should remain consistent from one year to another.

31. **Assertion** (A) A claim of a very big sum pending in a court of law against the enterprise should be brought to the notice of the users of financial statements, otherwise the statements would be misleading.

Reason (R) According to principle of full disclosure, all significant information relating to the economic affairs of the enterprise should be completely disclosed.

32. **Assertion** (A) Total assets are equal to owner's equity and outsider's liabilities.

Reason (R) Dual aspect is the foundation for the accounting equation.

33. **Assertion** (A) Cash basis of accounting is very simple.

Reason (R) Cash basis of accounting suits the organisations which mostly have cash transactions.

34. **Assertion** (A) Cash basis of accounting is that accounting which records only cash transactions, i.e. only those incomes and expenses are recorded which have been received and paid in cash respectively. Thus, cash basis of accounting violates GAAP.

Reason (R) Cash basis of accounting makes a distinction between capital and revenue items.

35. **Assertion** (A) Assets are recorded in the books of accounts at their cost to the firm.

Reason (R) According to the historical cost concept, assets are recorded at market value or book value whichever is lower.

36. **Assertion** (A) The goods supplied from Chennai to Lucknow would fetch Integrated GST.

Reason (R) Integrated GST is levied in the course of inter-state supply of goods and services.

Two Statements Based MCQs

Direction (Q.No. 37 to 43) *Read the following statements carefully and choose the correct alternative*

Alternatives

(a) Both the statements are correct
(b) Both the statements are incorrect
(c) Statement I is correct and Statement II is incorrect
(d) Statement I is incorrect and Statement II is correct

37. **Statement I** Accounting principles are man-made.

Statement II Accounting principles lack in universal applicability.

38. **Statement I** An accounting principle is called feasible when it is implemented without any complexity or cost.

Statement II An accounting principle is called relevant when it results in information that is meaningful and useful.

39. **Statement I** There should be reporting of all the significant information of economic affairs and it should be complete and understandable.

Statement II Reasons for low turnover due to natural calamities should not be disclosed as there is no requirement.

40. **Statement I** According to consistency concept, accounting principles should be changed year to year to benefit the organisation.

Statement II According to consistency concept, accounting principles or methods should remain same from year to year.

41. **Statement I** Accrual basis of accounting is complicated compared to cash basis of accounting.

Statement II The single entry system is also known as 'accounts from complete records'.

42. **Statement I** AS-1 is related with 'disclosure of accounting policies'.

Statement II AS-26 is related with 'intangible assets'.

43. **Statement I** Accounting Standards are not applicable to sole proprietor firms.

Statement II Accounting Standards are being converged with IFRS.

Matching

44. Match the following

Column I	Column II
A. Going concern concept	(i) Requires source documents on the basis of which, a transaction should be recorded
B. Consistency concept	(ii) States about the continuity of operations.
C. Accrual concept	(iii) States about the time when transaction is recorded
D. Verifiability objective concept	(iv) States about uniformity of policies and practices

Codes

	A	B	C	D		A	B	C	D
(a)	(ii)	(iv)	(iii)	(i)	(b)	(ii)	(iv)	(i)	(iii)
(c)	(iii)	(iv)	(ii)	(i)	(d)	(iii)	(iv)	(i)	(ii)

45. Match the following

Column I	Column II
A. GST paid reversed	(i) Depreciation
B. Reverse charge	(ii) Purchase return
C. GST is not levied	(iii) Payment of fee to lawyer
D. GST paid cannot to be set-off	(iv) Free gift to staff

Codes

	A	B	C	D		A	B	C	D
(a)	(ii)	(iii)	(i)	(iv)	(b)	(i)	(iii)	(ii)	(iv)
(c)	(ii)	(iii)	(iv)	(i)	(d)	(i)	(iii)	(iv)	(ii)

46. Match the column and relate with principles

Column I	Column II
A. Money measurement principle	(i) Quality of better staff cannot be recorded
B. Prudence principle	(ii) Date of sale is considered not the date of cash received.
C. Revenue recognition principle	(iii) Probability of expenses/loss can be anticipated
D. Historical cost principle	(iv) Market value is ignored

Codes

	A	B	C	D		A	B	C	D
(a)	(i)	(iii)	(ii)	(iv)	(b)	(ii)	(iii)	(i)	(iv)
(c)	(iii)	(iv)	(ii)	(i)	(d)	(iv)	(i)	(iii)	(ii)

47. Match the following

Column I	Column II
A. Quality of management is not recorded in books	(i) Full disclosure principle
B. Change in method of valuation of stock is shown in footnotes	(ii) Consistency concept
C. Making provision for likely bad debts should remain consistent with previous years	(iii) Money measurement principle
D. Provision should be made for pending law suit against firm	(iv) Principle of conservation

Codes

	A	B	C	D		A	B	C	D
(a)	(iii)	(ii)	(i)	(iv)	(b)	(i)	(ii)	(iii)	(iv)
(c)	(iii)	(ii)	(iv)	(i)	(d)	(iii)	(i)	(ii)	(iv)

Case Based MCQs

Direction *Read the following case study and answer the questions 48 and 49 on the basis of the same*

Arun and Rohan are two friends graduated from a top college of the country. After the college, they decide to build a startup in their hometown, Bengaluru. They decided to start a subscription service of fruits in the nearby cities.

For obtaining high quality fruits, they made 5 years contracts with farmers in and around Karnataka. They also decided to purchase machinery for cleansing and quality check of the fruits. The business of the company started booming.

Two years down the line, they had built a strong brand and reputation. To leverage the same, the company decided to venture into other states as well with the similar service line.

They first expanded to Tamil Nadu and got great demand. While accounting, company usually booked a normal loss to account for spoiled fruits that they might get. Moreover, they charged depreciation on the machinery to ensure that expenses are distributed over the years.

With all these good practices, after four more years of operations, the company attained a unicorn status.

48. **Which concept is highlighted in the fact that company made long-term contracts with the farmers?**

(a) Going concern concept (b) Accrual concept
(c) Consistency concept (d) Both (a) and (b)

49. **Which principle is highlighted in the line, "While accounting, company usually booked a normal loss to account for spoiled fruits that they might get"?**

(a) Business entity principle
(b) Prudence principle
(c) Materiality principle (d) Full disclosure principle

Direction *Read the following case study and answer the questions 50 and 51 on the basis of the same*

Golu Plastic Ltd. (GPL) is a leading plastic articles manufacturing company. It was listed on Indian stock market in 1999.

The founders and promoters of the company hold the highest number of shares of the company, approximately around 55%. All these founders belong to a single family. Unfortunately, all of them died in a car accident recently. However, the company continued to exist and grow.

In the year 2004, the company imported multiple machines for producing low-cost plastic sheets. The machines were recorded at the price prevailing in 2004 and have been subjected to depreciation year on year based on written down value method.

The depreciation is treated as a non-cash expense while preparing the cash flow statement. When GST was implemented in 2017, it benefitted the company by streaming the processes.

A single rate of GST was charged on the supply of the goods and the process of filing was very simple.

50. Which principle is highlighted in the fact that the company continued even after death of the founders?
(a) Business entity principle
(b) Money measurement principle
(c) Duality principle
(d) Historical cost principle

51. Which principle is highlighted in the line, "The machines were recorded at the price prevailing in 2004"?
(a) Full disclosure principle (b) Conservatism principle
(c) Duality principle
(d) Historical cost principle

Answers

1. (d) Both (a) and (c)
2. (a) Accrual concept
3. (c) Accounting entity principle
4. (b) Matching concept
5. (c) Full disclosure convention
6. (b) Materiality convention
7. (a) prudence
8. (c) Accrual
9. (a) Periodicity, accrual, matching
10. (c) Accounting period
11. (a) prudence
12. (b) full disclosure
13. (d) 4,50,000 – 1,30,000 = ₹ 3,20,000
14. (b) It requires expert knowledge to keep account under this system
15. (d) Either (b) or (c)
16. (a) Cash basis
17. (a) Net Profit as per Cash Basis = 5,00,000 – 3,60,000 = ₹ 1,40,000
18. (c) Net Profit = 6,00,000 + 3,60,000 – 1,20,000 – 80,000 = ₹ 7,60,000
19. (b) Provide basis of preparing financial statements
20. (c) Service tax
21. (d) All of the above
22. (d) India has followed a dual GST model (i.e. centre and states) and the list of exempted goods and services are common or the centre and the states.
23. (c) Transaction are recorded in the books on the assumption that it is a continuing enterprise as per going concern assumption.
24. (d) All are correct
25. (c) Cash basis of accounting is recognised by the Companies Act, 2013.
26. (d) All are correct
27. (a) Both Assertion (A) and Reason (R) are true and Reason (R) is the correct explanation of Assertion (A)
28. (d) As per prudence principle, it is stated that 'do not anticipate profits but provide for all probable losses'. Hence, accountant cannot anticipate the profits.
29. (a) Both Assertion (A) and Reason (R) are true and Reason (R) is the correct explanation of Assertion (A)
30. (b) Both Assertion (A) and Reason (R) are true, but Reason (R) is not the correct explanation of Assertion (A)
31. (a) Both Assertion (A) and Reason (R) are true and Reason (R) is the correct explanation of Assertion (A)
32. (a) Both Assertion (A) and Reason (R) are true and Reason (R) is the correct explanation of Assertion (A)
33. (b) Both Assertion (A) and Reason (R) are true, but Reason (R) is not the correct explanation of Assertion (A)
34. (c) Cash basis of accounting does not make distinction between capital and revenue items.
35. (c) As per historical cost concept, assets are recorded at cost subjected to depreciation.
36. (a) Both Assertion (A) and Reason (R) are true and Reason (R) is the correct explanation of Assertion (A)
37. (a) Both the statements are correct
38. (a) Both the statements are correct
39. (c) Reason for low turnover due to natural calamities should be disclosed as this is a significant information.
40. (d) According to consistency concept, the policies or method applied should not be changed year to year.

41. (c) The single entry system is known as 'accounts from incomplete records' as this system do not record both aspect of a transaction.
42. (a) Both the statements are correct
43. (d) Accounting Standards are applicable to all types of organisations except purely charitable organisations. Hence, Statement I is incorrect.
44. (a) (ii) (iv) (iii) (i)
45. (a) (ii) (iii) (i) (iv)
46. (a) (i) (iii) (ii) (iv)
47. (d) (iii) (i) (ii) (iv)
48. (a) Going concern concept
49. (b) According to prudence principle, company should not anticipate profits but provide for all possible losses.
50. (a) Business entity principle
51. (d) Historical cost principle

Subjective Questions

Short Answer Type Questions

1. What are accounting principles?

Ans. Accounting principles are a set of rules or guidelines which are developed to ensure uniformity and easy understanding of accounting information. They ensures comparability, consistency and transparency in financial reporting.

They provide the basis for preparing financial statements and ensure that users of financial information can rely on the information provided.

2. What do you mean by accounting concept?

Ans. Accounting concept refers to the necessary assumptions and ideas which are fundamental to accounting practice. These are the basic assumptions, rules and principles which work as the basis of recording of business transactions and preparing accounts.

These are the outcome of accounting practices or principles being followed by the enterprises over a period of time.

3. What do you understand by accounting conventions?

Ans. These are the outcome of accounting practices or principles being followed by the enterprises over a period of time.

Conventions may undergo a change with time to bring about improvement in the quality of accounting information.

4. A company purchased goods of ₹ 15,00,000 and sold 80% of such goods during the year. The market value of the remaining goods was ₹ 1,20,000. The company valued the closing stock at ₹ 3,00,000. Is this treatment correct? Competency Based Que

Ans. No, the principle of conservatism is being violated here as the closing stock should have been valued ₹ 1,20,000 i.e. lower of cost or market value, whichever is lower.

This principal states every potential loss must be recognised as soon as they are foreseeable. This principal states that "do not anticipate profit but provide all possible losses."

5. Arvind Ltd. purchased a machine for ₹ 20,00,000. At the end of year, the market value of such machine was ₹ 25,00,000. The company valued the machine at market value. Was it correct? Competency Based Que

Ans. No, company is violating historical cost principle according to which assets should be recorded at cost not at market value. As per this concept, assets are recorded at acquisition cost including transportation, installation fees, etc.

Except land and building fixed assets are subjected to depreciation. The value of fixed assets remain unchanged even when the market value fluctuates.

6. Due to a labour strike, in a factory the production had to stop for a week. The accountant estimated the loss of production and likely loss of profit and recorded it in the books of accounts. Is the accountant correct? Explain. Competency Based Que

Ans. No, as per the money measurement concept only those transactions and events, which can be recorded in money terms on the basis of documentary evidences are recorded in books of accounts.

In the given situation, labour strike cannot be measured in monetary terms hence it cannot be recorded.

7. Aashi Ltd. gets a contract of ₹ 200 crore to build a hospital to be completed in 4 years. The management of the company wants to ascertain profit or loss on this contract only when the contract is completed. Is the management correct? Competency Based Que

Ans. No, although the true profit or loss can be ascertained only after the completion of the contract but as per accounting period principle the contract period should be divided into time interval of twelve months for the ascertainment of profit of that period.

8. An accountant advised his client, who is a doctor to maintain his accounts on cash basis. Is the advice of accountant correct? Competency Based Que

Ans. Yes, the advice given by the accountant is correct as cash basis of accounting is more appropriate for a doctor as he receives his fee in cash.

9. Why is it necessary for accountants to assume that business entity will remain a going concern? NCERT

Ans. The concept of going concern assumes that a business firm would continue to carry out its operations indefinitely. Due to this concept distinction is made between capital and revenue expenditure and thus, assets and liabilities are recognised.

10. Give the advantages of following consistency concept.

Or **Why should a business follow principle of consistency?**

Ans. A business should follow this principle because of many advantages associated with it.

Advantages of following consistency concept are

(i) It helps the financial statements to be more understandable and comparable.

(ii) It is important when alternative accounting practices are available.

(iii) It eliminates personal bias and helps in achieving results that are comparable.

11. Principle of conservatism may lead to creation of secret reserves. Discuss in brief.

Ans. Yes, principle of conservatism has two effects

(i) Profit and loss account discloses lower profit in comparison to the actual profits.

(ii) Balance sheet will disclose understatement of assets and overstatement of liabilities.

These two effects result in creation of secret reserves.

12. How does matching principle apply to depreciation?

Ans. Matching principle states that the expenses of an accounting period are matched with the related revenue for correct determination of profit.

According to the matching principle, the purchase price of fixed asset is not related to the accounting period because the benefit derived from its use will be spread over a number of years.

Therefore, only depreciation related to the accounting period is considered for determination of profit.

13. When should revenue be recognised? Are there exceptions to the general rule? NCERT

Ans. Revenue should be recognised only when it is realised. Only such transactions should be recorded in accounting which have actually taken place not the ones which would take place in future.

Yes, there are certain exceptions to the general rule. In case of construction projects, revenue is generally realised before the contract is completed.

Similarly, when goods are sold on hire purchase, the amount collected in instalments, is treated as realised.

14. Explain verifiable objective concept or objectivity principle.

Ans. According to this principle, accounting information should be verifiable and should be free from personal bias. Every transaction should be based on source documents such as cash memo, invoices, sales bills, etc.

These evidences should be objective which means that they should state the facts as they are, without any bias towards either side.

15. Ashok & Co. has been charging depreciation @ 15% per annum on straight line method. It now wants to change the method to diminishing balance method, the rate of depreciation being 20% per annum. Can the company do so? Competency Based Que

Or **As per consistency concept a company cannot change an accounting policy. Does this holds true in all instances? Explain.**

Ans. Yes, the method and the rate of depreciation can be changed but only in the following circumstances

(i) The change is to comply with statutory regulations or

(ii) The change would help in better understanding of the true financial position of the business.

Also, the change and its effect on profit should be disclosed in the financial statements of the enterprise.

16. Name the accounting concept or convention associated with the following Competency Based Que

(i) Assets are recorded at cost, irrespective of the market price.

(ii) Life of a business should be divided into smaller periods.

(iii) Accounting transactions should be free from bias of accountants and others.

Ans. (i) **Historical Cost Concept**

Historical cost concept states that assets must be recorded at their acquisition cost, i.e. purchase price and this concept will remain unchanged irrespective of market price.

(ii) **Accounting Period Concept**

This concept states that financial statements of an entity should be prepared at fixed intervals i.e. usually one year. This time period is known as accounting period.

(iii) **Verifiable Objective Concept**

According to this concept, all financial transactions must be supported by source document such as invoice, receipts, etc. so that transactions can be verified when required.

17. Vijay, a Chartered Accountant earned ₹ 12,00,000 during the financial year 2024-25, out of which he received ₹ 10,50,000. He incurred expenses of ₹ 5,10,000, out of which ₹ 1,20,000 are outstanding.

He also received his fees relating to previous year ₹ 1,35,000 and also paid ₹ 60,000 due on expenses of last year. Find out Vijay's income for 2024-2025 following the cash basis and accrual basis of accounting. Competency Based Que

Ans. Cash Basis of Accounting

$$= 10{,}50{,}000 + 1{,}35{,}000 - 3{,}90{,}000$$
$$(5{,}10{,}000 - 1{,}20{,}000) - 60{,}000$$
$$= ₹\ 7{,}35{,}000$$

Accrual Basis of Accounting

$$= 12{,}00{,}000 - 5{,}10{,}000 = ₹\ 6{,}90{,}000$$

18. During the financial year, Aman had cash sales of ₹ 4,50,000 and credit sales of ₹ 3,00,000. Expenses incurred for the year were ₹ 3,50,000 out of which ₹ 1,50,000 are still to be paid. Competency Based Que

Find out Aman's income following

(i) Cash basis of accounting.

(ii) Accrual basis of accounting.

Ans. (i) Cash Basis of Accounting

$$= 4{,}50{,}000 - 2{,}00{,}000\ (3{,}50{,}000 - 1{,}50{,}000)$$
$$= ₹\ 2{,}50{,}000$$

(ii) Accrual Basis of Accounting

$$= 4{,}50{,}000 + 3{,}00{,}000 - 3{,}50{,}000$$
$$= ₹\ 4{,}00{,}000$$

19. What is the need for accounting standards?

Ans. The need for accounting standards arises from the following reasons

(i) They facilitate transparent and meaningful reporting of financial information.

(ii) They reduce accounting alternatives to reasonable and practical level.

(iii) They enhance comparability of financial statements.

(iv) They encourage consistency in accounting practices.

20. Differentiate between accrual basis and cash basis of accounting.

Ans. Differences between accrual and cash basis of accounting are

Basis	Accrual Basis of Accounting	Cash Basis of Accounting
Nature of Transactions	Both cash and credit transactions are recorded.	Only cash transactions are recorded.
Advance/ Outstanding Incomes and Expenses	These are adjusted in profit and loss account and shown in balance sheet.	These are not adjusted in profit and loss account nor shown in balance sheet.
Reliability of Profits	Correct profit or loss is ascertained because it records both cash and credit transactions.	Correct profit or loss is not ascertained because it records only cash transactions.
Accounting Knowledge	The accrual basis of accounting requires accounting knowledge, as many adjustments of advance, outstanding, capital and revenue are to be carried out in financial statements.	It does not require much of accounting knowledge, as only cash receipts and cash payments are considered for financial statements.
Legal Position	Accrual basis of accounting is recognised by the Companies Act, 2013.	Cash basis of accounting is not recognised by the Companies Act, 2013.
Acceptability	Accrual basis of accounting is more acceptable in business, as it reveals correct income and expense besides assets and liabilities.	Cash basis of accounting is not acceptable in business as it does not reveal the required information.

21. Differentiate between accounting standards and Indian accounting standards.

Ans. Differences between Accounting Standards (AS) and Indian Accounting Standards (Ind-AS) are

Basis	AS	Ind-AS
Basis	They are based on International Accounting Standards (IAS).	They are based on International Financial Reporting Standards (IFRS).
Rule/Principle Based	AS are rule based.	Ind-AS are principle based.
Language	They are drafted in technical language.	They are drafted in simple and clear language.
Concept	AS follow the concept of historical cost.	Ind-AS are based on the fair value of fixed asset.
Uniformity	They do not ensure uniformity in financial reporting.	They ensure uniformity in financial reporting.

22. State any ten transactions on which GST is not levied.

Ans. GST is not levied on following transactionsc

(i) Depreciation/Amortisation

(ii) Amount deposited into bank

(iii) Amount withdrawn from bank

(iv) Health services

(v) Payment of travelling expenses

(vi) Supply of services to the government

(vii) Cheque issued for purchase
(viii) Payment of electricity and water bills.
(ix) Advance received against sale
(x) Educational services

Long Answer Type Questions

23. Explain the features of accounting principles.

Ans. Features of accounting principles are as follows

(i) **Man-made**
Accounting principles are man-made. They are derived by men based on practical experience and reason. However, they lack in universal applicability as they are not laboratory tested like principles of physical and other natural sciences.

(ii) **Flexible**
Accounting principles are flexible and not rigid. They keep on changing with the passage of time and in response to changes in business practices and government policies. They also change according to the need of users of accounting information.

(iii) **Generally Accepted**
The general acceptance of the accounting principles or practices depends upon, how well they meet the following three criteria

- **Relevance** A principle is relevant to the extent, it results in information that is meaningful and useful to the user of the accounting information.
- **Objectivity** A principle is objective to the extent the accounting information is not influenced by personal bias or judgement of those who provide it.
It also implies verifiability which means that there is some way of ascertaining the correctness of the information reported.
- **Feasibility** A principle is feasible to the extent, it can be implemented without much complexity or cost.

24. "The accounting concepts and accounting standards are generally referred to as the essence of financial accounting." Comment. NCERT; Competency Based Que

Ans. Financial accounting is concerned with the preparation of financial statements and to provide financial information to various accounting users. It is performed according to the basic accounting concepts like business entity, money measurement, consistency, conservatism, etc.
However, these concepts allow various alternatives to treat the same transaction. This leads to wrong interpretation of financial results by external users due to the problem of inconsistency and incomparability of financial results among different business entities.
In order to remove inconsistency and incomparability and to bring uniformity in preparation of the financial statements, accounting standards are being issued in India by the Institute of Chartered Accountants of India.
Hence, accounting standards and accounting concepts are referred as the essence of financial accounting.

25. "It is assumed that business will be continued for a fairly long time."
Identify and explain practical implications of the concept referred by statement. Competency Based Que

Ans. The statement given states about going concern concept. According to this concept, it is assumed that the business firm would continue its operations for a fairly long period of time and would not be liquidated in the near future.
All the transactions are recorded in the books on the assumption that it is a continuing enterprise.
e.g. If a machinery is purchased which would last, for the next 10 years then, the cost of the machinery will be spread over the next 10 years for calculating the net profit or loss for each year.
The practical implications of this concept are

(i) This concept facilitates recording fixed assets on the basis of their cost value and maximum life. Market value of the assets is irrelevant for accounting of these assets.
(ii) It is due to this concept, that a distinction is made between capital and revenue expenditure.
(iii) It is due to this assumption profits are computed every year so that the performance of a business can be adjudged.
Expenses of a business are charged to its revenues, to find out profit.
(iv) It is due to this concept, that the total cost of the machinery is not to be treated as an expense in the year of purchase itself.

26. Why is it important to adopt a consistent basis for the preparation of financial statements? Explain. NCERT

Ans. For making the accounting information meaningful to its internal and external users, it is important that such information is reliable as well as comparable.
The comparability of information is required both to make inter-firm comparisons i.e. to see how a firm has performed as compared to the other firms, as well as to make inter-period comparison i.e. how it has performed as compared to the previous years.
This becomes possible only if the information provided by the financial statements is based on consistent accounting policies, principles and practices.

27. "A transaction is recorded at the time when it takes place not at the time when settlement is done." Identify the concept and explain. Competency Based Que

Ans. The given statement states about accrual concept. According to this concept, a transaction is recorded at the time, it takes place and not at the time when settlement is done.

In other words, revenue is recorded when sales are made or services are rendered and it is irrelevant as to when cash is received against such sales.

Similarly, expenses are recorded at the time when they are incurred and it is irrelevant as to when payment is made in cash for such expenses.

Thus, to find out correct profit and to show true financial position of an enterprise at the end of accounting period, all expenses and income belonging to that particular accounting period are shown whether cash has been paid or received or not.

e.g. Goods are sold to Raju on 1st January, 2022 on a credit of 3 months. In this instance, sale will be recorded on 1st January, 2022 although the amount will be received on 1st April, 2022.

28. "Capital is a liability for the business." Explain this statement with the principle applied. Competency Based Que

Or **Explain the business entity principle with the help of an example.**

Ans. According to business entity principle, business is treated as a separate entity distinct from its owners. Accounting information is recorded considering this principle.

All transactions are recorded from the point of view of business and not from the point of businessman/owner.

The capital introduced by the owner is treated as a liability from the point of view of business. Business owes money to the owner to the extent of his capital just like it owes money to lenders and creditors.

Due to this reason, interest on capital is treated as a business expense. Also, because of this principle, owner's personal property, investments, expenditures are kept separate from the recording of business transactions in the books.

e.g Ram started his business with cash. Purchased stock, machinery and furniture and deposited money into the bank account and also kept some cash in hand. From accounting point of view, cash introduced by Ram is a liability for the business and is referred to as capital.

The assets purchased are of the business and not of the owner.

Also, if the owner withdraws some money for his personal use, it will be termed as drawings and it will reduce the cash (assets) and capital at the same time.

29. What is the money measurement concept? Which one factor can make it difficult to compare the monetary values of one year with the monetary values of another year? NCERT

Or **Explain the money measurement principle.**

Ans. According to this principle, only those transactions which can be measured and expressed in terms of money are recorded in the books of accounts. Non-financial or non-monetary transactions do not find any place in the accounting records. e.g. Sale of goods or payment of expenses or receipt of income, etc. will be recorded as these can be expressed in monetary terms.

However, dispute among the owners or managers, appointment of a manager, efficiency of management, quality of product, etc. will not be recorded in the books of accounts simply because it cannot be converted or recorded in terms of money.

The factor which can make it difficult to compare the monetary values of one year with the monetary values of another year is inflation. Due to the changes in price, the value of money does not remain the same over a period of time. The value of rupee today on account of rise in price is much less than what it was, say ten years back.

30. "It refers to the span of time at the end of which financial statements are prepared." Identify and explain the concept. Competency Based Que

Ans. The statement here states about accounting period concept. Accounting period refers to the span of time at the end of which the financial statements (profit and loss account and balance sheet) of an enterprise are prepared, to know the profitability and financial position of the business.

It is also known as periodicity principle or time period principle. According to this principle, the life of a business is divided into smaller periods (usually one year), so that, its performance can be measured on regular basis or intervals.

According to the amended Income Tax Law, a business has to compulsorily adopt financial year beginning on 1st April and ending on 31st March in the next calendar year, as its accounting period.

Apart from this, companies whose shares are listed on the stock exchange, are required to publish quarterly results to ascertain the profitability and financial position at the end of every three months period.

31. Explain the full disclosure principle. Why should information be fully disclosed?

Ans. According to full disclosure principle, there should be reporting of all the significant information relating to the economic affairs of the business and it should be complete and understandable.

e.g. Reasons for low turnover or destruction of plant and machinery due to natural calamities should be disclosed.

Information should be fully disclosed because

(i) Since, one of the objectives of accounting information is to communicate accounting information to various users, it is important to provide complete information to them, so that they can take right decisions at the right time on the basis of the financial statements of the business.

(ii) Disclosure of complete and true information projects a correct picture of financial position of the business.

32. "Only those transactions should be recorded which are material and has ability to influence the decision of user." Explain the concept referred above with an example. Competency Based Que

Ans. The concept referred in given statement is materiality concept. According to this principle, only those transactions should be recorded which are material or relevant for the preparation of financial statements. All immaterial facts should be ignored.

An information is material, if it has the ability to influence or affect the decision-making of various parties interested in accounting information, contained in financial statements.

According to American Accounting Association (AAA), an item should be regarded as material if there is a reason to believe that knowledge of it would influence the decision of an informed investor.

e.g. ₹ 1,00,000 spent on advertising is material for a business having turnover of ₹ 3,00,000 whereas, it is immaterial for a business having turnover of ₹ 30,00,00,000.

33. Discuss the concept based on the premise 'do not anticipate profits but provide for all losses'. NCERT

Ans. The concept of conservatism (also called 'prudence') states that 'do not anticipate profits but provide for all losses'. In other words, this principle suggests that we should make provisions for probable future expenses but ignore any future probable gain, until it actually happens.

This approach of providing for the losses but not recognising the gains until realised is called conservation approach. e.g. Closing stock is valued at lower of cost or net realisable value, as per this concept only.

The merits of using this concept are

(i) It provides guidance for recording transactions in the books of accounts and is based on the policy of playing safe.

(ii) It ensures that the financial statements present a realistic picture of the working affairs of the business and does not present a picture which will mislead the users of accounting information.

However, excess use of this concept leads to creation of secret reserves because liabilities get overstated and assets get understated.

34. "According to this concept, adjustment of prepaid/ outstanding expenses and incomes are required." Discuss the concept referred in above statement. Competency Based Que

Ans. The statement refers to matching concept. According to this concept, expenses incurred in an accounting period should be matched with revenues during that period i.e. when a revenue is recognised in a period, then the cost related to that revenue also needs to be recognised in that period to enable calculation of correct profits of the business.

Business concerns should follow this concept because of the following reasons

(i) Due to this concept, adjustments are made for expenses not paid (outstanding expenses) or for those paid in advance (prepaid expenses).

(ii) This concept should be followed while preparing financial statements to have a true and fair view of the profitability and financial position of a business firm.

35. An accountant of ABC Ltd. recorded the revenue at the date when cash was received. Is he right? Give the valid reason for your answer explaining the relevent principle. Competency Based Que

Ans. No, accountant of ABC Ltd. has wrongly recognised the revenue. In the given situation, accountant has violated the principle of 'revenue recognition'. The concept of revenue recognition requires that the revenue for a business transaction should be recorded in the accounts only when it is realised. Revenue is assumed to be realised when a legal right to receive it arises i.e. the point of time when goods have been sold or service has been rendered.

In short, it is the sale or change of ownership which decides the revenue or expense and not the actual payment or receipt regarding such sale or expense.

e.g. If a business sells goods in January, 2022 and receives the amount from such sale in April, 2022 then revenue will be considered as recognised in January, 2022 when sale is made and not when payments is received from such sale.

Similarly, if a business receives advance in January, 2022 for a sale to happen in April, 2022, then revenue will be recognised when sale takes place i.e. April, 2022 and not when money was received.

03

CHAPTER

Source documents are evidence of a business transaction which provide the basis for recording entries in the books of accounts.

▼ **YOUR STUDY GOALS**

3.1 Source Documents
3.2 Vouchers
3.3 Accounting Equation

▼ **YOUR PRACTICE GOAL**

- Topicwise Solved Questions (20 Solved Questions)
- Numerical Questions [26 Questions (Unsolved)]
- Theoretical Questions [9 Questions (with answers)]
- Objective Questions (60 Qs ; MCQs, A-R, Statements, Matching, Case)

Source Documents and Accounting Equation

3.1 Source Documents

Various transactions are made everyday such as purchase and sale of goods and services, payment or receipt of cash, etc. All these transactions recorded in the books of accounts are evidenced by a document which is called source document or voucher.

Such documents contain details of transaction and are prepared at the time, a transaction is entered to. So, these documents are also known as supporting documents. e.g. Bills of purchase, invoices for sales, debit and credit notes, etc.

Most Common Source Documents

1. Cash Memo

- It is a written document prepared by the seller for the goods sold against cash.
- It includes details of goods sold, quantity, rate, amount received, date, etc. It does not contain party name usually to whom goods are sold.
- Cash transactions are recorded in the books of accounts on the basis of these cash memos.

Specimen of a Cash Memo

Cash Memo Tata Jewellers
225, MG Road, Delhi

No. Date : 10th February, 2024

Quantity	Descriptions	Rate (₹)	Amt (₹)	P
1	Silver Anklet	3,000	3,000	...
2	Gold Rings	15,000	30,000	...
			33,000	...
	(+) GST @ 12%		3,960	...
			36,960	...
	No. 340 Debit Purchases Credit Cash			

Goods once sold will not be taken back For Tata Jewellers

2. Invoice and Bill

- When a seller sells goods on credit, a sales invoice which contains the name of the party to whom goods are sold, is prepared. Apart the name of party, it contains rate, quantity and total amount of sale.
- Original copy is sent to purchaser and duplicate copy is kept by the seller for recording the transaction.
- For the seller, it means invoice of credit sale and for the purchaser, it means bill of credit purchase.

Specimen of an Invoice or a Bill

ABC Suppliers Ltd.
222, Begum Bridge, Meerut Cantt, 250001

No. 3978 Date : 10th April, 2024

Vikram Enterprises
Lodhi Road, Delhi ....Dr

Quantity	Particulars	Rate (₹)	Amt (₹)	P
1	Air Conditioner	30,000	30,000	...
2	Microwave	20,000	40,000	...
			70,000	...
	(+) GST @ 12%		8,400	...
			78,400	...
	(+) Forwarding and Delivery Charges		1,000	...
	Total		79,400	...

Rupees Seventy Nine Thousand Four Hundred Only
E.&.O.E. Sales Manager

3. Pay-in-Slip

- It is used for depositing cash or cheques into bank account.
- It has a counterfoil which is returned to the depositor with cashier's signature and bank's stamp as receipt.

Specimen of a Pay-in-Slip

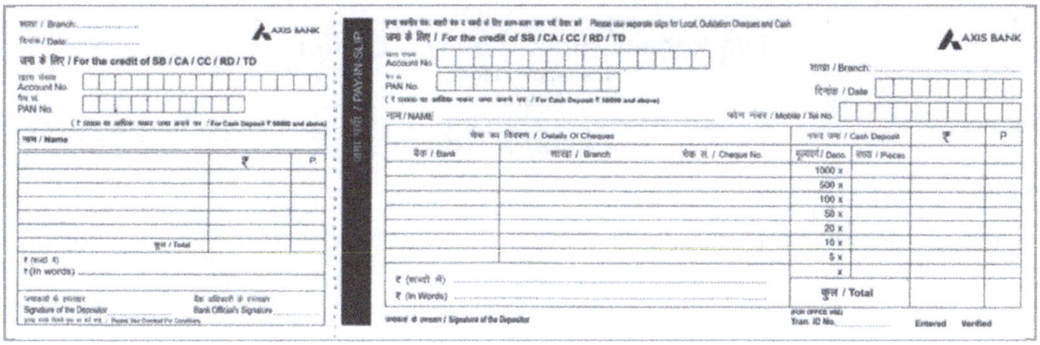

4. Cheque

- It is a document in writing drawn upon a specified banker and payable on demand.
- It must be dated and signed by the drawer.

Specimen of a Cheque

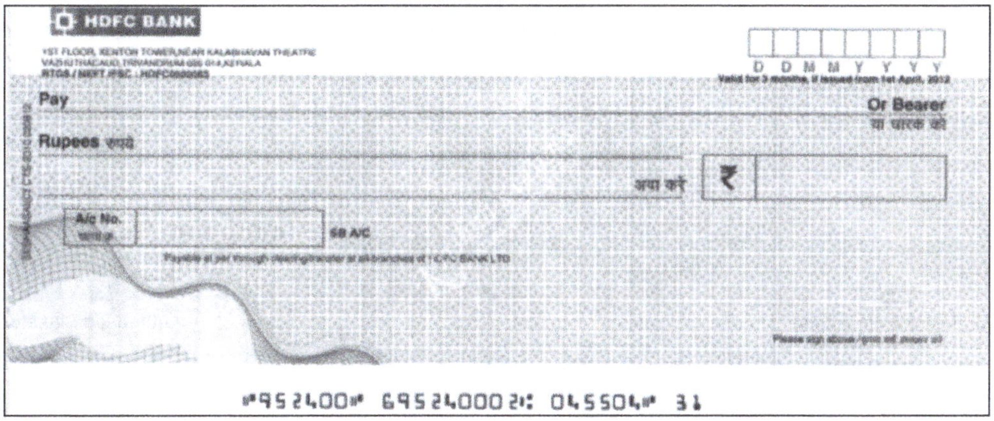

5. Debit Note

- A debit note is prepared by the buyer when he returns goods to the seller. It is sent to inform about debit made in the seller's account.
- A debit note contains the details of goods returned such as quantity, total amount, date of return, etc.

Specimen of a Debit Note

M/s Arihant Publications (India) Ltd.
Transport Nagar,
Meerut

No. : 5456 | **DEBIT NOTE** | 5th April, 2024

Against : **M/s Book Mart, New Delhi**
Goods returned as per delivery
Challan No. 387 ₹ 6,235
Rupees Six Thousand Two Hundred Thirty Five Only

TR Mani
Manager

6. Credit Note

- It is prepared by the seller and sent to buyer to inform that credit has been made in his account along with the reasons mentioned in it.
- It is an intimation to the buyer that goods returned by him has been received by seller.

Specimen of a Credit Note

M/s Arihant Publications (India) Ltd.
Transport Nagar,
Meerut

No. : 879

CREDIT NOTE

25th April, 2024

To
M/s Unique Books, Chandigarh
Goods received as per delivery challan
No. 4655 dated 22.2.2023 valued
at Rupees Eighteen Thousand Six Hundred Seventy Only

₹ 18,670
TR Mani
Manager

7. Receipt

- It is issued to the customer against cash received from him.
- Original copy is handed over to the customer and duplicate copy is kept for record.
- It contains all the details such as date, amount, party name and nature of payment.

Specimen of a Receipt

Sujata Watches
Abulane, Meerut

No. 15137

Date : 28.06.2024

Received with thanks from M/s Arihant Publications India Ltd, Meerut a sum of

Rupees Fifty Two Thousand Eight Hundred Seventy Four only in Cash/

Cheque No. 446546 dated 01.07.2024 drawn on State Bank of India, Baghpat Road, Meerut on

account of Invoice No. 54564 dated 28.06.2024

Note : Cheque are subject to realisation.

Authorised Signatory

3.2 Vouchers

Vouchers are documents evidencing a business transaction. They contain the details of the accounts to be debited and credited. Vouchers are prepared on the basis of source documents such as cash memo, invoice, receipts, pay-in-slip, cheque, debit and credit notes, etc.

Preparation of Vouchers

- There is no specific format of a voucher. Format depends upon nature, requirement and convenience of business.
- To distinguish various vouchers, different colour papers and different fonts of printing can be used.

Essential Elements

A standard voucher must contain the following essential elements

- It should be printed on a good quality paper.
- Name of the firm must be printed on the top.
- Date of transaction should be entered. Date of recording the transaction is irrelevant.
- The number of the voucher should be in a serial order.
- Name of the account to be debited or credited should be mentioned.
- Debit or credit amount should be written in figures against the amount.
- Description of the transaction should be given account wise.
- The person who prepares the voucher must mention his name alongwith signature.
- The name and signature of the authorised person are to be mentioned on the voucher.

Types of Vouchers

Type	Description
Supporting Vouchers	• These documents come into existence when a transaction is entered into. • These are also known as source vouchers or source documents. e.g. Cash memo, credit note, debit note, receipt, etc. • Its features are written document, contains details of transaction, proof of a transaction, signed by the maker.
Accounting Vouchers	• These are called secondary vouchers. • These are prepared on the basis of supporting vouchers for recording of a transaction. • These are prepared by an accountant and signed by an authorised person. • These vouchers are prepared for cash as well as non-cash transactions.

Types of Accounting Vouchers

Accounting vouchers may be classified into cash vouchers and non-cash vouchers.

1. **Cash Vouchers** These are prepared for cash transactions only. They include receipt and payment through cheques. Cash vouchers can be classified as debit vouchers and credit vouchers.

   (i) **Debit Vouchers**

   - These vouchers are prepared for transactions involving cash payments.
   - e.g. Cash paid to creditors, furniture purchased for cash, etc.
   - A format of debit voucher is shown below

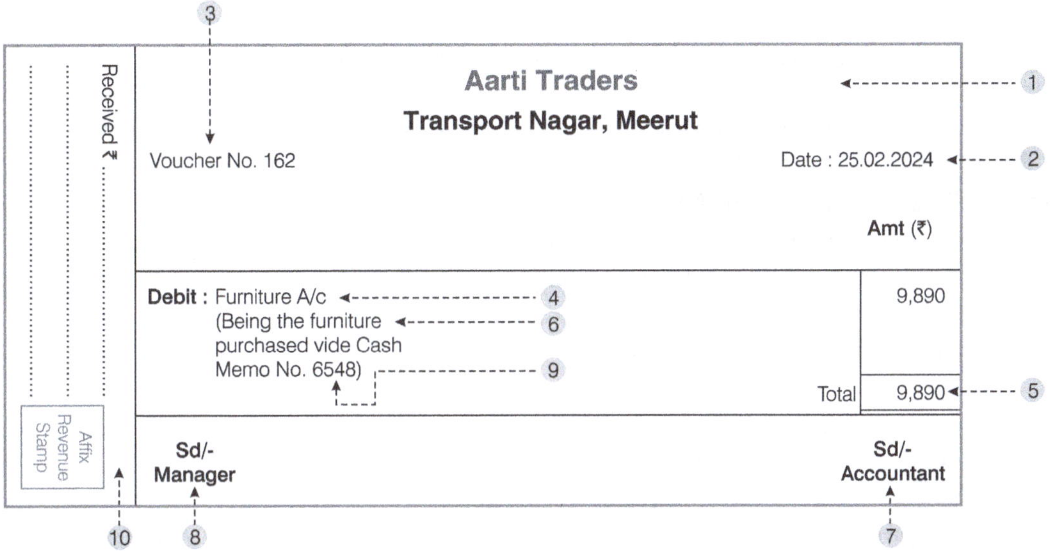

Contents

1 Name and address of the organisation	2 Date of preparing voucher
3 Accounting voucher number	4 Title of the account debited
5 Net amount of transaction	6 Narration (i.e. a brief description of the transaction)
7 Signature of the person preparing it	8 Signature of the authorised signatory
9 Supporting voucher number	10 A document in lieu of supporting voucher

   - If the supporting voucher is not available, then the receipt portion of the debit voucher is filled and is used as supporting voucher.

(ii) **Credit Vouchers**

- Credit vouchers are prepared to record the transactions involving cash receipts.
- e.g. Goods sold for cash, received commission in cash, etc.
- A format of credit voucher is shown below

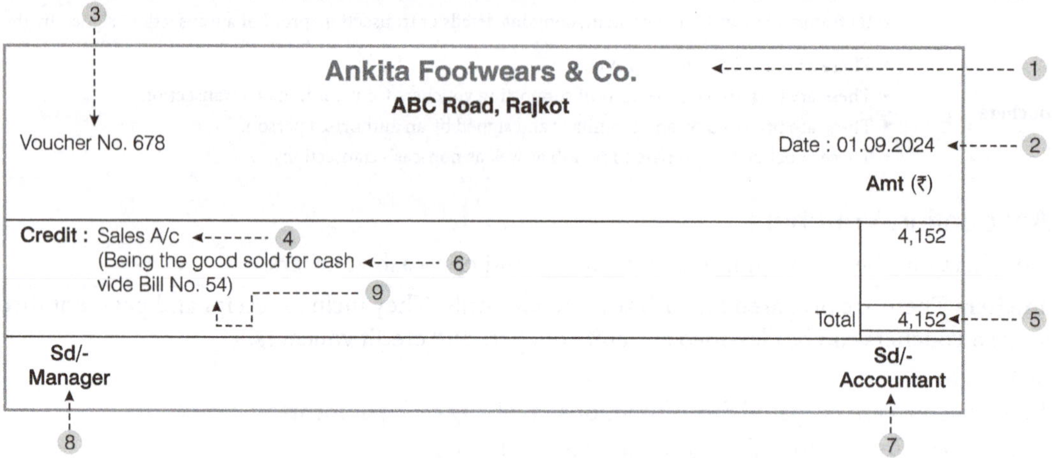

Contents

1. Name and address of the organisation
2. Date of preparing the voucher
3. Accounting voucher number
4. Title of the account credited
5. Net amount of transaction
6. Narration (i.e. a brief description of the transaction)
7. Signature of the person preparing it
8. Signature of the authorised signatory
9. Supporting voucher number

2. **Non-cash Vouchers or Transfer Vouchers**
   - These vouchers are prepared for non-cash transactions.
   - These vouchers are also known as transfer vouchers.
   - e.g Credit sale of goods, return of goods purchased, etc.
   - A format of non-cash voucher is shown below

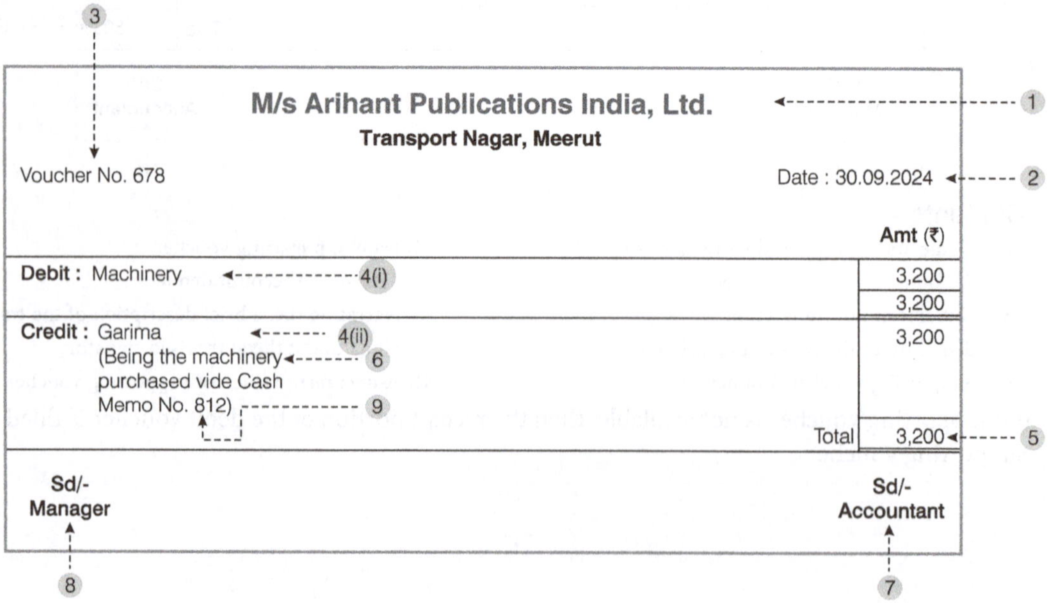

Contents

1 Name and address of the organisation
2 Date of preparing voucher
3 Accounting voucher number
4 (i) Title of account to be debited (ii) Title of account to be credited
5 Net amount of transaction
6 Narration (i.e. a brief description of the transaction)
7 Signature of the person preparing it
8 Signature of the authorised signatory
9 Supporting voucher number

Compound Voucher

A voucher which shows multiple debits and one credit or which shows multiple credits and one debit is called compound voucher.

A compound voucher may be of two types

- **Debit Voucher** Voucher showing transactions that contains multiple debits and one credit is called debit voucher.
- **Credit Voucher** Voucher showing transactions that contains multiple credits but one debit is called credit voucher.

3.3 Accounting Equation

It is based on **dual aspect** concept which states that every transaction has two aspects. It is a mathematical expression which shows that total **assets** are equal to total of **capital** and **liabilities**.

It is expressed as Assets = Capital + Liabilities

It is also known as **balance sheet** equation.

It is very important to know about a balance sheet before understanding an accounting equation. An example of balance sheet in T form is shown below

Balance Sheet

Capital and Liabilities		Amt (₹)	Assets	Amt (₹)
Capital		1,00,000	Cash and Bank	20,000
Liabilities			Stock	25,000
Creditors	10,000		Debtors	15,000
Outstanding Salary	5,000		Furniture	20,000
Bank Overdraft	15,000	30,000	Machine	50,000
		1,30,000		1,30,000

- In the above balance sheet, we can see that assets are recorded on right hand side and liabilities are recorded on the left hand side.
- Important point is to understand that both sides of balance sheet are always equal because assets are purchased either by the proprietors fund (capital) or from the external's parties funds (outsider's liabilities).
- The above balance sheet shows that assets worth ₹ 1,00,000 have been purchased from the capital and remaining assets of ₹ 30,000 have been purchased from the funds of external parties.

The above position can be expressed in the form of an accounting equation

Assets	=	Capital	+	Liabilities
₹ 1,30,000	=	₹ 1,00,000	+	₹ 30,000

or

Liabilities	=	Assets	−	Capital
₹ 30,000	=	₹ 1,30,000	−	₹ 1,00,000

or

Capital	=	Assets	−	Liabilities
₹ 1,00,000	=	₹ 1,30,000	−	₹ 30,000

Practical Steps involved in Developing an Accounting Equation

Step 1 Find out the affected accounts i.e. Cash A/c, Bank A/c, etc.
e.g. If goods are purchased for cash ₹ 20,000 then following accounts are affected in this transaction.
(i) Goods/Stock A/c (ii) Cash A/c

Step 2 Identify the type of accounts affected
In the above example, Goods A/c comes under assets and Cash A/c also comes under assets.

Step 3 Show the effect on the appropriate side of an equation and ensure total assets are equal to total of liabilities and capital.

Example Rohan purchased a machine worth ₹ 50,000 on credit from Anaya Ltd.

Sol. Due to the above transaction, following accounts are affected

1. Machine A/c (Asset) → Increase in the firm.
2. Anaya Ltd. (Liability) → Also increasing as machine is purchased on credit.

∴Accounting equation will be shown as follows

Assets	=	Capital	+	Liabilities
Machine	=	0	+	Anaya Ltd.
50,000				50,000

Effects of Various Transactions on Accounting Equation

Transaction	Account Affected	Nature	Remark
Commenced business with cash	Cash A/c (Increase) Capital A/c (Increase)	Asset Capital	Cash introduced by proprietor will increase cash and capital also.
Purchased goods/Fixed assets for cash	Stock/Fixed Assets A/c (Increase) Cash A/c (Decrease)	Asset Asset	Stock/Fixed assets will be increased and cash will be decreased.
Cash withdrawn for personal use	Cash A/c (Decrease) Capital A/c (Decrease)	Asset Capital	Withdrawn for personal use is called drawing. It is reduced from capital.
Purchased goods/Fixed assets on credit	Stock/Fixed Asset A/c (Increase) Liability (Increase) (Creditors)	Asset Liability	Purchasing on credit increases liability hence stock/fixed asset will be increased and liability will be also increased.
Purchased goods for cash as well as on credit	Stock A/c (Increase) Cash A/c (Decrease) Creditors A/c (Increase)	Asset Asset Liability	Purchasing goods for cash will reduce cash. Purchasing goods on credit will increase liability. Total stock will be added to assets.
Sold goods for cash	Cash A/c (Increase) Stock A/c (Decrease)	Asset Asset	As goods are sold hence stock will be decreased and cash will be increased.
Sold goods for cash at a profit	Cash A/c (Increase) Stock A/c (Decrease) Capital A/c (Increase) (With profit)	Asset Asset Capital	Profit is added to capital hence capital will be increased. As goods are sold out, its cost will be reduced from stock.
Sold goods for cash and some goods on credit	Cash A/c (Increase) Stock A/c (Decrease) Debtors A/c (Increase)	Asset Asset Asset	Selling goods on credit increases debtors i.e. asset. Cost of goods will be deducted from stock and whatever cash is received will be added.
Return of goods by a customer if goods were sold at profit	Stock A/c (Increase) Debtor A/c (Decrease) Capital A/c (Decrease)	Asset Asset Capital	Profit will be reduced back because it was added earlier. Stock will be increased at cost. Also debtor will be reduced.
Return of goods to a supplier	Stock A/c (Decrease) Creditors A/c (Decrease)	Asset Liability	Stock will be decreased at cost. Also liability will be decreased.
Goods destroyed by fire	Stock A/c (Decrease) Capital A/c (Decrease)	Asset Capital	As goods are lost, stock will be decreased by its cost. Capital will be reduced because loss are deducted from it.

Transaction	Account Affected	Nature	Remark
Payment received from a customer to whom discount was allowed	Cash A/c (Increase) Debtors A/c (Decrease) Capital A/c (Decrease)	Asset Asset Capital	Discount is an expense hence it is decreased from capital. Cash is received hence added to cash and debtors will be reduced.
Payment made to supplier who allowed cash discount	Cash A/c (Decrease) Creditors A/c (Decrease) Capital A/c (Increase)	Asset Liability Capital	Discount received is an income hence added to capital.
Loan taken	Cash/Bank A/c (Increase) Lender A/c (Increase)	Asset Liability	Cash or bank balance will be increased and liability will be also increased.
Repayment of a loan with interest	Cash/Bank A/c (Decrease) Lender A/c (Decrease) Capital A/c (Decrease)	Asset Liability Capital	Interest is an expense hence decreased from capital. Liability will be also decreased with the cash.
Expenses paid e.g. Salary, rent, etc.	Cash/Bank A/c (Decrease) Capital A/c (Decrease)	Asset Capital	Expenses are deducted from capital hence capital is decreased.
Expense due but not paid i.e. outstanding expenses	Outstanding Expense A/c (Increase) Capital A/c (Decrease)	Liability Capital	Expenses are deducted from capital and added to liabilities as these are to be paid.
Expense paid in advance	Cash/Bank A/c (Decrease) Prepaid Expenses A/c (Increase)	Asset Asset	Advance expenses are an asset. Cash will be reduced also.
Income received e.g. Rent received	Cash/Bank A/c (Increase) Capital A/c (Increase)	Asset Capital	Incomes are added to capital. Cash or bank will be increased with the amount also.
Income earned but not received i.e. accrued income	Accrued Income A/c (Increase) Capital A/c (Increase)	Asset Capital	Accrued income is to be received hence it is an asset. Capital will be increased because it is an income.
Income received in advance	Cash/Bank A/c (Increase) Advance Income A/c (Increase)	Asset Liability	Advance income is a liability hence liability will be increased. Cash or bank account will be increased with the amount.
Interest on drawings	Capital A/c (Increase) Capital A/c (Decrease)	Capital Capital	Interest on drawings is an income for the firm and charged from owner on his drawings. Hence, capital is reduced as well as increased.
Interest on capital	Capital A/c (Increase) Capital A/c (Decrease)	Capital Capital	Interest on capital is an income for owner and an expense for firm. Hence, it is added and deducted from capital.
Bad debts	Debtors A/c (Decrease) Capital A/c (Decrease)	Asset Capital	Bad debts are loss hence capital is reduced. Also debtor who has been insolvent is not able to pay. Hence, amount will be deducted from debtors.
Received amount against bad debt written-off last year	Cash/Bank A/c (Increase) Capital A/c (Increase)	Asset Capital	It is called bad debt recovered and it is an income in current year hence added to capital.
Depreciation charged on fixed asset	Fixed Asset A/c e.g. Furniture (Decrease) Capital A/c (Decrease)	Asset Capital	Depreciation is a fall in value of a fixed asset, hence, it is deducted from respective fixed asset. On the other hand, it is deducted from capital as it is an expense.
Goods destroyed by fire	Stock A/c (Decrease) Capital A/c (Decrease)	Asset Capital	As goods are lost by fire, hence, stock will be reduced at cost. On the other hand, it is deducted from capital as it as a loss.
Goods given as charity and sample	Stock A/c (Decrease) Capital A/c (Decrease)	Asset Capital	Goods given as charity is an expense hence it is decreased from capital. Stock will be reduced at cost also.

Mind Map

SOURCE DOCUMENTS AND ACCOUNTING EQUATION

1 Meaning of Source Documents

Various transactions are made everyday such as purchase and sale of goods and services, payment or receipt of cash, etc. All these transactions recorded in the books of accounts are evidenced by a document which is called source document or voucher.
Such documents contain details of transaction and are prepared at the time, a transaction is entered to. So, these documents are also known as supporting documents.

2 Most Common Source Documents

- **Cash Memo** It is a written document prepared by the seller for the goods sold against cash.
- **Invoice** It is prepared by the seller when he/she sells goods on credit.
- **Pay-in-slip** It is used for depositing cash or cheques into bank account.
- **Cheque** It is a document in writing drawn upon a specified banker and payable on demand.
- **Debit Note** It is prepared by the buyer when he returns goods to the seller.
- **Credit Note** It is prepared by the seller and sent to buyer to inform that credit has been made in his account along with the reasons mentioned in it.
- **Reciept** It is issued to the customer against cash received from him.

5 Accounting Equation

- It is based on dual aspect concept which states that every transaction has two aspects. It is a mathematical expression which shows that total assets are equal to total of capital and liabilities
- It is also known as balance sheet equation

Accounting Equation is expressed as
Assets = Capital + Liabilities

4 Types of Accounting Vouchers

Cash Vouchers These are prepared for cash transactions only. They can be classified as

- **Debit Vouchers** These vouchers are prepared for transactions involving cash payments.
- **Credit Vouchers** These vouchers are prepared to record the transactions involving cash receipts.

Non-cash Vouchers These vouchers are prepared for non-cash transactions.

3 Vouchers

- Vouchers are documents evidencing a business transaction. They contain the details of the accounts to be debited and credited. Vouchers are prepared on the basis of source documents such as cash memo, invoice, reciepts, etc
- There are two types of vouchers, i.e. supporting vouchers and accounting vouchers

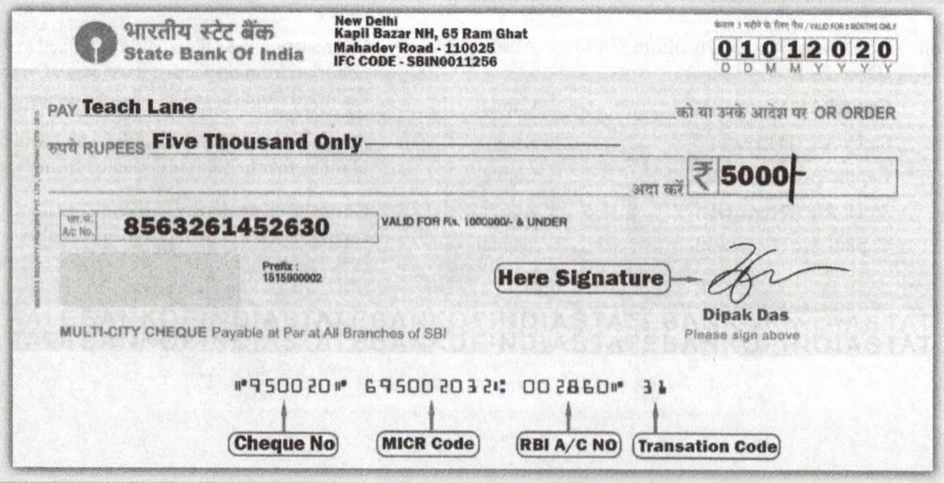

Topicwise Solved Questions

Vouchers

Solved Question 1 **Prepare debit vouchers on the basis of transactions given below for Aakash Traders, Delhi.**

Date	Particulars	Amt (₹)
2024		
May 20	Salary paid for the month of April, 2024	10,000
May 25	Purchased furniture for office by cash vide Cash Memo No. 1248	12,000

Sol. (i)

Received (₹) ....

Affix Revenue Stamp

Aakash Traders

Voucher No. 1	**Delhi**	**Date** : 20.05.2024

	Amt (₹)
Debit : Salary A/c (Being salary paid for the month of April, 2024)	10,000
Total	10,000

Sd/-
Manager

Sd/-
Accountant

(ii)

Received (₹) ....

Affix Revenue Stamp

Aakash Traders

Voucher No. 2	**Delhi**	**Date** : 25.05.2024

	Amt (₹)
Debit : Furniture A/c (Being furniture purchased for cash vide Cash Memo No. 1248)	12,000
Total	12,000

Sd/-
Manager

Sd/-
Accountant

Solved Question 2 **Prepare credit vouchers from the following information gathered from supporting vouchers of M/s Raghav Readymade Store, Kanpur.**

Date	Particulars	Amt (₹)
2024		
Jun 10	Received cash from Riya vide Cash Receipt No. 623	3,500
Jun 22	Sold goods vide Cash Memo No. 6528	6,000

Sol. (i)

M/s Raghav Readymade Store		
Voucher No. 1	Kanpur	Date : 10.06.2024
		Amt (₹)
Credit : Riya (Being the amount received vide Cash Receipt No. 623)		3,500
	Total	3,500
Sd/- Manager		Sd/- Accountant

(ii)

M/s Raghav Readymade Store		
Voucher No. 2	Kanpur	Date : 22.06.2024
		Amt (₹)
Credit : Sales A/c (Being goods sold for cash vide Cash Memo No. 6528)		6,000
	Total	6,000
Sd/- Manager		Sd/- Accountant

Solved Question 3 **On the basis of the following information, prepare non-cash voucher or transfer voucher for Tanya Electrical Co.**

Date	Particulars
2024	
Jul 27	Purchased 200 tubelights @ ₹ 100 each and 4 table fans @ ₹ 2,500 each on credit from Shakti Electrical Ltd.

Sol. (i)

M/s Tanya Electrical Co.		
Voucher No. 564	Vijay Nagar, Agra	Date : 27.07.2024
		Amt (₹)
Debit : Purchase A/c		30,000
Credit : Shakti Electricals Ltd. (Being 200 tubelights @ ₹ 100 each and 4 table fans @ ₹ 2,500 each purchased on credit vide Credit Bill No. 425)		30,000
	Total	30,000
Sd/- Manager		Sd/- Accountant

Accounting Equations

Solved Question 4 **Calculate total assets, if capital is ₹ 3,00,000 and creditors are ₹ 1,00,000.**

Sol. Capital = ₹ 3,00,000
Creditors = ₹ 1,00,000
Assets = ?
Assets = Capital + Liabilities = 3,00,000 + 1,00,000 = ₹ 4,00,000

Solved Question 5 **Calculate capital, if total assets amounted to ₹ 3,00,000 and liabilities ₹ 2,00,000.**

Sol. Assets = ₹ 3,00,000
Liabilities = ₹ 2,00,000
Capital = ?
Capital = Assets – Liabilities = 3,00,000 – 2,00,000 = ₹ 1,00,000

Solved Question 6 **Ramya started her business on 1st April, 2024 with capital of ₹ 1,20,000. On 31st March, 2025, her closing assets and closing liabilities were ₹ 1,50,000 and ₹ 30,000 respectively. Calculate closing capital and profit earned by Ramya for the year 2024-25.**

Sol. Opening Capital = ₹ 1,20,000 ; Closing Assets = ₹ 1,50,000
Closing Liabilities = ₹ 30,000
Profit = ? ; Closing Capital = ?
Closing Capital = Closing Assets – Closing Liabilities
= 1,50,000 – 30,000 = ₹ 1,20,000
Profit = Closing Capital – Opening Capital
= 1,20,000 – 1,20,000 = 0

Solved Question 7 **Suresh's opening capital was ₹ 9,00,000. During the year 2024-25, his revenue and expenses were ₹ 20,00,000 and ₹ 6,00,000 respectively. Find out total assets at the end of the year if**

(i) liabilities at the end are ₹ 5,00,000

(ii) expenses include ₹ 1,00,000 related with previous year.

Sol. Assets = Capital + Liabilities
= 9,00,000 + 5,00,000 + 15,00,000* = ₹ 29,00,000
*Income = Revenue – Expenses
= 20,00,000 – (6,00,000 – 1,00,000) = ₹ 15,00,000

Solved Question 8 **Vishakha & Bros. had its opening capital of ₹ 1,50,000 on 1st April, 2024. During the year, they borrowed ₹ 80,000 from Aarti Traders. Sales and expenses for the year 2024-25 were ₹ 1,50,000 and ₹ 1,20,000 respectively. Calculate (i) Profit (ii) Closing capital (iii) Total assets at the end of the year**

Sol. (i) Profit = Sales – Expenses = 1,50,000 – 1,20,000 = ₹ 30,000
(ii) Closing Capital = Opening Capital + Profit
= 1,50,000 + 30,000
= ₹ 1,80,000
(iii) Total Assets = Closing Capital + Closing Liabilities
= 1,80,000 + 80,000 = ₹ 2,60,000

Solved Question 9 **From the following balances, calculate closing capital.**

Closing Assets : Cash ₹ 60,000; Bank balance ₹ 90,000; Debtors ₹ 46,000; Machinery ₹ 1,30,000 ; Furniture ₹ 60,000; Bills receivable ₹ 1,10,000.

Closing Liabilities : Creditors ₹ 34,000; Bills payable ₹ 50,000.

Sol. Closing Assets = Closing Capital + Liabilities
Cash + Bank + Debtors + Machinery + Furniture + Bills Receivable = Closing Capital + Creditors + Bills Payable
60,000 + 90,000 + 46,000 + 1,30,000 + 60,000 + 1,10,000
= Closing Capital + 34,000 + 50,000
4,96,000 = Closing Capital + 84,000
Closing Capital = 4,96,000 – 84,000 = ₹ 4,12,000

Solved Question 10 **Calculate external equity in both cases**

(i) (a) Total assets ₹ 80,000 (b) Capital ₹ 40,000

(ii) (a) Opening capital ₹ 80,000
(b) Liabilities ₹ 40,000 (c) Profit earned ₹ 30,000
(d) Closing assets ₹ 2,00,000

Sol. (i) Total Assets = ₹ 80,000 ; Capital = ₹ 40,000
External Equity = ?
Liabilities = Total Assets – Capital = 80,000 – 40,000
= ₹ 40,000
(ii) Opening Capital = ₹ 80,000 ; Liabilities = ₹ 40,000
Profit during Year = ₹ 30,000
Closing Assets = ₹ 2,00,000 ; Closing Liabilities = ?
Closing Capital = Opening Capital + Profit
= 80,000 + 30,000 = 1,10,000
External Equity = Assets – Closing Capital
= 2,00,000 – 1,10,000 = ₹ 90,000

Solved Question 11 **Give an example for each of the following type of transaction**

(i) Increase in one asset, decrease in another asset.
(ii) Decrease in asset, decrease in liability.
(iii) Increase in liability, decrease in capital.
(iv) Increase in asset, increase in liability.
(v) Decrease in asset, decrease in capital
(vi) Increase in capital, decrease in capital
(vii) Increase in capital, decrease in asset, decrease in liability.
(viii) Increase in asset, increase in capital, decrease in asset.

Sol.

(i)	Cash deposited into bank account	Decrease in cash (Asset) and increase in bank (Asset)
(ii)	Payment made to creditors	Decrease in cash (Asset) and decrease in creditors (Liability)
(iii)	Outstanding salary	Increase in liability and decrease in capital
(iv)	Purchased stock on credit	Increase in stock (Asset) and increase in creditors (Liability)
(v)	Goods withdrawn for personal use	Decrease in stock (Asset) and decrease in capital
(vi)	Interest on capital or interest on drawings	Increase in capital and decrease in capital
(vii)	Paid ₹ 39,500 to Ramesh in full settlement of ₹ 40,000	Decrease in cash (Asset) decrease in creditor/Ramesh (Liability) and increase in capital by Income i.e. discount received
(viii)	Goods costing ₹ 500 sold at ₹ 700 for cash	Increase in cash (Asset) decrease in stock (Asset) and increase in capital by profit

Solved Question 12 Show the accounting equation on the basis of the following transaction **NCERT**

(i) Udit started business with cash ₹ 5,00,000 and goods ₹ 1,00,000.
(ii) Purchased building for cash ₹ 2,00,000.
(iii) Purchased goods from Himani ₹ 50,000.
(iv) Sold goods to Ashu (costing ₹ 25,000) ₹ 36,000.
(v) Paid insurance premium ₹ 3,000.
(vi) Rent outstanding ₹ 5,000.
(vii) Depreciation on building ₹ 8,000.
(viii) Rent received in advance ₹ 5,000.
(ix) Cash withdrawn for personal use ₹ 20,000.
(x) Cash paid to Himani on account ₹ 20,000.
(xi) Cash received from Ashu ₹ 30,000.

Sol.

Accounting Equation

Transaction		Assets							=	Capital	+	Liabilities				
		Cash	+	Stock	+	Building	+	Debtor	=	Capital	+	Adv. Rent	+	Outs. Rent	+	Creditors
(i)	Udit started business with cash and goods	5,00,000	+	1,00,000	+	0	+	0	=	6,00,000	+	0	+	0	+	0
	New equation	5,00,000	+	1,00,000	+	0	+	0	=	6,00,000	+	0	+	0	+	0
(ii)	Purchased building	(2,00,000)	+	0	+	2,00,000	+	0	=	0	+	0	+	0	+	0
	New equation	3,00,000	+	1,00,000	+	2,00,000	+	0	=	6,00,000	+	0	+	0	+	0
(iii)	Goods purchased from Himani	0	+	50,000	+	0	+	0	=	0	+	0	+	0	+	50,000
	New equation	3,00,000	+	1,50,000	+	2,00,000	+	0	=	6,00,000	+	0	+	0	+	50,000
(iv)	Sold goods to Ashu	0	+	(25,000)	+	0	+	36,000	=	11,000	+	0	+	0	+	0
	New equation	3,00,000	+	1,25,000	+	2,00,000	+	36,000	=	6,11,000	+	0	+	0	+	50,000
(v)	Paid insurance premium	(3,000)	+	0	+	0	+	0	=	(3,000)	+	0	+	0	+	0
	New equation	2,97,000	+	1,25,000	+	2,00,000	+	36,000	=	6,08,000	+	0	+	0	+	50,000
(vi)	Rent outstanding	0	+	0	+	0	+	0	=	(5,000)	+	0	+	5,000	+	0
	New equation	2,97,000	+	1,25,000	+	2,00,000	+	36,000	=	6,03,000	+	0	+	5,000	+	50,000
(vii)	Depreciation on building	0	+	0	+	(8,000)	+	0	=	(8,000)	+	0	+	0	+	0
	New equation	2,97,000	+	1,25,000	+	1,92,000	+	36,000	=	5,95,000	+	0	+	5,000	+	50,000
(viii)	Rent received in advance	5,000	+	0	+	0	+	0	=	0	+	5,000	+	0	+	0
	New equation	3,02,000	+	1,25,000	+	1,92,000	+	36,000	=	5,95,000	+	5,000	+	5,000	+	50,000
(ix)	Cash withdraw for personal use	(20,000)	+	0	+	0	+	0	=	(20,000)	+	0	+	0	+	0
	New equation	2,82,000	+	1,25,000	+	1,92,000	+	36,000	=	5,75,000	+	5,000	+	5,000	+	50,000
(x)	Cash paid to Himani on account	(20,000)	+	0	+	0	+	0	=	0	+	0	+	0	+	(20,000)
	New equation	2,62,000	+	1,25,000	+	1,92,000	+	36,000	=	5,75,000	+	5,000	+	5,000	+	30,000
(xi)	Cash received from Ashu	30,000	+	0	+	0	+	(30,000)	=	0	+	0	+	0	+	0
	Final equation	2,92,000	+	1,25,000	+	1,92,000	+	6,000	=	5,75,000	+	5,000	+	5,000	+	30,000

Solved Question 13 Show the effect of the following transactions on assets, liabilities and capital through accounting equation **NCERT**

(i) Started business with cash ₹ 1,20,000.
(ii) Rent received ₹ 10,000.
(iii) Invested in shares ₹ 50,000.
(iv) Received dividend ₹ 5,000.
(v) Purchase goods on credit from Ragani ₹ 35,000.
(vi) Paid cash for household expenses ₹ 7,000.
(vii) Sold goods for cash (costing ₹ 10,000) ₹ 14,000.
(viii) Cash paid to Ragani ₹ 35,000.
(ix) Deposited into bank ₹ 20,000.

Sol.

Accounting Equation

Transaction	Assets								=	Capital	+	Liabilities
	Cash	+	Investment	+	Stock	+	Bank		=	Capital	+	Creditors
(i) Started business with cash	1,20,000	+	0	+	0	+	0		=	1,20,000	+	0
New equation	1,20,000	+	0	+	0	+	0		=	1,20,000	+	0
(ii) Rent received	10,000	+	0	+	0	+	0		=	10,000	+	0
New equation	1,30,000	+	0	+	0	+	0		=	1,30,000	+	0
(iii) Investment in shares	(50,000)	+	50,000	+	0	+	0		=	0	+	0
New equation	80,000	+	50,000	+	0	+	0		=	130,000	+	0
(iv) Received dividend	5,000	+	0	+	0	+	0		=	5,000	+	0
New equation	85,000	+	50,000	+	0	+	0		=	1,35,000	+	0
(v) Purchased goods from Ragani	0	+	0	+	35,000	+	0		=	0	+	35,000
New equation	85,000	+	50,000	+	35,000	+	0		=	1,35,000	+	35,000
(vi) Paid household expense	(7,000)	+	0	+	0	+	0		=	(7,000)	+	0
New equation	78,000	+	50,000	+	35,000	+	0		=	1,28,000	+	35,000
(vii) Sold goods for cash	14,000	+	0	+	(10,000)	+	0		=	4,000	+	0
New equation	92,000	+	50,000	+	25,000	+	0		=	1,32,000	+	35,000
(viii) Cash paid to Ragani	(35,000)	+	0	+	0	+	0		=	0	+	(35,000)
New equation	57,000	+	50,000	+	25,000	+	0		=	1,32,000	+	0
(ix) Deposited into bank	(20,000)	+	0	+	0	+	20,000		=	0	+	0
Final equation	37,000	+	50,000	+	25,000	+	20,000		=	1,32,000	+	0

Solved Question 14 Show that an accounting equation always states that total assets are always equal to total of capital and liabilities in following transactions.

(i) Started business with cash ₹ 1,50,000 and machine ₹ 80,000.
(ii) Purchased goods for cash ₹ 30,000 and on credit ₹ 40,000 from Nancy.
(iii) Sold goods for cash costing ₹ 8,000 and on credit costing ₹ 10,000 both at a profit of 25% on cost.
(iv) Withdraw cash for personal use ₹ 5,000.
(v) Accrued interest ₹ 6,000.
(vi) Interest on capital provided @ 10% p.a.
(vii) Interest on drawings @ 5%.
(viii) Insurance premium paid in advance ₹ 1,000.
(ix) Deprecation on machinery charged ₹ 8,000.
(x) Bad debt recovered ₹ 2,000.

Sol. **Accounting Equation**

Transaction	Assets						=	Liabilities
	Cash +	Machine +	Stock +	Debtor +	Accrued Interest +	Prepaid Expenses =	Capital +	Creditors
(i) Started business with cash ₹ 1,50,000 and machine ₹ 80,000	1,50,000 +	80,000 +	0 +	0 +	0 +	0 =	2,30,000 +	0
New equation	1,50,000 +	80,000 +	0 +	0 +	0 +	0 =	2,30,000 +	0
(ii) Purchased goods for cash ₹ 30,000 and on credit ₹ 40,000 from Nancy	(30,000) +	0 +	70,000 +	0 +	0 +	0 =	0 +	40,000
New equation	1,20,000 +	80,000 +	70,000 +	0 +	0 +	0 =	2,30,000 +	40,000
(iii) Sold goods for cash costing ₹ 8,000 and on credit costing ₹ 10,000 both at a profit 25% on cost	10,000 +	0 +	(18,000) +	12,500 +	0 +	0 =	4,500 +	0
New equation	1,30,000 +	80,000 +	52,000 +	12,500 +	0 +	0 =	2,34,500 +	40,000
(iv) Withdraw cash for personal use ₹ 5,000	(5,000) +	0 +	0 +	0 +	0 +	0 =	(5,000) +	0
New equation	1,25,000 +	80,000 +	52,000 +	12,500 +	0 +	0 =	2,29,500 +	40,000
(v) Accrued interest ₹ 6,000	0 +	0 +	0 +	0 +	6,000 +	0 =	6,000 +	0
New equation	1,25,000 +	80,000 +	52,000 +	12,500 +	6,000 +	0 =	2,35,500 +	40,000
(vi) Interest on capital @ 10% p.a.	0 +	0 +	0 +	0 +	0 +	0 =	+23,000 (23,000) +	0
New equation	1,25,000 +	80,000 +	52,000 +	12,500 +	6,000 +	0 =	2,35,500 +	40,000
(vii) Interest on drawings @ 5%	0 +	0 +	0 +	0 +	0 +	0 =	+ 250 (250) +	0
New equation	1,25,000 +	80,000 +	52,000 +	12,500 +	6,000 +	0 =	2,35,500 +	40,000
(viii) Insurance premium paid in advance ₹ 1,000	(1,000) +	0 +	0 +	0 +	0 +	1,000 =	0 +	0
New equation	1,24,000 +	80,000 +	52,000 +	12,500 +	6,000 +	1,000 =	2,35,500 +	40,000
(ix) Depreciation on machinery ₹ 8,000	0 +	(8,000) +	0 +	0 +	0 +	0 =	(8,000) +	0
New equation	1,24,000 +	72,000 +	52,000 +	12,500 +	6,000 +	1,000 =	2,27,500 +	40,000
(x) Bad debts recovered ₹ 2,000	2,000 +	0 +	0 +	0 +	0 +	0 =	2,000 +	0
Final equation	1,26,000 +	72,000 +	52,000 +	12,500 +	6,000 +	1,000 =	2,29,500 +	40,000

Solved Question 15 **Prepare an accounting equation on the basis of following transactions for Ayushi Traders.**

(i) Started business with cash ₹ 3,00,000.
(ii) Deposited in firm's bank account ₹ 1,00,000.
(iii) Received commission ₹ 10,000.
(iv) Invested in shares of Reliance Ltd. ₹ 60,000.
(v) Purchased goods for cash from Anu ₹ 30,000.
(vi) Cash withdrawn for personal use ₹ 8,000.
(vii) Sold goods for cash costing ₹ 15,000 for ₹ 13,000.
(viii) Goods destroyed by fire ₹ 3,000.
(ix) Paid salary ₹ 10,000 to Payal. Half is in advance.
(x) Paid telephone bill by cheque ₹ 3,000.

Sol. **Accounting Equation**

Transaction	Assets					= Capital	+ Liabilities
	Cash +	Bank +	Investment +	Stock +	Prepaid Salary	= Capital	+ Liabilities
(i) Started business with cash ₹ 3,00,000	3,00,000 +	0 +	0 +	0 +	0	3,00,000 +	0
New equation	3,00,000 +	0 +	0 +	0 +	0	= 3,00,000 +	0
(ii) Deposited in firm's bank account ₹ 1,00,000	(1,00,000) +	1,00,000 +	0 +	0 +	0	= 0 +	0
New equation	2,00,000 +	1,00,000 +	0 +	0 +	0	= 3,00,000 +	0
(iii) Commission received ₹ 10,000	10,000 +	0 +	0 +	0 +	0	= 10,000 +	0
New equation	2,10,000 +	1,00,000 +	0 +	0 +	0	= 3,10,000 +	0
(iv) Invested in shares of Reliance Ltd. ₹ 60,000	0 +	(60,000) +	60,000 +	0 +	0	= 0 +	0
New equation	2,10,000 +	40,000 +	60,000 +	0 +	0	= 3,10,000 +	0
(v) Purchased goods on cash from Anu ₹ 30,000	(30,000) +	0 +	0 +	30,000 +	0	= 0 +	0
New equation	1,80,000 +	40,000 +	60,000 +	30,000 +	0	= 3,10,000 +	0
(vi) Withdrawn cash for personal use ₹ 8,000	(8,000) +	0 +	0 +	0 +	0	= (8,000) +	0
New equation	1,72,000 +	40,000 +	60,000 +	30,000 +	0	= 3,02,000 +	0
(vii) Sold goods for cash costing ₹ 15,000 for ₹ 13,000	13,000 +	0 +	0 +	(15,000) +	0	= (2,000) +	0
New equation	1,85,000 +	40,000 +	60,000 +	15,000 +	0	= 3,00,000 +	0
(viii) Goods destroyed by fire ₹ 3,000	0 +	0 +	0 +	(3,000) +		= (3,000) +	0
New equation	1,85,000 +	40,000 +	60,000 +	12,000 +	0	= 2,97,000 +	0
(ix) Paid salary ₹ 10,000 to Payal. Half is in advance	(10,000) +	0 +	0 +	0 +	5,000	= (5,000) +	0
New equation	1,75,000 +	40,000 +	60,000 +	12,000 +	5,000	= 2,92,000 +	0
(x) Paid telephone bill by cheque ₹ 3,000	0 +	(3,000) +	0 +	0 +	0	= (3,000) +	0
Final equation	1,75,000 +	37,000 +	60,000 +	12,000 +	5,000	= 2,89,000 +	0

Solved Question 16 **Prepare accounting equation from the following**

(i) Riya started business with cash ₹ 1,80,000, goods ₹ 80,000 and building ₹ 5,00,000.
(ii) Purchased goods from Yamini ₹ 45,000.
(iii) Sold goods costing ₹ 10,000 for ₹ 15,000 to Aditya.
(iv) Purchased goods for cash ₹ 40,000.
(v) Paid cash to Yamini in full settlement ₹ 44,000.
(vi) Salary paid ₹ 10,000.
(vii) Received cash from Aditya in full settlement ₹ 14,500.
(viii) Rent outstanding ₹ 2,000.
(ix) Taken a loan from SBI ₹ 80,000.
(x) Commission received ₹ 10,000.
(xi) Depreciation charged on building ₹ 8,000.
(xii) Additional capital introduced ₹ 40,000.
(xiii) Rent received in advance ₹ 4,000.

Sol. **Accounting Equation**

Transaction	Assets					= Capital +	Liabilities			
	Cash +	Stock +	Building +	Debtor +	Bank	= Capital +	Creditors +	Outsta. Exp. +	Adv. Rent +	SBI Loan
(i) Riya started business with cash ₹ 1,80,000, goods ₹ 80,000 and building ₹ 5,00,000	1,80,000 +	80,000 +	5,00,000 +	0 +	0	= 7,60,000 +	0 +	0 +	0 +	0

Transaction	Cash	Stock	Building	Debtor	Bank	Capital	Creditors	Outsta. Exp.	Adv. Rent	SBI Loan
	Assets					**= Capital +**	**Liabilities**			
New equation	1,80,000	80,000	5,00,000	0	0	7,60,000	0	0	0	0
(ii) Purchased goods from Yamini	0	45,000	0	0	0	0	45,000	0	0	0
New equation	1,80,000	1,25,000	5,00,000	0	0	7,60,000	45,000	0	0	0
(iii) Sold goods costing ₹ 10,000 for ₹ 15,000 to Aditya	0	(10,000)	0	15,000	0	5,000	0	0	0	0
New equation	1,80,000	1,15,000	5,00,000	15,000	0	7,65,000	45,000	0	0	0
(iv) Purchased goods for cash ₹ 40,000	(40,000)	40,000	0	0	0	0	0	0	0	0
New equation	1,40,000	1,55,000	5,00,000	15,000	0	7,65,000	45,000	0	0	0
(v) Paid cash to Yamini in full settlement ₹ 44,000	(44,000)	0	0	0	0	1,000	(45,000)	0	0	0
New equation	96,000	1,55,000	5,00,000	15,000	0	7,66,000	0	0	0	0
(vi) Salary paid ₹ 10,000	(10,000)	0	0	0	0	(10,000)	0	0	0	0
New equation	86,000	1,55,000	5,00,000	15,000	0	7,56,000	0	0	0	0
(vii) Received cash from Aditya in full settlement ₹ 14,500	14,500	0	0	(15,000)	0	(500)	0	0	0	0
New equation	1,00,500	1,55,000	5,00,000	0	0	7,55,500	0	0	0	0
(viii) Rent outstanding ₹ 2,000	0	0	0	0	0	(2,000)	0	2,000	0	0
New equation	1,00,500	1,55,000	5,00,000	0	0	7,53,500	0	2,000	0	0
(ix) Taken a loan from SBI ₹ 10,000	0	0	0	0	80,000	0	0	0	0	80,000
New equation	1,00,500	1,55,000	5,00,000	0	80,000	7,53,500	0	2,000	0	80,000
(x) Commission Received ₹ 10,000	10,000	0	0	0	0	10,000	0	0	0	0
New equation	1,10,500	1,55,000	5,00,000	0	80,000	7,63,500	0	2,000	0	80,000
(xi) Depreciation charged on building ₹ 8,000	0	0	(8,000)	0	0	(8,000)	0	0	0	0
New equation	1,10,500	1,55,000	4,92,000	0	80,000	7,55,500	0	2,000	0	80,000
(xii) Additional capital introduced ₹ 40,000	40,000	0	0	0	0	40,000	0	0	0	0
New equation	1,50,500	1,55,000	4,92,000	0	80,000	7,95,500	0	2,000	0	80,000
(xiii) Rent received in advance ₹ 4,000	4,000	0	0	0	0	0	0	0	4,000	0
Final equation	1,54,500	1,55,000	4,92,000	0	80,000	7,95,500	0	2,000	4,000	80,000

Solved Question 17 **Ananya had the following transactions. Prepare accounting equation to show their effect on her assets, liabilities and capital. Also, show the balance sheet on the basis of final equation.**

(i) Invested ₹ 3,50,000 in cash as capital and stock ₹ 60,000.

(ii) Purchased furniture for ₹ 40,000 in cash and stock ₹ 10,000 on credit.

(iii) Purchased a building for ₹ 4,00,000 giving ₹ 1,50,000 in cash and the balance through a loan from SBI bank.

(iv) Sold goods costing ₹ 5,000 for ₹ 4,000. **(v) Received cash as rent ₹ 8,000.**

(vi) Purchased an old car for ₹ 40,000 cash.

(vii) Paid ₹ 500 as interest.

(viii) Paid cash for household expenses ₹ 500.

(ix) Received cash for dividend on securities ₹ 3,000.

(x) Deposited ₹ 2,000 as a security for telephone connection.

Sol. **Accounting Equation**

Transaction	Assets						= Capital +	Liabilities	
	Cash +	Stock +	Furniture +	Building +	Car +	Security =	Capital +	Creditors +	Loan
(i) Invested ₹ 3,50,000 in cash and stock ₹ 60,000	3,50,000 +	60,000 +	0 +	0 +	0 +	0 =	4,10,000 +	0 +	0
New equation	3,50,000 +	60,000 +	0 +	0 +	0 +	0 =	4,10,000 +	0 +	0
(ii) Purchased furniture ₹ 40,000 for cash and stock ₹ 10,000 on credit	(40,000) +	10,000 +	40,000 +	0 +	0 +	0 =	0 +	10,000 +	0
New equation	3,10,000 +	70,000 +	40,000 +	0 +	0 +	0 =	4,10,000 +	10,000 +	0
(iii) Purchased a building for ₹ 4,00,000 giving ₹ 1,50,000 in cash and the balance through a loan from SBI	(1,50,000) +	0 +	0 +	4,00,000 +	0 +	0 =	0 +	0 +	2,50,000
New equation	1,60,000 +	70,000 +	40,000 +	4,00,000 +	0 +	0 =	4,10,000 +	10,000 +	2,50,000
(iv) Sold goods costing ₹ 5,000 for ₹ 4,000	4,000 +	(5,000) +	0 +	0 +	0 +	0 =	(1,000) +	0 +	0
New equation	1,64,000 +	65,000 +	40,000 +	4,00,000 +	0 +	0 =	4,09,000 +	10,000 +	2,50,000
(v) Received cash as rent ₹ 80,000	8,000 +	0 +	0 +	0 +	0 +	0 =	8,000 +	0 +	0
New equation	1,72,000 +	65,000 +	40,000 +	4,00,000 +	0 +	0 =	4,17,000 +	0 +	2,50,000
(vi) Purchased an old car for ₹ 40,000	(40,000) +	0 +	0 +	0 +	40,000 +	0 =	0 +	0 +	0
New equation	1,32,000 +	65,000 +	40,000 +	4,00,000 +	40,000 +	0 =	4,17,000 +	10,000 +	2,50,000
(vii) Paid ₹ 500 as interest	(500) +	0 +	0 +	0 +	0 +	0 =	(500) +	0 +	0
New equation	1,31,500 +	65,000 +	40,000 +	4,00,000 +	40,000 +	0 =	4,16,500 +	10,000 +	2,50,000
(viii) Paid cash for household expenses	(500) +	0 +	0 +	0 +	0 +	0 =	(500) +	0 +	0
New equation	1,31,000 +	65,000 +	40,000 +	4,00,000 +	40,000 +	0 =	4,16,000 +	10,000 +	2,50,000
(ix) Received cash for dividend on securities	3,000 +	0 +	0 +	0 +	0 +	0 =	3,000 +	0 +	0
New equation	1,34,000 +	65,000 +	40,000 +	4,00,000 +	40,000 +	0 =	4,19,000 +	10,000 +	2,50,000
(x) Deposited ₹ 2,000 as security for telephone connection	(2,000) +	0 +	0 +	0 +	0 +	2,000 =	0 +	0 +	0
Final equation	1,32,000 +	65,000 +	40,000 +	4,00,000 +	40,000 +	2,000 =	4,19,000 +	10,000 +	2,50,000

Balance Sheet
as at ...

Liabilities	Amt (₹)	Assets	Amt (₹)
Capital	4,19,000	Building	4,00,000
Creditors	10,000	Furniture	40,000
Loan	2,50,000	Car	40,000
		Stock	65,000
		Cash	1,32,000
		Security	2,000
	6,79,000		6,79,000

Solved Question 18 **Show the accounting equation on the basis of the following transactions and also prepare balance sheet of final equation.**

(i) Amit started business with cash ₹ 6,00,000, goods ₹ 1,20,000.
(ii) Purchased building for cash ₹ 2,50,000.
(iii) Purchased goods from Reema ₹ 60,000.
(iv) Sold 1/5th of the total stock of goods for ₹ 20,000.
(v) Paid insurance premium ₹ 4,000 out of which half relates to next year.
(vi) Rent outstanding ₹ 7,000.
(vii) Depreciation charged on building ₹ 10,000.
(viii) Cash withdrawn for personal use ₹ 30,000.
(ix) Paid outstanding rent by cash.
(x) Rent received in advance ₹ 7,000.
(xi) Cash paid to Reema on account ₹ 30,000.
(xii) Received interest ₹ 1,500.

Sol. **Accounting Equation**

Transaction	Assets				=	Capital	+	Liabilities	
	Cash +	Stock +	Building +	Prepaid Insurance	=	Capital	+ Creditors +	Outs. Rent+	Advance Rent
(i) Started business with cash and goods	6,00,000 +	1,20,000 +	0 +	0	=	7,20,000	+ 0 +	0 +	0
New equation	6,00,000 +	1,20,000 +	0 +	0	=	7,20,000	+ 0 +	0 +	0
(ii) Purchased building	(2,50,000) +	0 +	2,50,000 +	0	=	0	+ 0 +	0 +	0
New equation	3,50,000 +	1,20,000 +	2,50,000 +	0	=	7,20,000	+ 0 +	0 +	0
(iii) Purchased goods from Reema	0 +	60,000 +	0 +	0	=	0	+ 60,000 +	0 +	0
New equation	3,50,000 +	1,80,000 +	2,50,000 +	0	=	7,20,000	+ 60,000 +	0 +	0
(iv) Sold 1/5th goods for ₹ 20,000	20,000 +	(36,000) +	0 +	0	=	(16,000)	+ 0 +	0 +	0
New equation	3,70,000 +	1,44,000 +	2,50,000 +	0	=	7,04,000	+ 60,000 +	0 +	0
(v) Paid insurance premium ₹ 4,000. Half relates to next year	(4,000) +	0 +	0 +	2,000	=	(2,000)	+ 0 +	0 +	0
New equation	3,66,000 +	1,44,000 +	2,50,000 +	2,000	=	7,02,000	+ 60,000 +	0 +	0
(vi) Rent outstanding	0 +	0 +	0 +	0	=	(7,000)	+ 0 +	7,000 +	0
New equation	3,66,000 +	1,44,000 +	2,50,000 +	2,000	=	6,95,000	+ 60,000 +	7,000 +	0
(vii) Depreciation charged on building	0 +	0 +	(10,000) +	0	=	(10,000)	+ 0 +	0 +	0
New equation	3,66,000 +	1,44,000 +	2,40,000 +	2,000	=	6,85,000	+ 60,000 +	7,000 +	0
(viii) Cash withdraw for personal use	(30,000) +	0 +	0 +	0	=	(30,000)	+ 0 +	0 +	0

	Transaction	Assets				= Capital	+	Liabilities	
		Cash +	Stock +	Building +	Prepaid Insurance =	Capital	+ Creditors +	Outs. Rent +	Advance Rent
	New equation	3,36,000 +	1,44,000 +	2,40,000 +	2,000 =	6,55,000 +	60,000 +	7,000 +	0
(ix)	Paid outstanding rent	(7,000) +	0 +	0 +	0 =	0 +	0 +	(7,000) +	0
	New equation	3,29,000 +	1,44,000 +	2,40,000 +	2,000 =	6,55,000 +	60,000 +	0 +	0
(x)	Rent received in advance	7,000 +	0 +	0 +	0 =	0 +	0 +	0 +	7,000
	New equation	3,36,000 +	1,44,000 +	2,40,000 +	2,000 =	6,55,000 +	60,000 +	0 +	7,000
(xi)	Cash paid to Reema ₹ 30,000	(30,000) +	0 +	0 +	0 =	0 +	(30,000) +	0 +	0
	New equation	3,06,000 +	1,44,000 +	2,40,000 +	2,000 =	6,55,000 +	30,000 +	0 +	7,000
(xii)	Received interest ₹ 1,500	1,500 +	0 +	0 +	0 =	1,500 +	0 +	0 +	0
	Final equation	3,07,500 +	1,44,000 +	2,40,000 +	2,000 =	6,56,500 +	30,000 +	0 +	7,000

Balance Sheet

as at ...

Liabilities	Amt (₹)	Assets	Amt (₹)
Capital	6,56,500	Cash	3,07,500
Creditors	30,000	Stock	1,44,000
Rent received in Advance	7,000	Building	2,40,000
		Prepaid Insurance	2,000
	6,93,500		6,93,500

Missing Information

Solved Question 19 **On the basis of the following transactions, Sachin prepared on accounting equation and left some transactions unfilled in accounting equation. You are required to fill out those missing figures.**

	Transaction	Assets					= Capital	+ Liabilities
		Cash +	Stock +	Bank +	Furniture +	Security =	Capital +	Creditors
(i)	Started business with cash ₹ 2,00,000 and stock ₹ 50,000	2,00,000 +	50,000 +	0 +	0 +	0 =	2,50,000 +	0
	New equation	2,00,000 +	50,000 +	0 +	0 +	0 =	2,50,000 +	0
(ii)	Opened a bank account with ₹ 90,000	... +	... +	... +	... +	... =	... +	...
	New equation	... +	... +	... +	... +	... =	... +	...
(iii)	Purchased furniture for office ₹ 20,000 by cheque	0 +	0 +	(20,000) +	... +	0 =	0 +	0
	New equation	1,10,000 +	50,000 +	... +	... +	0 =	2,50,000 +	0
(iv)	Purchased goods for cash ₹ 40,000 and on credit ₹ 30,000	(...) +	70,000 +	0 +	0 +	0 =	0 +	30,000
	New equation	... +	1,20,000 +	... +	... +	0 =	2,50,000 +	30,000
(v)	Paid rent ₹ 10,000	(10,000) +	0 +	0 +	0 +	0 =	... +	...
	New equation	... +	1,20,000 +	... +	... +	0 =	... +	30,000
(vi)	Deposited security for electricity, connections	(20,000) +	0 +	0 +	0 +	20,000 =	0 +	0
	Final equation	... +	1,20,000 +	... +	... +	20,000 =	... +	30,000

Sol. **Accounting Equation**

Transaction	Assets									=	Capital	+	Liabilities
	Cash	+	Stock	+	Bank	+	Furniture	+	Security	=	Capital	+	Creditors
(i) Started business with cash ₹ 2,00,000 and stock ₹ 50,000	2,00,000	+	50,000	+	0	+	0	+	0	=	2,50,000	+	0
New equation	2,00,000	+	50,000	+	0	+	0	+	0	=	2,50,000	+	0
(ii) Opened a bank account with ₹ 90,000	**(90,000)**	+	**0**	+	**90,000**	+	**0**	+	**0**	=	**0**	+	**0**
New equation	**1,10,000**	+	**50,000**	+	**90,000**	+	**0**	+	**0**	=	**2,50,000**	+	**0**
(iii) Purchased furniture for office ₹ 20,000 by cheque	0	+	0	+	(20,000)	+	**20,000**	+	0	=	0	+	0
New equation	1,10,000	+	50,000	+	**70,000**	+	**20,000**	+	0	=	2,50,000	+	0
(iv) Purchased goods for cash ₹ 40,000 and on credit ₹ 30,000	**(40,000)**	+	70,000	+	0	+	0	+	0	=	0	+	30,000
New equation	**70,000**	+	1,20,000	+	**70,000**	+	**20,000**	+	0	=	2,50,000	+	30,000
(v) Paid rent ₹ 10,000	(10,000)	+	0	+	0	+	0	+	0	=	**(10,000)**	+	**0**
New equation	**60,000**	+	1,20,000	+	**70,000**	+	**20,000**	+	0	=	**2,40,000**	+	30,000
(vi) Deposited security for electricity connection	(20,000)	+	0	+	0	+	0	+	20,000	=	0	+	0
Final equation	**40,000**	+	1,20,000	+	**70,000**	+	**20,000**	+	20,000	=	**2,40,000**	+	30,000

Solved Question 20 **Based on incomplete accounting equation given below, fill the missing information**

Transaction	Assets			=	Capital	+	Liabilities
	Cash	+	Stock	=	Capital	+	Creditors
(i) Commenced business with cash ₹ 50,000	...	+	0	=	...	+	0
New equation	...	+	0	=	...	+	0
(ii)	0	+	20,000	=	0	+	20,000
New equation	...	+	...	=	...	+	20,000
(iii) Sold goods costing ₹ 2,000 for ₹ 1,500	1,500	+	...	=	...	+	0
New equation	...	+	...	=	...	+	20,000
(iv) Paid rent ₹ 500	(500)	+	0	=	...	+	0
New equation	...	+	...	=	...	+	20,000
(v) Paid to creditors ₹	(5,000)	+	0	=	0	+	(5,000)
Final equation	...	+	...	=	...	+	...

Sol. **Accounting Equation**

Transaction	Assets			=	Capital	+	Liabilities
	Cash	+	Stock	=	Capital	+	Creditors
(i) Commenced business with cash ₹ 50,000	50,000	+	0	=	**50,000**	+	0
New equation	**50,000**	+	0	=	**50,000**	+	0
(ii) **Purchased goods on credit ₹ 20,000**	0	+	20,000	=	0	+	20,000
New equation	**50,000**	+	**20,000**	=	**50,000**	+	20,000
(iii) Sold goods costing ₹ 2,000 for ₹ 1,500	1,500	+	**(2,000)**	=	**(500)**	+	0
New equation	**51,500**	+	**18,000**	=	**49,500**	+	20,000
(iv) Paid rent ₹ 500	(500)	+	0	=	**(500)**	+	0
New equation	**51,000**	+	**18,000**	=	**49,000**	+	20,000
(v) Paid to creditors ₹ **5,000**	(5,000)	+	0	=	0	+	(5,000)
Final equation	**46,000**	+	**18,000**	=	**49,000**	+	**15,000**

Numerical Questions

Vouchers

1. Prepare relevant vouchers on the basis of following transactions in the books of Arihant Publication India Ltd.

Date	Particulars	Amt (₹)
2024		
May 1	Purchased a machine from XYZ Ltd. for ₹ 1,00,000, paid by cheque vide Cash Memo No. 432	
May 3	Sold goods to Ajay for cash Cash Memo No. 432	20,000
May 5	Goods sold on credit to Payal & Bros Invoice No. 432	25,000

Ans. Following vouchers are to be prepared

(i) Debit voucher
(ii) Credit voucher
(iii) Transfer voucher

2. Prepare relevant vouchers from the following transactions

Date	Particulars	Amt (₹)
2024		
May 20	Paid ₹ 9,500 by cheque to Anuja & Sons in full settlement of ₹ 10,000	
30 May	Interest due but not paid on loan	1,000

Ans. Following vouchers will be prepared

(i) Compound voucher (credit)
(ii) Transfer voucher or non-cash voucher

Accounting Equation

3. If the capital of a business is ₹ 1,50,000 and outside liabilities amount to ₹ 30,000, calculate the total assets of the business.

Ans. Total assets = ₹ 1,80,000

4. Calculate the owner's equity if assets are ₹ 1,50,000 and liabilities are ₹ 70,000.

Ans. Owner's equity = ₹ 80,000

5. Raj started his business on 1st April, 2022 with a capital of ₹ 6,00,000. By 31st March, 2023, his assets were valued at ₹ 9,50,000, while liabilities stood at ₹ 80,000.

Determine his closing capital and the profit earned during the year.

Ans. Closing capital = ₹ 8,70,000; Profit = ₹ 2,70,000

6. If the total assets of a business are ₹ 1,50,000 and the net worth is ₹ 90,000, find the creditors.

Ans. Creditors = ₹ 60,000

7. Compute the total assets from the following details

Capital	=	₹ 50,000
Creditors	=	₹ 30,000
Revenue during the period	=	₹ 70,000
Expenses during the period	=	₹ 50,000

Ans. Total assets = ₹ 1,00,000

8. The owner's capital at the beginning is ₹ 18,000, revenue during the period is ₹ 20,000, expenses during the period are ₹ 18,000.

Compute the owner's capital at the end.

Ans. Owner's capital = ₹ 20,000

9. On 31st March, 2025 the total assets and external liabilities were ₹ 3,00,000 and ₹ 8,000, respectively. During the year, proprietor had introduced additional capital of ₹ 30,000 and withdrew ₹ 15,000 for personal use. He made a profit of ₹ 50,000 during the year.

Calculate the capital as on 1st April, 2024.

Ans. Opening capital = ₹ 2,27,000

10. (i) Rohan started a business on 1st April, 2024 with a capital of ₹ 30,000 and a loan of ₹ 15,000 borrowed from Anand. On 31st March, 2025, his assets were ₹ 70,000. Determine his capital as on 31st March, 2025 and calculate the profit or loss incurred during the year.

(ii) If in the above scenario, the proprietor had introduced additional capital of ₹ 15,000 and had withdrawn ₹ 10,000 for personal expenses, find the profit.

(iii) If in the case (i), on 31st March, 2025, apart from the loan, Rohan owes ₹ 7,000 to a supplier of goods, find his capital as on 31st March, 2025 and calculate the profit. **Competency Based Que**

Ans. (i) Closing capital = ₹ 55,000; Profit = ₹ 25,000

(ii) Profit = ₹ 20,000

(iii) Closing capital = ₹ 48,000; Profit = ₹ 18,000

11. Calculate the external equity as on 31st March, 2025 in the following scenarios **Competency Based Que**

(i) On 31st March, 2025, total assets and capital were ₹ 17,00,000 and ₹ 12,00,000 respectively.

(ii) On 1st April, 2024, Anita started business with a capital of ₹ 4,00,000 and a loan of ₹ 4,00,000 borrowed from a friend. During the year, she earned a profit of ₹ 2,00,000. On 31st March, 2025, the total assets were ₹ 10,00,000.

(iii) On 1st April, 2024, Rahul started business with a capital of ₹ 4,00,000 and a loan of ₹ 4,00,000 borrowed from a friend. During the year, he earned a profit of ₹ 2,00,000 introduced additional capital of ₹ 2,00,000 and had withdrawn ₹ 1,20,000 for personal use. On 31st March, 2025, the total assets were ₹ 11,00,000.

Ans. (i) External equity = 5,00,000
(ii) External equity = 4,00,000
(iii) External equity = 4,20,000

12. On 1st April, 2024, Anuj started his business of ready-made garments with ₹ 8,00,000. During the year, he took a loan of ₹ 2,00,000 from Punjab National Bank. On 1st October, 2024, he introduced ₹ 3,00,000 as an additional capital. Expenses for the year 2024-25 was recorded as ₹ 1,20,000. On 31st March, 2025, his total assets were ₹ 15,00,000.

Find the revenues of the year 2024-25. Competency Based Que

Ans. Revenues = ₹ 1,50,000

13. Asmit Brothers has total assets of ₹ 1,80,000 and liabilities ₹ 80,000 on 31st March, 2025. During the year 2024-25, Asmit withdrew ₹ 20,000 and introduced ₹ 35,000.

Calculate capital on 1st April, 2024, if he had made a profit of ₹ 15,000.

Ans. Opening capital = ₹ 70,000

14. Prepare the accounting equation from the following transactions

(i) Commenced business with cash ₹ 80,000.
(ii) Opened a bank account with ₹ 30,000.
(iii) Purchased goods for cash ₹ 30,000 and for ₹ 35,000 on credit.
(iv) Paid to creditors by cheque ₹ 35,000. Bank granted overdraft.
(v) Paid rent ₹ 500.
(vi) Purchased furniture for office ₹ 8,000.

Ans. Assets = Capital + Liabilities
84,500 = 79,500 + 5,000

15. From the following transactions, prepare the accounting equation Competency Based Que

(i) John invested ₹ 1,50,000 in his business and deposited out of it ₹ 75,000 in the firm's bank account.
(ii) Borrowed ₹ 50,000 from Axis Bank at interest rate of 10% p.a.
(iii) Deposited ₹ 30,000 through RTGS in the account of Ropoam & Sons for goods purchased on the same day.
(iv) Given goods costing ₹ 1,000 as salary.
(v) Paid rent in advance ₹ 500.
(vi) Withdrawn cash for office use ₹ 4,000.

Ans. Assets = Capital + Liabilities
1,99,000 = 1,49,000 + 50,000

16. Show the accounting equation on the basis of following transactions

(i) Opened a Kirana Store by Tina and invested ₹ 1,20,000 in the store.
(ii) Purchased the following for the purpose of resale
50 kg sugar @ ₹ 40 per kg
50 ltr mustard oil @ ₹ 100 per litre
50 masala packets @ ₹ 10 per packet
(iii) Opened a bank account in the name of the firm and deposited ₹ 20,000 out of firm's cash.
(iv) Purchased stationary for ₹ 500 by cheque.
(v) Sold 20 kg sugar @ ₹ 45 per kg for cash.

Ans. Assets = Capital + Liabilities
1,19,600 = 1,19,600 + 0

17. You are required to prepare accounting equation on the basis of the following information Competency Based Que

Anaya had a plan for starting business of buying and selling of honey. For this, she took a space for monthly rent of ₹ 1,000. She invested ₹ 5,00,000. Out of it, she purchased required furniture and equipments for ₹ 1,00,000 and Honey worth ₹ 3,00,000.

Half of balance was deposited in her firm's bank account that she had opened. She sold honey worth ₹ 50,000 for ₹ 80,000 and paid rent in advance ₹ 2,000.

Ans. Assets = Capital + Liabilities
5,30,000 = 5,30,000 + 0

18. Prakash had the following transactions. Prepare the accounting equation. Competency Based Que

(i) Commenced business with cash ₹ 70,000.
(ii) Purchased goods for cash ₹ 28,000 and on credit ₹ 40,000 from Vijay.
(iii) Sold goods for cash ₹ 55,000 costing ₹ 40,000. Only fifty percent cash was received.
(iv) Rent paid ₹ 8,000 and rent outstanding ₹ 1,500.
(v) Bought furniture ₹ 7,000 on credit.
(vi) Bought refrigerator for personal use ₹ 8,000. Half amount was paid by proprietor himself.
(vii) Purchasing building for cash ₹ 30,000.

Ans. Assets = Liabilities + Capital
1,20,000 = 48,500 + 71,500

19. Manav started a real estate agency business with a cash investment of ₹ 50,000. The following business transactions have been recorded Competency Based Que

(i) Paid 3 months advance rent for office accommodation ₹ 3,500.
(ii) Bought car for office ₹ 30,000.
(iii) Purchased office furniture ₹ 10,000.

(iv) Bought office typewriter from Astha's Ltd. ₹ 4,500.
(v) Sold extra office furniture at cost to Ramesh for ₹ 1,500. Ramesh paid ₹ 800 in cash and accepted a bill at 3 months for the balance.
(vi) Raj paid the amount of the bill at maturity and Manav paid the amount he owed to Astha's Ltd.
(vii) Collected ₹ 8,000 as commission.
(viii) Paid telephone bill amounting ₹ 300.

Prepare the accounting equation.

Ans. Assets = Liabilities + Capital
57,700 = 0 + 57,700

20. **Varun has the following transactions. Prepare accounting equation.**
(i) Commenced business with cash ₹ 2,00,000 and stock ₹ 50,000.
(ii) Purchased machinery on credit ₹ 50,000 from Mahi & Bros.
(iii) Purchased goods for cash ₹ 25,000.
(iv) Purchased motor cycle for personal use ₹ 90,000.
(v) Paid to Mahi & Bros. in full settlement ₹ 45,000.
(vi) Sold goods for cash costing ₹ 6,000 for ₹ 7,000.
(vii) Paid rent ₹ 1,500. Rent of ₹ 500 is still outstanding.
(viii) Commission received in advance ₹ 3,000.

Ans. Assets = Liabilities + Capital
1,67,500 = 3,500 + 1,64,000

21. **Show the accounting equation on the basis of the following transactions**
(i) Harish commenced business with cash ₹ 1,50,000.
(ii) Purchased goods on credit ₹ 50,000.
(iii) Withdrew for private use ₹ 3,500.
(iv) Goods purchased for cash ₹ 8,000.
(v) Paid wages ₹ 700 and rent ₹ 700.
(vi) Paid to creditors ₹ 30,000.
(vii) Sold goods on credit (cost price was ₹ 7,000) ₹ 10,000.
(viii) Sold goods for cash (cost price was ₹ 10,000) ₹ 12,000.
(ix) Purchased furniture ₹ 1,500.

Ans. Assets = Liabilities + Capital
1,70,100 = 20,000 + 1,50,100

22. **Prepare the accounting equation on the basis of the following and also prepare a balance sheet on the basis of the last new equation** **Competency Based Que**
(i) Started business with cash ₹ 2,00,000, goods ₹ 80,000, machinery ₹ 1,20,000 and furniture ₹ 7,000.
(ii) 1/4 of the above goods sold at a profit of 20% on cost and half of the payment is received in cash.
(iii) Cash withdrawn for personal use ₹ 2,000.
(iv) ₹ 1,000 was transferred out of the above withdrawn cash, into firm's bank account.
(v) Interest on drawings charged @ 5%.
(vi) Depreciation on machinery provided @ 10%.
(vii) Goods sold to Nikhil for ₹ 20,000 received a bill receivable for the same for 3 months.
(viii) Received ₹ 20,000 from Nikhil against the bill receivable on maturity.
(ix) Rent received in advance ₹ 800.

Ans. Assets = Liabilities + Capital
3,98,800 = 800 + 3,98,000
Balance Sheet Total = ₹ 3,98,800

23. **Prepare the accounting equation on the basis of the following and also prepare balance sheet on the basis of final equation.** **Competency Based Que**
(i) Started business with cash ₹ 5,00,000 and machinery ₹ 3,00,000.
(ii) Purchased goods from Sameer ₹ 70,000.
(iii) Accrued interest ₹ 2,000.
(iv) Commission received in advance ₹ 800.
(v) Interest on capital @ 10% (only on cash introduced as capital).
(vi) Proprietor paid the fee of his son ₹ 3,500 (withdrawn from business).
(vii) Received accrued interest in bank account.
(viii) Sold goods on credit (costing ₹ 8,000) for ₹ 9,000 to Rahul.
(ix) Bought furniture from Amit ₹ 9,000 and paid ₹ 4,000 in cash and for the balance, a bill was accepted.

Ans. Assets = Liabilities + Capital
8,75,300 = 75,800 + 7,99,500
Balance Sheet Total = ₹ 8,75,300

24. **Analyse the effect of each transaction and prove that the accounting equation (A = L + C) always remains balanced.** **Competency Based Que**
(i) Introduced ₹ 4,50,000 as cash and 1,20,000 by stock.
(ii) Purchased plant for ₹ 1,70,000 by paying ₹ 80,000 in cash and balance at a later date.
(iii) Deposited ₹ 3,50,000 into the bank.
(iv) Purchased office furniture for ₹ 60,000 and made payment by cheque.
(v) Goods amounting to ₹ 25,000 was sold for ₹ 35,000.
(vi) Goods costing ₹ 55,000 was sold for ₹ 65,000 on credit.
(vii) Cheque issued to the supplier of goods worth ₹ 20,000.
(viii) Cheque received from Ramesh amounting to ₹ 22,000.
(ix) Withdrawn by owner for personal use ₹ 14,000.

Ans. Assets = Liabilities + Capital
6,66,000 = 90,000 + 5,76,000

Missing Information

25. **On the basis of following transactions, an accountant prepared an accounting equation. He left some transactions incompleted. You are required to fill the incompleted/missing figures.** Competency Based Que

Accounting Equation

Transaction	Cash +	Bank +	Goods +	Advance Salary	=	Capital +	Liabilities
	Assets				=	Capital +	Liabilities
	Cash +	Bank +	Goods +	Advance Salary	=	... +	...
(i) Sujata started a business and invested ₹ 4,00,000 in cash	4,00,000 +	0 +	0 +	0	=	4,00,000 +	0
New equation	4,00,000 +	0 +	0 +	0	=	4,00,000 +	0
(ii) She opened a current account in the name of her firm and deposited ₹ 2,00,000	(2,00,000) +	... +	0 +	0	=	0 +	0
New equation	2,00,000 +	... +	0 +	0	=	4,00,000 +	0
(iii) Purchased goods ₹ 1,00,000. Paid equally by cash and bank	(50,000) +	(...) +	0 +	0	=	0 +	0
New equation	1,50,000 +	... +	... +	0	=	4,00,000 +	0
(iv) Travelled to Pune for business meeting and spent ₹ 8,000 from firm's account	0 +	(8,000) +	0 +	0	=	(8,000) +	0
New equation	1,50,000 +	... +	... +	0	=	3,92,000 +	0
(v) Paid ₹ 5,000 to manager as salary in advance	(5,000) +	0 +	0 +	5,000	=	... +	0
Final equation	1,45,000 +	... +	... +	5,000	=	3,92,000 +	0

Ans. Assets = Liabilities + Capital

3,92,000 = 0 + 3,92,000

26. **Accountant of Jay & Brothers left an accounting equation incompleted. You are required to fill the missing information.** Competency Based Que

Accounting Equation

Transaction	Cash +	Goods +	...	=	Capital +	Liabilities
	Assets			=	Capital +	Liabilities
	Cash +	Goods +	...	=	... +	...
(i) Started business with cash ₹ 50,000 and	50,000 +	20,000 +	...	=	70,000 +	0
New equation	50,000 +	20,000 +	...	=	70,000 +	0
(ii) Opened a bank account with ₹ 20,000	(20,000) +	0 +	20,000	=	0 +	0
New equation	30,000 +	20,000 +	20,000	=	70,000 +	0
(iii) Outstanding rent ₹ 500	0 +	0 +	0	=	(...) +	...
New equation	30,000 +	20,000 +	20,000	=	... +	...
(iv) Received a cheque from Ajay ₹ 2,000 for commission	0 +	0 +	...	=	... +	0
New equation	... +	20,000 +	...	=	... +	...
(v) Interest on capital provided ₹ 1,000	0 +	0 +	0	=	1,000 +	0
Final equation	... +	20,000 +	...	=	... +	...

Ans. Assets = Liabilities + Capital

72,000 = 500 + 71,500

Theoretical Questions

Short Answer Type Questions

1. Why is the evidence provided by source documents important to accounting? NCERT

Ans. The evidence provided by source document is important to accounting because of the reasons discussed below

(i) It provides evidence that a transaction has actually occurred.

(ii) It provides important and relevant information about date, amount, parties involved and other details of a particular transaction.

(iii) It acts as a proof in the court of law.

(iv) It helps in verifying transactions during the auditing process.

2. What is a compound voucher? What are its types?

Ans. Vouchers which record transactions with multiple debits/credits and one credit/debit are called compound vouchers.

Compound vouchers are of two types

(i) **Debit Voucher**
Voucher showing transactions that contain multiple debits and one credit is called debit voucher.

(ii) **Credit Voucher**
Voucher showing transactions that contain multiple credits but one debit is called credit voucher.

3. State the features of supporting vouchers.

Ans. Features of supporting voucher are as follows

(i) It is a written document.

(ii) It contains complete detail of the transaction.

(iii) It is a proof of a transaction having taken place.

(iv) It is generally prepared for a business transaction.

(v) It is signed by the maker.

4. State the features of accounting vouchers.

Ans. Features of accounting voucher are as follows

(i) It is a written document.

(ii) It is prepared on the basis of evidence of the transaction.

(iii) It is an analysis of a transaction.

(iv) It is prepared and signed usually by an accountant and countersigned by the authorised signatory.

(v) In the case of cash/bank voucher, it is a receipt.

5. "The accounting equation forms the foundation of double-entry bookkeeping and represents the relationship between assets, liabilities and owner's equity." In the light of the statement, mention the two basic purposes of accounting equation. Competency Based Que

Ans. The two basic purposes of an accounting equation are

(i) As the accounting equation is always equal, it ensures the accuracy in recording the business transaction.

(ii) It helps in the preparation of balance sheet.

6. "Jaibharat & Brothers sold goods costing ₹ 20,000 at 10% loss on cost. The account reduced the stock by ₹ 18,000." Is the accountant correct? Give answer with valid reasons. Competency Based Que

Ans. No, accountant of Jaibharat & Brothers is not correct because stock will be reduced by ₹ 20,000 not by ₹ 18,000. The right effect of the transaction will be as follows

(i) Stock will be reduced by ₹ 20,000.

(ii) Cash will be increased by ₹ 18,000 as the goods are sold at 10% loss.

(iii) Capital will be reduced by loss of ₹ 2,000.

7. Accounting equation (A = L + C) always holds good under all circumstances. Explain.

Or **"Accounting equation remains intact under all circumstances." Justify the statement with the help of an example.** NCERT; Competency Based Que

Ans. An accounting equation always remains intact with every change that occurs due to a transaction i.e. under all the circumstances. It is because dual aspect concept of accounting says that, every transaction simultaneously, has two effects of equal amount.

A transaction may affect either both sides of the equation by the same amount or one side of the equation only, by both increasing or decreasing it by equal amounts.

However, in any case, the equality of total assets with the total claims of the business (sum of capital and liabilities) is not disturbed. This equality is algebraically represented as "Assets = Liabilities + Capital"

e.g. "Purchased furniture for ₹ 50,000 from Anuj".

Two effects of this transaction will be

- Increase in asset as furniture.
- Increase in liability as creditor (Anuj).

8. Give an example for each of the following types of transaction. Competency Based Que

(i) Increase in one asset, decrease in another asset.

(ii) Increase in asset, increase in liability.

(iii) Increase in asset, increase in owner's capital.

(iv) Decrease in asset, decrease in liability.

(v) Decrease in asset, decrease in owner's capital.

(vi) Decrease in liabilities, increase in owner's capital.

(vii) Increase in one liability, decrease in another liability.
(viii) Increase in liabilities, decrease in owner's capital.

Ans. (i) Purchase of furniture for cash – Increase in furniture and decrease in cash.
(ii) Purchase of furniture on credit – Increase in furniture and increase in creditors.
(iii) Capital introduced by proprietor – Increase in cash and increase in capital.
(iv) Payment to creditors – Decrease in cash and decrease in creditors.
(v) Cash withdrawn by proprietor – Decrease in cash and decrease in capital.
(vi) Conversion of partner's loan into capital – Increase in capital and decrease in loan.
(vii) Bills payable accepted – Increase in bills payable and decrease in creditors.
(viii) Outstanding expenses provided – Increase in creditors for outstanding expenses and decrease in capital.

9. What is the difference between source documents and vouchers? NCERT

Ans. Differences between source documents and vouchers are

Basis	Source Documents	Vouchers
Support	It is a support to the voucher.	Voucher is supported by source document.
Purpose	It is not prepared to record transactions.	It is prepared for the purpose of recording of transactions.
Details	It contains full details of a transaction.	It puts emphasis on which account is to be debited and which account is to be credited.
Evidence	It is evidence of the transaction.	It is a document of correct recording of a transaction.

Objective Questions

Multiple Choice Questions (MCQs)

1. Debit vouchers are prepared to record the transactions involving ....
(a) cash payments (b) credit sale
(c) credit purchase (d) None of these

2. Arun purchased a machine worth ₹ 56,000 from Astha Enterprise on credit. Which voucher will be prepared by Arun? Competency Based Que
(a) Debit voucher (b) Credit voucher
(c) Transfer voucher (d) None of these

3. .... is a written document prepared by the seller for goods sold against cash.
(a) Cash memo (b) Pay-in-slip
(c) Debit note (d) Credit note

4. It is prepared when seller receives goods returned from the buyer.
(a) Debit note (b) Invoice
(c) Credit note (d) Receipt

5. Source vouchers are also known as
(a) supporting vouchers (b) source documents
(c) Both (a) and (b) (d) None of these

6. Accounting vouchers are prepared for ....
(a) cash transactions
(b) non-cash transactions
(c) cash as well as non-cash transactions
(d) None of the above

7. For which of the following transactions, a compound voucher will be prepared? Competency Based Que
(a) Paid ₹ 50,000 to Mohan in settlement of ₹ 51,000
(b) Received ₹ 10,000 from Krishna in full settlement of ₹ 10,500
(c) Purchased a machine ₹ 20,000 from Vijay. Paid 50% by cheque
(d) All of the above

8. Which of the following statement is/are correct?
(a) A debit voucher is prepared for a transaction involving outflow of cash
(b) Transfer voucher is prepared involving no inflow or outflow of cash
(c) Credit voucher is prepared where is inflow of cash
(d) All are correct

9. Voucher is prepared for NCERT
(a) cash received and paid (b) cash/credit sale
(c) cash/credit purchase (d) All of these

10. Voucher is prepared from NCERT
(a) documentary evidence (b) journal entry
(c) ledger account (d) All of these

11. Identify the transaction for which transfer voucher is prepared? Competency Based Que
I. A payment of ₹ 10,000 towards rent.
II. A receipt of ₹ 15,000 towards professional fee.
III. A credit sale of ₹ 5,000 to Ram.

Codes

(a) I and II (b) II and III
(c) Only III (d) Only II

12. At the time of preparing voucher of sales, the accountant of Arihant Publication requires original copy of sales bill. Identify the correct statement from the following. Competency Based Que

(a) No, the accountant is not correct with his stand
(b) Yes, the accountant is correct with his stand
(c) Somehow the accountant is correct
(d) None of the above

13. Which of these information is presented on invoice?

I. Party to whom goods are sold
II. Goods sold III. Total sale amount

Codes

(a) I and II (b) II and III
(c) I and III (d) All of these

14. Which of the following statements about original copy of invoice/bill is correct? Competency Based Que

(a) It is kept with seller for making records in books of accounts
(b) It is made for cash transactions
(c) It is sent to the purchaser
(d) All of the above

15. Due to the following transactions, the total of accounting equation will be Competency Based Que

(i) Started business with cash ₹ 50,000.
(ii) Deposited in bank account ₹ 20,000 out of ₹ 50,000.
(iii) Purchased goods on credit ₹ 20,000.

(a) ₹ 80,000 (b) ₹ 70,000
(c) ₹ 1,00,000 (d) ₹ 60,000

16. What are the main elements of accounting equation?

(a) Creditors, bank and bills payable
(b) Cash, bank and stock
(c) Assets, capital and liabilities
(d) Investments, prepaid expenses and drawing

17. If, there are no liabilities, assets of a business are equal to ....

(a) capital (b) creditors
(c) stock (d) None of these

18. Which of the following statement is incorrect? Competency Based Que

(a) Expenses are reduced from capital in an accounting equation
(b) Profit on sales is added to asset
(c) Payment of outsider's liabilities reduces the capital
(d) Both (b) and (c)

19. Choose the correct statement.

(a) Assets = Capital + Liabilities
(b) Assets = Total Liabilities
(c) Liabilities = Assets − Capital
(d) All of the above

20. "The company repays its bank loan". In the light of this statement, all the given statements are correct except one. Identify that wrong statement. Competency Based Que

(a) There is decrease in assets
(b) There is decrease in liability
(c) There is no effect on owner's equity
(d) There is increase in equity

21. For which of the following transactions, assets and capital will decrease by same amount? Competency Based Que

(a) Goods sold for cash
(b) Fixed asset purchased on credit
(c) Depreciation provided on fixed assets
(d) Goods sold for cash at a profit

22. When goods are returned to supplier, assets and ..... are ...... by same amount. Competency Based Que

(a) liabilities, increased (b) liabilities, decreased
(c) assets, increased (d) assets, decreased

23. Following are the steps involved in developing an accounting equation (in particular order). Arrange the steps in correct sequence.

(i) Find out the effect (in terms of increase or decrease) of a transaction on assets, capitals or liabilities.
(ii) Show the effect on appropriate side of an equation and ensure that the total of right hand side is equal to the total of left hand side.
(iii) Ascertain the variables (i.e. assets, liabilities or capital) involved in a transaction.

Codes

(a) (i), (ii), (iii) (b) (ii), (iii), (i)
(c) (iii), (i), (ii) (d) (iii), (ii), (i)

24. Which of the following transactions, decreases capital?

(a) Outstanding rent ₹ 500
(b) Accrued interest ₹ 1,000
(c) Interest on capital ₹ 800 (d) All of these

25. "Sold household furniture and amount received, deposited in saving account." How will this transaction be recorded in accounting equation? Competency Based Que

(a) Cash increases, capital increases
(b) Cash increases, furniture decreases
(c) Bank account increases, furniture decreases
(d) None of the above

26. **Tiya started her business with cash ₹ 40,000 and furniture of ₹ 30,000. She also borrowed from SBI Bank ₹ 35,000 during the year on which interest of ₹ 500 was outstanding at the year end.**

Closing assets at the year end were ₹ 1,40,000. What will be the closing capital? **Competency Based Que**

(a) ₹ 1,05,000 (b) ₹ 1,04,500
(c) ₹ 1,04,000 (d) ₹ 1,03,500

27. **Income tax paid will reduce**
(a) cash or bank balance (b) capital
(c) cash/bank balance and capital
(d) None of the above

28. **Dividend collected by bank will affect**
(a) bank account, capital account
(b) cash account, bank account
(c) dividend account, bank account
(d) None of the above

29. **Which of the following is correct?**
(a) Depreciation is reduced and amortisation is added to capital
(b) Goods sold costing ₹ 5,000 for ₹ 7,000 will reduce stock by ₹ 7,000
(c) Paid rent in advance will not change total assets
(d) Introduced from saving account ₹ 10,000 into the firm will increase stock as well as capital by ₹ 10,000

30. **As a result of the following transactions, the total of accounting equation will be** **Competency Based Que**
(i) started business with cash ₹ 80,000.
(ii) deposited cash into bank account ₹ 20,000.
(iii) purchased goods on credit ₹ 25,000.

(a) ₹ 1,05,000 (b) ₹ 80,000
(c) ₹ 1,00,000 (d) ₹ 1,20,000

31. **Raghav purchased furniture on credit ₹ 20,000 and paid rent in advance ₹ 1,000. As per final equation, total of capital and liabilities was ₹ 1,20,000. What will be the amount of cash in final equation?** **Competency Based Que**

(a) ₹ 1,00,000 (b) ₹ 99,000
(c) ₹ 1,20,000 (d) ₹ 90,000

32. **Purchased typewriter for personal use by the proprietor will ....**
(a) decrease cash as well as capital
(b) decrease cash and increase asset
(c) decrease cash and decrease asset
(d) decrease cash and increase liability

33. **Accounting equation is based on ....**
(a) dual aspect concept
(b) historical cost concept
(c) matching concept
(d) objectivity concept

Assertion-Reason

Direction (Q. No. 34 to 41) *Read the following Assertion (A) and Reason (R) and choose the correct alternative from the following*

Alternatives
(a) Both Assertion (A) and Reason (R) are true and Reason (R) is the correct explanation of Assertion (A)
(b) Both Assertion (A) and Reason (R) are true, but Reason (R) is not the correct explanation of Assertion (A)
(c) Assertion (A) is true, but Reason (R) is false
(d) Assertion (A) is false, but Reason (R) is true

34. **Assertion** (A) Cash memo is a source document.

Reason (R) It is prepared by seller when he/she sells goods for cash.

35. **Assertion** (A) If Jay sells goods on credit to Vijay, Jay will prepare a debit note.

Reason (R) A debit note is prepared by a person/firm who returns goods purchased earlier.

36. **Assertion** (A) A transfer voucher is prepared when deprecation is charged on machinery.

Reason (R) It does not involve cash.

37. **Assertion** (A) Auditors can easily vouch the vouchers and use them as documentary evidence in future.

Reason (R) A serial number is put on each voucher and the relative source documents are attached with the voucher.

38. **Assertion** (A) A business transaction may result in change in either assets, liabilities or capital of firm and as a result, the total assets might not equate with total of liabilities and capital.

Reason (R) If a business transaction results in increase of assets, there will also be a corresponding increase in amount of either capital or liabilities by same amount.

39. **Assertion** (A) In accounting equation, each transaction affects both sides of the equation, i.e. Assets side and Liabilities + Capital side.

Reason (R) Assets of a business are purchased either from the funds (capital) supplied by the proprietor or from the funds provided by external parties.

40. **Assertion** (A) If goods worth ₹ 4,000 are sold for ₹ 3,500 at credit, then assets will decrease, liabilities will be unchanged and capital will also decrease.

Reason (R) In case, goods are sold on credit, goods (assets) are decreased and debtors (assets) are increased. Also if goods are sold at a loss, the capital is reduced.

41. **Assertion** (A) The party to whom goods are sold on credit is shown at asset side as a debtor.

Reason (R) Debtor is the person or an institution from whom/which, amount is receivable against goods sold.

Two Statements Based MCQs

Direction (Q.No. 42 to 50) *Read the following statements carefully and choose the correct alternative*

Alternatives

(a) Both the statements are correct
(b) Both the statements are incorrect
(c) Statement I is correct and Statement II is incorrect
(d) Statement I is incorrect and Statement II is correct

42. **Statement I** Pay-in-slip is used to withdraw amount from bank account.

Statement II Cheque is a document drawn upon a specified banker and payable on a demand.

43. **Statement I** Cash memo acts as an evidence for a seller only.

Statement II An invoice does not contain party name.

44. **Statement I** Debit note is prepared by the buyer who returns the goods.

Statement II Credit note is prepared by seller who receives the goods returned from the buyer.

45. **Statement I** Source documents are required for audit and tax assessments.

Statement II Source documents do not serve as legal evidence in case of a dispute.

46. **Statement I** There is no change in total assets when goods are purchased for cash.

Statement II Payment received from debtors affects capital.

47. **Statement I** 'Interest on drawing' is reduced from capital as well as added to capital.

Statement II 'Loan taken from bank' is added to bank account and added to outsider's liabilities.

48. **Statement I** Assets = Capital + Liabilities.

Statement II Assets = Total Liabilities.

49. **Statement I** Sold goods costing ₹ 5,000 at 20% profit on sales will increase the capital with the amount of ₹ 1,000.

Statement II Depreciation charged on fixed asset is deducted from capital.

50. **Statement I** Accrued income is added to capital and also shown on asset side.

Statement II Outstanding salary will be reduced from capital and added to liabilities.

Matching

51. Match the following

Column I	Column II
A. Received cash against due from Raghav	(i) Invoice
B. Sold goods on credit	(ii) Receipt
C. Deposited cash into bank account	(iii) Cheque
D. Drawn upon a specified banker	(iv) Pay-in-slip

Codes

	A	B	C	D		A	B	C	D
(a)	(ii)	(iii)	(i)	(iv)	(b)	(ii)	(i)	(iv)	(iii)
(c)	(i)	(iii)	(ii)	(iv)	(d)	(i)	(iv)	(ii)	(iii)

52. Match the following

Column I	Column II
A. Cash memo	(i) Liability
B. Pay-in-slip	(ii) Asset
C. Loan	(iii) Supporting vouchers
D. Debtors	(iv) Depositing money in the bank

Codes

	A	B	C	D		A	B	C	D
(a)	(iii)	(iv)	(i)	(ii)	(b)	(i)	(iii)	(ii)	(iv)
(c)	(ii)	(i)	(iii)	(iv)	(d)	(iv)	(ii)	(i)	(iii)

53. Match the following

Column I	Column II
A. Owner's equity	(i) Capital
B. External equity	(ii) Creditors
C. Asset	(iii) Stock
D. Salary	(iv) Expense

Codes

	A	B	C	D		A	B	C	D
(a)	(i)	(ii)	(iii)	(iv)	(b)	(i)	(ii)	(iv)	(iii)
(c)	(ii)	(iii)	(iv)	(i)	(d)	(ii)	(iii)	(i)	(iv)

54. Match the following

Column I	Column II
A. Deposited cash into bank	(i) Capital (−), Liability (+)
B. Outstanding salary	(ii) Assets (−), Assets (+)
C. Purchased goods on credit	(iii) Assets (+), Liability (+)
D. Sold goods for cash	(iv) Assets (+), Assets (−)

Codes

	A	B	C	D		A	B	C	D
(a)	(ii)	(i)	(iii)	(iv)	(b)	(ii)	(i)	(iv)	(iii)
(c)	(iv)	(iii)	(i)	(ii)	(d)	(iv)	(iii)	(ii)	(i)

55. Match the following

Column I	Column II
A. Interest on drawings	(i) Assets (–), Capital (–)
B. Deprecation charged	(ii) Capital (–), Capital (+)
C. Cash withdrawn for office use	(iii) Assets (+), Assets (–)
D. Payment made to creditors	(iv) Assets (–), Liability (–)

Codes

	A	B	C	D
(a)	(ii)	(i)	(iii)	(iv)
(b)	(ii)	(i)	(iv)	(iii)
(c)	(i)	(ii)	(iii)	(iv)
(d)	(i)	(iii)	(ii)	(iv)

56. Match the following

Column I	Column II
A. Purchased goods for cash	(i) Assets and liabilities will decrease
B. Capital brought in	(ii) Assets and capital will decrease
C. Paid rent	(iii) Assets decrease as well as increase
D. Paid to creditors	(iv) Assets and capital will increase

Codes

	A	B	C	D
(a)	(iii)	(iv)	(ii)	(i)
(b)	(iv)	(iii)	(i)	(ii)
(c)	(iii)	(iv)	(i)	(ii)
(d)	(iii)	(i)	(iv)	(ii)

Case Based MCQs

Direction *Read the following case study and answer the questions 57 and 58 on the basis of the same*

Sohan & Bros started their new business with capital of ₹ 10,00,000 on 1st October, 2024. For smooth operations of business, they hired an expert for managing their business for the salary of ₹ 15,000 per month and paid him ₹ 10,000 against his salary. ₹ 5,00,000 was deposited in firm's current account opened in HDFC Bank. At the year ended 31st March, 2025, interest on capital was provided @ 10% per annum and on the same date rent of ₹ 5,000 was outstanding.

57. Which document will be prepared for cash deposited into bank in above case?

(a) Debit voucher (b) Credit voucher
(c) Transfer voucher (d) None of these

58. What will be the amount of interest on capital provided and its effect on accounting equation?

(a) ₹ 1,00,000; Capital (+), Capital (–)
(b) ₹ 1,00,000; Capital (+), Cash (–)
(c) ₹ 50,000; Capital (+), Capital (–)
(d) ₹ 50,000; Capital (+), Cash (–)

Direction *Read the following case study and answer the questions 59 and 60 on the basis of the same*

Chahar Opticals is a spectacles shop in Lucknow. The shop procures the frames from a local frame manufacturing firm. The shop arranges the lenses from Delhi as and when orders come in according to specifications by the customer.

After the pandemic, to boast the business further, it decided to enter into collaborations with hospital chains to provide the black spectacles required after the cataract surgery.

It shipped 20,000 units of ₹ 5 each of such spectacles to the local hospital. This transaction was on credit basis. However, the hospital returned 10,000 units as those units were found to be defective.

After 6 months, the hospital chain went bankrupt and the shop lost its money as bad debt. It decided to stop the credit policy altogether so that it prevents losses in the future.

At the end of the year, the company was left with ₹ 1,00,000 worth of goods and no debtors. The company also had a creditor of raw materials of ₹ 20,000 and a creditor of a small machinery (not written-off) ₹ 10,000.

59. Which document must have been prepared by Chahar Opticals in the line, "It shipped 20,000 units of ₹ 5 each of such spectacles to the local hospital. This transaction was on credit basis"?

(a) Cash memo (b) Invoice
(c) Debit note (d) None of these

60. What was the affect of the return by the hospitals on the accounting equation? [Use format : Assets = Liabilities + Capital]

(a) (50,000) = (50,000) + 0 (b) 50,000 = 50,000 + 0
(c) (50,000) + 50,000 = 0 + 0
(d) None of the above

Answers

1. (a) cash payments
2. (c) Transfer voucher
3. (a) Cash memo
4. (c) Credit note
5. (c) Both (a) and (b)
6. (c) cash as well as non-cash transactions
7. (d) All of the above
8. (d) All are correct
9. (d) All of these
10. (a) documentary evidence
11. (c) There is no involvement of cash at the time of credit sale. Hence non-cash voucher i.e. transfer voucher will be prepared.
12. (a) No, original copy is given to the buyer. It is not kept by the seller with himself. Only duplicate copy is retained for recording of transaction.
13. (d) All of these
14. (c) It is sent to the purchaser
15. (b) Total of accounting equation = Cash + Bank + Goods

$$= (50{,}000 - 20{,}000) + 20{,}000 + 20{,}000$$
$$= 30{,}000 + 20{,}000 + 20{,}000 = ₹\ 70{,}000$$

16. (c) Assets, capital and liabilities
17. (a) capital
18. (d) Profit is added to capital and payment to outsider's liabilities does not reduce the capital.
19. (d) All of the above
20. (d) Option (d) is wrong statement as on repayment on bank loan, balance from the bank account (assets) will be decreased and on the other hand liability (loan) will also be decreased. Hence there is no effect on owner's equity.
21. (c) Depreciation is charged on asset hence asset is decreased. On the other hand it is an expense therefore capital is also reduced.
22. (b) liabilities, decreased
23. (c) (iii), (i), (ii)
24. (a) Outstanding rent ₹ 500
25. (d) None of the above
26. (b) Closing Capital = Closing Assets – Closing Liabilities

$$= 1{,}40{,}000 - 35{,}000 \text{ (Loan)} - 500 \text{ (Outstanding interest)}$$
$$= ₹\ 1{,}04{,}500$$

27. (c) Cash/bank balance and capital
28. (a) Bank account, capital account
29. (c) Paid rent in advance will not change total assets
30. (a) Total of accounting equation

$$= 80{,}000 + 25{,}000 = ₹\ 1{,}05{,}000$$

31. (b)Final equation will be as follows

Cash + Furniture + Advance Rent = Capital + Liabilities

99,000 (Bal. Fig.) +20,000 + 1,000 = 1,00,000 + 20,000

32. (a) decrease cash as well as capital
33. (a) dual aspect concept
34. (a) Both Assertion (A) and Reason (R) are true and Reason (R) is the correct explanation of Assertion (A)
35. (d) If Jay sells goods on credit to Vijay then Jay will prepare invoice rather than debit note.
36. (a) Both Assertion (A) and Reason (R) are true and Reason (R) is the correct explanation of Assertion (A)
37. (a) Serial numbers make it easier for accountant to vouch the vouchers.
38. (d) As a result of any transaction, the change in assets and liabilities/capital will be equal. Therefore, the total of assets will be equal to total of liabilities and capital.
39. (d) In accounting equation, a transaction may affect only one side. For instance, goods purchased for cash will simultaneously increase and decrease the asset side by the same amount.
40. (a)

Assets			=	Liabilities	+	Capital
(4,000)	+	3,500	=	0	+	(500)
↓		↓				↓
Goods Decreased		Debtors Increased				Loss Deducted

41. (a) Both Assertion (A) and Reason (R) are true and Reason (R) is the correct explanation of Assertion (A)
42. (d) Pay-in-slip is used for depositing cash into bank account not for withdrawing cash from bank account.
43. (b) Cash memo acts as an evidence for seller and buyer both. Invoice contains party name also.
44. (a) Both the statements are correct
45. (c) Source documents are considered as an important evidence of transactions. Hence in case of dispute, it acts as an legal evidence.
46. (c) Payment received from debtors does not affect capital. It affects cash and debtors.
47. (a) Both the statement are correct
48. (a) Both the statements are correct
49. (d) As the rate of profit is given on sale amount, hence profit on cost will be 25%. Hence, capital will be increased by ₹ 1,250 (5,000 × 25%).
50. (a) Both the statements are correct
51. (b) (ii) (i) (iv) (iii)
52. (a) (iii) (iv) (i) (ii)
53. (a) (i) (ii) (iii) (iv)
54. (a) (ii) (i) (iii) (iv)
55. (a) (ii) (i) (iii) (iv)
56. (a) (iii) (iv) (ii) (i)
57. (a) As cash is deposited there is an outflow of cash hence debit voucher will be prepared.
58. (c) Interest on capital $= 10{,}00{,}000 \times \frac{10}{100} \times \frac{6}{12} = ₹\ 50{,}000$
59. (b) Invoice is prepared for credit sale.
60. (c)

Assets			=	Capital	+	Liabilities
50,000	+	(50,000)	=	0	+	0
↓		↓				
Stock Increased		Debtor Decreased				

04

CHAPTER

Journal and Ledger

Journal is a book of original entry in which transactions are recorded in systematic manner i.e. datewise. It provides a basis for ledger posting and keep record of each transaction at one place.

YOUR STUDY GOALS

4.1 Journal
4.2 Simple and Compound Journal Entries
4.3 Accounting Procedure for GST
4.4 Ledger

YOUR PRACTICE GOAL

- Topicwise Solved Questions (30 Solved Questions)
- Numerical Questions [36 Questions (Unsolved)]
- Theoretical Questions [12 Questions (with answers)]
- Objective Questions (57 Qs ; MCQs, A-R, Statements, Matching, Case)

On the basis of source documents, business transactions are recorded in two sets of books i.e. journal and ledger. Transactions are firstly recorded in the journal and thereafter these transactions are posted into ledger. Hence, journal is called the **book of original entry** and ledger as the **book of principal/final entry**.

4.1 Journal

- It is a book in which transactions are recorded in chronological order, i.e. datewise in the order in which they occur.
- The process of recording a transaction in journal is called 'journalising' and the entry recorded is called a 'journal entry'.
- If the business has large transactions, recording of transactions in the journal consumes more time and become tedicious process. Hence, journal is divided (in case of large business) into subsidiary books as given below

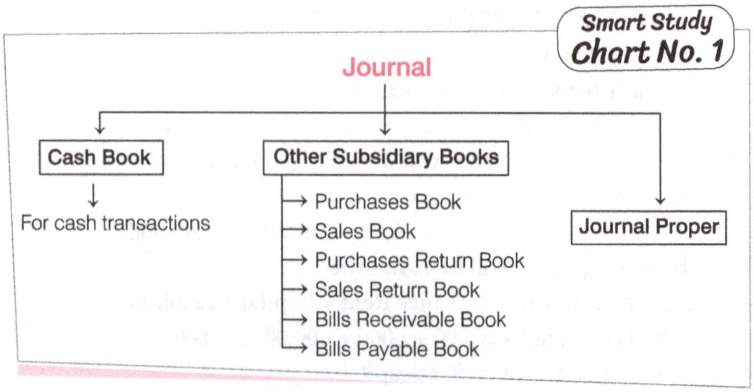

Note In this chapter, we are discussing only process of journalising and then posting into ledger. Subsidiary books have been discussed in the subsequent chapter.

Smart Study Chart No. 2

Aspects of Journal

Characteristics
- Contains day-to-day transactions in chronological order.
- Shows complete details of a transaction in one entry.
- Records both debit and credit aspects of a transaction.
- Provide brief explanation of transaction in 'Narration'.
- It is a daily accounting record, as transactions are recorded on same day.

Functions
- Maintains a chronological record of all transactions.
- Analyse that which accounts are to be debited and credited.
- Provide a basis for ledger posting.
- Keeps complete record of each transaction at one place.

Advantages
- Reduces possibility of ommission of a transaction.
- Easy to locate a particular transaction.
- Facilitates posting into ledger.
- Helps in cross checking of ledger, in case trial balance does not agree.
- Legally, it is more reliable evidence than ledger.

Limitations
- Due to large number of transactions, it becomes bulky.
- Does not provide information quickly.
- If does not facilitate an internal check system.
- In order to ascertain cash balance, cash transactions are recorded in cash book. Thus cash transactions are not recorded in journal.

Format of Journal

JOURNAL

Date	**Particulars**	**LF**	**Amt** (Dr)	**Amt** (Cr)
Records the date on which the transaction occur.	Records the journal entry. Account to be debited is written on first line beginning from the left hand corner along with the word 'Dr' on right hand corner. Account to be credited is written on second line leaving sufficient margin on left side with a prefix 'To'. Below journal entry, a brief description of the transaction is given, called **narration**.	Records the page number of ledger book on which relevant account appears. This column is filled up at the time of posting and not at the time of making journal entry.	The amount to be debited is entered in this column.	The amount to be credited is entered in this column.

Rules of Journalising

It can be studied under two approaches

- Traditional approach
- Modern approach

Smart Study Chart No. 3

Traditional Approach

Personal Accounts

These accounts relate to persons i.e. individuals, firms, companies, etc. Types of personal accounts are

- **Natural Personal Accounts** These accounts are related with human beings. e.g. Mohit, Dinesh, etc.
- **Artificial Personal Accounts** These accounts includes corporate bodies or institutions. e.g. Cooperative societies, company, bank, etc.
- **Representative Personal Accounts** These accounts represent a particular person or group of persons indirectly. e.g. Outstanding salary, capital account, etc.

Rule of Debit and Credit "Debit the receiver, credit the giver."

Impersonal Accounts

These are the accounts which are not personal such as cash account, rent account, etc. Types of impersonal accounts are

- **Real Accounts** These accounts relate to tangible and intangible assets of the firm. e.g. Machine, land, stock, goodwill, patent, etc.

Rule of Debit and Credit "Debit what comes in and credit what goes out."

- **Nominal Accounts** These accounts relate to expenses, losses, revenue, gain, income, etc. e.g. Rent account, purchases account, sales account, interest paid account, etc.

Rule of Debit and Credit "Debit all expenses and losses and credit all incomes and gain".

Smart Study Chart No. 4

Modern Approach

Assets Accounts
The accounts of assets and properties are termed as asset accounts. e.g. Building, plant, goodwill, cash/bank balance, etc.

Rule of Debit and Credit Debit when increase, credit when decrease

Capital Accounts
The accounts of partners or the proprietors, who have invested money in the business are termed as capital accounts.

Rule of Debit and Credit Debit when decrease, credit when increase

Expenses/Losses Accounts
The accounts which show the amount spent or lost in carrying on the business are termed as expenses/losses accounts. e.g. Purchases, wage paid, salary paid, etc.

Rule of Debit and Credit Debit the increase, credit the decrease

Liabilities Accounts
The accounts of lenders, creditors are termed as liabilities. e.g. Creditors, outstanding expenses, etc.

Rule of Debit and Credit Debit when decrease, credit when increase

Revenue/Gains Accounts
These are the accounts of income and gains of the business. e.g. Sales, interest received, discount received, etc.

Rule of Debit and Credit Debit the decrease, credit the increase

Rules for Debit and Credit According to Traditional Approach (A summarised view)

Type of Accounts	**Rule for Debit** (Dr)	**Rule for Credit** (Cr)
Personal Accounts	Dr the receiver	Cr the giver
Real Accounts	Dr what comes in	Cr what goes out
Nominal Accounts	Dr all expenses & losses	Cr all incomes and gains

Steps in Journalising

***Step* 1** Identify the accounts involved in a transaction.

***Step* 2** Identify the nature of accounts involved.

***Step* 3** Identify the rules of debit and credit that are applicable for each of the accounts involved.

***Step* 4** Identify which account is to be debited and which account is to be credited.

***Step* 5** Pass the necessary journal entry in the journal and also record the date and amount of transaction in the respective columns of the journal.

Important Points to Remember

- It is not necessary to use the word 'Account or A/c' after the personal accounts.
- Line should be drawn in particulars column after every journal entry.
- Transactions are recorded in a number of pages in journal book, hence, at the end of each page of journal book, amount columns are totalled and carried forward (c/f) to next page where such amounts are recorded as brought forward (b/f) balances.

4.2 Simple and Compound Journal Entries

A journal may be classified on the basis of number of accounts involved in a transaction as follows

1. **Simple Journal Entry** If there are only two accounts involved in a transaction, it is known as simple journal entry.
   e.g.

   Salary paid ₹ 5,000 → Involves only two accounts i.e. salary account and cash account → Salary A/c Dr / To Cash A/c

2. **Compound Journal Entry** It involves more than two accounts.

   e.g. Received ₹ 2,000 from Mohan, discount allowed ₹ 200 → Involves more than two accounts i.e. cash account, Mohan, discount allowed → Cash A/c Dr / Discount Allowed A/c Dr / To Mohan

Some Common Transactions and their Journal Entries as per Modern Rule

Transactions	Account Involved	Nature of Accounts	Effect on Accounts	Journal Entry	
Commenced business with cash	Cash A/c	Asset	Increase (Dr)	Cash A/c	Dr
	Capital A/c	Capital	Increase (Cr)	To Capital A/c	
Purchased goods for cash	Purchase A/c	Expense	Increase (Dr)	Purchase A/c	Dr
	Cash A/c	Asset	Decrease (Cr)	To Cash A/c	
Purchased goods on credit	Purchase A/c	Expense	Increase (Dr)	Purchase A/c	Dr
	Creditor A/c	Liability	Increase (Cr)	To Creditor A/c	
Sold goods for cash	Cash A/c	Asset	Increase (Dr)	Cash A/c	Dr
	Sales A/c	Revenue	Increase (Cr)	To Sales A/c	
Sold goods on credit	Debtor A/c	Asset	Increase (Dr)	Debtor A/c	Dr
	Sales A/c	Revenue	Increase (Cr)	To Sales A/c	
Purchased asset (furniture) **for cash**	Furniture A/c	Asset	Increase (Dr)	Furniture A/c	Dr
	Cash A/c	Asset	Decrease (Cr)	To Cash A/c	
Purchased furniture on credit from Ajay	Furniture A/c	Asset	Increase (Dr)	Furniture A/c	Dr
	Ajay (Creditor)	Liability	Increase (Cr)	To Ajay	
Cash received from Aryan	Cash A/c	Asset	Increase (Dr)	Cash A/c	Dr
	Aryan (Debtor)	Asset	Decrease (Cr)	To Aryan	
Cash withdrawn for personal use	Cash A/c	Asset	Decrease (Dr)	Drawings A/c	Dr
	Drawings A/c	Asset	Increase (Dr)	To Cash A/c	

Points to Remember for Transactions related to Sale and Purchase of Goods or Assets

- **Purchase** Purchase A/c is debited instead of Goods A/c because of the rule of "Debit all expenses and losses".
- **Sale** Sales A/c is credited instead of Goods A/c because of the rule of "Credit all income and gains."
- **Purchase Return A/c** Also known as Return Outward A/c, should always be credited because purchases (i.e. expenses) are reduced.
- **Sales Return A/c** Also known as Return Inward A/c, should always be debited because sales (i.e. income) are reduced.
- **Credit Transaction** If the name of seller or purchaser is given and it is not stated whether it is a cash or credit transaction, it is considered as credit transaction.
- **Cash Transaction** If the name of seller or purchaser is given alongwith cash or not given, it is considered as a cash transaction.

Some Banking Transactions

Transactions	Accounts Involved	Nature of Accounts	Effect on Accounts	Journal Entry	
Cash deposited into bank	Cash A/c	Asset	Decrease (Cr)	Bank A/c	Dr
	Bank A/c	Asset	Increase (Dr)	To Cash A/c	
Paid to Rahul by cheque	Rahul	Liability	Decrease (Dr)	Rahul	Dr
	Bank A/c	Asset	Decrease (Dr)	To Bank A/c	
Withdrew from bank for office use	Cash A/c	Asset	Increase (Dr)	Cash A/c	Dr
	Bank A/c	Asset	Decrease (Cr)	To Bank A/c	
Bank charges charged by the bank	Bank Charge A/c	Expense	Increase (Dr)	Bank Charges A/c	Dr
	Bank A/c	Asset	Decrease (Cr)	To Bank A/c	
Dividend collected by bank	Bank A/c	Asset	Increase (Dr)	Bank A/c	Dr
	Dividend A/c	Income	Increase (Cr)	To Dividend A/c	
Paid rent by cheque	Rent A/c	Expense	Increase (Dr)	Rent A/c	Dr
	Bank A/c	Asset	Decrease (Cr)	To Bank A/c	
Cheque deposited dishonoured	Debtor A/c	Asset	Increase (Dr)	Debtor A/c	Dr
	Bank A/c	Asset	Decrease (Cr)	To Bank A/c	

Some Specific Transactions

Transactions	Account Involved	Nature of Accounts	Effect on Accounts	Journal Entry
Amount not received due to insolvency of Rohan	Bad Debt A/c Rohan	Expense Asset	Increase (Dr) Decrease (Cr)	Bad Debt A/c Dr To Rohan
Recovered amount written-off as bad debt in last year	Cash A/c Bad Debt Recovered A/c	Asset Income	Increase (Dr) Increase (Cr)	Cash A/c Dr To Bad Debt Recovered A/c
Goods withdrawn by proprietor for personal use	Drawings A/c Purchases A/c	Asset Expense	Increase (Dr) Decrease (Cr)	Drawings A/c Dr To Purchases A/c
Goods given as charity/sample	Charity/Sample A/c Purchase A/c	Expense Asset	Increase (Dr) Decrease (Cr)	Charity/Sample A/c Dr To Purchase A/c
Loss of goods due to fire	Loss by Fire A/c Purchase A/c	Expense/Loss Asset	Increase (Dr) Decrease (Cr)	Loss by Fire A/c Dr To Purchase A/c
Paid installation expenses for a machinery purchased	Machinery A/c Cash A/c	Asset Asset	Increase (Dr) Decrease (Cr)	Machine A/c Dr To Cash A/c
Received ₹ 2,000 from Amit. Discount allowed ₹ 200	Cash A/c Discount Allowed A/c Amit (debtor)	Asset Expense Asset	Increase (Dr) Increase (Dr) Decrease (Cr)	Cash A/c Dr Discount Allowed Dr To Amit

Note

- Installation expenses are debited to machinery because it is a capital expenditure.
- Capital account can also be debited rather than drawings account.

Discount

It is a reduction in amount allowed by the seller to encourage prompt payment and purchase.

Smart Study Chart No. 5

Types of Discount

Trade Discount

- Allowed usually when purchase is made in large quantity.
- It is deducted from the list price and value is recorded after deduction from price.
- This discount is allowed both on credit as well as cash transactions.

Cash Discount

- Allowed by seller to receive immediate or early payment.
- It is allowed as a percentage of amount received.
- Discount allowed account is opened when payment is received. It is debited.
- Discount received account is opened when payment is made. It is credited.

Key Point

If trade discount and cash discount both are allowed, then cash discount is allowed. On the value after deducting trade discount from list price.

Rebate

- It is reduction in the value of goods allowed by the seller for reasons other than for which trade discount and cash discount are allowed.
- No separate entry is passed for rebate. But, if rebate is allowed after the entry for sale of goods has already been passed, then a separate entry will be required in the books of seller as well as purchaser.

In the books of sellers → Rebate Allowed A/c Dr
To Debtor A/c

In the books of purchaser → Creditor A/c Dr
To Rebate Received A/c

Opening Entry

- It is a journal entry by which various balances related to assets, liabilities and capital of the previous year are brought forward in the books of current year.
- While passing an opening entry, following points are to be considered
  - Assets accounts are debited and liabilities accounts are credited.
  - If total of credit side is less than total of debit sides, difference is entered as 'capital' on credit side.
  - If total of debit side is less than total of credit side difference is entered as 'goodwill' on debit side (if cash account or bank account already exists).

Adjustment Entries

These entries are passed at the end of the year to make adjustments in accounts, so that final accounts show true and fair view of the results of the business.

Accounts	Explanation/Entry for Adjustment
1. **Closing stock**	Goods lying unsold at the end of year are termed as closing stock. They are valued at cost or market value whichever is lower. These are usually given as additional information outside the trial balance. They should be brought into the books to determine correct gross profit or gross loss. **Entry** Closing Stock A/c Dr To Trading A/c
2. **Depreciation** (expense)	The fall in the value of fixed assets due to wear and tear, efflux of time or obsolescence is called depreciation. **Entry** Depreciation A/c Dr To Asset A/c
3. **Interest on capital** (expense)	Interest allowed on partner's capital is an expense for the firm. **Entry** Interest on Capital A/c Dr To Capital A/c
4. **Interest on drawings** (income)	Interest charged on drawings made by properietor is an income for the firm. **Entry** Drawings A/c Dr To Interest on Drawings A/c
5. **Outstanding expenses** (liability)	Expenses which have not been paid but have incurred are outstanding expenses. **Entry** Expense A/c Dr To Outstanding Expense A/c
6. **Prepaid expense** (asset)	Expenses which have been paid but benefit of which will be accrued in subsequent year are prepaid expenses. **Entry** Prepaid Expense A/c Dr To Expense A/c
7. **Accrued income or Income earned but not received** (asset)	Income which is earned, but not received is called accrued income. It is an asset for the firm. **Entry** Accrued Income A/c Dr To Income A/c
8. **Income received in advance or Unearned income** (liabilities)	Income which is received in advance but not earned during the accounting period. It is called unearned income. It is a liability for the firm. **Entry** Income A/c Dr To Unearned Income A/c or To Income received in Advance A/c

4.3 Accounting Procedure for GST

Following journal entries are required to be passed in accounting procedure for GST depending upon the different situations

1. For Purchase of Goods

- **For intra-state purchase**

Purchases A/c	Dr
Input CGST A/c	Dr
Input SGST A/c	Dr
To Cash/Bank A/c	(Cash Purchase)
To Creditor's A/c	(Credit Purchase)

- **For inter-state purchase**

Purchase A/c	Dr
Input IGST A/c	Dr
To Cash/Bank A/c	(Cash Purchase)
To Creditor's A/c	(Credit Purchase)

2. For Purchase of Assets

- **For intra-state purchase**

Assets A/c	Dr
Input CGST A/c	Dr
Input SGST A/c	Dr
To Cash/Bank A/c	(Against Payement)
To Vendor's A/c	(Credit Purchase)

- **For inter-state purchase**

Asset A/c	Dr
Input IGST A/c	Dr
To Cash/Bank A/c	(Against Payment)
To Vendors A/c	(Credit Purchase)

3. For Sale of Goods

- **For intra-state sale**

Cash/Bank A/c	Dr (Cash Sale)
Debtor's A/c	Dr (Credit Sale)
To Sales A/c	
To Output CGST A/c	
To Output SGST A/c	

- **For inter-state sale**

Cash/Bank A/c	Dr (Cash Sale)
Debtor's A/c	Dr (Credit Sale)
To Sales A/c	
To Output IGST A/c	

4. For Purchase Return

- **For return of intra-state credit purchase**

Creditor's A/c	Dr
To Purchases Return A/c	
To Input CGST A/c	
To Input SGST A/c	

- **For return of intra-state cash purchase**

Cash/Bank A/c	Dr
To Purchases Return A/c	
To Input CGST A/c	
To Input SGST A/c	

- **For return of inter-state credit purchase**

Creditor's A/c	Dr
To Purchases Return A/c	
To Input IGST A/c	

- **For return of inter-state cash purchase**

Cash/Bank A/c	Dr
To Purchases Return A/c	
To Input IGST A/c	

5. For Sales Return

- **For intra-state credit sale**

Sales Return A/c	Dr
Output CGST A/c	Dr
Output SGST A/c	Dr
To Debtor's A/c	

- **For intra-state cash sale**

Sales Return A/c	Dr
Output CGST A/c	Dr
Output SGST A/c	Dr
To Cash/Bank A/c	

- **For inter-state credit sale**

Sales Return A/c	Dr
Output IGST A/c	Dr
To Debtor's A/c	

- **For inter-state cash sale**

Sales Return A/c	Dr
Output IGST A/c	Dr
To Cash/Bank A/c	

6. For Expenses

- **For intra-state**

Expenses A/c	Dr
Input CGST A/c	Dr
Input SGST A/c	Dr
To Cash/Bank A/c	
To Expense Payable A/c	

- **For inter-state**

Expenses A/c	Dr
Input IGST A/c	Dr
To Cash/Bank A/c	
To Expense Payable A/c	

7. For Income

- **For intra-state**

Bank A/c	Dr (If Received)
Income Receivable A/c	Dr (If Receivable)
To Income Received A/c	
To Output CGST A/c	
To Output SGST A/c	

- **For inter-state**

Bank A/c	Dr (If Received)
Income Receivable A/c	Dr (If Receivable)
To Income Received A/c	
To Output IGST A/c	

8. For Goods taken by the Proprietor for Personal Use

- **If the goods were purchased intra-state**

Drawings A/c	Dr
To Purchases A/c	
To Input CGST A/c	
To Input SGST A/c	

- **If the goods were purchased inter-state**

Drawings A/c	Dr
To Purchases A/c	
To Input IGST A/c	

9. For Goods given as Free Sample,Donation/Charity, Loss of Goods by Fire or Theft

- **For intra-state**

Advertisement (Free sample) A/c	Dr
Donation/Charity A/c	Dr
Loss by Fire/Theft A/c	Dr
To Purchases A/c	
To Input CGST A/c / Input SGST A/c	

- **For inter-state**

Advertisement (Free sample) A/c	Dr
Donation/Charity A/c	Dr
Loss By Fire/Theft A/c	Dr
To Purchases A/c	
To Input IGST A/c	

Adjustment of IGST, CGST and SGST

From 1st Feb., 2019 onwards, set-off mechanism is

Firstly, Output IGST will be adjusted against Input IGST

Output IGST A/c	Dr
To Input IGST A/c	

After such adjustment, there may occur two situations, which are

- Input IGST may exceed Output IGST or
- Output IGST may exceed Input IGST

Case I If Input IGST Exceeds Output IGST

In such a situation, excess of Input IGST will be first adjusted against Output CGST and the balance, if any, will be applied to set off output SGST.

Output CGST A/c	Dr
Output SGST A/c	Dr
Input IGST A/c	

If the full amount of Output CGST has not been adjusted against Input IGST, then the remaining amount of Output CGST will be adjusted against Input CGST and the balance will be paid-off

Output CGST A/c	Dr
To Input CGST A/c	
To Bank A/c	

Similarly, remaining amount of Output SGST will be adjus- ted against Input SGST and the balance will be paid-off.

Output SGST A/c	Dr
To Input SGST A/c	
To Bank A/c	

Case II If Output IGST Exceeds Input IGST

In such a situation

- Firstly, entry for adjusting IGST will be passed

Output IGST A/c	Dr
To Input IGST A/c	

- Then, Input CGST will be adjusted against Output CGST
  Input SGST will be adjusted against Output SGST

Output CGST A/c	Dr
Output SGST A/c	Dr
To Input CGST A/c	
To Input SGST A/c	

- Thereafter, excess of Output IGST will be first adjusted against Input CGST and the balance, if any, will be applied to adjust Input SGST.

Output IGST A/c	Dr
To Input CGST A/c	
To Input SGST A/c	
To Bank A/c	

4.4 Ledger

- A ledger is the principal book of accounting which contains all the accounts related to assets, liabilities, revenues and expenses.
- All the transactions recorded in the journal are transferred to ledger.
- A trial balance is prepared from the ledger and there after financial statements are prepared. Thus, ledger is also called as the **book of final entry.**

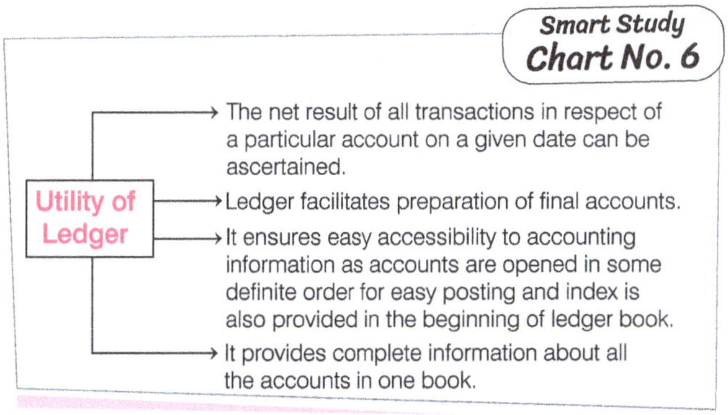

Format of Ledger Account

Each ledger account is the summary of transactions at one place, relating to a particular head. It records not only the amount of transactions but also their effect and direction.

The account is divided into two parts; the left hand side is the debit side and the right hand side is the credit side. The statement is prepared in 'T' shape, therefore sometimes it is called as 'T' account.

Dr **Name of the Account** Cr

Date	Particulars	JF	Amt (₹)	Date	Particulars	JF	Amt (₹)

A brief description of account is given below

1. **Title of the Account** The name of the item is written at the top of the format as the title of the account. The title of the account ends with suffix 'account'.
2. **Dr/Cr** Dr means debit side of the account i.e. left side and Cr means credit side of the account i.e. right side.
3. **Date** Year, month and date of transactions are posted in chronological order in this column.
4. **Particulars** Name of the item with reference to the original book of entry is written on debit/credit side of the account. An account is debited or credited according to the rules of debit and credit.
5. **Journal Folio** (JF) It records the page number of the original book of entry on which relevant transaction is recorded. This column is filled up at the time of posting.
6. **Amount** This column records the amount in numerical figure, corresponding to what has been entered in the amount column of the original book of entry.

Posting the Entries

- The process of transferring the entries from the books of original entry (journal) to the ledger is referred to as posting. Posting is the grouping of all the transactions, in respect to a particular account at one place, which facilitates meaningful conclusion.
- As per the requirements and convenience of the business, posting may be done periodically, weekly, fortnightly or monthly. But now-a-days, through accounting softwares, posting process is done automatically as the journal entry is passed.

Process of Posting from Journal to Ledger

The steps for posting of an account **debited** in a journal entry are

Step 1 Identify the account to be debited in the ledger.

Step 2 Enter the date of transaction in the date column on the debit side.

Step 3 In the 'particulars' column, write the name of the account credited in the journal on the debit side as "To...(name of the account credited)".

Step 4 Record the page number of the journal where the entry exists, in the 'Journal Folio (JF)'column.

Step 5 Enter the relevant amount in the 'amount' column on the debit side.

The steps for posting of an account **credited** in a journal entry are

Step 1 Identify the account to be credited in the ledger.

Step 2 Enter the date of transaction in the date column on the credit side.

Step 3 In the 'particulars' column, write the name of the account debited in the journal on the credit side as "By...(name of the account debited)".

Step 4 Record the page number of the journal where the entry exists, in the 'Journal Folio (JF)' column.

Step 5 Enter the relevant amount in the 'amount' column on the credit side.

An account is opened only once in the ledger and all the entries relating to a particular account are posted on the debit or credit side, as the case may be.

> ***Posting an Opening Entry***
>
> While passing an opening entry, all assets account are debited and all liabilities account are credited.
>
> So, in case of an account, which has been debited, it will be written on the debit side as 'To balance b/d' and in case of an account, which has been credited, it will be written on the credit side as 'By balance b/d'.

Balancing of Accounts

- It is the process of ascertaining the difference between total of debits and total of credits appearing in an account. The difference of amount will be recorded as 'Balance c/d'. It may be a debit balance or a credit balance or a nil balance.
- Balancing of an account is necessary to ascertain the net effect of all transactions posted to that account during a given period.
- Generally, **personal** and **real** accounts are balanced and **nominal** accounts are closed by transferring the balance to trading or profit and loss account. However, considering the scope of the present chapter, even nominal accounts have been balanced in some illustrations.

Procedure for Balancing a Ledger Account

***Step* 1** Total both the sides of a ledger account (i.e. the debit amount and credit amount column) and find out the difference in the totals.

***Step* 2** If the debit side total is more than the credit side total, write the difference on the credit side as 'By balance c/d'.
If the credit side total is more than the debit side total, write the difference on the debit side as 'To balance c/d'.

***Step* 3** Make the total of the debit side equal to the credit side and draw a double line after the totals.

***Step* 4** Bring forward the balance on the next date. If debit balance, write on the debit side as 'To Balance b/d'.
If credit balance, write on the credit side as 'By balance b/d'.

Balancing of a ledger account can be explained from the given ledger account

Dr **Kartik** Cr

Date	Particulars	JF	Amt (₹)	Date	Particulars	JF	Amt (₹)
2022				2022			
Jan 6	To Purchase Return A/c		16,000	Jan 1	By Purchases A/c		2,00,000
Jan 26	To Cash A/c		40,000				
Jan 31	To Bank A/c		60,000				
Jan 31	To Discount A/c		2,000				
Jan 31	To Balance c/d		82,000				
			2,00,000				2,00,000
				Feb 2022	By Balance b/d		82,000

Contents

1. Total the debit side = ₹ 1,18,000.
2. Total the credit side = ₹ 2,00,000.
3. Find out the difference = ₹ 82,000 (2,00,000 – 1,18,000).
   As the credit side total is more than the debit side total, write the difference on the debit side as 'To balance c/d' ₹ 82,000.
4. Make the total of the debit side equal to the credit side and draw a double line after the totals.
5. Bring forward the balance on the next date and since it is a credit balance, write on the credit side as 'By balance b/d' ₹ 82,000.

Mind Map

JOURNAL AND LEDGER

1 Meaning of Journal

- It is a book in which transactions are recorded in chronological order, i.e. datewise in the order in which they occur
- The process of recording a transaction in journal is called journalising and the entry recorded is called a journal entry

Format

JOURNAL

Date	Particulars	LF	Amt (Dr)	Amt (Cr)

2 Rules of Journalising

Rules of journalising can be studied under two approaches, i.e. traditional and modern approach

Modern Approach

According to modern approach, accounts are classified as

- **Assets Accounts** *"Debit when increase, credit when decrease."*
- **Liabilities Accounts** *"Debit when decrease, credit when increase."*
- **Capital Accounts** *"Debit when decrease, credit when increase."*
- **Revenue/Gains Accounts** *"Debit the decrease, credit the increase."*
- **Expenses/Losses Accounts** *"Debit the increase, credit the decrease."*

Traditional Approach

- **Personal Accounts** These accounts relate to persons i.e. individuals, firms, companies, etc. These accounts include natural personal, artificial personal and representative personal accounts.
  Rule *"Debit the reciever, credit the giver."*
- **Impersonal Accounts** These are the accounts which are not personal such as cash account, rent account, etc. These accounts include
  (i) **Real Accounts** These accounts relate to tangible and intangible assets, e.g. Machine, land, goodwill, etc.
  Rule *"Debit what comes in and credit what goes out."*
  (ii) **Nominal Accounts** These accounts relate to expenses, revenues, losses, gains, etc.
  Rule *"Debit all expenses and losses and credit all income and gain."*

3 Important Terms Related to Journal

- **Simple Journal Entry** It involves only two accounts in a transaction.
- **Compound Journal Entry** It involves more than two accounts.
- **Trade Discount** It is allowed usually when purchase is made in large quantity. It is deducted from the list price and value is recorded after deduction from price.
- **Cash Discount** It is allowed by seller to recieve immediate or early payment.
- **Opening Entry** It is a journal entry by which various balances related to assets, capital and liabilities of the previous year are brought forward in the books of current year.
- **Adjustment Entries** These entries are passed at the end of the year to make adjustments in accounts, so that final accounts show true and fair view of results of business.

4 Accounting Procedure of GST

- When there is intra-state purchase, Input CGST and Input SGST accounts are debited
- Where there is inter-state purchase, Input IGST account is debited
- For intra-state sale, Output CGST and Output SGST account are credited
- For inter-state sale, Output IGST account is credited
- In case of purchase return, drawing of goods by proprietor for personal use, goods given as charity, free sample and loss of goods by fire, Input GST is reversed with respective amount

5 Ledger

- A ledger is the principal book of accounting which contains all the accounts related to assets, liabilities, revenues and expenses
- All the transactions recorded in the journal are transferred to ledger
- It is also called as the book of final entry

Utility

- It facilitates preparation of final accounts
- It provides complete information about all the accounts in one book
- The net result of all transactions in respect of a particular account can be ascertained
- It ensures easy accessibility to accounting information

Format

Ledger

Dr | Cr

Date	Particulars	JF	Amt (₹)	Date	Particulars	JF	Amt (₹)

6 Posting Process from Journal to Ledger

- **Step 1** Identify the account to be debited/credited in the ledger.
- **Step 2** Enter date of transaction in the date column on debit/credit side.
- **Step 3** In 'particulars' column, write name of account credited/debited in journal on debit/credit side as To... (account credited)/By ... (account debited).
- **Step 4** Record page number of journal in 'Journal Folio (JF)' column.
- **Step 5** Enter relevant amount in 'amount' column on debit/credit side.

Topicwise Solved Questions

Journal

Solved Question 1 Write journal entries for the following transactions.

2024	
Jan 1	Amit commenced business with cash ₹ 50,000 and furniture ₹ 25,000.
Jan 3	He purchased goods worth ₹ 30,000 from Rahul. Out of it half was purchased on credit.
Jan 5	Sold goods to Priya ₹ 20,000.
Jan 10	Goods returned by Priya ₹ 3,000 (Sale value ₹ 4,000).
Jan 12	Goods purchased from Vishal ₹ 40,000.
Jan 15	Goods returned to Karan ₹ 8,000.
Jan 20	Bought goods for cash ₹ 10,000.
Jan 25	Paid cartage ₹ 500.
Jan 30	Paid interest on loan ₹ 2,000.

Sol. JOURNAL

Date	Particulars	LF	Amt (Dr)	Amt (Cr)
2024				
Jan 1	Cash A/c Dr		50,000	
	Furniture A/c Dr		25,000	
	To Capital A/c			75,000
	(Being capital introduced in cash and furniture)			
Jan 3	Purchase A/c Dr		30,000	
	To Cash A/c			15,000
	To Rahul			15,000
	(Being purchased goods, half on credit)			
Jan 5	Priya Dr		20,000	
	To Sales A/c			20,000
	(Being goods sold to Priya)			
Jan 10	Sales Return A/c Dr		4,000	
	To Priya			4,000
	(Being goods returned to Priya)			
Jan 12	Purchase A/c Dr		40,000	
	To Vishal			40,000
	(Being goods purchased on credit)			
Jan 15	Karan A/c Dr		8,000	
	To Purchase Return A/c			8,000
	(Being goods returned to Karan)			
Jan 20	Purchase A/c Dr		10,000	
	To Cash A/c			10,000
	(Being goods purchased for cash)			
Jan 25	Cartage A/c Dr		500	
	To Cash A/c			500
	(Being paid cartage)			
Jan 30	Interest on Loan A/c Dr		2,000	
	To Cash A/c			2,000
	(Being paid interest on loan)			
	Total		1,89,500	1,89,500

Solved Question 2 Write journal entries for the following transactions.

2024		Amt (₹)
(i)	Deposited into bank account	20,000
(ii)	Amount withdrawn from bank account	5,000
(iii)	Withdrawn from bank account for personal expenses	2,000
(iv)	Transferred from bank account to fixed deposit account	3,000
(v)	Goods bought from Arnav. Paid by cheque	2,000
(vi)	Paid salary ₹ 2,000, rent ₹ 1,000 and for a fan purchased ₹ 1,500	—
(vii)	Charged by bank for its services	200
(viii)	Interest allowed by bank	500

Sol. JOURNAL

Date	Particulars	LF	Amt (Dr)	Amt (Cr)
(i)	Bank A/c Dr		20,000	
	To Cash A/c			20,000
	(Being deposited in bank account)			
(ii)	Cash A/c Dr		5,000	
	To Bank A/c			5,000
	(Being withdrawn from bank account)			
(iii)	Drawings A/c Dr		2,000	
	To Bank A/c			2,000
	(Being withdrawn for personal expenses)			
(iv)	Fixed Deposit A/c Dr		3,000	
	To Bank A/c			3,000
	(Being transfer from bank account)			
(v)	Purchase A/c Dr		2,000	
	To Bank A/c			2,000
	(Being purchased goods and paid by cheque)			
(vi)	Salary A/c Dr		2,000	
	Rent A/c Dr		1,000	
	Fan A/c Dr		1,500	
	To Cash A/c			4,500
	(Being paid salary, rent and for fan)			

Date	Particulars		LF	Amt (Dr)	Amt (Cr)
(vii)	Bank Charge A/c	Dr		200	
	To Bank A/c				200
	(Being charged by bank)				
(viii)	Bank A/c	Dr		500	
	To Interest Received A/c				500
	(Being received interest by bank)				
	Total			37,200	37,200

Solved Question 3 Journalise the following.

2024

Jan 10 Bought goods on credit from Vijay ₹ 5,000.

Jan 12 Settled Vijay's dues by paying him a cheque of ₹ 4,500.

Jan 13 Bought a printer for ₹ 2,000 and spent ₹ 200 on its repairs. 50% amount was paid by cash and remaining by bank account.

Jan 14 Sold goods to Rahul ₹ 4,000. Received from him a cheque after banking hours.

Jan 15 Deposited Rahul's cheque in bank account.

Jan 20 Received a cheque of ₹ 2,000 from Amit.

Jan 25 Amit's cheque was returned dishonoured.

Jan 28 Amit settled his account by means a cheque of ₹ 2,050, ₹ 50 being for interest charged.

Sol. JOURNAL

Date	Particulars		LF	Amt (Dr)	Amt (Cr)
2024					
Jan 10	Purchase A/c	Dr		5,000	
	To Vijay				5,000
	(Being goods purchased from Vijay)				
Jan 12	Vijay A/c	Dr		5,000	
	To Bank A/c				4,500
	To Discount Received A/c				500
	(Being paid cheque in full settlement)				
Jan 13	Printer A/c	Dr		2,200	
	To Cash A/c				1,100
	To Bank A/c				1,100
	(Being printer purchased, half is paid by cash and remaining by cheque)				
Jan 14	Cheque in Hand A/c	Dr		4,000	
	To Sales A/c				4,000
	(Being received cheque after banking hour)				
Jan 15	Bank A/c	Dr		4,000	
	To Cheque in Hand A/c				4,000
	(Being cheque deposited in bank account)				
Jan 20	Bank A/c	Dr		2,000	
	To Amit				2,000
	(Being cheque received from Amit)				
Jan 25	Amit	Dr		2,000	
	To Bank A/c				2,000
	(Being cheque was dishonoured)				
Jan 28	Bank A/c	Dr		2,050	
	To Amit				2,000
	To Interest A/c				50
	(Being Amit settled his account)				
	Total			26,250	26,250

Solved Question 4 Write journal entries for the following transactions.

(i) Sold goods to Manav list price ₹ 50,000 less trade discount 10% plus 20% profit. Received only 3/4th amount and allowed him cash discount 5%.

(ii) Sold goods to Rachna list price ₹ 40,000 less trade discount 10% and cash discount 2%. Received 50% amount at the time of sale.

(iii) Received goods in return by Manav list price ₹ 4,000.

(iv) Rebate allowed to Manav ₹ 200.

(v) Received balance amount from Rachna.

Sol. JOURNAL

Date	Particulars		LF	Amt (Dr)	Amt (Cr)
(i)	Cash A/c	Dr		38,475	
	Discount Allowed A/c (WN1)	Dr		2,025	
	Manav	Dr		13,500	
	To Sales A/c				54,000
	(Being goods sold to Manav, 3/4th received and allowed cash discount)				
(ii)	Cash A/c	Dr		17,640	
	Discount Allowed A/c (WN2)	Dr		360	
	Rachna	Dr		18,000	
	To Sales A/c				36,000
	(Being goods sold to Rachna. 50% amount received, balance credit sale debited to Rachna)				
(iii)	Sales Return A/c (WN3)	Dr		4,320	
	To Manav				4,320
	(Being goods received as return from Manav)				
(iv)	Rebate Allowed A/c	Dr		200	
	To Manav				200
	(Being rebate allowed to Manav)				
(v)	Cash A/c	Dr		18,000	
	To Rachna				18,000
	(Being received balance amount from Rachna)				
	Total			1,12,520	1,12,520

Working Notes

1. Sale Value = Price − Trade Discount + Profit

$= 50{,}000 - 5{,}000 + (45{,}000 \times 20\%)$

$= 50{,}000 - 5{,}000 + 9{,}000 = ₹\ 54{,}000$

$\frac{3}{4}$th Value $= 54{,}000 \times \frac{3}{4} = ₹\ 40{,}500$

Cash Discount $= 40{,}500 \times \frac{5}{100} = ₹\ 2{,}025$

2. Sale Value = Price – Trade Discount (10% of price)

$= 40{,}000 - 4{,}000 = ₹\ 36{,}000$

50% Value $= \frac{36{,}000}{2} = ₹\ 18{,}000$

Cash Discount $= 18{,}000 \times 2\% = ₹\ 360$

3. Value of Goods returned by Manav

$= 4{,}000 - 400 + (3{,}600 \times 20\%)$

$= 3{,}600 + 720 = ₹\ 4{,}320$

Solved Question 5 **Enter the following transactions in the journal book of Narmada & Co.**

2024

Oct 1 **Purchased goods from Vandana of the list price ₹ 30,000 at 10% trade discount.**

Oct 5 **Returned goods to Vandana of the list price of ₹ 10,000.**

Oct 7 **Paid cash to Vandana ₹ 17,700 in full settlement of her account.**

Oct 10 **Sold goods to Aradhana list price ₹ 20,000 less 10% trade discount. Cash discount of 5% was allowed on immediate payment of any amount. Received only 50% cash immediately and balance at a later date.**

Oct 15 **Received due amount from Aradhana in cash.**

Sol. **In the Books of Narmada & Co.**
JOURNAL

Date	Particulars	LF	Amt (Dr)	Amt (Cr)
2024				
Oct 1	Purchase A/c Dr		27,000	
	To Vandana			27,000
	(Being goods purchased on credit from Vandana)			
Oct 5	Vandana Dr		9,000	
	To Purchase Return A/c			9,000
	(Being goods returned to Vandana)			
Oct 7	Vandana A/c Dr		18,000	
	To Cash A/c			17,700
	To Discount Received A/c			300
	(Paid cash to Vandana, discount received ₹ 300)			
Oct 10	Cash A/c Dr		8,550	
	Discount Allowed A/c (WN) Dr		450	
	Aradhana Dr		9,000	
	To Sales A/c			18,000
	(Being goods sold to Aradhana, 50% on credit, discount allowed on 50% cash sale)			
Oct 15	Cash A/c Dr		9,000	
	To Aradhana			9,000
	(Being received balance due from Aradhana)			
	Total		81,000	81,000

Working Note

Sale Value = Price – Trade Discount

$= 20{,}000 - 2{,}000\ (20{,}000 \times 10\%) = ₹\ 18{,}000$

Cash Discount $= \frac{18{,}000}{2} \times 5\% = ₹\ 450$

Solved Question 6 **Following balances appear in the books of Hari & Sons on 31st March, 2024.**

Assets : Cash at bank ₹ 5,500, cash in hand ₹ 4,500, sundry debtors (Ram ₹ 1,500; Shyam ₹ 2,000), closing stock ₹ 10,000, plant and machinery ₹ 8,000.

Liabilities : Creditors ₹ 5,000 (Parul & Sons)

Pass the opening entry as on 1st April, 2024.

Sol. **Opening Journal Entry**

Date	Particulars	LF	Amt (Dr)	Amt (Cr)
2024				
Apr 1	Bank A/c Dr		5,500	
	Cash A/c Dr		4,500	
	Sundry Debtors A/c Dr		3,500	
	(Ram 1,500			
	Shyam 2,000)			
	Stock A/c Dr		10,000	
	Plant and Machinery A/c Dr		8,000	
	To Parul & Sons			5,000
	To Capital A/c (Balancing figure)			26,500
	(Being balances of assets, liabilities and capital brought forward)			
	Total		31,500	31,500

Solved Question 7 **Journalise the following transactions in the journal of Shri Laxman**

(i) **Paid cash to Ramit (after receiving discount ₹ 500) ₹ 5,000.**

(ii) **Received cash from Rahul ₹ 5,600 and discount allowed ₹ 600.**

(iii) **Goods sold to Mohan ₹ 2,000 and Mohan returned goods ₹ 500 later.**
Received cash from Mohan in full settlement ₹ 1,400.

(iv) **Goods sold to Rakesh list price ₹ 20,000 at 10% trade discount plus 20% profit.**

(v) **Purchased goods from Indu list price ₹ 10,000 at 10% trade discount.**

(vi) **Sold goods costing ₹ 50,000 to Suresh at a profit of 25% on cost less 20% trade discount. Paid cartage ₹ 500 (to be charged from customer).**

Sol. **In the Books of Shri Laxman**
JOURNAL

Date	Particulars	LF	Amt (Dr)	Amt (Cr)
(i)	Ramit Dr		5,500	
	To Cash A/c			5,000
	To Discount Received A/c			500
	(Being paid cash, discount received)			

Date	Particulars	LF	Amt (Dr)	Amt (Cr)
(ii)	Cash A/c Dr		5,600	
	Discount Allowed A/c Dr		600	
	To Rahul			6,200
	(Being cash received from Rahul and discount allowed)			
(iii)	Mohan Dr		2,000	
	To Sales A/c			2,000
	(Being goods sold to Mohan)			
	Sales Return A/c Dr		500	
	To Mohan			500
	(Being goods returned by Mohan)			
	Cash A/c Dr		1,400	
	Discount Allowed A/c Dr		100	
	To Mohan's			1,500
	(Being received cash after allowing discount)			
(iv)	Rakesh Dr		21,600	
	To Sales A/c			21,600
	(Being goods sold to Rakesh at 20% profit and less 10% trade discount)			
(v)	Purchase A/c Dr		9,000	
	To Indu			9,000
	(Being goods purchased from Indu 10% trade discount)			
(vi)	Suresh Dr		50,000	
	To Sales A/c			50,000
	(Being goods sold to Suresh)			
	Cartage A/c Dr		500	
	To Cash A/c			500
	(Being paid for cartage)			
	Suresh Dr		500	
	To Cartage A/c			500
	(Being cartage charged from Suresh)			
	Total		97,300	97,300

Solved Question 8 **Pass journal entries for the following transactions**

2024

Dec 1 **Bought goods from Vimal list price ₹ 60,000 at 10% trade discount and 2% cash discount. Paid full amount at the time of purchase equally by cash and a cheque.**

Dec 5 **Bought goods from Kartik list price ₹ 1,00,000 at 10% trade discount and 5% cash discount. Only half amount was paid by a cheque.**

Dec 10 **Sold goods to Prince list price ₹ 60,000 at 10% trade discount and 5% cash discount. Half amount was received equally by cash and a cheque.**

Dec 12 **Sold goods to Amrita list price ₹ 40,000 at trade discount 10% and 2% cash discount (if payment is received in 10 days). 70% amount was received on 20th December and remaining amount was received on 28th December.**

Sol. **JOURNAL**

Date	Particulars	LF	Amt (Dr)	Amt (Cr)
2024				
Dec 1	Purchase A/c Dr		54,000	
	To Cash A/c			26,460
	To Bank A/c			26,460
	To Discount Received A/c			1,080
	(Being goods bought price ₹ 60,000 less trade discount 10% and cash discount 2%, paid equally by cash and a cheque)			
Dec 5	Purchase A/c Dr		90,000	
	To Bank A/c			42,750
	To Discount Received A/c			2,250
	To Kartik			45,000
	(Being goods bought price ₹ 1,00,000 at 10% trade discount and 5% cash discount. Only half paid by cheque)			
Dec 10	Cash A/c Dr		12,825	
	Bank A/c Dr		12,825	
	Prince Dr		27,000	
	Discount Allowed A/c Dr		1,350	
	To Sales A/c			54,000
	(Being sold goods price ₹ 60,000 less 10% trade discount 5% cash discount, half on credit and half was received equally by cash and a cheque)			
Dec 12	Amrita Dr		36,000	
	To Sales A/c			36,000
	(Being goods sold to Amrita)			
Dec 20	Cash A/c Dr		24,696	
	Discount Allowed A/c Dr		504	
	To Amrita			25,200
	(Being 70% amount received and discount allowed 2%)			
Dec 28	Cash A/c Dr		10,800	
	To Amrita			10,800
	(Being remaining amount received)			

Solved Question 9 **Journalise the following transactions in the books of Shree Nimesh.**

(i) Received cash from Jaya for a bad debt written-off last year ₹ 400.

(ii) Manu who owed us ₹ 5,000 is declared insolvent and 65 paise in a rupee is received from his estate.

(iii) ₹ 1,000 due from Rohit are now bad debts.

(iv) Goods worth ₹ 2,000 were used by the proprietor.

(v) Paid income tax ₹ 5,000.

(vi) Purchased furniture worth ₹ 20,000 and tools worth ₹ 4,000.

(vii) Paid to Nishant out of business funds for repair of Shree Nimesh's house ₹ 8,000.

Sol. In the Books of Shree Nimesh

JOURNAL

Date	Particulars	LF	Amt (Dr)	Amt (Cr)
(i)	Cash A/c Dr		400	
	To Bad Debts Recorvered A/c			400
	(Being the bad debts written-off last year, now recovered)			
(ii)	Cash A/c (5,000 × 0.65) Dr		3,250	
	Bad Debts A/c Dr		1,750	
	To Manu			5,000
	(Being cash received and bad debts written-off)			
(iii)	Bad Debts A/c Dr		1,000	
	To Rohit			1,000
	(Being ₹ 1,000 due from Rohit is bad debts now)			
(iv)	Drawings A/c Dr		2,000	
	To Purchases A/c			2,000
	(Being goods worth ₹ 2,000 used by the proprietor)			
(v)	Drawings A/c / Capital A/c Dr		5,000	
	To Cash A/c			5,000
	(Being the income tax paid)			
(vi)	Furniture A/c Dr		20,000	
	Tools A/c Dr		4,000	
	To Cash A/c			24,000
	(Being furniture and tools purchased)			
(vii)	Drawings A/c Dr		8,000	
	To Cash A/c			8,000
	(Being amount paid for repairs of Shree Nimesh's residential house)			
	Total		45,400	45,400

Solved Question 10 Journalise the following transactions.

(i) Paid rent of building ₹ 30,000, half of the building is used by the proprietor for residential use.
(ii) Paid fire insurance of the above building ₹ 2,500.
(iii) Salary due to clerk ₹ 1,250.
(iv) Charge depreciation on furniture @ 10% per annum for 1 month (furniture ₹ 30,000).
(v) Provide interest on capital (₹ 1,50,000) at 15% per annum for 6 months.
(vi) Charge interest on drawings (₹ 25,000) at 18% per annum for 6 months.
(vii) Interest on loan from Ram (₹ 2,50,000) at 18% per annum for 2 months is outstanding.
(viii) Interest on loan to Shyam (₹ 5,00,000) at 18% per annum for 2 months is outstanding.
(ix) Received commission ₹ 2,500 half of which is in advance.
(x) Brokerage due to us ₹ 1,250.
(xi) Salaries remaining unpaid ₹ 15,000 and rent due to landlord ₹ 2,000.

Sol. **JOURNAL**

Date	Particulars	LF	Amt (Dr)	Amt (Cr)
(i)	Rent A/c Dr		30,000	
	To Cash A/c			30,000
	(Being the rent paid for building)			
	Drawings A/c (30,000 × 50%) Dr		15,000	
	To Rent A/c			15,000
	(Being the rent for half building charged to proprietor)			
	In place of the two entries, one single entry can also be passed			
	Rent A/c Dr		15,000	
	Drawings A/c Dr		15,000	
	To Cash A/c			30,000
(ii)	Fire Insurance Premium A/c Dr		2,500	
	To Cash A/c			2,500
	(Being the fire insurance premium paid for building)			
	Drawings A/c Dr		1,250	
	To Fire Insurance Premium A/c			1,250
	(Being the fire insurance premium for half building charged to proprietor)			
	In place of two entries, one single entry can also be passed			
	Drawings A/c Dr		1,250	
	Fire Insurance Premium A/c Dr		1,250	
	To Cash A/c			2,500
(iii)	Salary A/c Dr		1,250	
	To Outstanding Salary A/c			1,250
	(Being salary due to clerk)			
(iv)	Depreciation A/c Dr $\left(30{,}000 \times \frac{10}{100} \times \frac{1}{12}\right)$		250	
	To Furniture A/c			250
	(Being the depreciation on furniture provided)			
(v)	Interest on Capital A/c Dr $\left(1{,}50{,}000 \times \frac{15}{100} \times \frac{6}{12}\right)$		11,250	
	To Capital A/c			11,250
	(Being the interest on capital provided @ 15% per annum for 6 months)			

Date	Particulars	LF	Amt (Dr)	Amt (Cr)
(vi)	Capital A/c / Drawings A/c Dr		2,250	
	To Interest on Drawings A/c $\left(25{,}000 \times \frac{18}{100} \times \frac{6}{12}\right)$			2,250
	(Being the interest on drawings charged @ 18% per annum for 2 months)			
(vii)	Interest on Loan from Ram A/c Dr $\left(2{,}50{,}000 \times \frac{18}{100} \times \frac{2}{12}\right)$		7,500	
	To Outstanding Interest on Loan from Ram A/c			7,500
	(Being the interest on loan from Ram provided @ 18% per annum for 2 months)			
(viii)	Accrued Interest on Loan to Shyam A/c Dr		15,000	
	To Interest on Loan to Shyam A/c $\left(5{,}00{,}000 \times \frac{18}{100} \times \frac{2}{12}\right)$			15,000
	(Being the interest on loan to Shyam charged @ 18% per annum 2 months)			
(ix)	Cash A/c Dr		2,500	
	To Commission A/c			2,500
	(Being the commission received)			
	Commission A/c Dr		1,250	
	To Commission Received in Advance A/c (2,500 × 50%)			1,250
	(Being the commission received in advance adjusted)			
(x)	Accrued Brokerage A/c Dr		1,250	
	To Brokerage A/c			1,250
	(Being the brokerage due to us adjusted)			
(xi)	Salaries A/c Dr		15,000	
	To Outstanding Salaries A/c			15,000
	(Being salaries due)			
	Rent A/c Dr		2,000	
	To Outstanding Rent A/c			2,000
	(Being rent due but not paid)			
	Total		1,08,250	1,08,250

Solved Question 11 Write journal entries for the following transactions.

(i) Proprietor withdrew ₹ 5,000 for making payment of his son's tuition fees.

(ii) Proprietor withdrew goods cost ₹ 600, sales price ₹ 800 for his personal use.

(iii) Goods of ₹ 10,000 were distributed to red cross society as a charity.

(iv) Stolen by Ramesh, an employee, goods worth ₹ 200.

(v) Goods worth ₹ 5,000 were destroyed by fire. Goods were not insured.

(vi) Goods worth ₹ 6,000 were destroyed by fire goods were insured and company accepted insurance claim of ₹ 5,000.

Sol. JOURNAL

Date	Particulars	LF	Amt (Dr)	Amt (Cr)
(i)	Drawing A/c Dr		5,000	
	To Cash A/c			5,000
	(Being withdrew for payment of his son's tuition fees)			
(ii)	Drawing A/c Dr		600	
	To Purchase A/c			600
	(Being withdrew goods for personal use)			
(iii)	Charity A/c Dr		10,000	
	To Purchase A/c			10,000
	(Being goods were distributed for charity)			
(iv)	Loss by Theft A/c Dr		200	
	To Purchase A/c			200
	(Being stolen by Ramesh)			
(v)	Loss by Fire A/c Dr		5,000	
	To Purchase A/c			5,000
	(Being goods destroyed by fire)			
(vi)	Loss by Fire A/c Dr		6,000	
	To Purchase A/c			6,000
	Insurance Claim A/c Dr		5,000	
	To Loss by Fire A/c			5,000
	Profit and Loss A/c Dr		1,000	
	To Loss by Fire A/c			1,000
	(Being goods were destroyed by fire, goods were insured accepted insurance claim)			
	Total		32,800	32,800

Solved Question 12 Journalise the following transactions.

2024

Jun 1 Paid rent ₹ 5,000 of building. Half is related with proprietor's residence.

Jun 4 Paid insurance premium of ₹ 4,000 (home insurance) for above building.

Jun 7 Salary outstanding to Rashika ₹ 5,000.

Jun 10 Charged depreciation for 2 months @ 10% p.a. on furniture of ₹ 50,000.

Jun 10 Provide interest on capital @ 5% p.a on capital ₹ 2,00,000 for 6 months.

Jun 15 Interest on loan @ 10% p.a. loan amount is ₹ 20,000 taken on 1st October, 2023 from SBI. Books are closed on 31st March.

Jun 20 Interest on drawings ₹ 500.

Jun 27 Received commission ₹ 10,000. Half is related with next year.

Jun 29 Paid ₹ 5,000 for security deposit for telephone connection.

Jun 30 Rent paid ₹ 10,000. Half is in advance.

Sol. JOURNAL

Date	Particulars	LF	Amt (Dr)	Amt (Cr)
2024				
Jun 1	Rent A/c Dr		2,500	
	Drawings A/c Dr		2,500	
	To Cash A/c			5,000
	(Being paid rent half of which is for proprietor's residence)			
Jun 4	Drawings A/c Dr		4,000	
	To Cash A/c			4,000
	(Being paid insurance premium home insurance)			
Jun 7	Salary A/c Dr		5,000	
	To Outstanding Salary A/c			5,000
	(Being salary outstanding)			
Jun 10	Depreciation A/c Dr		833	
	To Furniture A/c			833
	(Being depreciation charged on furniture $50{,}000 \times \frac{10}{100} \times \frac{2}{12} = ₹\ 833$)			
Jun 10	Interest on Capital A/c Dr		5,000	
	To Capital A/c			5,000
	(Being provided interest on capital @ 5% for 6 months)			
Jun 15	Interest on Loan A/c Dr		1,000	
	To Loan from SBI A/c			1,000
	(Being interest on loan @ 10% p.a. charged for 6 months)			
Jun 20	Drawings A/c Dr		500	
	To Interest on Drawings A/c			500
	(Being interest on drawings charged)			
Jun 27	Cash A/c Dr		10,000	
	To Commission Received A/c			5,000
	To Commission Received in Advance A/c			5,000
	(Being commission received half of which is advance)			
Jun 29	Security Deposit A/c Dr		5,000	
	To Cash A/c			5,000
	(Being paid security deposit for telephone connection)			
Jun 30	Rent A/c Dr		5,000	
	Prepaid Rent A/c Dr		5,000	
	To Cash A/c			10,000
	(Being paid rent half of which is advance)			
	Total		46,333	46,333

Solved Question 13 Pass journal entries for the following transactions

(i) Received final amount ₹ 15,000 out of ₹ 25,000 from Raghav who became insolvent.

(ii) Received ₹ 5,000 from Anushka written-off as bad debt previous year.

(iii) Salary paid ₹ 10,000. Out of which ₹ 2,000 was related to next year.

(iv) Outstanding rent (rent due but not paid) ₹ 1,000.

(v) Charged 5% depreciation on furniture costing ₹ 50,000.

(vi) Provide 10% interest on capital amounting to ₹ 5,00,000.

(vii) Charged interest on drawings ₹ 1,000.

Sol. JOURNAL

Date	Particulars	LF	Amt (Dr)	Amt (Dr)
(i)	Cash A/c Dr		15,000	
	Bad Debt A/c Dr		10,000	
	To Raghav			25,000
	(Being received cash from Raghav in full settlement on account of his insolvency)			
(ii)	Cash A/c Dr		5,000	
	To Bad Debt Recovered A/c			5,000
	(Being bad debt written-off last year received)			
(iii)	Salary A/c Dr		8,000	
	Prepaid Salary A/c Dr		2,000	
	To Cash A/c			10,000
	(Being paid salary, ₹ 2,000 in advance)			
(iv)	Rent A/c Dr		1,000	
	To Outstanding Rent A/c			1,000
	(Being rent outstanding recorded)			
(v)	Depreciation A/c Dr		2,500	
	To Furniture A/c			2,500
	(Being depreciation charged on furniture)			
(vi)	Interest on Capital A/c Dr		50,000	
	To Capital A/c			50,000
	(Being interest on capital provided)			
(vii)	Drawings A/c Dr		1,000	
	To Interest on Drawings A/c			1,000
	(Being interest charged on drawings)			
	Total		94,500	94,500

Solved Question 14 Record the following items in the books of Thakur & Sons.

(i) Purchased stock/goods on cash ₹ 40,000 from Kartik and also paid ₹ 500 for their carriage.

(ii) Purchased a machine by giving a cheque of ₹ 2,00,000. Paid cash ₹ 5,000 for installation expense of machine.

(iii) Purchased an old machine ₹ 50,000 and spent ₹ 4,000 on its carriage and ₹ 5,000 for its urgent repairing.

(iv) Paid ₹ 1,500 for repairing the office furniture.

Sol. In the Books of Thakur & Sons

JOURNAL

Date	Particulars		LF	Amt (Dr)	Amt (Cr)
(i)	Purchase A/c	Dr		40,000	
	Carriage A/c	Dr		500	
	To Cash A/c				40,500
	(Being purchased goods and paid carriage)				
(ii)	Machine A/c	Dr		2,05,000	
	To Bank A/c				2,00,000
	To Cash A/c				5,000
	(Being machine purchased by cheque and paid installation expense debited to machine account)				
(iii)	Machine A/c	Dr		59,000	
	To Cash A/c				59,000
	(Being purchased an old machine for ₹ 50,000 and spent ₹ 4,000 and ₹ 5,000 on carriage and repairing)				
(iv)	Repairs A/c	Dr		1,500	
	To Cash A/c				1,500
	(Being cash paid for repairing)				
	Total			3,06,000	3,06,000

Solved Question 15 Journalise the following transactions.

		Amt (₹)
(i)	Commenced business with cash	25,000
(ii)	Purchased furniture for cash	2,000
(iii)	Stationery purchased	150
(iv)	Cash paid for installation of machine	500
(v)	Goods given as charity	2,000
(vi)	Drawings by the proprietor for household expenses	400
(vii)	Bought from Salil	2,600
(viii)	Interest charge on capital @ 7% per annum when total capital were	70,000
(ix)	Received ₹ 1,200 of a bad debts written-off last year	
(x)	Sold to Mathur on credit	4,000
(xi)	Goods destroyed by fire	2,000
(xii)	Cash paid to Salil after deduction of discount ₹ 130	2,470
(xiii)	Rent outstanding	1,000
(xiv)	Interest on drawings	900
(xv)	Purchase of office equipment for cash	1,250
(xvi)	Mathur returned goods	200
(xvii)	Sudhir Kumar owed ₹ 3,000. He paid only 45 paise in a rupee in full settlement due to his insolvency.	
(xviii)	Salary paid to clerk	2,000
(xix)	Commission received in advance	7,000

Sol. JOURNAL

Date	Particulars		LF	Amt (Dr)	Amt (Cr)
(i)	Cash A/c	Dr		25,000	
	To Capital A/c				25,000
	(Being amount brought in as capital)				
(ii)	Furniture A/c	Dr		2,000	
	To Cash A/c				2,000
	(Being furniture purchased for cash)				
(iii)	Stationery A/c	Dr		150	
	To Cash A/c				150
	(Being stationery purchased)				
(iv)	Machinery A/c	Dr		500	
	To Cash A/c				500
	(Being ₹ 500 installation charges for machinery paid)				
(v)	Charity A/c	Dr		2,000	
	To Purchases A/c				2,000
	(Being goods given as charity)				
(vi)	Drawings A/c	Dr		400	
	To Cash A/c				400
	(Being drawings in cash made by proprietor)				
(vii)	Purchases A/c	Dr		2,600	
	To Salil				2,600
	(Being goods purchased from Salil)				
(viii)	Interest on Capital A/c (70,000 ×7%)	Dr		4,900	
	To Capital A/c				4,900
	(Being interest @ 7% charged on capital of ₹ 70,000)				
(ix)	Cash A/c	Dr		1,200	
	To Bad Debts Recovered A/c				1,200
	(Being ₹ 1,200 bad debts recovered)				
(x)	Mathur	Dr		4,000	
	To Sales A/c				4,000
	(Being sales to Mathur on credit)				
(xi)	Loss by Fire A/c	Dr		2,000	
	To Purchases A/c				2,000
	(Being goods destroyed by fire)				
(xii)	Salil	Dr		2,600	
	To Cash A/c				2,470
	To Discount Received A/c				130
	(Being cash paid to Salil and discount received from him)				

Date	Particulars	LF	Amt (Dr)	Amt (Cr)
(xiii)	Rent A/c Dr		1,000	
	To Outstanding Rent A/c			1,000
	(Being outstanding rent recorded in books)			
(xiv)	Drawings A/c Dr		900	
	To Interest on Drawings A/c			900
	(Being interest on drawings charged)			
(xv)	Office Equipment A/c Dr		1,250	
	To Cash A/c			1,250
	(Being equipment purchased for cash)			
(xvi)	Sales Return A/c Dr		200	
	To Mathur			200
	(Being goods returned by Mathur)			
(xvii)	Cash A/c (3,000 × 0.45) Dr		1,350	
	Bad Debts A/c Dr		1,650	
	To Sudhir			3,000
	(Being 45 paise in a rupee received from Sudhir who owed ₹ 3,000)			
(xviii)	Salary A/c Dr		2,000	
	To Cash A/c			2,000
	(Being salary paid)			
(xix)	Cash A/c Dr		7,000	
	To Commission Received in Advance A/c			7,000
	(Being commission received in advance)			
	Total		62,700	62,700

Solved Question 16 Record the following transactions in the books of Himalaya & Co.

2024

Apr 1 Himalaya & Co. started business with cash ₹ 2,00,000, furniture ₹ 50,000 and goods ₹ 40,000.

Apr 3 Purchased goods list price ₹ 50,000 less 10% trade discount from Arman.

Apr 4 Sold goods to Ananya list price ₹ 30,000 less 10%. trade discount and 5% cash discount. Received the amount immediately.

Apr 6 Purchased on old furniture of ₹ 15,000.

Apr 7 Returned goods to Arman list price ₹ 10,000.

Apr 10 Sold a part of the furniture for ₹ 3,000.

Apr 15 Sold goods to Vishal ₹ 10,000.

Apr 17 Introduced additional capital of ₹ 1,50,000.

Apr 20 Purchased goods ₹ 50,000 and a computer for office ₹ 25,000.

Apr 22 Paid the due of Arman after receiving cash discount of ₹ 300.

Apr 24 Paid ₹ 5,000 for rent. 3/4th area was occupied by the proprietor as his residence.

Apr 26 Paid for telephone connection, a security deposit ₹ 10,000.

Apr 27 Received commission ₹ 2,000. Half was received as an advance.

Sol. JOURNAL

Date	Particulars	LF	Amt (Dr)	Amt (Cr)
2024				
Apr 1	Cash A/c Dr		2,00,000	
	Furniture A/c Dr		50,000	
	Goods A/c Dr		40,000	
	To Capital A/c			2,90,000
	(Being cash, furniture and goods invested in business)			
Apr 3	Purchase A/c Dr		45,000	
	To Arman			45,000
	(Being goods purchased on credit list price ₹ 50,000 less 10% trade discount)			
Apr 4	Cash A/c Dr		25,650	
	Discount Allowed A/c Dr		1,350	
	To Sales A/c			27,000
	(Being sold goods for cash, list price ₹ 30,000 less 10% trade discount, 5% cash discount)			
Apr 6	Furniture A/c Dr		15,000	
	To Cash A/c			15,000
	(Being furniture purchased for cash)			
Apr 7	Aman Dr		9,000	
	To Purchase Return A/c			9,000
	(Being goods returned to Arman)			
Apr 10	Cash A/c Dr		3,000	
	To Furniture A/c			3,000
	(Being furniture sold for cash)			
Apr 15	Vishal Dr		10,000	
	To Sales A/c			10,000
	(Being goods sold to Vishal)			
Apr 17	Cash A/c Dr		1,50,000	
	To Capital A/c			1,50,000
	(Being additional capital was introduced)			
Apr 20	Purchase A/c Dr		50,000	
	Computer A/c Dr		25,000	
	To Cash A/c			75,000
	(Being goods and computer purchased for cash)			
Apr 22	Arman Dr		36,000	
	To Discount Received A/c			300
	To Cash A/c			35,700
	(Being dues paid to Arman after receiving discount)			
Apr 24	Drawings A/c Dr		3,750	
	Rent A/c Dr		1,250	
	To Cash A/c			5,000
	(Being rent paid, 3/4th of residence)			
Apr 26	Security Deposit A/c Dr		10,000	
	To Cash A/c			10,000
	(Being deposit for security made by cash)			
Apr 27	Cash A/c Dr		2,000	
	To Commission Received A/c			1,000
	To Advance Commission A/c			1,000
	(Being cash received for commission, half was advance)			
	Total		6,77,000	6,77,000

Solved Question 17 The following balances appeared in the books of Anu Departmental Stores on 1st April, 2024.

Assets : Cash ₹ 2,00,000, bank balance ₹ 80,000, stock ₹ 60,000, furniture ₹ 4,600, debtors ₹ 30,000 (X ₹ 15,000, Y ₹ 10,000 and Z ₹ 5,000).

Liabilities : Loan from bank ₹ 40,000, creditors ₹ 10,000 (Vijay ₹ 6,000; Suresh ₹ 4,000).

Following transactions took place during April, 2024

Apr 1	Bought goods from Kunal for ₹ 60,000 at a trade discount of 10% and cash discount of 2%. Paid 70% amount immediately.
Apr 3	Sold goods to X for ₹ 16,000.
Apr 4	Paid to Vijay ₹ 5,000 by transferring in his account.
Apr 5	Additional cash ₹ 1,00,000 introduced and deposited into bank account as capital.
Apr 7	Cheque received from Z in full settlement ₹ 4,600.
Apr 8	Payment made to Suresh by cheque ₹ 3,700 in full settlement.
Apr 10	Cheque issued to Suresh dishonoured.
Apr 12	Old newspapers sold for ₹ 250.
Apr 15	Y became insolvent. Only 80% amount was received from his estate in the form of a cheque after banking hours.
Apr 20	Anu (proprietor) withdrew ₹ 10,000 from cash and ₹ 2,000 from bank for personal use.
Apr 22	Anu returned cash of ₹ 2,000 from the drawings made on 20th April.
Apr 24	Paid salaries by cash ₹ 15,000.
Apr 30	Opened another account in Punjab National Bank in the name of firm and deposited ₹ 30,000 from cash borrowed from her brother Anuj.

Journalise.

Sol. In the Books of Anu Departmental Stores

JOURNAL

Date	Particulars		LF	Amt (Dr)	Amt (Cr)
2024					
Apr 1	Cash A/c	Dr		2,00,000	
	Bank A/c	Dr		80,000	
	Stock A/c	Dr		60,000	
	Furniture A/c	Dr		4,600	
	X	Dr		15,000	
	Y	Dr		10,000	
	Z	Dr		5,000	
	To Vijay				6,000
	To Suresh				4,000
	To Loan from Bank A/c				40,000
	To Capital A/c				3,24,600
	(Being balance of accounts opened)				
Apr 1	Purchase A/c	Dr		54,000	
	To Cash A/c				37,044
	To Discount Received A/c				756
	To Kunal A/c				16,200
	(Being bought goods from Kunal)				
Apr 3	X	Dr		16,000	
	To Sale A/c				16,000
	(Being goods sold to X on credit)				
Apr 4	Vijay	Dr		5,000	
	To Bank A/c				5,000
	(Being payment made to Vijay)				
Apr 5	Bank A/c	Dr		1,00,000	
	To Capital A/c				1,00,000
	(Being additional capital introduced)				
Apr 7	Bank A/c	Dr		4,600	
	Discount Allowed A/c	Dr		400	
	To Z				5,000
	(Being received cheque in full settlement)				
Apr 8	Suresh	Dr		4,000	
	To Discount Received A/c				300
	To Bank A/c				3,700
	(Being payment made to Suresh in full settlement)				
Apr 10	Bank A/c	Dr		3,700	
	Discount Received A/c	Dr		300	
	To Suresh				4,000
	(Being cheque issued to Suresh dishonoured)				
Apr 12	Cash A/c	Dr		250	
	To Newspaper A/c				250
	(Being newspaper sold)				
Apr 15	Cheque in Hand A/c	Dr		8,000	
	Bad Debt A/c	Dr		2,000	
	To Y				10,000
	(Being Y became insolvent, only 80% received by cheque after banking hours)				
Apr 20	Drawings A/c	Dr		12,000	
	To Cash A/c				10,000
	To Bank A/c				2,000
	(Being drawings made for personal use)				
Apr 22	Cash A/c	Dr		2,000	
	To Drawings A/c				2,000
	(Being drawings reversed)				
Apr 24	Salary A/c	Dr		15,000	
	To Cash A/c				15,000
	(Being paid salary by cash)				
Apr 30	Bank A/c	Dr		30,000	
	To Capital A/c				30,000
	(Being capital introduced)				

Solved Question 18 The following balances are given on 1st April, 2024 in the books of Rohit Garments.

Assets : Cash ₹ 20,000, bank ₹ 30,000, stock ₹ 20,000, furniture ₹ 5,000, debtors ₹ 21,000 (Arun ₹ 6,000, Varun ₹ 10,000, Tarun ₹ 5,000).

Liabilities : Loan from PNB ₹ 12,000, creditors ₹ 15,000 (Sita ₹ 2,500, Rita ₹ 12,500).

Following transactions took place during April, 2024

- Apr 1 Sold goods to Arun for ₹ 5,000 at trade discount of 10% and cash discount of 2%. Received 80% amount immediately.
- Apr 2 Bought goods from Sita ₹ 3,000 at trade discount of 10%. Paid 50% by cheque.
- Apr 4 Received cash from Arun in full settlement after allowing him discount ₹ 200.
- Apr 5 Cash deposited into bank account ₹ 2,000.
- Apr 6 Received a cheque from Varun ₹ 4,000.
- Apr 7 Cheque received from Varun deposited into bank account.
- Apr 9 Cash sales ₹ 8,000. Half deposited into bank.
- Apr 12 Tarun settled his account by paying cash after allowing him cash discount of ₹ 300.
- Apr 18 Salary paid ₹ 1,000.
- Apr 20 ₹ 500 received from a debtor Arman written-off as bad debt last year.
- Apr 22 Purchased goods from Vijay ₹ 4,000.
- Apr 24 Sold half of goods purchased from Vijay above at 20% profit on cost, received cash.
- Apr 25 Paid rent in advance ₹ 500.
- Apr 27 Paid trade expenses ₹ 500. Half from bank account.

Journalise.

Sol. **In the Books of Rohit Garments**

JOURNAL

Date	Particulars		LF	Amt (Dr)	Amt (Dr)
2024					
Apr 1	Cash A/c	Dr		20,000	
	Bank A/c	Dr		30,000	
	Stock A/c	Dr		20,000	
	Furniture A/c	Dr		5,000	
	Arun	Dr		6,000	
	Varun	Dr		10,000	
	Tarun	Dr		5,000	
	To Loan from PNB A/c				12,000
	To Sita				2,500
	To Rita				12,500
	To Capital A/c (Balancing figure)				69,000
	(Being opening entry passed and difference credited to capital account)				
Apr 1	Cash A/c	Dr		3,528	
	Arun	Dr		900	
	Discount Allowed A/c	Dr		72	
	To Sales A/c				4,500
	(Being goods sold to Arun, 80% received, allowed 2% cash discount)				
Apr 2	Purchase A/c	Dr		2,700	
	To Bank A/c				1,350
	To Sita				1,350
	(Being bought goods price ₹ 3,000 less 10% trade discount, 50% paid by cheque)				
Apr 4	Cash A/c	Dr		6,700	
	Discount Allowed A/c	Dr		200	
	To Arun				6,900
	(Being cash received in full settlement against total due ₹ 6,900)				
Apr 5	Bank A/c	Dr		2,000	
	To Cash A/c				2,000
	(Being deposited into bank account)				
Apr 6	Cheque in Hand A/c	Dr		4,000	
	To Varun				4,000
	(Being received cheque)				
Apr 7	Bank A/c	Dr		4,000	
	To Cheque in Hand A/c				4,000
	(Being cheque deposited into bank account)				
Apr 9	Bank A/c	Dr		4,000	
	Cash A/c	Dr		4,000	
	To Sales A/c				8,000
	(Being half deposited in bank account)				
Apr 12	Cash A/c	Dr		4,700	
	Discount Allowed A/c	Dr		300	
	To Tarun				5,000
	(Being Tarun settled his account, discount allowed ₹ 300)				
Apr 18	Salary A/c	Dr		1,000	
	To Cash A/c				1,000
	(Being salary paid in cash)				
Apr 20	Cash A/c	Dr		500	
	To Bad Debt Recovered A/c				500
	(Being received amount as bad debt written-off last year)				
Apr 22	Purchase A/c	Dr		4,000	
	To Vijay				4,000
	(Being goods bought from Vijay)				
Apr 24	Cash A/c	Dr		2,400	
	To Sales A/c				2,400
	(Being goods sold for cash)				
Apr 25	Advance Rent A/c	Dr		500	
	To Cash A/c				500
	(Being rent paid in advance)				

Date	Particulars		LF	Amt (Dr)	Amt (Dr)
Apr 27	Trade Expenses A/c	Dr		500	
	To Cash A/c				250
	To Bank A/c				250
	(Being trade expenses paid)				
	Total			1,42,000	1,42,000

Journal (GST)

Solved Question 19 *(Intra-state)* **Pass entries in the books of Nirbhay & Sons, assuming all transactions have been entered within the state of West Bengal, charging CGST and SGST @ 6% each.**

2024

Apr 1 Purchased goods for ₹ 1,50,000 from Kim.
Apr 6 Sold goods for ₹ 2,50,000 to Tim.
Apr 8 Returned goods to Kim for ₹ 10,000.
Apr 15 Tim returned goods for ₹ 8,000.
Apr 18 Printing and stationery expenses of ₹ 5,000 paid in cash.
Apr 24 Goods withdrawn by proprietor for personal use ₹ 20,000.
Apr 27 Goods destroyed by fire ₹ 15,000.
Apr 30 Payment made of balance amount of GST.

Sol. **In the Books of Nirbhay & Sons**
JOURNAL

Date	Particulars		LF	Amt (Dr)	Amt (Cr)
2024					
Apr 1	Purchase A/c	Dr		1,50,000	
	Input CGST A/c	Dr		9,000	
	Input SGST A/c	Dr		9,000	
	To Kim				1,68,000
	(Being purchased goods on credit)				
Apr 6	Tim	Dr		2,80,000	
	To Sales A/c				2,50,000
	To Output CGST A/c				15,000
	To Output SGST A/c				15,000
	(Being sale of goods on credit)				
Apr 8	Kim	Dr		11,200	
	To Purchase Return A/c				10,000
	To Input CGST A/c				600
	To Input SGST A/c				600
	(Being goods returned and GST reversed)				
Apr 15	Sales Return A/c	Dr		8,000	
	Output CGST A/c	Dr		480	
	Output SGST A/c	Dr		480	
	To Tim				8,960
	(Being sales return and GST reversed)				
Apr 18	Printing and Stationery A/c	Dr		5,000	
	Input CGST A/c	Dr		300	
	Input SGST A/c	Dr		300	
	To Cash A/c				5,600
	(Being paid for printing and stationery)				
Apr 24	Drawings A/c	Dr		22,400	
	To Purchases A/c				20,000
	To Input CGST A/c				1,200
	To Input SGST A/c				1,200
	(Being goods withdrawn for personal use and GST reversed)				
Apr 27	Loss by Fire A/c	Dr		16,800	
	To Purchases A/c				15,000
	To Input CGST A/c				900
	To Input SGST A/c				900
	(Being goods destroyed by fire and GST reversed)				
Apr 30	Output CGST A/c	Dr		14,520	
	Output SGST A/c	Dr		14,520	
	To Input CGST A/c				6,600
	To Input SGST A/c				6,600
	To Bank A/c (7,920 + 7,920)				15,840
	(Being adjustment of GST and payment of balance amount)				
	Total			5,42,000	5,42,000

Working Note

Total Input CGST = 9,000 − 600 + 300 − 1,200 − 900 = ₹ 6,600
Total Input SGST = 9,000 − 600 + 300 − 1,200 − 900 = ₹ 6,600
Total Output CGST = 15,000 − 480 = ₹ 14,520
Total Output SGST = 15,000 − 480 = ₹ 14,520
Net CGST Paid = 14,520 − 6,600 = ₹ 7,920
Net SGST Paid = 14,520 − 6,600 = ₹ 7,920

Solved Question 20 **Enter the following transactions in the books of PQP Traders assuming that all transactions have taken place in the state of Rajasthan. Assume CGST @ 9% and SGST @ 9%.**

2024

Mar 5 Purchased goods for ₹ 50,000 from Zen Traders, at 20% trade discount.
Mar 10 Sold goods to Verma Bros. for ₹ 32,000.
Mar 15 Received from Verma Bros. a cheque for ₹ 20,000 on account. Cheque is sent to bank.
Mar 18 Purchased furniture for ₹ 5,000 and payment made by cheque.
Mar 20 Advertisement charges of ₹ 2,000 paid by cheque.
Mar 22 Sold goods for ₹ 10,000 and received a cheque for the same. Cheque is sent to bank.
Mar 25 Commission of ₹ 1,000 received in cash.
Mar 31 Output GST adjusted against input GST.

Sol. **In the Books of PQP Traders**
JOURNAL

Date	Particulars		LF	Amt (Dr)	Amt (Cr)
2024					
Mar 5	Purchases A/c	Dr		40,000	
	Input CGST A/c	Dr		3,600	
	Input SGST A/c	Dr		3,600	
	To Zen Traders				47,200
	(Being purchase of goods for ₹ 5,00,000 at 20% trade discount)				

Date	Particulars		LF	Amt (Dr)	Amt (Cr)
Mar 10	Verma Bros.	Dr		37,760	
	To Sales A/c				32,000
	To Output CGST A/c				2,880
	To Output SGST A/c				2,880
	(Being sale of goods on credit)				
Mar 15	Bank A/c	Dr		20,000	
	To Verma Bros.				20,000
	(Being payment received by cheque)				
Mar 18	Furniture A/c	Dr		5,000	
	Input CGST A/c	Dr		450	
	Input SGST A/c	Dr		450	
	To Bank A/c				5,900
	(Being furniture purchased)				
Mar 20	Advertisement Expenses A/c	Dr		2,000	
	Input CGST A/c	Dr		180	
	Input SGST A/c	Dr		180	
	To Bank A/c				2,360
	(Being payment of advertisement expenses)				
Mar 22	Bank A/c	Dr		11,800	
	To Sales A/c				10,000
	To Output CGST A/c				900
	To Output SGST A/c				900
	(Being sold goods and received a cheque)				
Mar 25	Cash A/c	Dr		1,180	
	To Commission Received A/c				1,000
	To Output CGST A/c				90
	To Output SGST A/c				90
	(Being commission received)				
Mar 31	Output CGST A/c	Dr		3,870	
	Output SGST A/c	Dr		3,870	
	To Input CGST A/c (WN)				3,870
	To Input SGST A/c				3,870
	(Being adjustment of GST)				
	Total			1,33,940	1,33,940

Working Note

Total Input CGST = 3,600 + 450 + 180 = ₹ 4,230

Total Input SGST = 3,600 + 450 + 180 = ₹ 4,230

Total Output CGST = 2,880 + 900 + 90 = ₹ 3,870

Total Ouput SGST = 2,880 + 900 + 90 = ₹ 3,870

Since Input GST is more than Output GST, there is no tax liability to be paid to the government. Excess of Input GST is called input tax credit. It will be carried forward and shown on the assets side of balance sheet and will be adjusted in the next month.

Input Tax Credit = Input CGST − Ouput CGST

= 4,230 − 3,870 = ₹ 360

Input SGST − Ouput SGST = 4,230 − 3,870 = ₹ 360

Input tax credit of 360 + 360 = ₹ 720 will be carried forward and will be adjusted in the next month.

Solved Question 21 ***(Inter-state)*** **Pass entries in the books of Raj of Kerala assuming CGST @ 9% and SGST @ 9%.**

2022

Apr 1 Purchased goods for ₹ 3,00,000 from Amit of Chennai (Tamil Nadu).

Apr 3 Purchased goods for ₹ 50,000 from Vivek of Ernakulam (Kerala).

Apr 10 Sold goods costing ₹ 80,000 to Veer of Hyderabad (Telangana) at a profit of 25% on cost less trade discount 10%.

Apr 15 Sold goods at Kottayam (Kerala) costing ₹ 2,50,000 at 60% profit less trade discount 15% against cheque which was deposited into bank.

Apr 16 Advertisement charges of ₹ 8,000 paid in cash.

Apr 20 Purchased a computer for office use for ₹ 30,000 and payment made by cheque.

Apr 25 Proprietor withdrew ₹ 10,000 for his personal use.

Apr 30 Payment made of balance amount of GST.

Sol.

In the Books of Raj
JOURNAL

Date	Particulars		LF	Amt (Dr)	Amt (Cr)
2022					
Apr 1	Purchases A/c	Dr		3,00,000	
	Input IGST A/c*	Dr		54,000	
	To Amit				3,54,000
	(Being purchased goods from outside the state)				
Apr 3	Purchases A/c	Dr		50,000	
	Input CGST A/c	Dr		4,500	
	Input SGST A/c	Dr		4,500	
	To Vivek				59,000
	(Being purchased goods within the state)				
Apr 10	Veer	Dr		1,06,200	
	To Sales A/c (WN 1)				90,000
	To Output IGST A/c				16,200
	(Being sale of goods outside the state)				
Apr 15	Bank A/c	Dr		4,01,200	
	To Sales A/c (WN 2)				3,40,000
	To Output CGST A/c				30,600
	To Output SGST A/c				30,600
	(Being sale of goods within the state)				
Apr 16	Advertisement Expenses A/c**	Dr		8,000	
	Input CGST A/c	Dr		720	
	Input SGST A/c	Dr		720	
	To Cash A/c				9,440
	(Being paid for advertisement)				

Date	Particulars	LF	Amt (Dr)	Amt (Cr)
Apr 20	Office Equipment A/c Dr		30,000	
	Input CGST A/c Dr		2,700	
	Input SGST A/c Dr		2,700	
	To Bank A/c			35,400
	(Being computer purchasesd)			
Apr 25	Drawings A/c Dr		10,000	
	To Cash A/c			10,000
	(Being withdrew for personal use)			
Apr 30	Output IGST A/c (WN 3) Dr		16,200	
	To Input IGST A/c			16,200
	(Being adjustment of IGST)			
Apr 30	Output CGST A/c (WN 4) Dr		30,600	
	To Input IGST A/c			30,600
	(Being adjustment of CGST)			
Apr 30	Output SGST A/c (WN 5) Dr		30,600	
	To Input IGST A/c			7,200
	To Input SGST A/c			7,920
	To Bank A/c			15,480
	(Being final payment)			
	Total		10,52,640	10,52,640

*In case CGST is 9% and SGST is 9%, IGST will be 9% + 9% = 18%

**If nothing is stated, it will be assumed that the transaction is entered within the same state.

Working Notes Amt (₹)

	Amt (₹)
1. Cost	80,000
(+) Profit 25% on ₹ 80,000	20,000
	1,00,000
(−) Trade Discount 10% on ₹ 1,00,000	(10,000)
Total	90,000
2. Cost	2,50,000
(+) Profit 60% on ₹ 2,50,000	1,50,000
	4,00,000
(−) Trade Discount 15% on ₹ 4,00,000	(60,000)
Total	3,40,000

3. First of all, IGST will be ajdusted against Input IGST

Input IGST	54,000
(−) Output IGST	(16,200)
Balance of Input IGST	37,800

4. This balance of ₹ 37,800 on Input IGST will be first applied to set-off Output CGST and the balance will be adjusted to set-off Output SGST.

Total Output CGST	30,600
(−) Adjusted against Input IGST	(30,600)
	—

Since sufficient Input IGST was available, Input CGST amounting to ₹ 7,920 has not been used here. It will be carried forward to next period.

5. Balance of Input IGST was ₹ 37,800, out of which ₹ 30,600 has been adjusted against Output CGST. The balance of Input IGST ₹ 7,200 (i.e. 37,800 − 30,600) will be adjusted against Output SGST.

Total Output SGST	30,600
(−) Adjusted against Input IGST	(7,200)
	23,400
(−) Adjusted against Input SGST (4,500 + 720 + 2,700)	(7,920)
Balance Paid-off	15,480

Solved Question 22 **Pass entries in the books of Den of Gujarat for the following transactions.**

2022

Feb 2 Purchased goods from Ven of Gujarat for ₹ 25,000. (CGST @ 9% and SGST @ 9%)

Feb 5 Purchased goods from Ren of Rajasthan for ₹ 30,000. (IGST @ 12%)

Feb 10 Sold goods of Sen of Gujarat for ₹ 20,000. (CGST @ 9% and SGST @ 9%)

Feb 12 Paid railway freight ₹ 1,500. (CGST @ 9% and SGST @ 9%)

Feb 16 Purchased computer printer for office for ₹ 8,000 from Froyo Ltd. on credit. (CGST @ 6% and SGST @ 6%)

Feb 24 Sold goods to Pen of UP goods for ₹ 42,000 against cheque which is deposited into the bank. (IGST @ 18%)

Feb 25 Paid for broad-band services ₹ 1,000 by cheque. (CGST @ 6% and SGST @ 6%)

Feb 28 Payment made of balance amount of GST.

Sol. **In the Books of Den**
JOURNAL

Date	Particulars	LF	Amt (Dr)	Amt (Cr)
2022				
Feb 2	Purchases A/c Dr		25,000	
	Input CGST A/c Dr		2,250	
	Input SGST A/c Dr		2,250	
	To Ven			29,500
	(Being purchased goods within the state)			
Feb 5	Purchases A/c Dr		30,000	
	Input IGST A/c Dr		3,600	
	To Ren			33,600
	(Being purchased goods from outside the state)			
Feb 10	Sen Dr		23,600	
	To Sales A/c			20,000
	To Output CGST A/c			1,800
	To Output SGST A/c			1,800
	(Being sale of goods within the state)			

Date	Particulars		LF	Amt (Dr)	Amt (Cr)
Feb 12	Freight A/c	Dr		1,500	
	Input CGST A/c	Dr		135	
	Input SGST A/c	Dr		135	
	To Cash A/c				1,770
	(Being paid railway freight)				
Feb 16	Computer Printer A/c	Dr		8,000	
	Input CGST A/c	Dr		480	
	Input SGST A/c	Dr		480	
	To Froyo Ltd.				8,960
	(Being purchases computer printer)				
Feb 24	Bank A/c	Dr		49,560	
	To Sales A/c				42,000
	To Output IGST A/c				7,560
	(Being sale of goods outside the state)				
Feb 25	Internet Charges A/c	Dr		1,000	
	Input CGST A/c	Dr		60	
	Input SGST A/c	Dr		60	
	To Bank A/c				1,120
	(Being paid for broad-band services)				
Feb 28	Output IGST A/c (WN1)	Dr		3,600	
	To Input IGST A/c				3,600
	(Being adjustment of IGST)				
Feb 28	Output CGST A/c (WN2)	Dr		1,800	
	Output SGST A/c	Dr		1,800	
	To Input CGST A/c				1,800
	To Input SGST A/c				1,800
	(Being adjustment of CGST and SGST)				
Feb 28	Output IGSTA/c (WN2)	Dr		3,960	
	To Input CGST A/c				1,125
	To Input SGST A/c				1,125
	To Bank A/c				1,710
	(Being final payment)				
	Total			1,59,270	1,59,270

Working Notes

1. First of all, Output IGST will be adjusted against Input IGST

	Amt (₹)
Output IGST	7,560
Input IGST	(3,600)
Excess of Output IGST	3,960

Excess of Output IGST of ₹ 3,960 is a liability payable to the government while making this payment, adjustment shall be made for CGST and SGST.

	CGST (₹)	SGST (₹)
2. Input (2,250 + 135 + 480 + 60)	2,925	2,925
Output	1,800	1,800
	1,125	1,125

Excess of Output IGST	—	3,960
(–) Adjusted for Input CGST	(1,125)	—
Adjusted for Input SGST	(1,125)	(2,250)
Net amount payable to government	—	1,710

Solved Question 23 **Pass journal entries in the books of Mr. Yogesh assuming CGST and SGST 9% each.**

(i) Yogesh purchased goods for ₹ 2,00,000 from outside the state. Payment made by chque.

(ii) He sold goods for ₹ 1,50,000 outside the state on credit.

(iii) He sold goods for ₹ 2,00,000 locally on credit.

(iv) Paid telephone bill for ₹ 8,000 by cheque.

(v) Purchased an office equipment for his office for ₹ 30,000.

(vi) Payment made balance of GST.

Sol.

In the Books of Yogesh

JOURNAL

Date	Particulars		LF	Amt (Dr)	Amt (Cr)
(i)	Purchase A/c	Dr		2,00,000	
	Input IGST A/c	Dr		36,000	
	To Bank A/c				2,36,000
	(Being purchased goods out of the state)				
(ii)	Debtor A/c	Dr		1,77,000	
	To Sales A/c				1,50,000
	To Output IGST A/c				27,000
	(Being sold goods out of the state)				
(iii)	Debtor A/c	Dr		2,36,000	
	To Sales A/c				2,00,000
	To Output CGST A/c				18,000
	To Output SGST A/c				18,000
	(Being sold goods locally on credit)				
(iv)	Telephone Expenses A/c	Dr		8,000	
	Input CGST A/c	Dr		720	
	Input SGST A/c	Dr		720	
	To Bank A/c				9,440
	(Being paid telephone bill)				
(v)	Office Equipment A/c	Dr		30,000	
	Input CGST A/c	Dr		2,700	
	Input SGST A/c	Dr		2,700	
	To Bank A/c				35,400
	(Being purchased office equipment by cheque)				
(vi)	Output IGST A/c	Dr		27,000	
	To Input IGST A/c				27,000
	(Being IGST adjusted)				

Date	Particulars		LF	Amt (Dr)	Amt (Cr)
	Output CGST A/c	Dr		18,000	
	To Input IGST A/c				9,000
	To Input CGST A/c				3,420
	To Bank A/c				5,580
	(Being adjustment of CGST and balance paid)				
	Output SGST A/c	Dr		18,000	
	To Input SGST A/c				3,420
	To Bank A/c				14,580
	(Being adjusted Output SGST and balance paid)				
	Total			7,56,840	7,56,840

Working Note

Input IGST = ₹ 36,000

Output IGST = ₹ 27,000

Input CGST = 720 + 2,700 = ₹ 3,420

Input SGST = 720 + 2,700 = ₹ 3,420

Output CGST = ₹ 18,000

Output SGST = ₹ 18,000

1. Firstly, Output IGST will be adjusted against Input IGST. Balance of Input IGST = 36,000 − 27,000 = ₹ 9,000
2. Balance of Input IGST will be first applied to Output CGST then balance in Output CGST if any will be applied to set-off Input CGST.

	Amt (₹)
Balance of Output CGST	18,000
(−) Input IGST	(9,000)
	9,000
(−) Input CGST	(3,420)
Paid-off	5,580

3. Balance of Output SGST = 18,000 − 3,420 = ₹ 14,580 after adjustment of input SGST.

Solved Question 24 (*Set-off of GST*) **House Cleaning Enterprise has following balances in its GST accounts as on 31st March, 2024. Show, how GST will be set-off.**

Particulars	IGST (₹)	CGST (₹)	SGST (₹)
Input GST	7,50,000	4,00,000	4,00,000
Output GST	6,25,000	3,00,000	3,00,000

Sol.

Particulars	IGST (₹)	CGST (₹)	SGST (₹)
Output GST	(6,25,000)	3,00,000	3,00,000
(−) Input IGST	(7,50,000)	—	—
Balance	1,25,000	(3,00,000)	(3,00,000)
(−) Balance of Input IGST set-off against Output CGST	(1,25,000)	1,25,000	—
Balance	—	(1,75,000)	(3,00,000)
(−) Input CGST/SGST set-off against Output CGST/SGST	—	4,00,000	4,00,000
	Nil	2,25,000 Dr	1,00,000 Cr

Ledger

Solved Question 25 **Pass the opening entry as on 1st April, 2024. Also, post the opening entry.**

1st April, 2022	Amt (₹)
Cash in Hand	50,000
Cash at Bank	60,000
Stock of Goods	1,00,000
Furniture	35,000
Building	8,50,000
Sundry Debtors	26,000
Sundry Creditors	3,20,000

Sol.

JOURNAL

Date	Particulars		LF	Amt (Dr)	Amt (Cr)
2024 Apr 1	Cash A/c	Dr		50,000	
	Bank A/c	Dr		60,000	
	Stock A/c	Dr		1,00,000	
	Furniture A/c	Dr		35,000	
	Building A/c	Dr		8,50,000	
	Sundry Debtors A/c	Dr		26,000	
	To Sundry Creditors A/c				3,20,000
	To Capital A/c (Balancing figure)				8,01,000
	(Being balances carried forward from last year)				

Dr **Cash Account** Cr

Date	Particulars	JF	Amt (₹)	Date	Particulars	JF	Amt (₹)
2024 Apr 1	To Balance b/d		50,000				

Dr **Bank Account** Cr

Date	Particulars	JF	Amt (₹)	Date	Particulars	JF	Amt (₹)
2024 Apr 1	To Balance b/d		60,000				

Dr **Stock Account** Cr

Date	Particulars	JF	Amt (₹)	Date	Particulars	JF	Amt (₹)
2024 Apr 1	To Balance b/d		1,00,000				

Dr **Furniture Account** Cr

Date	Particulars	JF	Amt (₹)	Date	Particulars	JF	Amt (₹)
2024 Apr 1	To Balance b/d		35,000				

Dr **Building Account** Cr

Date	Particulars	JF	Amt (₹)	Date	Particulars	JF	Amt (₹)
2024 Apr 1	To Balance b/d		8,50,000				

Dr **Sundry Debtors Account** Cr

Date	Particulars	JF	Amt (₹)	Date	Particulars	JF	Amt (₹)
2024 Apr 1	To Balance b/d		26,000				

Dr **Sundry Creditors Account** Cr

Date	Particulars	JF	Amt (₹)	Date	Particulars	JF	Amt (₹)
				2024 Apr 1	By Balance b/d		3,20,000

Dr **Capital Account** Cr

Date	Particulars	JF	Amt (₹)	Date	Particulars	JF	Amt (₹)
				2024 Apr 1	By Balance b/d		8,01,000

Solved Question 26 **Journalise the following transactions and post in ledger accounts in the books of Radhey Bros.**

2024		Amt (₹)
Aug 1	Vimal started business with cash	3,50,000
Aug 2	Bought goods for cash	76,250
Aug 3	Opened bank account with cash	1,25,000
Aug 4	Sold goods for cash	80,000
Aug 7	Bought goods from Jaya on credit	75,000
Aug 10	Sold goods to Prateek on credit	62,500
Aug 15	Purchased plant and machinery and payment is made by cheque	51,000
Aug 19	Paid to Jaya in cash	25,000
Aug 21	Received loan from Vineet and deposited the same into bank	20,000
Aug 23	Goods returned to Jaya	2,500

2024		Amt (₹)
Aug 26	Withdrew from bank for personal use	12,500
Aug 27	Paid to Jaya by cheque	20,000
Aug 29	Received cash from Prateek	25,000
Aug 30	Purchased stationery by cash	1,000
Aug 30	Paid wages and salaries	35,000

Sol. **In the Books of Radhey Bros.**

JOURNAL

Date	Particulars		LF	Amt (Dr)	Amt (Cr)
2024 Aug 1	Cash A/c	Dr		3,50,000	
	To Capital A/c				3,50,000
	(Being the business started with capital of ₹ 3,50,000 brought in cash)				
Aug 2	Purchases A/c	Dr		76,250	
	To Cash A/c				76,250
	(Being the goods purchased for cash)				
Aug 3	Bank A/c	Dr		1,25,000	
	To Cash A/c				1,25,000
	(Being the bank account opened by depositing cash into bank)				
Aug 4	Cash A/c	Dr		80,000	
	To Sales A/c				80,000
	(Being the goods sold for cash)				
Aug 7	Purchases A/c	Dr		75,000	
	To Jaya				75,000
	(Being the goods purchased on credit from Jaya)				
Aug 10	Prateek	Dr		62,500	
	To Sales A/c				62,500
	(Being the goods sold to Prateek on credit)				
Aug 15	Plant and Machinery A/c	Dr		51,000	
	To Bank A/c				51,000
	(Being the plant and machinery purchased by cheque)				
Aug 19	Jaya	Dr		25,000	
	To Cash A/c				25,000
	(Being the amount paid to Jaya in cash)				
Aug 21	Bank A/c	Dr		20,000	
	To Vineet's Loan A/c				20,000
	(Being the loan from Vineet received and deposited into bank)				
Aug 23	Jaya	Dr		2,500	
	To Return Outwards A/c				2,500
	(Being the goods returned to Jaya)				
Aug 26	Drawings A/c	Dr		12,500	
	To Bank A/c				12,500
	(Being the amount withdrawn from bank for personal use)				
Aug 27	Jaya	Dr		20,000	
	To Bank A/c				20,000
	(Being the amount paid to Jaya by cheque)				
Aug 29	Cash A/c	Dr		25,000	
	To Prateek				25,000
	(Being the cash received from Prateek)				

Date	Particulars		LF	Amt (Dr)	Amt (Cr)
Aug 30	Stationery A/c	Dr		1,000	
	To Cash A/c				1,000
	(Being the stationery purchased for cash)				
Aug 30	Wages and Salaries A/c	Dr		35,000	
	To Cash A/c				35,000
	(Being the wages and salaries paid in cash)				
	Total			9,60,750	9,60,750

Dr **Cash Account** Cr

Date	Particulars	JF	Amt (₹)	Date	Particulars	JF	Amt (₹)
2024				2024			
Aug 1	To Capital A/c		3,50,000	Aug 2	By Purchases A/c		76,250
Aug 4	To Sales A/c		80,000	Aug 3	By Bank A/c		1,25,000
Aug 29	To Prateek		25,000	Aug 19	By Jaya		25,000
				Aug 30	By Stationery A/c		1,000
				Aug 30	By Wages and Salaries A/c		35,000
				Aug 30	By Balance c/d		1,92,750
			4,55,000				4,55,000

Dr **Capital Account** Cr

Date	Particulars	JF	Amt (₹)	Date	Particulars	JF	Amt (₹)
2024				2024			
Aug 30	To Balance c/d		3,50,000	Aug 1	By Cash A/c		3,50,000
			3,50,000				3,50,000

Dr **Purchases Account** Cr

Date	Particulars	JF	Amt (₹)	Date	Particulars	JF	Amt (₹)
2024				2024			
Aug 2	To Cash A/c		76,250	Aug 30	By Balance c/d		1,51,250
Aug 7	To Jaya		75,000				
			1,51,250				1,51,250

Dr **Bank Account** Cr

Date	Particulars	JF	Amt (₹)	Date	Particulars	JF	Amt (₹)
2024				2024			
Aug 3	To Cash A/c		1,25,000	Aug 15	By Plant and Machinery A/c		51,000
Aug 21	To Vineet's Loan A/c		20,000	Aug 26	By Drawings A/c		12,500
				Aug 27	By Jaya		20,000
				Aug 30	By Balance c/d		61,500
			1,45,000				1,45,000

Dr **Sales Account** Cr

Date	Particulars	JF	Amt (₹)	Date	Particulars	JF	Amt (₹)
2024				2024			
Aug 30	To Balance c/d		1,42,500	Aug 4	By Cash A/c		80,000
				Aug 10	By Prateek		62,500
			1,42,500				1,42,500

Dr **Jaya** Cr

Date	Particulars	JF	Amt (₹)	Date	Particulars	JF	Amt (₹)
2024				2024			
Aug 19	To Cash A/c		25,000	Aug 7	By Purchases A/c		75,000
Aug 23	To Return Outwards A/c		2,500				
Aug 27	To Bank A/c		20,000				
Aug 30	To Balance c/d		27,500				
			75,000				75,000

Dr **Prateek** Cr

Date	Particulars	JF	Amt (₹)	Date	Particulars	JF	Amt (₹)
2024				2024			
Aug 10	To Sales A/c		62,500	Aug 29	By Cash A/c		25,000
				Aug 30	By Balance c/d		37,500
			62,500				62,500

Dr **Plant and Machinery Account** Cr

Date	Particulars	JF	Amt (₹)	Date	Particulars	JF	Amt (₹)
2024				2024			
Aug 15	To Bank A/c		51,000	Aug 30	By Balance c/d		51,000
			51,000				51,000

Dr **Vineet's Loan Account** Cr

Date	Particulars	JF	Amt (₹)	Date	Particulars	JF	Amt (₹)
2024				2024			
Aug 30	To Balance c/d		20,000	Aug 21	By Bank A/c		20,000
			20,000				20,000

Dr **Return Outwards Account** Cr

Date	Particulars	JF	Amt (₹)	Date	Particulars	JF	Amt (₹)
2024				2022			
Aug 30	To Balance c/d		2,500	Aug 23	By Jaya		2,500
			2,500				2,500

Dr **Drawings Account** Cr

Date	Particulars	JF	Amt (₹)	Date	Particulars	JF	Amt (₹)
2024				2024			
Aug 26	To Bank A/c		12,500	Aug 30	By Balance c/d		12,500
			12,500				12,500

Dr **Stationery Account** Cr

Date	Particulars	JF	Amt (₹)	Date	Particulars	JF	Amt (₹)
2024				2024			
Aug 30	To Cash A/c		1,000	Aug 30	By Balance c/d		1,000
			1,000				1,000

Dr **Wages and Salaries Account** Cr

Date	Particulars	JF	Amt (₹)	Date	Particulars	JF	Amt (₹)
2024				2024			
Aug 30	To Cash A/c		35,000	Aug 30	By Balance c/d		35,000
			35,000				35,000

Solved Question 27 (*With GST*) **Journalise the following transactions of Adhiraj, Delhi for April, 2024, post them in ledger accounts and balance them**

Date	Particulars	Amt (₹)
2024		
Apr 1	Adhiraj started business with cash*	2,00,000
Apr 2	Bought goods for cash	60,000
Apr 3	Opened bank account with cash*	1,00,000
Apr 4	Sold goods for cash	80,000
Apr 7	Bought goods from Amrit, Kanpur on credit	60,000
Apr 10	Solds goods to Aryan, Delhi on credit	50,000
Apr 15	Purchased machinery costing ₹ 40,000 from Bhalla Bros. Patiala (Punjab) and payment is made by cheque	
Apr 19	Paid to Amrit in cash on account*	40,000
Apr 23	Goods returned to Amrit	10,000
Apr 27	Paid to Amrit by cheque in full settlement*	15,000
Apr 29	Received cash from Aryan*	20,000

CGST and SGST is leived @ 6% each on intra-state transactions and IGST @12% on inter-state transactions. GST is not levied on transactions marked with (*).

Sol.

JOURNAL

Date	Particulars		LF	Amt (Dr)	Amt (Cr)
2024					
Apr 1	Cash A/c	Dr		2,00,000	
	To Capital A/c				2,00,000
	(Being the business started with capital of ₹ 2,00,000 brought in cash)				
Apr 2	Purchases A/c	Dr		60,000	
	Input CGST A/c	Dr		3,600	
	Input SGST A/c	Dr		3,600	
	To Cash A/c				67,200
	(Being the intra-state purchase of goods for cash, paid CGST and SGST @ 6% each)				
Apr 3	Bank A/c	Dr		1,00,000	
	To Sales A/c				1,00,000
	(Being bank account opened)				
Apr 4	Cash A/c	Dr		89,600	
	To Sales A/c				80,000
	To Output CGST A/c				4,800
	To Output SGST A/c				4,800
	(Being the intra-state of goods, charged CGST and SGST @ 6% each)				
Apr 7	Purchases A/c	Dr		60,000	
	Input IGST A/c	Dr		7,200	
	To Amrit				67,200
	(Being the inter-state purchase of goods on credit from Amrit plus IGST @ 12%)				
Apr 10	Aryan	Dr		56,000	
	To Sales A/c				50,000
	To Output CGST A/c				3,000
	To Output SGST A/c				3,000
	(Being the intra-state sale of goods on credit to Aryan, charged CGST and SGST @ 6% each)				
Apr 15	Machinery A/c	Dr		40,000	
	Input IGST A/c	Dr		4,800	
	To Bank A/c				44,800
	(Being the machinery purchased, plus IGST @ 12% and payment made by cheque)				
Apr 19	Amrit	Dr		40,000	
	To Cash A/c				40,000
	(Being the amount paid to Surya in cash)				

Date	Particulars		LF	Amt (Dr)	Amt (Cr)
Apr 23	Amrit	Dr		11,200	
	To Returns Outward A/c				10,000
	To Input IGST A/c				1,200
	(Being the goods returned to Amrit, Input IGST reversed)				
Apr 27	Amrit	Dr		16,000	
	To Bank A/c				15,000
	To Discount Received A/c				1,000
	(Being the amount paid to Amrit by cheque and discount received)				
Apr 29	Cash A/c	Dr		20,000	
	To Aryan				20,000
	(Being the cash received from Aryan)				
	Total			6,12,000	6,12,000

Dr **Cash Account** Cr

Date	Particulars	JF	Amt (₹)	Date	Particulars	JF	Amt (₹)
2024				2024			
Apr 1	To Capital A/c		2,00,000	Apr 2	By Purchases A/c		60,000
Apr 4	To Sales A/c		80,000	Apr 2	By Input CGST A/c		3,600
Apr 4	To Output CGST A/c		4,800	Apr 2	By Input SGST A/c		3,600
Apr 4	To Output SGST A/c		4,800	Apr 3	By Bank A/c		1,00,000
Apr 29	To Aryan		20,000	Apr 19	By Amrit		40,000
				Apr 30	By Balance c/d		1,02,400
			3,09,600				3,09,600
May 1	To Balance b/d		1,02,400				

Dr **Capital Account** Cr

Date	Particulars	JF	Amt (₹)	Date	Particulars	JF	Amt (₹)
2024				2024			
Apr 30	To Balance c/d		2,00,000	Apr 1	By Cash A/c		2,00,000
			2,00,000				2,00,000
				May 1	By Balance b/d		2,00,000

Dr **Purchases Account** Cr

Date	Particulars	JF	Amt (₹)	Date	Particulars	JF	Amt (₹)
2024				2024			
Apr 2	To Cash A/c		60,000	Apr 30	By Balance c/d		1,20,000
Apr 7	To Amrit		60,000				
			1,20,000				1,20,000
May 1	To Balance b/d		1,20,000				

Dr **Bank Account** Cr

Date	Particulars	JF	Amt (₹)	Date	Particulars	JF	Amt (₹)
2024				2024			
Apr 3	To Cash A/c		1,00,000	Apr 15	By Machinery A/c		40,000
				Apr 15	By Input IGST A/c		4,800
				Apr 27	By Amrit		15,000
				Apr 30	By Balance c/d		40,200
			1,00,000				1,00,000
May 1	To Balance b/d		40,200				

Dr — Sales Account — Cr

Date	Particulars	JF	Amt (₹)	Date	Particulars	JF	Amt (₹)
2024				2024			
Apr 30	To Balance c/d		1,30,000	Apr 4	By Cash A/c		80,000
				Apr 10	By Aryan		50,000
			1,30,000				1,30,000
				May 1	By Balance b/d		1,30,000

Dr — Amrit — Cr

Date	Particulars	JF	Amt (₹)	Date	Particulars	JF	Amt (₹)
2024				2024			
Apr 19	To Cash A/c		40,000	Apr 7	By Purchases A/c		60,000
Apr 23	To Returns Outward A/c		10,000	Apr 7	By Input IGST A/c		7,200
Apr 23	To Input IGST A/c		1,200				
Apr 27	To Bank A/c		15,000				
Apr 27	To Discount Received A/c		1,000				
			67,200				67,200

Dr — Aryan — Cr

Date	Particulars	JF	Amt (₹)	Date	Particulars	JF	Amt (₹)
2024				2024			
Apr 10	To Sales A/c		50,000	Apr 29	By Cash A/c		20,000
Apr 10	To Output CGST A/c		3,000	Apr 30	By Balance c/d		36,000
Apr 10	To Output SGST A/c		3,000				
			56,000				56,000
May 1	To Balance b/d		36,000				

Dr — Machinery Account — Cr

Date	Particulars	JF	Amt (₹)	Date	Particulars	JF	Amt (₹)
2024				2024			
Apr 15	To Bank A/c		40,000	Apr 30	By Balance c/d		40,000
			40,000				40,000
May 1	To Balance b/d		40,000				

Dr — Returns Outward Account — Cr

Date	Particulars	JF	Amt (₹)	Date	Particulars	JF	Amt (₹)
2024				2024			
Apr 30	To Balance c/d		10,000	Apr 23	By Amrit		10,000
			10,000				10,000
				May 1	By Balance b/d		10,000

Dr — Input CGST Account — Cr

Date	Particulars	JF	Amt (₹)	Date	Particulars	JF	Amt (₹)
2024				2024			
Apr 2	To Cash A/c (Purchases)		3,600	Apr 30	By Balance c/d		3,600
			3,600				3,600

Dr **Input SGST Account** Cr

Date	Particulars	JF	Amt (₹)	Date	Particulars	JF	Amt (₹)
2024				2024			
Apr 2	To Cash A/c (Purchases)		3,600	Apr 30	By Balance c/d		3,600
			3,600				3,600

Dr **Output CGST Account** Cr

Date	Particulars	JF	Amt (₹)	Date	Particulars	JF	Amt (₹)
2024				2024			
Apr 30	To Balance c/d		7,800	Apr 4	By Cash A/c (Sales)		4,800
				Apr 10	By Aryan (Sales)		3,000
			7,800				7,800

Dr **Output SGST Account** Cr

Date	Particulars	JF	Amt (₹)	Date	Particulars	JF	Amt (₹)
2024				2024			
Apr 30	To Balance c/d		7,800	Apr 4	By Cash A/c (Sales)		4,800
				Apr 10	By Aryan (Sales)		3,000
			7,800				7,800

Dr **Input IGST Account** Cr

Date	Particulars	JF	Amt (₹)	Date	Particulars	JF	Amt (₹)
2024				2024			
Apr 7	To Amrit (Purchases)		7,200	Apr 23	By Amrit (Returns Outward)		1,200
Apr 15	To Bank A/c (Machinery)		4,800	Apr 30	By Balance c/d		10,800
			12,000				12,000

Dr **Discount Received Account** Cr

Date	Particulars	JF	Amt (₹)	Date	Particulars	JF	Amt (₹)
2024				2024			
Apr 30	To Balance c/d		1,000	Apr 27	By Amrit		1,000
			1,000				1,000

Solved Question 28 Prepare journal entries of the following postings.

(i)

Dr **Bank Account** Cr

Particulars	Amt (₹)	Particulars	Amt (₹)
To Sales A/c	50,000		
To Output CGST A/c	4,500		
To Output SGST A/c	4,500		

(ii)

Dr **Discount Received Account** Cr

Particulars	Amt (₹)	Particulars	Amt (₹)
		By Ajay	500

(iii)

Dr **Outstanding Salary Account** Cr

Particulars	Amt (₹)	Particulars	Amt (₹)
		By Salary A/c	1,500

(iv)

Dr **Suresh Account** Cr

Particulars	Amt (₹)	Particulars	Amt (₹)
To Bank A/c	2,000		
To Discount Received A/c	5,00		

Sol. **JOURNAL**

Date	Particulars	LF	Amt (Dr)	Amt (Cr)
(i)	Bank A/c Dr		59,000	
	To Sales A/c			50,000
	To Output CGST A/c			4,500
	To Output SGST A/c			4,500
	(Bding sold goods and charged GST)			
(ii)	Ajay Dr		500	
	To Discount Received A/c			500
	(Being discount received from Ajay)			
(iii)	Salary A/c Dr		1,500	
	To Outstanding Salary A/c			1,500
	(Being salary outstanding)			

Date	Particulars	LF	Amt (Dr)	Amt (Cr)
(iv)	Suresh Dr		2,500	
	To Bank A/c			2,000
	To Discount Received A/c			500
	(Being payment made to Suresh by cheque and discount received)			

Missing Information

Solved Question 29

JOURNAL

Date	Particulars	LF	Amt (Dr)	Amt (Cr)
2024				
Apr 3	.... Dr		...	
	To			...
	To			...
	(Being salary paid ₹ 5,000 equally by cash and cheque)			
Apr 5	.... Dr		...	
	To			...
	(Being goods sold to Neha costing ₹ 10,000 at 20% profit on cost less 10%, trade discount)			
Apr 10	.... Dr		...	
	To			...
	(Being goods lost by theft ₹ 5,000)			
Apr 11	.... Dr		...	
	To			...
	(Being interest on drawings charged ₹ 200)			
Apr 15	.... Dr		...	
	.... Dr		...	
	To			...
	(Being rent paid ₹ 2,000. 25% is in advance)			
Apr 18	.... Dr		...	
	To			...
	(Being ₹ 10,000 transferred to firms current account from saving account)			
Apr 30	.... Dr		...	
	To			...
	(Being salary outstanding ₹ 2,000)			

Sol. **JOURNAL**

Date	Particulars	LF	Amt (Dr)	Amt (Cr)
2024				
Apr 3	**Salary A/c** Dr		**5,000**	
	To Cash A/c			**2,500**
	To Bank A/c			**2,500**
	(Being salary paid ₹ 5,000 equally by cash and cheque)			
Apr 5	**Neha** Dr		**10,800**	
	To Sales A/c			**10,800**
	(Being goods sold to Neha costing ₹ 10,000 at 20% profit on cost less 10%, trade discount)			
Apr 10	**Loss by Theft A/c** Dr		**5,000**	
	To **Purchase A/c**			**5,000**
	(Being goods lost by theft ₹ 5,000)			
Apr 11	**Drawings A/c** Dr		**200**	
	To **Interest on Drawings A/c**			**200**
	(Being interest on drawing charged ₹ 200)			
Apr 15	**Prepaid Rent A/c** Dr		**500**	
	Rent A/c Dr		**1,500**	
	To **Cash**			**2,000**
	(Being rent paid ₹ 2,000, 25% is in advance)			
Apr 18	**Bank A/c** Dr		**10,000**	
	To **Capital A/c**			**10,000**
	(Being ₹ 10,000 transferred to firms current account from saving account)			
Apr 30	**Salary A/c** Dr		**2,000**	
	To **Outstanding Salary**			**2,000**
	(Being salary outstanding ₹ 2,000)			

Solved Question 30

Complete the missing information.

JOURNAL

Date	Particulars	LF	Amt (Dr)	Amt (Cr)
2022				
Apr 3	.... Dr		...	
	To			...
	To			...
	(Being goods of the list price of ₹ 4,000 purchased at 20% trade discount and 5% cash discount)			
Apr 8	.... Dr		...	
	To			...
	(Being goods costing ₹ 7,500 sold at profit of $33\frac{1}{3}$% on cost)			
Apr 10	.... Dr		...	
	To			...
	(Being goods costing ₹ 2,000 destroyed by fire)			
Apr 16	.... Dr		...	
	To			...
	(Being plant purchased for ₹ 50,000 and installation charges paid ₹ 1,000)			
Apr 20	Bank A/c Dr		1,500	
	.... Dr		...	
	To			...
	(Being 40 paise per rupee received from the estate of Mohan on his insolvency)			

Date	Particulars		LF	Amt (Dr)	Amt (Cr)
Apr 22	....	Dr		15,000	
	....	Dr		5,000	
	To Bank A/c				20,000
	(Being purchase of a computer for ₹ 15,000 and an electric fan for ₹ 5,000)				
Apr 30	....	Dr		...	
	To				...
	To				...
	(Being salary paid ₹ 20,000 and due ₹ 5,000)				

Sol. **JOURNAL**

Date	Particulars		LF	Amt (Dr)	Amt (Cr)
2022					
Apr 3	**Purchases A/c**	Dr		**3,200**	
	To Cash A/c				**3,040**
	To Discount Received A/c				**160**
	(Being goods for ₹ 4,000 purchased at 20% trade discount and 5% cash discount)				
Apr 8	**Cash A/c**	Dr		**10,000**	
	To Sales A/c				**10,000**
	(Being goods costing ₹ 7,500 sold at a profit of $33\frac{1}{3}$% on cost)				
Apr 10	**Loss by Fire A/c**	Dr		**2,000**	
	To Purchases A/c				**2,000**
	(Being goods destroyed by fire)				
Apr 16	**Plant A/c**	Dr		**51,000**	
	To Cash A/c				**51,000**
	(Being plant purchased for ₹ 50,000 and installation charges paid ₹ 1,000)				
Apr 20	Bank A/c	Dr		1,500	
	Bad Debts A/c	Dr		**2,250**	
	To Mohan				**3,750**
	(Being the receipt of 40 paise per rupee)				
Apr 22	**Computer A/c**	Dr		15,000	
	Fixtures A/c	Dr		5,000	
	To Bank A/c				20,000
	(Being purchases of a computer for ₹ 15,000 and an electric fan for ₹ 5,000)				
Apr 30	**Salary A/c**	Dr		**25,000**	
	To Cash A/c				**20,000**
	To Outstanding Salary A/c				**5,00**
	(Being salary paid and due)				

Numerical Questions

Journal

1. Journalise the following transactions.

Apr 1	Rohit started business with cash ₹ 1,50,000 and furniture of ₹ 80,000.
Apr 3	Goods purchased for cash ₹ 30,000.
Apr 5	Purchased goods from Vishal ₹ 20,000.
Apr 8	Sold goods for cash ₹ 25,000.
Apr 15	Sold goods to Arman ₹ 15,000.
Apr 22	Purchased furniture for cash ₹ 20,000.
Apr 25	Purchased a machine on credit from Anjana ₹ 25,000.
Apr 26	Received cash from Arman ₹ 15,000 and paid to Vishal.

Ans. Total of Journal = ₹ 3,95,000

2. Write journal entries in the books of Tarun & Bros. for the following transactions.

2024	
Jul 1	Paid cash to Suresh ₹ 9,800 after receiving discount ₹ 200 from him.
Jul 3	Received cash from Akhil ₹ 4,800 after allowing discount of ₹ 200 to him.
Jul 6	Sold goods to Tanya ₹ 40,000.
Jul 12	Tanya returned goods ₹ 12,000.
Jul 15	Received cash from Tanya ₹ 27,000 in full settlement of her account.
Jul 20	Sold goods to Gopal list price of ₹ 40,000 at 10% trade discount plus 20% profit.
Jul 28	Purchased goods from Vijay valued ₹ 10,000 after deducting trade discount of ₹ 2,000.

Ans. Total of Journal = ₹ 1,48,200

3. Below are given the transactions of Madhuri. Journalise.

Date	Particulars	Amt (₹)
Apr 1	Started business with cash	5,00,000
Apr 4	Purchased goods for cash	1,00,000
Apr 8	Bought goods from Pranav	30,000
Apr 13	Sold goods to Sumdhi	40,000
Apr 15	Received 50% of amount due from Sunidhi	
Apr 17	Paid cash to Pranav	15,000
Apr 20	Cash sales for the month	25,000
Apr 25	Paid salary to Ram on behalf of Shyam	8,000
Apr 30	Goods were returned to Pranav	5,000

Ans. Total of Journal = ₹ 7,43,000

4. Pass journal entries for the following transactions.

2024		Amt (₹)
Feb 1	Deposited into bank for opening a current account	70,000
Feb 3	Transferred into fixed deposit account	10,000
Feb 5	Sold goods for cash ₹ 40,000, out of this ₹ 30,000 deposited into bank account	
Feb 8	Deposited ₹ 3,000 as school fees of proprietor son's	
Feb 9	Withdrawn from bank for office use	5,000
Feb 10	Received a cheque of ₹ 2,500 from Vijay after banking hours	
Feb 12	Deposited Vijay's cheque into bank account	
Feb 15	Cheque deposited of Vijay dishonoured	

Ans. Total of Journal = ₹ 1,65,500

5. Record the following transactions in Vishnu Stores.

2024

Aug 1 Started business with cash ₹ 5,00,000, paid into bank ₹ 2,00,000.

Aug 3 Purchased furniture ₹ 50,000 and paid 2% commission on the cost.

Aug 5 Sold goods to Tarun for ₹ 2,50,000. Tarun paid one-fourth in cash only.

Aug 7 Received a cheque from Tarun in full settlement. Discount allowed @ 2%.

Aug 9 Paid life insurance premium of ₹ 5,000 of the proprietor.

Aug 10 Goods lost by fire ₹ 4,000.

Aug 15 Paid for advertisement ₹ 5,000.

Ans. Total of Journal = ₹ 12,02,500

6. Write journal entries in the journal book of Shyama Bros.

(i) Radhey who owed us ₹ 25,000 is declared insolvent and 75 paise in a rupee is received as final dividend from her estate by cheque.

(ii) Purchased goods list price ₹ 40,000 less 10% trade discount from Amar.

(iii) Goods of ₹ 10,000 is given to the manager against his salary.

(iv) Sold goods costing ₹ 6,000 at 20% profit on cost to Bharat.

(v) Received from Bharat ₹ 7,000 in full settlement.

Ans. Total of Journal = ₹ 85,400

7. Write journal entries for the following transactions.

(i) ₹ 15,000 due from Amrit are not recoverable.

(ii) Goods worth ₹ 10,000 were withdrawn by the proprietor for personal use.

(iii) Provided interest on capital at 10% p.a. Commenced business with ₹ 8,00,000 on 1st October, 2024. Books are closed on 31st March every year.

(iv) Goods costing ₹ 40,000 sold to Pankaj for ₹ 60,000.

(v) Rishabh paid ₹ 58,500 in full settlement on behalf of Pankaj.

(vi) Rent paid to Murarilal ₹ 3,000.

(vii) Accrued interest ₹ 500 received in bank account.

Ans. Total of Journal = ₹ 1,88,500

8. Journalise the following transactions in the books of Dev & Sons, dealing in electricals.

(i) Received a cheque of ₹ 6,750 from Ajay. Allowed him discount ₹ 250.

(ii) Due to defect in goods which were purchased, Brahma Electricals allowed rebate of ₹ 300.

(iii) Issued a cheque of ₹ 3,500 in favour of M/s Narmada Electricals Ltd.

(iv) Purchased a machine (second hand) ₹ 50,000 and spent ₹ 5,000 on its overhauling to get started.

(v) Purchased goods for ₹ 50,000 from Mahesh & Co. and supplied its fourty percent plus 20% profit to Anand for cash.

Ans. Total of Journal = ₹ 1,39,800

9. Journalise the following transactions. **Competency Based Que**

(i) Sold goods to Koa for ₹ 40,000 at 15% trade discount and 4% cash discount. Received 75% amount immediately through a cheque.

(ii) Bought goods from Pia for ₹ 1,00,000 at terms 5% cash discount and 20% trade discount. Paid 3/4th of the amount in cash at the time of purchase.

(iii) Bought goods for cash of the list price of ₹ 40,000 at 10% trade discount and 2½ cash discount.

Ans. Total of Journal = ₹ 1,50,000

10. On 31st March, 2024, Kushal's assets and liabilities stood as under **Competency Based Que**

Assets Building ₹ 3,00,000, machinery ₹ 10,000, furniture ₹ 2,000, bills receivable ₹ 5,000, sundry debtors ₹ 12,000, stock ₹ 9,000, cash at bank ₹ 15,000, cash in hand ₹ 2,000.

Liabilities Bills payable ₹ 4,000, Twinkle's loan ₹ 15,000, sundry creditors ₹ 20,000. Write an opening entry on 1st April, 2024.

Ans. Capital (Balancing figure) = ₹ 3,16,000

11. Write journal entries for the following transactions

2024

Apr 1 Anil invested ₹ 45,000 in business.

Apr 2 Deposited in firm's current account ₹ 25,000.

Apr 3 Bought goods ₹ 5,000 and paid ₹ 100 for cartage.

Apr 5 Purchased goods ₹ 5,000 on credit from Sumit.

Apr 8 Purchased a machine ₹ 2,000 and spent ₹ 100 on its installation.

Apr 10 Payment made to Sumit by cheque in full settlement. Received discount ₹ 200.

Apr 12 Deposited by Anil in firm's current account from his saving account ₹ 20,000.

Apr 14 Withdrawn from bank account ₹ 10,000. Half for personal use of Anil.

Apr 16 Sold goods costing ₹ 6,000 at 25% profit on sales.

Ans. Total of Journal = ₹ 1,25,200

12. Journalise the following transactions.

(i) Rohit borrowed ₹ 2,00,000 from his wife's brother for commencing a business and transferred ₹ 1,00,000 out of it into firm's current account.

(ii) Purchased a machine for ₹ 15,000 and paid ₹ 500 on its installation.

(iii) Appointed a manager at salary of ₹ 10,000 per month.

(iv) Charged depreciation @ 10% p.a. on above machines.

(v) Goods purchased ₹ 40,000 from Sanaya and accepted a bill for the same.

(vi) Goods costing ₹ 2,000, was given to manager against his salary.

(vii) Paid wages to a worker ₹ 4,000 out of which wages of ₹ 2,000 was outstanding in previous year.

(viii) Paid manager's due salary by cheque.

(ix) Introduced additional cash ₹ 50,000.

(x) Taken a loan of ₹ 1,00,000 from IDBI at interest 10% p.a.

Ans. Total of Journal = ₹ 3,21,050

Hint Appointment of a manager is not a transaction.

13. Journalise the following transactions in the books of Kartik Enterprises.

2024

Apr 1 Purchased equipment worth ₹ 10,000.

Apr 4 Opened a bank account with ₹ 20,000 and transferred ₹ 5,000 into proprietor's personal account for meeting travelling expenses for business purpose.

Apr 5 Banked ₹ 2,00,000.

Apr 6 Withdrawn from bank ₹ 20,000 and paid to Kanha Bros.

Apr 8 Bought debentures of Reliance Ltd. for ₹ 40,000 and brokerage paid ₹ 500. Payment is made by cheque.

Apr 9 Paid for stamps ₹ 500.

Apr 12 Rent due to landlord ₹ 2,000 was paid by cheque.

Apr 15 Received commission ₹ 5,000. It includes accrued commission of ₹ 2,000 of previous year i.e. 2023-24.

Ans. Total of Journal = ₹ 3,23,000

14. Journalise the following transactions in the books of Pihu.

(i) Opened a current account with Punjab National Bank ₹ 1,00,000.

(ii) Received a cheque of ₹ 12,900 from Sita and allowed discount ₹ 300 to her. The cheque was deposited into bank on the same day.

(iii) Purchased machinery for ₹ 1,00,000, payment made by cheque. Installation charge of machinery ₹ 6,000 paid in cash.

(iv) Purchased a horse for business for ₹ 20,000.

(v) Sold goods to Gita at a list price of ₹ 4,000. Trade discount @ 10% and cash discount @ 5%. He paid the amount on the same day and availed the cash discount.

(vi) Purchased goods for ₹ 10,000 and paid ₹ 400 for carriage on these goods.

(vii) Additional cash introduced by the proprietor ₹ 40,000.

(viii) Purchased stationery ₹ 800 and postal stamps ₹ 100.

(ix) Withdrawn from bank ₹ 20,000.

(x) Received an order to supply goods of ₹ 40,000 from Mia and received ₹ 10,000 as an advance together with the order.

(xi) Cash ₹ 10,000 and goods worth ₹ 40,000 were stolen.

(xii) Purchased goods from Dia for ₹ 40,000 and the payment was made by cheque.

(xiii) Sold 1/4th of the above goods at a profit of @ 25% for cash.

Ans. Total of Journal = ₹ 4,26,600

15. Following balances appeared in the books of Ira Bros. as on 1st April, 2022. Competency Based Que

Assets Cash ₹ 8,000, cash at bank ₹ 7,000, stock ₹ 30,000, debtors ₹ 36,000 (Miya ₹ 10,000, Siya ₹ 12,000, Diya ₹ 14,000), furniture ₹ 5,000, building ₹ 25,000.

Liabilities Creditors (Tiya ₹ 5,000; Piya ₹ 6,000).

In April, 2024, the following transactions took place

Date	Particulars	Amt (₹)
2024		
Apr 2	Bought goods of the list price of ₹ 6,000 from Zen Bros. less 15% trade discount and 2% cash discount and paid 40% price at the same time	
Apr 3	Received a draft from Miya in full settlement and deposited it into bank	9,750
Apr 5	Purchased goods from Riya of the list price of ₹ 8,000 at 20% trade discount and paid by cheque	
Apr 8	Sold goods and received a cheque	25,000
Apr 10	Deposited the above cheque into bank	
Apr 12	Siya deposited in our bank account	4,000
Apr 16	Paid income tax by cheque	5,600
Apr 20	Received a cheque from Siya and sent to bank	7,800
	Discount allowed	200
Apr 21	Withdrew from bank for office	2,000
	for private use	4,000
Apr 23	Sent a cheque to Tiya in full settlement of her account	4,900
Apr 27	Cheque of Siya returned by the bank as dishonoured	
Apr 28	Diya was declared insolvent and a payment of 60 paise in a rupee received from her estate by a cheque	
Apr 30	Bank allowed interest	350
Apr 30	Paid for rent by cheque	1,500
Apr 30	Paid for travelling expenses by cheque	500

Pass journal entries for the above transactions.

Ans. Capital = ₹ 1,00,000; Total of Journal = ₹ 2,35,450

16. **Give journal entries in the books of Narayan & Co. for the following transactions.**

Date	Particulars	Amt (₹)
2024		
Apr 3	Cash purchase	50,000
Apr 5	Sold goods to Sudama	20,000
Apr 7	Sudama found some goods defective. Rebate allowed to him ₹ 500	
Apr 10	Received cash from Sudama	15,000
Apr 15	Vinay sold goods to Narayan & Co.	10,000
Apr 20	Kaushal purchased goods from us	8,000
Apr 25	Received cash from Sudama in full settlement	4,000
Apr 27	Paid life insurance premium of proprietor's wife	1,000
Apr 28	Paid fire insurance premium by cheque	1,500
Apr 28	Paid cash to Vinay ₹ 9,800 after discount of ₹ 200	
Apr 29	Paid advertisement expenses ₹ 1,000 and salaries ₹ 4,000	
Apr 30	Received interest ₹ 300 and commission ₹ 500	

Ans. Total of Journal = ₹ 1,26,300

17. **Journalise the following transactions in the journal of Gupta & Sons.**

(i) Paid income tax ₹ 3,000 by cheque.

(ii) Joya who owed us ₹ 10,000 becomes insolvent and nothing is received from her estate.

(iii) Purchased building ₹ 1,50,000 and incurred expenses of ₹ 12,000 on its purchase.

(iv) Proprietor visited Pune and paid ₹ 20,000 for expenses incurred for business purpose, from his personal account. Amount was not reimbursed by the firm.

(v) Paid rent ₹ 5,000 in advance.

(vi) Goods of ₹ 2,400 (cost + 20% profit on cost) given as charity.

(vii) Proprietor took a loan for education expenses for his son ₹ 1,00,000 from SBI. Amount received in his personal account.

Ans. Total of Journal = ₹ 2,02,000

Journal (GST)

18. **Write journal entries in the books of Gupta & Sons assuming all transactions take place within the state of Rajasthan. Assume CGST and SGST 9% each.**

2024

Feb 1 Purchased goods for ₹ 5,00,000 from Mittal Bros.

Feb 4 Sold goods for ₹ 6,00,000 to Singhal & Bros.

Feb 8 Paid for advertisement expenses ₹ 20,000 by cheque.

Feb 12 Purchased a computer for office ₹ 30,000. Payment made by cheque.

Feb 20 Paid for stationery ₹ 1,000.

Feb 29 Payment made of balance amount of GST.

Ans. Total of Journal = ₹ 14,66,180

19. **Pass entries in the books of Gopal & Bros. assuming CGST and SGST 9% each.** **Competency Based Que**

(i) Gopal & Bros. purchased goods for ₹ 90,000 from out of the state. Payment was made by cash.

(ii) Sold goods for ₹ 59,000 including GST outside the state on credit.

(iii) Sold goods for ₹ 30,000 within the state on credit.

(iv) Paid telephone bill for ₹ 2,000 by cheque.

(v) Purchased an office equipment for office for ₹ 20,000.

20. Pass entries in the books of Sanjay Pratap & Son assuming all transactions have been entered within the state of West Bengal, charging CGST and SGST @ 6% each.

2024

Apr 1	Purchased goods for ₹ 90,000 from Akhil Bhatia.
Apr 5	Sold goods to Vishal for ₹ 1,20,000.
Apr 10	Returned goods to Akhil Bhatia for ₹ 10,000.
Apr 16	Vishal returned goods for ₹ 6,000.
Apr 20	Paid for stationery ₹ 2,000 in cash.
Apr 24	Goods withdrawn for personal use ₹ 10,000.
Apr 27	Goods destroyed by fire ₹ 10,000.
Apr 30	Payment made of balance amount of GST.

Ans. Total of Journal = ₹ 2,91,440

21. Enter the following transactions in the books of Mittal & Sons assuming that all transactions have taken place in the state of Uttar Pradesh. Assume CGST and SGST @ 9% each. Competency Based Que

2024

Sep 05	Purchased goods ₹ 60,000 from Goyal & Bros. at 20% trade discount.
Sep 08	Sold goods to Singhal traders for ₹ 25,000.
Sep 10	Received a cheque from Singhal Traders for ₹ 18,000.
Sep 14	Purchased furniture for ₹ 4,000 by cheque.
Sep 20	Advertisement expenses of ₹ 1,000 paid by cheque.
Sep 24	Sold goods for ₹ 6,000 and received a cheque.
Sep 28	Received commission of ₹ 1,500.
Sep 30	Output GST adjusted against input GST.

Ans. Total of Journal = ₹ 1,24,740

22. Write journal entries in the books of Gandhi & Sons (Madhya Pradesh), assuming all transactions have been entered within the state, charging CGST and SGST 9% each.

2024

Apr 4	Bought goods ₹ 1,00,000 from Nehru & Bros.
Apr 6	Good returned to Nehru & Bros. ₹ 40,000.
Apr 8	Sold goods to Aftab & Sons for ₹ 1,50,000.
Apr 10	Goods returned by Aftab & Sons for ₹ 30,000.
Apr 15	Goods withdrawn by proprietor for personal use ₹ 8,000.
Apr 20	Goods lost by fire ₹ 4,000.
Apr 25	Paid advertisement expenses ₹ 10,000.
Apr 30	Payment made of balance amount of GST.

Ans. Total of Journal = ₹ 4,25,160

23. Write journal entries in the books of Raghav & Sons (Agra) assuming all transactions take place out of state, charging GST 18%.

(i) Purchased goods for ₹ 3,00,000 by cheque.
(ii) Sold goods to Radhika & Sons ₹ 1,50,000.
(iii) Purchased goods for ₹ 60,000 on credit.
(iv) Sold goods ₹ 3,00,000. Received cheque and deposited into bank.
(v) Received rent ₹ 10,000.

Ans. Total of Journal = ₹ 9,67,600

24. Journalise the following

(i) Purchased goods list price ₹ 50,000 less 10%. Trade discount plus CGST and SGST 9% each.
(ii) Purchased goods list price ₹ 50,000 less 10% trade discount and 5% cash discount. CGST and SGST will be levied 9% each.
(iii) Purchased goods list price ₹ 20,000 less 10% trade discount. CGST and SGST will be levied 9% each. Paid half amount by cheque and availed 5% cash discount.
(iv) Sold goods list price ₹ 50,000 to Vijay less 10% trade discount and 5% cash discount plus CGST and SGST 9% each. Vijay paid 1/2th amount only. Competency Based Que

Ans. Total of Journal = ₹ 1,79,851

25. Journalise the following Competency Based Que

(i) Purchased goods list price ₹ 50,000 less 10% trade discount and 5% cash discount with CGST and SGST 9% each. Payment made by cheque.
(ii) Purchased goods list price ₹ 1,00,000 less 20% trade discount and 3% cash discount with CGST and SGST 9% each. 50% amount paid by cheque immediately.
(iii) Sold goods to Aryan list price ₹ 60,000 less 10% trade discount and 2% cash discount with CGST and SGST 9% each. Amount was received by cheque immediately.
(iv) Sold goods to Dev list price ₹ 70,000 less 10% trade discount and 2% cash discount with CGST and SGST 9% each. Three-fourth amount was received by cheque immediately.

Ans. Total of Journal = ₹ 2,84,574

26. Write journal entries for the following transactions.

(i) Goods returned to Das & Sons ₹ 11,800 including GST. Goods were purchased at CGST and SGST 9% each.
(ii) Goods of ₹ 10,000 excluding GST were withdrawn by proprietor for personal use. (IGST 18% was charged at the time of purchase).

(iii) Distributed goods costing ₹ 8,000 as free samples. (CGST and SGST 9% each was charged at the time of purchase).

(iv) Goods for ₹ 10,000 given as charity. (Purchased with IGST 18%). **Competency Based Que**

Ans. Total of Journal = ₹ 44,840

27. Journalise the following transactions in the books of Rahul Traders, Pune. **Competency Based Que**

2024

Oct 3	Purchased goods Vijaya & Sons list price of ₹ 2,00,000 at 20%, trade discount and 5% cash discount on purchase price. Paid CGST and SGST @ 9% each. Payment was made immediately by cheque.
Oct 10	Sold to Samiran & Sons, goods of list price ₹ 2,50,000 at 20% trade discount and 3% cash discount on sale price. Charged CGST and SGST @ 9% each. Full payment received by cheque at the time of sale.
Oct 20	Sold goods to Kakuli & Bros. list price ₹ 50,000 at 20% trade discount and 3% cash discount on sale price. CGST and SGST @ 9% each was charged. 80% of amount was received by cheque immediately.
Oct 31	Payment made of balance amount of GST.

Ans. Total of Journal = ₹ 5,11,252

28. Pass entries in the books of Murari of Maharashtra assuming CGST and SGST 9% each.

Competency Based Que

2024

Apr 1	Purchased goods for ₹ 2,00,000 from Girdhari of Vadodra (Gujarat).
Apr 4	Purchased goods for ₹ 60,000 from Tanhaji of Pune (Maharashtra).
Apr 6	Sold goods costing ₹ 60,000 to Arun from Uttar Pradesh at a profit of 25% on cost less 10% trade discount.
Apr 8	Sold goods to Thapa (Maharashtra) costing ₹ 20,000 at 50% profit less 10% trade discount cheque which was deposited into bank.
Apr 15	Paid to a newspaper agency for an advertisement ₹ 5,000.
Apr 25	Bought a computer for office ₹ 30,000 and payment made by cheque.
Apr 30	Proprietor withdrew ₹ 5,000 for his personal use.

Ans. Total of Journal = ₹ 4,05,510

29. Write journal entries for the following transactions assuming goods were purchased at CGST 6% and SGST 6%.

(i) Goods ₹ 10,000 withdrawn by proprietor for personal use.

(ii) Goods ₹ 15,000 were given as charity.

(iii) Goods lost by fire ₹ 5,000.

(iv) Goods of ₹ 20,000 were distributed as free samples.

(v) Goods of ₹ 5,000 were stolen by employees.

Ans. Total of Journal = ₹ 61,600

30. Prachi Departmental Store has following balances in its GST accounts as on 31st March, 2024.

Competency Based Que

Particulars	IGST (₹)	CGST (₹)	SGST (₹)
Input GST	3,00,000	4,00,000	4,50,000
Output GST	6,00,000	2,50,000	2,75,000

Show how Input GST will be adjusted against Output GST and also show that which accounts have balance.

31. Write journal entries for the following transactions assume CGST and SGST @ 9% each was claimed as input. **Competency Based Que**

(i) Goods returned to Niketan ₹ 10,000.

(ii) Goods ₹ 5,000 taken by proprietor for personal use.

(iii) Goods of ₹ 2,000 given as charity.

(iv) Goods distributed as free samples ₹ 6,000.

Ans. Total of Journal = ₹ 27,140

Ledger

32. Journalise the following transactions, post them into ledger accounts and balance them.

		Amt (₹)
(i)	Business started with	
	(a) Cash	1,50,000
	(b) Goods	50,000
(ii)	Purchased computers and paid by cheque	2,50,000
(iii)	Goods returned to Ritika	2,000
(iv)	Stationery purchased for cash	3,000
(v)	Goods returned by Krishna	2,000
(vi)	Cheque given to Ritika	28,000
(vii)	Cheque received from Krishna	8,000
(viii)	Cash deposited into bank	20,000
(ix)	Goods given as charity	2,000
(x)	Paid sundry expenses	200
(xi)	Cash paid to Harish in full settlement of account (amount due ₹ 15,000)	14,700
(xii)	Cartage paid	200

Ans. Total of Journal = ₹ 5,30,400

33. **Sanjay of Delhi started his business on 1st April, 2024 with cash ₹ 5,00,000 and machinery of ₹ 2,50,000. Transactions for the month of April, 2024 are given below. Prepare ledger accounts after journalising.**

2024		Amt (₹)
Apr 2	Purchased goods for cash from Delhi	50,000
Apr 3	Purchased goods from Dev from Chandigarh (Haryana)	60,000
Apr 4	Sold goods for cash in Delhi	80,000
Apr 6	Cash deposited into firm's bank account	70,000
Apr 10	Purchased machinery for cash	40,000
Apr 14	Sold goods to Gupta & Bros.	65,000
Apr 20	Paid salary for the month of April	8,000
Apr 25	Received interest in bank account	1,500
Apr 30	Rent outstanding	1,200

CGST and SGST will be received @ 9% each on intra-state transactions and IGST 18% on inter-state purchase and sale of goods.

34. **Prepare journal entries of the following postings.**

Competency Based Que

(i) Dr **Sales Account** Cr

Particulars	Amt (₹)	Particulars	Amt (₹)
		By Cash A/c	2,000
		By Varun	3,000

(ii) Dr **Rent Account** Cr

Particulars	Amt (₹)	Particulars	Amt (₹)
To Cash A/c	3,000		
To Outstanding Rent A/c	2,000		

(iii) Dr **Interest Account** Cr

Particulars	Amt (₹)	Particulars	Amt (₹)
		By Accrued Interest A/c	2,000

(iv) Dr **Purchases Account** Cr

Particulars	Amt (₹)	Particulars	Amt (₹)
To Pramod	5,000		

Missing Information

35. **Complete the missing information.**

Competency Based Que

Date	Particulars	LF	Amt (Dr)	Amt (Cr)
(i)	.... Dr		...	
	.... Dr		...	
	To			...
	(Being goods of the list price of ₹ 2,500 sold at 10% trade discount and 2% cash discount)			
(ii)	.... Dr		...	
	To			...
	(Being the purchase of motor car for ₹ 40,000 and the payment of ₹ 2,500 as repair charges on it. Entire payment is made by cheque)			
(iii)	Prashant Dr		2,500	
	To Cash A/c			...
	To			...
	(Being Prashant's account settled, cash discount @ 3%)			
(iv)	Bank A/c Dr		...	
	.... Dr		...	
	To			4,200
	(Being 70 paise per rupee received from the estate of Ashok on his insolvency)			
(v)	.... Dr		1,500	
	To			1,500
	(Being goods used by proprietor for personal use)			
(vi)	.... Dr		1,000	
	To			1,000
	(Being rent due to landlord)			

36. **Fill in the missing figures. Assume CGST and SGST 9% each.**

Competency Based Que

In the Books of Goyal Bros.
JOURNAL

Date	Particulars	LF	Amt (Dr)	Amt (Cr)
(i)	.... A/c Dr		...	
	Input CGST A/c Dr		18,000	
	.... A/c Dr		...	
	To Malhotra & Sons			...
	(Being purchased goods within state)			
(ii)	Debtors A/c Dr		3,54,000	
	To			...
	To			...
	To			...
	(Being sale of goods within state)			
(iii)	.... Dr		...	
	.... Dr		...	
	.... Dr		...	
	To Bank A/c			11,800
	(Being rent paid)			

Theoretical Questions

Short Answer Type Questions

1. When an account is said to have a debit balance and credit balance?

Ans. An account shows a debit balance when the debit side exceeds the credit side. It shows a credit balance when the credit side exceeds the debit side. e.g. If cash account's total of debit side is ₹ 50,000 and total of credit side is ₹ 30,000 then it will show debit balance of ₹ 20,000.

2. Describe the features of a journal.

Ans. The main features of a journal are

(i) It records day-to-day business transactions in the order in which they happen.

(ii) It provides a complete record of each transaction in a single entry.

(iii) It follows the double entry system, recording both debit and credit aspects of each transaction.

(iv) Every journal entry is accompanied by a brief description or narration of the transaction.

3. Why is it necessary to sub-divide a journal? **Competency Based Que**

Ans. When a business grows, recording every transaction in one place becomes cumbersome and time consuming. To make the process more efficient, the journal is divided into multiple specialised books, such as

(i) Cash book (ii) Journal proper
(iii) Purchase book (iv) Sales book
(v) Purchases returns book
(vi) Sales returns book (vii) Bills receivable book
(viii) Bills payable book

4. What are the advantages of maintaining a journal?

Ans. The benefits of keeping a journal include

(i) Reduces the chances of missing a transaction since all entries are recorded when they happen.

(ii) Makes it easier to locate specific transactions since they are recorded in chronological order.

(iii) Simplifies posting entries into the ledger, as transactions are systematically classified into debits and credits.

(iv) Helps in verifying ledger entries through trial balance checks.

(v) Provides reliable legal evidence of transactions compared to the ledger.

5. Despite its benefits, a journal has certain limitations. Discuss these limitations.

Ans. The limitations of a journal include

(i) As the business grows, the journal becomes bulky and harder to manage due to the increasing number of transactions.

(ii) It does not provide instant information about a transaction.

(iii) Since a journal is often handled by only one person, it limits the implementation of an internal control system.

(iv) Cash transactions are usually recorded in a separate cash book, not in the journal itself.

6. Imagine you're starting a small business and need to keep track of every financial transaction, from purchase to sale and you want to record these transactions in an organised manner. Describe the process involved in documenting transactions in a journal. Additionally, explore how journal differ from ledger? **Competency Based Que**

Ans. The process of recording in a journal begins by documenting transactions in chronological order. For each transaction, the date, the accounts involved and whether they are debited or credited are recorded.

A brief description or narration of the transaction follows, explaining the nature of the entry. The journal serves as the initial record before the transactions are transferred into the ledger.

The difference between a journal and a ledger is that a journal captures day-to-day transactions as they occur, while the ledger classifies these transactions under their respective accounts.

The journal is used for recording, whereas the ledger summarises these records to create the final accounts, helping in the preparation of financial statements.

7. Distinguish between the following types of accounts

(i) Real accounts and nominal accounts
(ii) Personal accounts and real accounts
(iii) Nominal accounts and personal accounts

Ans. (i) Real accounts deal with permanent assets such as buildings, land and machinery, which carry balances into the next accounting period. Nominal accounts, however, deal with income, expenses, gains and losses and are closed at the end of each financial year.

(ii) Personal accounts relate to individuals, companies or organisations the business interacts with, like customers and suppliers.

Real accounts, in contrast, involve tangible or intangible assets the business owns, such as cash, land or trademarks.

(iii) Nominal accounts track the business's performance by recording its income and expenses.

These accounts are temporary and are closed each period. Personal accounts, however, represent amounts due from or owed to individuals and entities and they are carried forward to the next accounting period.

8. Explain how debit and credit rules are applied to various types of accounts.

Ans. The rules for debits and credits vary depending on the type of account

(i) For assets and expenses, debit entries increase the account balance, while credit entries decrease it.

(ii) For liabilities, equity and income, credits increase the account balance and debits decrease it.

These rules form the foundation of the double entry accounting system, ensuring that every transaction maintains the balance between debits and credits.

9. What do you mean by 'debit' and 'credit'? Explain with examples.

Ans. 'Debit' refers to entries on the lefthand side of an account, which usually indicate an increase in assets or expenses or a decrease in liabilities or equity. 'Credit' on the other hand, appears on the right-hand side of an account and represents an increase in liabilities or equity, or a decrease in assets or expenses.

For instance, if a business buys equipment worth ₹ 10,000, the equipment account is debited by ₹ 10,000 (asset increase) and the cash account is credited by ₹ 10,000 (asset decrease).

10. Differentiate between trade discount and cash discount.

Ans. A trade discount is a reduction in the price of goods given to buyers, typically to encourage bulk purchasing and it is not recorded in the books of accounts. It is deducted from the invoice before the transaction is recorded. In contrast, a cash discount is an incentive offered to customers for prompt payment and is recorded in the books. This discount reduces the total amount payable if payment is made within a specific period, helping businesses improve cash flow.

11. What is a 'ledger' and why is it important? Explain the role of a ledger in financial accounting.

Ans. A ledger is an accounting book where transactions are classified and summarised by account, consolidating all journal entries.

Its importance lies in the fact that it provides a detailed overview of all accounts, allowing the company to track financial performance, assets, liabilities and equity.

The ledger is crucial for preparing key financial statements like the balance sheet and income statement and ensures that every transaction has been appropriately categorised.

12. Classify these commonly used accounts into assets, liabilities, capital, revenue and expense. NCERT; Competency Based Que

(i) Building (ii) Wages (iii) Credit sales (iv) Credit purchases (v) Electricity charges due but not yet paid (outstanding electricity bills) (vi) Godown rent paid in advance (prepaid godown rent) (vii) Sales (viii) Fresh capital introduced (ix) Drawings (x) Discount paid

Ans.

Assets	Liabilities	Capital	Revenue	Expense
Building, Godown rent paid in advance	Credit purchases, Electricity charges due but not paid	Fresh capital introduced	Sales, Credit sales	Wages, Drawings, Discount paid

Objective Questions

Multiple Choice Questions (MCQs)

1. Journal is called a book of

(a) original entry
(b) prime entry
(c) Both (a) and (b)
(d) None of these

2. From the following, which account is a nominal account?

(a) Drawings account
(b) Capital account
(c) Purchase account
(d) Bank account

3. Outstanding salary account is

(a) natural personal account
(b) artificial personal account
(c) real account
(d) nominal account

4. Rule of 'debit the receiver and credit the giver' applies to

(a) personal account
(b) real account
(c) nominal account
(d) None of these

5. 'Debit all expenses and losses and credit the incomes and gains' applies to

(a) cash account
(b) purchase account
(c) machine account
(d) None of these

6. The journal entry to record the sale of services on credit should include NCERT

(a) debit to debtors and credit to capital
(b) debit to cash and credit to debtors
(c) debit to fees income and credit to debtors
(d) debit to debtors and credit to fees income

7. **Recording of transactions in journal is called** NCERT
(a) costing (b) posting
(c) journalising (d) recordly

8. **The journal entry to record payment of monthly bill will include** Competency Based Que
(a) debit monthly bill and credit capital
(b) debit capital and credit cash
(c) debit monthly bill and credit cash
(d) debit monthly bill and credit creditors

9. **What will be the journal entry recorded for the following transaction?** Competency Based Que
"Received ₹ 2,000 interest accrued in the previous year."

(a) Cash A/c	Dr	2,000	
To Interest Received A/c			2,000
(b) Cash A/c	Dr	2,000	
To Accrued Interest A/c			2,000
(c) Accrued Interest A/c	Dr	2,000	
To Interest A/c			2,000
(d) Bank A/c	Dr	2,000	
To Interest Received A/c			2,000

10. **Sold goods to Rahim ₹ 10,000 plus CGST and SGST 6% each. Allowed cash discount 5%. On what amount GST will be levied?** Competency Based Que
(a) ₹ 10,000 (b) ₹ 9,500
(c) ₹ 9,000 (d) None of these

11. **Opening balance in the account of a creditor Raj is ₹ 80,000. During the year, credit purchase from Raj was ₹ 70,000 and payment made to him was ₹ 30,000. What will be closing balance in the account of Raj?** Competency Based Que
(a) ₹ 1,80,000 (b) ₹ 40,000
(c) ₹ 1,20,000 (d) ₹ 1,50,000

12. **GST paid on which of the following cannot be set-off against GST collected?**
(a) Educational services
(b) Goods distributed as free sample
(c) Health services (d) Free gift to staff

13. **"Income tax paid ₹ 2,000." Which accounts are to be debited and credited?** Competency Based Que
(a) Income Tax A/c (Dr), Cash A/c (Cr)
(b) Drawings A/c (Dr), Cash A/c (Cr)
(c) Capital A/c (Dr), Cash A/c (Cr)
(d) Either (a), (b) or (c)

14. **If the GST rate is 18% then rate of CGST will be in case of sale/purchase of goods and services within the state.**
(a) 10% (b) 9%
(c) 12% (d) None of these

15. **"Rent A/c Dr**
To Outstanding Rent A/c"
Why 'outstanding rent account' is credited in above journal entry? Competency Based Que
(a) Because outstanding rent is an income
(b) Because outstanding rent is a liability
(c) Because outstanding rent is an asset
(d) None of the above

16. **Which of following is incorrect?**
(a) Nominal accounts are related to debtors and creditors
(b) Real accounts are related to assets and liabilities
(c) Journal records the transactions in a chronological order
(d) Outstanding expenses is a representative personal account

17. **Payment for brokerage on purchase of a machine will be recorded as**
(a) debit machinery account and credit brokerage account
(b) debit cash account and credit brokerage account
(c) debit machinery account and credit cash account
(d) debit brokerage account and credit cash account

18. **Purchased goods price ₹ 50,000 plus CGST and SGST 6% each. Payment made immediately and received 2% cash discount. Calculate the amount which is paid.** Competency Based Que
(a) ₹ 56,000 (b) ₹ 55,880
(c) ₹ 54,880 (d) ₹ 54,000

19. **What will be the journal entry for interest earned but not received ₹ 5,000?** Competency Based Que

(a) Accrued Interest A/c	Dr	5,000	
To Interest A/c			5,000
(b) Interest A/c	Dr	5,000	
To Accrued Interest A/c			5,000
(c) Accrued Interest A/c	Dr	5,000	
To Cash A/c			5,000

(d) None of the above

20. **Cash of ₹ 2,000 was received from Ajay on behalf of Vijay. Choose the correct option.** Competency Based Que
(a) Cash A/c Dr ₹ 2,000, Vijay Cr ₹ 2,000
(b) Cash A/c Dr ₹ 2,000, Ajay Cr ₹ 2,000
(c) Ajay Dr ₹ 2,000, Cash A/c Cr ₹ 2,000
(d) Vijay Dr ₹ 2,000, Cash A/c Cr ₹ 2,000

21. **₹ 5,000 returned to accountant by the proprietor, which were withdrawn for personal use earlier, will be credited to**
(a) cash account (b) drawing account
(c) capital account (d) Either (b) or (c)

22. **Rohit purchased goods list price ₹ 10,000 less 10% trade discount and paid 90% amount of the bill. Cash discount was availed 5% on the payment. What will be the amount of credit purchase?** Competency Based Que
(a) ₹ 1,000 (b) ₹ 810
(c) ₹ 900 (d) ₹ 2,000

23. **"Paid security deposit for a telephone connection." Security deposit will be considered as**
(a) an expense (b) an asset
(c) a liability (d) capital

24. **What will be the journal entry recorded for the following transaction?** Competency Based Que

"Jyoti sold goods list price ₹ 50,000 less trade discount 10%. CGST and SGST charged @ 9% each."

(a)	Jyoti Dr	53,100	
	To Sales A/c		45,000
	To Output CGST A/c		4,050
	To Output SGST A/c		4,050
(b)	Cash A/c Dr	59,000	
	To Sales A/c		50,000
	To Output CGST A/c		4,500
	To Output SGST A/c		500
(c)	Cash A/c Dr	53,100	
	To Sales A/c		45,000
	To Output CGST A/c		4,050
	To Output SGST A/c		4,050

(d) None of the above

25. **Purchased goods costing ₹ 5,000 less 10% trade discount plus 20% profit. 3/4th amount paid only. Goods bought on credit for ....** Competency Based Que
(a) ₹ 1,250 (b) ₹ 4,050
(c) ₹ 1,350 (d) None of these

26. **In which book, all accounts are opened?**
(a) Journal (b) Ledger
(c) Cash book (d) Journal proper

27. **When credit side of an account is less than that of its debit side it is called**
(a) credit balance (b) debit balance
(c) income (d) expenses

28. **If an account shows debit balance, it may be .... depending upon the nature of the account.** Competency Based Que
(a) profits and incomes (b) expense or asset
(c) income or liability (d) None of the above

29. **Goods sold to Aditi will be posted to the .... side of her account.**
(a) credit (b) debit
(c) debit side of sales account
(d) None of the above

30. **Goods returned to Malhotra & Sons will be posted to the**
(a) credit of Malhotra & Sons
(b) credit of purchase return
(c) debit of sales return (d) None of the above

Assertion-Reason

Direction (Q. No. 31 to 40) *Read the following Assertion (A) and Reason (R) and choose the correct alternative from the following*

Alternatives
(a) Both Assertion (A) and Reason (R) are true and Reason (R) is the correct explanation of Assertion (A)
(b) Both Assertion (A) and Reason (R) are true, but Reason (R) is not the correct explanation of Assertion (A)
(c) Assertion (A) is true, but Reason (R) is false
(d) Assertion (A) is false, but Reason (R) is true

31. **Assertion** (A) 'Machine purchased for ₹ 5,000'. Machine account will be debited.
Reason (R) Machine account relates to real account hence rule will apply "Debit what comes in and credit what goes out."

32. **Assertion** (A) 'Salary paid in advance'. Advance salary account will be debited.
Reason (R) Expenses paid in advance is an asset hence debited.

33. **Assertion** (A) Received ₹ 2,000 from Ram for commission will be credited to Ram.
Reason (R) Commission received from Ram will be credited to commission account as it is an income.

34. **Assertion** (A) Trade discount is not recorded in the books of account.
Reason (R) Trade discount is provided by the seller on the purchase in bulk. It is allowed as deduction from the sale value and sale is recorded at new amount i.e. sale less trade discount.

35. **Assertion** (A) Both the credit and debit aspects are recorded in a journal entry.
Reason (R) Transactions are recorded according to the double entry system.

36. **Assertion** (A) Trade discount is not recorded in the books of account.
Reason (R) Trade discount is allowed when a buyer buy goods in bulk.

37. **Assertion** (A) When there is loss of goods by fire, purchase account is credited.
Reason (R) Purchase account is credited because as a result of loss of goods, net purchase is reduced.

38. **Assertion** (A) "Received cash ₹ 2,000 from Ruchika after allowing discount of ₹ 200." Discount received is credited in this transaction.
Reason (R) Discount received is an income hence it is credited.

39. **Assertion** (A) GST is called as value added tax.

Reason (R) Since Input GST is set-off against output GST, hence GST is levied on the incremental value only.

40. **Assertion** (A) Input IGST will be credited when there is loss by fire of goods purchased with IGST.

Reason (R) Input GST is allowed to be reversed i.e. credited when there is loss of goods by fire.

Two Statements Based MCQs

Direction (Q.No. 41 to 50) *Read the following statements carefully and choose the correct alternative*

Alternatives

(a) Both the statements are correct
(b) Both the statements are incorrect
(c) Statement I is correct and Statement II is incorrect
(d) Statement I is incorrect and Statement II is correct

41. **Statement I** Insurance claim paid by insurance company is debited to cash/bank account.

Statement II Bad debt recovered account is credited as it is an income.

42. **Statement I** Purchase return account is always debited.

Statement II Sale return account is always debited.

43. **Statement I** Sale of goods to Neelam will be credited to Neelam account.

Statement II Cash sales for the month will be debited to cash account.

44. **Statement I** "Cheque received on 5th February, 2024, deposited into bank on 8th February, 2024."
Journal entry will be

Bank A/c Dr
  To Party A/c

Statement II "Discount received from Priya."
Journal entry will be

Priya Dr
  To Discount Received A/c

45. **Statement I** Cash paid to Diya on behalf of Arjun will be debited to Arjun.

Statement II Received commission from Abhishek will be debited to Abhishek.

46. **Statement I** When sale or purchase is made within the state, CGST and SGST is levied.

Statement II Input GST is reversed in case of drawing of goods by owner for personal use.

47. **Statement I** Commission received from Kalki will be posted to the credit of Kalki.

Statement II Interest on capital provided is posted to the credit side of capital account.

48. **Statement I** Brokerage paid for purchase of a machine will be debited to brokerage account.

Statement II Installation expenses paid for a machine will be debited to machine account.

49. **Statement I** Real accounts relate to tangible and intangible assets.

Statement II Rule of real account is 'debit the receiver, credit the giver'.

50. **Statement I** Capital account is a representative personal account.

Statement II Drawing account is a representative personal account.

Matching

51. Match the following

Column I	Column II
A. Rent account	(i) Real account
B. Cash account	(ii) Nominal account
C. Outstanding rent account	(iii) Representative personal account

Codes

	A	B	C
(a)	(i)	(ii)	(iii)
(b)	(ii)	(i)	(iii)
(c)	(iii)	(i)	(ii)
(d)	(i)	(iii)	(ii)

52. Match the following

Column I	Column II
A. Cash received from Shyam	(i) Debited to cash account
B. Amount paid for rent	(ii) Credited to cash account
C. Discount allowed to Ram	(iii) Debited to discount allowed account
D. Purchased goods from Rohit	(iv) Credited to Rohit

Codes

	A	B	C	D
(a)	(i)	(ii)	(iii)	(iv)
(b)	(i)	(ii)	(iv)	(iii)
(c)	(ii)	(i)	(iii)	(iv)
(d)	(iv)	(iii)	(i)	(ii)

53. Match the following

Column I	Column II
A. Cash purchase	(i) Debit cash account, credit sales account
B. Credit purchase	(ii) Debit purchase account, credit creditor account
C. Cash sales	(iii) Debit purchase account, credit cash account
D. Goods returned by a customer	(iv) Debit customer account credit purchase return account

Codes

	A	B	C	D
(a)	(iii)	(ii)	(i)	(iv)
(b)	(iii)	(iv)	(i)	(ii)
(c)	(iv)	(iii)	(i)	(ii)
(d)	(iv)	(ii)	(iii)	(i)

54. Match the following

Column I	Column II
A. Compound entry	(i) Preparing financial statements
B. Opening entry	(ii) Debit or credit multiple accounts
C. Closing entry	(iii) Recording opening balances
D. Transfer entry	(iv) Movement between two ledger accounts

Codes

	A	B	C	D
(a)	(i)	(iii)	(ii)	(iv)
(b)	(ii)	(iii)	(i)	(iv)
(c)	(ii)	(iii)	(iv)	(i)
(d)	(i)	(iv)	(ii)	(iii)

55. Match the following

Column I	Column II
A. Purchased goods from same state	(i) Input IGST debit
B. Purchased goods from other state	(ii) Input CGST and Input SGST will be debited
C. Sales within same state	(iii) Output CGST and Output SGST will be credited
D. Return of goods purchased from same state with GST	(iv) Input CGST and SGST will be credited

Codes

	A	B	C	D
(a)	(ii)	(i)	(iii)	(iv)
(b)	(i)	(ii)	(iii)	(iv)
(c)	(iii)	(iv)	(ii)	(i)
(d)	(iv)	(iii)	(ii)	(i)

Case Based MCQs

Direction *Read the following case study and answer the questions 56 and 57 on the basis of the same*

Dev is the owner of a trading firm with a capital of ₹ 25,000. During the year 2021, he bought goods at the list price of ₹ 1,00,000 from Rani less 20% trade discount and 2% cash discount and paid 40% by cheque. He sold goods to Preeti at the list price of ₹ 2,00,000 less 20% trade discount and 2% cash discount and she paid 50% by cheque.

He also sold goods to Tanu for ₹ 40,000 allowing her a trade discount of 5% and cash discount of 10%. She paid 1/4th of the amount in cash at the time of purchase. He received cash from Jaya for a bad debt written-off last year amounting to ₹ 400.

56. How is a trade discount different from cash discount?

I. Trade discount is allowed when goods are purchased in a specified quantity whereas cash discount is allowed when payment is made on or before a specified date.

II. Trade discount is not recorded separately in the books of account whereas cash discount is separately recorded in the books of account.

Codes

(a) Only I (b) Only II
(c) Both I and II (d) Neither I nor II

57. What is the amount paid to Rani by cheque?

(a) ₹ 40,000 (b) ₹ 32,000
(c) ₹ 31,360 (d) None of these

Answers

1. (c) Both (a) and (b)
2. (c) Purchase account
3. (b) artificial personal account
4. (a) personal account
5. (b) purchase account
6. (d) debit to debtors and credit to fees income
7. (c) journalising
8. (c) debit monthly bill and credit cash
9. (b) Cash A/c Dr 2,000
   To Accrued Interest A/c 2,000
10. (b) GST will be levied on ₹ 9,500 calculated as
    10,000 – (10,000 × 5%) = ₹ 9,500

11. (c) Closing balance = 80,000 + 70,000 – 30,000
= ₹ 1,20,000

12. (d) Free gift to staff

13. (d) Either (a), (b) or (c)

14. (b) 9%

15. (b) Because outstanding rent is a liability

16. (a) Nominal accounts are related to debtors and creditors

17. (c) Debit machinery account and credit cash account

18. (c) Amount paid = 49,000 (50,000 – 50,000 × 2%)
+ GST i.e. 49,000 × 12%
= ₹ 54,880

19. (a)

Accrued Interest A/c	Dr	5,000	
To Interest A/c			5,000

20. (a) Cash A/c Dr ₹ 2,000, Vijay Cr ₹ 2,000

21. (d) Either (b) or (c)

22. (c) Credit purchase = 9,000 – (9,000 × 90%) = ₹ 900

23. (b) an asset

24. (a)

Jyoti	Dr	53,100	
To Sales A/c			45,000
To Output CGST A/c			4,050
To Output SGST A/c			4,050

25. (c) Purchase Value = 5,000 – (5,000 × 10%) + 20% Profit (4,500 × 20%)
= ₹ 5,400

Credit Purchase = 5,400 – 4,050 = ₹ 1,350

26. (b) Ledger

27. (b) debit balance

28. (b) expense or asset

29. (b) debit

30. (b) credit of purchase return

31. (a) Both Assertion (A) and Reason (R) are true and Reason (R) is the correct explanation of Assertion (A)

32. (a) Both Assertion (A) and Reason (R) are true and Reason (R) is the correct explanation of Assertion (A)

33. (d) Assertion (A) is false, but Reason (R) is true

34. (a) Both Assertion (A) and Reason (R) are true and Reason (R) is the correct explanation of Assertion (A)

35. (a) Both Assertion (A) and Reason (R) are true and Reason (R) is the correct explanation of Assertion (A)

36. (b) Both Assertion (A) and Reason (R) are true, but Reason (R) is not the correct explanation of Assertion (A)

37. (a) Both Assertion (A) and Reason (R) are true and Reason (R) is the correct explanation of Assertion (A)

38. (d) Assertion (A) is false, but Reason (R) is true

39. (b) Both Assertion (A) and Reason (R) are true, but Reason (R) is not the correct explanation of Assertion (A)

40. (a) Both Assertion (A) and Reason (R) are true and Reason (R) is the correct explanation of Assertion (A)

41. (a) Both the statements are correct

42. (d) Purchase return account is always credited.

43. (d) Sale of goods to Neelam will be credited to sales account rather than Neelam.

44. (d) Cheque received on 5th, February, 2024 deposited on 8th February, 2024 will be recorded as

Bank A/c	Dr
To Cheque in Hand A/c	

45. (c) Received commission from Abhishek will be debited to cash account rather than Abhishek.

46. (a) Both the statements are correct

47. (d) Commission received from Kalki will be posted to credit of 'commission received account'.

48. (d) Brokerage paid for purchase of a machine will be debited to machine account.

49. (c) Rule of real account is "debit what comes in, credit what goes out".

50. (a) Both the statements are correct

51. (b) (ii) (i) (iii)

52. (a) (i) (ii) (iii) (iv)

53. (a) (iii) (ii) (i) (iv)

54. (b) (ii) (iii) (i) (iv)

55. (a) (ii) (i) (iii) (iv)

56. (c) Both I and II

57. (c) Purchase Value = 1,00,000 – 20,000 = ₹ 80,000

40% Value = $80{,}000 \times \frac{40}{100}$ = ₹ 32,000

Cash Discount = $32{,}000 \times \frac{2}{100}$ = ₹ 640

Paid Amount = 32,000 – 640 = ₹ 31,360

05

CHAPTER

Special Purpose Books

Special purpose books/Subsidiary books are prepared when it becomes difficult for business to record each transaction in journal. Each subsidiary book e.g. Sales book, purchase return book, sales return book, etc. records transactions of similar nature.

YOUR STUDY GOALS

YOUR PRACTICE GOAL

- Topicwise Solved Questions (25 Solved Questions)
- Numerical Questions [35 Questions (Unsolved)]
- Theoretical Questions [17 Questions (with answers)]
- Objective Questions (65 Qs ; MCQs, A-R, Statements, Matching, Case)

5.1 Introduction

For a small business, it is easy to record all transactions in one book only i.e. the journal. But as the business expands, the number of transactions become large. Thus, it may become difficult to record each transaction in journal.

Hence, journal is required to be sub-divided into **special purpose books/subsidiary books/special journals.**

Each subsidiary book is meant for recording transactions of similar nature. e.g. All cash transactions are recorded in cash book, credit purchase is recorded in purchase book, etc.

Smart Study Chart No. 1

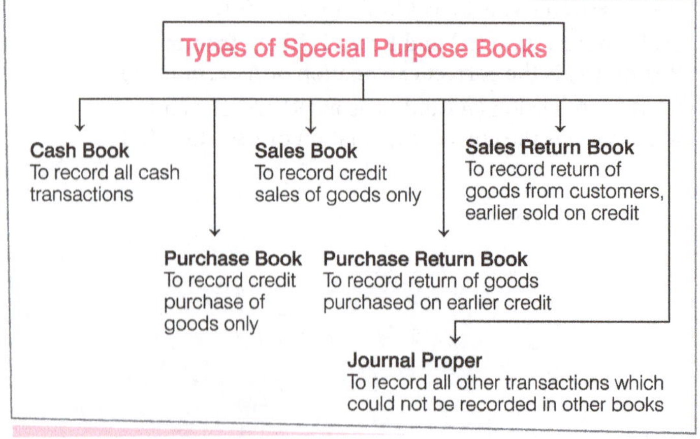

5.2 Cash Book

- Cash book is used for recording only cash transactions, i.e. all receipts and payments in cash.
- It is a book of **prime entry** since transactions are recorded in it for the first time from the source documents.
- It has two sides, i.e. debit and credit. Cash receipts are recorded on debit side and cash payments are recorded on credit side.
- In the cash book, balance of cash will always show a debit balance because cash payments can never exceed cash receipts and cash in hand at the beginning.

Similarities of Cash Book

With Journal	With Ledger
Just like journal, • transactions in cash book are recorded for the first time from source documents. • transactions in cash book are recorded datewise, i.e. in a chronological order. • transactions from cash book are posted to the relevant accounts (except cash account) in the ledger. • a cash book also contains a ledger folio column.	• Form of cash book closely resembles to a ledger account having two equally divided sides with identical column. • Cash book itself serves as a cash account also and as such when a cash book is maintained, cash account is not opened in the ledger. The cash book, hence is a part of ledger also. • Just like a ledger account, the words 'To' and 'By' are used in a cash book also. • It is balanced just like a ledger account.

Cash Book – Both a Subsidiary Book (Journal) and a Principal Book (Ledger)

Cash book serves both purposes i.e. of a subsidiary book and of a principal book.

- Cash transactions are first recorded in cash book and thereafter ledger posting is done from cash book. Thus, it is called a **subsidiary book** or book of original entry.
- Cash book itself serves the purpose of cash account. Therefore, the cash book is also a part of ledger. Hence, it is also a **principal book.**

Advantages of Cash Book

- It prevents the size of ledger from becoming too voluminous.
- Both cash and bank transactions can be entered in cash book.
- Businessman can know the balance of cash and bank at any point of time.
- It gives information about daily receipts, payments and closing balance at the end of each day.

Types of Cash Book

Cash book may be of three types

- Single column cash book
- Double column cash book
- Petty cash book

I. Single Column Cash Book or Simple Cash Book

This cash book records all cash transactions of the business in a chronological order. It has one column on each side. All cash receipts are recorded on the debit side and all cash payments on the credit side. Single column cash book is nothing but a cash account. Format of single column cash book is shown below

Dr **Single Column Cash Book** Cr

Date	Particulars	V.No.	LF	Amt (₹)	Date	Particulars	V.No.	LF	Amt (₹)
Records the date of transaction.	Records the name of the account under which cash has been *received.*	Records the serial number of the voucher certifying the *receipt.*	Records the page number of the ledger.	Records amount *received.*	Records the date of transaction.	Records the name of the account under which cash has been *paid.*	Records the serial number of the voucher certifying the *payment.*	Records the page number of the ledger.	Records amount *paid.*

Receipts (Debit side) **Payments** (Credit side)

Points to Consider

- Single column cash book does not record cash discount allowed or received and cheques received or given.
- Discount allowed, discount received and cancellation of discount received or discount allowed, in case of dishonour of cheque, will be recorded through journal proper.
- When an entry is recorded in cash book, a corresponding entry is recorded in the ledger.

Balancing of Single Column Cash Book

The cash book is balanced in the same way as an account is balanced in the ledger.

- The total of the receipts column (debit side) will always be greater than the total of the payments column (credit side).
- The difference will be written on the credit side as 'By Balance c/d'. This will make the total of the two sides equal and the total will be written in the two columns opposite one another.
- The closing balance becomes opening balance of cash in hand at the beginning of the next period and is written on the debit side as 'To Balance b/d'.

Smart Study Chart No. 2

Ledger Posting from Single Column Cash Book

Debit Side

The accounts appearing on the debit side of the cash book are credited to their respective ledger accounts by writing 'By Cash' in the particulars column because cash has been received in respect of them.

Credit Side

The accounts appearing on the credit side of the cash book are debited to the ledger accounts by entering 'To Cash' in the particulars column as cash/cheque has been paid in respect of them.

II. Double Column or Two Column Cash Book (Cash Book with Cash and Bank Column)

It is a cash book which has two columns of amount on each side; one for cash and one for bank transactions. As cash and bank account are both asset account (as per modern classification), therefore cash and bank transactions are recorded, following the **rule** "debit the increase in asset and credit the decrease in asset". All the cash receipts/deposits into the bank are recorded on debit side and all cash payments/withdrawals from bank are recorded on credit side.

Format of double column cash book is shown below

Dr **Double Column Cash Book** Cr

Date	Particulars	LF	Cash (₹)	Bank (₹)	Date	Particulars	LF	Cash (₹)	Bank (₹)
	↓ Receipts					↓ Payments			

Some Important Points and Transactions related to Double Column Cash Book

1. **Bank Account**
   It is a personal account and rule applicable to personal account is followed while recording transactions in the bank column of cash book. Thus, cash deposited is debited while cash withdrawn from bank is credited, in the bank column of cash book.
2. **Opening Balance**
   Opening balance of bank column of cash book may be debit or credit. If it is debit balance, it will be written as 'To Balance b/d' on the debit side. If credit balance (or overdraft balance) is given, it will be written as 'By Balance b/d'. Cash column of cash book always show a debit balance, thus it will be written as 'To Balance b/d'.
3. **Payment made by Cheque**
   When a payment is made by cheque, it is recorded on the credit side in the bank column, thus true bank balance can be ascertained.

4. **Bank Charges**

These are amount charged from customer for the services provided by bank. They are recorded on credit side as 'By Bank Charges' and amount is recorded in bank column.

Point to Remember
Bank charges on dishonoured cheques are added into the amount of dishonoured cheque itself.

5. **Cash Discount Allowed or Received is Recorded by Means of a Journal Entry**

- Cash discount may be received/allowed when payment is made/received by cheque/ cash.

For Discount Allowed

Discount Allowed A/c	Dr
To Debtors A/c	

For Discount Received

Creditors A/c	Dr
To Discount Received A/c	

- In case cheque is dishonoured, discount received /allowed is also written back by passing a entry in journal proper.

For Reversal of Discount Allowed

Debtors A/c	Dr
To Discount Allowed A/c	

For Reversal of Discount Received

Discount Received A/c	Dr
To Creditors A/c	

6. **Contra Entries**

In a double column cash book, there are some transactions that relate to both cash and bank. Such transactions are entered on both sides of the cash book and known as contra entries. These entries are not posted into the ledger.

Against such entries, letter 'C' is written in the LF column to indicate that these are contra transactions. Contra entries are required to be passed in following cases

- **Cash Deposited into Bank**

Bank A/c	Dr
To Cash A/c	

- **Cash Withdrawn from Bank for Office Use**

Cash A/c	Dr
To Bank A/c	

Key Point
Amount withdrawn for personal use from bank is not a contra transaction, it will only affect the bank column of cash book. It will be recorded on credit side as 'By Drawings A/c' and amount will be written in bank column.

7. **Cheques Received Deposited into Bank on Same Date**

It is recorded in the debit side of cash book in the bank column. In this case, following entry is passed

Bank A/c	Dr
To Debtors	

8. **Cheques Received and Deposited on Different Dates**

In this case, following entries are passed

- **When Cheque is Received**

Cheques in Hand A/c	Dr
To Debtors	

- **When Cheque received is Deposited**

Bank A/c	Dr
To Cheques in Hand A/c	

Note This entry will not be recorded in cash book

It is recorded on the debit side of cash book in the bank column.

In this manner, the balance in cheques in hand account will become nil.

9. **Cheque Received, Endorsed in Favour of a Creditor**
In case a business firm endorses the cheque received from a debtor in favour of a creditor, then the following entries are passed

- **When Cheque is Received**

Cheques in Hand A/c	Dr
To Debtor	

- **When Cheque is Endorsed**

Creditor	Dr
To Cheques in Hand A/c	

These entries will not be recorded in cash book.

10. **Cheque Deposited into Bank Dishonoured**
There can be two possible conditions

- When cheque was deposited in bank on the day on which it was received.
In this case the following entry is passed

Debtor	Dr
To Bank A/c	

It is recorded on the credit side of cash book in the bank column.

- When cheque was not deposited in bank on the day on which it was received, following entries are passed

Cheques in Hand A/c	Dr
To Bank A/c	
Debtor	Dr
To Cheques in Hand A/c	

It is recorded on the credit side of cash book in the bank column.

11. **Amount Deposited into Our Bank Account by a Customer Directly**
Sometimes, customers deposit the amount directly into our bank account. When we receive information about such deposit, it is recorded in cash book on the debit side of bank column. In this case, following entry is passed

Bank A/c	Dr
To Customer/Debtor	

Balancing of Double Column Cash Book

- Cash columns are balanced in the same way as in case of single column cash book.
- The process of balancing the bank column is also the same. However, it is possible that the bank column may either have a debit balance or credit balance.
- Debit balance indicates bank balance shown as asset in balance sheet.
- Credit balance indicates negative balance considered as a liability which is known as bank overdraft.

Smart Study Chart No. 3

Ledger Posting of Double Column Cash Book

Debit Side

Transactions written in cash and bank column on debit side are credited to their respective ledger account by writing 'By Cash' (for cash transactions) and 'By Bank' (for bank transactions) in particulars column. Discount allowed is individually posted to credit of debtor's account and to debit of discount allowed account.

Credit Side

Transactions written in cash and bank column on credit side are debited to their respective ledger accounts by writing 'To Cash' (for cash transactions) and 'To Bank' (for bank transactions) in particulars column. Discount received is individually posted to debit of creditor's account and to credit of discount received account.

III. Petty Cash Book

It is the book which is used for the purpose of recording the payment of petty cash expenses. For transferring cash to petty cash account, cash account is credited and petty cash account is debited.

Advantages of Petty Cash Book

- Maintaining petty cash book is simple and does not require any specialised knowledge of accounting.
- Petty cash book is maintained by the petty cashier, therefore efforts and time of the chief/head cashier is saved.

- The chances of fraud minimises, as each petty expense is supported by a voucher.
- Petty expenses are maintained within the limit of imprest amount so the petty cashier can never spend more than the available petty cash with him.
- Head cashier can keep a close watch time to time on the amount paid to petty cashier and all payments made by him.

Impress System of Petty Cash Book

Under this system, the petty cashier is given a fixed sum of money at the beginning of a certain period. This amount is called **imprest amount.** The petty cashier makes all small payments out of this imprest amount which is reimbursed to him from the head cashier. Thus, he again has the full imprest amount in the beginning of the next period.

Advantages of Imprest System of Petty Cash

- Control over mistakes can be easily maintained, as the petty cash book is regularly examined by the chief cashier.
- As petty cashier can never spend more than available petty cash, petty expenses are kept within the limit of imprest.
- As the petty cashier is not allowed to draw cash as and when he desires, misappropriation and frauds are kept within the limits of imprest.

Format of Petty Cash Book

This cash book has one amount column on its debit side and a number of columns on its credit side relating to most common petty expenses. Each payment is recorded on it twice, one on total amount column and next on individual expense column.

The total amount column is balanced and individual expense columns are totalled. The total of different columns for payments equals the totals in the 'total payment column'.

Dr **Analytical Petty Cash Book** Cr

Receipts		**Payments**								
Receipt (₹)	**Date**	**Voucher No.**	**Particulars**	**Total Payment (₹)**	**Postage/ Telegram (₹)**	**Conveyance/ Travelling (₹)**	**Staff Welfare/ Entertainment (₹)**	**Cartage (₹)**	**Printing and Stationery (₹)**	**Misce-llaneous Items (₹)**

Posting the Petty Cash Book

- Entries in petty cash book are posted into the ledger accounts at the end of specified period i.e. monthly or quarterly or as the case may be.
- Petty cash book is not posted directly in the ledger, instead a petty cash account is opened in the ledger.
- When petty cash is advanced to the petty cashier the following journal entry is passed

Petty Cash A/c	Dr
To Cash A/c	

It is recorded by chief cashier on credit side of petty cash book as 'By Petty Cash A/c'.

- At the end of specified period, the following journal entry is first prepared on the basis of the petty cash book, debiting each expense account individually and crediting the petty cash account with the total expenditure.

Expenses A/c	Dr
To Petty Cash A/c	

Thus, in the ledger, there is a petty cash account as well as separate ledger account for each expense.

Thereafter, posting is made to the debit of each expense account by writing 'To Petty Cash A/c.'

5.3 Other Special Purpose Books

In addition to cash transactions, there are a number of non-cash transactions. These non-cash transactions can be recorded in separate books popularly known as 'other special purpose books' such as purchases book, purchases return book, sales book, sales return book and journal proper.

Purchases (Journal) Book

This book records all credit purchases of goods (i.e. goods in which the enterprise deals in). This book is prepared on the basis of invoices or bills received by the firm from the suppliers of the goods with the amount net of trade discount/quantity discount. It is also known as **invoice book/bought book/purchase day book/purchase journal/ supplier's journal**. Format of a purchases book is shown below

Purchases Book

Date	Particulars (A/c to be credited)	Invoice No.	LF	Details (₹)	Purchase (₹)	Input CGST (₹)	Input SGST (₹)	Input IGST (₹)	Total Amt (₹)
Transaction date is written.	Name of supplier, articles and quantities purchased are written.	Invoice number of goods purchased is written.	Page number of ledger is written while posting to ledger.	Amount of each article is written alongwith trade discount, shown as deduction.	Net amount of purchase (i.e. purchase less trade discount) is written.	Tax paid on purchase within the same State (intra-state) is written. Total of this column is posted to debit of input CGST account, in ledger.	Tax paid on purchase within the same State (intra-state) is written. Total of this column is posted to debit of input SGST account, in ledger.	Tax paid on purchase from outside the State (inter-state) is written.	Total of each transaction is recorded. The total in this column will show 'total credit purchases' made in a period.

Ledger Posting from Purchases Book

- Individual amounts are daily posted to the credit of supplier's accounts by writing 'By Purchases A/c' in the particulars column.
- Periodic total is posted to the debit of purchases account by writing 'To Sundries as per Purchases Book' in the particulars column.

Key Point

Freight/Carriage/Packing and Forwarding Charges These charges are incurred on purchase of goods. With the introduction of GST, it is not appropriate to provide a separate column for freight in the purchase book, as GST is levied on purchase of goods at a different rate, whereas as per GST Act, GST on freight is charged at a fixed rate of 18%.

Sales (Journal) Book

This book records all credit sales of merchandise (i.e. the goods in which the firm deals in). The source documents for recording entries in the sales journal are sales invoice or bill issued by the firm to the customers with the amount net of trade discount/ quantity discount. It is also known as **sales day book/sales journal/customer journal.**

Format of a sales book is shown below

Sales Book

Date	Particulars (A/c to be debited)	Invoice No.	LF	Details (₹)	Sale (₹)	Output CGST (₹)	Output SGST (₹)	Output IGST (₹)	Total Amt (₹)
Transaction date is written.	Name of customer, articles and quantities sold are written.	Invoice number of goods sold is written.	Page number of ledger is written while posting to ledger.	Individual items sold are written alongwith trade discount, shown as deduction.	Net amount of sale (i.e. sale less trade discount) is written.	Tax collected by seller on sale within the same State (i.e. intra-state) is recorded. Total of this column is posted to credit of output CGST account in ledger.	Tax collected by seller on sale within the same State (i.e. intra-state) is recorded. Total of this column is posted to credit of output SGST account in ledger.	Tax collected by seller on sale outside the State (i.e. inter-state) is recorded.	Total of each transaction is recorded. The total in this column will show 'total credit sales' made in a period.

Ledger Posting from Sales Book

- Individual amounts are daily posted to the debit of customer's accounts by writing 'To Sales A/c' in the particulars column.
- Periodic total is posted to the credit of sales account by writing 'By Sundries as per Sales Book' in the particulars column.

Purchases Return (Journal) Book

In this book, purchase return of goods is recorded. It does not record the returns of goods purchased on cash basis nor the returns of purchases other than the goods in which the firm deals in.

The entries are usually made in purchases return book on the basis of **debit notes** issued to suppliers and credit notes received from suppliers. It is also known as **return outwards book.**

Format of a purchases return book is shown below

Purchases Return Book

Date	Particulars (Account to be debited)	Debit Note No.	LF	Details (₹)	Purchase Return (₹)	Input CGST (₹)	Input SGST (₹)	Input IGST (₹)	Total Amt (₹)

Note The format of a purchases return book is similar to the purchases book except that instead of a column for 'Invoice No.' it has a column for 'Debit Note No.'.

Ledger Posting from Purchases Return Book

- Individual amounts are debited to the supplier's account by writing 'To Purchases Return A/c' in the particulars column.
- Periodic total is credited to the purchases return account by writing 'By Sundries as per Purchases Returns Book' in the particulars column.

Sales Return (Journal) Book

This subsidiary book is used to record return of goods by customers that had been sold on credit. It does not record the return of goods sold on cash basis nor the return of any asset other than the goods in which the firm deals in.

The source documents for recording entries in sales return journal are the **credit notes** issued to customers or debit notes issued by customers. It is also known as **return inwards book.**

Format of a sales return book is shown below

Sales Return Book

Date	Particulars (Account to be credited)	Credit Note No.	LF	Details (₹)	Sales Return (₹)	Output CGST (₹)	Output SGST (₹)	Output IGST (₹)	Total Amt (₹)

Note The format of a sales return book is similar to the sales book except that instead of a column for 'Invoice No.' it has a column for 'Credit Note No.'.

Ledger Posting from Sales Return Book

- Individual amounts are credited to the customer's accounts by writing 'By Sales Returns A/c' in the particulars column.
- Periodic total is debited to the sales return account by writing 'To Sundries as per Sales Return Book' in the particular column.

Journal Proper or General Journal

In journal proper book, only those transactions are recorded which cannot be recorded in any other subsidiary book.

For example, if furniture is purchased on credit, it can neither be recorded in the purchase book nor in cash book because cash book records only the cash transactions and purchase book records only credit purchase of goods, but not the purchase of an asset. Hence, purchase of furniture on credit being purchase of an asset, which will be recorded in journal proper.

The following types of transactions are recorded in journal proper

Types of Entries	Explanation
Opening Entry	This entry is passed to bring the balances of accounts appearing in the balance sheet of previous accounting period to the current accounting period.
Closing Entries	At the end of accounting period, nominal accounts are closed by transferring their balances to trading and profit and loss account for ascertaining net profit or net loss. These entries are called closing entries.
Transfer Entries	These entries are passed for transferring the balance of one account to another account. e.g. The balance of drawings account to capital account.
Adjustment Entries	Certain items are adjusted at the time of preparation of final accounts, such as closing stock, outstanding expenses, prepaid expenses, etc. Entries for these adjustments are called adjustment entries.
Rectifying Entries	These entries are passed for rectification of errors occurred at the time of journalising, posting, totalling, balancing, etc.
Miscellaneous Entries	In addition, following entries are passed in the journal proper • Purchase of an asset on credit. • Sale of an asset on credit. • Loss of goods by fire, accident, etc. • Writing-off bad debts, etc. • Depreciation charged on asset. • Goods withdrawn for personal use. • Discount allowed and discount received.

Mind Map

SPECIAL PURPOSE BOOKS

1 Meaning of Special Purpose Book

- As the business expands, the number of transactions become large Thus, it may become difficult to record each transaction in journal
- Hence, journal is required to be sub-divided into special purpose books/subsidiary books/special journals
- Each subsidiary book is meant for recording transactions of similiar nature. e.g. All cash transactions are recorded in cash book, credit purchase is recorded in purchase book, etc

2 Cash Book

- Cash book is used for recording only cash transactions, i.e. all receipts and payments in cash
- It is a book of prime entry since transactions are recorded in it for the first time from the source documents
- In the cash book, balance of cash will always show a debit balance because cash payments can never exceed cash receipts and cash in hand at the beginning

Both a Subsidiary Book and a Principal Book

- Cash transactions are first recorded in cash book and thereafter ledger posting is done from cash book. So, it is called a subsidiary book or book of original entry
- Cash book itself serves the purpose of cash account
- Thus, cash book is also a part of ledger. Hence, it is also a principal book

Types of Cash Book

- **Single Column Cash Book** It has only one column on each side, i.e. cash column on debit and credit side.
- **Double Column Cash Book** It has two columns on each side, one for cash and one for bank.
- **Petty Cash Book** It is prepared for the purpose of recording the payment of petty cash expenses of small amounts.

  The **advantages** of petty cash book are
  - It does not require any specialised knowledge of accounting
  - It is maintained by the petty cashier, therefore time of the chief cashier is saved
  - The chances of fraud minimises, as such petty expense is supported by a voucher
  - Head cashier can keep a close watch time to time on the amount paid to petty cashier and all payments made by him

  Imprest System of Petty Cash Book
  - Under this system, the petty cashier is given a fixed sum of money at the beginning of a certain period. This amount is called impres amount
  - The petty cashier makes all small payments out of this imprest amount
- The amount spent in a particular period is reimbursed from the head cashier

3 Purchases Book

- This book records all credit purchases of goods
- Cash purchase, purchase of assets and purchase of stationey for office use are not recorded in this book
- It is also known as invoice book/bought book/purchase day book/purchase journal/supplier's journal

4 Sales Book

- This book records all credit sales of goods
- It does not record cash sales of goods and sale of fixed assets
- It is also known as sales day book/sales journal/customer journal

5 Purchases Return Book

- In this book, purchase return of goods is recorded
- It does not record the return of goods purchased on cash basis nor the return of purchases other than the goods in which the firm deals
- The entries are made on the basis of debit notes issued to the suppliers and credit notes received from the suppliers

6 Sales Return Book

- In this book, return of goods by the customers that had been sold on credit, is recorded
- It does not record the return of goods sold on cash basis nor the return of any asset other than the goods in which the firm deals
- The entries are made in this book on the basis of credit notes issued to the customers or debit notes issued by the customers

7 Journal Proper

- In this book, only those transactions are recorded which cannot be recorded in any other subsidiary book
- Opening entry, closing entries, transfer entries, adjustment entries, rectifying entries and other miscellaneous entries are recorded in this book

Topicwise Solved Questions

Preparation of Cash Book

Solved Question 1 **Prepare single column cash book for the month of April, 2024 of Vishal, a trader, from the following particulars and also post them into ledger.**

Date	Particulars	Amt (₹)
2024		
Apr 1	Cash in hand	65,000
Apr 2	Cash sales	6,80,000
Apr 3	Deposited cash into bank	5,50,000
Apr 3	Paid cheque to creditors of ₹ 1,49,700 after deducting cash discount of ₹ 9,300	
Apr 4	Wages paid in cash	55,500
Apr 4	Cash sales of ₹ 5,40,000 of which ₹ 4,50,000 were banked on 7th April	
Apr 9	Paid cash to transport corporation of India ₹ 13,500 against their bill number 265	
Apr 15	Cash sales ₹ 4,50,000 of which ₹ 3,60,000 were banked on 16th April	
Apr 17	Paid to cleaner in cash	5,600
Apr 19	Cash sales	4,52,000
Apr 20	Deposited cash into bank	3,25,000
Apr 20	Paid cash for window cleaning	5,400
Apr 21	Purchased goods on credit	45,000
Apr 25	Paid cash for rent	1,08,000
Apr 26	Cash sales	5,76,000
Apr 28	Paid cash to Dharma, a creditor after deducting discount ₹ 1,500	28,500
Apr 29	Paid electricity bill in cash	27,000
Apr 30	Cash collected from Karun (debtor) ₹ 1,35,000 after allowing discount of ₹ 7,500	

Sol. Dr **Cash Book** (Single Column) Cr

Date	Particulars	LF	Amt (₹)	Date	Particulars	LF	Amt (₹)
2024				2024			
Apr 1	To Balance b/d		65,000	Apr 3	By Bank A/c		5,50,000
Apr 2	To Sales A/c		6,80,000	Apr 4	By Wages A/c		55,500
Apr 4	To Sales A/c		5,40,000	Apr 7	By Bank A/c		4,50,000
Apr 15	To Sales A/c		4,50,000	Apr 9	By Transport Corporation of India		13,500
Apr 19	To Sales A/c		4,52,000	Apr 16	By Bank A/c		3,60,000
Apr 26	To Sales A/c		5,76,000	Apr 17	By Office Expenses A/c		5,600
Apr 30	To Karun		1,35,000	Apr 20	By Bank A/c		3,25,000
				Apr 20	By Office Expenses A/c		5,400
				Apr 25	By Rent A/c		1,08,000
				Apr 28	By Dharma		28,500
				Apr 29	By Electricity Expenses A/c		27,000
				Apr 30	By Balance c/d		9,69,500
			28,98,000				28,98,000
May 1	To Balance b/d		9,69,500				

Ledger Posting of Single Column Cash Book

Dr **Wages Account** Cr

Date	Particulars	JF	Amt (₹)	Date	Particulars	JF	Amt (₹)
2024							
Apr 4	To Cash A/c		55,500				

Dr **Sales Account** Cr

Date	Particulars	JF	Amt (₹)	Date	Particulars	JF	Amt (₹)
				2024			
				Apr 2	By Cash A/c		6,80,000
				Apr 4	By Cash A/c		5,40,000
				Apr 15	By Cash A/c		4,50,000
				Apr 19	By Cash A/c		4,52,000
				Apr 26	By Cash A/c		5,76,000

Dr **Transport Corporation Account** Cr

Date	Particulars	JF	Amt (₹)	Date	Particulars	JF	Amt (₹)
2024							
Apr 9	To Cash A/c		13,500				

Dr **Office Expenses Account** Cr

Date	Particulars	JF	Amt (₹)	Date	Particulars	JF	Amt (₹)
2024							
Apr 17	To Cash A/c		5,600				
Apr 20	To Cash A/c		5,400				

Dr **Rent Account** Cr

Date	Particulars	JF	Amt (₹)	Date	Particulars	JF	Amt (₹)
2024							
Apr 25	To Cash A/c		1,08,000				

Dr **Dharma** Cr

Date	Particulars	JF	Amt (₹)	Date	Particulars	JF	Amt (₹)
2024							
Apr 28	To Cash A/c		28,500				

Dr **Electricity Expenses Account** Cr

Date	Particulars	JF	Amt (₹)	Date	Particulars	JF	Amt (₹)
2024							
Apr 29	To Cash A/c		27,000				

Dr **Karun** Cr

Date	Particulars	JF	Amt (₹)	Date	Particulars	JF	Amt (₹)
				2024			
				Apr 30	By Cash A/c		1,35,000

Working Notes

1. Credit purchases are not recorded in the cash book since the cash book is maintained to record only cash transactions.
2. Cheque issued to creditors ₹1,49,700 on 3rd April, is not recorded in single column cash book.
3. Cheque deposited into bank is not a cash transaction.

4. Discount allowed to Karun ₹ 7,500 and discount received from Dharma ₹ 1,500 shall be recorded through journal entry as

Date	Particulars		LF	Amt (Dr)	Amt (Dr)
(i)	Dharma	Dr		1,500	
	To Discount Received A/c				1,500
	(Being the cash discount received from Dharma)				
(ii)	Discount Allowed A/c	Dr		7,500	
	To Karun				7,500
	(Being the discount allowed to Karun)				

Solved Question 2 *(With GST)* **Enter the following transactions in a single column cash book and post them into the ledger.**

2024

Apr 1 Cash in hand ₹ 1,00,000

Apr 5 Cash purchases of ₹ 20,000 plus CGST and SGST @ 9% each

Apr 8 Cash sales of ₹ 16,000 plus CGST and SGST @ 9% each

Apr 15 Purchased furniture for ₹ 10,000 plus CGST and SGST @ 9% each

Apr 25 Received commission ₹ 2,000 plus CGST and SGST @ 9% each

Apr 30 Paid rent ₹ 12,000 plus CGST and SGST @ 9% each

Sol.

Dr **Cash Book** Cr

Date	Particulars	V. No.	LF	Amt (₹)	Date	Particulars	V.No.	LF	Amt (₹)
2024					2024				
Apr 1	To Balance b/d			1,00,000	Apr 5	By Purchases A/c			20,000
Apr 8	To Sales A/c			16,000	Apr 5	By Input CGST A/c			1,800
Apr 8	To Output CGST A/c			1,440	Apr 5	By Input SGST A/c			1,800
Apr 8	To Output SGST A/c			1,440	Apr 15	By Furniture A/c			10,000
Apr 25	To Commission Received A/c			2,000	Apr 15	By Input CGST A/c			900
Apr 25	To Output CGST A/c			180	Apr 15	By Input SGST A/c			900
Apr 25	To Output SGST A/c			180	Apr 30	By Rent A/c			12,000
					Apr 30	By Input CGST A/c			1,080
					Apr 30	By Input SGST A/c			1,080
					Apr 30	By Balance c/d			71,680
				1,21,240					1,21,240

Dr **Purchases Account** Cr

Date	Particulars	JF	Amt (₹)	Date	Particulars	JF	Amt (₹)
2024							
Apr 5	To Cash A/c		20,000				

Dr **Sales Account** Cr

Date	Particulars	JF	Amt (₹)	Date	Particulars	JF	Amt (₹)
				2024			
				Apr 8	By Cash A/c		16,000

Dr **Furniture Account** Cr

Date	Particulars	JF	Amt (₹)	Date	Particulars	JF	Amt (₹)
2024							
Apr 15	To Cash A/c		10,000				

Dr **Commission Received Account** Cr

Date	Particulars	JF	Amt (₹)	Date	Particulars	JF	Amt (₹)
				2024			
				Apr 25	By Cash A/c		2,000

Dr **Rent Account** Cr

Date	Particulars	JF	Amt (₹)	Date	Particulars	JF	Amt (₹)
2024							
Apr 30	To Cash A/c		12,000				

Dr **Input CGST Account** Cr

Date	Particulars	JF	Amt (₹)	Date	Particulars	JF	Amt (₹)
2024							
Apr 5	To Cash A/c (Purchase)		1,800				
Apr 15	To Cash A/c (Furniture)		900				
Apr 30	To Cash A/c (Rent)		1,080				
			3,780				

Dr **Input SGST Account** Cr

Date	Particulars	JF	Amt (₹)	Date	Particulars	JF	Amt (₹)
2024							
Apr 5	To Cash A/c (Purchase)		1,800				
Apr 15	To Cash A/c (Furniture)		900				
Apr 30	To Cash A/c (Rent)		1,080				
			2,780				

Dr **Output CGST Account** Cr

Date	Particulars	JF	Amt (₹)	Date	Particulars	JF	Amt (₹)
				2024			
				Apr 8	By Cash A/c (Sales)		1,440
				Apr 25	By Cash A/c (Commission Received)		180
							1,620

Dr **Output SGST Account** Cr

Date	Particulars	JF	Amt (₹)	Date	Particulars	JF	Amt (₹)
				2024			
				Apr 8	By Cash A/c (Sales)		1,440
				Apr 25	By Cash A/c (Commission)		180
							1,620

Solved Question 3 **Prepare single column cash book of Mr. Raman.**

2024

Jan 1 Cash balance ₹ 8,500
Jan 3 Sold goods for ₹ 3,000 to Ram for cash less 2% cash discount
Jan 5 Bought goods ₹ 3,000
Jan 7 Received cash from Sunil ₹ 6,000, discount allowed ₹ 300
Jan 10 Paid to Ram Store ₹ 4,300 and discount received ₹ 200
Jan 12 Bought goods from Mohan for ₹ 6,000 for cash less 2% cash discount
Jan 15 Bought furniture on credit ₹ 2,500
Jan 18 Paid wages ₹ 2,000 and rent ₹ 1,000
Jan 21 Received cash from Gopal after deducting 2% cash discount ₹ 4,900
Jan 25 Received interest ₹ 200 and commission ₹ 300

Sol. Dr **Cash Book** Cr

Date	Particulars	V.No.	LF	Amt (₹)	Date	Particulars	V.No.	LF	Amt (₹)
2024					2022				
Jan 1	To Balance b/d			8,500	Jan 5	By Purchases A/c			3,000
Jan 3	To Sales A/c			2,940	Jan 10	By Ram Store			4,300
Jan 7	To Sunil			6,000	Jan 12	By Purchases A/c			5,880
Jan 21	To Gopal			4,900	Jan 18	By Wages A/c			2,000
Jan 25	To Interest			200	Jan 18	By Rent A/c			1,000
Jan 25	To Commission			300	Jan 31	By Balance c/d			6,660
				22,840					22,840
Feb 1	To Balance b/d			6,660					

Working Notes

1. Entries for discount received and discount allowed will be recorded in journal proper.
2. Jan 5 Bought goods for ₹ 4,000 : It will be treated as cash transaction because the name of the party is not given.
3. Jan 15 Bought furniture on credit will not be recorded in cash book. It will be recorded in journal.

Solved Question 4 **Prepare a single column cash book for the month of August, 2024 for Tanya & Bros.**

2024	
Aug 1	**Cash in hand ₹ 80,000.**
Aug 2	**Deposited in bank ₹ 60,000.**
Aug 4	**Purchased goods from Aditya ₹ 25,000.**
Aug 6	**Sold goods to Shubham for cash ₹ 40,000.**
Aug 8	**Payment made ₹ 24,500 to Aditya in full settlement by cheque.**
Aug 12	**Additional capital introduced in cash ₹ 70,000.**
Aug 20	**Purchased a computer for office ₹ 30,000. 60% amount was paid by cash only, balance by cheque.**
Aug 22	**Loan taken in cash from Tanmay ₹ 20,000.**
Aug 24	**Commission received in cash ₹ 2,000.**
Aug 28	**Withdrawn from bank ₹ 5,000.**

Sol. Dr **Single Column Cash Book** Cr

Date	Particulars	V. No.	LF	Amt (₹)	Date	Particulars	V. No.	LF	Amt (₹)
2024					2024				
Aug 1	To Balance b/d			80,000	Aug 2	By Bank A/c			60,000
Aug 6	To Sales A/c			40,000	Aug 20	By Computer A/c			18,000
Aug 12	To Capital A/c			70,000	Aug 31	By Balance c/d			1,39,000
Aug 22	To Loan from Tanmay A/c			20,000					
Aug 24	To Commission Received A/c			2,000					
Aug 28	To Bank A/c			5,000					
				2,17,000					2,17,000
Sept 1	To Balance b/d			1,39,000					

Solved Question 5 **Enter the following transactions in the cash book with cash and bank column.**

Date	Particulars	Amt (₹)
2024		
Jul 1	Cash in hand	22,000
Jul 1	Bank overdraft	8,000
Jul 3	Introduced additional capital in cash by proprietor	8,000
Jul 4	Deposited cash into bank account	40,000
Jul 6	Purchased a furniture for office, paid by cheque	10,000
Jul 8	Purchased goods on credit from Ramya	24,500
Jul 9	Sold goods, payment received by cheque	18,500
Jul 12	Returned goods to Ramya	4,500
Jul 13	A debtor (Mohit) became insolvent, received ₹ 2,000 against dues of ₹ 4,500 from his estate only	
Jul 15	Withdrew for office use from bank	8,000
Jul 17	Paid for stationary ₹ 500, postage ₹ 800	
Jul 20	Received cash from salesman	10,000
Jul 23	Received a cheque for commission earned after banking hours	2,000
Jul 24	Cheque received on 23rd July endorsed to a creditor Rohan	
Jul 28	Bank charges for its services	400

Sol. Dr **Double Column Cash Book** Cr

Date	Particulars	LF	Cash (₹)	Bank (₹)	Date	Particulars	LF	Cash (₹)	Bank (₹)
2024					2024				
Jul 1	To Balance b/d		22,000	—	Jul 1	By Balance b/d		—	8,000
Jul 3	To Capital A/c		8,000	—	Jul 4	By Bank A/c	C	40,000	—
Jul 4	To Cash A/c	C	—	40,000	Jul 6	By Furniture A/c		—	10,000
Jul 9	To Sales A/c		—	18,500	Jul 15	By Cash A/c	C	—	8,000
Jul 13	To Mohit		2,000	—	Jul 17	By Stationery A/c		500	—
Jul 15	To Bank A/c	C	8,000	—	Jul 28	By Postage A/c		800	—
Jul 20	To Sales A/c		10,000	—	Jul 31	By Bank Charges A/c		—	400
						By Balance c/d		8,700	32,100
			50,000	58,500				50,000	58,500
Aug 1	To Balance b/d		8,700	32,100					

Solved Question 6 **Enter the following transactions in the cash book with cash and bank columns**

2024

Apr 1 Balance of cash in hand ₹ 10,000, overdraft at bank ₹ 35,000.
Apr 4 Invested further capital ₹ 50,000 out of which ₹ 20,000 deposited into the bank.
Apr 5 Sold goods for cash ₹ 15,000 plus CGST and SGST @ 9% each.
Apr 10 Purchased goods ₹ 25,000 plus CGST and SGST @ 9% each and issued a cheque for the same.
Apr 11 Paid to Zen, a creditor ₹ 12,500; discount allowed by him ₹ 500.
Apr 14 Rent of ₹ 5,000 plus CGST and SGST @ 9% each paid by cheque.
Apr 15 Office furniture purchased and a cheque of ₹ 17,700 issued for the same including CGST and SGST @ 9% each.
Apr 16 Drew cheque for personal use ₹ 2,500.
Apr 18 Collection from Ram ₹ 15,000, deposited in the bank on 19th April.
Apr 20 Goods sold to Kia for ₹ 40,000 plus CGST and SGST @ 9% each.
Apr 25 Received a cheque of ₹ 46,000 from Kia in full settlement of his account; deposited into bank on 28th April.
Apr 29 Drew from the bank for salary of the office staff ₹ 12,500.
Apr 29 Paid salary to the manager by cheque ₹ 5,000.

Sol. Dr **Double Column Cash Book** Cr

Date	Particulars	LF	Cash (₹)	Bank (₹)	Date	Particulars	LF	Cash (₹)	Bank (₹)
2024					2024				
Apr 1	To Balance b/d		10,000	—	Apr 1	By Balance b/d		—	35,000
Apr 4	To Capital A/c		30,000	20,000	Apr 10	By Purchase A/c		—	25,000
Apr 5	To Sales A/c		15,000	—	Apr 10	By Input CGST A/c		—	2,250
Apr 5	To Output CGST A/c		1,350	—	Apr 10	By Input SGST A/c		—	2,250
Apr 5	To Output SGST A/c		1,350	—	Apr 11	By Zen		12,500	—
Apr 19	To Cheque in Hand (Ram's cheque)		—	15,000	Apr 14	By Rent A/c		—	5,000
					Apr 14	By Input CGST A/c		—	450
Apr 28	To Cheque in Hand A/c (Kia's cheque)		—	46,000	Apr 14	By Input SGST A/c		—	450
					Apr 15	By Furniture A/c		—	15,000
Apr 29	To Bank A/c		12,500	—	Apr 15	By Input CGST A/c		—	1,350
Apr 30	To Balance c/d		—	27,100	Apr 15	By Input SGST A/c		—	1,350
					Apr 16	By Drawings A/c		—	2,500
					Apr 29	By Cash A/c		—	12,500

Date	Particulars	LF	Cash (₹)	Bank (₹)	Date	Particulars	LF	Cash (₹)	Bank (₹)
					Apr 29	By Salary A/c		12,500	5,000
					Apr 30	By Balance c/d		45,200	—
			70,200	1,08,100				70,200	1,08,100

Solved Question 7 **Prepare two column cash book from the following transactions of M/s Laxman for the month of April, 2024. Also prepare any five related ledger accounts and pass journal entries related to discount received and discount allowed.**

Date	Particulars	Amt (₹)
2024		
Apr 1	Cash in hand	60,000
	Bank overdraft	56,000
Apr 2	Cash purchases ₹ 8,000 less trade discount @ 10%	
Apr 3	Sold goods to Raja on credit	3,500
	Purchased goods on credit from Rajesh	7,000
Apr 4	Wages paid	5,000
Apr 5	Cash sales	80,000
Apr 7	Purchased goods from Karuna for ₹ 61,250 paid by cheque in full settlement	60,000
Apr 9	Purchased furniture for cash	40,000
Apr 10	Cash paid to Sarika discount received ₹ 500	25,000
Apr 11	Cheque issued to Karuna was dishonoured	
Apr 13	Cash sales	20,500
Apr 16	Bank charged interest on overdraft	2,500
Apr 18	Deposited into bank	33,000
Apr 20	Paid telephone bill by cheque	3,000
Apr 25	Sold goods for ₹ 1,17,500 to Sachin and received cheque in full settlement (Deposited same day)	1,15,000
Apr 27	Paid rent	3,500
Apr 29	Drew cash for personal use	5,000
Apr 30	Paid salary	8,000
Apr 30	Interest collected by bank	12,500

Sol. Dr **Double Column Cash Book** Cr

Date	Particulars	LF	Cash (₹)	Bank (₹)	Date	Particulars	LF	Cash (₹)	Bank (₹)
2024					2024				
Apr 1	To Balance b/d		60,000	—	Apr 1	By Balance b/d		—	56,000
Apr 5	To Sales A/c		80,000	—	Apr 2	By Purchases A/c		7,200	—
Apr 11	To Karuna		—	60,000	Apr 4	By Wages A/c		5,000	—
Apr 13	To Sales A/c		20,500	—	Apr 7	By Karuna		—	60,000
Apr 18	To Cash A/c	C	—	33,000	Apr 9	By Furniture A/c		40,000	—
Apr 25	To Sales A/c		—	1,15,000	Apr 10	By Sarika		25,000	—
Apr 30	To Interest A/c		—	12,500	Apr 16	By Interest on Bank Overdraft A/c		—	2,500
					Apr 18	By Bank A/c	C	33,000	—
					Apr 20	By Telephone Expenses A/c		—	3,000
					Apr 27	By Rent A/c		3,500	—
					Apr 29	By Drawings A/c		5,000	—
					Apr 30	By Salary A/c		8,000	—
					Apr 30	By Balance c/d		33,800	99,000
			1,60,500	2,20,500				1,60,500	2,20,500
May 1	To Balance b/d		33,800	99,000					

Note Trade discount is not recorded separately in the books of accounts. Net amount 8,000 − 800 = ₹ 7,200 is credited to cash account and debited to purchases account. Transactions of 3rd April are not recorded being credit transactions.

JOURNAL

Date	Particulars		LF	Amt (Dr)	Amt (Cr)
2024					
Apr 7	Karuna	Dr		1,250	
	To Discount Received A/c				1,250
	(Being the cash discount received from Manisha)				
Apr 10	Sarika	Dr		500	
	To Discount Received A/c				500
	(Being the cash discount received from Sarika)				
Apr 11	Discount Received A/c	Dr		1,250	
	To Karuna				1,250
	(Being the discount received reversed on cheque being dishonoured)				
Apr 25	Discount Allowed A/c	Dr		2,500	
	To Sachin				2,500
	(Being the cash discount allowed to Sachin)				

Dr **Wages Account** Cr

Date	Particulars	JF	Amt (₹)	Date	Particulars	JF	Amt (₹)
2024							
Apr 4	To Cash A/c		5,000				

Dr **Sales Account** Cr

Date	Particulars	JF	Amt (₹)	Date	Particulars	JF	Amt (₹)
				2024			
				Apr 5	By Cash A/c		80,000
				Apr 13	By Cash A/c		20,500

Dr **Karuna** Cr

Date	Particulars	JF	Amt (₹)	Date	Particulars	JF	Amt (₹)
2024				2024			
Apr 7	To Bank A/c		60,000	Apr 11	By Bank A/c		60,000
Apr 7	To Discount Received A/c		1,250	Apr 25	By Discount Allowed A/c		2,500

Dr **Discount Allowed Account** Cr

Date	Particulars	JF	Amt (₹)	Date	Particulars	JF	Amt (₹)
2024							
Apr 25	To Sachin		2,500				

Dr **Discount Received Account** Cr

Date	Particulars	JF	Amt (₹)	Date	Particulars	JF	Amt (₹)
2024				2024			
Apr 11	To Karuna		1,250	Apr 7	By Karuna		1,250
				Apr 10	By Sarika		500

Solved Question 8 Prepare a double column cash book (Cash and Bank) from the following transactions. Also pass the necessary journal entries.

2024

Aug 1	Cash in hand ₹ 1,200; overdraft at bank ₹ 15,000.
Aug 3	Further capital introduced ₹ 20,000 out of which ₹ 16,000 deposited in the bank.
Aug 4	Purchased goods from Vrijesh Traders amounting to ₹ 3,000 and they allowed trade discount ₹ 200. The amount was paid by cheque.
Aug 4	Goods purchased for cash ₹ 4,000.
Aug 5	Sold goods to Varun on credit ₹ 5,000.
Aug 6	Received cheque from Siddhartha ₹ 2,450. Allowed him discount ₹ 50.
Aug 10	Cheque received from Siddhartha deposited into bank.
Aug 11	Settled the account of Superstar Printers ₹ 750 by paying cash ₹ 680.
Aug 12	Cash received from Varun ₹ 4,750 in full settlement of his account of ₹ 5,000.
Aug 16	An amount of ₹ 1,000 due from Kartik Brothers written-off as bad debts in the previous year, now recovered.
Aug 17	Received from Kunal on behalf of Karan ₹ 200.
Aug 19	Received a cheque for ₹ 800 from Adarsh, which was endorsed to Parth on 24th August.
Aug 20	Sale of old furniture, payment received in cash for ₹ 720.
Aug 25	Cashed a cheque for ₹ 3,000.
Aug 25	Drew from bank for household expenses ₹ 1,000 and for income tax ₹ 500.
Aug 28	Amit who owed ₹ 400 became bankrupt and paid 60 paise in a rupee.
Aug 28	Received repayment of a loan ₹ 3,000 and deposited out of it ₹ 2,500 into the bank.
Aug 30	Interest debited by bank ₹ 375.
Aug 30	Deposited with the bank the entire balance after retaining ₹ 2,000 at office.

Sol. Dr **Double Column Cash Book** Cr

Date	Particulars	LF	Cash (₹)	Bank (₹)	Date	Particulars	LF	Cash (₹)	Bank (₹)
2024					2024				
Aug 1	To Balance b/d		1,200	—	Aug 1	By Balance b/d		—	15,000
Aug 3	To Capital A/c		4,000	16,000	Aug 4	By Purchases A/c (3,000 – 200)		—	2,800
Aug 10	To Cheques in Hand A/c		—	2,450	Aug 4	By Purchases A/c		4,000	—
Aug 12	To Varun		4,750	—	Aug 11	By Superstar Printers		680	—
Aug 16	To Bad Debts Recovered A/c		1,000	—	Aug 25	By Cash A/c	C	—	3,000
Aug 17	To Karan		200	—	Aug 25	By Drawings A/c (1,000 + 500)		—	1,500
Aug 20	To Furniture A/c		720	—		By Interest A/c		—	375
Aug 25	To Bank A/c (WN 3)	C	3,000	—	Aug 30	By Bank A/c (WN 4)	C	8,930	—
Aug 28	To Amit		240	—	Aug 30	By Balance c/d		2,000	7,205
Aug 28	To Loan A/c		500	2,500					
Aug 30	To Cash A/c (WN 4)	C	—	8,930					
			15,610	29,880				15,610	29,880
Sep 1	To Balance b/d		2,000	7,205					

JOURNAL

Date	Particulars		LF	Amt (Dr)	Amt (Cr)
2024					
Aug 6	Cheques in Hand A/c	Dr		2,450	
	Discount Allowed A/c	Dr		50	
	To Siddhartha's A/c				2,500
	(Being the cheque received from Siddhartha's and allowed him discount. Cheque received was not deposited the same day)				
Aug 11	Superstar Printers	Dr		70	
	To Discount Received A/c				70
	(Being the discount received on payment made to Superstar Printers)				
Aug 12	Discount Allowed A/c	Dr		250	
	To Varun				250
	(Being the cash discount allowed to Varun against payment received)				
Aug 19	Cheques in Hand A/c	Dr		800	
	To Adarsh				800
	(Being the cheque received from Adarsh not deposited but endorsed) (WN2)				
Aug 24	Parth	Dr		800	
	To Cheques in Hand A/c				800
	(Being the cheque received from Adarsh endorsed in favour of Parth) (WN2)				

Working Notes

1. Goods sold to Varun on 5th August, will not be recorded in the cash book, it being credit sale.
2. When a cheque is received but endorsed in favour of a creditor, the transaction is recorded through a journal entry. It is recorded through the journal and not cash book because cheque has neither been deposited in the bank nor has been issued to the third party. In this case, we shall pass two entries one for receiving cheque from Adarsh on 19th August, 2022 and later for endorsing the cheque in favour of Parth on 24th August, 2022.
3. On 25th August, a cheque encashed for ₹ 3,000 is treated as cash withdrawn from bank for business.
4. 15,610 – (4,000 + 680 + 2,000) = ₹ 8,930.
5. ₹ 8,930 is deposited into bank after retaining ₹ 2,000 at office on 30th August, 2022.

Solved Question 9 ***(With GST)*** **Enter the following transactions in a cash book with cash and bank columns**

Date	Particulars	Amt (₹)
2024		
Jan 1	Commenced business with cash	20,000
Jan 2	Opened a current account in Central Bank and deposited	12,000
Jan 3	Further capital introduced ₹ 5,000, out of which ₹ 4,000 deposited into the bank	
Jan 3	Goods purchased for ₹ 6,000 plus CGST and SGST @ 9% each and issued a cheque for the same	
Jan 4	Sold goods for ₹ 4,000 plus CGST and SGST @ 9% each. Cheque received which was immediately deposited into bank	
Jan 8	Sold goods to Tom on credit plus CGST and SGST @ 9% each	1,500
Jan 10	Received cheque from Tom in full settlement of his account	1,650
Jan 12	Cheque received on 10th June deposited into bank	
Jan 15	Paid rent by cheque plus CGST and SGST @ 9% each	400
Jan 16	Paid commission by cheque including CGST and SGST @ 9% each	1,180
Jan 18	Drew cheque for personal use	200
Jan 25	Withdrew from bank for office use	1,000
Jan 25	Received a cheque for Zen and endorsed it to Ben on 29th June	600
Jan 30	Paid salary	800

Sol.

Dr **Double Column Cash Book** Cr

Date	Particulars	V. No.	LF	Cash (₹)	Bank (₹)	Date	Particulars	V. No.	LF	Cash (₹)	Bank (₹)
2024						2024					
Jun 2	To Capital A/c			20,000	—	Jun 2	By Bank A/c		C	12,000	—
Jun 2	To Cash A/c		C	—	12,000	Jun 3	By Purchases A/c			—	6,000
Jun 3	To Capital A/c			1,000	4,000	Jun 3	By Input CGST A/c			—	540
Jun 4	To Sales A/c			—	4,000	Jun 3	By Input SGST A/c			—	540
Jun 4	To Output CGST A/c			—	360	Jun 15	By Rent A/c			—	400
Jun 4	To Output SGST A/c			—	360	Jun 15	By Input CGST A/c			—	36
Jun 12	To Cheques-in-hand A/c			—	1,650	Jun 15	By Input SGST A/c			—	36
Jun 25	To Bank A/c		C	1,000	—	Jun 16	By Commission A/c			—	1,000
						Jun 16	By Input CGST A/c			—	90
						Jun 16	By Input SGST A/c			—	90
						Jun 18	By Drawings A/c			—	200
						Jun 25	By Cash A/c			—	1,000
						Jun 30	By Salary A/c			800	—
						Jun 30	By Balance c/d			9,200	12,438
				22,000	22,370					22,000	22,370
Jul 1	To Balance b/d			9,200	12,438						

Working Notes

1. On 8th June, entry for credit sale of ₹ 1,500 plus CGST and SGST @ 9% each will be recorded in journal.
2. Cheque received from Tom on 10th June, 2022 will be recorded in the journal as follows

Cheques in Hand A/c	Dr	1,650	
Discount Allowed A/c	Dr	120	
To Tom			1,770

When the above cheque is deposited into bank on 12th June, 2024, it will be recorded in the cash book on the debit side in bank column.

3. The receipt as well as endorsement of cheque will not be recorded in cash book. It will be recorded in journal as follows

Jun 25	Cheque in Hand A/c	Dr		600	
	To Zen				600
	(Being cheque received from Zen)				
Jun 29	Ben	Dr		600	
	To Cheques in hand A/c				600
	(Being cheque received from Zen endorsed to Ben)				

Solved Question 10 **Following are the transactions given for the month of October, 2024. You are required to prepare a double column cash book (with cash and bank column). On 1st October, 2024, balance of cash and bank account were ₹ 80,000 and ₹ 60,000 respectively.**

2024	
Oct 1	**Purchased goods list price ₹ 20,000 less trade discount 10% with CGST and SGST @ 9% each. Cash discount of 3% was received on the payment by cheque immediately.**
Oct 3	**Paid for rent by cash ₹ 1,500 which will become due on 31st October, 2024.**
Oct 5	**Sold goods list price ₹ 15,000 less 5% trade discount plus CGST and SGST @ 9% each. Received cash immediately.**
Oct 8	**Paid for stationary ₹ 500 and received commission ₹ 21,000.**
Oct 10	**Withdrawn from bank for personal use ₹ 2,000.**
Oct 15	**Paid ₹ 2,500 for insurance premium by a cheque.**
Oct 18	**Purchased a refrigerator by proprietor for personal use. Amount was paid from saving account.**
Oct 20	**Goods returned to Ajay list price ₹ 1,000 purchased on 1st October, 2024.**
Oct 24	**Received a cheque of ₹ 2,000 from Aditya and transferred it to Yash & Bros.**

Sol. Dr **Double Column Cash Book** Cr

Date	Particulars	V.No.	LF	Cash (₹)	Bank (₹)	Date	Particulars	V.No.	LF	Cash (₹)	Bank (₹)
2024						2024					
Oct 1	To Balance b/d			80,000	60,000	Oct 1	By Purchase A/c			—	17,460
Oct 5	To Sales A/c			14,250	—	Oct 1	By Input CGST A/c			—	1,571
Oct 5	To Output CGST A/c			1,282	—	Oct 1	By Input SGST A/c			—	1,571
Oct 5	To Output SGST A/c			1,282	—	Oct 3	By Advance Rent A/c			1,500	—
Oct 8	To Commission A/c			1,000	—	Oct 8	By Stationery A/c			500	—
						Oct 10	By Drawings A/c			—	2,000
						Oct 15	By Insurance Premium A/c			—	2,500
							By Balance c/d			95,814	34,898
				97,814	60,000					97,814	60,000

Working Notes

1. Transaction on 18th October is a personal transaction, hence it will not be recorded.
2. Transaction on 20th October and 24th October are non-cash/bank transactions, hence will not be entered in cash book.

Solved Question 11 **Prepare a petty cash book on the imprest system from the following particulars.**

2024

Jul 1 Received ₹ 5,000 from the cashier.
Jul 3 Purchased stationery ₹ 400.
Jul 6 Paid for wages ₹ 250, for charity ₹ 150.
Jul 7 Purchased soap ₹ 100, paid for newspaper bill ₹ 350.
Jul 9 Paid taxi fare ₹ 400, cartage ₹ 100.
Jul 12 Paid postal expenses ₹ 300.
Jul 14 Paid auto fare ₹ 190, paid for courier services ₹ 35.
Jul 25 Speed post charges ₹ 200, wages ₹ 300.
Jul 26 Paid cartage ₹ 225.
Jul 27 Refreshment expenses ₹ 400, photostating charges ₹ 200.
Jul 28 Pen/Pencils ₹ 375.
Jul 29 Wages ₹ 150.
Jul 31 Loading charges ₹ 75.

Sol.

Dr **Petty Cash Book** Cr

Amount Received (₹)	Date	Particulars	V. No.	Total Payments (₹)	Postage and Courier (₹)	Wages (₹)	Conveyance (₹)	Cartage (₹)	Stationery (₹)	Miscellaneous Expenses (₹)
	2024									
5,000	Jul 1	To Cash A/c		—	—	—	—	—	—	—
	Jul 3	By Stationery		400	—	—	—	—	400	—
	Jul 6	By Wages		250	—	250	—	—	—	—
	Jul 6	By Charity		150	—	—	—	—	—	150
	Jul 7	By Soap		100	—	—	—	—	—	100
	Jul 7	By Newspapers		350	—	—	—	—	—	350
	Jul 9	By Taxi Fare		400	—	—	400	—	—	—
	Jul 9	By Cartage		100	—	—	—	100	—	—
	Jul 12	By Postal Expenses		300	300	—	—	—	—	—
	Jul 14	By Auto Fare		190	—	—	190	—	—	—
	Jul 14	By Courier Services		35	35	—	—	—	—	—
	Jul 25	By Speed Post Charges		200	200	—	—	—	—	—
	Jul 25	By Wages		300	—	300	—	—	—	—
	Jul 26	By Cartage		225	—	—	—	225	—	—
	Jul 27	By Refreshment		400	—	—	—	—	—	400
	Jul 27	By Photostating Charges		200	—	—	—	—	—	200

Amount Received (₹)	Date	Particulars	V. No.	Total Payments (₹)	Postage and Courier (₹)	Wages (₹)	Conveyance (₹)	Cartage (₹)	Stationery (₹)	Miscellaneous Expenses (₹)
	Jul 28	By Pen/Pencils		375	—	—	—	—	375	—
	Jul 29	By Wages		150	—	150	—	—	—	—
	Jul 31	By Loading Charges		75	—	—	—	75	—	—
		Total Payments		4,200	535	700	590	400	775	1,200
	Jul 31	By Balance c/d		800						
5,000				5,000						
800	Aug 1	To Balance b/d								
4,200	Aug 1	To Cash A/c								

Solved Question 12 Prepare petty cash book from the following transactions. The imprest amount is ₹ 2,000.

NCERT Modified

Date	Particulars	Amt (₹)	Date	Particulars	Amt (₹)
2024			Jan 15	Taxi fare to manager	70
Jan 1	Paid cartage	50	Jan 18	Stationery	65
Jan 2	STD charges	40	Jan 20	Bus fare	10
Jan 2	Bus fare	20	Jan 22	Fax charges	30
Jan 3	Postage	30	Jan 25	Telegram charges	35
Jan 4	Refreshment for employees	80	Jan 27	Postage stamps	200
Jan 6	Courier charges	30	Jan 29	Repair of furniture	105
Jan 8	Refreshment of customer	50	Jan 30	Laundry expenses	115
Jan 10	Cartage	35	Jan 31	Miscellaneous expenses	100

Sol. Dr **Petty Cash Book** Cr

Amount Received (₹)	Date	Particulars	V. No.	Total Payment (₹)	Cartage (₹)	Postage (₹)	Telephone and Telegram (₹)	Conveyance (₹)	Stationery (₹)	Miscellaneous (₹)
	2024									
2,000	Jan 1	To Cash Received		—	—	—	—	—	—	—
	Jan 1	By Cartage		50	50	—	—	—	—	—
	Jan 2	By STD Charges		40	—	—	40	—	—	—
	Jan 2	By Bus Fare		20	—	—	—	20	—	—
	Jan 3	By Postage		30	—	30	—	—	—	—
	Jan 4	By Refreshment for Employees		80	—	—	—	—	—	80
	Jan 6	By Courier Charges		30	—	30	—	—	—	—
	Jan 8	By Refreshment of Customer		50	—	—	—	—	—	50
	Jan 10	By Cartage		35	35	—	—	—	—	—
	Jan 15	By Taxi Fare		70	—	—	—	70	—	—
	Jan 18	By Stationery		65	—	—	—	—	65	—
	Jan 20	By Bus Fare		10	—	—	—	10	—	—
	Jan 22	By Fax Charges		30	—	—	30	—	—	—
	Jan 25	By Telegram Charges		35	—	—	35	—	—	—
	Jan 27	By Postage Stamps		200	—	200	—	—	—	—
	Jan 29	By Repair of Furniture		105	—	—	—	—	—	105
	Jan 30	By Laundry Expenses		115	—	—	—	—	—	115

Amount Received (₹)	Date	Particulars	V. No.	Total Payment (₹)	Cartage (₹)	Postage (₹)	Telephone and Telegram (₹)	Conveyance (₹)	Stationery (₹)	Miscellaneous (₹)
	Jan 31	By Miscellaneous Expenses		100	—	—	—	—	—	100
				1,065	85	260	105	100	65	450
	Jan 31	By Balance c/d		935						
2,000				2,000						
935	Feb 1	To Balance b/d								
1,065	Feb 1	To Cash A/c								

Ledger Posting of Petty Cash Book

Dr **Cartage Account** Cr

Date	Particulars	JF	Amt (₹)	Date	Particulars	JF	Amt (₹)
Jan 31	To Petty Cash A/c		85				

Dr **Postage Account** Cr

Date	Particulars	JF	Amt (₹)	Date	Particulars	JF	Amt (₹)
Jan 31	To Petty Cash A/c		260				

Dr **Telephone and Telegram Account** Cr

Date	Particulars	JF	Amt (₹)	Date	Particulars	JF	Amt (₹)
Jan 31	To Petty Cash A/c		105				

Dr **Conveyance Account** Cr

Date	Particulars	JF	Amt (₹)	Date	Particulars	JF	Amt (₹)
Jan 31	To Petty Cash A/c		100				

Dr **Stationery Account** Cr

Date	Particulars	JF	Amt (₹)	Date	Particulars	JF	Amt (₹)
Jan 31	To Petty Cash A/c		65				

Dr **Miscellaneous Expenses Account** Cr

Date	Particulars	JF	Amt (₹)	Date	Particulars	JF	Amt (₹)
Jan 31	To Petty Cash A/c		450				

Dr **Petty Cash Account** Cr

Date	Particulars	JF	Amt (₹)	Date	Particulars	JF	Amt (₹)
2024				2024			
Jan 1	To Cash A/c		2,000	Jan 31	By Cartage A/c		85
				Jan 31	By Postage A/c		260
				Jan 31	By Telephone and Telegram A/c		105
				Jan 31	By Conveyance A/c		100
				Jan 31	By Stationery A/c		65
				Jan 31	By Miscellaneous Expenses A/c		450
				Jan 31	By Balance c/d		935
			2,000				2,000
Feb 1	To Balance b/d		935				
Feb 1	To Cash A/c		1,065				

Purchase Book

Solved Question 13 **Record the following transactions in purchases book and prepare purchases account and M/s Sudha Electronics account.**

2024

Apr 4 **Purchased from M/s Sudha Electronics (Invoice no. 3250). 20 mini-size TV @ ₹ 1,500 per piece, 15 tape recorders @ ₹ 12,500 per piece. Trade discount @ 20%.**

Apr 10 **Bought from M/s Pawan Electronics (Invoice no. 8260). 10 video cassettes @ ₹ 150 per piece, 20 tape recorders @ ₹ 1,650 per piece. Trade discount @ 10%.**

Apr 18 **Purchased from M/s Northern Electronics (Invoice no. 4256). 15 northern stereos @ ₹ 4,000 per piece, 20 northern colour TV @ ₹14,500 per piece. Trade discount @ 12.5%.**

Apr 26 **Purchased from M/s Sudha Electronics (Invoice no. 3294). 10 mini-size TV @ ₹ 1,000 per piece, 5 colour TV @ ₹ 12,500 per piece. Trade discount @ 20%.**

Apr 29 **Bought from M/s Pawan Electronics (Invoice No. 8281). 20 video cassettes @ 150 per piece, 25 tape recorders @ ₹ 1,600 per piece. Trade discount @ 10%.**

Sol.

Purchases Book

Date	Particulars	Invoice No.	LF	Details (₹)	Total Amt (₹)
2024					
Apr 4	**Sudha Electronics**	3250			
	20 Mini-Size TV @ ₹ 1,500 per Piece			30,000	
	15 Tape Recorders @ ₹ 12,500 per Piece			1,87,500	
				2,17,500	
	(−) Trade Discount @ 20%			(43,500)	1,74,000
Apr 10	**Pawan Electronics**	8260			
	10 Video Cassettes @ ₹ 150 per Piece			1,500	
	20 Tape Recorders @ ₹ 1,650 per Piece			33,000	
				34,500	
	(−) Trade Discount @ 10%			(3,450)	31,050
Apr 18	**Northern Electronics**	4256			
	15 Northern Stereos @ ₹ 4,000 per Piece			60,000	
	20 Northern Colour TV @ 14,500 per Piece			2,90,000	
				3,50,000	
	(−) Trade Discount @ 12.5%			(43,750)	3,06,250
Apr 26	**Sudha Electronics**	3294			
	10 Mini-Size TV @ ₹ 1,000 per Piece			10,000	
	5 Colour TV @ ₹ 12,500 per Piece			62,500	
				72,500	
	(−) Trade Discount @ 20%			(14,500)	58,000
Apr 29	**Pawan Electronics**	8281			
	20 Video Cassettes @ ₹ 150 per Piece			3,000	
	25 Tape Recorders @ ₹ 1,600 per Piece			40,000	
				43,000	
	(−) Trade Discount @ 10%			(4,300)	38,700
Apr 31	Purchases A/c Dr				6,08,000

Ledger Posting of Purchases Book

Dr **Sudha Electronics Account** Cr

Date	Particulars	JF	Amt (₹)	Date	Particulars	JF	Amt (₹)
				2024			
				Apr 4	By Purchases A/c		1,74,000
				Apr 26	By Purchases A/c		58,000

Dr **Purchases Account** Cr

Date	Particulars	JF	Amt (₹)	Date	Particulars	JF	Amt (₹)
2024							
Apr 31	To Sundries as per Purchases Book		6,08,000				

Solved Question 14 ***(With GST)*** **Prepare the purchases book for the month of February, 2024 in the books of Agarwal and Sons.**

2024

Feb 1 **Purchased from M/s White & Co., Aligarh**
5 gross pencils @ ₹ 500 per gross
2 dozen registers @ ₹ 250 per dozen
Less : Trade Discount @ 10%, IGST @ 18%

Feb 5 **Purchased for cash from the Teacher's Mart**
20 dozen exercise books @ ₹ 150 per dozen

Feb 10 **Purchased from Howme, Delhi**
8 reams of white paper @ ₹ 250 per ream
10 reams of ruled paper @ ₹ 300 per ream
Less Trade Discount @ 10%, CGST and SGST @ 9% each

Feb 20 **Purchased 80 Reynolds Pens @ ₹ 10 each from M/s Thakur Bros., Delhi**
CGST and SGST is levied @ 9% each.

Sol.

Purchases Book

Date	Particulars	Invoice No.	LF	Details (₹)	Cost (₹)	Input CGST (₹)	Input SGST (₹)	Input IGST (₹)	Total Amt (₹)
2024									
Feb 1	**White & Co., Aligarh**								
	5 gross Pencils @ ₹ 500 per gross			2,500					
	2 dozen Registers @ ₹ 250 per dozen			500					
				3,000					
	(–) Trade Discount @ 10%			(300)					
				2,700					
	(+) IGST @ 18%			486					
				3,186	2,700	—	—	486	3,186
Feb 10	**Howme, Delhi**								
	8 reams White Paper @ ₹ 250 each			2,000					
	10 reams Ruled Paper @ ₹ 300 each			3,000					
				5,000					
	(–) Trade Discount @ 10%			(500)					
				4,500					
	(+) CGST @ 9%			405					
	SGST @ 9%			405					
				5,310	4,500	405	405	—	5,310
Feb 20	**M/s Thakur Bors., Delhi**								
	80 Reynolds Pens @ ₹ 10 each			800					
	(+) CGST @ 9%			72					
	SGST @ 9%			72					
				944	800	72	72	—	944
Feb 28	Purchases A/c Dr				8,000	477	477	486	9.440

Sales Book

Solved Question 15 Enter the following transactions in sales book

(i) 2 water purifiers @ ₹ 2,100 each and 5 buckets @ ₹ 100 each to M/s Aman Traders (Invoice no. 178 dated 6th April, 2024) less trade discount @ 10%.

(ii) 5 road side containers @ ₹ 4,200 each to M/s Nutan Enterprises (Invoice no. 180 dated 9th April, 2024).

(iii) 100 big buckets @ ₹ 850 each to M/s Raman Traders (Invoice no. 209, dated 28th April, 2024).

(iv) Sold old furniture to Rajesh & Co. on credit ₹ 1,000.

Record the above transactions in sales book and prepare sales account and Raman Trader's account.

Sol.

Sales Book

Date	Particulars	Invoice No.	LF	Details (₹)	Total Amt (₹)
2024					
Apr 6	**Aman Traders**	178			
	2 Water Purifiers @ ₹ 2,100 each			4,200	
	5 Buckets @ ₹ 100 each			500	
				4,700	
	(−) Trade Discount @ 10%			(470)	4,230
Apr 9	**Nutan Enterprises**	180			
	5 Road Side Containers @ ₹ 4,200 each				21,000
Apr 28	**Raman Traders**	209			
	100 Big Buckets @ ₹ 850 each				85,000
Apr 30	Sales A/c Cr				1,10,230

Ledger Posting of the Sales Book

Dr **Raman Traders Account** Cr

Date	Particulars	JF	Amt (₹)	Date	Particulars	JF	Amt (₹)
2024							
Apr 28	To Sales A/c		85,000				

Dr **Sales Account** Cr

Date	Particulars	JF	Amt (₹)	Date	Particulars	JF	Amt (₹)
				2022			
				Apr 30	By Sundries as per Sales Book		1,10,230

Working Note

Sale of old furniture is not recorded in the sales book as the firm does not deal in furniture.

Solved Question 16 *(With GST)* From the following transactions of M/s Vijay Sales, Bengaluru, prepare sales book.

2024

Mar 1 Sold to M/s Karishma Tea, Darjeeling, vide Invoice no. 1008, 3 chests of tea ₹ 15,000 per chest less trade discount @ 5% and IGST is charged @ 18%.

Mar 4 Sold to M/s Madhurkar and Sons, Bangalore vide Invoice no. 1010, 20 kg Amul Butter @ ₹ 750 per kg less trade discount @ 5% and charged CGST and SGST @ 9% each.

Mar 5 Sold to M/s Samuel Sons, Delhi vide Invoice no. 1012, 20 kg Assam Tea @ ₹ 1,800 per kg less trade discount @ 5%, charged IGST @ 18%.

Sol.

M/s Vijay Sales, Bengaluru
Sales Book

Date	Particulars	Invoice No.	LF	Details (₹)	Sale Value (₹)	Output CGST (₹)	Output SGST (₹)	Output IGST (₹)	Total Amt (₹)
2024									
Mar 1	**M/s Karishma Tea, Assam**	1008							
	3 Chests Tea @ ₹ 15,000 per chest			45,000					
	(–) Trade Discount @ 5%			(2,250)					
				42,750					
	(+) IGST @ 18%			7,695					
				50,445	42,750	—	—	7,695	50,445
Mar 4	**M/s Madhurkar and Sons, Bangalore**	1010							
	20 kg Amul Butter @ ₹ 750 per kg			15,000					
	(–) Trade Discount @ 5%			(750)					
				14,250					
	(+) CGST @ 9%			1,282					
	SGST @ 9%			1,282					
				16,814	14,250	1,282	1,282	—	16,814
Mar 5	**M/s Samuel Sons, Delhi**	1012							
	20 kg Assam Tea @ ₹ 1,800 per kg			36,000					
	(–) Trade Discount @ 5%			(1,800)					
				34,200					
	(+) IGST @ 18%			6,156	34,200	—	—	6,156	40,356
				40,356	—	—	—	—	40,356
Mar 31	Sales A/c Cr				91,200	1,282	1,282	13,851	1,07,615

Purchase Return Book

Solved Question 17 **Record the following transactions in purchases return book**

(i) 2 Banarsi sarees @ ₹ 2,000 each and 2 Kanjivaram sarees @ ₹ 12,500 each were bought from Neema Mills, trade discount on all items @ 20%. However, on delivery these sarees were found defective and were returned back with Debit Note no. 100.

(ii) Returned to Payal Mills, Surat-5 polyster sarees @ ₹ 200 each. Trade discount @ 10% (Debit Note no. 101)

(iii) Garg Mills, Kota accepted the returns of goods (which were purchased for cash) from us, 5 Kota sarees @ ₹ 80. (Debit Note no. 102)

(iv) Returned to Mittal Mills, Bangalore, 5 Silk sarees @ ₹ 520 each. Trade discount @ 10% (Debit Note no. 103)

(v) Returned one typewriter (being defective)@ ₹ 7,000 to Bansal & Co.

Also prepare purchase return account and Neema Mills account.

Sol.

Purchases Return Book

Date	Particulars	Debit Note No.	LF	Details (₹)	Total Amt (₹)
	Neema Mills	100			
	2 Banarsi Sarees @ ₹ 2,000 each			4,000	
	2 Kanjivaram Sarees @ ₹ 12,500 each			25,000	
				29,000	
	(–) Trade Discount @ 20%			(5,800)	23,200
	Payal Mills, Surat	101			
	5 Polyster Sarees @ 200 each			1,000	
	(–) Trade Discount @ 10%			(100)	900

Date	Particulars		Debit Note No.	LF	Details (₹)	Total Amt (₹)
	Mittal Mills, Bangalore		103			
	5 Silk Sarees @ 520 each				2,600	
	(–) Trade Discount @ 10%				(260)	2,340
	Purchases Return A/c	Cr				26,440

Important Problem Solving Point

Return of Kota sarees will be recorded in the cash book and return of typewriter will be recorded in the general journal (journal proper) since in the purchases return book, only the return of merchandise purchased on credit are recorded.

Ledger Posting of Purchase Return Book

Dr **Neema Mills Account** Cr

Date	Particulars	JF	Amt (₹)	Date	Particulars	JF	Amt (₹)
	To Purchases Return A/c		23,200				

Dr **Purchases Return Account** Cr

Date	Particulars	JF	Amt (₹)	Date	Particulars	JF	Amt (₹)
					By Sundries as per Purchases Return Book		26,440

Solved Question 18 *(With GST)* **Record the following in purchases return book.**

2024

Mar 10 **Returned 2 washing machines purchased from M/s Sudhakar Electronics at the list price of ₹ 21,000 per machines less trade discount 20%, CGST and SGST was paid @ 9% each.**

Mar 24 **Returned 6 pendrives to M/s Monika Electronics purchased @ ₹ 3,000 each plus IGST @ 18%**

Sol. **Purchases Return Book**

Date	Particulars		Invoice No.	LF	Details (₹)	Cost (₹)	Input CGST (₹)	Input SGST (₹)	Input IGST (₹)	Total Amt (₹)
2022										
Mar 10	**M/s Sudharkar Electronics**									
	2 Washing Machines @ ₹ 21,000 each				42,000					
	(–) Trade Discount @ 20%				(8,400)					
					33,600					
	(+) CGST @ 9%				3,024					
	SGST @ 9%				3,024					
					39,648	33,600	3,024	3,024	—	39,648
Mar 24	**M/s Monika Electronics**									
	6 Pendrives @ ₹ 3,000 each				18,000					
	(+) IGST @ 18%				3,240					
					21,240	18,000	—	—	3,240	21,240
Mar 31	Purchase Return A/c	Cr				51,600	3,024	3,024	2,160	60,888

Sales Return Book

Solved Question 19 *(With GST)* **Prepare sales return book in the books of Lal and Co., Delhi from the following transactions and write journal entry.**

2024

Apr 6 Goods returned by Komalika and Co., Delhi
2 Table Fans @ ₹ 4,000 each
Less : Trade Discount @ 15%
Add : CGST and SGST @ 9% each

Apr 12 Sehgal Electricals, Agra returned defective Room Cooler ₹ 21,250 plus IGST @ 18%

Sol.

Lal and Co., Delhi
Sales Return Book

Date	Particulars	Credit Note No.	LF	Details (₹)	Value (₹)	Output CGST (₹)	Output SGST (₹)	Output IGST (₹)	Total Amt (₹)
2024									
Apr 6	**Komalika and Co., Delhi**								
	2 Table Fans @ ₹ 4,000 each			8,000					
	(–) Trade Discount @ 15%			(1,200)					
				6,800					
	(+) CGST @ 9%			612					
	SGST @ 9%			612					
				8,024	6,800	612	612	—	8,024
Apr 12	**Sehgal Electricals, Agra**								
	1 Room Cooler			21,250					
	(+) IGST @ 12%			3,825					
				25,075	21,250	—	—	3,825	25,075
Apr 30	Sales Return A/c Dr				28,050	612	612	3,825	33,099

JOURNAL

Particulars		LF	Amt (Dr)	Amt (Cr)
Sales Return A/c	Dr		28,050	
Output CGST A/c	Dr		612	
Output SGST A/c	Dr		612	
Output IGST A/c	Dr		3,825	
To Komalika & Co.				8,024
To Sehgal Electricals				25,075
(Being sales return recorded for April)				

Solved Question 20 **Prepare sales return book of M/s Balwan & Sons, Mathura from the following transactions and post them in ledger**

2024

Jul 1 Return by Shiv Shankar, Kolkata
50 Shirts @ ₹ 600 per shirt
30 t-shirts @ ₹ 400 per t-shirt

Jul 8 Return by Ankit & Co., Mumbai
15 Jeans @ ₹ 2,000 each
20 Trousers @ 200 each
Less : Trade discount @ 10%

Jul 11 Return by Prema Stores, Ahmedabad
25 Kurti @ ₹ 150 each
40 Saree @ 2,000 each
Less: Trade discount @ 10%

Jul 15 Return by Kratika Stores, Mumbai
10 overcoat @ ₹ 1,000 each

Sol.

M/s Balwan & Sons, Mathura
Sales Return Book

Date	Particulars	Credit Note No.	Details (₹)	Total Amt (₹)
2024				
Jul 1	**Shiv Shankar, Kolkata**			
	50 Shirts @ ₹ 600 per shirt		30,000	
	30 T-shirts @ ₹ 400 per t-shirt		12,000	42,000
Jul 8	**Ankit & Co., Mumbai**			
	15 Jeans @ ₹ 2,000 each		30,000	
	20 Trousers @ ₹ 200 each		4,000	
			34,000	
	(–) Trade Discount @ 10%		(3,400)	30,600
Jul 11	**Prema Stores, Ahmedabad**			
	25 Kurti @ ₹ 150 each		3,750	
	40 Saree @ ₹ 2,000 each		80,000	
			83,750	
	(–) Trade Discount @ 10%		(8,375)	75,375
Jul 15	**Kratika Stores, Mumbai**			
	10 Overcoat @ ₹ 1,000 each			10,000
Jul 31	Sales Return A/c Dr			1,57,975

JOURNAL

Date	Particulars	LF	Amt (Dr)	Amt (Cr)
2024				
Jul 31	Sales Return A/c Dr		1,57,975	
	To Shiv Shankar, Kolkata			42,000
	To Ankit & Co., Mumbai			30,600
	To Prema Stores, Ahmedabad			75,375
	To Kratika Stores, Mumbai			10,000
	(Being sales return for the month of July, 2024)			

Ledger Posting of Sales Return Book

Dr **Sales Return Account** Cr

Date	Particulars	JF	Amt (₹)	Date	Particulars	JF	Amt (₹)
2024							
Jul 31	To Sundry for the Month of July		1,57,975				

Dr **Shiv Shankar, Kolkata** Cr

Date	Particulars	JF	Amt (₹)	Date	Particulars	JF	Amt (₹)
				2024			
				Jul 1	By Sales Return A/c		42,000

Dr **Ankit & Co., Mumbai** Cr

Date	Particulars	JF	Amt (₹)	Date	Particulars	JF	Amt (₹)
				2024			
				Jul 8	By Sales Return A/c		30,600

Dr **Prema Stores, Ahmedabad** Cr

Date	Particulars	JF	Amt (₹)	Date	Particulars	JF	Amt (₹)
				2024			
				Jul 11	By Sales Return A/c		75,375

Dr **Kratika Stores, Mumbai** Cr

Date	Particulars	JF	Amt (₹)	Date	Particulars	JF	Amt (₹)
				2024 Jul 15	By Sales Return A/c		10,000

Journal Proper

Solved Question 21 Write necessary adjustment entries for the following transactions in the books of Palvender at the end of accounting year on 31st March, 2024.

(i) For March, 2024, salary of ₹ 5,000 is outstanding.
(ii) Prepaid insurance ₹ 3,000.
(iii) Closing stock ₹ 50,000.
(iv) Depreciate machine by ₹ 6,000.
(v) Accrued interest on fixed deposits ₹ 1,000.
(vi) Commission in advance ₹ 2,000.

Sol. **JOURNAL PROPER**

Date	Particulars	LF	Amt (Dr)	Amt (Cr)
(i)	Salary A/c Dr		5,000	
	To Outstanding Salary A/c			5,000
	(Being adjustment of salary due but not paid)			
(ii)	Prepaid Insurance A/c Dr		3,000	
	To Insurance A/c			3,000
	(Being adjusted prepaid insurance)			
(iii)	Closing Stock A/c Dr		50,000	
	To Trading A/c			50,000
	Or			
	Closing Stock A/c Dr		50,000	
	To Purchase A/c			50,000
	(Being closing stock adjusted)			
(iv)	Depreciation A/c Dr		6,000	
	To Machine A/c			6,000
	(Being depreciation charged on machine)			
(v)	Accrued Interest A/c Dr		1,000	
	To Interest A/c			1,000
	(Being accrued interest recorded)			
(vi)	Commission Received A/c Dr		2,000	
	To Advance Commission A/c			2,000
	(Being advance commission adjusted)			

Solved Question 22 Record the following transactions in the 'journal proper' of Shree Krishna Traders.

2024

(i) An old machinery was sold to Laxmi for ₹ 10,000 on credit.
(ii) Anil who owed us ₹ 50,000 was declared insolvent and 40% is received as full and final payment.
(iii) Goods worth ₹ 60,000 were destroyed by fire.
(iv) Insurance company admitted a fire insurance claim of ₹ 30,000.
(v) Proprietor withdrew for personal use cash ₹ 10,000 and goods ₹ 8,000.
(vi) A bill receivable for ₹ 20,000 was endorsed to Mr. Sharma.
(vii) Debtors include ₹ 5,000 due from Ajay, whereas creditors include ₹ 2,000 due to Ajay.
(viii) Salary and wages of ₹ 10,000 remain outstanding.
(ix) Insurance is prepaid to the extent of ₹ 1,500.
(x) Provide depreciation on furniture for ₹ 2,500.
(xi) Interest accrued on investment ₹ 400.

Sol.

Shri Krishna Traders
JOURNAL PROPER

Date	Particulars		LF	Amt (Dr)	Amt (Cr)
(i)	Laxmi	Dr		10,000	
	To Machinery A/c				10,000
	(Being old machinery sold on credit)				
(ii)	Bad Debts A/c	Dr		30,000	
	To Anil				30,000
	(Being bad debts written-off on Anil's insolvency)				
(iii)	Loss by Fire A/c	Dr		60,000	
	To Purchases A/c				60,000
	(Being goods destroyed by fire)				
(iv)	Insurance Company	Dr		30,000	
	To Loss by Fire A/c				30,000
	(Being insurance claim admitted by insurance company)				
(v)	Drawings A/c	Dr		8,000	
	To Purchases A/c				8,000
	(Being goods withdrawn for personal use)				
(vi)	Mr. Sharma	Dr		20,000	
	To Bills Receivable A/c				20,000
	(Being bills receivable endorsed to Mr. Sharma)				
(vii)	Creditors A/c	Dr		2,000	
	To Debtor's A/c				2,000
	(Being amount transferred from creditor to debtor account)				
(viii)	Salaries and Wages A/c	Dr		10,000	
	To Outstanding Salaries and Wages A/c				10,000
	(Being adjustment of salaries due but not paid)				
(ix)	Prepaid Insurance A/c	Dr		1,500	
	To Insurance A/c				1,500
	(Being adjustment of prepaid insurance premium)				
(x)	Depreciation A/c	Dr		2,500	
	To Furniture A/c				2,500
	(Being depreciation provided on furniture)				
(xi)	Accrued Interest A/c	Dr		400	
	To Interest A/c				400
	Being interest accrued on investment)				

Comprehensive Illustration

Solved Question 23 **Enter the following transactions in the proper subsidiary books, show the ledgers of Dishant, Raghav, Ronak & Co., Anuj and purchases account and balance the ledger account. The accounts are to be closed on 31st March, 2024.**

The following balances existed in the books of Khandelwal & Sons on 1st March, 2024

Assets : Cash in hand ₹ 1,50,000; Cash at bank ₹ 2,10,000; Debtors (Karun ₹ 60,000; Geeta ₹ 40,000); Stock ₹ 3,20,000 and Machinery ₹ 4,00,000.

Liabilities : Creditors (Avinash & Co. ₹ 70,000).

The following transactions took place during the month of March, 2024

Mar 2	**Deposited into bank ₹ 25,000.**
Mar 4	**Purchased from Raghav goods of the list price of ₹ 60,000 at 10% trade discount.**
Mar 5	**Returned to Raghav goods worth ₹ 8,000 (after deducting 10% trade discount).**
Mar 7	**Issued a cheque to Raghav in full settlement of his account after deducting cash discount @ 5%.**

Mar 10 Sold to Dishant goods worth ₹ 90,000.
Mar 12 Received cash ₹ 60,000 and cheque ₹ 8,000 from Dishant. The cheque was sent to bank on the same day. Discount allowed ₹ 1,000.
Mar 14 Purchased machinery from Ronak & Co. on credit for ₹ 45,000.
Mar 16 Khandelwal withdrew goods for his personal use ₹ 20,000
Mar 18 Sold to Anuj goods valued ₹ 32,000.
Mar 19 Issued cheque to Ronak & Co. ₹ 45,000.
Mar 20 Returned by Anuj goods worth ₹ 4,000.
Mar 21 Purchased goods from Gaurav for ₹ 80,000. Trade discount @ 10%.
Mar 22 Accepted a bill drawn by Gaurav for ₹ 72,000 at 1 month.
Mar 27 Received from Anuj ₹ 20,000. Discount allowed ₹ 100.
Mar 27 Goods purchased for cash ₹ 60,000.
Mar 28 Withdrew from bank ₹ 30,000.
Mar 29 Paid salaries by cheque ₹ 10,000.
Mar 30 Paid rent ₹ 6,600.
Mar 31 Received commission in cash ₹ 3,200.

Sol. Dr **Cash Book** Cr

Date	Particulars	LF	Cash (₹)	Bank (₹)	Date	Particulars	LF	Cash (₹)	Bank (₹)
2024					2024				
Mar 1	To Balance b/d		1,50,000	2,10,000	Mar 2	By Bank A/c	C	25,000	—
Mar 2	To Cash A/c	C	—	25,000	Mar 7	By Raghav (Note)		—	43,700
Mar 12	To Dishant		60,000	8,000	Mar 19	By Ronak & Co.		—	45,000
Mar 27	To Anuj		20,000	—	Mar 27	By Purchases A/c		60,000	—
Mar 28	To Bank A/c	C	30,000	—	Mar 28	By Cash A/c	C	—	30,000
Mar 31	To Commission A/c		3,200	—	Mar 29	By Salaries A/c		—	10,000
					Mar 30	By Rent A/c		6,600	—
					Mar 31	By Balance c/d		1,71,600	1,14,300
			2,63,200	2,43,000				2,63,200	2,43,000

Working Note		**Amt (₹)**
(Mar 7)	List Price	60,000
	(–) Trade Discount	(6,000)
	Net Price	54,000
	(–) Goods Returned	(8,000)
		46,000

Cash Discount = 46,000 × 5/100 = ₹ 2,300; Net Amount Paid = 46,000 – 2,300 = ₹ 43,700

Purchases Book

Date	Particulars	Invoice No.	LF	Details (₹)	Total Amt (₹)
2024					
Mar 4	Raghav			60,000	
	(–) Trade Discount @ 10%			(6,000)	54,000
Mar 21	Gaurav			80,000	
	(–) Trade Discount @ 10%			(8,000)	72,000
Jan 31	Purchases A/c Dr				1,26,000

Sales Book

Date	Particulars	Invoice No.	LF	Details (₹)	Total Amt (₹)
2024					
Mar 10	Dishant				90,000
Mar 18	Anuj				32,000
Mar 31	Sales A/c Cr				1,22,000

Purchases Return Book

Date	Particulars		Debit Note No.	LF	Details (₹)	Total Amt (₹)
2024						
Mar 5	Raghav					8,000
Mar 31	Purchases Return A/c	Cr				8,000

Sales Return Book

Date	Particulars		Credit Note No.	LF	Details (₹)	Total Amt (₹)
2024						
Mar 20	Anuj					4,000
Mar 31	Sales Return A/c	Dr				4,000

JOURNAL

Date	Particulars		LF	Amt (Dr)	Amt (Cr)
2024					
Mar 1	Cash A/c	Dr		1,50,000	
	Bank A/c	Dr		2,10,000	
	Karun	Dr		60,000	
	Geeta	Dr		40,000	
	Stock A/c	Dr		3,20,000	
	Machinery A/c	Dr		4,00,000	
	To Avinash & Co.				70,000
	To Capital A/c (Balancing Figure)				11,10,000
	(Being the last year's balances brought forward)				
Mar 7	Raghav	Dr		2,300	
	To Discount Received A/c				2,300
	(Being the discount received on payment made to Raghav)				
Mar 12	Discount Allowed A/c	Dr		1,000	
	To Dishant				1,000
	(Being the discount allowed to Dishant against payment received)				
Mar14	Machinery A/c	Dr		45,000	
	To Ronak & Co.				45,000
	(Being the machinery purchased on credit)				
Mar 16	Drawings A/c	Dr		20,000	
	To Purchases A/c				20,000
	(Being the goods withdrawn by the proprietor for personal use)				
Mar 22	Gaurav	Dr		72,000	
	To Bills Payable A/c				72,000
	(Being the bills accepted for 1 month tenure)				
Mar 27	Discount Allowed A/c	Dr		100	
	To Anuj				100
	(Being the discount allowed to Anuj against payment received)				

Ledger Posting

Dr **Dishant** Cr

Date	Particulars	JF	Amt (₹)	Date	Particulars	JF	Amt (₹)
2024				2024			
Mar 10	To Sales A/c		90,000	Mar 12	By Cash A/c		60,000
				Mar 12	By Bank A/c		8,000
				Mar 12	By Discount Allowed A/c		1,000
				Mar 31	By Balance c/d		21,000
			90,000				90,000
Apr 1	To Balance b/d		21,000				

Dr **Raghav** Cr

Date	Particulars	JF	Amt (₹)	Date	Particulars	JF	Amt (₹)
2024				2024			
Mar 5	To Purchases Return A/c		8,000	Mar 4	By Purchases A/c (60,000 – 6,000)		54,000
Mar 7	To Bank A/c		43,700				
Mar 7	To Discount Received A/c		2,300				
			54,000				54,000

Dr **Ronak & Co.** Cr

Date	Particulars	JF	Amt (₹)	Date	Particulars	JF	Amt (₹)
2024				2024			
Mar 19	To Sales A/c		45,000	Mar 14	By Machinery A/c		45,000
			45,000				45,000

Dr **Anuj** Cr

Date	Particulars	JF	Amt (₹)	Date	Particulars	JF	Amt (₹)
2024				2024			
Mar 18	To Sales A/c		32,000	Mar 20	By Sales Return A/c		4,000
				Mar 27	By Cash A/c		20,000
				Mar 27	By Discount Allowed A/c		100
				Mar 31	By Balance c/d		7,900
			32,000				32,000
Feb 1	To Balance b/d		7,900				

Dr **Purchases Account** Cr

Date	Particulars	JF	Amt (₹)	Date	Particulars	JF	Amt (₹)
2024				2024			
Mar 27	To Cash A/c		60,000	Mar 16	By Drawings A/c		20,000
Mar 31	To Sundries as per Purchases Book		1,26,000	Mar 31	By Balance c/d		1,66,000
			1,86,000				1,86,000

Missing Information

Solved Question 24 **An accountant of Samanta & Bros. prepared a cash book on the basis of following transactions. He left cash book incompleted. You are required to complete the cash book.**

2024

Apr 1	**Cash in hand ₹ 80,000 and cash at bank ₹ 60,000**
Apr 3	**Purchased goods worth ₹ 20,000. Paid only 50% by cash**
Apr 5	**Sold goods for ₹ 8,000. Received a cheque of ₹ 6,000 and balance in cash**
Apr 8	**Paid advance rent ₹ 500**
Apr 10	**Received a cheque of ₹ 4,000 after allowance of discount ₹ 300 from Aditya**
Apr 15	**Cash withdrawn ₹ 5,000 from bank, out of which ₹ 2,000 was for personal use**

Dr **Cash Book** (Double Column) Cr

Date	Particulars	Cash (₹)	Bank (₹)	Date	Particulars	Cash (₹)	Bank (₹)
2024				2024			
Apr 1	To Balance b/d	80,000	60,000	Apr 3	By ……	……	…
Apr 5	To ……	……	……	Apr 8	By ……	500	…
Apr 10	To Aditya	……	……	Apr 15	By ……	…	…
Apr 15	To ……	……	……	……	By ……	…	…
				Apr 30	By Balance c/d	…	…
		……	……			…	…

Sol.

Dr **Cash Book** (Double Column) Cr

Date	Particulars	Cash (₹)	Bank (₹)	Date	Particulars	Cash (₹)	Bank (₹)
2024				2024			
Apr 1	To Balance b/d	80,000	60,000	Apr 3	By **Purchase A/c**	**10,000**	—
Apr 5	To **Sales A/c**	**2,000**	**6,000**	Apr 8	By **Advance Rent A/c**	500	—
Apr 10	To Aditya	—	**4,000**	Apr 15	By **Cash A/c**	—	**3,000**
Apr 15	To **Bank A/c**	**3,000**	—	Apr 15	By **Drawings A/c**	—	**2,000**
				Apr 30	By **Balance c/d**	**74,500**	**65,000**
		85,000	**70,000**			**85,000**	**70,000**

Note Name of some accounts may be used by other names e.g. Advance rent as rent in advance, etc.

Solved Question 25 **Fill out the missing figures.**

Sales Book

Date	Particulars	Invoice No.	LF	Details (₹)	Sale Value (₹)	Output CGST (₹)	Output SGST (₹)	Output IGST (₹)	Total Amt (₹)
2024									
Apr 1	**Aditya & Sons**								
	100 pkts of Bread @ ₹ 10 each			1,000					
	(–) … Trade Discount			(100)					
				900					
	(+) 9% CGST			81					
	9% SGST			……					
				……	……	……	……	……	……
Apr 10	**Suman General Stores**								
	200 pkts of Toast @ ₹ 30 each			……					
	(–) 10% Trade Discount			(……)					
				……					
	(+) …… % CGST			486					
	…… % SGST			486					
				……	……	……	……	……	……
Apr 30	By Sales A/c Cr				……	……	……	……	……

Sol.

Sales Book

Date	Particulars	Invoice No.	LF	Details (₹)	Sale Value (₹)	Output CGST (₹)	Output SGST (₹)	Output IGST (₹)	Total Amt (₹)
2024									
Apr 1	**Aditya & Sons**								
	100 pkts of Bread @ ₹ 10 each	**115**		1,000					
	(–) **10%** Trade Discount			(100)					
				900					
	(+) 9% CGST			81					
	9% SGST			**81**					
				1,062	**900**	**81**	**81**	—	**1,062**
Apr 10	**Suman General Stores**								
	200 pkts of Toast @ ₹ 30 each			**6,000**					
	(–) 10% Trade Discount			**(600)**					
				5,400					
	(+) **9%** CGST			486					
	9% SGST			486					
				6,372	**5,400**	**486**	**486**	—	**6,372**
Apr 30	By Sales A/c Cr				**6,300**	**567**	**567**	—	**7,434**

Numerical Questions

Cash Book

1. **Enter the following transactions in Ayushi's single column cash book.**

2024

Apr 1	Cash in hand ₹ 40,000
Apr 3	Goods purchased ₹ 10,000
Apr 4	Goods sold ₹ 8,000
Apr 6	Sold goods on credit to Milky ₹ 6,000
Apr 8	Purchased goods from Seema ₹ 12,000
Apr 10	Received from Milky ₹ 5,800 in full settlement
Apr 15	Paid to Seema, ₹ 11,500 in full settlement
Apr 25	Paid office rent ₹ 6,000
Apr 30	Deposited cash into bank account in excess of ₹ 10,000

Ans. Total = ₹ 53,800; Deposited into bank = ₹ 16,300

2. **Enter the following transactions in a single column cash book.**

2024

Sept 1	Balance of cash ₹ 1,00,000
Sept 3	Bought a computer on credit from Ramya & Bros. ₹ 25,000
Sept 4	Purchased goods from Priyansh ₹ 20,000 with CGST and SGST @ 9% each
Sept 6	Advance paid for rent ₹ 8,000
Sept 8	Sold goods to Tarun for ₹ 50,000 and charged CGST and SGST @ 9% each
Sept 12	Paid ₹ 12,000 to Priyansh
Sept 15	Received ₹ 40,000 in cash and balance by a cheque from Tarun
Sept 17	Paid for travelling expenses ₹ 1,500
Sept 22	Loan taken from Bank of India ₹ 50,000. Received in bank account
Sept 26	Paid to Ramya & Bros. ₹ 24,500 in full settlement
Sept 30	Withdrawn from bank ₹ 5,000 for personal use and ₹ 45,000 for office use

Ans. Balance of cash = ₹ 1,39,000

3. **Enter the following transactions in a single column cash book.**

2024		**Amt (₹)**
Apr 1	Cash in hand	30,000
Apr 7	Cash sales	2,00,000
Apr 9	Purchase furniture	50,000
Apr 12	Deposited cash into bank	80,000
Apr 15	Purchase stationery	700
Apr 17	Advertisement expense paid in cash	1,000
Apr 20	Telephone expense paid in cash	2,000
Apr 22	Cash received from Radhika (a debtor)	40,000
Apr 25	Salary paid in cash	5,000
Apr 27	Cash withdrew for personal use	800

Ans. Balance of cash = ₹ 1,30,500

4. **Enter the following transactions in a single column cash book.**

2024

Mar 1	Mrs. Sonali commenced business with cash ₹ 3,00,000
Mar 2	Opened a bank account and deposited cash ₹ 80,000
Mar 5	Purchased typewriter ₹ 40,000
Mar 7	Bought goods against cash ₹ 70,000
Mar 10	Paid rent for ₹ 5,000
Mar 15	Commission received in cash ₹ 10,000
Mar 19	Cash sales ₹ 7,000
Mar 22	Withdrew cash from bank ₹ 8,000
Mar 28	Paid electricity bill ₹ 3,000
Mar 29	Paid wages in cash ₹ 10,000

Ans. Balance of cash = ₹ 1,17,000

5. **Enter the following transactions in a single column cash book of Ajay Traders.** Competency Based Que

2024		**Amt (₹)**
Apr 1	Cash in hand	22,500
Apr 2	Cash sales (CGST 9%, SGST 9%)	30,000
Apr 4	Received from Ram on behalf of Shyam	2,000
Apr 9	Paid to Laxman	4,500
	Discount received	50
Apr 12	Received from Bharat	4,900
	and discount allowed	100
Apr 20	Bought goods for cash (CGST 9%, SGST 9%)	15,000
Apr 21	Paid cartage (CGST 9%, SGST 9%)	1,000
Apr 23	Remitted to Supriya and discount	940
	allowed by Supriya	60
Apr 25	Received cash from Sunita	250
Apr 27	Borrowed from Vir	3,750
Apr 29	Received from Kabir	1,950
	discount allowed	50
Apr 30	Paid to Vish ₹ 1,350 in full settlement of his account of ₹ 1,500	

Ans. Cash balance = ₹ 45,080

6. Enter the following transactions in two column cash book with cash and bank column. Competency Based Que

2024		Amt (₹)
Apr 1	Cash in hand	70,000
Apr 1	Bank overdraft	15,000
Apr 2	Appointed a salesman for salary of ₹ 5,000 per month. Paid advance ₹ 2,000	
Apr 3	Rent paid ₹ 10,000 out of which 75% relates to proprietor's residence	
Apr 5	Purchased goods from Aryan	18,000
Apr 7	Received a cheque from Anuj after banking hours	16,000
Apr 10	Sold goods to Rohan for ₹ 22,000. Only half amount received by cheque	
Apr 15	Paid rent in advance	6,000
Apr 18	Proprietor withdrew ₹ 3,000 for travelling expense (personal) from bank account	
Apr 20	Cheque received from Anuj deposited into bank account	
Apr 22	Paid fire insurance premium ₹ 6,000. Out of which ₹ 1,500 belongs to next year	
Apr 30	Deposited cash into bank in excess of ₹ 20,000	

Ans. Cash balance = ₹ 20,000; Bank balance = ₹ 29,000

7. Prepare two column cash book from the following transactions. Consider CGST and SGST @ 9% each on sale and purchase of goods. Competency Based Que

2024	
Oct 1	Commenced business with cash ₹ 2,00,000
Oct 2	Deposited in current account ₹ 1,40,000
Oct 3	Bought goods by cheque ₹ 35,000
Oct 4	Purchased a machine for ₹ 10,000 and spent ₹ 1,000 on its installation
Oct 6	Transfer from bank account into petty cash account ₹ 2,000
Oct 8	Sold goods for cash ₹ 12,000 and cheque ₹ 8,000
Oct 10	Deposited above cheque into bank
Oct 12	Purchased goods from Soma ₹ 18,000
Oct 15	Settled Soma's account by cheque ₹ 17,400
Oct 18	Rent received in advance ₹ 3,000
Oct 20	Loan taken from Punjab National Bank ₹ 2,00,000. Amount received in bank account
Oct 26	Purchased debentures of ₹ 50,000 of Reliance Ltd. Payment was made from bank Account

Ans. Cash balance = ₹ 66,160 ; Bank balance = ₹ 2,38,020

8. Enter the following transactions in a cash book with cash and bank columns. Charge CGST and SGST @ 9% each on purchase and sale of goods. Competency Based Que

2024	
Feb 1	Cash in hand ₹ 30,000, bank ₹ 32,000
Feb 2	Sold goods for ₹ 16,000, received a cheque after allowing discount of 5%
Feb 3	Purchased goods from Aniket list price ₹ 40,000 less trade discount @ 20%and cash discount @ 5%. Paid only 50% amount by cash
Feb 5	Cheque received on 2nd February, deposited into bank
Feb 7	Received electricity bill of ₹ 2,000
Feb 9	Issued a demand draft of ₹ 3,000 in favour of Ramlal. Bank charged ₹ 100
Feb 11	Sold goods list price ₹ 20,000 less trade discount @ 10%. Received cheque and deposited into bank on 12th February
Feb 15	Withdrawn from bank for personal use ₹ 1,500
Feb 17	Received a cheque from Bhanu ₹ 2,000 against bad debt written-off in 2022-23
Feb 20	Paid to landlord Aakash, rent ₹ 3,000 by cash
Feb 24	Purchased goods from Garima Bros. for ₹ 10,000
Feb 28	Settled account of Garima Bros. by issuing a cheque

Ans. Cash balance = ₹ 9,064; Bank = ₹ 56,776

Hint Received electricity bill is assumed as outstanding.

9. Enter the following transactions in a double column cash book having cash and bank columns.

2024		Amt (₹)
May 1	Cash in hand	10,000
May 1	Cash at bank	16,000
May 3	Purchased goods by paying 60% by cheque and remaining by cash	12,000
May 5	Sold goods for cash to Ram	14,000
May 7	Returned goods to a creditor (Mohan)	1,000
May 8	Received a cheque for commission	2,000
May 10	Rent paid to Himani by cheque	500
May 14	Paid for telephone bill	300
May 16	Purchased goods from Varun	3,000
May 20	Paid to Varun in full settlement by cheque	2,800
May 23	Withdrew from bank for office use	1,000
May 25	Received commission in advance by a cheque	4,000
May 28	Paid charity	150
May 31	Outstanding telephone bill paid	200

Ans. Cash balance = ₹ 19,550; Bank balance = ₹ 10,500

10. Enter the following transactions in double column cash book.

2024		Amt (₹)
Jan 1	Cash in hand	1,50,000
Jan 1	Cash at bank	90,000
Jan 5	Bought goods including CGST and SGST 9% each	1,06,200
Jan 9	Bought machine against cheque	10,000
Jan 12	Sold goods for cash including CGST and SGST 9% each	11,800
Jan 17	Cash deposited into bank	50,000
Jan 19	Paid travelling expense by cheque	800
Jan 20	Purchase calculator	600
Jan 21	Paid salary	3,000
Jan 25	Paid wages by cheque	10,000
Jan 28	Withdrew from bank	30,000

Ans. Cash balance = ₹ 2,000; Bank balance = 1,19,200

11. From the following cash and bank transactions of Mr. Samrat, owner of Samrat Stationery House, prepare a two column cash book and post them into ledger. Competency Based Que

2024		Amt (₹)
Apr 1	Cash in hand	32,000
	Cash at bank	46,500
Apr 3	Purchased goods from M/s Arun for ₹ 5,000 and paid by cheque	
Apr 9	Cash purchases ₹ 4,000 less trade discount @ 5%	
Apr 10	Purchased postage stamps	250
Apr 12	Proceeds of cash sales of ₹ 35,000 deposited into bank	
Apr 14	Drew cash for personal use	3,500
Apr 15	Received from Manan cash ₹ 1,500 and cheque ₹ 2,500, both deposited into bank allowed ₹ 250 as cash discount	
Apr 15	Withdrew from bank for office use	3,500
Apr 16	Paid wages ₹ 1,500 and rent ₹ 2,500	
Apr 19	Paid M/s Vrijesh by cheque, cash discount allowed by him ₹ 500	12,000
Apr 23	Received a cheque from Nitin for sale of old goods	4,000
Apr 25	Paid M/s Arun cash ₹ 3,750 and ₹ 1,800 by a cheque, received cash discount ₹ 125	
Apr 26	Karan, a customer, deposited into bank	4,000
Apr 29	Withdrew from bank for personal use	1,000
Apr 30	Bank charged commission	1,000
Apr 30	Withdrew from bank for paying income tax	2,500

Ans. Cash balance = ₹ 20,200; Bank balance = ₹ 66,700

12. Prepare a petty cash book on the imprest system from the following

2024		Amt (₹)
Apr 1	Received for petty cash	10,000
Apr 2	Paid metro fare	100
Apr 3	Paid cartage	250
Apr 4	Paid for postage	600
Apr 5	Paid for stationery	200
Apr 5	Paid wages for casual labourers	500
Apr 6	Paid auto charges	100
Apr 7	Paid bus fare	150
Apr 7	Paid for repairs of chairs	400
Apr 8	Paid cartage	600
Apr 9	Paid for conveyance charges	800
Apr 9	Paid telephone bill	400
Apr 9	Paid for postage	200

Ans. Petty cash in hand = ₹ 5,700

13. Prepare a petty cash book.

2024		Amt (₹)
Jul 1	Received for petty cash book	10,000
Jul 3	Paid cartage	800
Jul 4	Paid bus fare,	400
	Speed post	200
Jul 6	Paid for stationery	700
Jul 7	Paid for courier services	300
Jul 9	Paid for taxi fare,	800
	Wages	300
Jul 10	Paid for wages,	400
	Charity	500
Jul 11	Paid for newspaper bill	600
Jul 15	Paid for Soap,	320
	Postage	300
Jul 16	Paid for postage	780
Jul 17	Paid for repair	500
Jul 19	Paid for refreshment to customers	900

Ans. Balance = ₹ 2,200

Purchase Book

14. Enter the following transactions in the purchase book of ABC Cloth House, Agra. Competency Based Que

2024	
Apr 5	Purchased from XYZ & Sons, Agra vide invoice no. 220
	200 metre silk cloth @ ₹ 300 per metre
	100 metre cotton cloth @ ₹ 400 per metre
	Trade discount @ 10% and CGST and SGST @ 6% each
Apr 12	Purchased from Manipal & Bros, Agra vide invoice no. 340
	100 five lining shirts @ ₹ 500 per shirt
	200 trousers fabric @ ₹ 600 per trouser
	Trade discount @ 20%, CGST and SGST @ 6% each
Apr 18	Purchased from Divya Traders, Agra
	10 tubelights for showroom @ ₹ 200 per tubelight
Apr 24	Purchased from Sunder & Sons for cash
	50 metre woolen cloth @ ₹ 200 per metre

Ans. Total purchase = ₹ 2,26,000; Total = ₹ 2,53,120

15. Enter the following transactions in purchase book of Brahma & Bros dealing in electrical items, Gurugram (Haryana), assuming CGST and SGST @ 6% each.

2024	
Jul 1	Purchased following items from PQ Electric Store, Gurugram on credit (Invoice no. 320)
	20 table fans @ ₹ 2,500 each
	100 bulbs ₹ 40 each
	Trade discount @ 10%

Jul 9 Bought goods from AB Lights, XYZ Road, Gurugram on credit (Invoice no. 1140)
15 ceiling fans @ ₹ 2,000 each
20 electric irons @ ₹ 500 each
Trade discount @ 20%

Jul 15 Bought goods from Sujata & Sons, Gurugram for cash
10 ceiling fans @ 2,000 each

Jul 24 Bought from Khushbu Traders, Gurugram on credit (Invoice no. 4450)
10 chairs @ ₹ 500 each

Ans. Purchase = ₹ 1,00,600; Total = ₹ 1,12,672

16. Enter the following transactions in the purchase journal (book) of M/s Gupta Stationery Traders of July, 2024. Competency Based Que

Jul 1 Bought from Rahul Traders as per Invoice no. 20041
40 registers @ ₹ 60 each
80 gel pens @ ₹ 15 each
50 note books @ ₹ 20 each
Trade discount @ 10%

Jul 15 Bought from Global Stationers as per Invoice no. 1132
40 ink pads @ ₹ 8 each
50 files @ ₹ 10 each
20 colour books @ ₹ 20 each
Trade discount @ 5%

Jul 23 Purchased from Lamba Furniture as per Invoice no. 3201
2 chairs @ ₹ 600 per chair
1 table @ 1,000 per table

Jul 25 Bought from Mumbai Traders as per Invoice no. 1111
10 paper rim @ ₹ 100 each
400 drawing sheets @ 3 each
20 packet water colour @ 40 each

Jul 26 Bought from Mona Lamp, Saket, for cash (Invoice no. 705)
5 Electric irons @ ₹ 175 each

Jul 28 Bought from Innovation Furniture Co. Kankerkhera on credit (Invoice no. 3450)
12 chairs @ ₹ 200 each
2 tables @ 1,000 each

Ans. Total purchase = ₹ 8,299

17. Prepare a purchase book in the books of M/s XYZ Furnitures, Meerut (UP) from the following transactions assuming CGST @6% and SGST @ 6%.

2024

Apr 5 Bought from Zen & Co., Agra (UP)
20 chairs @ ₹ 2,000 each
5 tables @ ₹6,000 each
Trade discount @ 20%

Apr 10 Purchased from Ram & Sons, Lucknow (UP)
5 almirahs @ ₹ 12,000 each
2 revolving chairs @ ₹ 20,000 each
Trade discount @ 10%

Apr 14 Purchased form Surya Traders, Meerut (UP)
80 desks @ ₹ 2,500 each
10 sofa sets @ ₹ 20,000 each
Trade discount @ 15%

Apr 20 Purchased for cash from Veer & Co, Mumbai
4 tables @ ₹ 5,000 each

Apr 25 Bought furniture for office use from Delhi on credit
5 chairs @ ₹ 2,500 each
2 tables @ ₹ 5,000 each

Ans. Purchase = ₹ 3,86,000; Total = ₹ 4,32,320

18. Enter the following transactions in purchase book of the M/s Gupta Furniture, Mumbai and pass the journal entry of purchase book.

2024

Apr 1 Purchase goods from Shree Furniture, Kanpur on credit (Invoice no. 510)
20 chairs @ ₹ 400, plus CGST and SGST @ 6% each.
30 desk chairs @ ₹ 200 each, plus CGST and SGST @ 6% each. Trade discount @ 10%

Apr 10 Purchase furniture from Birla Furniture, Delhi vide Invoice no. 210.
10 dresser @ ₹ 500 each, trade discount @ 10%, plus IGST @ 12%
20 bed @ ₹ 2,000 each, trade discount @ 10% and plus IGST @ 12%

Apr 16 Purchase furniture from Vishal Furniture, Kota vide Invoice no. 125
5 fans @ ₹ 200 each plus IGST @ 12%
20 book-self @ ₹ 3,000 each plus IGST @ 12%
Trade discount @ 10%

Ans. Purchase = ₹ 1,08,000; Input CGST = ₹ 756; Input SGST = ₹ 756; Input IGST = ₹ 11,448; Total = ₹ 1,20,960

Sales Book

19. From the following transaction of M/s Sharma Sales, Mumbai. Prepare sales book.

2024

Mar 1 Sold to M/s Rakesh Garment, vide Invoice no. 2005
6 t-shirts for ₹ 2,000 per t-shirt less trade discount @ 5% and IGST is charged 12%

Mar 4 Sold to M/s Suresh Garment, Kolkata vide Invoice no. 2006
20 jeans @ ₹ 500 per jeans less trade discount @ 5% and charged CGST and SGST @ 6% each

Mar 5 Sold to M/s Sohan Garments, Delhi Invoice no. 2007
10 trousers @ ₹ 200 per trouser less trade discount @ 5% charged IGST @ 12%

Also, show the journal entry for the entries recorded in the sales book.

Ans. Sales = ₹ 22,800; Output CGST = ₹ 570 ; Output SGST = ₹ 570; Output IGST = ₹ 1,596; Total = ₹ 25,536

20. **Prepare the sales book from the following transaction of M/s Hari & Co., Delhi**

2024

Jun 1 Sold to M/s Sharma Furniture House, Chandigarh
80 chairs @ ₹ 800 per chairs
50 tables @ ₹ 600 per tables
Trade discount @ 10%

Jun 4 Sold to M/s Ajit Singh & Sons, Kolkata
100 desks @ ₹ 1,000 per desk
120 chairs @ ₹ 1,500 per chair
Trade discount @ 5%

Jun 10 Sold to M/s Puran Chand Furniture House, Ahmedabad.
20 sofa sets @ ₹ 75,000 each
10 almirahs @ 2,000 each
25 round tables @ 4,000 each
Trade discount @ 20%

Ans. Total of sales = ₹ 16,46,600

21. **Record the following transactions in the sales book of Bablu Electronics, Patna (Bihar) assuming CGST and SGST @ 6% each.** **Competency Based Que**

2024

Aug 1 Sold to Alok Electricals, Patna
300 metre cable @ ₹ 20 per metre
100 holders @ ₹ 10 per holder
Trade discount @ 5%

Aug 5 Sold to Gagan Shop of Electricals, Agra (UP)
10 ceiling fans @ ₹ 1,000 each
6 table fans @ ₹ 500 each
Trade discount @ 5%

Aug 18 Sold a chair of office to Raman & Co. on credit for ₹ 2,000

Aug 20 Sold for cash 100 bulbs @ ₹ 50 each to Garima & Bros.

Ans. Sales = ₹ 19,000; Total = ₹ 21,820

Purchase Return Book

22. **Write up purchase return book of Aradhana Stores, Delhi for July 2024.**

2024

Jul 4 Returned goods to Shubham Brothers, Delhi, purchased for ₹ 10,000

Jul 8 Returned goods to JK & Sons, Aligarh of ₹ 8,000

Jul 12 Returned goods to Aniket & Bros. of ₹ 4,000

Ans. Total of purchase return = ₹ 22,000

23. **Record the following in purchase return book and post them in ledger book.**

2024

May 10 Returned 4 computer purchased from M/s Shiva Electronics at the list price of ₹ 5,000 per machine less trade discount @ 20%, CGST and SGST was paid @ 6% each

May 24 Returned 5 air conditioner from M/s Ganesh Electronic @ ₹ 30,000 each plus IGST @ 12%

Ans. Total = ₹ 1,85,920 ; Purchase return = ₹ 1,66,000; Input CGST = ₹ 960 ; Input SGST = ₹ 960; Input IGST = ₹ 18,000

Sales Return Book

24. **Record the following transaction of Shyam & Co. Delhi in the return inward book and post these transaction into the ledger account.**

2024

Jan 1 Manav & Co., Mumbai returned 500 paper sheet sold @ ₹ 50 per sheet. Less trade discount @ 10% and plus IGST @ 12%

Jan 25 Shivam and Co., Ghaziabad returned 300 pen @ ₹ 55 per pen, plus CGST and SGST @ 6% each

Ans. Sales return = ₹ 39,000; Output CGST = ₹ 990 ; Output SGST = ₹ 990; Output IGST = ₹ 2,700 ; Total = ₹ 43,680

25. **Prepare sales return book in the books of Hariom Das & Co. Rajkot, Gujarat from the following transactions, assuming CGST and SGST @ 6% each.**

2024

Nov 1 Goods returned by Krishna & Bros, Surat (Gujarat)
100 shirts @ ₹ 200 per shirt less trade discount @ 15%

Nov 6 Goods returned being defective by Radhey & Sons for ₹ 5,000

Nov 20 Allowance allowed to Murari & Sons, Jamnagar (Gujarat) on account of mistake in the invoice ₹ 1,500

Ans. Sales return = ₹ 23,500; Total = ₹ 26,320

Journal Proper

26. **From the following information available on 31st March, 2024, pass necessary adjustment entries for the year ending on that date.**

(i) Accrued interest ₹ 600.
(ii) Wages for March, 2024 was outstanding ₹ 9,000.
(iii) Insurance prepaid ₹ 2,000.
(iv) Commission due to manager @ 5% on net profit after charging such commission. The profit before charging such commission was ₹ 1,26,000.
(v) Interest due on loan taken from SBI amounted to ₹ 2,000 was outstanding.

Ans. Total of journal proper = ₹ 19,600

27. Write journal entries in 'journal proper' of Tanmay & Bros.

2024

Apr 5 A machinery worth ₹ 60,000 was purchased on credit from Aniket.

Apr 7 Vijay who owed us ₹ 20,000 was declared insolvent and 60% is received as final settlement.

Apr 8 Depreciation charged on machinery ₹ 5,000.

Apr 9 Goods worth ₹ 8,000 was destroyed by fire.

Apr 10 A bills receivable for ₹ 5,000 endorsed to Mr. Kamal.

Apr 15 Salary outstanding ₹ 4,000.

Apr 17 Insurance prepaid at the end of the year was ₹ 2,500.

Apr 20 Goods costing ₹ 4,000 withdrawn for personal use.

Apr 22 Insurance company accepted a claim of ₹ 8,000.

Apr 25 Goods costing ₹ 7,500 was given as charity.

Ans. Total = ₹ 1,12,000

28. Enter the following transactions in journal proper of Komal Sharma (Proprietor). **Competency Based Que**

(i) Interest accrued ₹ 5,000.

(ii) Rent not paid (Rent outstanding) ₹ 1,000.

(iii) Wages for March, 2016 outstanding ₹ 20,000.

(iv) Goods withdrawn by proprietor for personal use ₹ 5,000.

(v) Insurance prepaid ₹ 3,000.

(vi) Purchase of machine on credit for ₹ 10,000 from Ram Sons.

(vii) Rent received in advance ₹ 6,000.

(viii) Depreciate motor car with book value ₹ 1,00,000 @ 10% per annum for one year.

(ix) Depreciation on furniture ₹ 10,000.

(x) Commission due to Manager 6% on net profit after charging such commission. The profit before charging such commission was ₹ 2,12,000.

(xi) Interest due on loan but not paid. Loan of ₹ 3,00,000 was taken at 9% per annum; 9 months before end of the year.

Ans. Total = ₹ 96,250

Hint Entry (vii) will not be recorded in journal proper. It will be recorded in cash book.

$$\text{Commission} = ₹\ 2,12,000 \times \frac{6}{100} = ₹\ 12,000$$

Comprehensive Questions

29. Record the following transactions of Zen Bros. in the proper books, post them into a ledger and balance the ledger account **Competency Based Que**

2022

Jan 1 **Assets** Cash in hand ₹ 8,500; Cash at bank ₹ 1,40,000; Stock of goods ₹ 2,20,000; Due from Mia ₹ 30,000 and Deep Chand ₹ 24,000; Furniture and equipment ₹ 3,00,000

Liabilities Due to Sia ₹ 15,000

Jan 2 Withdrawn from bank ₹ 20,000

Jan 4 Paid salaries ₹ 22,000

Jan 6 Sold goods to Tia
60 metres silk @ ₹ 150 per metre
100 metres cotton @ ₹ 70 per metre
Trade discount @ $12\frac{1}{2}$%

Jan 8 Tia returned 40 metres cotton

Jan 9 Received full payment from Mia by cheque, sent it to bank, discount allowed 3%

Jan 10 Purchased from Kia
300 metres cotton @ ₹ 60 per metre
500 metres silk @ ₹ 120 per metre
Trade discount @ 10%

Jan 12 Sold goods to Kia for cash ₹ 16,000

Jan 13 Accepted a bill for ₹ 25,000 for 30 days drawn by Kia

Jan 15 Gave cheque to Kia for ₹ 45,000, discount allowed by him ₹ 200

Jan 18 Paid to Sia ₹ 14,850 after receiving discount of 1%

Jan 20 Zen took away 5 metres silk costing ₹ 100 per metre for his personal use

Jan 24 Paid rent by cheque ₹ 2,000

Jan 25 Received from Tia ₹ 11,000 in full settlement of his account

Jan 27 Old newspapers sold for cash ₹ 400

Jan 27 Paid for stationery and postage ₹ 500

Jan 28 Sold 400 metres silk @ ₹ 160 per metre to Zen

Jan 31 Received cash ₹ 40,000 from Zen and also received a B/R from him for the balance amount due from him for 2 months

Ans. Cash balance = ₹ 58,550; Bank = ₹ 1,02,100; Total of purchase book = ₹ 70,200; Sales book = ₹ 78,000; Sales return book = ₹ 2,450; Journal proper = ₹ 7,73,800

30. On 1st July, 2024, Vignesh of Meerut started business with a capital of ₹ 1,00,000 and entered into following transactions.
Pass the following transactions through proper books to the ledger. The cash book must be balanced.

Competency Based Que

2024		Amt (₹)
Jul 1	Opened a bank account and deposited	22,000
	Purchased goods for cash	12,000
	Purchased a computer for office from Kiran	22,500
	Purchased furniture for shop	12,000
	Sold goods to Aman, Agra	8,000
July 3	Bought goods from Mohan, Delhi	12,000
Jul 5	Bought stationery and paid by cash	500
Jul 7	Received cash from Aman, Agra	7,700
	Discount allowed to him	300
Jul 10	Sold goods to Samiran, Jaipur	6,500
Jul 12	Samiran returned goods supplied on 10th July	1,200
Jul 14	Paid cash into bank	2,000
Jul 16	Paid wages	3,500

Jul 18	Bought a table for office from Raghav Furniture Co.	1,600
Jul 20	Paid salaries	1,800
Jul 21	Paid to Mohan by cheque in full settlement	11,800
Jul 22	Sold goods to Kunal, Delhi	8,000
Jul 23	Received balance amount from Samiran by cheque	
Jul 24	Bought goods from Kapil, Mathura	4,000
Jul 26	Withdrew from bank for personal use	900
Jul 28	Salary outstanding	600

Ans. Cash balance = ₹ 53,900; Bank balance = ₹ 16,600 ; Purchase = ₹ 16,000; Sales = ₹ 22,500; Sales return = ₹ 1,200; Journal proper = ₹ 25,200

31. Record the following transactions of Madhav & Sons (oil trader) in the proper books. **Competency Based Que**

2024

Feb 1 **Assets** Cash in hand ₹ 13,000; Cash at bank ₹ 80,000; Stock ₹ 40,000; Debtors (Aavya ₹ 15,000, Kavya ₹ 16,000); Furniture ₹ 1,20,000.
Liabilities Creditors (Vandana ₹ 17,500; Preeti ₹ 12,500); Outstanding salary ₹ 4,500.

Feb 3 Withdrawn from bank for personal use ₹ 2,500 and for office use ₹ 20,000.

Feb 5 Paid for stationeries ₹ 800.

Feb 7 Sold goods to Moon Traders.
100 litre mustard oil @ ₹ 150 per litre
50 litre refined oil ₹ 200 per litre
Trade discount @ 10%

Feb 9 Moon Traders returned 20 litres mustard oil.

Feb 10 Paid to Vandana ₹ 16,500 in full settlement by cheque.

Feb 12 Received cash from Aavya ₹ 14,500 in full settlement. Cash deposited in bank account on same day.

Feb 15 Purchased from Alka Traders
100 packs of refined oil @ ₹ 180 per pack
50 litres mustard oil @ ₹ 130 per litre
Trade discount @ 10%

Feb 16 Sold goods to Megha for cash ₹ 3,000.

Feb 17 A bill for ₹ 4,000 drawn by Alka Traders accepted.

Feb 18 Paid to Preeti ₹ 6,000 by cheque.

Feb 19 Paid rent ₹ 2,500 by cash.

Feb 20 Received the amount due from Kavya after allowing cash discount @ 2%

Feb 21 Sold an old furniture for ₹ 4,000

Feb 23 Sold 20 packs of refined oil @ ₹ 220 per pack to Ajay Kirana Store.

Feb 28 Purchased stationery on credit ₹ 500 from Raghav & Bros.

Ans. Capital = ₹ 2,49,500; Cash balance = ₹ 52,380; Bank balance = ₹ 49,500 ; Sales book = ₹ 26,900 ; Sales return book = ₹ 2,700; Purchase book = 22,050; Journal proper total = 2,90,320

32. Prepare returns inward and returns outward books of Varun, Agra from the following transactions. **Competency Based Que**

2024

Sept 1 Kishore & Sons, Agra returned
10 pairs of sandals being not as per order @ ₹ 500 per pair
Trade discount @ 10%

Sept 5 Returned to Raghav Shoes Pvt. Ltd, Mathura
50 pairs of leather shoes @ ₹ 400 per pair
Trade discount @ 10%

Sept 15 Ahuja & Sons, Aligarh returned 20 pairs of chappals sold to them @ ₹ 1,000 per pair
Trade discount @ 10%

Sept 24 Returned to Kataria Shoes Pvt. Ltd, Delhi
200 pairs of sports shoes @ ₹ 500 per pair
Trade discount @ 10%

Ans. Sales return = ₹ 22,500; Purchase return = ₹ 1,08,000

33. Prepare return books of Karma & Bros, Agra (UP) from the following transactions and assuming CGST and SGST @ 6% each.

2024

Apr 5 Returned to Aman & Co., Mathura (UP)
4 bags of wheat @ ₹ 300 each
10 bags of rice @ ₹ 500 each
Trade discount @ 10%

Apr 8 Goods received as return from Shyama Kirana Store, Agra (UP)
5 bags of rice @ ₹ 600 each

Apr 10 Returned to Vijay & Sons, Haridwar (UP)
20 bags of wheat @ ₹ 300 each
Trade discount @ 10%

Apr 25 Anil, Aligarh returned to Karma & Bros.
5 bags of rice @ 600 each

Ans. Purchase return = ₹ 10,980; Sales return = ₹ 6,000

Missing Information

34. Complete the given cash book prepared by an accountant of a firm. Transactions are given below **Competency Based Que**

2024

Jun 1 Cash in hand ₹ 45,000
Cash at bank ₹ 30,000

Jun 4 Purchased goods for cash ₹ 15,000 and a computer from Kiran ₹ 28,000

Jun 6 Additional capital introduced by proprietor in cash ₹ 65,000

Jun 8 Deposited in bank account ₹ 40,000

Jun 12 Paid cash for stamps ₹ 600

Jun 14 Paid salary in advance by cheque ₹ 2,500

Jun 16 Sold goods list price ₹ 20,000, less trade discount @ 10% and cash discount @ 5%. Only 1/4th amount was received by cheque

Jun 20 Paid to Kiran in full settlement, discount received 5%

Cash Book

Dr | | | | | | | Cr

Date	Particulars	Cash (₹)	Bank (₹)	Date	Particulars	Cash (₹)	Bank (₹)
2024				2024			
Jun 1	To Balance b/d	45,000	30,000	Jun 4	By ...	15,000	...
Jun 6	To ...	65,000	...	Jun 8	By ...	40,000	...
Jun 8	To ...	...	40,000	Jun 12	By Stamps A/c	600	...
Jun 16	To ...	...	...	Jun 14	By Advance Salary A/c	...	...
				Jun 20	By Kiran	...	...
				June 30	By Balance c/d	...	...
		...	...			...	...

Ans. Cash balance = 32,075; Bank balance = ₹ 45,000

35. Fill out the missing figures. **Competency Based Que**

Purchase Book

Date	Particulars	Invoice No.	LF	Details (₹)	Sale Value (₹)	Input CGST (₹)	Input SGST (₹)	Total Amt (₹)
2024								
Feb 1	**Ram & Bros.**							
	20 jeans @ 1,000 each	120		20,000				
	(−) 10% trade discount			(...)				
	(+) 9% CGST			...				
	9% SGST			...				
				...	...	...	...	...
Feb 5	**Damini Garments**							
	100 shirts @ ₹ 250 each	118		25,000				
	(−) 10% trade discount			(...)				
	(+) 9% CGST			...				
	9% SGST			...	...	...	...	...
				...				
Feb 29	To ... A/c Dr			...	...	...	...	...

Ans. Purchase = ₹ 40,500; Total = ₹ 47,790

Theoretical Questions

Short Answer Type Questions

1. What are special purpose books? **NCERT**

Ans. Special purpose subsidiary books are those books in which the transactions of similar nature are recorded. For a large business organisation it is not possible to journalise each transaction, thus, journal is sub-divided into subsidiary books in which transactions of similar nature are recorded.

These books are also called books of original entry as ledger accounts are prepared from the transactions recorded in these books and for these transactions journal entry is not passed. All the transactions of purchases, sales, cash are recorded in their respective books, such as purchase book, sales book, etc.

2. Explain the need for drawing up the special purpose books. NCERT

Ans. The needs for drawing up the special purpose books are as follows

(i) **Quick and Efficient Recording**
It is a time consuming process to record all the transactions in a journal. If there are separate books, then recording of transactions can be done more efficiently and timely. So, the need of special purpose books arises.

(ii) **Repetitive Nature**
In every business, some transactions are similar and repetitive in nature. It will be more convenient to record all similar transactions at one place. e.g. All credit sales are recorded in the sales book.

(iii) **Economical**
It is more economical as recording through the special purpose books saves time and also enhances the efficiency of accountants and clerks.

(iv) **Easy Posting**
If similar transactions are recorded at one place, positing becomes easier.

(v) **Complete Information at One Place**
All information related to purchases, sales, cash receipts, payments, etc. are easily available.

3. Describe the advantages of sub-dividing the journal. NCERT

Ans. The various advantages of sub-dividing the journal are

(i) **Division of Work**
In place of one journal, many special journals are prepared. This results in division of work among various executives.

(ii) **Specialisation**
If a particular task is handled by a particular executive, then this leads to specialisation and increases efficiency.

(iii) **Time Saving**
Dividing journal into different categories means different executives can work simultaneously on different journals. This will increase the speed of work and will save time.

(iv) **Easy Access to Desired Information**
Transactions are recorded on the basis of their nature i.e. purchase transactions in purchase book, sales transactions in sales book, etc. This facilitates easy and quick accessibility to particular type of transactions.

(v) **Quick Checking**
In case of errors in recording, it is easier to find out the reasons of errors.

4. Define the purpose of maintaining subsidiary journal. NCERT

Ans. The purpose of maintaining subsidiary journal are given below

(i) It saves time and efforts in recording.

(ii) It enables division of work, leading to an enhancement of efficiency and effectiveness, as particular accountant takes care of particular books.

(iii) It also makes each accountant more responsible and accountable for the books assigned to them.

(iv) It records routine and repetitive transactions at one place, which leads to easy accessibility of information.

5. Briefly state how the cash book is both journal and a ledger. NCERT; Competency Based Que

Or **Explain the statement 'cash book is a journalised ledger'.**

Ans. Cash book is a journal since the transactions are recorded in it for the first time from the source documents and from there these are posted to the respective accounts in the ledger.

The cash book is also a ledger in the sense that it serves the purpose of a cash account also. When a cash book is prepared, no separate cash account is opened in the ledger. As such, the cash book is a journal, as well as, a ledger and hence it may be called a journalised ledger.

6. How does a cash book serves a dual purpose?

Or **"Cash book is both a subsidiary book and principal book." Comment.** Competency Based Que

Ans. Cash book achieves a dual purpose. It is both a subsidiary book (book of original entry) and principal book. When a cash book is maintained, transactions of cash are not recorded in the journal. As all the cash transactions are recorded for the first time in the cash book, it is therefore a book of original entry.

Also, when a cash book is prepared, cash account in the ledger is not prepared. In this way, cash book represents the cash accounts and hence, becomes the principal book of accounts. As such, the cash book is a subsidiary book as well as principal book.

7. What are the advantages of having a cash book?

Ans. (i) Both cash and bank transactions can be entered in the cash book.

(ii) It enables a businessman to know the balance of cash in hand and at bank at any point of time.

(iii) It gives information about daily receipts, payments and the closing cash and bank balance at the end of each day.

(iv) Since cash account is not opened in the ledger, it prevents the size of ledger from becoming two voluminous.

8. In financial accounting there is a specific type of entry that affects both the cash and bank columns within a double column cash book. Explain. Also how does this entry impacts the overall balancing of the book? Competency Based Que

Or **What is contra entry? How can you deal with this entry while preparing double column cash.** NCERT

Ans. Contra entries mean entries that are made on both sides of cash book. In a two column cash book, there are some transactions that relate to both cash and bank. Such transactions are entered on both sides of the cash book. Such entries are known as contra entries and are not posted into the ledger. Against such entries, the letter 'C' is written in the LF column to indicate that these are contra transactions. e.g. Cash deposited into the bank.

As the cash book with cash and bank columns is a combined cash and bank account, both the aspects of the transaction will be entered in the same book. On the debit side 'To Cash A/c' will be entered in the particulars column and the amount will be entered in the bank column. On the credit side 'By Bank A/c' will be entered in the particulars column and the amount will be entered in the cash column.

9. What is petty cash book? How is it prepared? NCERT

Ans. It is the book which is used for the purpose of recording the payment of petty cash expenses.

Petty cash book is prepared by petty cashier to record petty expenses (expenses of small amounts). This book is prepared to save valuable time of main (head) cashier from bothering about small and irrelevant cash expenses. Petty cash book can be prepared according to the ordinary system or according to the imprest system.

10. Write the advantages of petty cash book. NCERT

Ans. Some advantages of petty cash book are as follows

(i) Maintaining petty cash book is simple and does not require any specialised, knowledge of accounting.

(ii) Petty cash book is maintained by the petty cashier, therefore efforts and time of the chief/head cashier is saved.

(iii) The chances of fraud minimises, as each petty expense is supported by a voucher.

(iv) Petty expenses are maintained within the limit of imprest amount so the petty cashier can never spend more than the available petty cash with him.

(v) Head cashier can keep a close watch time to time on the amount paid to petty cashier and all payment made by him.

11. Name the books of original entry where the following transactions will be recorded with reasons thereof Competency Based Que

(i) Goods purchased from Ram Lal for ₹ 5,000 on credit.

(ii) Provision for doubtful debts created @ 5% on debtors with books value of ₹ 10,000.

(iii) Defective goods sold to Babita on credit worth ₹ 4,000 were returned by her.

(iv) Purchased furniture on credit from Mr Ratan Singh for ₹ 15,000 for use in the business.

Ans. (i) Purchases book because it is credit purchase of goods.

(ii) Journal proper because it will not be recorded in any other subsidiary books.

(iii) Sales return book because it is return of goods sold.

(iv) Journal proper because it is credit purchase of asset.

12. Mention the subsidiary books in which following transactions are recorded along with reason thereof Competency Based Que

(i) Purchase of furniture on credit for use in shop

(ii) Sale of goods on credit

(iii) Goods returned by debtors

(iv) Purchase of stock on credit

(v) Providing for interest on capital to proprietor

(vi) Goods returned to creditors

(vii) Sale of goods for cash

Ans. (i) Journal proper because purchase of fixed assets on credit is recorded in journal proper.

(ii) Sales book because sales book records credit sales of goods.

(iii) Sales return book because goods returned by customer are recorded in sales return book.

(iv) Purchases book because purchases book records credit purchases of goods.

(v) Journal proper because it is an adjustment entry and adjustment entries are recorded in journal proper.

(vi) Purchases return book because it records goods returned by the firm to its suppliers.

(vii) Cash book because cash book records cash receipts and cash payments.

13. Is it correct that total of the purchase invoices recorded in the purchases book is posted to debit side of the purchases account in the ledger and credited to the accounts of suppliers? Competency Based Que

Ans. Yes, purchase is an expense account therefore, following the rule 'increase in expenses is debited', purchases account is debited.

Since, the purchases book contains records of credit purchases, the suppliers account is credited following the rule applicable to liabilities accounts i.e. 'increase in liabilities is credited'.

14. Distinguish between sales book and sales account.

Ans. The differences between sales book and sales account are

Sales Book	Sales Account
Sales book is a part of journal book.	Sales account is a part of a ledger.
Sales book does not have debit and credit columns like a ledger account.	Sales account has debit and credit columns.

Sales Book	Sales Account
In a sales book, only credit sales of goods are recorded.	In a sales account, credit as well as cash sales of goods are recorded.
Total amount of sales book is posted to the sales account periodically.	Balance in the sales account is transferred to the trading account.

15. Distinguish between special journal and general journal.

Ans. The differences between special journal and general journal are

Special Journal (Subsidiary Books)	General Journal (Journal Proper)
It records transactions of similar nature e.g. purchase book records only credit purchase.	It does not record transactions of a similar nature.
It is in the form of a statement.	It is in the form of a journal.
A business unit may not have a special journal.	A business unit must have a journal proper.
Each transaction is not recorded in the ledger separately.	Each transaction is recorded in the ledger separately.
A mistake in the journal proper is not recitified by a special journal.	A mistake in a special journal is recitified by the journal proper.

16. Write the difference between return inwards and return outwards. NCERT

Ans. The differences between return inwards and return outwards are

Basis	Return Inwards	Return Outwards
Meaning	Goods sold to customers, are returned by them.	Goods purchased are returned to the suppliers.
Balance	It has debit balance.	It has credit balance.
Treatment	It is deducted from sales in the trading account.	It is deducted from purchases in trading account.
Issued	Credit note is prepared by the seller.	Debit note is prepared by the buyer.
Reduction	It reduces the payment from the debtors.	It reduces the payment made to the creditors.
Term	It is also termed as sales return.	It is also termed as purchases return.

17. What is the difference between cash account and cash book?

Ans. The differences between cash account and cash book are

Cash Account	Cash Book
It is an account in the ledger.	It is a separate book maintained for recording cash transactions.
It records only one aspect of a transaction i.e. cash.	It records both the aspects of a transaction.
Cash account is opened in the ledger and posting is done in this account from journal.	It is a book of original entry because all cash transactions are first of all recorded in cash book and then posted from cash book to various accounts in the ledger.
When transactions of cash are recorded in journal, it is necessary to open a cash account in the ledger.	When transactions of cash are recorded in cash book, there is no necessity to open a cash account in the ledger.

Objective Questions

Multiple Choice Questions (MCQs)

1. Which of the following is an advantage of special purpose books?
(a) Increases efficiency
(b) Protect from frauds
(c) Flexibility
(d) All of these

2. Subsidiary books include
(a) purchase return book
(b) sales return book
(c) bills payable book
(d) All the these

3. There is no need to maintain .... when cash book is maintained.
(a) journal proper
(b) purchase return book
(c) sales book
(d) cash and bank accounts in the ledger

4. Since cash account is not opened in the ledger, it .... the size of ledger becoming two voluminous.
(a) increases
(b) enlarge
(c) prevents
(d) Both (a) and (b)

5. Sold goods list price ₹ 1,00,000 less trade discount 10%. How much amount will be recorded in cash book and on which side? Competency Based Que
(a) Debit side; ₹ 90,000
(b) Debit side; ₹ 1,00,000
(c) Credit side; ₹ 90,000
(d) Debit side; ₹ 1,00,000

6. On 1st April, 2024, cash book shows bank overdraft of ₹ 30,000. On 2nd April, 2024, goods list price ₹ 80,000 were sold at 10%, trade discount to Ramit for cash. The balance of bank account will be Competency Based Que
(a) ₹ 1,02,000 (Dr)
(b) ₹ 42,000 (Dr)
(c) ₹ 30,000 (Cr)
(d) ₹ 50,000 (Dr)

7. Purchased a machine at ₹ 50,000. Amount was paid only 50% by cheque. In which subsidiary books, this transaction will be recorded? Competency Based Que

(a) Single column cash book; Journal proper
(b) Double column cash book; Journal proper
(c) Single column cash book; Purchase book
(d) Double column cash book; Purchase book

8. Sukanya Traders have bank overdraft of ₹ 30,000. On 1st April, 2024 following transactions are incurred thereafter Competency Based Que

(i) Taken a loan from PNB ₹ 40,000, received in bank account.
(ii) Paid insurance premium of ₹ 2,000 by bank as per standing instructions.
(iii) Withdrawn from bank for office use ₹ 3,000.

What will be the balance in bank account after considering above transaction?

(a) ₹ 5,000
(b) ₹ 7,000
(c) ₹ 10,000 (d) ₹ 8,000

9. A cheque of ₹ 5,500 received after banking hours from Ajay on 1st June, 2024, will be recorded in cash book on the same date on Competency Based Que

(a) debit side of bank column
(b) credit side of bank column
(c) debit side of cash column
(d) None of the side in cash book

10. "Payment made in full settlement ₹ 15,500 by cheque, discount received ₹ 200." Bank column will be credited with Competency Based Que

(a) ₹ 15,700 (b) ₹ 15,500
(c) ₹ 15,300 (d) None of these

11. Which of the following may have either debit balance or credit balance? Competency Based Que

(a) Bank column of cash book
(b) Cash column of cash book
(c) Both cash and bank column
(d) Neither bank column nor cash column

12. Wages due for the month of March will be recorded on

(a) debit side of cash column
(b) credit side of bank column
(c) credit side of cash column
(d) will not be recorded in cash book

13. When a firm maintains a cash book, it need not maintain NCERT

(a) journal proper
(b) purchases (journal) book
(c) sales (journal) book
(d) bank and cash account in the ledger

14. Sold goods list price ₹ 50,000 less 10% trade discount plus CGST and SGST 9% each. 5% cash discount was allowed on sale price.
What amount of GST will be received and where it will be recorded? Competency Based Que

(a) ₹ 7,695; Debit column of cash in cash book
(b) ₹ 8,100; Debit column of cash in cash book
(c) ₹ 7,695; Debit column of bank in cash book
(d) ₹ 8,100; Debit column of bank in cash book

15. Credit balance of bank account in cash book shows

(a) overdraft NCERT
(b) cash deposited in our bank
(c) cash withdrawn from bank
(d) None of the above

16. Cash book is considered as both ...... and ...... book.

(a) primary, subsidiary (b) subsidiary, principal
(c) tertiary, principal (d) None of these

17. What is the journal entry passed (at the time of receipt of cheques) if cheques received are deposited on different dates?

(a) Cheques in Hand A/c Dr
To Debtors A/c
(b) Debtors A/c Dr
To Cheques in Hand A/c
(c) Bank A/c Dr
To Debtors A/c
(d) None of the above

18. If a cheque of ₹ 25,000 is deposited on the same day, it is received and eventually the cheque is dishonoured, it will be recorded as Competency Based Que

(a) Debtor A/c Dr 25,000
To Bank A/c 25,000
(b) Bank A/c Dr 25,000
To Debtor A/c 25,000
(c) Debtor A/c Dr 25,000
To Cash A/c 25,000
(d) None of the above

19. Identify contra entry from the following.

(a) Salary paid ₹ 20,000
(b) Cash received from P ₹ 10,000
(c) Cash deposited into bank ₹ 25,000
(d) Cash withdrawn from bank for personal use ₹ 5,000

20. Cash deposited into bank ₹ 50,000 will be recorded as Competency Based Que

(a) debit of bank column with ₹ 50,000 and credit of cash column with ₹ 50,000
(b) debit of cash column with ₹ 50,000 and credit of bank column with ₹ 50,000
(c) debit of bank column with ₹ 50,000 and also debit of cash column with ₹ 50,000
(d) debit of cash column with ₹ 50,000 also credit of cash column with ₹ 50,000

21. If cheque of ₹ 3,000 is received from A, what will be the journal entry? **Competency Based Que**

(a) Cash A/c Dr 3,000
  To A 3,000
(b) Bank A/c Dr 3,000
  To A 3,000
(c) A Dr 3,000
  To Bank A/c 3,000
(d) None of the above

22. On 1st April, 2020, the balance of cash column of cash book stood at ₹ 50,000. After paying salaries of ₹ 20,000, receiving ₹ 20,000 from debtors and giving a cheque of ₹ 5,000 to a creditor S, balance of cash will be **Competency Based Que**

(a) ₹ 45,000 (b) ₹ 50,000
(c) ₹ 70,000 (d) ₹ 85,000

23. Given-Imprest amount = ₹ 10,000. What will be the amount of reimbursement, if following expenses were incurred by the petty cashier during the month? Wages = ₹ 1,900 , Tiffin = ₹ 1,200, Small repairs = ₹ 900, General expenses = ₹ 450. **Competency Based Que**

(a) ₹ 1,900 (b) ₹ 2,100
(c) ₹ 4,000 (d) ₹ 4,450

24. Which of the following is/are advantage(s) of maintaining petty cash book?

I. Saving of time and efforts of chief cashier.
II. Effective control over cash disbursements.
III. Convenient recording. **Competency Based Que**

Codes
(a) I and II (b) I and III
(c) Only I (d) I, II and III

25. Which cash book is prepared to book small amounts by cashier to save valuable time of main cashier?
(a) Three column cash book (b) Two column cash book
(c) Petty cash book (d) None of these

26. A column for 'debit note' is made in
(a) sales book (b) purchase book
(c) sales return book (d) purchase return book

27. Which of the following transactions will be recorded in purchase book?
(a) Goods purchased for cash
(b) Machine purchased on credit
(c) Goods purchased on credit
(d) Stationery purchased on credit

28. The total of purchase book is posted to
(a) purchase account (debit)
(b) sales account (credit)
(c) purchase account (crebit)
(d) sales account (dedit)

29. Purchase book is also known as
(a) invoice book (b) bought book
(c) sales book (d) Both (a) and (b)

30. Which of the following is/are not recorded in purchase book? **Competency Based Que**

I. Cash purchase of goods worth ₹ 5,000.
II. Purchase of furniture on credit worth ₹ 75,000.
III. Purchase of stationery of ₹ 3,000 on credit.

Codes
(a) Only I (b) II and III
(c) I and III (d) I, II and III

31. If XYZ Electronics Ltd. purchases 20 TV @ ₹ 2,000 per piece and 15 tape recorders @ ₹ 12,500 per piece. There was a trade discount of 20%. What will be the amount recorded in purchase book? **Competency Based Que**

(a) ₹ 40,000 (b) ₹ 1,87,500
(c) ₹ 2,27,500 (d) ₹ 1,82,000

32. Credit note is used to prepare
(a) sales return book (b) purchase book
(c) sales book (d) purchase return book

33. Sales book is a part of
(a) journal (b) journal proper
(c) ledger (d) balance sheet

34. Goods sold for cash ₹ 23,000 plus CGST and SGST @ 6% each. Sales account will be credited by **Competency Based Que**

(a) ₹ 23,000 (b) ₹ 25,760
(c) ₹ 25,000 (d) ₹ 24,760

35. Goods received from a debtor for list price ₹ 4,000 sold at 10% trade discount, will be recorded in .... at amount of .... **Competency Based Que**

(a) purchase return book, ₹ 3,600
(b) sales return book, ₹ 3,600
(c) purchase return book, ₹ 4,000
(d) sales return book, ₹ 4,000

36. The source document for recording entries in the sales return book is generally the ....
(a) credit note (b) debit note
(c) trial balance (d) None of these

37. 'Depreciation charged on machinery' should be recorded in
(a) cash book (b) purchase book
(c) sales book (d) journal proper

38. Which of the following entries are recorded in journal proper? **Competency Based Que**

I. Purchase of items on credit other than goods
II. Goods withdrawn by the owner for personal use

III. Endorsement and dishonour of bills of exchange

Codes

(a) I and II (b) I and III
(c) Only I (d) I, II and III

39. **If Razi paid ₹ 9,900 in settlement of her account of ₹ 10,000, then the discount allowed of ₹ 100 will be recorded in** **Competency Based Que**

(a) journal proper book (b) cash book
(c) Both (a) and (b) (d) None of these

40. **Where would a second hand motor car purchased on credit from Mr XYZ be recorded?**

(a) Purchase return book (b) Purchase book
(c) Journal proper (d) Cash book

Assertion-Reason

Direction (Q. No. 41 to 49) *Read the following Assertion (A) and Reason (R) and choose the correct alternative from the following.*

Alternatives

(a) Both Assertion (A) and Reason (R) are true and Reason (R) is the correct explanation of Assertion (A)
(b) Both Assertion (A) and Reason (R) are true, but Reason (R) is not the correct explanation of Assertion (A)
(c) Assertion (A) is true, but Reason (R) is false
(d) Assertion (A) is false, but Reason (R) is true

41. **Assertion** (A) Discount received from Ajay will not be recorded in bank or cash column.

Reason (R) The transactions i.e. discount received from Ajay does not involve cash or bank account.

42. **Assertion** (A) All credit purchases of goods are recorded in the purchases journal.

Reason (R) Cash purchases of goods are recorded in cash book.

43. **Assertion** (A) Imprest system is maintained for petty cash book.

Reason (R) Petty cash book can be of two types i.e. simple and analytical.

44. **Assertion** (A) In large businesses, journal is sub-divided into special journals.

Reason (R) Special journals prove economical and make division of labour possible in accounting work.

45. **Assertion** (A) Petty cash book records repetitive large expenses.

Reason (R) Petty cash book is maintained so that the cash book does not become bulky due to repetitive transactions.

46. **Assertion** (A) Sales return book is used to record return of goods by customers sold to them on credit.

Reason (R) As the sales book records only credit sale of goods, hence sales return book keeps only record of returned goods which were sold on credit.

47. **Assertion** (A) Rent due ₹ 300 will be recorded in journal proper.

Reason (R) In journal proper, those transactions are recorded which can't be recorded in cash book and purchase book.

48. **Assertion** (A) In case, Aarti returned goods to Himani, Aarti will prepare credit note.

Reason (R) Credit note is prepared when goods are received as return.

49. **Assertion** (A) Transferring salary account to profit and loss account is a closing entry.

Reason (R) Closing entry is the one which is passed to transfer the balance of one account to another.

Two Statements Based MCQs

Direction (Q. No. 50 to 55) *Read the following statements carefully and choose the correct alternative*

Alternatives

(a) Both the statements are correct
(b) Both the statements are incorrect
(c) Statement I is correct and Statement II is incorrect
(d) Statement I is incorrect and Statement II is correct

50. **Statement I** Cash book serves the purpose of both journal as we as the ledger (cash) account.

Statement II When a cash book is maintained, transactions of cash are not recorded in the journal and no separated account for cash or bank is required in the ledger.

51. **Statement I** Rajan, who owed us ₹ 10,000 became bankrupt and paid 50 paise in a rupee. ₹ 10,000 will be recorded on debit side of cash column in above case.

Statement II Paid ₹ 2,000 by cheque for furniture purchased. It will be recorded on credit side of bank column as 'By Purchase A/c.'

52. **Statement I** Cheque received after banking hours will be debited to bank column in cash book.

Statement II Cash withdrawn for personal use by the proprietor is recorded as contra entry.

53. **Statement I** Assets sold on credit are recorded in journal proper.

Statement II Recording is made in journal proper only for assets bought on credit.

54. **Statement I** Purchase day book has debit balance.
Statement II Sales day book has credit balance.

55. **Statement I** Sales book is prepared for keeping record of cash sales and credit sales.
Statement II Sales return book is a part of sales book.

Matching

56 **Match the following**

Column I	Column II
A. Single column cash book	(i) Small expenses
B. Double column cash book	(ii) Only cash account
C. Petty cash book	(iii) Both cash and bank account

Codes

	A	B	C		A	B	C
(a)	(i)	(iii)	(ii)	(b)	(ii)	(iii)	(i)
(c)	(i)	(ii)	(iii)	(d)	(iii)	(i)	(ii)

57. **Match the following**

Column I	Column II
A. Single column cash book	(i) Record both cash and bank transactions
B. Double column cash book	(ii) Only records cash transactions
C. Triple column cash book	(iii) Records, cash, discount and bank transactions
D. Petty cash book	(iv) Records small regular cash payments

Codes

	A	B	C	D		A	B	C	D
(a)	(i)	(iii)	(ii)	(iv)	(b)	(ii)	(i)	(iii)	(iv)
(c)	(ii)	(i)	(iv)	(iii)	(d)	(i)	(ii)	(iv)	(iii)

58. **Match the following**

Column I	Column II
A. Petty cash book	(i) Records small regular expenses
B. Single column cash book	(ii) Only records cash transactions
C. Contra entry	(iii) Transactions involving cash and bank
D. Purchase book	(iv) Record all credit purchase of goods

Codes

	A	B	C	D		A	B	C	D
(a)	(i)	(ii)	(iii)	(iv)	(b)	(i)	(ii)	(iv)	(iii)
(c)	(i)	(iii)	(iv)	(ii)	(d)	(i)	(iv)	(iii)	(ii)

59. **Match the following**

Column I	Column II
A. Cash sales	(i) Journal proper
B. Goods returned to creditor	(ii) Cash book
C. Writing-off bad debts	(iii) Purchase book
D. Purchased goods on credit	(iv) Purchase return book

Codes

	A	B	C	D		A	B	C	D
(a)	(i)	(ii)	(iii)	(iv)	(b)	(ii)	(iv)	(i)	(iii)
(c)	(ii)	(iv)	(iii)	(i)	(d)	(i)	(ii)	(iv)	(iiii)

60. **Match the following**

Column I	Column II
A. Defective goods returned by Taksh	(i) Journal proper
B. Providing interest on capital	(ii) Purchase return book
C. Bill accepted by proprietor from creditor	(iii) Sales return book
D. Received credit note from Khushi	(iv) Bills payable book

Codes

	A	B	C	D		A	B	C	D
(a)	(iii)	(i)	(iv)	(ii)	(b)	(i)	(ii)	(iii)	(iv)
(c)	(iv)	(iii)	(ii)	(i)	(d)	(iii)	(iv)	(i)	(ii)

61. **Match the following**

Column I	Column II
A. Purchase of goods on credit	(i) Purchase book
B. Sales of goods on credit	(ii) Sales return book
C. Cash received from debtors	(iii) Cash book
D. Goods returned by debtors	(iv) Sales book

Codes

	A	B	C	D		A	B	C	D
(a)	(i)	(iii)	(iv)	(ii)	(b)	(i)	(iv)	(iii)	(ii)
(c)	(iii)	(iv)	(i)	(ii)	(d)	(iii)	(ii)	(i)	(iv)

Case Based MCQs

Direction *Read the following case study and answer the questions 62 and 63 on the basis of the same*

Amit Bros. is a manufacturing firm. Following information about it is available

Assets Cash in hand ₹ 1,00,000; Cash at bank ₹ 1,10,000; Debtors (Aman ₹ 90,000; Ankush ₹ 50,000); Stock ₹ 3,20,000 and Machinery ₹ 4,00,000.

Liabilities Creditors: Sumit & Sons ₹ 70,000.

The following transactions took place during the month of September, 2024.

Date	Particulars
2022	
Sep 2	Deposited into bank ₹ 30,000.
Sep 4	Purchased from M goods of the list price of ₹ 70,000 at 10% trade discount.

Date	Particulars
Sep 5	Returned to M goods of list price ₹ 8,000.
Sep 7	Issued a cheque to M in full settlement of their account after deducting cash discount @ 5%.
Sep 10	Sold to S goods worth ₹ 80,000.
Sep 12	Received cash ₹ 60,000 and cheque ₹ 8,000 from S. The cheque was sent to bank on the same day. Discount allowed₹ 1,000.
Sep 14	Purchased machinery from XYZ Co. on credit for ₹ 50,000.
Sep 16	Amit withdrew goods for his personal use ₹ 20,000.
Sep 18	Sold to A goods valued ₹ 32,000.
Sep 19	Issued cheque to XYZ Co. ₹ 50,000.
Sep 20	Returned by A goods worth ₹ 4,000.
Sep 21	Purchased goods from P for ₹ 80,000. Trade discount 10%.
Sep 22	Accepted a bill drawn by P for ₹ 72,000 at 1 month.
Sep 27	Received from A ₹ 20,000. Discount allowed ₹ 100.
Sep 27	Goods purchased for cash ₹ 60,000.
Sep 28	Withdrew from bank ₹ 40,000.
Sep 29	Paid salaries by cheque ₹ 10,000.
Sep 30	Paid rent ₹ 5,600.
Sep 30	Received commission in cash ₹ 3,200.

62. **Purchase of goods from M on 4th September will be recorded on that date in**
(a) cash book (b) purchase book
(c) journal proper (d) None of these

63. **What amount is finally paid to M on 7th September?**
(a) ₹ 62,000 (b) ₹ 63,000
(c) ₹ 55,000 (d) ₹ 53,010

Direction *Read the following case study and answer the questions 64 and 65 on the basis of the same*

Karim & Co., a saree dealer has the following transactions for the month of January.

Date	Particulars
Jan 4	Returned to Mohan Mills, Kerala,10 polyester sarees @ ₹ 1,600 each. (−) Trade discount @ 10% (Debit note no. 101).
Jan 8	Srimala Mills, Kota accepted the returns of goods (which were purchased for cash) from us, 8 Kota sarees @ ₹ 640 each (Debit note no. 102).
Jan 12	Returned to Sonica Mills, Bombay, 12 silk sarees @ ₹ 1,040 each. (−) Trade discount @ 10% (Debit note no. 103).
Jan 30	Returned one typewriter (being defective) @ ₹ 7,200 to Vishaka & Co.

64. **What will the total amount recorded in the purchase returns book relating to the returns to Mohan Mills on 4th January?**
(a) ₹ 16,000
(b) ₹ 14,400
(c) ₹ 17,600
(d) None of the above

65. **In which of the following books, will the return of Kota Sarees on 8th January be recorded?**
(a) Purchase returns book
(b) Journal
(c) Cash book
(d) None of the above

Answers

1. (d) All of these **2.** (d) All of these
3. (d) cash and bank accounts in the ledger
4. (c) prevents
5. (a) Total cash received = 1,00,000 − 10,000 = ₹ 90,000 (Dr)
6. (c) ₹ 30,000 (Cr)
7. (b) Double column cash book; Journal proper
8. (a) Balance in bank account
= (30,000) + 40,000 − 2,000 − 3,000 = ₹ 5,000
9. (d) On the same date, cheque in hand account will be debited and Ajay will be credited because cheque is received after banking hours.
10. (b) ₹ 15,500
11. (a) Bank column of cash book
12. (d) will not be recorded in cash book
13. (d) bank and cash account in the ledger
14. (a) GST will be levied upon sale price i.e.
= 50,000 − 5,000 (Trade discount) − (45,000 × 5%)
= ₹ 42,750
GST = 42,750 × 18% = ₹ 7,695
15. (a) overdraft
16. (b) subsidiary, principal
17. (a) Cheques in hand A/c Dr
To Debtors A/c
18. (a) Debtor A/c Dr 25,000
To Bank A/c 25,000
19. (c) Cash deposited into bank ₹ 25,000
20. (a) debit of bank column with ₹ 50,000 and credit of cash column with ₹ 50,000
21. (b) Bank A/c Dr 3,000
To A 3,000

22. (b) Balance in cash column = 50,000 − 20,000 (Salary) + 20,000 (Received from debtors) = ₹ 50,000

23. (d) Total expenses incurred = 1,900 + 1,200 + 900 + 450 = ₹ 4,450 will be reimbursed

24. (d) I, II and III

25. (c) Petty cash book

26. (d) purchase return book

27. (c) Goods purchased on credit

28. (a) purchase account (debit)

29. (d) Purchase book records all invoices or bills received by the firm. All the goods bought on credit are recorded in this book.

30. (d) I, II and III

31. (d)

Amount of TV purchased (20 × 2,000)	= ₹ 40,000
Amount of tape recorder (15 × 12,500)	= ₹ 1,87,500
Total	= ₹ 2,27,500
(−) 20% Trade discount	= ₹ (45,500)
	₹ 1,82,000

32. (a) sales return book

33. (a) journal

34. (a) ₹ 23,000

35. (b) sales return book, ₹ 3,600

36. (a) credit note

37. (d) journal proper

38. (d) I, II and III

39. (a) journal proper book

40. (c) Journal proper is a book that records transactions which cannot be recorded in any other subsidiary book, i.e. cash book, purchase book, sales book, etc. Purchase/Sale of items on credit other than goods are recorded into journal proper only.

41. (a) Both Assertion (A) and Reason (R) are true and Reason (R) is the correct explanation of Assertion (A)

42. (b) Both Assertion (A) and Reason (R) are true, but Reason (R) is not the correct explanation of Assertion (A)

43. (b) Both Assertion (A) and Reason (R) are true, but Reason (R) is not the correct explanation of Assertion (A)

44. (a) A small business may be able to record all its transactions in one book only, i.e. the journal.

But as the business expands and the number of transactions becomes large, it may become cumbersome to journalise each transaction. For quick, efficient and accurate recording of business transactions, journal is sub-divided into special journals.

45. (d) Petty cash book records small and repetitive expenses.

46. (a) Both Assertion (A) and Reason (R) are true and Reason (R) is the correct explanation of Assertion (A)

47. (a) Both Assertion (A) and Reason (R) are true and Reason (R) is the correct explanation of Assertion (A)

48. (d) In case Aarti returns goods to Himani, Aarti will prepare a debit note and Himani will prepare a credit note.

49. (c) Closing entry is an entry which is recorded to close the accounts. e.g. Transfer of accounts related with income and expenses to trading and profit and loss account etc.

50. (a) Both the statements are correct

51. (b) Both the statements are incorrect

52. (b) Both the statements are incorrect

53. (c) Statement I is correct and Statement II is incorrect

54. (a) Both the statements are correct

55. (b) Both the statements are incorrect

56. (b) (ii) (iii) (i)

57. (b) (ii) (i) (iii) (iv)

58. (a) (i) (ii) (iii) (iv)

59. (b) (ii) (iv) (i) (iii)

60. (a) (iii) (i) (iv) (ii)

61. (b) (i) (iv) (iii) (ii)

62. (b) purchase book

63. (d)

Purchase =	63,000
(−) Return	(7,200)
	55,800

Amount paid = 55,800 − (55,800 × 5%) = ₹ 53,010

64. (b) ₹ 14,400

65. (a) Purchase returns book

06

CHAPTER

Trial balance is an important statement in the accounting process as it shows the final position of all accounts and helps in preparing the final statements.

Trial Balance

▼ **YOUR STUDY GOALS**

▼ **YOUR PRACTICE GOAL**

- Solved Questions (8 Solved Questions)
- Numerical Questions [12 Questions (Unsolved)]
- Theoretical Questions [6 Questions (with answers)]
- Objective Questions (66 Qs ; MCQs, A-R, Statements, Matching, Case)

6.1 Concept of Trial Balance

Trial balance is a statement which incorporates the balances of all ledger accounts.

It consists of debit column which records debit balances of ledger accounts and a credit column which records credit balances of ledger accounts.

If the total of the debit column equals that of the credit column, then this proves the arithmetical accuracy of the accounts maintained.

According to **William Pickles**, "The statement prepared with the help of ledger balances, at the end of the financial year (or at any other date) to find out whether debit total agrees with credit total is called trial balance."

Format of Trial Balance

Trial Balance
as on ...

Name of Accounts	LF	Debit Balance (₹)	Credit Balance (₹)
Name of account is written.	Page number of ledger where the balance appears is written.	Debit balance (if any) is entered.	Credit balance (if any) is written.
Total			

Characteristics/Features of Trial Balance

- It contains list of all ledger accounts including cash account.
- It is a statement, not an account.
- It is not a part of the double entry system of bookkeeping, it is just a working paper.
- It can be prepared at any time during the accounting period.
- It is prepared to check the arithmetical accuracy of the ledger accounts.
- It is prepared on a particular date and not for a particular period.

Objectives/Functions/Purpose of Preparing Trial Balance

- Ascertain the arithmetical accuracy of the ledger accounts.
- Helps in the detection or location of errors.
- Offers a summary of the ledger accounts.
- Provides a basis for preparation of final accounts.
  It is considered as the connecting link between accounting records and the preparation of financial statements.

Limitations of Trial Balance

- It only confirms that the total of all debit balances matches the total of all credit balances.
- It gives only condensed information of each account.
- Total of trial balance may agree inspite of errors.
- Following errors are not disclosed by trial balance
  - Error of complete omission
  - Error of principles
  - Compensating errors
  - Incorrect amount entered in journal
  - Posting to the wrong account
  - An entry posted twice in the ledger

6.2 Steps to Prepare a Trial Balance

Step 1 The balances of each account in the ledger are ascertained. The balance of an account is the difference between the total of the debit entries and the total of the credit entries in an account. If the total of debit entries is greater, it is called **debit balance**. Likewise, if the total of credit entries is greater, it is called **credit balance**.

Step 2 List each account and place its balance in the debit or credit column (If an account does not have a balance, it is ignored).

Step 3 Compute the total of debit balances column.

Step 4 Compute the total of the credit balances column.

Step 5 Verify that the sum of the debit balances equals the sum of credit balances. If they do not tally, it indicates that there are some errors. So, one must check the correctness of the balances of all accounts.

Rules for Preparing Trial Balance from the Given List of Ledger Balances

- The balances of all (a) assets accounts (b) expenses and losses accounts (c) drawings (d) cash and bank balances (e) purchases (f) sales return are placed in the debit column of the trial balance.
- The balances of all (a) liabilities accounts (b) income and profit accounts (c) capital (d) sales (e) purchases return are placed in the credit column of the trial balance.
- All expenses and losses show debit balances, so they should be written on debit side of the trial balance.
- All incomes and profits show credit balances, so they should be written on credit side of the trial balance.

Treatment of Closing Stock

- Generally, **closing stock** does not appear in the trial balance. It is usually given outside the trial balance as an additional information or adjustment. Following entry is passed

  Closing Stock A/c Dr
  To Trading A/c
- In case, it appears in the trial balance, it means that it has already been adjusted through purchases. Following entry is passed

  Closing Stock A/c Dr
  To Purchases A/c
- It can also appear in trial balance
  - if trading account is prepared before preparing trial balance or
  - if trial balance is prepared after passing adjustment entries.

6.3 Methods of Preparation of Trial Balance

There are three methods used for the preparation of a trial balance.

- Total Method
- Balance Method
- Total-cum-balance Method

Note As per the syllabus, only 'balance method' is discussed.

Balance Method of Preparing Trial Balance

- This is the most commonly used method of preparing trial balance.
- Under this method, the balances of all the accounts are incorporated in the trial balance.
- The debit and credit columns of the trial balance are totalled and they must be equal.
- It should be remembered that trial balance can be prepared under balance method, only when all the ledger accounts have been balanced.
- Account balances are used because the balance summarises the net effect of all transactions relating to an account.
- It helps in preparation of financial statements.

Steps to Locate or Detect the Errors

If the trial balance does not agree, we need to locate the errors. The following steps may be taken to locate the errors

Step 1 Recheck the total of debit and credit columns of trial balance.

Step 2 Calculate the exact figure of difference. After this, check subsidiary books and see if any item of that amount remains unposted. e.g. If the difference is of ₹ 6,200, all the entries of ₹ 6,200 should be checked to ensure whether they have been duly posted.

Step 3 The difference should be halved to find out if some figure equal to half the difference has been posted on the wrong side of an account.
e.g. If the total of debit side of the trial balance exceeds by ₹ 5,000, it is possible that a credit item of ₹ 2,500 may have been posted to the debit side of a ledger account.

Step 4 Divide the difference in trial balance by 9. If difference is completely divisible, it can be a mistake of transposition of figures. e.g. If the figure of ₹ 48 is written as ₹ 84, the difference is ₹ 36. This is completely divisible by 9. Likewise, if '0' is added against a figure, the difference will also be divisible by 9. If the figure of 23 is written as 230 then the difference of 207 which will be completely divisible by 9.

Step 5 If difference is in a round figure, i.e. ₹ 1, ₹ 10, ₹ 100, etc., there can be a possibility of wrong totalling or wrong carry forwards of the total of subsidiary books or there may be an error in balancing of an account. Hence, check the totalling and balancing.

Step 6 Check whether the balance of each and every account including cash and bank balances have been included in the trial balance on the correct side with correct amounts.

Step 7 Check all closing balances from the previous year's balance sheet whether they have been correctly carried forward and recorded in respective ledger accounts.

Step 8 Check the figures which are not clearly written.

Step 9 If difference is of a very big amount, it is possible that balance of certain ledger account may not have been included in the trial balance. To detect this, compare the trial balance of previous year and current year.

Step 10 If inspite of all above efforts, there is still a difference in the trial balance, then a complete checking of the posting of all the entries will be crucial.

Note Numericals related to locating and rectification of errors are covered in Chapter-9 ahead.

Mind Map

TRIAL BALANCE

1 Concept of Trial Balance

- Trial balance is a statement which incorporates the balances of all ledger accounts
- It consists of debit column which records debit balances of ledger accounts and a credit column which records credit balances of ledger accounts

Format →

Trial Balance
as on...

Name of Accounts	LF	Debit Balance (₹)	Credit Balance (₹)
Total			

2 Features of Trial Balance

- Contains list of all ledger accounts including cash account
- It is a statement, not an account
- Not a part of the double entry system of bookkeeping
- Can be prepared at any time during the accounting period
- Prepared to check the arithmetical accuracy of the ledger accounts
- Prepare on a particular date and not for a particular period

3 Objectives of Trial Balance

- Ensures the arithmetical accuracy of the ledger accounts
- Helps in the detection or location of errors
- Offers a summary of the ledger accounts
- Considered as the connecting link between accounting records and the preparation of financial statements

4 Limitations of Trial Balance

- Only confirms that the total of all debit balances matches the total of all credit balances
- Gives only condensed information of each account
- Total of trial balances may agree inspite of errors
- Following errors are not disclosed by the trial balance
  - Error of complete omission
  - Errors of principles
  - Compensating errors
  - Incorrect amount entered in journal
  - Posting to the wrong account
  - An entry posted twice in the ledger

5 Steps to Prepare a Trial Balance

- **Step 1** The balances of each account in the ledger are ascertained. The balance of an account is the difference between the total of the debit entries and the total of the credit entries in an account. If the total of debit entries is greater, it is called debit balance. Likewise, if the total of credit entries is greater, it is called credit balance.
- **Step 2** List each account and place it's balance in debit or credit column.
- **Step 3** Compute the total of debit column and credit column.
- **Step 4** Verify that sum of the debit balance equals the sum of the credit balance. If they do not tally, it indicates that there are some errors. So, one must check the correctness of the balances of all accounts.

6 Rule for Treatment of Closing Stock

- If closing stock is given outside of trial balance, then it appears on credit side of trading account and on asset side of balance sheet
- If closing stock appears in trial balance, it means it is adjusted with purchases. Hence in this case, it does not appear on credit side of trading account and only appears on the asset side of balance sheet

7 Method of Preparing Trial Balance

Balance Method

- This is the most common method of preparation of trial balance
- Under this method, balances of all accounts are incorporated under trial balance
- The debit and credit balance of trial balance is totalled and must be equal
- It helps in preparation of financial statements

Solved Questions

Solved Question 1 **Given below is a ledger extract relating to the business of Viren and Co as on 31st March, 2024. You are required to prepare the trial balance by balance method.**

Dr **Cash Account** Cr

Date	Particulars	JF	Amt (₹)	Date	Particulars	JF	Amt (₹)
	To Capital A/c		1,00,000		By Furniture A/c		30,000
	To Veer		2,50,000		By Salaries A/c		25,000
	To Sales A/c		5,000		By Arjun		2,10,000
					By Purchases A/c		10,000
					By Capital A/c		5,000
					By Balance c/d		75,000
			3,55,000				3,55,000

Dr **Furniture Account** Cr

Date	Particulars	JF	Amt (₹)	Date	Particulars	JF	Amt (₹)
	To Cash A/c		30,000		By Balance c/d		30,000
			30,000				30,000

Dr **Salaries Account** Cr

Date	Particulars	JF	Amt (₹)	Date	Particulars	JF	Amt (₹)
	To Cash A/c		25,000		By Balance c/d		25,000
			25,000				25,000

Dr **Arjun** Cr

Date	Particulars	JF	Amt (₹)	Date	Particulars	JF	Amt (₹)
	To Cash A/c		2,10,000		By Purchases A/c (Credit purchases)		2,50,000
	To Purchases Return A/c		5,000				
	To Balance c/d		35,000				
			2,50,000				2,50,000

Dr **Purchases Account** Cr

Date	Particulars	JF	Amt (₹)	Date	Particulars	JF	Amt (₹)
	To Cash A/c		10,000		By Balance c/d		2,60,000
	To Arjun (As per purchases book-credit purchases)		2,50,000				
			2,60,000				2,60,000

Dr **Purchases Return Account** Cr

Date	Particulars	JF	Amt (₹)	Date	Particulars	JF	Amt (₹)
	To Balance c/d		5,000		By Arjun (As per purchases return book)		5,000
			5,000				5,000

Dr **Veer** Cr

Date	Particulars	JF	Amt (₹)	Date	Particulars	JF	Amt (₹)
	To Sales A/c (Credit sales)		3,00,000		By Sales Return A/c		1,000
					By Cash A/c		2,50,000
					By Balance c/d		49,000
			3,00,000				3,00,000

Dr **Sales Account** Cr

Date	Particulars	JF	Amt (₹)	Date	Particulars	JF	Amt (₹)
	To Balance c/d		3,05,000		By Cash A/c		5,000
					By Veer (As per sales book-credit sales)		3,00,000
			3,05,000				3,05,000

Dr **Sales Return Account** Cr

Date	Particulars	JF	Amt (₹)	Date	Particulars	JF	Amt (₹)
	To Veer (As per sales return book)		1,000		By Balance c/d		1,000
			1,000				1,000

Dr **Capital Account** Cr

Date	Particulars	JF	Amt (₹)	Date	Particulars	JF	Amt (₹)
	To Cash A/c		5,000		By Cash A/c		1,00,000
	To Balance c/d		95,000				
			1,00,000				1,00,000

Key Point
Students should keep in mind that balancing amount on the credit side signifies debit balance and balancing amount on the debit side signifies credit balance.

Sol.

Trial Balance
as on 31st March, 2024

Name of Accounts	LF	Debit Balance (₹)	Credit Balance (₹)
Cash		75,000	—
Furniture		30,000	—
Salaries		25,000	—
Arjun's		—	35,000
Purchases		2,60,000	—
Purchases Return		—	5,000
Veer's		49,000	—
Sales		—	3,05,000
Sales Return		1,000	—
Capital		—	95,000
Total		4,40,000	4,40,000

Solved Question 2 **From the following list of balances extracted from the books of Shri Ram, prepare a trial balance as on 31st March, 2024.**

Name of Accounts	Amt (₹)	Name of Accounts	Amt (₹)
Stock on 1st April, 2023	40,000	Discount Received	25,000
Purchases	2,57,500	Long-term Borrowings	1,65,000
Sales	3,61,800	Provision for Doubtful Debts	5,000
Carriage Inwards	300	Provision for Depreciation on Machinery	5,000
Carriage Outwards	120	Bad Debts	400
Return Inwards	23,500	Stationery	620
Return Outwards	2,000	Insurance	340
Debtors	14,000	Wages and Salaries	18,500
Creditors	17,400	Investment	30,000
Building	2,00,000	Interest on Investment	2,700
Equipment	1,60,000	Cash and Bank Balance	1,240
Repairs to Equipment	2,000	Vehicle	55,000
Depreciation	8,000	Furniture and Fixtures	19,000
Bills Receivable	840	Miscellaneous Expenses	520
Bills Payable	480	Miscellaneous Income	140
Bank Overdraft	1,40,000	Loan from SBI	25,000
Interest on Overdraft	640	Interest on Loan	3,000
Purchases Return	60,000	Capital	70,000
Discount Allowed	3,000	Proprietor's Withdrawals (Drawings)	6,000
Salaries	11,000	Computers	9,000
		Goodwill	15,000
		Stock on 31st March, 2024 (not adjusted)	31,000

Sol.

Trial Balance
as on 31st March, 2024

Name of Accounts	LF	Debit Balance (₹)	Credit Balance (₹)
Stock on 1st April, 2023		40,000	—
Purchases		2,57,500	—
Sales		—	3,61,800
Carriage Inwards		300	—
Carriage Outwards		120	—
Return Inwards		23,500	—
Return Outwards		—	2,000
Debtors		14,000	—
Creditors		—	17,400
Building		2,00,000	—
Equipment		1,60,000	—
Repairs to Equipment		2,000	—
Depreciation		8,000	—
Bills Receivable		840	—
Bills Payable		—	480
Bank Overdraft		—	1,40,000
Interest on Overdraft		640	—
Purchases Return		—	60,000
Discount Allowed		3,000	—
Salaries		11,000	—
Discount Received		—	25,000
Long-term Borrowings		—	1,65,000
Provisions for Doubtful Debts		—	5,000
Provision for Depreciation on Machinery		—	5,000
Bad Debts		400	—
Stationery		620	—
Insurance		340	—
Wages and Salaries		18,500	—
Investment		30,000	—
Interest on Investment		—	2,700
Cash and Bank Balance		1,240	—
Vehicle		55,000	—
Furniture and Fixtures		19,000	—
Miscellaneous Expenses		520	—
Miscellaneous Income		—	140
Loan from SBI		—	25,000
Interest on Loan		3,000	—
Capital		—	70,000
Proprietor's Withdrawals (Drawings)		6,000	—
Computers		9,000	—
Goodwill		15,000	—
Total		8,79,520	8,79,520

Note Closing stock is not adjusted with purchases, hence it will not be shown in trial balance.

Solved Question 3 *(With GST)* **Prepare trial balance from the following balances of accounts in the books of Madhuri & Sons as on 31st March, 2024.**

Name of Accounts	Amt (₹)	Name of Accounts	Amt (₹)
Stock (1st April, 2023)	60,000	Discount Allowed	6,000
Purchases	2,10,800	Cash at Bank	15,000
Sales	2,60,000	Bad Debts	7,000
Carriage Inwards	12,000	Debtors	44,400
Cash	26,000	Creditors	49,000
Furniture and Fixtures	26,000	Provision for Doubtful Debts	2,800
Depreciation	8,000		
Drawings	15,000	Input CGST	8,000
Return Outwards	6,400	Output CGST	12,000
Return Inwards	2,000	Input SGST	8,000
		Output SGST	12,000

Sol.

Trial Balance
as on 31st March, 2024

Name of Accounts	LF	Debit Balance (₹)	Credit Balance (₹)
Stock on (1st April, 2023)		60,000	—
Purchases		2,10,800	—
Sales		—	2,60,000
Carriage Inwards		12,000	—
Input CGST		8,000	—
Input SGST		8,000	—
Cash		26,000	—
Furniture		26,000	—
Depreciation		8,000	—
Drawings		15,000	—
Output CGST		—	12,000
Output SGST		—	12,000
Return Outwards		—	6,400
Return Inwards		2,000	—
Discount Allowed		6,000	—
Cash at Bank		15,000	—
Bad Debts		7,000	—
Debtors		44,400	—
Creditors		—	49,000
Provision for Doubtful Debts		—	2,800
Capital (Balancing figure)		—	1,06,000
Total		4,48,200	4,48,200

Solved Question 4 **The following trial balance has been prepared by an inexperienced accountant. You are required to identify the errors and prepare the trial balance in a correct form.**

Name of Accounts	LF	Debit Balance (₹)	Credit Balance (₹)
Cash in Hand		10,000	—
Fixed Assets		—	12,500
Capital		—	38,600
Purchases		22,500	—
Sales		10,250	—
Discount Allowed		—	250
Return Inwards		—	500
Return Outwards		700	—
Wages and Salaries		5,000	—
Debtors		1,340	—
Creditors		—	4,700
Drawings		—	1,000
Discount Received		—	350
Bills Receivable		1,170	—
Bills Payable		—	2,160
Rent		1,500	—
Interest Paid		—	1,000
Total		52,460	61,060

Sol. Following errors are identified in the above trial balance

(i) Fixed assets are shown in the credit column, which is wrong. Assets have a debit balance and as such, they should be shown in the debit column.

(ii) Sales have been shown in the debit column. Sales are revenue for a business and therefore should be shown in the credit column.

(iii) Discount allowed has been shown in the credit column, which is wrong. Discount allowed is an expense for the business and should therefore be shown in the debit column.

(iv) Return inwards have been entered in the credit column and return outwards have been entered in the debit column, which is not correct. Return inwards should be recorded in debit column and return outwards in the credit column.

(v) Drawings have been recorded in the credit column, which is wrong. Drawings reduce the capital and should therefore be recorded in the debit column.

(vi) Interest paid has been recorded in the credit column. This is not correct. Interest paid is an expense for the business and should therefore be recorded in debit column.

Redrafted trial balance is given below

Trial Balance

as on...

Name of Accounts	LF	Debit Balance (₹)	Credit Balance (₹)
Cash in Hand		10,000	—
Fixed Assets		12,500	—
Capital		—	38,600
Purchases		22,500	—
Sales		—	10,250
Discount Allowed		250	—
Return Inwards		500	—
Return Outwards		—	700
Wages and Salaries		5,000	—
Debtors		1,340	—
Creditors		—	4,700
Drawings		1,000	—
Discount Received		—	350
Bills Receivable		1,170	—
Bills Payable		—	2,160
Rent		1,500	—
Interest Paid		1,000	—
Total		56,760	56,760

Solved Question 5 **Following is the trial balance of Sudhir Chaudhary as on 31st March, 2024.**

Name of Accounts	LF	Debit Balance (₹)	Credit Balance (₹)
Capital		—	10,00,000
Plant and Machinery		13,40,000	—
Furniture		2,40,000	—
Cash in Hand		60,000	—
Bank Overdraft		—	1,10,000
Purchases		22,40,000	—
Sales		—	34,80,000
Debtors		10,20,000	—
Creditors		—	5,00,000
Rent		1,76,000	—
General Expenses		14,000	—
Total		50,90,000	50,90,000

Following transactions were entered into but were not recorded in the books of accounts

(i) Goods worth ₹ 20,000 were purchased on credit.

(ii) Received a cheque of ₹ 58,000 from a debtor in full settlement of his account of ₹ 60,000.

(iii) Goods amounting to ₹ 6,000 were returned by a customer.

(iv) Paid rent for the month ₹ 14,000 by cheque.

Required

(a) Pass journal entries for the above mentioned transactions and post them into the ledger.

(b) Redraft the trial balance.

Sol. (a) **JOURNAL**

Date	Particulars	LF	Amt (Dr)	Amt (Cr)
(i)	Purchases A/c Dr To Creditors A/c (Being goods purchased on credit)		20,000	20,000

Date	Particulars		LF	Amt (Dr)	Amt (Cr)
(ii)	Bank A/c	Dr		58,000	
	Discount Allowed A/c	Dr		2,000	
	To Debtors A/c				60,000
	(Being amount received from debtors and discount allowed)				
(iii)	Sales Return A/c	Dr		6,000	
	To Debtors A/c				6,000
	(Being goods returned by a debtor)				
(iv)	Rent A/c	Dr		14,000	
	To Bank A/c				14,000
	(Being rent paid by cheque)				

Ledger

Purchases Account

Dr | Cr

Date	Particulars	JF	Amt (₹)	Date	Particulars	JF	Amt (₹)
	To Balance b/d		22,40,000		By Balance c/d		22,60,000
	To Creditors A/c		20,000				
			22,60,000				22,60,000

Creditors Account

Dr | Cr

Date	Particulars	JF	Amt (₹)	Date	Particulars	JF	Amt (₹)
	To Balance c/d		5,20,000		By Balance b/d		5,00,000
					By Purchases A/c		20,000
			5,20,000				5,20,000

Bank Account

Dr | Cr

Date	Particulars	JF	Amt (₹)	Date	Particulars	JF	Amt (₹)
	To Debtors A/c		58,000		By Balance b/d		1,10,000
	To Balance c/d		66,000		By Rent A/c		14,000
			1,24,000				1,24,000

Discount Allowed Account

Dr | Cr

Date	Particulars	JF	Amt (₹)	Date	Particulars	JF	Amt (₹)
	To Debtors A/c		2,000		By Balance c/d		2,000
			2,000				2,000

Debtors Account

Dr | Cr

Date	Particulars	JF	Amt (₹)	Date	Particulars	JF	Amt (₹)
	To Balance b/d		10,20,000		By Bank A/c		58,000
					By Discount Allowed A/c		2,000
					By Sales Return A/c		6,000
					By Balance c/d		9,54,000
			10,20,000				10,20,000

Sales Return Account

Dr | Cr

Date	Particulars	JF	Amt (₹)	Date	Particulars	JF	Amt (₹)
	To Debtors A/c		6,000		By Balance c/d		6,000
			6,000				6,000

Dr **Rent Account** Cr

Date	Particulars	JF	Amt (₹)	Date	Particulars	JF	Amt (₹)
	To Balance b/d		1,76,000		By Balance c/d		1,90,000
	To Bank A/c		14,000				
			1,90,000				1,90,000

(b) **Trial Balance**
as on 31st March, 2024

Name of Accounts	LF	Debit Balance (₹)	Credit Balance (₹)
Capital		—	10,00,000
Plant and Machinery		13,40,000	—
Furniture		2,40,000	—
Cash in Hand		60,000	—
Bank Overdraft		—	66,000
Purchases		22,60,000	—
Discount Allowed		2,000	—
Sales		—	34,80,000
Debtors		9,54,000	—
Creditors		—	5,20,000
Sales Return		6,000	—
Rent		1,90,000	—
General Expenses		14,000	—
Total		50,66,000	50,66,000

Solved Question 6 **Prepare a trial balance from the following balances as on 31st March, 2025.**

Name of Accounts	Amt (₹)
Capital	1,17,000
Machinery	1,80,000
Purchases	2,00,000
Sales	2,50,000
Wages Due	15,000
Rent Received	5,000
Input CGST	18,000
Input SGST	18,000
Output CGST	18,000
Output SGST	18,000
Factory Wages	6,830
Travelling Expenses	2,000
Outstanding Electricity Bill	10,630
Printing	4,000
Transportation	1,000
Postage	800
Sales Return	7,000
Purchases Return	4,000

***Closing stock (31st March, 2025) was valued at ₹ 1,72,000 (not adjusted).**

Sol. **Trial Balance**
as on ...

Name of Accounts	LF	Debit Balance (₹)	Credit Balance (₹)
Capital		—	1,17,000
Machinery		1,80,000	—
Purchases		2,00,000	—
Sales		—	2,50,000
Wages Due		—	15,000
Rent Received		—	5,000
Input CGST		18,000	—
Input SGST		18,000	—
Output CGST			18,000
Output SGST			18,000
Factory Wages		6,830	—
Travelling Expenses		2,000	—
Outstanding Electricity Bill		—	10,630
Printing		4,000	—
Transportation		1,000	—
Postage		800	—
Purchases Return		—	4,000
Sales Return		7,000	—
Total		4,37,630	4,37,630

*Closing stock will not be shown in the trial balance because it is not adjusted with purchases.

Missing Information

Solved Question 7 **Following are balances of accounts extracted from the books of Rohan & Bros. and an incomplete trial balance prepared by an inexperienced accountant. You are required to complete the trial balance.**

Name of Accounts	Amt (₹)	Name of Accounts	Amt (₹)
Stock (1st April, 2024)	50,800	Discount Allowed	6,000
Purchases	2,20,000	Cash at Bank	16,000
Sales	2,80,000	Bad Debts	6,000
Carriage	12,000	Debtors	44,400
Cash	16,000	Creditors	49,000
Furniture	36,000	Provision for Doubtful Debts	2,800
Depreciation	8,000		
Drawings	13,000	Input CGST	9,000
Return Outwards	6,400	Output CGST	10,000
Return Inwards	4,000	Input SGST	9,000
		Output SGST	10,000

Trial Balance
as on ...

Name Accounts	Debit Balance (₹)	Credit Balance (₹)
Stock (1st April, 2024)	50,800	......
Purchases	2,20,000	......
Sales	......	2,80,000
Carriage	12,000	......
Cash	16,000	......
Furniture	36,000	......
Depreciation	......	......
Drawings	13,000	......
Return Outwards	......	......
Return Inwards	......	......
Discount Allowed	6,000	......
Cash at Bank	16,000	......
Bad Debts	6,000	......
Debtors	44,400	......
Creditors	......	49,000
Provision for Doubtful Debts	......	......
Input CGST	......	......
Output SGST	......	......
Input SGST	......	......
Output SGST	......	......
Total	......	......

Sol. **Trial Balance**
as on ...

Name of Accounts	LF	Debit Balance (₹)	Credit Balance (₹)
Stock (1st April, 2024)		50,800	—
Purchases		2,20,000	—
Sales		—	2,80,000
Carriage		12,000	—
Cash		16,000	—
Furniture		36,000	—
Depreciation		**8,000**	—
Drawings		13,000	—
Return Outwards		—	**6,400**
Return Inwards		**4,000**	—
Discount Allowed		6,000	—
Cash at Bank		16,000	—
Bad Debts		6,000	—
Debtors		44,400	—
Creditors		—	49,000
Provision for Doubtful Debts		—	**2,800**
Input CGST		**9,000**	—
Output SGST		—	**10,000**
Input SGST		**9,000**	—
Output SGST		—	**10,000**
Capital		—	**92,000**
Total		4,50,200	4,50,200

Solved Question 8 **Suresh, an accountant of the firm prepared a trial balance from the following balances which is incomplete. You are required to complete the given trial balance.**

Name of Accounts	Amt (₹)	Name of Accounts	Amt (₹)
Bank	85,000	Purchases	4,45,000
Sales	8,10,000	Cash in Hand	8,500
Purchases Return	22,500	Creditors	2,15,000
Debtors	4,00,500	Sales Return	15,750
Wages	96,000	Equipment	25,000
Capital	...	Opening Stock	3,00,500

Trial Balance
as on ...

Name of Accounts	Debit Balance (₹)	Credit Balance (₹)
Bank Overdraft	85,000	...
Sales	...	...
Purchases Return	...	22,500
Debtors	4,00,500	...
Wages	96,000	...
Capital	...	...
Purchases	4,45,000	...
Cash in Hand	8,500	...
Creditors	...	...
Sales Return	...	...
Equipment	...	...
Opening Stock	...	...
Total	...	...

Sol. **Trial Balance**
as on ...

Name of Accounts	LF	Debit Balance (₹)	Credit Balance (₹)
Bank Overdraft		85,000	—
Sales		—	**8,10,000**
Purchases Return		—	22,500
Debtors		4,00,500	—
Wages		96,000	—
Capital		—	**3,28,750**
Purchases		4,45,000	—
Cash in Hand		8,500	—
Creditors		—	**2,15,000**
Sales Return		**15,750**	—
Equipment		**25,000**	—
Opening Stock		**3,00,500**	—
Total		**13,76,250**	**13,76,250**

Numerical Questions

Trial Balance

1. **From the following balances, prepare a trial balance.**

Name of Accounts	Amt (₹)
Furniture	1,50,000
Capital	1,40,000
Electricity Charges	9,000
Drawings	500
Inventory	9,000
Computer	90,000
Telephone Expenses	500
Stationery	800
Bad Debts	1,900
Bad Debts Recovered	700
Outstanding Wages	5,000
Rent Received in Advance	56,500
Loan	50,000
Outstanding Interest	500
Creditors	9,000

Ans. Total of trial balance = ₹ 2,61,700

2. **Following are given balances of accounts. You are required to prepare trial balance.**

Name of Accounts	Amt (₹)
Building	3,00,000
Capital	2,70,000
Purchases	40,000
Sales	55,000
Debtors	50,000
Creditors	80,000
Bills Payable	21,000
Bills Receivable	10,000
Bank Overdraft	8,000
Cash in Hand	5,000
Opening Stock (1st April, 2024)	8,500
Wages	18,000
Bad Debts	3,000
Outstanding Salary	500

Ans. Total of trial balance = ₹ 4,34,500

3. **From the following balance extracted from the books of Varun Traders, prepare a trial balance as at 31st March, 2024. Difference in credit side, if any, should be entered as capital.**

Name of Accounts	Amt (₹)	Name of Accounts	Amt (₹)
Purchases	2,20,000	Bad Debts	3,000
Stock (1st April, 2023)	80,000	Bad Debts Recovered	1,500
Stock (31st March, 2024) (not adjusted)	40,000	Advance Commission (Cr)	2,200
Sales	5,50,000	Furniture	35,000
Repairs	2,000	Loan to Aditya	15,000
Office Equipments	12,000	Bank Balance	25,000
Investments	18,000	Cash Balance	45,000
Premises	3,50,000	Debtors	28,000
Depreciation	2,000	Bills Receivable	18,000
Loss by Fire	1,800	Bills Payable	32,000
Drawings	4,400	Discount Received	3,400
		Interest Received	6,600

Ans. Total of trial balance = ₹ 8,59,200; Capial = ₹ 2,63,500

4. **Prepare a trial balance of Mukul & Sons from the following balances as at 31st March, 2024. Difference will be considered as capital.**

Name of Accounts	Amt (₹)	Name of Accounts	Amt (₹)
Opening Stock	40,000	Creditors	18,000
Purchases	1,20,000	Bills Receivable	8,000
Purchases Returns	10,000	Bank Overdraft	12,000
Rent	2,000	Outstanding Rent	1,600
Salaries	5,000	Drawings	15,000
Sales	1,85,000	Input CGST	8,100
Sales Returns	5,500	Input SGST	8,100
Accrued Interest	1,200	Output CGST	9,000
Discount Received	550	Output SGST	9,000
Furniture	12,000	Postage	600
Machine	65,000	Carriage	400
Debtors	46,000		

Ans. Total of trial balance = ₹ 3,36,900; Capital = ₹ 91,750

5. **Prepare a trial balance from the following account balances.** **Competency Based Que**

Name of Accounts	Amt (₹)
Capital	37,43,000
Inventory	20,00,000
Cash at Bank	3,500
Interest Received	1,00,000
Discount Allowed	50,000
Discount Received	45,000
Purchases	1,00,000
Sales	2,00,000
Opening Stock (1st April, 2024)	12,00,000
Carriage and Freight	70,000
Delivery Van	30,000
Rates, Taxes, Insurance	20,000
Advanced Loan	6,00,000
Telephone Bill Charges	15,000
Purchases Return	1,000
Sales Return	500
Input IGST	9,000
Output IGST	9,000
Closing Stock (not adjusted)	3,00,000

Ans. Total of trial balance = ₹ 40,98,000

6. **Given below is a cash book and ledger extracts relating to the books of M/s Rahul Bros. as at 31st January, 2024. You are required to prepare a trial balance.** **Competency Based Que**

Dr **Cash Account** Cr

Date	Particulars	LF	Cash (₹)	Bank (₹)	Date	Particulars	LF	Cash (₹)	Bank (₹)
2024					2024				
Jan 1	To Capital A/c		50,000	—	Jan 2	By Bank A/c	C	43,000	—
Jan 2	To Cash A/c	C	—	43,000	Jan 3	By Purchases A/c		—	4,200
Jan 10	To Sales A/c		3,600	—	Jan 20	By Mia		—	55,200
Jan 12	To Sales A/c		—	2,000	Jan 27	By Rent A/c		800	—
Jan 15	To Nia		—	47,000	Jan 31	By Balance c/d		9,800	59,100
Jan 18	To Pia		—	26,500					
			53,600	1,18,500				53,600	1,18,500
Feb 1	To Balance b/d		9,800	59,100					

Dr **Capital Account** Cr

Date	Particulars	JF	Amt (₹)	Date	Particulars	JF	Amt (₹)
2024				2024			
Jan 31	To Balance c/d		50,000	Jan 1	By Cash A/c		50,000
				Feb 1	By Balance b/d		50,000

Dr **Purchases Account** Cr

Date	Particulars	JF	Amt (₹)	Date	Particulars	JF	Amt (₹)
2024							
Jan 3	To Bank A/c		4,200				
Jan 31	To Sundries as per Purchase Book		64,000				

Dr **Purchases Return Account** Cr

Date	Particulars	JF	Amt (₹)	Date	Particulars	JF	Amt (₹)
				2024			
				Jan 31	By Sundries as per Purchase Return Book		1,000

Dr **Sales Account** Cr

Date	Particulars	JF	Amt (₹)	Date	Particulars	JF	Amt (₹)
				2024			
				Jan 10	By Cash A/c		3,600
				Jan 12	By Bank A/c		2,000
				Jan 31	By Sundries as per Sales Book		92,500

Dr **Sales Return Account** Cr

Date	Particulars	JF	Amt (₹)	Date	Particulars	JF	Amt (₹)
2024							
Jan 31	To Sundries as per Sales Return Book		1,500				

Dr **Mia** Cr

Date	Particulars	JF	Amt (₹)	Date	Particulars	JF	Amt (₹)
2024				2024			
Jan 7	To Purchase Return A/c		1,000	Jan 6	By Purchases A/c		64,000
Jan 20	To Bank A/c		55,200				
Jan 31	To Balance c/d		7,800				
			64,000				64,000
				Feb 1	By Balance b/d		7,800

Dr **Nia** Cr

Date	Particulars	JF	Amt (₹)	Date	Particulars	JF	Amt (₹)
2024				2024			
Jan 13	To Sales A/c		60,000	Jan 15	By Bank A/c		47,000
				Jan 31	By Balance c/d		13,000
			60,000				60,000
Feb 1	To Balance b/d		13,000				

Dr **Pia** Cr

Date	Particulars	JF	Amt (₹)	Date	Particulars	JF	Amt (₹)
2024				2024			
Jan 14	To Sales A/c		32,500	Jan 15	By Sales Return A/c		1,500
				Jan 18	By Bank A/c		26,500
				Jan 31	By Balance c/d		4,500
			32,500				32,500
Feb 1	To Balance b/d		4,500				

Dr **Rent Account** Cr

Date	Particulars	JF	Amt (₹)	Date	Particulars	JF	Amt (₹)
2024							
Jan 27	To Cash A/c		800				

7. Prepare a trial balance from the following balances of M/s Sharma and Sons as at 31st March, 2024

Name of Accounts	Amt (₹)	Name of Accounts	Amt (₹)
Opening Stock	10,000	Creditors	6,375
Purchases	42,500	Bills Receivable	2,300
Purchases Returns	2,500	Bills Payable	1,250
Sales	80,000	Cash in Hand	5,610
Sales Returns	3,100	Bank Overdraft	5,000
Rent	600	Interest on Overdraft	900
Salaries	2,850	Capital	25,000
Advertisement	440	Drawings	3,900
Commission Received	720	Input CGST	2,500
Discount (Cr)	355	Input SGST	2,500
Furniture	3,000	Output CGST	4,000
Machinery	31,000	Output SGST	4,000
Debtors	18,000		

Ans. Total of trial balance = ₹ 1,29,200

8. **The following is the trial balance prepared by an inexperienced accountant. Identify the errors and redraft it in a correct form.** **Competency Based Que**

Trial Balance
for the year ending 31st March, 2024

Name of Accounts	LF	Debit Balance (₹)	Credit Balance (₹)
Sundry Debtors		6,100	—
Sundry Creditors		—	4,600
Opening Stock		7,800	—
Purchases		26,750	—
Purchases Returns		1,050	—
Cash in Hand		5,500	—
Machinery		20,100	—
Goodwill		—	5,000
Sales		—	43,100
Sales Returns		—	3,900
Loan from Ram		10,000	—
Interest on Ram's Loan		1,500	—
Bills Receivable		—	3,200
Capital		—	28,500
Life Insurance Premium		2,500	—
Carriage		300	—
Advertisement		1,250	—
Discount Received		750	—
Investments		4,000	—
Interest on Investments		400	—
Total		88,000	88,300

Ans. Total of trial balance = ₹ 88,400

9. **Following is the trial balance of Raj Nayak as on 31st March, 2024.** **Competency Based Que**

Name of Accounts	LF	Debit Balance (₹)	Credit Balance (₹)
Capital		—	6,40,000
Fixed Assets		3,60,000	—
Drawings		1,20,000	—
Debtors		4,80,000	—
Creditors		—	3,60,000
Purchases		14,20,000	—
Sales		—	21,00,000
Bank Balance		90,000	—
Cash in Hand		60,000	—
Salaries		3,30,000	—
Rent		2,40,000	—
Total		31,00,000	31,00,000

Having prepared the trial balance, it was discovered that following transactions remained unrecorded

(i) Goods were sold on credit amounting to ₹ 70,000.
(ii) Paid to creditors ₹ 34,000 by cheque.
(iii) Goods worth ₹ 8,000 were returned to a supplier.
(iv) Paid salary ₹ 25,000 by cheque.

Required

(a) Pass journal entries for the above mentioned transactions and post them into ledger.
(b) Redraft the trial balance.

Ans. (b) Total of trial balance = ₹ 31,36,000

10. **The following trial balance is prepared by an inexperienced accountant. Redraft it correctly.**

Trial Balance
for the year ending 31st March, 2024

Name of Accounts	LF	Debit Balance (₹)	Credit Balance (₹)
Cash in Hand		28,000	—
Stock (Opening)		22,500	—
Machinery		68,000	—
Purchases		85,000	—
Carriage Inwards		4,200	—
Sundry Debtors		26,000	—
Bills Payable		31,000	—
Outstanding Salary		800	—
Rent Paid		6,600	—
Advertisement		6,400	—
Discount Received		2,200	—
Bank Overdraft		—	18,500
Capital		—	60,000
Goodwill		—	9,000
Creditors		—	9,200
Sales		—	1,40,000
Returns Inward		—	4,000
Drawings		—	2,500
Investments		—	3,000
Returns Outward		—	3,500
Total		2,80,700	2,49,700

Ans. Total of trial balance = ₹ 2,65,200

Missing Information

11. **From the following balances extracted on 31st March, 2024, Ajay prepared an incomplete trial balance. You are required to complete the same.** **Competency Based Que**

Name of Accounts	Amt (₹)	Name of Accounts	Amt (₹)
Purchases	2,12,500	Drawings	9,625
Stock (1st April, 2023)	30,000	Return Inwards	4,375
Sales	1,31,250	Premises	6,60,000
Sundry Debtors	29,750	Sundry Creditors	20,125

Name of Accounts	Amt (₹)	Name of Accounts	Amt (₹)
Discount Received	4,375	Discount Allowed	3,500
Carriage Outwards	875	Carriage Inwards	1,750
Cash in Hand	4,375	Cash at Bank	21,875
Machinery	1,55,625	General Expenses	2,625
Provision for Depreciation on Machinery	30,250	Bad Debts Written-off	3,065
		Provision for Doubtful Debts	2,975

Trial Balance
as at 31st March, 2024

Name of Accounts	Debit Balance (₹)	Credit Balance (₹)
Purchases	2,12,500	...
Stock (1st April, 2023)	...	...
Sales	...	1,31,250
Sundry Debtors	29,750	...
Discount Received	...	4,375
Carriage Outwards	...	...
Cash in Hand	4,375	...
Machinery	1,55,625	...
Provision for Depreciation on Machinery	...	...
Drawings	...	...
Return Inwards	...	...
Premises	6,60,000	...
Sundry Creditors	...	...
Discount Allowed	3,500	...
Carriage Inwards	1,750	...
Cash at Bank	21,875	...
General Expenses	2,625	...
Bad Debts Written-off	3,065	...
Provision for Doubtful Debts	...	...
Capital	...	...
Total	...	...

Ans. Total of trial balance = ₹ 11,39,940

12. **From the following balances, an accountant prepared an incomplete trial balance. You are required to complete the same.** **Competency Based Que**

Name of Accounts	Amt (₹)	Name of Accounts	Amt (₹)
Cash	10,700	Sundry Creditors	40,000
Capital	80,000	Investment	8,000
Purchases	85,000	Plant and Machinery	15,000
Sales	1,08,400	Building	20,000
Purchases Return	6,000	Postage	400
Sales Return	4,000	Drawings	8,000
Transportation	1,800	Salaries	6,000
Discount Allowed	500		
Printing	5,000		
Sundry Debtors	70,000		

Trial Balance
as on ...

Name of Accounts	Debit Balance (₹)	Credit Balance (₹)
Cash	10,700	...
Capital	...	...
Purchases	85,000	...
Sales	...	1,08,400
Purchases Return	...	...
Sales Return	...	...
Transportation	1,800	...
Discount Allowed	500	...
Printing	...	...
Creditors	...	40,000
Investment	8,000	...
Plant and Machinery	15,000	...
Building	20,000	...
Postage	...	...
Drawings	...	...
Salaries	6,000	...
Debtors	70,000	...
Total	...	...

Ans. Total of trial balance = ₹ 2,34,700

Theoretical Questions

Short Answer Type Questions

1. **State any four functions of a trial balance.**

Or **Describe the purpose for the preparation of a trial balance.** **NCERT**

Or **What are the objectives or functions or importance of a trial balance?**

Ans. The objectives/functions/purpose of a trial balance are

(i) **Ascertain the Arithmetical Accuracy of the Ledger Accounts**

The trial balance ensures the arithmetical accuracy of the ledger accounts. When the debit and credit balances in the trial balance are equal, it is assumed that the posting to the ledger accounts is arithmetically correct i.e. all debits and corresponding credit have been properly recorded in ledger.

(ii) **Helps in Locating Errors**

A trial balance helps in the detection or location of errors. However, all the errors are not disclosed, but only arithmetical errors are disclosed.

(iii) **Summary of the Ledger Accounts**

Trial balance offers a summary of the ledger. It enables to know the assets, liabilities, expenses, incomes, etc.

(iv) **Helps in the Preparation of Final Accounts**
Trial balance is considered as the connecting link between accounting records and the preparation of financial statements. As trial balance is a list of summary of all ledger accounts, it provides a basis for, preparation of final accounts (trading and profit and loss account and balance sheet).

2. State the characteristics/features of a trial balance.

Ans. The characteristics/features of a trial balance are as follows

(i) Trial balance contains a list of all ledger accounts including cash account.
(ii) It is a statement, not an account.
(iii) It is just a working paper, it is not a part of the double entry system of bookkeeping.
(iv) It can be prepared at any time during the accounting period, i.e. at the end of any chosen period which may be monthly, quarterly, half-yearly or annually depending upon the requirements.
(v) It is prepared to check the arithmetical accuracy of the ledger accounts.
(vi) It is not an absolute proof of the accuracy of accounting records.
(vii) It is always prepared on a particular date and not for a particular period.

3. "Trial balance is a link between the ledger and final accounts." Explain. Competency Based Que

Ans. Trial balance is a connecting link between the accounting records and the preparation of financial statements. The availability of a tallied trial balance is the first step in the preparation of financial statements, as it contains the balances of all the accounts.

All revenue and expenses account, which appear in the trial balance are transferred to the trading and profit and loss account and all liabilities, capital and assets accounts are transferred to the balance sheet.

4. "Trial balance only confirms that the total of all debit balances matches the total of all credit balances. There are some errors inspite of those, a trial balance may agree." Defend or refute the statement with valid reason. Competency Based Que

Ans. The statement is defended that a trial balance only confirms that both side are equal. There may be errors which cannot be detected by a trial balance.

Following errors are not disclosed by a trial balance
(i) Error of complete omission
(ii) Error of principles (iii) Compensating errors

5. Following are some accounts given below. State the side (debit or credit) in which the balance of these accounts will be shown in trial balance.
Furniture account, machine account, sales account, purchase account, sales return account, carriage inward account, carriage outward account, drawings account, input CGST account, opening stock, loss by fire account. Competency Based Que

Ans.

Accounts	Side	Accounts	Side
Furniture A/c	Debit	Carriage outward A/c	Debit
Machine A/c	Debit	Drawings A/c	Debit
Sales A/c	Credit	Input CGST A/c	Debit
Purchase A/c	Debit	Opening stock	Debit
Sales return A/c	Debit	Loss by fire A/c	Debit
Carriage inward A/c	Debit		

6. State the steps to prepare a trial balance.

Ans. Following are the steps to be taken to prepare a trial balance

Step 1 The balance of each account in the ledger is ascertained.

Step 2 List each account and place its balance in the debit or credit column of trial balance.

Step 3 Compute the total of debit column.

Step 4 Compute the total of credit column.

Step 5 Verify that the sum of the debit balances equals the sum of credit balances.

Objective Questions

Multiple Choice Questions (MCQs)

1. What is the trial balance?
(a) An account (b) A statement
(c) A subsidiary book (d) A principal book

2. Trial balance is ..... .
(a) a real account
(b) a nominal account
(c) an artificial personal account
(d) not an account

3. The basis on which a trial balance is prepared is
(a) the subsidiary books (b) the ledger
(c) cash book (d) journal

4. Trial balance shows
(a) real accounts (b) nominal accounts
(c) balances of accounts (d) None of these

5. What is shown by trial balance?
(a) Final position of accounts
(b) Standard position of accounts
(c) Beginning position of accounts
(d) None of the above

6. Preparation of the trial balance is not ....
(a) compulsory (b) mandatory
(c) Both (a) and (b) (d) None of these

7. Which of the following is a limitation of trial balance?
(a) It offers a summary of the ledger accounts
(b) It is not a part of double entry system
(c) Gives only condensed information of each account
(d) None of the above

8. A trial balance is prepared **NCERT**
(a) after preparation financial statement
(b) after recording transactions in subsidiary books
(c) after posting to ledger is complete
(d) after posting to ledger is complete and accounts have been balanced

9. Trial balance is considered as the connecting link between accounting records and preparation of financial statements. It provides a basis for **Competency Based Que**
(a) auditing accounting reports
(b) accuracy of the ledger account
(c) further processing of accounting data
(d) All of the above

10. Agreement of trial balance is affected by **NCERT**
(a) one sided errors only (b) two sided errors only
(c) Both (a) and (b) (d) None of these

11. Which is not a trial balance method?
(a) Balance method
(b) Total method
(c) Balance cum total method
(d) Grand total method

12. One of the trader is preparing trial balance and it has maintained all the books of accounts properly. What is the best method you suggest to prepare trial balance? **Competency Based Que**
(a) Balance total method
(b) Total method
(c) Balance method
(d) None of the above

13. Trial balance can be prepared under balance method, only when
(a) all the entries are made in journal
(b) all the subsidiary books are maintained
(c) all the ledger accounts have been balanced
(d) all the balances have been transferred to final accounts

14. A trader has prepared the trial balance and total doesn't tie. Which approach the trader should follow? **Competency Based Que**
(a) He should recheck all the ledger
(b) He should recheck the total of trial balance
(c) He should open the suspense account
(d) All of the above

15. Which of the following error is disclosed by trial balance?
(a) Error of complete ommission
(b) Error of principle
(c) Error of partial ommission
(d) Compensating error

16. Trial balance helps in preparation of ....
(a) profit and loss account
(b) balance sheet
(c) Both (a) and (b)
(d) None of the above

17. The purpose of trial balance is to ascertain
(a) whether all debits and credits are properly recorded or not
(b) all accounts have been correctly balanced
(c) arithmetical accuracy of all ledger accounts
(d) All of the above

18. Trial balance can be prepared by .... method.
(a) total method (b) balance method
(c) total cum balance method
(d) All of the above

19. Which of the following statement is correct? **Competency Based Que**
(a) Trial balance can be prepared by total method
(b) Trial balance is not a connection link between accounting records and the preparation of financial statements
(c) Accounting accuracy is ensured if the totals of debit and credit balances are equal
(d) All of the above

20. Which of the following is correct in regard to objective of preparing the trial balance?
(a) It ascertains the arithmetical accuracy of the ledger accounts
(b) It helps in locating errors
(c) It helps in preparation of financial statements
(d) All of the above

21. Which of the following is a correct statement? Competency Based Que

(a) Under total method, total of each side of the ledger is shown in the trial balance
(b) Under balance method, balance of account is shown in respective column
(c) Total cum balance method is a combination of total methods and balances method
(d) All of the above

22. Trial balance is prepared

(a) monthly (b) quarterly
(c) half yearly (d) on any date

23. Identify the incorrect objective of preparing trial balance. Competency Based Que

(i) To prepare financial statements.
(ii) To locate errors.
(iii) To communicate accounting information to the users.
(iv) To ascertain arithmetical accuracy of ledger accounts.

Codes
(a) (i) and (ii) (b) (i), (iii), (iv)
(c) Only (iii) (d) (ii) and (iv)

24. Identify the incorrect characteristic of trial balance. Competency Based Que

(a) It shows balances of all ledger accounts and cash book
(b) It shows final position of all accounts
(c) It is a part of double entry system of bookkeeping
(d) It can be prepared anytime

25. Trial balance does not include

(a) opening stock (b) closing stock
(c) drawings (d) capital

26. Which of the following account's balance will be shown on credit side of trial balance?

(a) Machinery (b) Purchases
(c) Purchases return (d) Sales return

27. Which balance of account from the following will be placed in credit side of trial balance?

(a) Carriage outwards (b) Carriage inwards
(c) Rebate received (d) Freight inwards

28. You are given the following journal entries Competency Based Que

(i) Bank A/c	**Dr 20,000**	
To Cash A/c		**20,000**
(ii) Bank A/c	**Dr 15,000**	
To Sales A/c		**15,000**
(iii) Carriage A/c	**Dr 500**	
To Bank A/c		**500**

On the basis of the above journal entries, state the balance and column on which bank account will be shown.

(a) ₹ 35,000; debit column (b) ₹ 34,500; debit column
(c) ₹ 30,000; credit column (d) ₹ 35,500; debit column

29. "Purchased a machine for ₹ 25,000 from Randhawa & Bros." For the above transaction, accountant wrongly posted the amount in debit side of 'Randhawas & Bros.' account in the ledger.
With what amount and which column of trial balance will be affected? Competency Based Que

(a) ₹ 25,000; credit column (short)
(b) ₹ 25,000; debit column (short)
(c) ₹ 50,000; credit column (short)
(d) ₹ 50,000; debit column (short)

30. If the trial balance agrees, it implies that NCERT

(a) there is no error in books
(b) there may be two sided errors in the book
(c) there may be one sided error in the books
(d) there may be both two sided and one sided errors in the books

31. Sundry creditors worth ₹ 50,000 will be shown

(a) ₹ 50,000 in debit column of trial balance
(b) ₹ 50,000 in credit column of trial balance
(c) ₹ 50,000 as an adjustment at the end
(d) None of the above

32. Interest received worth ₹ 1,000 and sales worth ₹ 5,00,000 are shown Competency Based Que

(a) in debit column and credit column respectively of trial balance
(b) in credit column and debit column respectively of trial balance
(c) in credit column of trial balance
(d) in debit column of trial balance

33. The given below are the balances of the accounts. You are required to find out the total of the trial balance.
Capital ₹ 3,00,000, cash ₹ 1,80,000, creditors ₹ 2,00,000, sales ₹ 2,00,000, cash at bank ₹ 70,000, debtors ₹ 4,00,000, bank loan ₹ 1,00,000, purchases ₹ 1,50,000. Competency Based Que

(a) ₹ 10,00,000 (b) ₹ 8,00,000
(c) ₹ 7,00,000 (d) ₹ 9,00,000

34. The following trial balance as on 31st March, 2022 is extracted by Ramesh's CA. Choose the correct option on the basis of the trial balance. Competency Based Que

Name of Accounts	LF	Debit Balance (₹)	Credit Balance (₹)
Furniture		—	30,000
Debtors		2,00,000	—
Machinery		40,000	—
Goodwill		—	50,000
Creditors		60,000	—
Discount Received		—	5,000
Capital		—	95,000
Bank Loan		—	1,20,000
Total		3,00,000	3,00,000

(a) Furniture and machinery should appear in debit column of trial balance
(b) Creditors should appear in credit column of trial balance
(c) Goodwill should appear in debit column of trial balance
(d) All of the above

35. **Bank overdraft of ₹ 5,000 will be shown**
(a) in debit column of trial balance
(b) in credit column of trial balance
(c) as an adjustment at the end
(d) None of the above

36. **Trial Balance**

Name of Accounts	LF	Debit Balance (₹)	Credit Balance (₹)
Prepaid Expenses		—	5,000
Outstanding Expenses		—	2,000
Bad Debts Recovered		—	4,000
Interest on Investment		—	1,000
Machinery		8,000	—
Investment		4,000	—
Total		12,000	12,000

Which of the following is incorrect? **Competency Based Que**
(a) Prepaid expenses should appear in credit column of trial balance
(b) Outstanding rent should appear in credit column of trial balance
(c) Interest on investment should appear in credit column of trial balance
(d) All of the above

37. **Choose correct journal entry when closing stock is adjusted with purchase account** **Competency Based Que**
(a) Purchase A/c Dr
  To Closing Stock A/c
(b) Closing Stock A/c Dr
  To Purchase A/c
(c) Closing Stock A/c Dr
  To Opening Stock A/c
(d) None of the above

38. **Accrued commission ₹ 5,000 and purchase ₹ 30,000 will be shown** **Competency Based Que**
(a) in debit column and credit column respectively of trial balance
(b) in credit column and debit column respectively of trial balance
(c) in credit column of trial balance
(d) in debit column of trial balance

39. **Find out the total of trial balance.**
Capital ₹ 50,000, cash ₹ 20,000, furniture ₹ 30,000, creditors ₹ 15,000, purchases ₹ 15,000; bank loan ₹ 10,000, debtors ₹ 10,000. **Competency Based Que**
(a) ₹ 70,000 (b) ₹ 60,000
(c) ₹ 75,000 (d) ₹ 65,000

40. **What will be the effect on trial balance if cash received from Ramesh ₹ 2,000 was omitted to be posted in Ramesh account?** **Competency Based Que**
(a) Debit side will exceed credit side by ₹ 2,000
(b) Credit side will exceed debit side by ₹ 2,000
(c) Debit and credit side will be equal
(d) None of the above

41. **If opening stock, closing stock, purchase and cost of goods sold are given then which items will be appeared in trial balance?** **Competency Based Que**
(a) Opening stock and purchase
(b) Closing stock and cost of goods sold
(c) Either (a) or (b) (d) None of the above

42. **If closing stock is shown in trial balance, it means**
(a) it is adjusted against opening stock
(b) it is adjusted against purchases
(c) Both (a) and (b)
(d) None of the above

43. **After the trial balance had been prepared and balance of purchase account ₹ 2,20,000 was placed, following transactions were discovered which were not recorded.** **Competency Based Que**
(i) Purchased goods for ₹ 30,000 from Kamakhya.
(ii) Return of goods by a debtor earlier sold (cost price ₹ 2,000) sale price ₹ 3,000.
What will be correct amount of purchase should be shown in trial balance?
(a) ₹ 2,50,000 (b) ₹ 2,47,000
(c) ₹ 2,53,000 (d) ₹ 1,90,000

Assertion-Reason

Direction (Q.No. 44 to 51) *Read the following Assertion (A) and Reason (R) and choose the correct alternative from the following*

Alternatives
(a) Both Assertion (A) and Reason (R) are true and Reason (R) is the correct explanation of Assertion (A)
(b) Both Assertion (A) and Reason (R) are true, but Reason (R) is not the correct explanation of Assertion (A)
(c) Assertion (A) is false, but Reason (R) is true
(d) Assertion (A) is true, but Reason (R) is false

44. **Assertion** (A) The trial balance does not help in detecting certain types of errors made in ledger accounts.
Reason (R) The trial balance only checks the arithmetical accuracy of accounts and does not ensure that all transactions are correctly recorded.

45. **Assertion** (A) A trial balance ensures that no transactions are omitted from books of accounts.
Reason (R) A trial balance does not detect errors of omission or compensating errors.

46. **Assertion** (A) Closing stock does not appear in trial balance.

Reason (R) When closing stock is not adjusted with purchase account it is not shown in trial balance.

47. **Assertion** (A) Rent received is shown in credit column of trial balance.

Reason (R) All incomes and profits are shown in credit column of trial balance.

48. **Assertion** (A) Owner's wife loan to the business is shown in credit column of trial balance.

Reason (R) All assets are shown in credit column of trial balance.

49. **Assertion** (A) Trial balance is not a conclusive proof of accuracy of accounts.

Reason (R) Error of commission do not affect trial balance.

50. **Assertion** (A) Furniture and fixtures is shown in debit column of trial balance.

Reason (R) All assets are shown in debit column of trial balance.

51. **Assertion** (A) Trial balance total will not agree if there is any error.

Reason (R) Various errors like errors of principle, errors of complete omission are not disclosed by trial balance.

Two Statements Based MCQs

Direction (Q.No. 52 to 59) *Read the following statements carefully and choose the correct alternatives*

Alternatives

(a) Both the statements are correct
(b) Both the statements are incorrect
(c) Statement I is correct and Statement II is incorrect
(d) Statement I is incorrect and Statement II is correct

52. **Statement I** A trial balance is a statement showing the balance of all the accounts in the ledger.

Statement II Trial balance helps in preparing the final statements.

53. **Statement I** A trial balance does not ascertain the arithmetical accuracy of the ledger accounts.

Statement II Trial balance help in locating errors.

54. **Statement I** Balance of capital account is shown in credit column of trial balance.

Statement II Balance of bills receivable is shown in credit column in trial balance.

55. **Statement I** Trial balance is prepared with the help of all accounts and cash book.

Statement II Trial balance is prepared only at the end of financial or calendar year.

56. **Statement I** Trial balance is not a conclusive proof of the accuracy of the accounts.

Statement II It ensures that all debits and corresponding credits have been properly recorded in the ledger.

57. **Statement I** Trial balance can be prepared by total method, balances method and total cum balances method.

Statement II Balance method of preparing trial balance is most widely used method in practice.

58. **Statement I** Rent from subletting account balance is shown in credit column of trial balance.

Statement II "Rent due to landlord account's, balance is shown in debit column" of trial balance.

59. **Statement I** 'Loan from SBI bank' is a liability, hence it is shown in credit column of trial balance.

Statement II 'Loan to Suresh' is an asset, hence it is shown in debit column of trial balance.

Matching

60. Match the following

Column I		Column II
A. Carriage inward and carriage outward	(i)	Credit and debit column respectively
B. Returns inward and returns outwards	(ii)	Both in debit column
C. Interest received and rent received	(iii)	Debit and credit column respectively
D. Creditors and loan advanced	(iv)	Both in credit column

Codes

	A	B	C	D		A	B	C	D
(a)	(ii)	(iii)	(i)	(iv)	(b)	(ii)	(iii)	(iv)	(i)
(c)	(i)	(iv)	(iii)	(ii)	(d)	(iii)	(ii)	(i)	(iv)

61. **Match the column in respects of steps for preparation of trial balance**

Column I	Column II
A. Step 1	(i) List each account and place its balance in debit and credit column
B. Step 2	(ii) The balances of each account in the ledger are ascertained
C. Step 3	(iii) Compute the total of debit column
D. Step 4	(iv) Compute the total of credit column

Codes

	A	B	C	D		A	B	C	D
(a)	(ii)	(i)	(iii)	(iv)	(b)	(ii)	(iii)	(iv)	(i)
(c)	(iv)	(iii)	(ii)	(i)	(d)	(i)	(ii)	(iii)	(iv)

62. **Match the following**

Column I	Column II
A. Closing stock	(i) Does not affect the total of trial balance
B. Suspense account	(ii) Used to locate errors in a trial balance
C. Compensating error	(iii) Recorded on the asset side of balance sheet
D. List of ledger balances	(iv) Basis for preparing a trial balance

Codes

	A	B	C	D		A	B	C	D
(a)	(i)	(ii)	(iii)	(iv)	(b)	(iii)	(ii)	(i)	(iv)
(c)	(iii)	(ii)	(iv)	(i)	(d)	(ii)	(iii)	(i)	(iv)

Case Based MCQs

Direction Read *the following case study and answer the questions 63 and 64 on the basis of the same*

Mr. Gupta is a sole proprietor who lives near Daryaganj. He started his business on 1st April, 2024 with capital of ₹ 1,40,000. His daughter, Reena who is in class 11th of ABC school prepares his trial balance as on 31st March, 2025. Mr. Gupta is a penny pincher who does not want to appoint a CA to prepare his financial statements. Following is extract of trial balance prepared by Reena.

Name of Accounts	LF	Debit Balance (₹)	Credit Balance (₹)
Cash in Hand		10,000	—
Machinery		—	50,000
Mr. Gupta's Wife Loan		30,000	—
Drawings		—	15,000
Purchases		25,000	—
Return Inwards		—	500
Return Outwards		600	—
Sundry Expenses		100	—
Rent		1,200	—
Debtors		1,140	—
Creditors		—	10,000
Total		68,040	75,500

63. **Reena has shown machinery in credit balance of trial balance. According to you, where it should be shown?**

(a) In credit balance (b) In debit balance
(c) As an adjustment
(d) Should be adjusted against cash

64. **Identify the item(s) that has/have been shown incorrectly by Reena.**

I. Mr. Gupta's wife loan **II. Cash in hand**
III. Drawings **IV. Purchases**

Codes

(a) Only I (b) Only II
(c) Both I and III (d) Both IV and II

Direction *Read the following case study and answer the questions 65 and 66 on the basis of the same*

Manuj Jindal, dropout UPSC aspirant has now started his own Edtech Company 'MJ Enterprises', where he sell UPSC, RBI and SEBI exam courses books. To maintain his books of accounts, he hired his friend Sahil, who has just passed IPCC group II. After preparing following trial balance, Sahil discovered that some transactions were not recorded.

Trial Balance
as on ......

Name of Accounts	LF	Debit Balance (₹)	Credit Balance (₹)
Furniture		2,00,000	—
Capital		—	2,00,000
Drawings		1,00,000	—
Debtors		1,80,000	—
Creditors		—	1,95,000
Purchases		2,00,000	—
Sales		—	5,00,000
Bank		60,000	—
Cash in Hand		85,000	—
Rent		70,000	—
Total		8,95,000	8,95,000

Following transactions were not recorded

(i) Books worth ₹ 5,000 purchased on credit.
(ii) Manuj withdraws ₹ 10,000 for personal use.
(iii) Purchased from M/s Kamran Furniture costing ₹ 20,000.

65. **Which journal entry reflects the correct accounting treatment of transaction "Manuj withdraws ₹ 10,000 for personal use"?**

(a) Drawings A/c	Dr	10,000	
To Cash A/c			10,000
(b) Manuj A/c	Dr	10,000	
To Cash A/c			10,000
(c) Capital A/c	Dr	10,000	
To Cash A/c			10,000
(d) MJ Enterprises A/c	Dr	10,000	
To Cash A/c			10,000

66. **Which of the following will be the amount of purchases shown in trial balance?**

(a) ₹ 2,15,000 (b) ₹ 2,25,000
(c) ₹ 1,95,000 (d) ₹ 2,05,000

Answers

1. (b) A statement
2. (d) not an account
3. (b) the ledger
4. (c) balances of accounts
5. (a) Final position of accounts
6. (c) Both (a) and (b)
7. (c) Gives only condensed information of each account
8. (d) after posting to ledger is complete and accounts have been balanced
9. (c) further processing of accounting data
10. (a) one sided errors only
11. (d) Grand total method
12. (c) Balance method
13. (c) all the ledger accounts have been balanced
14. (d) All of the above
15. (c) Error of partial ommission
16. (c) Both (a) and (b)
17. (d) All of the above
18. (d) All of the above
19. (a) Trial balance can be prepared by total method.
20. (d) All of the above
21. (d) All of the above
22. (d) on any date
23. (c) All others are correct objective of preparing trial balance except communicating accounting information to the users.
24. (c) Trial balance is not a part of double entry system of bookkeeping. It is a result of double entry system of bookkeeping.
25. (b) Trial balance does not include closing stock when it is not adjusted with purchases.
26. (c) Purchases return
27. (c) Rebate received is an income hence it has credit balance. All other accounts given are expenses which have debit balance.
28. (b) ₹ 34,500; debit column
29. (c) Amount is posted to debit side instead of credit of Randhawa & Bros. account, hence credit side will be affected short by ₹ 50,000.
30. (b) there may be two sided errors in the book
31. (b) ₹ 50,000 in credit column of trial balance
32. (c) Interest received account and sales account, both have credit balance.
33. (b) Total of Trial Balance = Capital + Creditors + Sales + Bank Loan

    = 3,00,000 + 2,00,000 + 2,00,000 + 1,00,000

    = ₹ 8,00,000
34. (d) All of the above
35. (b) Bank overdraft is a liability for the business, hence it is shown in credit column of trial balance.
36. (a) Prepaid expenses are asset, hence they are placed in debit column of trial balance.
37. (b) Closing Stock A/c Dr

    To Purchase A/c
38. (d) in debit column of trial balance
39. (c) ₹ 75,000
40. (a) Debit side will exceed credit side by ₹ 2,000
41. (c) Either (a) or (b)
42. (b) Usually, closing stock does not appear in trial balance when it's information is given outside the trial balance. However, if it is adjusted against purchases, it will be shown in trial balance.
43. (a) Correct amount of purchase = 2,20,000 + 30,000

    = ₹ 2,50,000
44. (a) Both Assertion (A) and Reason (R) are true and Reason (R) is the correct explanation of Assertion (A)
45. (c) A trial balance does not detect errors of ommission and compensating errors.

    Errors of ommission affect both debit and credit side hence it is not detected even trial balance agree.

    Errors of compensating means an error in one account is compensated by an error in another account.
46. (a) Both Assertion (A) and Reason (R) are true and Reason (R) is the correct explanation of Assertion (A)
47. (a) Both Assertion (A) and Reason (R) are true and Reason (R) is the correct explanation of Assertion (A)
48. (d) Assets have debit balance hence these are shown in debit column of trial balance.
49. (a) Both Assertion (A) and Reason (R) are true and Reason (R) is the correct explanation of Assertion (A)
50. (a) Both Assertion (A) and Reason (R) are true and Reason (R) is the correct explanation of Assertion (A)
51. (c) When there are errors of wrong casting, errors of partial ommission, etc., trial balance does not agree.
52. (a) Both the statements are correct
53. (d) Trial balance is prepared to ascertain arithmetical accuracy of the ledger accounts.
54. (c) Bills receivable is an asset hence it is shown in debit column of trial balance.
55. (c) Trial balance is prepared normally at the end of financial year. It means it is not compulsory to prepare trial balance at the end of the year only. It can be prepared at any time.
56. (a) Both the statements are correct
57. (a) Both the statements are correct
58. (c) Rent due to landlord is a liability, therefore it will be shown in credit column rather than debit column.
59. (a) Both the statements are correct
60. (b) (ii) (iii) (iv) (i)
61. (a) (ii) (i) (iii) (iv)
62. (b) (iii) (ii) (i) (iv)
63. (b) In debit balance
64. (c) Both I and III
65. (a) Drawings A/c Dr 10,000

    To Cash A/c 10,000
66. (d) ₹ 2,05,000 (2,00,000 + 5,000)

07

CHAPTER

Bank Reconciliation Statement

Bank reconciliation statement is a statement showing the reasons or causes of differences between bank statement and cash book.

YOUR STUDY GOALS

7.1 Meaning of Bank Reconciliation Statement
7.2 Reasons of Differences in Cash Book and Passbook Balances
7.3 Preparation of Bank Reconciliation Statement

YOUR PRACTICE GOAL

- Topicwise Solved Questions (14 Solved Questions)
- Numerical Questions [22 Questions (Unsolved)]
- Theoretical Questions [6 Questions (with answers)]
- Objective Questions (61 Qs ; MCQs, A-R, Statements, Matching, Case)

7.1 Meaning of Bank Reconciliation Statement

Bank reconciliation statement is a statement which is prepared mainly to reconcile (tally) the difference between the bank balance as shown by the cash book and passbook.

Features of Bank Reconciliation Statement

- It is prepared for the reconciliation of cash book balance with passbook balance.
- It is prepared by the customer having an account with the bank.
- It is prepared on the basis of bank statement supplied by the bank.
- It is prepared on a particular date.

Need and Importance of Bank Reconciliation Statement

- It helps in locating and rectifying the errors or omissions committed either by the firm or by the bank.
- It helps the firm to keep track of the cheques issued and also helps to check the accuracy of the cash book.
- It shows the undue delay in the collection and clearing of the cheques by the bank.
- It reduces the chances of fraud by the staff of the firm or bank.
- It facilitates the preparation of amended or revised cash book.
- It helps to assure the customer about the correctness of the bank balance shown by the passbook.

7.2 Reasons of Differences in Cash Book and Passbook Balances

The difference between cash book and passbook balances is caused by following reasons

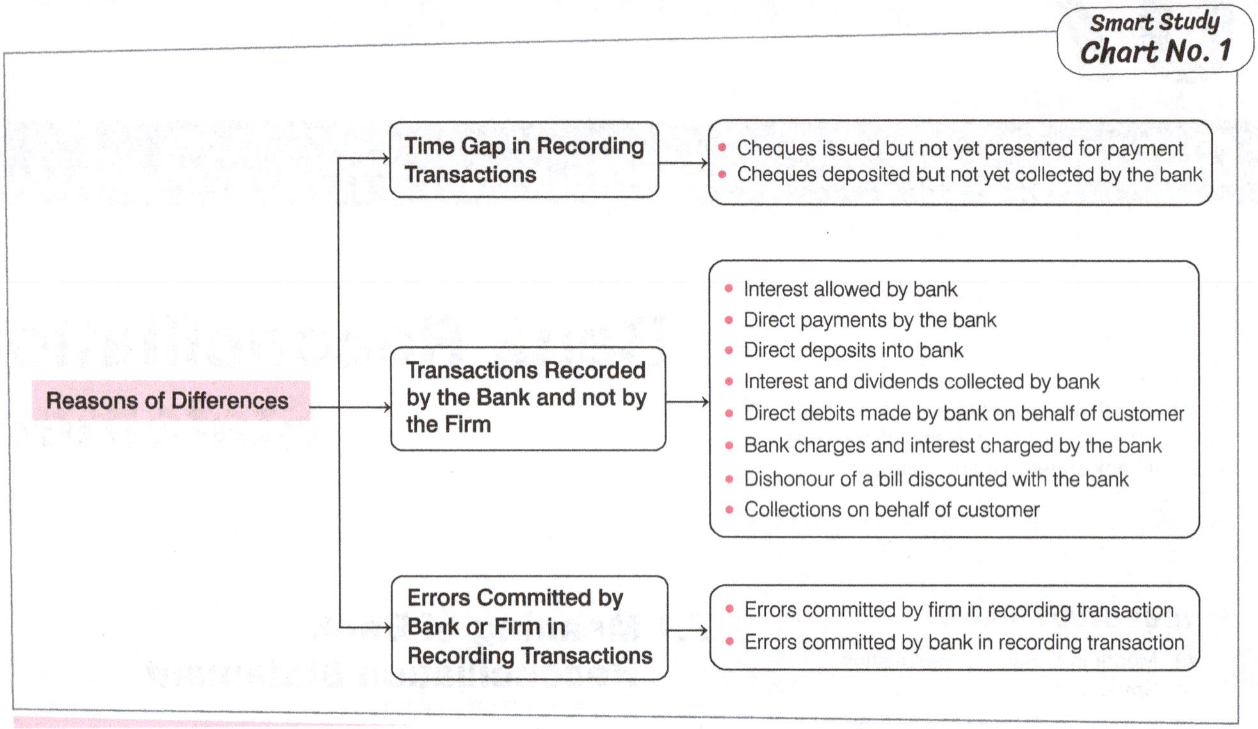

7.3 Preparation of Bank Reconciliation Statement

- Tally the debit side of the cash book and the credit side of the passbook and *vice-versa* and note the point of differences.
- A bank reconciliation statement is prepared by taking either the balance of passbook or cash book as the starting point.
- If the starting point is balance as per cash book, the answer arrived at will be the balance as per passbook and *vice-versa*.

Bank Reconciliation Statement
as on ......

Particulars	Plus (₹)	Minus (₹)

Points to be Remembered

- If it is not clearly stated that the balance as per cash book is debit or credit, it will be treated as a debit balance.
- If it is not clearly stated that the balance as per passbook is debit or credit, it will be treated as a credit balance.
- 'Balance as per ledger account' indicates the 'Balance as per cash book'.
- 'Balance as per bank book' or 'Balance as per bank statement' indicates 'Balance as per passbook'.

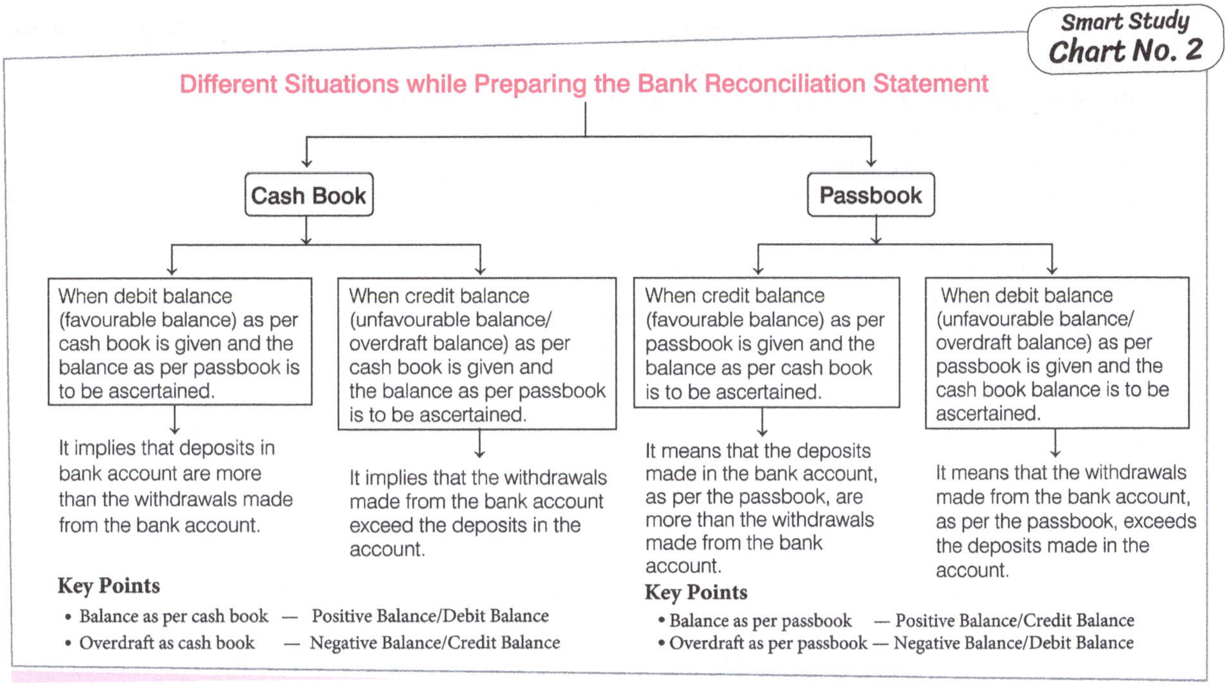

Preparation of BRS when Balance as per Cash Book is Given

While preparing BRS when balance as per cash book is given, following points should be considered

Items that should be entered in the Plus Column

- Starting point is debit balance as per cash book*.
- Cheques issued but not yet presented for payment.
- Credit made by the bank.
- Amount directly deposited by the customer in firm's bank account.
- Interest and dividend collected by the bank.
- Cheques paid into bank, but omitted to be recorded in the cash book.

Items that should be entered in the Minus Column

- Starting point is credit balance as per cash book*.
- Cheques sent to bank for collection but not yet credited by the bank.
- Cheques sent to bank for collection are dishonoured.
- Direct payment made by bank on behalf of customers.
- Debits made by the bank for bank charges, interest, etc.
- Cheques issued but omitted to be recorded in the cash book.

**Either debit or credit balance will appear*

Bank Reconciliation Statement

as on ......

Particulars	Plus (₹)	Minus (₹)
Bank Balance as per Cash Book (Favourable i.e. Debit Balance)	...	
or Overdraft as per Cash Book (Unfavourable i.e. Credit Balance)		...
Add Transactions having the Effect of Higher Balance in Passbook		
(a) Cheques deposited into the bank but not recorded in cash book	...	
(b) Cheques issued but not yet presented for payment	...	
(c) Interest allowed in passbook only	...	
(d) Bills receivable directly collected by bank	...	
(e) Direct payment by a customer into bank but not recorded in cash book	...	
(f) 'Cheques issued' returned on technical grounds	...	
(g) A wrong credit given by bank in passbook	...	

Particulars	Plus (₹)	Minus (₹)
Less Transactions having the Effect of Lower Balance in Passbook		
(a) Cheques received and recorded in bank column but not yet sent to bank for collection		...
(b) Cheques deposited but not yet collected by bank		...
(c) Bank charges, interest on overdraft debited in passbook only		...
(d) Insurance premium paid directly by bank under standing advice		...
(e) Cheques deposited for collection, returned dishonoured and recorded in passbook only		...
(f) Discounted bills dishonoured but not recorded in cash book		...
(g) A wrong debit given by bank in passbook		...
Balance (favourable) as per Passbook (If Total of Plus Items > Total of Minus Items)		...
or		
Overdraft (unfavourable) as per Passbook (If Total of Plus Items < Total of Minus Items)	...	
	...	...

Point to Remember

When there is unfavourable (credit) balance as per cash book, in this case, only the balance as per the cash book is in the minus column instead of plus column and everything else remains the same.

Preparation of BRS When Balance as per Passbook is Given

While preparing BRS when balance as per passbook is given, following points should be considered

Items that should be entered in the Plus Column

- Starting point is credit balance as per passbook*.
- Cheques sent to bank for collection, but not yet credited by the bank.
- Cheques sent to bank for collection are dishonoured.
- Direct payment made by the bank on behalf of customers.
- Debits made by the bank for bank charges, interest etc.
- Cheques issued but omitted to be recorded in the cash book.

Items that should be entered in the Minus Column

- Starting point is debit balance as per passbook*.
- Cheques issued but not yet presented for payment.
- Credit made by the bank.
- Amount directly deposited by the customer in firm's bank account.
- Interest and dividend collected by the bank.
- Cheques paid into bank, but omitted to be recorded in the cash book.

**Either credit or debit balance will appear.*

Bank Reconciliation Statement

as on ......

Particulars	Plus (₹)	Minus (₹)
Bank Balance as per Passbook (Favourable i.e. Credit Balance)	...	
or		
Overdraft as per Passbook (Unfavourable i.e. Debit Balance)		...
Add Transactions having the Effect of Lower Balance in Cash Book		
(a) Cheques received and recorded in bank column but not yet sent to bank for collection		...
(b) Cheques deposited but not yet collected by bank		...
(c) Bank charges, interest on overdraft debited in passbook only		...
(d) Insurance premium paid directly by bank under standing advice		...
(e) Cheques deposited for collection, returned dishonoured and recorded in passbook only		...
(f) Discounted bills dishonoured but not recorded in cash book		...
(g) A wrong debit given by bank in passbook		...

Particulars	Plus (₹)	Minus (₹)
Less Transactions having the Effect of Higher Balance in Cash Book		
(a) Cheques deposited into the bank but not recorded in cash book	...	
(b) Cheques issued but not yet presented for payment	...	
(c) Interest allowed in passbook only	...	
(d) Bills receivable directly collected by bank	...	
(e) Direct payment by a customer into bank but not recorded in cash book	...	
(f) 'Cheques issued' returned on technical grounds	...	
(g) A wrong credit given by bank in passbook	...	
Balance (Favourable) as per Cash Book (If Total of Plus Items > Total of Minus Items)		...
or		
Overdraft (Unfavourable) as per Cash Book (If Total of Plus Items < Total of Minus Items)	...	
	...	...

Point to Remember

When there is unfavourable balance as per passbook, in this case, only the balance as per the passbook is in the minus column instead of plus column and everything else remains the same.

A Summarised View of Transactions Related to BRS

Items	Balance (Favourable/ Unfavourable) as per	
	Cash Book	Passbook
1. Cheques issued but not yet presented for payment	+	−
2. Cheques etc. sent to the bank for collection but not yet collected	−	+
3. Interest allowed by the bank but not written in the cash book	+	−
4. Bank charges and interest on overdraft charged by the bank but not written in the cash book	−	+
5. Payment received by bank but not written in the cash book	+	−
6. Payments made by the bank but not written in the cash book	−	+
7. Money directly deposited by a customer in our bank account	+	−
8. Cheques etc. sent to the bank for collection but dishonoured	−	+
9. Cheques etc. debited in the cash book but not sent to the bank	−	+
10. Cheques issued and dishonoured but no entry made in cash book for dishonour	+	−
11. Any wrong entry in debit side of the passbook	−	+
12. Any wrong entry in credit side of the passbook	+	−
13. Interest or dividend collected by bank from investment	+	−
14. Cheque deposited into bank but not written in cash book	+	−

Mind Map

1 Meaning of Bank Reconciliation Statement

It is a statement which is prepared mainly to reconcile the difference between the bank balance as shown by the cash book and passbook.

Format →

Bank Reconciliation Statement
as on...

Particulars	Plus (₹)	Minus (₹)

2 Features of Bank Reconciliation Statement

- It is prepared for the reconciliation of cash book balance with passbook balance
- It is prepared by the customer having an account with the bank
- It is prepared on the basis of bank statement supplied by the bank
- It is prepared on a particular date

BANK RECONCILIATION STATEMENT

3 Importance of Bank Reconciliation Statement

- It helps in locating and rectifying the errors committed either by the firm or by the bank
- It helps to keep track of the cheques issued and also helps to check the accuracy of the cash book
- It shows the undue delay in the collection and clearing of the cheques by the bank
- It reduces the chances of fraud by the staff of the firm or bank
- It facilitates the preparation of revised cash book
- It helps to assure the customer about the correctness of the bank balance shown by the passbook

4 Reasons of Difference in Cash Book and Passbook Balance

1. **Time Gap in Recording Transactions**
   - Cheques issued but not yet presented for payment
   - Cheques deposited but not yet collected by the bank
2. **Transactions Recorded by the Bank and not by the Firm**
   - Interest allowed by bank
   - Direct payments by the bank
   - Direct deposits into bank
   - Interest and dividends collected by bank
   - Direct debits made by bank on behalf of customer
   - Bank charges and interest charged by bank
   - Dishonour of a bill discounted with the bank
   - Collection on behalf of customer
3. **Errors Committed by Bank or Firm in Recording Transactions**
   - Errors committed by firm in recording transactions
   - Errors committed by bank in recording transactions

5 Preparation of Bank Reconciliation Statement

- Tally the debit side of the cash book and credit side of the passbook and *vice-versa* and note the point of differences
- A bank reconciliation statement is prepared by taking either the balance of passbook or cash book as the starting point
- If the starting point is balance as per cash book, the answer arrived at will be the balance as per passbook and *vice-versa*

When Balance as per Passbook is Given

1. **Items that should be entered in Plus Column**
   - If starting point is credit balance as per passbook
   - Cheques sent to bank for collection, but not yet credited by the bank
   - Cheques sent to bank for collection are dishonoured
   - Payment made by bank on behalf of customers
   - Debit made by bank for bank charges, interest, etc
   - Cheques issued but omitted to be recorded in the cash book
2. **Items that should be entered in the Minus Column**
   - If starting point is debit balance as per passbook
   - Cheques issued but not yet presented for payment
   - Credit made by the bank
   - Amount directly deposited by the customer in firm's bank account
   - Interest and dividend collected by the bank
   - Cheques paid into bank, but omitted to be recorded in the cash book

When Balance as per Cash Book is Given

1. **Items that should be entered in Plus Column**
   - If starting point is debit balance as per cash book
   - Cheques issued but not yet presented for payment
   - Credits made by the bank
   - Amount directly deposited by the customer in firm's bank account
   - Interest and dividend collected by the bank
   - Cheques paid into bank, but omitted to be recorded in the cash book
2. **Items that should be entered in the Minus Column**
   - If starting point is credit balance as per cash book
   - Check sent to bank for collection but not yet credited by the bank
   - Cheques sent to bank for collection are dishonoured
   - Payment made by bank on behalf of customers
   - Debit made by bank for bank charges, interest, etc
   - Cheques issued but omitted to be recorded in the cash book

Topicwise Solved Questions

Favourable i.e. Debit Balance as per Cash Book

Solved Question 1 Prepare a bank reconciliation statement from the following particulars on 31st March, 2023.

(i) Debit balance as per bank column of the cash book is ₹ 7,44,000.
(ii) Cheques of ₹ 1,44,000 issued to creditors, but not yet presented to the bank for payment.
(iii) Dividend of ₹ 10,000 received by the bank, but not entered in the cash book.
(iv) Interest of ₹ 2,500 allowed by the bank.
(v) Cheques amounting to ₹ 30,800 are deposited into bank for collection, but not collected by bank upto this date.
(vi) Bank charges are ₹ 400.
(vii) A cheque of ₹ 640 was deposited into bank was dishonoured but no intimation was received for the same.
(viii) Bank paid house tax of ₹ 700 on our behalf, but no information received from bank for the same.

Sol.

Reconciliation Statement
as on 31st March, 2023

Particulars	Plus (₹)	Minus (₹)
Debit/Favourable Balance as per Cash Book	7,44,000	
Add Cheques issued, but not yet presented for payment	1,44,000	
Dividend received by the bank not entered in the cash book	10,000	
Interest allowed by the bank not entered in the cash book	2,500	
Less Cheques deposited into bank, but not collected by bank upto this date		30,800
Bank charges not entered in the cash book		400
Cheque deposited into bank but dishonoured		640
Payment of house tax by bank on our behalf not entered in the cash book		700
Credit/Favourable Balance as per Passbook		8,67,960
	9,00,500	9,00,500

Solved Question 2 On 31st March, 2023, on comparing the cash book with passbook of Saahil, it is found that, bank balance of ₹ 81,920 showed by the cash book differs from the bank balance with regard to the following

(i) Bank charges ₹ 200 on 31st March, 2023, are not entered in the cash book.
(ii) Cheques totalling ₹ 25,960 were issued by Saahil and duly recorded in the cash book before 31st March, 2023 but had not been presented at the bank for payment upto that date.
(iii) On 21st March, 2023, a debtor paid ₹ 4,000 into Saahil's bank account in settlement of his dues, but no entry was made in the cash book in respect of this.
(iv) A bill for ₹ 13,800 discounted with the bank is entered in the cash book without recording the discount charges of ₹ 1,600.
(v) ₹ 7,040 is entered in the cash book as paid into bank on 31st March, 2023, but not credited by the bank.
(vi) No entry has been made in the cash book to record the dishonour on 15th March, 2023 of a cheque for ₹ 1,300 received from Shiv.

Prepare a reconciliation statement as on 31st March, 2023.

Sol.

Bank Reconciliation Statement
as on 31st March, 2023

Particulars	Plus (₹)	Minus (₹)
Debit/Favourable Balance as per Cash Book.*	81,920	
Add Cash deposited by debtor directly in bank account	4,000	
Cheque issued, but not presented for payment	25,960	
Less Bank charges not entered in cash book		200
Discount charges recorded in bank		1,600
Cash deposited in bank but not credited		7,040
Cheque of Shiv dishonoured		1,300
Credit/Favourable Balance as per Passbook		1,01,740
	1,11,880	1,11,880

**If nothing is mentioned regarding the balance being a debit balance or credit balance, it is to be assumed to have a favourable balance.*

Unfavourable i.e. Credit (Overdraft) Balance as Per Cash Book

Solved Question 3 **On 30th September, 2023, there was an overdraft of ₹ 15,400 as per the cash book of a businessman. When it was compared with passbook, it was discovered that**

(i) Cheques amounting to ₹ 7,000 were paid into bank, but those for only ₹ 2,000 were credited in passbook so far.
(ii) Cheques amounting to ₹ 13,000 were issued in September but only cheques of ₹ 5,300 were presented for payment.
(iii) A cheque for ₹ 4,000 was entered in the cash book, but was not sent to the bank at all.
(iv) There is a debit in the passbook for ₹ 130 for bank charges and ₹ 70 for interest.
(v) ₹ 4,800 have been directly deposited into bank by somebody. It does not appear in the cash book.
(vi) Insurance premium has been paid by the bank ₹ 3,000 under his standing instructions.

Prepare bank reconciliation statement as on 30th September, 2023.

Sol.

Bank Reconciliation Statement
as on 30th September, 2023

Particulars	Plus (₹)	Minus (₹)
Overdraft as per Cash Book		15,400
Add Cheques issued, but not encashed till date (13,000 – 5,300)	7,700	
Amount directly deposited by some customer	4,800	
Less Cheques deposited, but not cleared (7,000 – 2,000)		5,000
Cheque entered in cash book, but not sent to bank		4,000
Bank charges		130
Interest charged by bank		70
Insurance premium paid by bank understanding instructions		3,000
Overdraft as per Passbook	15,100	
	27,600	27,600

Solved Question 4 **On 30th September, 2023, Rahul's cash book (bank column of account number 1) showed a bank overdraft of ₹ 1,97,400. After going through the bank passbook for reconciling the balance, he found the following**

(i) Out of cheques drawn on 26th September, those for ₹ 14,800 were cashed by the bankers on 2nd October.
(ii) A crossed cheque for ₹ 3,000 given to Nihal was returned by him and a bearer cheque was issued to him in lieu on 1st October.
(iii) Cash and cheques amounting to ₹ 13,600 were deposited in the bank on 29th September, but cheques worth ₹ 5,200 were cleared by the bank on 1st October and one cheque for ₹ 1,000 was returned by them as dishonoured on the later date.

(iv) According to his standing instructions, the bankers on 30th September, paid ₹ 1,280 as interest to his creditors, paid quarterly premium on his policy amounting to ₹ 640 and have paid a second call of ₹ 2,400 on shares held by him and lodged with the bankers for safe custody.

(v) Bank have also received ₹ 600 as dividend on his shares and recovered an insurance claim of ₹ 3,200 and their charges and commission on the above being ₹ 60. On receipt of information of the above transactions, he passed necessary entries in his cash book on 1st October.

(vi) His bankers seem to have given him a wrong credit for ₹ 2,000 paid in by him in account number 2 and a wrong debit in respect of a cheque for ₹ 1,200 drawn against his account number 2.

Prepare a bank reconciliation statement as on 30th September, 2023.

Sol.

Bank Reconciliation Statement
as on 30th September, 2023

Particulars		Plus (₹)	Minus (₹)
Overdraft/Credit/Unfavourable Balance as per Cash Book			1,97,400
Add Cheques issued but not presented for payment		14,800	
Crossed cheque issued to Nihal not presented for payment		3,000	
Amounts collected by the bank on my behalf, but not entered in the cash book			
Dividend	600		
Insurance claim (3,200 – 60)	3,140	3,740	
Amount paid in account number 2 credited by the bank wrongly to this account		2,000	
Less Cheques deposited in the bank, but not cleared (5,200 + 1,000)			6,200
Payments made by the bank on my behalf, but not entered in the cash book			
Interest	1,280		
Premium	640		
Second call	2,400		4,320
Cheques issued against account number 2, but wrongly debited by the bank to this account			1,200
Overdraft/Debit/Unfavourable Balance as per Passbook		1,85,580	
		2,09,120	2,09,120

Favourable i.e. Credit Balance as Per Passbook

Solved Question 5 **On 31st March, 2023, bank passbook of Suresh showed a balance of ₹ 32,750 on his credit. Prepare the bank reconciliation statement with the following information**

(i) Out of total cheques amounting to ₹ 21,000, cheques aggregating ₹ 12,000 were credited upto 31st March, 2023.

(ii) Before that date, he had issued cheques amounting to ₹ 6,500, of which cheques amounting to ₹ 3,000 have been presented for payment so far.

(iii) Cheque for ₹ 2,300 drawn on his savings deposit account has been shown as drawn on current account in cash book.

(iv) Bills payable amounting to ₹ 1,000 paid by bank, but it has not been entered in the cash book and a bill receivable amounting to ₹ 1,500 which was discounted with the bank was dishonoured by the drawer on due date.

(v) A bill for ₹ 6,600 was retired by the bank under rebate of ₹ 100, but the full amount of bill was credited in the bank column of the cash book.

(vi) Amount wrongly debited by bank ₹ 450.

(vii) Bank has debited the account with bank charges ₹ 365.

Sol. **Bank Reconciliation Statement**
as on 31st March, 2023

Particulars	Plus (₹)	Minus (₹)
Credit Balance as per Passbook	32,750	
Add Cheques deposited, but not credited (21,000 – 12,000)	9,000	
Bills payable paid by bank, but it has not been entered in the cash book	1,000	
Bills receivable discounted with the bank was dishonoured by the drawer on due date	1,500	
Amount wrongly debited by bank	450	
Bank has debited the account with bank charges	365	
Less Cheques issued but not presented for payment (6,500 – 3,000)		3,500
Cheque drawn on his savings deposit account has been shown as drawn on current account in cash book		2,300
Rebate on bill not entered in the cash book		100
Debit Balance as per Cash Book		39,165
	45,065	45,065

Solved Question 6 **Prepare a bank reconciliation statement in the books of Somil as on 30th April, 2023.**

(i) Balance as per passbook on 30th April, 2023 ₹ 24,000.

(ii) Out of total cheques amounting to ₹ 1,50,000 drawn by Mr. Rohil, cheques aggregating ₹ 20,000 were encashed in April, 2023, cheques aggregating ₹ 16,000 were encashed in May 2023 and the rest have not been presented at all.

(iii) Out of total cheques amounting to ₹ 48,000 deposited, cheques aggregating ₹ 30,000 were credited in April, 2023, cheques aggregating ₹ 8,000 were credited in May, 2023 and the rest have not been collected at all.

(iv) Bank has charged ₹ 108 as its commission for collecting outstation cheques and has allowed interest ₹ 1,320 on his bank balance.

(v) Amount wrongly debited by bank ₹ 9,600.

(vi) A cheque of ₹ 4,800 was entered in the cash book in April, 2023, but was sent to the bank in May, 2023.

(vii) A cheque of ₹ 53,200 paid into the bank was returned dishonoured but no intimation was received from the bank till April, 2023.

Sol. **Bank Reconciliation Statement**
as on 30th April, 2023

Particulars	Plus (₹)	Minus (₹)
Balance as per Passbook* (Credit/Favourable)	24,000	
Add Cheques deposited, but not credited upto April, 2023 (48,000 – 30,000)	18,000	
Commission charged by bank	108	
Amount wrongly debited by bank	9,600	
Cheque entered in the cash book, but not yet sent to bank	4,800	
Cheque returned dishonoured	53,200	
Less Cheques drawn, but not presented for payment upto April, 2023 (1,50,000 – 20,000)		1,30,000
Interest allowed by bank		1,320
Overdraft as per Cash Book	21,612	
	1,31,320	1,31,320

**If nothing is mentioned regarding the balance being a debit balance or credit balance, it is to be assumed to have a favourable balance.*

Unfavourable i.e. Debit (Overdraft) Balance as Per Passbook

Solved Question 7 **Prepare bank reconciliation statement from details given below, to find out balance as per cash book of Mr. Anil as on 31st October, 2023.**

(i) Passbook of Mr. Anil shows an overdraft of ₹ 53,970.

(ii) Bank wrongly credited Mr. Anil's account with ₹ 17,070.

(iii) Bank paid annual subscription to Chamber of Commerce ₹ 6,000 on Mr. Anil's standing order which was not recorded in cash book.

(iv) Payment side, bank column of cash book was undercast ₹ 350.

(v) Interest on overdraft charged by bank was ₹ 1,530.

(vi) Cash deposit of ₹ 23,000 on 31st October, 2023 was not recorded in the passbook.

(vii) Cheques issued, but not presented to bank for payment ₹ 40,000.

Sol.

Bank Reconciliation Statement
as on 31st October, 2023

Particulars	Plus (₹)	Minus (₹)
Bank Overdraft as per Passbook		53,970
Add Annual subscription of Chamber of Commerce paid by bank not recorded in cash book	6,000	
Payment side of cash book (bank column) was undercast	350	
Interest on overdraft debited in passbook only	1,530	
Cash deposit was not recorded in passbook	23,000	
Less Wrong credit given by bank in passbook		17,070
Cheques issued, but not presented to bank for payment		40,000
Bank Overdraft as per Cash Book	80,160	
	1,11,040	1,11,040

Solved Question 8 **On 31st March, 2023, there is an overdraft of ₹ 15,000 in the passbook of Sh. Sandeep Gupta. On comparison with the cash book, it was found that**

(i) The bank has charged interest on overdraft for ₹ 600.

(ii) Cheques for ₹ 80,000 were issued and out of these cheques only for ₹ 8,000 has been encashed.

(iii) Cheques for ₹ 4,500 were deposited into bank, but cheques for ₹ 500 only were cleared.

(iv) The bank collected interest on his investments ₹ 600 and a direct payment was made into his account by some debtor of for ₹ 900.

(v) He had received a cheque for ₹ 1,200 which he entered in the cash book but he forgot to send the cheque to the bank.

Prepare bank reconciliation statement.

Sol.

Bank Reconciliation Statement
as on 31st March, 2023

Particulars	Plus (₹)	Minus (₹)
Overdraft as per Passbook		15,000
Add Interest on overdraft	600	
Cheques deposited, but not cleared and collected (4,500 – 500)	4,000	
Cheques entered in cash book but not sent to bank	1,200	
Less Cheques issued, but not presented for payment (80,000 – 8,000)		72,000
Interest collected by the bank		600
Direct payment into the bank		900
Overdraft as per Cash Book	82,700	
	88,500	88,500

Comprehensive

Solved Question 9 **Passbook of Tarun, on 31st March, 2023, showed a balance of ₹ 2,040. On comparing with the cash book, it was noted that**

(i) Bills collected by bank were ₹ 2,600.
(ii) Interest allowed by bank ₹ 460.
(iii) Insurance premium was paid by bank ₹ 1,200.
(iv) Debit side of bank column is overcast by ₹ 3,150.
(v) Cheques issued, but not encashed were ₹ 6,800.
(vi) A bills receivable discounted with the bank was dishonoured on due date ₹ 1,200.
(vii) A cash receipt of ₹ 3,800 was recorded in the bank column of the cash book by mistake.
(viii) Cheques issued, but returned dishonoured were ₹ 3,820 for technical reasons.
(ix) A wrong credit was given by the bank in the passbook ₹ 730.
(x) Cash book was underbalanced by ₹ 1,480.

Prepare bank reconciliation statement.

Sol.

Bank Reconciliation Statement
as on 31st March, 2023

Particulars	Plus (₹)	Minus (₹)
Overdraft as per Passbook	2,040	
Add Insurance premium paid by bank	1,200	
A wrong debit in passbook	3,150	
A discounted bill receivable dishonoured on due date	1,200	
A cash receipt recorded by mistake in bank column of cash book	3,800	
Less Cheques issued but not encashed		6,800
Bills collected by bank		2,600
Interest allowed by bank		460
Cheques issued, but returned dishonoured for technical reasons		3,820
A wrong credit in the passbook		730
A direct payment into bank		1,480
Overdraft as per Cash Book	4,500	
	15,890	15,890

Solved Question 10 **On 31st December, 2023, Singla has two accounts (I and II) with ABC Bank, his ledger shows a balance of ₹ 10,000 in account I and an overdraft of ₹ 4,500 in account II. On verification of the ledger entries with the respective bank statement, the following mistakes were noticed**

(i) Deposit of ₹ 3,000 made in account I on 20th December has been entered in the ledger in account II.
(ii) Withdrawal of ₹ 1,000 from account I on 20th November, has been entered in the ledger in account II.
(iii) Two cheques of ₹ 1,000 and ₹ 1,500 deposited in account I on 1st December (and entered in the books in account II) have been dishonoured by the bankers. The entries for dishonour of these cheques have been entered in the books in account II.
(iv) In accounts I and II, Singla has issued on 29th December, cheques for ₹ 20,000 and ₹ 2,000 respectively and these have not been encashed till 31st December.
(v) Incidental charges of ₹ 20 and ₹ 50 charged in accounts I and II respectively, have not been entered in the books.
(vi) The bank has credited interest of ₹ 100 for account I and has charged interest of ₹ 550 for account II, which have not been recorded in the books.
(vii) Deposits of ₹ 10,000 and ₹ 7,000 made into accounts I and II respectively, both on 30th December, have not been credited by the bank till 31st December.

Prepare a bank reconciliation statement for the above accounts.

Sol.

Bank Reconciliation Statement Account I
as on 31st December, 2023

Particulars	Plus (₹)	Minus (₹)
Debit/Favourable Balance as per Cash Book	10,000	
Add Cheque deposited, but entered in account II	3,000	
Cheques issued, but not presented	20,000	
Interest credited by bank	100	

Particulars	Plus (₹)	Minus (₹)
Less Incidental charges		20
Cheques deposited, but not credited		10,000
Withdrawal from account I but entered in account II		1,000
Credit/Favourable Balance as per Passbook		22,080
	33,100	33,100

Bank Reconciliation Statement Account II
as on 31st December, 2023

Particulars	Plus (₹)	Minus (₹)
Overdraft/Credit/Unfavourable Balance as per Cash Book		4,500
Add Withdrawal from I account, but entered in account II	1,000	
Cheque issued but not presented	2,000	
Less Cheque deposited with account I, but entered in account II		3,000
Incidental charges		50
Interest charged by bank		550
Cheques deposited, but not credited		7,000
Overdraft/Debit/Unfavourable Balance as per Passbook	12,100	
	15,100	15,100

Solved Question 11 **Prepare bank reconciliation statement from details given below, to find out balance as per passbook of Mr. Saman as on 31st March, 2023, the cash book shows a debit balance of ₹ 15,000.**

(i) A cheque for ₹ 750 issued in favour of Sia has not been presented till 31st March.

(ii) A sum of ₹ 1,500 deposited in the bank has been credited as ₹ 150 in the passbook.

(iii) Payment side of cash book has been undercast by ₹ 200.

(iv) A bill receivable for ₹ 1,500, discounted with the bank in February. 2023 was dishonoured on 31st March, 2023, but the dishonour was not recorded in the cash book.

(v) On 30th March, 2023 a cheque of ₹ 1,570 received by him was paid into bank but the same was omitted to be entered in the cash book.

(vi) There was a credit of ₹ 100 for interest on current account and a debit of ₹ 25 for bank charges in the passbook.

(vii) A bill for ₹ 1,050 retired by bank on our behalf under a rebate of ₹ 25, the full amount of the bill was credited in cash book.

(viii) A cheque for ₹ 495 deposited in bank has been dishonoured.

Sol.

Bank Reconciliation Statement
as on 31st March, 2023

Particulars	Plus (₹)	Minus (₹)
Debit/Favourable Balance as per Cash Book	15,000	
Add Cheque issued but not presented for payment	750	
Rebate on payment of a bill by bank not recorded in cash book (WN)	25	
Cheque received was paid into bank but not entered in the cash book	1,570	
Interest credited on current account	100	
Less Cheque deposited but dishonoured		495
Deposit credited by bank with lesser amount (1,500 – 150)		1,350
Payment side of cash book undercast		200
Bill receivable dishonoured		1,500
Bank charges		25
Credit/Favourable Balance as per Passbook		13,875
	17,445	17,445

Working Note

Bank received a rebate of ₹ 25 while making payment of the bill payable on our behalf. Hence, bank has paid only ₹ 1,025 whereas amount recorded on the payment side of cash book was ₹ 1,050. Hence, ₹ 25 will be recorded in plus column.

Solved Question 12 **From the following particulars, prepare a bank reconciliation statement in the books of Sanjay as on 31st March, 2023. Sanjay's passbook showed a balance of on 31st March, 2023 ₹ 36,000.**

(i) Premium on life policy of Sanjay paid by the bank on standing advice for ₹ 1,000.

(ii) Out of total cheques amounting to ₹ 90,000 drawn by Mr. Raj, cheques aggregating ₹ 30,000 were encashed in March, 2023, cheques aggregating ₹ 24,000 were encashed in April, 2023 and the rest have not been presented at all.

(iii) A payment of ₹ 25,000 was received from customers directly by the bank.

(iv) Out of total cheques amounting to ₹ 72,000 deposited, cheques aggregating ₹ 45,000 were credited in March, 2023, cheques aggregating ₹ 12,000 were credited in April, 2023 and the rest have not been collected at all.

(v) He also received a cheque of ₹ 25,500 which although entered by him in the bank column of cash book, was omitted to be paid into the bank.

(vi) Bank has charged ₹ 150 as its commission for collecting outstation cheques.

(vii) Bank has allowed interest ₹ 330 on his bank balance.

(viii) Amount wrongly debited by bank ₹ 8,800.

(ix) A cheque of ₹ 12,400 was entered in the cash book in March, 2023, but was sent to the bank in April, 2023.

(x) A cheque of ₹ 6,600 paid into the bank was returned dishonoured but no intimation was received from the bank till March, 2023.

Sol.

Bank Reconciliation Statement
as on 31st March, 2023

Particulars	Plus (₹)	Minus (₹)
Balance as per Passbook (Credit/Favourable)	36,000	
Add Cheques deposited but not credited upto (72,000 – 45,000)	27,000	
Amount wrongly debited by bank	8,800	
Cheque entered in the cash book but not yet sent to bank	12,400	
Commission charged by bank	150	
Cheque returned dishonoured	6,600	
Premium on life policy of Sanjay paid by the bank on standing advice	1,000	
Cheque omitted to be paid into the bank	25,500	
Less Payment received from customers directly by the bank		25,000
Cheques drawn but not presented for payment (90,000 – 30,000)		60,000
Interest allowed by bank		330
(Credit/Favourable) as per Cash Book		32,120
	1,17,450	1,17,450

Missing Information

Solved Question 13 **Determine the missing amounts of the following bank reconciliation statement.**

Bank Reconciliation Statement
as on 31st October, 2023

Particulars	Plus (₹)	Minus (₹)
Overdraft as per Cash Book		35,000
(i) Cheques for ₹ 8,000 were issued in March, but were not presented for payment	8,000	
(ii) Cheques for ₹ 12,000 were deposited into bank, but were not cleared so far	...	...
(iii) A cheque received from a debtor for 8,500 was deposited into bank, but the same has been dishonoured	...	...
(iv) The bank has collected a bills receivable for ₹ 25,000, but the same was not credited to the cash book	...	...
(v) Bank charges debited by bank only are ₹ 3,750		3,750
(vi) Interest allowed by bank on a fixed deposit was ₹ 5,000 credited in passbook	...	...
Overdraft as per Passbook	...	...
	59,250	59,250

Sol.

Bank Reconciliation Statement
as on 31st October, 2023

Particulars	Plus (₹)	Minus (₹)
Overdraft as per Cash Book		35,000
(i) Cheques for ₹ 8,000 were issued in March, but were not presented for payment	8,000	
(ii) Cheques for ₹ 12,000 were deposited into bank, but were not cleared so far		**12,000**
(iii) A cheque received from a debtor for ₹ 8,500 was deposited into bank but the same has been dishonoured		**8,500**
(iv) The bank has collected a bills receivable for ₹ 25,000 but the same was not credited to the cash book	**25,000**	
(v) Bank charges debited by bank only are ₹ 3,750		3,750
(vi) Interest allowed by bank on a fixed deposit was ₹ 5,000 credited in passbook	**5,000**	
Overdraft as per Passbook	**21,250**	
	59,250	59,250

Solved Question 14 **In the following bank reconciliation statement, determine the missing amounts.**

Bank Reconciliation Statement
as on 31st March, 2022

Particulars	Plus (₹)	Minus (₹)
Balance as per Cash Book (Debit)	32,000	
(i) Cheques of ₹ 60,000 deposited into bank but cheques of ₹ 35,000 only cleared	...	...
(ii) Cheques of ₹ 80,000 issued, but cheques of ₹ 42,000 presented for payment	...	...
(iii) Receipt column of cash book overcast by ₹ 1,000	...	...
(iv) Interest on investment collected by bankers	1,200	
(v) Bank charges debited by bank		800
(vi) Direct deposit made by the customer ₹ 800	...	...
Balance as per Passbook	...	...
	72,000	72,000

Sol.

Bank Reconciliation Statement
as on 31st March, 2022

Particulars	Plus (₹)	Minus (₹)
Balance as per Cash Book (Debit)	32,000	
(i) Cheques of ₹ 60,000 deposited into bank but cheques of ₹ 35,000 only cleared		**25,000**
(ii) Cheques of ₹ 80,000 issued but cheques of ₹ 42,000 presented for payment	**38,000**	
(iii) Receipt column of cash book overcast by ₹ 1,000		**1,000**
(iv) Interest on investment collected by bankers	1,200	
(v) Bank charges debited by bank		800
(vi) Direct deposit made by the customer ₹ 800	**800**	
Balance as per Passbook (Credit) (72,000 – 26,800)		**45,200**
	72,000	72,000

Numerical Questions

Favourable i.e. Debit Balance as Per Cash Book

1. From the following particulars, prepare the bank reconciliation statement as on 31st January, 2023

(i) Debit balance as per cash book ₹ 24,000.
(ii) Cheque of ₹ 18,500 was deposited and collected by the bank but not recorded in cash book.
(iii) Cash deposit of ₹ 13,100 was recorded in cash column of cash book.
(iv) Purchased furniture and payment by debit card ₹ 12,500, was not recorded in cash book.
(v) Online transfer was made to our creditors account ₹ 13,350, for which no entry was made in cash book.
(vi) Telephone bill ₹ 3,625 and electricity bill ₹ 4,125 paid through online banking, was not recorded in the cash book.
(vii) Cheque received from Vinod for ₹ 14,300 paid into bank was dishonoured on 27th January, 2023 but advice was received only on 4th February, 2023.

Ans. Bank balance as per passbook = ₹ 7,700

2. Prepare a bank reconciliation statement in the books of Bharti as on 31st January, 2023

(i) Balance as per cash book as on 31st January, 2023 was ₹ 33,705.
(ii) Cheque of ₹ 17,800 was issued by her on 28th January, 2023 but this was not presented for payment till 31st January, 2023.
(iii) A cheque of ₹ 4,000 issued to Mr Rahim, was taken in the cash column.
(iv) A cheque of ₹ 15,000 was paid into bank, but was omitted to be entered in the cash book.
(v) The bank has charged ₹ 55 as its commission and has allowed interest ₹ 50.

Ans. Balance as per passbook as on 31st January, 2023 was = ₹ 62,500

3. From the following particulars, prepare a bank reconciliation statement as at 31st December, 2023 of Ramya Ltd. who had cash at bank as per cash book ₹ 10,500 and as per passbook ₹ 12,350

(i) The following cheques were deposited on 30th and 31st December, but were not collected by 31st December, 2023.
(a) ₹ 300   (b) ₹ 500
(c) ₹ 200
(ii) The following cheques were issued, but not cashed by 31st December, 2023.
(a) ₹ 600   (b) ₹ 200   (c) ₹ 489   (d) ₹ 50
(iii) The bank allowed interest ₹ 20 and a commission was charged ₹ 9 on 31st December, 2023.
(iv) The bank collected a bill of ₹ 1,500 on the 31st December, 2023, but the intimation was received by the firm on 1st January, 2024.

4. On comparing the cash book of Mr.Akash with his passbook it was found that Competency Based Que

(i) His cash book showed a balance of ₹ 21,450 as on 31st March, 2023.
(ii) Out of ₹ 12,500 deposited in cash and by cheques on 25th March, cheques for ₹ 2,500 were collected only on 4th April, 2023.
(iii) Cheques and cash amounting to ₹ 12,350 were deposited on 29th March, but the bank had given a credit of only ₹ 2,350 by mistake.
(iv) Out of cheques drawn for ₹ 14,850 in March, cheques for ₹ 4,850 were presented on 2nd April, 2023.
(v) A cheque for ₹ 600 entered in cash book on 26th March, was omitted to be banked.
(vi) A cheque for ₹ 360 was deposited in bank on 28th March and cleared, but it was omitted to be recorded in cash book.
(vii) A bill receivable for ₹ 1,800 which was discounted sometime back has been dishonoured on due date.
(viii) A cheque for ₹ 380 issued on 26th March, has been entered twice in the cash book.

Prepare bank reconciliation statement as on 31st March, 2023.

Ans. Balance as per passbook = ₹ 12,140

Unfavourable i.e. Credit Balance as per Cash Book

5. From the following particulars, ascertain the balance that would appear in the bank passbook of Sh.Rakesh Bansal on 31st December, 2023 Competency Based Que

(i) The bank overdraft as per cash book on 31st December, 2023 is ₹ 12,680.
(ii) Interest on overdraft for 6 months ending 31st December, 2023, ₹ 320, is entered into the passbook.
(iii) Bank charges of ₹ 60 for the above period are debited in the passbook.

(iv) Cheques issued, but not presented prior to 31st December 2023, amounted to ₹ 2,336.
(v) Cheques paid into the bank, but not cleared before 31st December, 2023 were for ₹ 4,340.
(vi) Interest on investments collected by the bank and credited in the passbook ₹ 2,400.

Ans. Overdraft as per passbook = ₹ 12,664

6. Prepare a bank reconciliation statement as on 31st March, 2023 from the following information

(i) Cash book balance (overdraft) ₹ 12,500.
(ii) Cheque deposited, but not recorded in cash book ₹ 2,000.
(iii) Cheque received, but not sent to bank ₹ 1,500.
(iv) Credit side of the bank column has been overcast ₹ 60.
(v) Bank charges entered in passbook twice ₹ 75.
(vi) Bills receivable directly collected by the bank ₹ 4,000.
(vii) Deposited cheques returned dishonoured by bank ₹ 1,700.
(viii) Electricity bill paid by the bank as per instruction ₹ 800.
(ix) Cheques issued, but not presented for payment ₹ 5,400.
(x) Cheques deposited, but not cleared ₹ 3,200.

Ans. Overdraft balance as per passbook = ₹ 8,315

7. From the following information, find out the balance or overdraft as per passbook of Amit as on 31st March, 2023

(i) Overdraft as per cash book ₹ 31,680.
(ii) Interest on overdraft ₹ 1,020.
(iii) Bank charges ₹ 580.
(iv) A cheque for ₹ 1,000 was issued to Nitin, but the same was not written in cash book. The cheque has been encashed.
(v) A bill receivable discounted was dishonoured on due date ₹ 9,000.
(vi) A cheque for ₹ 420 deposited in the bank has been credited in the passbook as ₹ 240.

Prepare bank reconciliation statement as on 31st March, 2023.

Ans. Overdraft as per passbook = ₹ 43,460

8. On 31st December, 2023, the bank column of cash book of Aneja & Co showed an overdraft of ₹ 38,538. On the basis of the following particulars, prepare a bank reconciliation statement

(i) Cheques issued before 31st December, 2023, but not yet presented for payment amounted to ₹ 10,500.
(ii) Cheques paid into the bank but a cheque amounting to ₹ 7,800, has not been collected yet.
(iii) Interest on loan amounting to ₹ 1,662 directly debited by the bank did not appear in the cash book.
(iv) ₹ 14,400 directly deposited by the customer entered in the passbook but not in cash book.

Ans. Overdraft as per passbook = ₹ 23,100

Favourable i.e. Credit Balance as per Passbook

9. On 31st March, 2023, Mohan's passbook showed a credit balance of ₹ 1,00,000. **Competency Based Que**

(i) On 25th March, 2023, he had issued cheques for ₹ 73,000 out of which cheques for ₹ 15,400 have been presented for payment so far.
(ii) A cheque for ₹ 14,800 deposited into bank on 28th March, 2023 has not been cleared so far.
(iii) A cheque for ₹ 10,960 received by him has been entered in the cash book, but the same has not been deposited into bank.
(iv) On 28th March, 2023, a cheque for ₹ 11,500, received by him was paid into the bank, but it was not entered into cash book. The cheque has been cleared and collected.
(v) The bank has credited an interest of ₹ 910 and has also debited the account with bank charges of ₹ 300.
(vi) The cash book shows a bank balance of ₹ 56,050.

Prepare Mohan's bank reconciliation statement to reconcile the bank passbook balance with his cash book balance.

10. On 31st March, 2023 the passbook of Narayan showed a credit balance of ₹ 3,300. On comparing it with the cash book, it was noted

(i) The cheques sent to bank in March were for ₹ 700 which were not collected by the bank.
(ii) Three cheques for ₹ 200, ₹ 250 and ₹ 300 were issued in March, but were not presented for payment.
(iii) A bills payable for ₹ 1,500 was paid by bank, but there was no record in cash book.
(iv) A bill receivable for ₹ 800 which was discounted from the bank, has been dishonoured.
(v) The bank has allowed interest of ₹ 25.
(vi) The commission charged by the bank amounted to ₹ 45 on collection of cheques.

Ans. Balance as per cash book = ₹ 5,570

11. From the following particulars, prepare a bank reconciliation statement showing the balance as per cash book **Competency Based Que**

(i) The following cheques were paid into the bank in December 2023, but were credited by bank in January, 2024
Seema – ₹ 3,500, Sangita – ₹ 2,500, Sonia – ₹ 2,000

(ii) The following cheques were issued by the firm in December, 2023, but were presented in January, 2024
Arti – ₹ 4,000, Bharti – ₹ 4,500

(iii) A cheque for ₹ 1,000, which was received from a customer, was entered in the bank column of cash book in December, 2023, but was omitted to be banked in December, 2023.

(iv) The passbook shows a debit of ₹ 1,000 for bank charges and a credit of ₹ 2,000 for interest.

(v) Interest on investments, ₹ 2,500, collected by bank appeared in the passbook.

The bank balance as per passbook was ₹ 20,000 on 31st December, 2023.

Ans. Balance as per cash book = ₹ 17,000

12. From the following particulars, prepare a bank reconciliation statement as on 31st March, 2021

Competency Based Que

(i) Credit/Favourable balance as per passbook ₹ 1,35,290.

(ii) A cheque for ₹ 10,000 deposited, but not recorded in the cash book. Bank has collected and credited this cheque.

(iii) A bank deposit of ₹ 2,000 was recorded in the cash book as if there is no bank column therein.

(iv) A cheque issued for ₹ 2,500 was recorded as ₹ 2,050 in the cash column. Bank has made the payment of this cheque.

(v) The debit balance of ₹ 15,000 as on the previous day was brought forward as a credit balance.

(vi) The payment side of the cash book (bank column) was undercast by ₹ 1,000.

(vii) A cash discount allowed of ₹ 1,120 was recorded as ₹ 1,210 in the debit of bank column.

(viii) A cheque of ₹ 5,000 received from a debtor was recorded in the cash book but not deposited in the bank for collection.

(ix) One outgoing cheque of ₹ 3,000 was recorded twice in the cash book.

Ans. Favourable balance as per cash book = ₹ 1,00,000

Unfavourable i.e. Debit Balance as per Passbook

13. Prepare a bank reconciliation statement

(i) Overdraft shown as per passbook on 31st December, 2023 ₹ 26,490.

(ii) Bank charges for the above period also debited in the passbook ₹ 300.

(iii) Interest on overdraft for six months ending 31st December, 2016 ₹ 1,140 debited in the passbook.

(iv) Cheques issued, but not encashed prior to 31st December, 2016 amounted to ₹ 6,450.

(v) Interest on investment collected by the bank and credited in the passbook ₹ 1,800.

(vi) Cheques paid into bank, but not cleared before 31st December, 2016 were ₹ 3,300.

Ans. Balance as per cash book (credit) = ₹ 30,000

14. Prepare bank reconciliation statement as on 31st December, 2023

(i) Debit balance as per passbook ₹ 16,000.

(ii) Customer directly deposited in our bank account by internet banking ₹ 8,000.

(iii) Cheques deposited into bank, but not credited by bank ₹ 10,500.

(iv) Passbook shows debit entry for bank commission ₹ 300, not recorded in cash book.

(v) A bill of exchange of ₹ 3,500 discounted with the bank in December, 2023, returned dishonoured in January, 2023.

(vi) As per standing instructions bank paid telephone bill ₹ 650, not recorded in cash book.

(vii) Cheque of ₹ 975 deposited into bank, but wrongly recorded on ₹ 795 in cash book.

Ans. Overdraft as per cash book = ₹ 16,230

15. On 31st March, 2023, passbook of Nihal Garg shows a debit balance of ₹ 40,000. From the following, prepare a bank reconciliation statement

Competency Based Que

(i) Cheques amounting to ₹ 32,000 drawn on 25th March, 2023 of which cheques of ₹ 20,000 were encashed on 2nd April, 2023.

(ii) Cheques paid into the bank for collection ₹ 20,000 but cheques of ₹ 8,800 could only be collected in March, 2023.

(iii) Bank charges ₹ 100 and dividend of ₹ 1,400 on investments collected by the bank could not be shown in the cash book.

(iv) A bill of ₹ 40,000 was retired by the bank under rebate of ₹ 600 but the full amount was credited in the cash book.

(v) The payment of a cheque for ₹ 2,200 was recorded twice in the passbook.

(vi) Withdrawal column of the passbook undercast by ₹ 800.

(vii) ₹ 2,000 in respect of dishonoured cheque were entered in the passbook, but not in the cash book.

Ans. Overdraft/Credit/Unfavourable balance as per cash book = ₹ 47,300

16. Prepare bank reconciliation statement of Sh. Siv Das as on 31st December, 2023 from the following information.

(i) Overdraft as per passbook ₹ 26,300.
(ii) Cheques deposited but not recorded in cash book ₹ 15,000.
(iii) Cheques received and entered in cash book, but not sent to bank ₹ 10,500.
(iv) Credit side of cash book was overcast by ₹ 2,200.
(v) Bank charges entered twice in passbook ₹ 250.
(vi) Bills directly collected by bank without intimation to Sh. Shiv Das ₹ 28,500.
(vii) Deposited cheque returned by bank due to technical reasons ₹ 21,500.
(viii) Cheques issued, but not presented for payment ₹ 28,000.
(ix) Cheques deposited in bank, but not cleared till 31st December, 2023 ₹ 26,000.

Ans. Overdraft as per cash book = ₹ 39,900

Comprehensive

17. Prepare bank reconciliation statement of Mr. Shikhar Bansal as on 31st December, 2023 from the following information

(i) Overdraft as per passbook ₹ 26,300.
(ii) Cheques received and entered in cash book, but not sent to bank for ₹ 10,500.
(iii) Cheques deposited, but not recorded in cash book ₹ 15,000.
(iv) Bank charges for ₹ 50 entered twice in passbook.
(v) Credit side of cash book was overcast by ₹ 200.
(vi) Bills directly collected by bank without intimation to Mr. Shikhar Bansal for ₹ 8,500.
(vii) Cheques issued, but not presented for payment for ₹ 8,000.
(viii) Cheques deposited in bank, but not cleared till 31st December, 2023 were for ₹ 6,000.
(ix) Deposited cheque returned by bank due to technical reasons ₹ 1,500.

Ans. Overdraft as per cash book = ₹ 39,900

18. From the following particulars, prepare the bank reconciliation statement Competency Based Que

(i) Bank overdraft as per the cash book ₹ 16,200.
(ii) A cheque deposited as per bank statement, but not recorded in the cash book ₹ 700.
(iii) Debit side of the bank column undercast by ₹ 100.
(iv) A cheque for ₹ 5,000 deposited, but collection as per the bank statement was only ₹ 4,996.
(v) A cheque of ₹ 530 returned dishonoured.
(vi) Bills collected directly by the bank ₹ 3,500.
(vii) Bank charges recorded twice in the cash book ₹ 25.
(viii) A bill for ₹ 8,000 discounted for ₹ 7,960 returned dishonoured by the bank, noting charges being ₹ 15.
(ix) Cheques deposited, but not yet collected by the bank ₹ 2,320.
(x) Cheques issued, but not yet presented for encashment ₹ 1,250.

Ans. Bank overdraft as per the passbook (debit) = ₹ 21,494

19. On 31st March, 2023, the balance as per passbook of a trader was ₹ 2,040. On comparing with the cash book, it was noted that Competency Based Que

(i) Cheques deposited into bank but not recorded in cash book ₹ 9,200.
(ii) Cheques issued but not encashed were ₹ 6,800.
(iii) Cheques issued but returned dishonoured were ₹ 3,820 for technical reasons.
(iv) A wrong credit was given by the bank in the pass book ₹ 730.
(v) Cheques received were recorded in cash book but not sent to bank ₹ 4,100.
(vi) Cheques for ₹ 2,300 were deposited but were not collected by bank.
(vii) Cheques for ₹ 8,900 were deposited but were returned dishonoured.
(viii) Debit side bank column is overcast by ₹ 3,150.
(ix) A bill receivable discounted with the bank was dishonoured on due date ₹ 1,200.
(x) A cash receipt of ₹ 3,800 was by mistake recorded in the bank column of the cash book.

Prepare bank reconciliation statement.

Ans. Debit balance as per cash book = ₹ 4,940

20. The following particulars relate to the business of Shri Ajay Bansal on 31st March, 2023

Particulars	Amt (₹)
(i) Cheques issued, but not presented for payment	34,500
(ii) Cheques paid into the bank, but not yet collected	7,500
(iii) Interest credited by the bank, but not entered in the cash book	1,650
(iv) Bank charges debited in the passsook, but not entered in the cash book	105
(v) Credit balance as shown by the passbook	1,06,590
(vi) Debit balance as shown by the cash book	78,045

Prepare

(a) Statement reconciling the bank balance as per cash book with that shown by the bank passbook as on 31st March, 2023.
(b) Statement reconciling the bank balance as per passbook with that shown by the cash book as on 31st March, 2023.

Missing Information

21. In the following bank reconciliation statement, determine the missing amounts. Competency Based Que

Bank Reconciliation Statement
as on 31st March, 2023

Particulars	Plus (₹)	Minus (₹)
Credit Balance as per Passbook	3,60,000	
(i) Cheques of ₹1,20,000 issued, but a cheque of ₹72,000 not yet presented for payment	......	......
(ii) Cheques of ₹3,00,000 deposited into bank, but cheque of ₹1,56,000 not credited by bank	......	......
(iii) Interest credited by bank, but not recorded in cash book	......	5,100
(iv) Cheque deposited into bank, but not entered in cash book ₹60,000	......	......
Debit Balance as per Cash Book	......	......
	5,16,000	5,16,000

Ans. Debit balance as per cash book = ₹ 3,78,900

22. Determine the missing amounts. Competency Based Que

Bank Reconciliation Statement
as on 31st March, 2023

Particulars	Plus (₹)	Minus (₹)
Debit/Favourable Balance as per Cash book	16,980	—
(i) Cheque received and recorded in the cash book, but not sent to bank ₹1,200	......	......
(ii) Credit side of the cash book bank column cast short ₹200	—	200
(iii) Insurance premium not recorded in the cash book ₹600	......	......
(iv) Cheque received entered twice in the cash book ₹1,000	—	1,000
(v) Bill discounted dishonoured, not recorded in the cash book ₹5,000	......	......
(vi) Cheque deposited into the bank, but not recorded in the cash book ₹500	......	......
(vii) Bank charges entered twice in the cash book ₹20	......	......
(viii) Cheque issued, but not presented for payment ₹500	......	......
Credit/Favourable Balance as per Passbook	......	......
	18,000	18,000

Ans. Credit balance as per passbook = ₹ 10,000

Theoretical Questions

Short Answer Type Questions

1. State the reasons when the cash book balance will be higher than the passbook balance. Competency Based Que

Ans. The reasons when cash book balance will be higher than the passbook balance are

(i) Cheques paid into the bank but not yet collected.
(ii) Direct debits made by the bank on behalf of the customers.
(iii) Direct payment made by the bank on behalf of the customers.
(iv) Cheques deposited/bill discounted dishonoured.

2. Briefly explain the term favourable balance as per cash book. NCERT

Ans. The favourable balance as per cash book means, balance of deposits held at the bank. It is also known as debit balance as per the cash book.

Such a balance will be a credit balance as per passbook. This type of balance exist when the deposits made by the firm are more than its withdrawals.

3. Briefly explain the statement 'wrongly debited by the bank' with the help of an example. NCERT

Ans. Amount wrongly debited by the bank implies a situation when the bank wrongly debits a passbook.

e.g. A firm issued a cheque of ₹ 1,500 to its creditor and it is presented for payment and paid by the bank but in place of ₹ 1,500 bank debited it wrongly by ₹ 15,000.

The above error may be opposite too but in every situation, the balance of cash book and passbook will not tally. The term used for it will be wrongly debited by the bank. It generally happens at the time of posting the transaction.

4. If you proceed to start with the bank column with 'debit' cash book balance, how would you deal with the following Competency Based Que

(i) Cheques issued but not presented for payment.
(ii) Amount directly deposited by the customer in firm's bank account.
(iii) Cheques deposited but not yet credited.

Ans. (i) **Cheques Issued but not Presented for Payment**
This transaction reduces the cash book balance, but the passbook balance is more. Therefore, it should be entered in the plus column to reconcile the cash book with the passbook.

(ii) **Amount directly Deposited by the Customer in Firm's Bank Account**
This transaction increases the balance at bank, but the cash book balance is less.

Therefore, the amount corresponding to this transaction should be entered in the plus column to reconcile the cash book with the passbook.

(iii) **Cheques Deposited but not yet Ccredited**
This transaction increases the cash book balance, but the passbook balance is less. Therefore, amounts corresponding to this transaction should be entered in the minus column to reconcile the cash book with the passbook.

Long Answer Type Questions

5. What is bank reconciliation statement? Why is it prepared? NCERT

Or

State the need for the preparation of bank reconciliation statement. NCERT

Ans. Bank reconciliation statement is a statement which is prepared mainly to reconcile (tally) the difference between the bank balance as shown by the cash book and bank passbook.

In day-to-day affairs, an individual or organisation makes numerous transactions through bank. Along with the copy of bank statement (i.e., the passbook), an individual or organisation needs to maintain a separate book (cash book) for recording the banking transactions.

Bank reconciliation statement is important for many reasons.

They are listed as below

(i) It helps in locating any error, that may have been committed either in the cash book or in the passbook.

(ii) It helps in bringing out the unnecessary delay in the collection of cheques by the bank.

(iii) Misappropriation of funds are avoided by regular periodic reconciliation.

(iv) The customer is assured of the correctness of the bank balance shown by the passbook, by preparing a bank reconciliation statement.

(v) It helps the management to keep a track of cheques, which have been sent to the bank for collection.

6. Explain the reasons where the balance shown by the passbook does not agree with the balance as shown by the bank column of the cash book.
NCERT; Competency Based Que

Ans The reasons where the balance shown by the passbook does not agree with the balance as shown by the bank column of the cash book are as follows

(i) **Differences Due to Timing on Recording Any Transaction**
When a comparison is made between the balance of the cash book with the balance of the bank passbook, there is often a difference which is caused due to the time gap in recording the transactions relating either to payments or receipts. The transactions affecting time gap includes

- Cheques issued by the bank but not yet presented for payment.
- Cheques paid/deposited into the bank but not yet collected.

(ii) **Transactions Recorded by the Bank**
There are transactions, which are recorded by the bank and are not known to the customer/account holder. The account holder comes to know about such transactions after receiving the bank passbook. Such transactions can take the following forms

- Direct debits made by the bank on behalf of the customer.
- Amounts directly deposited in the bank account by the customer.
- Interest and dividend collected by the bank.
- Direct payments made by the bank on behalf of the customers.
- Interest credited by the bank but not recorded in the cash book.
- Cheque deposited/bills discounted dishonoured.

(iii) **Differences Caused by Errors**
Sometimes, there may be a difference between the balance as per cash book and the balance as per passbook on account of an error on the part of the bank or an error in the cash book of the business.

- Errors committed in recording transactions by the firm.
- Errors committed in recording transactions by the bank.

Objective Questions

Multiple Choice Questions (MCQs)

1. Bank reconciliation statement is prepared by NCERT

(a) debtors (b) creditors
(c) accountholder in a bank (d) landlord

2. Debit balance in cash book means

(a) overdraft (b) favourable balance
(c) amount deposited (d) amount due from bank

3. Unfavourable bank balance means NCERT

(a) credit balance in passbook
(b) credit balance in cash book
(c) debit balance in cash book
(d) None of the above

4. Bank reconciliation statement is prepared

(a) at the end of each week (b) at the end of each month
(c) at the end of accounting year
(d) when a bank statement is received

5. Which of the following statements is incorrect? Competency Based Que

(a) The bank column of cash book represents bank account
(b) Bank statement enables accountholder to prepare bank reconciliation statement
(c) Cheques issued for payment, but not presented to bank appears in cash book only
(d) Bank reconciliation statement is prepared only during the year end

6. Which of the following statements is correct? Competency Based Que

(a) A bank reconciliation statement is mainly prepared to reconcile the cash balance of cash book
(b) Businessman can prepare bank reconciliation statement only with cash book balance
(c) When overdraft as per cash book is given, bank charges debited in passbook only, is to be subtracted
(d) Bank statement is sent by businessman to bank

7. When balance as per passbook is given, direct debits made by the bank on behalf of the customer will be .... in bank reconciliation statement.

(a) added to bank balance
(b) deducted from bank balance
(c) deducted from the cash book balance
(d) added to cash book balance

8. In the bank statement, the debit balance means that there is an ....

(a) overdraft (b) positive balance
(c) zero balance (d) None of these

9. Passbook is a statement of

(a) all cash transactions in the bank
(b) receipts and payments of the bank
(c) all bank transactions in the cash book
(d) customer's account prepared by the bank

10. The customer's account is .... when he/she withdraws the amount from the bank.

(a) debited (b) credited
(c) No effect (d) None of these

11. Unfavourable cash book balance implies

(a) credit balance in the cash book
(b) debit balance in the cash book
(c) credit balance in the passbook
(d) debit balance in the passbook

12. The differences between the cash book and the bank passbook is caused by Competency Based Que

I. timing differences in recording of the transactions.
II. errors made by the business or by the bank.

Codes

(a) Only I
(b) Only II
(c) Both I and II
(d) Neither I nor II

13. Bank reconciliation statement helps in

(a) locating any error, that may have been committed either in the cash book or in the passbook
(b) bringing out the unnecessary delay in the collection of cheques by the bank
(c) avoiding embezzlements or misappropriation of funds by regular periodic reconciliation
(d) All of the above

14. Cheque deposited by firm is recorded in the books on the date of deposit while bank records when the cheque has been cleared.

The reason for this may be due to

(a) recording of transaction gap
(b) firm and bank gap
(c) timing gap
(d) receipt and payment gap

15. Passbook is a copy of

(a) copy of customer account
(b) bank column of cash book
(c) cash column of cash book
(d) copy of receipts and payments

16. **Difference caused due to bank charges amounting to ₹ 1,900, is an example of**
(a) timing differences in recording of transactions
(b) errors made by the business
(c) errors made by the bank
(d) None of the above

17. **"Sam issued cheques amounting to ₹ 32,000 out of which cheques amounting to ₹ 12,800 have so far been presented for payment. " What will be the amount deducted from the balance of passbook to reconcile it with the balance of cash book?** **Competency Based Que**
(a) ₹ 32,000
(b) ₹ 12,800
(c) ₹ 19,200 (d) None of the above

18. **A cheque of ₹ 6,000 deposited into bank, but was not recorded in the cash book. It will be .... if the balance as per cash book is given.**
(a) deducted from the balance as per passbook
(b) deducted from the balance as per cash book
(c) added to the balance as per passbook
(d) added to the balance as per cash book

19. **The balance (debit) at bank in Singh's cash book on 30th April, 2023 is ₹ 35,000. However a cheque for 3,000 received from Hemant and a cheque for ₹ 2,000 paid to Aman appear in the cash book, but not on the bank statement. Also, bank charges of ₹ 500 have not been entered in the cash book. What will be the balance as per passbook?** **Competency Based Que**
(a) ₹ 33,500 (b) ₹ 34,000
(c) ₹ 36,500 (d) ₹ 36,000

20. **Interest collected by bank from investments amounts to ₹ 5,000. How will it be treated for the purpose of bank reconciliation statement?**
(a) It will be deducted from the balance as per cash book
(b) It will be added to the balance as per passbook
(c) It will be added to the balance as per cash book
(d) None of the above

21. **Bank paid house tax on accountholder's behalf, but no information was received from the bank will lead to**
(a) balance in cash book more than the balance of passbook
(b) balance in cash book less than the balance of passbook
(c) balance in passbook more than the balance of cash book
(d) None of the above

22. **If the balance as per the cash book is taken as the starting point, then a wrong entry on the debit side of the passbook for ₹ 1,510 is to be .... in the bank reconciliation statement.**
(a) deducted (b) added
(c) No effect (d) None of these

23. **Which of the following is an example of difference caused due to errors in cash book and passbook?** **Competency Based Que**
(a) Cheques issued by the firm to suppliers worth ₹ 10,000 not yet presented by supplier to the bank
(b) Cheques paid into the bank of ₹ 36,000, but not yet collected
(c) Cheque collection charges worth ₹ 75,000 levied by bank
(d) Wrong totalling as ₹ 5,50,000 instead of ₹ 3,30,000 by the accountant of the firm

24. **₹ 900 were collected as dividend by bank from investments. This amount will be .... from the balance as per passbook.**
(a) added (b) deducted (c) No effect (d) None of these

25. **Overdraft as per cash book is ₹ 90,000. Cheques deposited, but not credited ₹ 22,500. Cheques issued but not encashed ₹ 31,500. What is the balance as per passbook?** **Competency Based Que**
(a) ₹ 90,000 (b) ₹ 81,000
(c) ₹ 1,02,500 (d) ₹ 1,21,500

26. **If bank balance as per cash book is ₹ 1,00,000, cheques issued, but not presented for payment of ₹ 12,000 and bank charges of ₹ 800 were not entered in the cash book, then balance as per passbook will be** **Competency Based Que**
(a) ₹ 1,00,000 (b) ₹ 1,11,200
(c) ₹ 1,02,200 (d) ₹ 1,22,000

27. **After preparing bank reconciliation statement the debit balance as per cash book of Mr. Rehaan was ₹ 1,86,000. He found a cheque deposited in bank, but not collected by bank for ₹ 7,700 also ₹ 2,500 received as dividend for which no entry in cash book was passed. What will be the balance as per passbook?**
(a) ₹ 1,86,000 (b) ₹ 1,88,000 (c) ₹ 1,96,200 (d) ₹ 1,80,800

28. **Cheques issued by the firm to suppliers, but not presented by supplier to the bank for payment immediately. It is an example of difference caused due to** **Competency Based Que**
(a) timing differences in recording of transactions
(b) errors made by the business
(c) errors made by the bank (d) None of the above

29. **The bank balance in the cash book of Sarika on 31st December, 2023 is ₹ 45,300 (credit), but the passbook shows difference due to the following reason**
A cheque (post dated) for ₹ 500 has been debited in bank column of cash book, but not presented for payment. Cheque totalling ₹ 750 deposited in bank yet not collected. What will be the balance as per passbook? **Competency Based Que**
(a) ₹ 31,200 (b) ₹ 45,550
(c) ₹ 44,050 (d) ₹ 45,050

30. **If balance as per cash book is ₹ 54,000 and ₹ 100 for bank incidental charges are debited to Pratibha and Co. account, but not recorded in cash book and cheques for ₹ 5,400 were deposited in the bank, but not yet collected by the bank, then what will be the balance in the passbook?** Competency Based Que

(a) ₹ 48,500 (b) ₹ 59,500
(c) ₹ 59,300 (d) None of these

31. **The bank passbook of Sand Ltd. had an overdraft of ₹ 40,000. Interest on overdraft was ₹ 4,000. Insurance premium paid by the bank was ₹ 400. What is the balance as per cash book?** Competency Based Que

(a) ₹ 24,400 overdraft
(b) ₹ 42,200 favourable balance
(c) ₹ 35,600 overdraft
(d) ₹ 35,600 favourable balance

32. **On 31st March, 2023, the bank column of the cash book of Mr. Srijan showed a credit balance of ₹ 1,18,100. Cheques received and recorded in the cash book, but not sent to the bank for collection of ₹ 12,400. Payment received from a customer directly by the bank of ₹ 27,300, but no entry was made in the cash book. What will be the balance as per bank passbook?** Competency Based Que

(a) ₹ 1,03,200 overdraft
(b) ₹ 1,33,000 overdraft
(c) ₹ 1,03,200 favourable balance
(d) ₹ 1,33,000 favourable balance

Assertion-Reason

Direction (Q. No. 33 to 42) *Read the following Assertion (A) and Reason (R) and choose the correct alternative from the following*

Alternatives

(a) Both Assertion (A) and Reason (R) are true and Reason (R) is the correct explanation of Assertion (A)
(b) Both Assertion (A) and Reason (R) are true, but Reason (R) is not the correct explanation of Assertion (A)
(c) Assertion (A) is true, but Reason (R) is false
(d) Assertion (A) is false, but Reason (R) is true

33. **Assertion** (A) Bank reconciliation statement is prepared by the bank.

Reason (R) Bank reconciliation statement is prepared to reconcile the difference between bank balance as shown by passbook and cash book.

34. **Assertion** (A) If the starting point is cash book balance then the ending point will be passbook balance.

Reason (R) If the starting point is passbook balance then the ending point will be the balance as per cash book.

35. **Assertion** (A) If a businessman commits an error while recording the transactions in the bank column of the cash book, the balance of the cash book will not agree with the balance of the passbook.

Reason (R) If the bank commits an error, the balance of the passbook will not agree with the balance of cash book.

36. **Assertion** (A) When a comparison is made between the balance of the cash book with the balance of the passbook, there is often a difference.

Reason (R) The differences between the cash book and the bank passbook are caused by either timing differences in recording of the transactions or errors made by the business or by the bank.

37. **Assertion** (A) When cheques are issued for payment by the firm to the suppliers/creditors of the firm, they are immediately credited in the bank column of the cash book. However, it is recorded by the bank only when it is presented for payment.

Reason (R) There may be a gap between the issue of a cheque and its presentation to the bank, which may cause the difference.

38. **Assertion** (A) When bank allows interest, it credits the amount in the customers account immediately.

Reason (R) Sometimes the passbook balance will be higher than the cash book balance.

39. **Assertion** (A) Bank statement is usually prepared by the bank to keep a record of customer's transactions with the bank and to ascertain the balance in the account of the customer.

Reason (R) Bank statement is a copy of the customer's account in the books of a bank.

40. **Assertion** (A) A reconciliation statement facilitates the preparation of a revised cash book.

Reason (R) It helps in locating any error, that may have been committed either in the cash book or in the passbook.

41. **Assertion** (A) When direct debits are made by the bank on behalf of the customer, the balance in the passbook will be more when compared to the cash book.

Reason (R) If an entry of payment has been recorded in the passbook, but not in the cash book, then the balance of passbook will be less than of cash book.

42. **Assertion** (A) When a bill receivable discounted is dishonoured on presentation then the passbook balance will be higher than the cash book balance.

Reason (R) When a bill receivable discounted is dishonoured on presentation, the bank immediately deducts (debits) the amount of the bill out of the customer's account.

Two Statements Based MCQs

Direction (Q. No. 43 to 50) *Read the following statements carefully and choose the correct alternative*

Alternatives
(a) Both the statements are correct
(b) Both the statements are incorrect
(c) Statement I is correct and Statement II is incorrect
(d) Statement I is incorrect and Statement II is correct

43. **Statement I** There may be a gap of some days between some transactions in the cash book and in the passbook.

Statement II The entry in the cash book is made at the time of issue of cheque only while entry will be made by the bank when the cheque is presented for payment.

44. **Statement I** There are various transactions which the bank carries out by itself without intimating the customer.

Statement II There will be no effect if a transaction is carried out without intimating the accountholder.

45. **Statement I** Mistakes or errors made in preparing the accounts either by the bank or the customer can also result in disagreement of the two statements.

Statement II Rectification of errors is required to be done in both the statements before preparing any bank reconciliation statement.

46. **Statement I** Bank reconciliation statement is a very important tool for internal control of cash flows.

Statement II It helps in detecting errors, frauds and irregularities occurred, if any.

47. **Statement I** Overdraft is one where the bank account becomes positive and the businesses in effect have borrowed from the bank.

Statement II Overdraft is one where the bank account becomes negative and the businesses in effect have borrowed from the bank.

48. **Statement I** Cheques deposited into bank, but not yet cleared appears in the passbook only.

Statement II Direct deposit made by debtors into businessman's bank account is recorded on the credit side of passbook.

49. **Statement I** On dishonour of a cheque, the bank does not credit the amount to the account of the customer.

Statement II On dishonour of a cheque, the customer credit his/her bank account in his books.

50. **Statement I** If the starting point is cash book balance, the amount of the cheques issued but not presented for payment will be added to match it with passbook.

Statement II If the starting point is passbook balance the amount of the cheques issued but not presented for payment will be added to match it with cash book.

Matching

51. Match the following

Column I		Column II	
A.	₹ 300 interest debited in passbook only	(i)	₹ 300 will be added to cashbook
B.	₹ 400 direct deposit made by customer in bank recorded in passbook	(ii)	₹ 400 will be deducted from passbook
C.	Cheque of ₹ 300 issued, but not yet presented	(iii)	₹ 400 will be added to passbook
D.	Cheque for ₹ 400 deposited into bank is dishonoured	(iv)	₹ 300 will be deducted from cashbook

Codes

	A	B	C	D
(a)	(i)	(ii)	(iii)	(iv)
(b)	(ii)	(iii)	(iv)	(i)
(c)	(iv)	(ii)	(i)	(iii)
(d)	(i)	(iii)	(ii)	(iv)

52. Match the following

Column I		Column II	
A.	Favourable cash book balance	(i)	Debit balance as per passbook
B.	Favourable passbook balance	(ii)	Debit balance as per cash book
C.	Unfavourable cash book balance	(iii)	Credit balance as per passbook
D.	Unavourable cash book balance	(iv)	Credit balance as per cash book

Codes

	A	B	C	D		A	B	C	D
(a)	(i)	(ii)	(iii)	(iv)	(b)	(ii)	(iii)	(iv)	(i)
(c)	(iv)	(iii)	(ii)	(i)	(d)	(i)	(iii)	(ii)	(iv)

53. Match the following

Column I		Column II	
A.	Cheque issued, but not presented for payment	(i)	Error by the firm
B.	Bank charges deducted by bank	(ii)	Time gap
C.	Bank column in cash book is undercasted	(iii)	Recorded by bank only

Codes

	A	B	C		A	B	C
(a)	(i)	(ii)	(iii)	(b)	(ii)	(iii)	(i)
(c)	(i)	(iii)	(ii)	(d)	(iii)	(i)	(ii)

54. **Match the following**

Column I	Column II
A. Credit balance of cash book shows	(i) Negative balance
B. Passbook is a copy of	(ii) Bank overdraft
C. Debit balance of passbook means	(iii) Favourable balance
D. Credit balance of passbook shows	(iv) Customer's account

Codes

	A	B	C	D		A	B	C	D
(a)	(i)	(ii)	(iii)	(iv)	(b)	(ii)	(iii)	(iv)	(i)
(c)	(iv)	(iii)	(ii)	(i)	(d)	(i)	(iv)	(ii)	(iii)

Case Based MCQs

Direction *Read the following case study and answer the questions 55 and 56 on the basis of the same*

On 30th June, 2023, the cash book of Galaxy Ltd, showed a balance of ₹ 400 at bank. They had sent cheques amounting to ₹ 2,000 sent to the bank before 30th June, but it appears from the passbook that cheques worth only ₹ 800 had been credited before that date.

Similarly, out of cheques of ₹ 1,000 issued during the month of June, cheques for ₹ 50 were presented and paid in July. The passbook also showed the following payments

(i) ₹ 64 as premium on the life policy according to standing instructions.

(ii) ₹ 400 against a pro-note, as per instructions.

The passbook showed that the bank had collected ₹ 120 as interest on government securities. The bank had charged interest ₹ 10 and bank charges ₹ 4. There was no entry in the cash book for the payments, interest, etc.

55. **On 30th June, 2023, cheques of amounting to ₹ 2,000 sent to the bank, but it appears from the passbook that cheques worth only ₹ 800 had been credited before that date is an example of**

(a) timing differences in recording of transactions
(b) errors made by the business
(c) errors made by the bank
(d) None of the above

56. **Out of cheques of ₹ 1,000 issued during the month of June, cheques for ₹ 50 were presented and paid in July. What will be the amount deducted/added from the balance of cashbook to reconcile it with the balance of passbook?**

(a) Add ₹ 50 (b) Add ₹ 950
(c) Less ₹ 50 (d) Less ₹ 950

Direction *Read the following case study and answer the questions 57 and 58 on the basis of the same*

Sakhi, on 1st April, 2023 joined in the accounting department of Sanjay Ltd. which is an apparel firm. Her manager Mr. Shanu ask her to prepare a bank reconciliation statement. Sakhi, on the other hand is new to this statement and is not aware about the need and importance of preparing the bank reconciliation statement. Mr. Shanu explains to her the procedure and the importance of preparing the bank reconciliation statement. She still has a few queries which she ask from her manager Shanu.

57. **What type of document does she needs to prepare bank reconciliation statement?**

(a) Passbook of Sanjay Ltd. (b) Cash book of Sanjay Ltd.
(c) Both (a) and (b) (d) None of these

58. **Using which of the following statements, Mr. Shanu have explained the importance of bank reconciliation statement to Sakhi?**

(a) It helps in bringing out the unnecessary delay in the collection of cheques by the bank
(b) It helps the management to keep a track of cheques, which have been sent to the bank for collection
(c) It helps in avoiding embezzlements or misappropriation of funds by regular periodic reconciliation
(d) All of the above

Direction *Read the following case study and answer the questions 59 to 61 on the basis of the same*

Cash book of Sagar Ltd. showed a bank balance of ₹ 1,86,000 on 31st March, 2023. It did not match with the balance shown in his passbook. A closer analysis revealed that there were cheques issued to creditors, but not yet presented to the bank for payment amounted to ₹ 36,000. Dividend of ₹ 2,500 was received by the bank, but not entered in the cash book. Interest of ₹ 625 was allowed by the bank. Cheques worth ₹ 7,700 were deposited into bank for collection but not collected by bank upto this date. Bank charges amounted to ₹ 100.

59. **Difference caused due to bank charges amounting to ₹ 100, is an example of**

(a) timing differences in recording of transactions
(b) errors made by the business
(c) errors made by the bank (d) None of the above

60. **Cheques of ₹ 7,700 deposited into bank for collection but not yet collected by bank will be**

(a) added to debit balance of cash book
(b) deducted from debit balance of cash book
(c) there will be no treatment (d) None of the above

61. **The balance of passbook on 31st March, 2023 will be**

(a) ₹ 2,17,325 (b) ₹ 2,25,125
(c) ₹ 1,86,000 (d) None of these

Answers

1. (c) accountholder in a bank
2. (b) favourable balance
3. (b) credit balance in cash book
4. (d) when a bank statement is received
5. (d) Bank reconciliation statement is prepared only during the year end
6. (c) When overdraft as per cash book is given, bank charges debited in passbook only, is to be subtracted
7. (a) added to bank balance
8. (a) overdraft
9. (d) customer's account prepared by the bank
10. (a) debited
11. (a) credit balance in the cash book
12. (c) Both I and II
13. (d) All of the above
14. (c) timing gap
15. (a) copy of customer account
16. (a) timing differences in recording of transactions
17. (c) Amount deducted will be (32,000 – 12,800) = ₹ 19,200
18. (b) deducted from the balance as per cash book
19. (a) ₹ 33,500 (35,000 + 2,000 –3,000 –500)
20. (c) It will be added to the balance as per cash book
21. (a) balance in cash book more than the balance of passbook
22. (a) deducted
23. (d) Wrong totalling as ₹ 5,50,000 instead of ₹ 3,30,000 by the accountant of the firm
24. (b) deducted
25. (b) ₹ 81,000 (90,000 + 22,500 –31,500)
26. (b) ₹ 1,11,200 (1,00,000 + 12,000 – 800)
27. (d) ₹ 1,80,800 (1,86,000 + 2,500 – 7,700)
28. (a) timing differences in recording of transactions
29. (b) ₹ 45,550 (45,300 + 750 –500)
30. (a) ₹ 48,500 (54,000 –100 –5,400)
31. (c) ₹ 35,600 overdraft (40,000 – 4,000 – 400)
32. (a) ₹ 1,03,200 overdraft (1,18,100 + 12,400 –27,300)
33. (d) Assertion (A) is false, but Reason (R) is true
34. (b) Both Assertion (A) and Reason (R) are true, but Reason (R) is not the correct explanation of Assertion (A)
35. (b) Both Assertion (A) and Reason (R) are true, but Reason (R) is not the correct explanation of Assertion (A)
36. (a) Both Assertion (A) and Reason (R) are true and Reason (R) is the correct explanation of Assertion (A)
37. (a) Both Assertion (A) and Reason (R) are true and Reason (R) is the correct explanation of Assertion (A)
38. (b) Both Assertion (A) and Reason (R) are true, but Reason (R) is not the correct explanation of Assertion (A)
39. (a) Both Assertion (A) and Reason (R) are true and Reason (R) is the correct explanation of Assertion (A)
40. (a) Both Assertion (A) and Reason (R) are true and Reason (R) is the correct explanation of Assertion (A)
41. (d) Assertion (A) is false, but Reason (R) is true
42. (d) Assertion (A) is false, but Reason (R) is true
43. (a) Both the statements are correct
44. (c) There will be a effect even if a transaction is carried out with intimating the accountholder.
45. (a) Both the statements are correct
46. (a) Both the statements are correct
47. (d) Statement I is incorrect and Statement II is correct
48. (d) Statement I is incorrect and Statement II is correct
49. (a) Both the statements are correct
50. (c) If the starting point is passbook balance, the amount of the cheques issued but not presented for payment will be deducted to match it with cash book.
51. (c) (iv) (ii) (i) (iii)
52. (b) (ii) (iii) (iv) (i)
53. (b) (ii) (iii) (i)
54. (d) (i) (iv) (ii) (iii)
55. (a) timing differences in recording of transactions
56. (b) Add ₹ 950
57. (c) Both (a) and (b)
58. (d) All of the above
59. (a) timing differences in recording of transactions
60. (b) deducted from debit balance of cash book
61. (a) ₹ 2,17,325 (1,86,000 + 36,000 + 2,500 + 625 –7,700 – 100)

08

CHAPTER

Depreciation, Provisions and Reserves

Depreciation is the diminution in intrinsic value of the asset due to use and/or lapse of time.
- ICMA

YOUR STUDY GOALS

8.1 Depreciation
- Methods of Providing Depreciation
- Methods of Recording Depreciation

8.2 Provisions

8.3 Reserves

YOUR PRACTICE GOAL

- Topicwise Solved Questions (22 Solved Questions)
- Numerical Questions [30 Questions (Unsolved)]
- Theoretical Questions [13 Questions (with answers)]
- Objective Questions (65 Qs ; MCQs, A-R, Statements, Matching, Case)

8.1 Depreciation

Depreciation means decline in the value of fixed assets on account of usage and various other factors such as passage of time or obsolescence.

As per Schedule II under the **Companies Act, 2013**, "Depreciation is the systematic allocation of the depreciable amount of an asset over its useful life. The depreciable amount of an asset is the cost of an asset minus its residual value."

Terms related to Depreciation

- **Depletion**
  It is used in relation to natural resources or where depleting assets are involved such as mines, oil wells, timber, trees, etc. As the resource is extracted or removed, its asset value will be reduced or exhausted. This reduction in value or expiration of cost of asset resulting from production is called depletion.
- **Amortisation**
  It refers to the process of writing-off the cost of an intangible asset over a future period covering its expected useful life. This applies to patents, goodwill, copyrights, etc.

Characteristics/Features of Depreciation

- It is decline in the book value of property, plant and equipment (fixed assets) except land.
- It is a continuing process.

- It is charged on permanent basis, i.e. it reduces the value of asset permanently.
- It includes loss of value of assets due to effluxion of time, usage or obsolescence.
- It is an expired cost and must be deducted before calculating taxable profit.
- It is a non-cash expense and does not result in any cash outflow.
- It decreases only book value of asset, not market value.

Need for Providing Depreciation

- To calculate true profit or loss.
- For correct assessment of income tax.
- To provide funds for replacement of assets.
- To show the true and fair financial position.
- To ascertain the accurate cost of production.
- To prevent payment of dividend out of capital.

Smart Study Chart No. 1

Causes and Factors affecting Depreciation

Causes of Depreciation

- Physical wear and tear (constant use)
- Passage of time
- Accidents
- Changes in economic environment
- Obsolescence
- Depletion of assets
- Expiry of intellectual property rights or legal rights

Factors affecting Depreciation

- Cost of asset
- Estimated useful life of an asset
- Estimates scrap or residual value of an asset
- Depreciable cost

Methods of Providing Depreciation

- Straight Line Method
- Written Down Value Method
- Depreciation Fund Method
- Annuity Method
- Insurance Policy Method
- Revaluation Method
- Depletion Method
- Machine Hour Rate Method

Note As per the syllabus, only straight line method and written down value method are discussed.

Straight Line Method

This method is also known as **fixed instalment method** or **original cost method**. It is based on the assumption of equal usage of time over asset's whole useful life.

As per this method, a fixed and equal amount is charged as depreciation in every accounting period, during the life time of an asset.

Advantages and Disadvantages of Straight Line Method

Advantages	Disadvantages
• Simple and easy to apply. • Assets can be depreciated fully or upto the scrap value over the life of the asset. • Since, the depreciation amount is same every year, hence there is a same effect on the profit and loss account every year. • The book value of the assets becomes zero or equal to scrap value after passage of its useful life. Thus, the asset can be completely written-off. • Useful for those assets where the useful life can be estimated regularly.	• Assumes that asset is utilised consistently over the life of asset which is practically not correct in most cases. • Reduces the book value of an asset to zero, although the asset may still be in existence. • If some additions are made to the asset, fresh calculations are to be made. • It does not take into account, the interest on investment in fixed assets. • It is very difficult to estimate exact residual value.

Suitability of Straight Line Method

This method is suitable in case of those assets whose repair charges are less, the possibility of obsolescence is less and for those assets whose useful life can be predicted accurately.

Smart Study Chart No. 2

Calculation of Amount of Depreciation under Straight Line Method

By Using Formula

$$\text{Yearly Depreciation} = \frac{(\text{Original Cost of Asset} - \text{Estimated Scrap Value})}{\text{Estimated Useful Life of Asset}}$$

As a Percentage of Original Cost

$$\text{Yearly Depreciation} = \frac{\text{Cost of Acquisition} \times \text{Rate of Depreciation}}{100}$$

Written Down Value (WDV) Method

This method is also known as **diminishing balance method** or **reducing balance method**. In this method, depreciation is charged on the book value (written down value) of the asset by a fixed rate of percentage. Thus, as the value of asset keeps going down year by year, depreciation also goes down in proportion.

Advantages and Disadvantages of WDV Method

Advantages	Disadvantages
• It is easy to apply and understand. • The balance of this asset is never reduced to zero. • As a large portion of cost is written-off in earlier years, loss due to obsolescence gets reduced. • It is an approved method of depreciation by income tax authorities.	• Even if the asset looses it utility, it still appears in the books of accounts. • The fact of loss of interest is ignored under this method. • The rate of depreciation to be provided cannot be easily determined under this method.

Suitability of WDV Method

This method is suitable in case of those assets which are affected by technological changes and require more repair expenses as they become old, e.g. Machinery.

Calculation of Amount of Depreciation under WDV Method

- Yearly Depreciation = Book Value of Asset $\times \dfrac{\text{Rate of Depreciation}}{100}$
- Calculating Rate of Depreciation (if not given)

$$R = \left[1 - \sqrt[n]{\frac{S}{C}}\right] \times 100$$

Where, R = Rate of depreciation
n = Expected useful life
S = Scrap value ; C = Cost of an asset

Distinction between Straight Line and WDV Method

Basis	Straight Line Method	Written Down Value Method
Basis of Charging Depreciation	It is calculated on the original cost of the asset.	It is calculated on the book value or the written down value of the asset.
Rate of Depreciation	Rate of depreciation is kept low.	Rate of depreciation is normally kept high.
Amount of Depreciation	The amount of depreciation on the asset remains fixed every year.	The amount of depreciation goes on diminishing every year.
Book Value of Asset	At the end of the life of the asset, its balance is zero.	Under this method, the asset is never reduced to zero.
Recognised by Income Tax Law	It is not recognised.	It is recognised.
Effect of Depreciation and Repairs on Profit and Loss	Burden of repairs and depreciation is unequal year after year, i.e. it will be lighter in earlier years and will increase in later years.	Burden to total cost of running the asset is almost equal every year.

Methods of Recording Depreciation

In the books of account, there are two types of arrangements for recording depreciation of fixed assets. These are

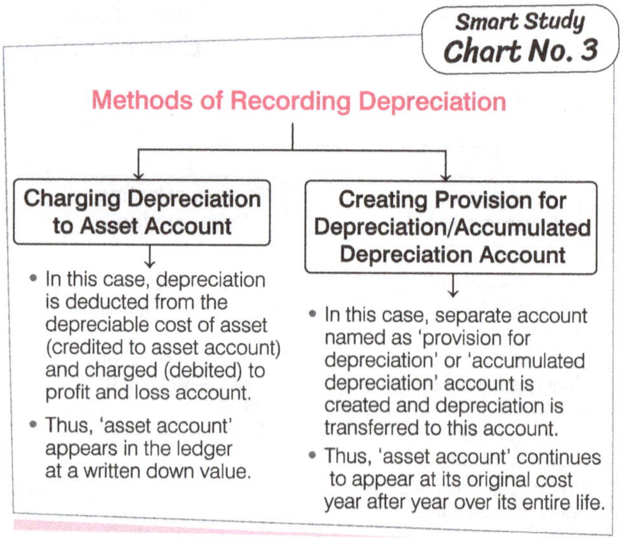

Journal Entries and Balance Sheet Treatment

I. In Case of Charging Depreciation to Asset Account

Journal Entries

(i) To record purchase of asset	Asset A/c To Cash/Bank A/c (Being the asset purchased)	Dr
(ii) To provide depreciation	Depreciation A/c To Asset A/c (Being the depreciation provided)	Dr
(iii) To transfer depreciation	Profit and Loss A/c* To Depreciation A/c (Being the transfer of depreciation to profit and loss account)	Dr

In case of a company, 'Statement of Profit and Loss' will be used.

Balance Sheet

Liabilities	Amt (₹)	Assets	Amt (₹)
		Asset ... (−) Depreciation (...)	...

II. In Case of Creating Provision for Depreciation/ Accumulated Depreciation Account

Journal Entries

(i) For recording purchase of asset	Asset A/c Dr To Bank/Cash/Vendor A/c
(ii) For providing depreciation	Depreciation A/c Dr To Provision for Depreciation A/c
(iii) For closure of depreciation account	Profit and Loss A/c Dr To Depreciation A/c

Balance Sheet

Liabilities	Amt (₹)	Assets	Amt (₹)
		Asset ... (−) Provision for Depreciation (...)	...

or

Balance Sheet

Liabilities	Amt (₹)	Assets	Amt (₹)
Provision for Depreciation	...	Asset	...

Disposal of Asset

It implies that the asset has been sold or has been discarded. Generally, to record the disposal of asset, an **asset disposal account** is opened. This account provides a complete and clear view of all the transactions involved in the sale of asset under one account head.

It can be treated as under

I. Disposal of Assets when the Provision for Depreciation Account is not Maintained

Journal Entries

(i) To record depreciation upto the date of sale	Depreciation A/c Dr To Asset A/c (Being depreciation charged)
(ii) To transfer asset to asset disposal account	Asset Disposal A/c Dr To Asset A/c
(iii) To record sale of asset	Cash/Bank A/c Dr To Asset Disposal A/c (Being the asset sold)
(iv) To record profit/loss on sale • In case of profit	Asset Disposal A/c Dr To Gain/Profit on Sale of Assets A/c (Profit and Loss A/c) (Being the transfer of profit on sale of asset)
• In case of loss	Loss on Sale of Asset A/c Dr (Profit and Loss A/c) To Asset Disposal A/c (Being the transfer of loss on sale of asset)
(v) To transfer depreciation	Profit and Loss A/c Dr To Depreciation A/c (Being depreciation transferred to profit and loss account)

II. Disposal of Assets when the Provision for Depreciation Account is Maintained

Journal Entries

(i) For transfer of original cost of asset disposed-off	Asset Disposal A/c Dr To Asset A/c
(ii) For transfer of accumulated depreciation on asset disposed-off	Provision for Depreciation A/c Dr To Asset Disposal A/c
(iii) For recording sale proceeds	Cash/Bank A/c Dr To Asset Disposal A/c
(iv) For transfer of the balance in asset disposal account • In case of profit	Asset Disposal A/c Dr To Gain on Sale on Asset A/c (Profit and Loss A/c)
• In case of loss	Loss on Sale of Asset A/c Dr (Profit and Loss A/c) To Asset Disposal A/c

Format of Asset Disposal Account

Dr **Asset Disposal Account** Cr

Date	Particulars	Amt (₹)	Date	Particulars	Amt (₹)
	To Asset A/c	...		By Prov. for Dep. A/c	...
				By Bank A/c (Sale)	...
	To Gain on Sale of Asset A/c (Profit and Loss A/c)* [Bal. fig. (Profit)]	...		By Loss on Sale of Assets A/c (Profit and Loss A/c)* [Balancing figure (Loss)]	...

**Any one will appear*

8.2 Provisions

A provision is that part of profit which is retained or kept aside to meet some known and expected contingencies, the amount of which cannot be ascertained with reasonable accuracy.

Examples of Provisions

- Provision for depreciation
- Provision for repairs and renewals
- Provision for taxation
- Provision for bad and doubtful debts
- Provision for discount on debtors

Features of Provisions

- It is created to meet a known liability.
- Provision is a charge to profit and loss account.
- The liability is known but the amount of such liability cannot be ascertained with reasonable accuracy.
- Creation of provision ensures proper matching of revenue and expenses.

Accounting Treatment and Disclosure of Provisions

Provision is a charge against the profits and is created by debiting profit and loss account before calculating net profit.

In the balance sheet, the amount of provision may be shown either

- on the **assets** side, by way of deduction from the concerned asset. e.g. Provision for doubtful debts is shown as deduction from the amount of sundry debtors, etc.
- on the **liability** side, along with the current liabilities. e.g. Provision for taxes and provision for repairs and renewals.

8.3 Reserves

Reserve is that part of profit which is retained or kept aside to meet some unknown and unexpected contingencies in future. Firm create reserves to secure their future. Reserves are also referred to as undistributed or accumulated profits by the companies.

Examples of Reserves

- General reserve
- Workmen compensation fund
- Investment fluctuation fund
- Capital reserve
- Dividend equalisation reserve

Features of Reserves

- Reserves are created out of net profits/divisible profits.
- Amount of reserve when invested in outside securities, it is known as 'reserve fund'.
- Creation of reserve is not a legal necessity.
- Reserves are created for meeting an unknown liability/loss in the future and not for meeting any known liability.

Objectives of Reserves

- To strengthen the financial position.
- To meet unforeseen and unexpected losses in future.
- To provide funds out of profits for expansion and modernisation.
- To meet legal requirements as required under the Companies Act.
- To pay dividends in the years when profits are not sufficient.

Difference between Provisions and Reserves

Basis	Provisions	Reserves
Meaning	It is created to meet some known contingencies.	It is created to meet some unknown contingencies.
Basic Nature	It is charge against profits.	It is an appropriation of profits.
Purpose	It is created for specific liability.	It is created to strengthen the financial position.
Mode of Creation	It is created through profit and loss account.	It is created through profit and loss appropriation account.
Presenting in Balance Sheet	It is shown as an item of deduction from its related asset or shown on liability side.	It is always shown on the liabilities side in the balance sheet.

Basis	Provisions	Reserves
Use for Payment of Dividend	It cannot be used for dividend distribution.	It can be used for dividend distribution.
Effect on Taxable Profit	It reduces the taxable profit.	It has no effect on taxable profit.
Compulsion	Creation of provision is necessary.	Creation of reserve is at the discretion of management.

Smart Study **Chart No. 4**

Types of Reserves

Revenue Reserves

These reserves are created by companies out of profits which arise out of the normal operating activities of business and are available for dividend.
It is very useful to increase financial soundness of business.

Capital Reserves

These reserves are created out of capital profits. Capital profits are generally not available for paying dividend.
Capital reserves are used to meet capital losses.

Types of Revenue Reserves

1. **General Reserve** It is the amount set aside out of profits without any specific purpose. It is available to strengthen the financial position or expansion of business. It is also known as **free reserve** or **contingency reserve**.
2. **Specific Reserve** This is created for specific purpose and can be utilised only for that purpose. It is shown on the debit side of profit and loss account.

   Examples of specific reserves are

   - Workmen compensation reserve
   - Debentures redemption reserve
   - Investment fluctuation reserve
   - Dividend equalisation reserve

Examples of Capital Reserves

- Profit prior to incorporation
- Premium on issue of shares or debentures
- Profit on redemption of debentures
- Profit on forfeiture of shares, re-issue of shares
- Profit on sale of property, plant and equipment
- Capital redemption reserve
- Profit on revaluation of fixed assets and liabilities
- Profit on the sale of land and buildings

Difference between Revenue Reserve and Capital Reserve

Basis	Revenue Reserve	Capital Reserve
Source of Creation	It is created out of revenue profits.	It is created out of capital profits.
Purpose	It is created for meeting unforeseen losses and for strengthening financial position of business.	It is used for writing-off the capital losses or to comply with legal requirements.
Usage	It can be used to give dividend to shareholders or for any other purpose. Specific reserve can be used for a specific purpose.	It can be used for giving dividend to members. Only on the fulfilment of certain conditions as prescribed by the Companies Act.

Secret Reserve

It is defined as any reserve which does not appear in the balance sheet. It is also called as **inner reserve** or **internal reserve** or **hidden reserve**.

It is a result of understatement of assets or overstatement of liabilities and corresponding understatement of capital.

With the existence of secret reserves, the finanical position of the company is better than it appears from the balance sheet. Creation of secret reserve is prohibited as per Companies Act.

Mind Map

DEPRECIATION, PROVISIONS AND RESERVES

1 Depreciation, Depletion and Amortisation

- Depreciation means decline in the value of fixed assets on account of usage and other factors such as passage of time or obsolescence
- The term depletion is used in relation to natural resources or where depleting assets are involved such as mines, trees, etc
- Amortisation is the process of writing-off the cost of an intangible asset over a future period covering its expected useful life

2 Causes and Factors Affecting Depreciation

- **Causes** Physical wear and tear, passage of time, accidents, changes in economic environment, obsolescence, depletion of assests, etc.
- **Factors** Cost of asset, estimated useful life of an asset, estimated scrap value and depreciable cost.

3 Straight Line Method of Depreciation

- This method is also known as fixed installment method or original cost method. It is based on the assumption of equal usage of time over asset's whole useful life
- As per this method, a fixed and equal amount is charged as depreciation in every accounting period, during the life time of an asset
- Depreciation amount under this method is calculated
  - By using formula

$$\text{Yearly Depreciation} = \frac{(\text{Original Cost of Asset} - \text{Estimated Scrap Value})}{\text{Estimated Useful Life of Asset}}$$

  - As a percentage of original cost

$$\text{Yearly Deprecation} = \frac{\text{Cost of Acquisition} \times \text{Rate of Depreciation}}{100}$$

4 Written Down Value Method of Depreciation

- This method is also known as diminishing balance method or reducing balance method
- In this method, depreciation is charged on the book value of asset by a fixed rate of percentage. Thus, the value of asset keeps going down year by year, depreciation also goes down in proportion
- Depreciation amount under this method is calculated as
  - Yearly Depreciation = Book Value of Asset × $\frac{\text{Rate of Depreciation}}{100}$
  - Calculating Rate of Depreciation (if not given)

$$R = \left[1 = \sqrt[n]{\frac{S}{C}}\right] \times 100$$

5 Methods of Recording Depreciation

Charging Depreciation to Asset Account

- In this case, depreciation is deducted from depreciable cost of asset and charged to profit and loss account.
- Asset account appears in the ledger at a written down value.

Creating Provision for Depreciation Account

- In this case, seperate account named 'provision for depreciation' account is created and depreciation is transferred to this account.
- Asset account continues to appear at its original cost year after year over its entire life.

6 Disposal of Asset

- It implies that the asset has been sold or has been discarded
- Generally, to record the disposal of asset, an asset diposal account is opened
- This account provides a complete and clear view of all the transactions involved in the sale of asset under one account head

7 Provisions

Provision is that part of profit which is kept aside to meet known and expected contingencies, the amount of which cannot be ascertained with reasonable accuracy. e.g. Provision for depreciation, provision for repairs, etc.

Features

- It is created to meet known liability
- It is a charge to profit and loss account
- It ensures proper matching of revenue and expenses

Accounting Treatment and Disclosure

- It is charge against profit and is created by debiting profit and loss account before calculating net profit
- It is shown on the asset side of balance sheet by way of deduction from the concerned asset
- Alternatively, on the liability side of balance sheet

8 Reserves

It is that part of profit which is retained or kept aside to meet some unknown and unexpected contingencies in future. e.g. General reserve, investment fluctuation reserve, etc.

Types

- **Revenue Reserves** These reserves are created out of revenue profits and classified into general reserves and specific reserves.
- **Capital Reserves** These reserves are created out of capital profits. Capital profits are not available for paying dividend. These reserves are created to meet capital losses.

Topicwise Solved Questions

Straight Line Method

Solved Question 1 *(When expected working life is given)* **Zenith Ltd. purchased a machine for ₹ 9,80,000 and spent ₹ 20,000 on installation on 1st April, 2021. Estimated effective life of the machine is 10 years and the salvage value at the end will be ₹ 1,00,000. Pass the necessary journal entries and prepare the machinery account of Zenith Ltd. for three years. The books are closed on 31st March every year and the depreciation is charged as per straight line method.**

Sol.

In the Books of Zenith Ltd.
JOURNAL

Date	Particulars		LF	Amt (Dr)	Amt (Cr)
2021 Apr 1	Machinery A/c	Dr		10,00,000	
	To Bank A/c				10,00,000
	(Being machinery purchase for ₹ 9,80,000 and installation paid ₹ 20,000)				
2022 Mar 31	Depreciation A/c [(10,00,000 – 1,00,000)/10]	Dr		90,000	
	To Machinery A/c				90,000
	(Being depreciation charged)				
Mar 31	Statement of Profit and Loss	Dr		90,000	
	To Depreciation A/c				90,000
	(Being depreciation transferred to profit and loss account)				
2023 Mar 31	Depreciation A/c	Dr		90,000	
	To Machinery A/c				90,000
	(Being depreciation charged)				
Mar 31	Statement of Profit and Loss	Dr		90,000	
	To Depreciation A/c				90,000
	(Being depreciation transferred to profit and loss account)				
2024 Mar 31	Depreciation A/c	Dr		90,000	
	To Machinery A/c				90,000
	(Being depreciation charged)				
Mar 31	Statement of Profit and Loss	Dr		90,000	
	To Depreciation A/c				90,000
	(Being depreciation transferred to profit and loss account)				

Dr **Machinery Account** Cr

Date	Particulars	Amt (₹)	Date	Particulars	Amt (₹)
2021 Apr 1	To Bank A/c (9,80,000 + 20,000)	10,00,000	2022 Mar 31	By Depreciation A/c	90,000
			Mar 31	By Balance c/d	9,10,000
		10,00,000			10,00,000
2022 Apr 1	To Balance b/d	9,10,000	2023 Mar 31	By Depreciation A/c	90,000
			Mar 31	By Balance c/d	8,20,000
		9,10,000			9,10,000

Date	Particulars	Amt (₹)	Date	Particulars	Amt (₹)
2023			2024		
Apr 1	To Balance b/d	8,20,000	Mar 31	By Depreciation A/c	90,000
			Mar 31	By Balance c/d	7,30,000
		8,20,000			8,20,000

Solved Question 2 *(When percentage is given)* **On 1st October, 2021, Rahul purchased a truck for ₹ 2,00,000. Another truck was purchased for ₹ 1,20,000 on 1st April, 2023. Depreciation is charged @ 10% p.a. of the original cost every year. The books are closed on 31st March every year. Prepare truck account and depreciation account upto 31st March, 2024.**

Sol. Dr **Truck Account** Cr

Date	Particulars	Amt (₹)	Date	Particulars		Amt (₹)
2021			2022			
Oct 1	To Bank A/c (Truck A)	2,00,000	Mar 31	By Depreciation (Truck A) $\left(2,00,000 \times \frac{10}{100} \times \frac{6}{12}\right)$		10,000
			Mar 31	By Balance c/d		1,90,000
		2,00,000				2,00,000
2022			2023			
Apr 1	To Balance b/d	1,90,000	Mar 31	By Depreciation A/c (Truck A)		20,000
			Mar 31	By Balance c/d		1,70,000
		1,90,000				1,90,000
2023			2024			
Apr 1	To Balance b/d	1,70,000	Mar 31	By Depreciation A/c		
Apr 1	To Bank A/c (Truck B)	1,20,000		Truck A	20,000	
				Truck B	12,000	32,000
			Mar 31	By Balance c/d		
				Truck A	1,50,000	
				Truck B	1,08,000	2,58,000
		2,90,000				2,90,000

Dr **Depreciation Account** Cr

Date	Particulars	Amt (₹)	Date	Particulars	Amt (₹)
2022			2022		
Mar 31	To Truck A/c	10,000	Mar 31	By Profit and Loss A/c	10,000
2023			2023		
Mar 31	To Truck A/c	20,000	Mar 31	By Profit and Loss A/c	20,000
2024			2024		
Mar 31	To Truck A/c	32,000	Mar 31	By Profit and Loss A/c	32,000

Solved Question 3 *(When the asset is sold)* **On 1st April, 2020, Rashi Ltd. purchased a plant of ₹ 1,00,000. The life of plant is estimated to be 8 years and the salvage value is estimated as ₹ 4,000. On 1 January, 2023, entire plant is sold for ₹ 70,000. The firm closes its books on 31st March every year and follows straight line method of depreciation. Prepare plant account upto 31st March, 2023.**

Sol. Dr **Plant Account** Cr

Date	Particulars	Amt (₹)	Date	Particulars	Amt (₹)
2020			2021		
Apr 1	To Bank A/c	1,00,000	Mar 31	By Depreciation A/c (WN1)	12,000
			Mar 31	By Balance c/d	88,000
		1,00,000			1,00,000

Date	Particulars	Amt (₹)	Date	Particulars	Amt (₹)
2021			2022		
Apr 1	To Balance b/d	88,000	Mar 31	By Depreciation A/c	12.000
			Mar 31	By Balance c/d	76,000
		88,000			88,000
2022			2023		
Apr 1	To Balance b/d	76,000	Jan 1	By Depreciation A/c	9,000
	To Profit on Sale A/c (WN2)	3,000	Jan 1	By Bank A/c	70,000
		79,000			79,000

Working Notes

1. **Calculation of Depreciation**

$$\text{Depreciation} = \frac{\text{Cost of an Asset} - \text{Scrap Value}}{\text{Estimated Life of an Asset}} = \frac{1,00,000 - 4,000}{8} = \frac{96,000}{8} = ₹\ 12,000$$

2. **Calculation of Profit or Loss on Sale of Plant** = 1,00,000 (Cost) – [(12,000 + 12,000 + 9,000) Dep.] – 70,000 (Sale) = ₹ (3,000)

Solved Question 4 *(When the asset is sold)* **On 1st July, 2021, Sunita Ltd. purchased a machinery for ₹ 5,00,000 plus IGST @ 12%. On 1st October, 2023, it was sold for ₹ 1,50,000 plus IGST @ 12%. Depreciation is charged @ 10% per annum on straight line method. Prepare machinery account for three years. Books are closed on 31st March every year.**

Sol. Dr **Machinery Account** Cr

Date	Particulars	Amt (₹)	Date	Particulars	Amt (₹)
2021			2022		
Jul 1	To Bank A/c	5,00,000	Mar 31	By Depreciation A/c (WN1)	37,500
			Mar 31	By Balance c/d	4,62,500
		5,00,000			5,00,000
2022			2023		
Apr 1	To Balance b/d	4,62,500	Mar 31	By Depreciation A/c	50,000
			Mar 31	By Balance c/d	4,12,500
		4,62,500			4,62,500
2023			2023		
Apr 1	To Balance b/d	4,12,500	Oct 1	By Depreciation A/c	25,000
			Oct 1	By Bank A/c	1,50,000
			Oct 1	By Loss on Sale of MachineryA/c	2,37,500
		4,12,500			4,12,500

Working Notes

1.

Particulars	Amt (₹)
Original Cost of Machinery on 1st July, 2021	5,00,000
(–) Depreciation on 31st March, 2022 $\left(5,00,000 \times \frac{10}{100} \times \frac{9}{12}\right)$	(37,500)
	4,62,500
(–) Depreciation on 31st March, 2023 $\left(5,00,000 \times \frac{10}{10}\right)$	(50,000)
	4,12,500
(–) Depreciation on 1st October, 2023 $\left(5,00,000 \times \frac{10}{100} \times \frac{6}{12}\right)$	(25,000)
Book Value of Machinery on 1st October, 2023	3,87,500
(–) Sales Proceeds	(1,50,000)
Loss on Sale of Asset	2,37,500

2. Entry for purchase of machinery

Machinery A/c	Dr	5,00,000	
Input IGST A/c	Dr	60,000	
To Bank A/c			5,60,000
(Being machinery purchased and inter-state IGST paid @12%)			

Since machinery account is debited by ₹ 5,00,000 excluding IGST, there will be no effect of IGST on machinery account. It is not a cost of machinery as IGST paid can be set off against IGST, CGST and SGST collected.

3. Entry for sale of machinery

Bank A/c	Dr	1,68,000	
To Machinery A/c			1,50,000
To Output IGST A/c			18,000
(Being machinery sold and IGST collected)			

Since machinery account is credited by ₹ 1,50,000 excluding IGST, there will be no effect of Output IGST on machinery account.

Solved Question 5 ***(When a part of asset sold)*** **Nitya Ltd. purchased a machinery costing ₹ 45,000 on 1st April, 2021. An additional machinery on 1st October, 2021, was purchased for ₹ 30,000. On 1st January, 2023, one-third of the machinery purchased on 1st April, 2021, was sold for ₹ 4,500. Depreciation is charged @ 10% p.a. on straight line method.**

Prepare machinery account for three years if the books are closed on 31st December every year.

Sol. Dr **Machinery Account** Cr

Date	Particulars		Amt (₹)	Date	Particulars		Amt (₹)
2021				2021			
Apr 1	To Bank A/c (Machine A)		45,000	Dec 31	By Depreciation A/c		
Oct 1	To Bank A/c (Machine B)		30,000		Machine A	2,250	
					Machine B	1,125	
					Machine C	750	4,125
				Dec 31	By Balance c/d		
					Machine A	27,750	
					Machine B	13,875	
					Machine C	29,250	70,875
			75,000				75,000
2022				2022			
Jan 1	To Balance b/d			Dec 31	By Depreciation A/c		
	Machine A	27,750			Machine A	3,000	
	Machine B	13,875			Machine B	1,500	
	Machine C	29,250	70,875		Machine C	3,000	7,500
				Dec 31	By Balance c/d		
					Machine A	24,750	
					Machine B	12,375	
					Machine C	26,250	63,375
			70,875				70,875
2023				2023			
Jan 1	To Balance b/d			Jan 1	By Bank A/c (Machine B)		4,500
	Machine A	24,750		Jan 1	By Loss on Sale of Machinery A/c		7,875
	Machine B	12,375					
	Machine C	26,250	63,375				
				Dec 31	By Depreciation A/c		
					Machine A	3,000	
					Machine C	3,000	6,000
				Dec 31	By Balance c/d		
					Machine A	21,750	
					Machine C	23,250	45,000
			63,375				63,375

Working Note

Since a part i.e. one-third of the machinery is sold, we will split the machinery purchased on 1st April, 2021 for ₹ 45,000 likewise i.e. ₹ 30,000 (A) and ₹ 15,000 (B).

Particulars	A (₹)	B (₹)	C (₹)
Machinery Purchased on 1st April, 2021	30,000	15,000	—
Machinery Purchased on 1st October, 2021	—	—	30,000
Depreciation on Machinery A, B, C on 31st December, 2021 $\left[30{,}000 \times \frac{10}{100} \times \frac{9}{12}\right], \left[15{,}000 \times \frac{10}{100} \times \frac{9}{12}\right], \left[30{,}000 \times \frac{10}{100} \times \frac{3}{12}\right]$	(2,250)	(1,125)	(750)
Book Value of Machines on 1st January, 2022	27,750	13,875	29,250
(–) Depreciation on Machines A, B, C on 31st December, 2022	(3,000)	(1,500)	(3,000)
Book Value of Machines A, B, C on 1st January, 2023	24,750	12,375	26,250
(–) Machine Sold on 1st January, 2023	—	(4,500)	—
Loss on Sale of Machine	—	7,875	—
(–) Depreciation on 31st December, 2023	(3,000)	—	(3,000)
Book Value of 1st April, 2024	21,750	—	23,250

Solved Question 6 *(When a part of asset is sold)* **Sambit limited purchased on 1st April, 2020, a machinery for ₹ 100,000. Another machinery was purchased on 1st January, 2021 for ₹ 5,000 and on 1st October 2021 for ₹ 10,000. On 1st July, 2022, a machinery whose book value was ₹ 15,000 on 1st April, 2020 was sold for ₹ 8,000. Depreciation had been charged at 10% per annum on straight line method.**

Accounts are closed on 31st March every year. You are required to prepare machinery account upto 31st March, 2023.

Sol. Dr **Machinery Account** Cr

Date	Particulars		Amt (₹)	Date	Particulars		Amt (₹)
2020				2021			
Apr 1	To Bank A/c (A)		1,00,000	Mar 31	By Depreciation A/c		
2021					A	10,000	
Jan 1	To Bank A/c (B)		5,000		B	125	10,125
				Mar 31	By Balance c/d		
					A	90,000	
					B	4,875	94,875
			1,05,000				1,05,000
2021				2022			
Apr 1	To Balance b/d			Mar 31	By Depreciation A/c		
	A	90,000			A	10,000	
	B	4,875	94,875		B	500	
Oct 1	To Bank A/c (C)		10,000		C	500	11,000
				Mar 31	By Balance c/d		
					A	80,000	
					B	4,375	
					C	9,500	93,875
			1,04,875				1,04,875
2022				2022			
Apr 1	To Balance b/d			Jul 1	By Bank A/c		8,000
	A	80,000		Jul 1	By Depreciation A/c		375
	B	4,375		Jul 1	By Loss on Sale of Machinery A/c		3,625
	C	9,500	93,875				
				2023			
				Mar 31	By Depreciation A/c		
					A (WN 2)	8,500	
					B	500	
					C	1,000	10,000

Date	Particulars	Amt (₹)	Date	Particulars		Amt (₹)
			Mar 31	By Balance c/d		
				A	59,500	
				B	3,875	
				C	8,500	71,875
		93,875				93,875

Working Notes

1. **Calculation of Loss on Sale of Machinery Purchased on 1st April, 2020**

	Amt (₹)
Book value of machinery on 1st April, 2020	15,000
(−) Depreciation @ 10% : 31st March, 2021 & 31st March, 2022	(3,000)
Book value on 31st March, 2022	12,000
(−) Depreciation (@ 10% for 3 months) till 1st July, 2022	(375)
(−) Sale	(8,000)
Loss on Sale of Machinery	3,625

2. **Calculation of Balance of Machinery Purchased on 1st April, 2020**

Book value of machinery (1,00,000 − 15,000)	85,000
(−) Depreciation @ 10% (8,500 × 3)	(25,500)
	59,500

Solved Question 7 *(When assets are purchased and sold on different dates and depreciation is charged on SLM)*

On 1st April, 2020, Rauneek Bros. purchased a machinery for ₹ 1,00,000. Maintenance on this machine during the year was ₹ 15,000. An additional machinery was puchased on 1st July, 2021, for ₹ 50,000. On 1st April, 2022, machinery purchased on 1st April, 2020 became obsolete and it was sold for ₹ 55,000. A new machine was purchased for ₹ 75,000 on 1st October, 2022. Depreciation is charged @ 10% p.a. on Straight Line Method (SLM). Prepare the machinery account for four years when books are closed 31st March, 2023.

Sol. Dr **Machinery Account** Cr

Date	Particulars		Amt (₹)	Date	Particulars		Amt (₹)
2020				2021			
Apr 1	To Bank A/c (Machine A)		1,00,000	Mar 31	By Depreciation A/c		10,000
				Mar 31	By Balance c/d		90,000
			1,00,000				1,00,000
2021				2022			
Apr 1	To Balance b/d (Machine A)		90,000	Mar 31	By Depreciation A/c		
Jul 1	To Bank A/c (Machine B)		50,000		Machine A	10,000	
					Machine B	3,750	13,750
					$\left(50,000 \times \frac{10}{100} \times \frac{9}{12}\right)$		
				Mar 31	By Balance c/d		
					Machine A	80,000	
					Machine B	46,250	1,26,250
			1,40,000				1,40,000
2022				2022			
Apr 1	To Balance b/d			Apr 1	By Bank A/c		55,000
	Machine A	80,000		Apr 1	By Loss on Sale of Machinery A/c (WN1)		25,000
	Machine B	46,250	1,26,250				
				2023			
				Mar 31	By Depreciation A/c		
Oct 1	To Bank A/c (Machine C)		75,000		Machine B	5,000	
					Machine C	3,750	8,750
					$\left(75,000 \times \frac{10}{100} \times \frac{6}{12}\right)$		

Date	Particulars		Amt (₹)	Date	Particulars		Amt (₹)
				Mar 31	By Balance c/d		
					Machine B	41,250	
					Machine C	71,250	1,12,500
			2,01,250				2,01,250
2023				2024			
Apr 1	To Balance b/d			Mar 31	By Depreciation A/c		
	Machine B	41,250			Machine B	5,000	
	Machine C	71,250	1,12,500		Machine C	7,500	12,500
				Mar 31	By Balance c/d		
					Machine B	36,250	
					Machine C	63,750	1,00,000
			1,12,500				1,12,500

Working Notes

1. Book Value of Machine A Sold on 1st April, 2022 (1,00,000 – 10,000 – 10,000) 80,000

Book Value of Machine A Sold on 1st April, 2022 (1,00,000 – 10,000 – 10,000)	80,000
(–) Depreciation	—
(–) Sales Proceeds	(55,000)
Loss on Sale of Machine A	25,000

2. Maintence of machinery is a revenue expenditure and thus, will not effect machinery account.

Written Down Value Method

Solved Question 8 *(When asset is purchased)* **A plant was purchased by Parana Ltd. on 1st October, 2020 at a cost of ₹ 16,000 and spent on installation ₹ 4,000. The scrap value of the plant at the end of its estimated life of 2.5 years is ₹ 15,390. The depreciation is charged @ 10% p.a. on written down value method. The books are closed on 31st March every year. Prepare necessary ledger accounts.**

Sol.

Dr **Plant Account** Cr

Date	Particulars	Amt (₹)	Date	Particulars	Amt (₹)
2020			2021		
Apr 1	To Bank A/c (16,000 + 4,000)	20,000	Mar 31	By Depreciation A/c $\left(20{,}000 \times \frac{10}{100} \times \frac{6}{12}\right)$	1,000
			Mar 31	By Balance c/d	19,000
		20,000			20,000
2021			2022		
Apr 1	To Balance b/d	19,000	Mar 31	By Depreciation A/c (19,000 × 10%)	1,900
			Mar 31	By Balance c/d	17,100
		19,000			19,000
2022			2023		
Apr 1	To Balance b/d	17,100	Mar 31	By Depreciation (17,100 × 10%)	1,710
			Mar 31	By Balance c/d	15,390
		17,100			17,100

Dr **Depreciation Account** Cr

Date	Particulars	Amt (₹)	Date	Particulars	Amt (₹)
2021			2021		
Mar 31	To Plant A/c	1,000	Mar 31	By Statement of Profit and Loss	1,000
2022					
Mar 31	To Plant A/c	1,900	Mar 31	By Statement of Profit and Loss	1,900
2023			2023		
Mar 31	To Plant A/c	1,710	Mar 31	By Statement of Profit and Loss	1,710

Solved Question 9 **(*IGST*) On 1st April, 2021, Sagar Ltd. purchased a machinery for ₹ 1,60,000. Another machinery was purchased on 1st July, 2022, for ₹ 96,000. Machinery purchased on 1st April, 2021, was sold for ₹ 84,000 on 1st December, 2023. On the same date, another machinery was purchased for ₹ 1,50,000. Depreciation is provided @ 10% on written down value method. The company closes its accounts on 31st March every year. IGST is charged @ 12% on purchase and sale of machinery. You are required to prepare the machinery account.**

Sol. Dr **Machinery Account** Cr

Date	Particulars		Amt (₹)	Date	Particulars		Amt (₹)
2021				2022			
Apr 1	To Bank A/c		1,60,000	Mar 31	By Depreciation A/c		16,000
				Mar 31	By Balance c/d (A)		1,44,000
			1,60,000				1,60,000
2022				2023			
Apr 1	To Balance b/d		1,44,000	Mar 31	By Depreciation A/c		
Jul 1	To Bank A/c		96,000		A	14,400	
					B	7,200	21,600
				Mar 31	By Balance c/d		
					A	1,29,600	
					B	88,800	2,18,400
			2,40,000				2,40,000
2023				2023			
Apr 1	To Balance b/d			Dec 1	By Bank A/c		84,000
	A	1,29,600		Dec 1	By Depreciation A/c		8,640
	B	88,800	2,18,400	Dec 1	By Loss on Sale of Machinery A/c		36,960
Dec 1	To Bank A/c		1,50,000	2024			
				Mar 31	By Depreciation A/c		
					B	8,880	
					C	5,000	13,880
				Mar 31	By Balance c/d		
					B	79,920	
					C	1,45,000	2,24,920
			3,68,400				3,68,400

Working Notes

1.

Particulars	A (₹)	B (₹)	C (₹)
Cost of Machine Purchased on 1st April, 2021	1,60,000	—	—
(−) Depreciation (31st March, 2022)	(16,000)	—	—
Book Value on 1st April, 2022	1,44,000	—	—
Machinery Purchased on 1st July, 2022	—	96,000	—
(−) Depreciation (31st March, 2023)	(14,400)	(7,200)	—
Book value on 1st April, 2023	1,29,600	88,800	—
(−) Depreciation on Machinery A for 8 months on 1st December, 2023	(8,640)	—	—
	1,20,960	—	—
(−) Sales Price	(84,000)	—	—
Loss on Sale of Machinery on 1st December	36,960	—	—
Machinery Purchased on 1st December, 2023	—	—	1,50,000
(−) Depreciation (31st March, 2024)	—	(8,880)	(5,000)
Book Value of Machines on 31st March, 2024	—	79,920	1,45,000

2. Machinery account is debited by ₹ 1,60,000 and credited by ₹ 84,000 as IGST paid on purchase of machinery is not the cost of machinery as it is to be set-off against GST collected on sale of goods and assets.

Solved Question 10 ***(When another asset is purchased on different date)*** **A truck was purchased by Saras Ltd. on 1st April, 2020 for ₹ 30,00,000. Another truck was purchased on 1st October, 2020 for ₹ 18,00,000. The rate of depreciation is charged @ 10% p.a. on the written down value. Prepare truck account for three years, if the accounts are closed on 31st March every year.**

Sol. Dr **Truck Account** Cr

Date	Particulars		Amt (₹)	Date	Particulars		Amt (₹)
2020				2021			
Apr 1	To Bank A/c (Truck A)		30,00,000	Mar 31	By Depreciation A/c		
Oct 1	To Bank A/c (Truck B)		18,00,000		Truck A	3,00,000	
					Truck B	90,000	3,90,000
				Mar 31	By Balance c/d		
					Truck A	27,00,000	
					Truck B	17,10,000	44,10,000
			48,00,000				48,00,000
2021				2022			
Apr 1	To Balance b/d			Mar 31	By Depreciation A/c		
	Truck A	27,00,000			Truck A	2,70,000	
	Truck B	17,10,000	44,10,000		Truck B	1,71,000	4,41,000
				Mar 31	By Balance c/d		
					Truck A	24,30,000	
					Truck B	15,39,000	39,69,000
			44,10,000				44,10,000
2022				2023			
Apr 1	To Balance b/d			Mar 31	By Depreciation A/c		
	Truck A	24,30,000			Truck A	2,43,000	
	Truck B	15,39,000	39,69,000		Truck B	1,53,900	3,96,900
				Mar 31	By Balance c/d		
					Truck A	21,87,000	
					Truck B	13,85,100	35,72,100
			39,69,000				39,69,000

Working Note

Particulars	Truck A (₹)	Truck B (₹)
Cost of Truck on 1st April, 2020	30,00,000	—
Cost of Truck on 1st October, 2020	—	18,00,000
(–) Depreciation on 31st March, 2021 @ 10%	(3,00,000)	(90,000)
	27,00,000	17,10,000
(–) Depreciation on 31st March, 2022 @ 10%	(2,70,000)	(1,71,000)
	24,30,000	15,39,000
(–) Depreciation on 31st March, 2023	(2,43,000)	(1,53,900)
Book Value on 31st March, 2023	21,87,000	13,85,100

Solved Question 11 **Anjana Ltd. bought a plant for ₹ 3,00,000 on 1st April, 2019. The plant included a boiler worth ₹ 30,000. The boiler got damaged on 1st April, 2023 and sold for ₹ 6,000. Depreciation is charged on written down value method @ 10% p.a. The books are closed on 31st March. You are required to prepare plant account.**

Sol. Dr **Plant Account** Cr

Date	Particulars	Amt (₹)	Date	Particulars		Amt (₹)
2019			2020			
Apr 1	To Bank A/c (A)	2,70,000	Mar 31	By Depreciation A/c		
Apr 1	To Bank A/c (B) (Boiler)	30,000		A	27,000	
				B	3,000	30,000
			Mar 31	By Balance c/d		
				A	2,43,000	
				B	27,000	2,70,000
		3,00,000				3,00,000

Date	Particulars		Amt (₹)	Date	Particulars		Amt (₹)
2020				2021			
Apr 1	To Balance b/d			Mar 31	By Depreciation A/c		
	A	2,43,000			A	24,300	
	B	27,000	2,70,000		B	2,700	27,000
				Mar. 31	By Balance c/d		
					A	2,18,700	
					B	24,300	2,43,000
			2,70,000				2,70,000
2021				2022			
Apr 1	To Balance b/d			Mar 31	By Depreciation A/c		
	A	2,18,700			A	21,870	
	B	24,300	2,43,000		B	2,430	24,300
				Mar 31	By Balance c/d		
					A	1,96,830	
					B	21,870	2,18,700
			2,43,000				2,43,000
2022				2023			
Apr 1	To Balance b/d			Mar 31	By Depreciation A/c		
	A	1,96,830			A	19,683	
	B	21,870	2,18,700		B	2,187	21,870
				Mar 31	By Balance c/d		
					A	1,77,147	
					B	19,683	1,96,830
			2,18,700				2,18,700
2023				2023			
Apr 1	To Balance b/d			Apr 1	By Bank A/c		6,000
	A	1,77,147		Apr 1	By Loss on Sale of Plant A/c (WN)		13,683
	B	19,683	1,96,830	2024			
				Mar 31	By Depreciation A/c (WN)		17,715
				Mar 31	By Balance c/d		1,59,432
			1,96,830				1,96,830

Working Note

A part of plant (boiler) worth ₹ 30,000 was sold, so we will spilt it likewise

Particulars	A (₹)	B (₹)
Cost of Plant bought on 1st April, 2019	2,70,000	30,000
(–) Depreciation on 31st March, 2020	(27,000)	(3,000)
Book Value on 1st April, 2020	2,43,000	27,000
(–) Depreciation on 31st March, 2021	(24,300)	(2,700)
Book Value on 1st April, 2021	2,18,700	24,300
(–) Depreciation on 31st March, 2022	(21,870)	(2,430)
Book Value on 1st April, 2022	(1,96,830)	21,870
(–) Depreciation on 31 March, 2023	(19,683)	(2,187)
Book Value on 1st April, 2023	1,77,147	19,683
(–) Sales on 1st April, 2023	—	(6,000)
Loss on Sale	1,77,147	13,683
(–) Depreciation on 31st March, 2024	(17,715)	—
Book value on 31st March, 2024	1,59,432	—

Solved Question 12 ***(When a part of asset is sold on later date)*** **On 1st January, 2020, Satya Limited purchased a machinery for ₹ 12,00,000. Another machinery was purchased on 1st July, 2021 for ₹ 2,00,000. On 31st March, 2022, machinery costing ₹ 50,000 purchased 1st January, 2020, become obsolete and was sold as scrap for ₹ 5,000. On same date, another machine was purchased for ₹ 80,000. Books are closed on 31st December every year and depreciation is charged @ 15% p.a. on diminishing balance method.**

Prepare machinery account for 3 years.

Sol.

Dr **Machinery Account** Cr

Date	Particulars		Amt (₹)	Date	Particulars		Amt (₹)
2020				2020			
Jan 1	To Bank A/c (Machine A)		12,00,000	Dec 31	By Depreciation A/c		
					Machine A	1,72,500	
					Machine B	7,500	1,80,000
				Mar 31	By Balance c/d		10,20,000
			12,00,000				12,00,000
2021				2021			
Jan 1	To Balance b/d		10,20,000	Dec 31	By Depreciation A/c		
Jul 1	To Bank A/c		2,00,000		Machine A	1,46,625	
					Machine B	6,375	
					Machine C	15,000	1,68,000
				Dec 31	By Balance c/d		
					Machine A	8,30,875	
					Machine B	36,125	
					Machine C	1,85,000	10,52,000
			12,20,000				12,20,000
2022				2022			
Jan 1	To Balance b/d			Mar 31	By Bank A/c (Sales)		5,000
	Machine A	8,30,875		Mar 31	By Depreciation (Machine B)		1,355
	Machine B	36,125		Mar 31	By Loss on Sale of Machine A/c		29,770
	Machine C	1,85,000	10,52,000	Dec 31	By Depreciation A/c		
Mar 31	To Bank A/c		80,000		Machine A	1,24,631	
					Machine C	27,750	
					Machine D	9,000	1,61,381
				Dec 31	By Balance c/d		
					Machine A	7,06,244	
					Machine C	1,57,250	
					Machine D	71,000	9,34,494
			11,32,000				11,32,000

Working Note

A part of machinery is being sold so we will split it likewise into A (₹ 11,50,000) and B (₹ 50,000).

Particulars	A (₹)	B (₹)	C (₹)	D (₹)
Cost of Machine purchased on 1st January, 2020	11,50,000	50,000	—	—
(–) Depreciation (31st December, 2020)	(1,72,500)	(7,500)	—	—
Book Value on (1st January, 2021)	9,77,500	42,500	—	—
Machinery Purchased on (1st July, 2021)	—	—	2,00,000	—
(–) Depreciation on 31st December, 2021	(1,46,625)	(6,375)	(15,000)	—
Book Value on 1st January, 2022	8,30,875	36,125	1,85,000	—
(–) Machinery Sold on 31st March, 2022	—	(5,000)	—	—

Particulars	A (₹)	B (₹)	C (₹)	D (₹)
(–) Depreciation till 31st March, 2022	—	(1,355)	—	—
New Machinery Purchase on 31st March, 2022	—	—	—	80,000
Loss on Sale of Machinery	—	29,770	—	—
(–) Depreciation on 31st December, 2022	(1,24,631)	—	(27,750)	(9,000)
	7,06,244	—	1,57,250	71,000

Solved Question 13 ***(When a part of machinery gets damaged)*** **On 1st January, 2019, A Ltd. company purchased machinery for ₹ 20,00,000. Depreciation is provided @ 15% per annum on diminishing balance method. On 1st March, 2021, 1/4 of machinery was damaged by fire and ₹ 40,000 were received from the insurance company in full settlement. On 1st September, 2021 another machinery was purchased by the company for ₹ 15,00,000.**

Write up the machinery account from 2021 to 2022. Books are closed on 31st December, every year. **NCERT Modified**

Sol. Dr **Machinery Account** Cr

Date	Particulars		JF	Amt (₹)	Date	Particulars		JF	Amt (₹)
2021					2021				
Jan 1	To Balance b/d (WN1)				Mar 1	By Bank A/c (Insurance)			40,000
	A	10,83,750			Mar 1	By Depreciation A/c (B) (WN 2)			9,031
	B	3,61,250		14,45,000	Mar 1	By Profit and Loss A/c			3,12,219
Sep 1	To Bank A/c (C)			15,00,000	Dec 31	By Depreciation A/c			
						A	1,62,562		
						C	75,000		2,37,562
					Dec 31	By Balance c/d			
						A	9,21,188		
						C	14,25,000		23,46,188
				29,45,000					29,45,000
2022					2022				
Jan 1	To Balance b/d				Dec 31	By Depreciation A/c			
	A	9,21,188				A	1,38,178		
	C	14,25,000		23,46,188		C	2,13,750		3,51,928
					Dec 31	By Balance c/d			
						A	7,83,010		
						C	12,11,250		19,94,260
				23,46,188					23,46,188

Working Notes

1. Since a part $\left(\text{i.e. } \frac{1}{4}\text{th}\right)$ of the machinery is damaged we will split the cost of machinery as A ₹ (15,00,000) and B ₹ (5,00,000)

2.

Particulars	A (₹)	B (₹)
Value of Machinery	15,00,000	5,00,000
(–) Depreciation for 2019	(2,25,000)	(75,000)
Written Down Value	12,75,000	4,25,000
(–) Depreciation for 2020	(1,91,250)	(63,750)
Written Down Value	10,83,750	3,61,250

3. Depreciation on Part B in 2021 $= 3,61,250 \times \frac{15}{100} \times \frac{2}{12} =$ ₹ 9,031

Provision for Depreciation Account

Solved Question 14 **On 1st April, 2020, a machinery was purchased by Nanda Ltd. for ₹ 10,00,000. On 1st October, 2023, the plant became obsolete and was sold for ₹ 4,00,000. The company provides depreciation @ 10% by straight line method and the books are closed on 31st March every year. Prepare necassary accounts if the provision for depreciation account is maintained.**

Sol.

Dr **Machinery Account** Cr

Date	Particulars	Amt (₹)	Date	Particulars	Amt (₹)
2020			2021		
Apr 1	To Bank A/c	10,00,000	Mar 31	By Balance c/d	10,00,000
2021			2022		
Apr 1	To Balance b/d	10,00,000	Mar 31	By Balance c/d	10,00,000
2022			2023		
Apr 1	To Balance b/d	10,00,000	Mar 31	By Balance c/d	10,00,000
2023			2023		
Apr 1	To Balance b/d	10,00,000	Oct 1	By Bank A/c	4,00,000
			Oct 1	By Provision for Depreciation A/c	3,50,000
			Oct 1	By Loss on Sale of Plant A/c	2,50,000
		10,00,000			10,00,000

Dr **Provision for Depreciation Account** Cr

Date	Particulars	Amt (₹)	Date	Particulars	Amt (₹)
2021			2021		
Mar 31	To Balance c/d	1,00,000	Mar 31	By Depreciation A/c	1,00,000
2022			2021		
Mar 31	To Balance c/d	2,00,000	Apr 1	By Balance b/d	1,00,000
			2022		
			Mar 31	By Depreciation A/c	1,00,000
		2,00,000			2,00,000
2023			2022		
Mar 31	To Balance c/d	3,00,000	Apr 1	By Balance b/d	2,00,000
			2023		
			Mar 31	By Depreciation A/c	1,00,000
		3,00,000			3,00,000
2023			2023		
Oct 1	To Plant A/c	3,50,000	Apr 1	By Balance b/d	3,00,000
			Oct 1	By Depreciation A/c	50,000
		3,50,000			3,50,000

Solved Question 15 **Mahima Ltd. purchased a plant on 1st April, 2021, for ₹ 60,00,000. On 1st October, 2023, a part of costing ₹ 4,00,000 was sold for ₹ 2,25,000. Another plant was purchased on the same date for ₹ 7,90,000. Depreciation is charged @ 10% on diminishing balance method.**

Show the necessary ledger accounts when

(i) Provision for depreciation accounts is not maintained, and (ii) Provision for depreciation account is maintained.

Sol. (i) When provision for depreciation account is not maintained.

Dr **Plant Account** Cr

Date	Particulars	Amt (₹)	Date	Particulars	Amt (₹)
2021			2022		
Apr 1	To Bank A/c	60,00,000	Mar 31	By Depreciation A/c	6,00,000
			Mar 31	By Balance c/d	54,00,000
		60,00,000			60,00,000

Date	Particulars	Amt (₹)	Date	Particulars	Amt (₹)
2022			2023		
Apr 1	To Balance b/d	54,00,000	Mar 31	By Depreciation A/c	5,40,000
			Mar 31	By Balanced c/d	48,60,000
		54,00,000			54,00,000
2023			2023		
Apr 1	To Balance b/d	48,60,000	Oct 1	By Bank A/c (Sale)	2,25,000
Oct 1	To Bank A/c	7,90,000	Oct 1	By Loss on Sale of Plant A/c	82,800
			Oct 1	By Depreciation (On Plant Sold)	16,200
			Mar 31	By Depreciation A/c	4,93,100
			Mar 31	By Balance c/d	48,32,900
		56,50,000			56,50,000

(ii) When provision for depreciation account is maintained.

Dr **Plant Account** (Original cost) Cr

Date	Particulars	Amt (₹)	Date	Particulars	Amt (₹)
2021			2022		
Apr 1	To Bank A/c	60,00,000	Mar 31	By Balance c/d	60,00,000
		60,00,000			60,00,000
2022			2023		
Apr 1	To Balance b/d	60,00,000	Mar 31	By Balance c/d	60,00,000
		60,00,000			60,00,000
2023			2023		
Apr 1	To Balance b/d	60,00,000	Oct 1	By Bank A/c (Sale)	2,25,000
Oct 1	To Bank A/c (C)	7,90,000	Oct 1	By Provision for Depreciation A/c	92,200
			Oct 1	By Loss on Sale of Plant A/c	82,800
			2024		
			Mar 31	By Balance c/d	63,90,000
		67,90,000			67,90,000

Dr **Provision for Depreciation Account** Cr

Date	Particulars	Amt (₹)	Date	Particulars	Amt (₹)
2022			2022		
Mar 31	To Balance c/d	6,00,000	Mar 31	By Depreciation A/c	6,00,000
2023			2023		
Mar 31	To Balance c/d	11,40,000	Apr 1	By Balance b/d	6,00,000
			2023		
			Mar 31	By Depreciation A/c	5,40,000
		11,40,000			11,40,000
2023			2023		
Oct 1	To Machinery A/c	92,200	Apr 1	By Balance b/d	11,40,000
2024			Oct 1	By Depreciation A/c	16,200
Mar 31	To Balance c/d	15,57,100	2024		
			Oct 31	By Depreciation A/c	4,93,100
		16,49,300			16,49,300

Working Notes

1. Since a part of plant is sold we will split the cost likewise A (₹ 56,00,000) and B (₹ 4,00,000).

Particulars	A (₹)	B (₹)	C (₹)
Cost of Plant on 1st April, 2021	56,00,000	4,00,000	—
(–) Depreciation on 31st March, 2022	(5,60,000)	(40,000)	—
Book Value on 1st April, 2022	50,40,000	3,60,000	—
(–) Depreciation on 31st March, 2023	(5,04,000)	(36,000)	—

Particulars	A (₹)	B (₹)	C (₹)
Book Value on 1st April 2023	45,36,000	3,24,000	—
(–) Depreciation on Plant Sold on 1st October, 2023	—	(16,200)	—
	—	3,07,800	—
(–) Sales Proceeds	—	(2,25,000)	—
Loss on Sale of Plant	—	82,800	—
New Plant Purchased on 1st October, 2023	—	—	(7,90,000)
(–) Depreciation on 31st March, 2024	(4,53,600)	—	(39,500)
	40,82,400	—	7,50,500

2. Accumulated depreciation on asset sold = 40,000 + 36,000 + 16,200 = ₹ 92,200

Asset Disposal Account

Solved Question 16 ***(When assets are purchased and sold on different dates and depreciation is charged on written down value basis, when provision for depreciation account is maintained)*** **On 1st April, 2020, X Ltd purchased a machinery for ₹ 12,00,000. On 1st October, 2022 a part of the machinery purchased on 1st April, 2020 for ₹ 80,000 was sold for ₹ 45,000 and a new machinery at the cost of ₹ 1,58,000 was purchased and installed on the same date. The company has adopted the method of providing 10% per annum depreciation on the diminishing balance of the machinery.**

Show the necessary ledger accounts assuming that provision for depreciation account and machinery disposal account is maintained. The accounting year ends on 31st March.

Sol. Dr **Machinery Account** (At Original Cost) Cr

Date	Particulars		JF	Amt (₹)	Date	Particulars		JF	Amt (₹)
2020					2021				
Apr 1	To Bank A/c				Mar 31	By Balance c/d			
	A	11,20,000				A	11,20,000		
	B	80,000		12,00,000		B	80,000		12,00,000
				12,00,000					12,00,000
2021					2022				
Apr1	To Balance b/d				Mar 31	By Balance c/d			
	A	11,20,000				A	11,20,000		
	B	80,000		12,00,000		B	80,000		12,00,000
				12,00,000					12,00,000
2022					2022				
Apr 1	To Balance b/d				Oct 1	By Machinery Disposal A/c			80,000
	A	11,20,000							
	B	80,000		12,00,000	2023				
Oct 1	To Bank A/c (C)			1,58,000	Mar 31	By Balance c/d			
						A	11,20,000		
						C	1,58,000		12,78,000
				13,58,000					13,58,000

Dr **Provision for Depreciation Account** Cr

Date	Particulars		JF	Amt (₹)	Date	Particulars		JF	Amt (₹)
2021					2021				
Mar 31	To Balance c/d				Mar 31	By Depreciation A/c			
	A	1,12,000				A	1,12,000		
	B	8,000		1,20,000		B	8,000		1,20,000
				1,20,000					1,20,000
2022					2021				
Mar 31	To Balance c/d				Apr 1	By Balance c/d			
	A	2,12,800				A	1,12,000		
	B	15,200		2,28,000		B	8,000		1,20,000

Date	Particulars		JF	Amt (₹)	Date	Particulars		JF	Amt (₹)
					2022				
					Mar 31	By Depreciation A/c			
						A	1,00,800		
						B	7,200		1,08,000
				2,28,000					2,28,000
2022					2022				
Oct 1	To Machinery Disposal A/c (B) (15,200+3,240)			18,440	Apr 1	By Balance b/d			
						A	2,12,800		
						B	15,200		2,28,000
2023					Oct 1	By Depreciation A/c (B) (WN)			3,240
Mar 31	To Balance c/d				2023				
	A	3,03,520			Mar 31	By Depreciation A/c			
	C	7,900		3,11,420		A	90,720		
						C	7,900		98,620
				3,29,860					3,29,860

Dr **Machinery Disposal Account** Cr

Date	Particulars	JF	Amt (₹)	Date	Particulars	JF	Amt (₹)
2022				2022			
Oct 1	To Machinery A/c		80,000	Oct 1	By Provision for Depreciation A/c		18,440
					By Bank A/c		45,000
					By Statement of Profit and Loss (Loss on sale) (WN 1)		16,560
			80,000				80,000

Working Note

Calculation of Profit/Loss on Sale of Machinery	**Amt (₹)**
Original cost as on 1st April, 2020	80,000
(−) Depreciation @ 10% per annum for 2020-21	(8,000)
Book value as on 1st April, 2021	72,000
(−) Depreciation @ 10% per annum for 2021-22	(7,200)
Book value as on 1st April, 2022	64,800
(−) Depreciation @ 10% per annum upto date of sale (64,800 × 10/100 × 6/12)	(3,240)
Book value as on 1st October, 2022	61,560
(−) Sale proceeds	(45,000)
Loss on sale of machinery	16,560

Solved Question 17 **On 1st April, 2021, Samarth Ltd. purchased a truck for ₹ 3,50,000. On 1st January, 2023, the truck was found unsuitable and was sold for ₹ 2,10,000. Depreciation is charged @ 10% p.a. on straight line basis and accounts are closed on 31st March every year. Shown the truck account, depreciation account and truck disposal account.**

Sol. Dr **Truck Account** Cr

Date	Particulars	Amt (₹)	Date	Particulars	Amt (₹)
2021			2022		
Apr 1	To Bank A/c	3,50,000	Mar 31	By Depreciation A/c	35,000
			Mar 31	By Balance c/d	3,15,000
		3,50,000			3,50,000

Date	Particulars	Amt (₹)	Date	Particulars	Amt (₹)
2021			2023		
Apr 1	To Balance b/d	3,15,000	Jan 1	By Depreciation A/c (WN)	26,250
			Jan 1	By Truck Disposal A/c	2,88,750
		3,15,000			3,15,000

Dr **Depreciation Account** Cr

Date	Particulars	Amt (₹)	Date	Particulars	Amt (₹)
2022			2022		
Mar 31	To Truck A/c	35,000	Mar 31	By Statement of Profit and Loss	35,000
		35,000			35,000
2023			2023		
Jan 1	To Truck A/c	26,250	Jan 1	By Statement of Profit and Loss	26,250
		26,250			26,250

Dr **Truck Disposal Account** Cr

Date	Particulars	Amt (₹)	Date	Particulars	Amt (₹)
2023			2023		
Jan 1	To Truck A/c	2,88,750	Jan 1	By Bank A/c (Sale)	2,10,000
			Jan 1	By Loss on Sale of Machinery A/c	78,750
		2,88,750			2,88,750

Working Notes

Depreciation till the time of sale on 1st January, 2023 will be for 9 months $= 3{,}50{,}000 \times \frac{10}{100} \times \frac{9}{12} =$ ₹ 26,250

Solved Question 18 ***(When a part of machinery is sold and depreciation)*** **Mahavir Ltd. purchased a machinery for ₹ 75,000 on 1st April, 2020. A part of this machine puchased for ₹ 15,000, was sold for ₹ 12,500 on 1st April, 2021. Depreciation was provided @ 10% p.a. on original cost of the machinery. Accounts are closed on 31st March every year. Prepare machine account, machine disposal account and provision for depreciation account for two years.**

Sol. Dr **Machine Account** Cr

Date	Particulars	Amt (₹)	Date	Particulars	Amt (₹)
2020			2021		
Apr 1	To Bank A/c	75,000	Mar 31	By Balance c/d	75,000
		75,000			75,000
2021			2021		
Apr 1	To Balance b/d	75,000	Apr 1	By Machine Disposal A/c	15,000
			Mar 31	By Balance c/d	60,000
		75,000			75,000

Dr **Provision for Depreciation Account** Cr

Date	Particulars	Amt (₹)	Date	Particulars	Amt (₹)
2021			2021		
Mar 31	To Balance c/d	7,500	Mar 31	By Depreciation A/c	7,500
		7,500			7,500
2021			2021		
Apr 1	To Machine Disposal A/c	1,500	Apr 1	By Balance b/d	7,500
2022			2022		
Mar 31	To Balance c/d	12,000	Mar 31	By Depreciation A/c	6,000
		13,500			13,500

Dr **Machine Disposal Account** Cr

Date	Particulars	Amt (₹)	Date	Particulars	Amt (₹)
2021			2021		
Apr 1	To Machine A/c	15,000	Apr 1	By Provision for Depreciation	1,500
			Apr 1	By Bank (Sale)	12,500
			Apr 1	By Loss on Sale of Machine A/c	1,000
		15,000			15,000

Working Notes

	Particulars	Amt (₹)
1.	Cost of Machinery on 1st April, 2020	15,000
	(–) Depreciation provided on 31st March, 2021	(1,500)
	Book Value of Machinery on 1st April, 2021	13,500
	(–) Sales Proceeds	(12,500)
	Loss on Sale of Machine	1,000
2.	Depreciation for Remaining Machine	
	Depreciation on Original Cost	7,500
	(–) Depreciation on Machine Sold	(1,500)
	Depreciation on remaining Machine	6,000

Solved Question 19 ***(When machinery is sold and purchased)*** **Sanjana Ltd. purchased a machinery on 1st April, 2021 for ₹ 5,00,000 and ₹ 1,00,000 were spent on installation. On 1st September, 2021 one-third of machine purchased on 1st April, 2021 was sold for ₹ 30,000. A new machinery costing ₹ 4,00,000 was purchased on the same date. The firm charges depreciation on its machinery @ 15% p.a. on straight line method. Prepare machinery account provision for depreciation account and machinery disposal account. The accounts are closed on 31st March every year.**

Sol. Dr **Machinery Account** Cr

Date	Particulars	Amt (₹)	Date	Particulars	Amt (₹)
2021			2022		
Apr 1	To Bank A/c (5,00,000 + 1,00,000)	6,00,000	Mar 31	By Balance c/d	6,00,000
		6,00,000			6,00,000
2022			2023		
Apr 1	To Balance b/d	6,00,000	Mar 31	By Balance c/d	6,00,000
		6,00,000			6,00,000
2023			2023		
Apr 1	To Balance b/d	6,00,000	Sep 1	By Machinery Disposal A/c	2,00,000
Sep 1	To Bank A/c	4,00,000	2024		
			Mar 31	By Balance c/d	8,00,000
		10,00,000			10,00,000

Dr **Provision for Depreciation Account** Cr

Date	Particulars	Amt (₹)	Date	Particulars	Amt (₹)
2022			2022		
Mar 1	To Balance c/d	90,000	Mar 31	By Depreciation A/c	90,000
		90,000			90,000

Date	Particulars	Amt (₹)	Date	Particulars	Amt (₹)
2023			2022		
Mar 1	To Balance c/d	1,80,000	Apr 1	By Balance b/d	90,000
			2023		
			Mar 31	By Depreciation A/c	90,000
		1,80,000			1,80,000
2023			2023		
Sep 1	To Machinery Disposal A/c	72,500	Apr 1	By Balance b/d	1,80,000
2024			Sep 1	By Depreciation A/c	12,500
Mar 31	To Balance c/d	2,15,000	2024		
			Mar 31	By Depreciation A/c (WN2)	95,000
		2,87,500			2,87,500

Dr **Machinery Disposal Account** Cr

Date	Particulars	Amt (₹)	Date	Particulars	Amt (₹)
2023			2023		
Sep 1	To Machinery A/c	2,00,000	Sep 1	By Provision for Depreciation A/c	72,500
			Sep 1	By Bank A/c	30,000
			Sep 1	By Loss on Sale of Machine A/c	97,500
		2,00,000			2,00,000

Working Notes

Particulars		Amt (₹)
1. Cost of One-third machinery on 1st April, 2021		2,00,000
(–) Depreciation for the Years ending 31st March, 2022	(30,000)	
2023	(30,000)	
[For 5 Months (till 1st September)] $\left(30,000 \times \frac{5}{12}\right)$ 2024	(12,500)	(72,500)
Book Value of Machinery Sold on 1st September, 2023		1,27,500
(–) Sales Proceeds		(30,000)
Loss on Sale		97,500
2. Depreciation on Remaining Machinery 2023-24		
On Previous Machinery $\left(4,00,000 \times \frac{15}{100}\right)$		60,000
On New Machinery $\left(4,00,000 \times \frac{15}{100} \times \frac{7}{12}\right)$		35,000
		95,000

Solved Question 20 ***(When a part of asset is sold and new is purchased)*** **Sahni Bros. purchased a plant on 1st October, 2019 for ₹ 18,00,000. A part of this plant worth ₹ 2,40,000 was sold for ₹ 90,000 on 31st May, 2021. Another plant was purchased on 31st May, 2021 for ₹ 4,50,000. Prepare a plant account, provision for depreciation account and plant disposal account. Depreciation is provided @ 20% per year on the writen down value method and the books are closed on 31st March every year.**

Sol. Dr **Plant Account** Cr

Date	Particulars	Amt (₹)	Date	Particulars	Amt (₹)
2019			2020		
Oct 1	To Bank A/c	18,00,000	Mar 31	By Balance c/d	18,00,000
		18,00,000			18,00,000

Date	Particulars	Amt (₹)	Date	Particulars	Amt (₹)
2020			2021		
Apr 1	To Balance b/d	18,00,000	Mar 31	By Balance c/d	18,00,000
		18,00,000			18,00,000
2021			2021		
Apr 1	To Balance b/d	18,00,000	May 1	By Plant Disposal A/c	2,40,000
Sep 1	To Bank A/c	4,50,000	2022		
			Mar 31	By Balance c/d	20,10,000
		22,50,000			22,50,000

Dr **Provision for Depreciation Account** Cr

Date	Particulars	Amt (₹)	Date	Particulars	Amt (₹)
2020			2020		
Mar 31	To Balance c/d	1,80,000	Mar 31	By Depreciation A/c	1,80,000
		1,80,000			1,80,000
2021			2020		
Mar 31	To Balance c/d	5,04,000	Apr 1	By Balance b/d	1,80,000
			2021		
			Mar 31	By Depreciation A/c	3,24,000
		5,04,000			5,04,000
2021			2021		
May 31	To Plant Disposal A/c	72,960	Apr 1	By Balance b/d	5,04,000
2022			May 31	By Depreciation A/c (WN 1)	5,760
Mar 31	To Balance c/d	7,36,440	2022		
			Mar 31	By Depreciation (WN 3)	2,99,640
		8,09,400			8,09,400

Dr **Plant Disposal Account** Cr

Date	Particulars	Amt (₹)	Date	Particulars	Amt (₹)
2021			2021		
May 31	To Plant A/c	2,40,000	May 31	By Provision for Depreciation A/c	72,960
			May 31	By Bank A/c	90,000
			May 31	By Loss on Sale of Plant A/c	77,040
		2,40,000			2,40,000

Working Notes

1. Depreciation on plant purchased on 1st October, 2019 @ 20%

Particulars	Remaining (₹)	Sold (₹)
	18,00,000	
Original Cost on 1st October, 2019	15,60,000	2,40,000
(–) Depreciation for 2019-20 6 Months	(1,56,000)	(24,000)
	14,04,000	2,16,000
(–) Depreciation for 2020-21	(2,80,800)	(43,200)
	11,23,200	1,72,800
(–) Depreciation for 2021-22	(2,24,640)	(5,760)
	8,98,560	1,67,040

Particulars	Amt (₹)
2. **Book Value of Plant Sold on 31st May, 2021**	1,67,040
(–) Sales Proceeds	(90,000)
Loss on Sale of Plant	77,040
3. **Total Depreciation for 2021-22**	
Depreciation on Remaining Plant	2,24,640
(+) Depreciation on New Plant for 10 Months	75,000
	2,99,640

Solved Question 21 **The following balances appear in the books of Crystal Ltd. on 1st January, 2022.**

Particulars	Amt (₹)
Machinery Account	15,00,000
Provision for Depreciation Account	5,50,000

On 1st April, 2022, a machinery which was purchased on 1st January, 2019 for ₹ 2,00,000 was sold for ₹ 75,000. A new machine was purchased on 1st July, 2022 for ₹ 6,00,000. Depreciation is provided on machinery at 20% per annum on straight line method and books are closed on 31st December every year. Prepare the machinery account and provision for depreciation account for the year ending 31st December, 2022. NCERT Modified

Sol.

Dr **Machinery Account** Cr

Date	Particulars	JF	Amt (₹)	Date	Particulars	JF	Amt (₹)
2022				2022			
Jan 1	To Balance b/d (13,00,000 + 2,00,000)		15,00,000	Apr 1	By Machinery Disposal A/c		2,00,000
Jul 1	To Bank A/c		6,00,000	Dec 1	By Balance c/d		19,00,000
			21,00,000				21,00,000

Dr **Provision for Depreciation Account** Cr

Date	Particulars	JF	Amt (₹)	Date	Particulars	JF	Amt (₹)
2022				2022			
Apr 1	To Machinery Disposal A/c		1,30,000	Jan 1	By Balance b/d		5,50,000
Dec 31	To Balance c/d		7,50,000	Apr 1	By Depreciation A/c		10,000
				Dec 31	By Depreciation A/c (2,60,000 + 60,000)		3,20,000
			8,80,000				8,80,000

Dr **Machinery Disposal Account** Cr

Date	Particulars	JF	Amt (₹)	Date	Particulars	JF	Amt (₹)
2022				2022			
Apr 1	To Machinery A/c		2,00,000	Apr 1	By Provision for Depreciation A/c		1,30,000
Apr 1	To Statement of Profit and Loss (Profit)		5,000	Apr 1	By Bank A/c		75,000
			2,05,000				2,05,000

Working Note

Depreciation charged on machinery costing ₹ 2,00,000 in past 3 years

2019 @ 20% = ₹ 40,000

2020 @ 20% = ₹ 40,000

2021 @ 20% = ₹ 40,000

2022 @ 20% = ₹ 10,000 (for 3 months)

Total depreciation charged = ₹ 1,30,000

Missing Information

Solved Question 22 **Fill up the missing information in the machinery account given below. You are informed that on 30th June, 2021, the company sold the first machines purchased in 2019 for ₹ 19,250. Depreciation is provided at 20% p.a. on the original cost each year. Accounts are closed on 31st March every year.**

Dr **Machinery Account** Cr

Date	Particulars		Amt (₹)	Date	Particulars		Amt (₹)
2019				2020			
Aug 1	To Bank A/c		30,000	Mar 31	By Depreciation A/c		...
				Mar 31	By Balance c/d		...
			...				...
2020				2021			
Apr 1	To Balance b/d		...	Mar 31	By Depreciation A/c		
Oct 1	To Bank A/c		10,000		(i)	...	
					(ii)	...	...
				Mar 31	By Balance c/d		
					(i)	...	
					(ii)	...	...
			...				...
2021				2021			
Apr 1	To Balance b/d			Jun 30	By Bank A/c		...
	(i)	...		Jun 30	By Depreciation A/c		...
	(ii)	...	...	2022			
				Mar 31	By Depreciation A/c		...
Jun 30	To Gain on Sale of Machinery A/c		...	Mar 31	By Balance c/d		...
			...				...

Sol. Dr **Machinery Account** Cr

Date	Particulars		Amt (₹)	Date	Particulars		Amt (₹)
2019				2020			
Aug 1	To Bank A/c		30,000	Mar 31	By Depreciation A/c (for 8 months)		**4,000**
				Mar 31	By Balance c/d		**26,000**
			30,000				**30,000**
2020				2021			
Apr 1	To Balance b/d		**26,000**	Mar 31	By Depreciation A/c		
Oct 1	To Bank A/c		10,000		(i)	**6,000**	
					(ii)	**1,000**	**7,000**
				Mar 31	By Balance c/d		
					(i)	**20,000**	
					(ii)	**9,000**	**29,000**
			36,000				**36,000**
2021				2021			
Apr 1	To Balance b/d			Jun 30	By Bank A/c		**19,250**
	(i)	**20,000**		Jun 30	By Depreciation A/c (for 3 months)		**1,500**
	(ii)	**9,000**	**29,000**	2022			
Jun 30	To Gain on Sale of Machinery A/c (19,250 + 1,500 – 20,000)		**750**	Mar 31	By Depreciation A/c		**2,000**
				Mar 31	By Balance c/d		**7,000**
			29,750				**29,750**

Numerical Questions

Straight Line Method

1. On 1st January, 2020, a trader bought a plant for ₹ 1,00,000. The useful life of this plant was 10 years and scrap value is 10% of cost. On 1st September, 2021 another plant was purchased for ₹ 80,000 with a useful life of 8 years and a scrap value of 10%.

On 1st July, 2022, another plant was bought for ₹ 50,000 with a useful life of 3 years and a scrap value of 10%. Depreciation is charged on straight line method.

Prepare plant account for upto 31st December, 2023.

Ans. Balance of machine account = ₹ 1,50,500

2. On 1st July, 2020 Ashok Ltd. purchased a machine for ₹ 1,08,000 and spent ₹ 12,000 on its installation. At the time of purchase, it was estimated that the effective commerical life of the machine will be 12 years and after 12 years, its salvage value will be ₹ 12,000.

Pass necessary journal entries and prepare machinery account and depreciation account in the books of Ashok Ltd. for first 3 years, if depreciation is written-off according to straight line method. The accounts are closed on 31st December, every year.

NCERT Modified; Competency Based Que

Ans. Balance of machinery account = ₹ 97,500

3. Amit purchased a machine on 1st April, 2020 for 5,00,000. Another machine was purchased for ₹ 3,00,000 on 1st October, 2020. The salvage value of both the machines were ₹ 20,000 and ₹ 10,000 respectively. The company follows original cost method @ 10% per annum.

You are required to prepare machinery account for the 2 years.

Ans. Balance of machine = ₹ 6,55,000

4. A machine was purchased for ₹ 45,000 on 1st April, 2023 and another ₹ 5,000 were spent on its erection. The effective life of the machine is 10 years and the scrap value is ₹ 2,000. Calculate the amount of depreciation according to straight line method.

Prepare machine account for three years. Accounts are closed on 31st March every year.

Ans. Balance of machine account = ₹ 35,600

5. Surbhi Ltd. on 1st July, 2021, purchased a plant for ₹ 15,00,000 plus IGST @ 12%. On 1st October, 2023, the plant become obsolete and was sold for ₹ 4,00,000 plus IGST @ 12%. The company follows the straight line method @ 15%. The books are closed on 31st December every year.

Prepare plant account for three years.

Ans. Loss on sale of plant = ₹ 5,93,750

6. On 1st April, 2022 Mr. Singh purchased three machines for ₹ 40,000 each. Another machine was purchased on 1st October, 2022 for ₹ 40,000.

On 1st July, 2023, one of the machines purchased on 1st April, 2022 was found defective and was sold for ₹ 30,000 and a new machine was purchased on the same date for ₹ 80,000. Depreciation is charged at 10% (straight line method).

Prepare machine account for the year 2022 and 2023. The company closes its books on 31st December.

Competency Based Que

Ans. Balance of machine account = ₹ 1,77,000
Loss on sale of machinery = ₹ 5,000

7. Trackzee Ltd. purchased a plant on 1st April, 2021 costing ₹ 90,000. On 1st October, 2023, one-third of the plant (which included a boiler) become obsolete was sold for ₹ 9,000. Depreciation is charged @ 10% p.a. on fixed installment method.

Show the plant account if the books are closed on 31st December every year.

Ans. Balance of plant account = ₹ 43,500
Loss on sale of plant = ₹ 14,250

8. Shiva Ltd. purchased on 1st April, 2020, 5 trucks of ₹ 60,000 each. 1 truck out of these 5 trucks was sold for ₹ 48,000 on 30th June, 2021. Another truck was sold for ₹ 45,000 on 31st December, 2022. On 30th September, 2023, a new truck was purchased for ₹ 64,000.

Depreciation is provided @ 10% p.a. on straight line method. Company closes its books on 31st March every year.

You are required to prepare truck account for three years.

Competency Based Que

Ans. Balance of truck account = ₹ 1,68,800
Loss on sale of truck sold on 30th June, 2021 = ₹ 4,500
Loss on sale of truck sold on 31st December, 2021 = ₹ 1,500

9. A company purchased the following machines on different dates as stated against each of them

(i) On 1st April, 2021 for ₹ 90,000.
(ii) On 1st October, 2021 for ₹ 60,000.
(iii) On 1st July, 2022 for ₹ 30,000.

The firm charges depreciation at the rate of 10% p.a. on fixed instalment method. On 1st February, 2023 it sold one third of first machine which was bought on 1st April, 2021 for ₹ 9,000 because it became old and obsolete.

Prepare machinery account upto 31st December, 2023.

Competency Based Que

Ans. Balance of machine account = ₹ 1,15,500

Written Down Value Method

10. Nandini purchased a machine for ₹ 4,00,000 on credit from Raghav on 1st July, 2020. She paid installation expenses through cheque of ₹ 50,000.

Rate of depreciation followed is @ 10% per annum and written down value method is being followed.

Prepare machinery and depreciation account if the books are closed on 31st December every year.

Ans. Balance of machinery account = ₹ 3,46,275

11 On 1st April, 2020, a machine was purchased for ₹ 20,00,000. Another new machine was purchased for ₹ 12,00,000 on 1st October, 2020. The company follows written down value method @ 10% p.a.

Prepare necessary accounts for two years. The books are closed on 31st March every year.

Ans. Balance of machinery account = ₹ 26,46,000

12. Param has balance of ₹ 2,70,000 on 1st April, 2021 (purchased on 1st April, 2020). He purchased additional machine of ₹ 1,50,000 on 1st October, 2022. On 1st January, 2023, he sold 1/4th part of machine purchased on 1st October, 2022, for ₹ 30,000.

Prepare machine account for 2021-22 and 2022-23. Depreciation is charged @ 10% p.a. written down value method.

Ans. Balance in machinery account = ₹ 3,19,950
Loss on sale = ₹ 4,688

13. Sandhya Ltd. bought a machine for ₹ 1,00,000 and a boiler for ₹ 20,000 on 1st January, 2020. Depreciation has been charged at 10% on reducing balance method. On 1st July, 2022, the boiler became useless and was sold for ₹ 8,000.

Prepare machine account for five years, ending on 31st December, 2024.

Ans. Balance of machine account = ₹ 59,049
Loss on sale of machinery = ₹ 7,390

14. Saakh Ltd. purchased a second hand plant on 1st January, 2021 for ₹ 72,000 and spent ₹ 8,000 on installation.

The firm purchased another plant on 1st July, 2021 for ₹ 40,000. Plant purchased on 1st January, 2021 was sold on 1st July, 2023, for ₹ 24,000. A new plant was purchased on the same date.

Show the plant account for these two years if the depreciation is provided @ 10% per annum on the written down value method. Competency Based Que

Ans. Balance of plant account = ₹ 1,52,380
Loss on sale of plant = ₹ 37,560

15. Abhaas Ltd. purchased a plant for ₹ 10,00,000 which includes a boiler worth ₹ 1,00,000. The company follows diminishing value method @ 10%. In the beginning of the 5th year, the boiler become obsolete and was sold for ₹ 20,000.

Show the plant account for the 5 years.

Ans. Balance of plant account at the end of 5th year = ₹ 5,31,440
Loss on sale of boiler = ₹ 45,610

16. On 1st April, 2020, a machine was purchased for ₹ 24,000; another machine was purchased for ₹ 16,000 on 1st September, 2021.

On 28th February, 2022, one machine costing ₹ 6,000 purchased on 1st April, 2020 was sold for ₹ 2,800. Depreciation rate is 10% on diminishing balance method.

Prepare machine account for three years ending 31st March, 2024. Competency Based Que

Ans. Balance of machine account = ₹ 26,682
Loss on sale of machinery = ₹ 1,614

17. On 1st January, 2019, A Ltd. company purchased machinery for ₹ 20,00,000. Depreciation is provided @ 15% per annum on diminishing balance method. On Ist March, 2021, 1/4 of machinery was damaged by fire and ₹ 40,000 were received from the insurance company in full settlement. On 1st September, 2021, another machinery was purchased by the company for ₹ 15,00,000.

Write up the machinery account from 2021 to 2022. Books are closed on 31st December, every year.

NCERT; Competency Based Que

18. ABC Ltd. purchased a plant on 1st April, 2017 for ₹ 2,40,000. It bought another plant on 1st July, 2018 for ₹ 1,60,000.

On 1st January, 2018, plant bought on 1st April, 2017 was sold for ₹ 1,60,000 and a fresh plant was purchased on the same date. Payment of this plant will be made as under

1st January, 2020 for ₹ 40,000
1st January, 2021 for ₹ 48,000
1st January, 2022 for ₹ 44,000

Payment made in 2021 and 2022 include interest of ₹ 8,000 and ₹ 4,000 respectively. Depreciation is charged at 10% p.a. on the diminishing balance method.

Show the plant account for three years ended 31st March, 2018 to 31st March, 2020. Competency Based Que

Ans. Balance of plant account = ₹ 2,50,200

Provision for Depreciation

19. Nand Goel bought a machine for ₹ 1,80,000 on 31st May, 2022. He paid installation charges of ₹ 60,000.

Another machine was bought for 80,000 on 30th June, 2023 and ₹ 20,000 was paid as freight. Depreciation is charged at 10% straight line method.

Prepare machine account and depreciation provision account upto 31st December, 2024.

Ans. Balance of Plant account = ₹ 3,40,000
Provision for depreciation = ₹ 77,000

20. A trader bought a machine on 1st January, 2022 for ₹ 36,000 and spent ₹ 34,000 on its erection.

He bought another machine for ₹ 20,000 on 30th September, 2023. Depreciation is charged at 20% on diminishing balance method.

Prepare machine account and depreciation provision account for three years ending 31st December, 2024 .

Ans. Balance of plant account = ₹ 60,000
Provision for depreciation = ₹ 24,320

21. Narendra Ltd. purchased 5 trucks at the cost of ₹ 4,00,000 each on 1st April, 2022. The company writes-off depreciation @ 20% p.a. on original cost and closes its books on 31st December every year.

On 1st October, 2024, one of the trucks is involved in an accident and is completely destroyed. Insurance company has agreed to pay ₹ 1,40,000 in full settlement of the claim. On the same date, the company purchased a second hand truck for ₹ 2, 00,000 and spent ₹ 40,000 on its overhauling.

Prepare truck account and provision for depreciation account for the three years ended on 31st december, 2024. Also prepare truck disposal account.

Competency Based Que

Ans. Balance of plant account = ₹ 18,40,000
Provision for depreciation = ₹ 8,92,000

22. On 1st April, 2020, a firm purchased a machinery for ₹ 2,00,000. On 1st August, 2023, the machinery became obsolete and was auctioned for ₹ 90,000. The firm provides depreciation on its machinery @ 10% per annum on written down value method. The books are closed on 31st March of every year.

Show the necessary ledger accounts assuming that

(i) **Provision for depreciation account is not maintained**

(ii) **Provision for depreciation account is maintained.**

Competency Based Que

Ans. (i) Loss on sale of machinery account = ₹ 50,940
(ii) Provision for depreciation = ₹ 59,060

Asset Disposal Account

23. On 1st January, 2019, Raj Ltd. purchased a plant for ₹ 2,00,000. Its residual value is estimated to be ₹ 20,000 after around 4 years. This plant was sold for ₹ 25,000 at the end of 4 years.

Prepare the plant account, provision for depreciation account and plant disposal account if company follows SLM.

Ans. Balance of plant account = ₹ 2,00,000
Loss on sale of plant = ₹ 5,000

24. On 1st October, 2019, Saanchi Ltd. purchased a plant for ₹ 13,10,000. The firm purchased another plant for ₹ 4,80,000 and sold-off the plant purchased on 1st October, 2019 for ₹ 10,48,000 on 1st July, 2021. The firm follows straight line method of depreciation @ 10% every year.

Prepare the necessary account along with the disposal account.

Ans. Balance of plant account = ₹ 4,80,000
Loss on sale of plant = ₹ 32,750

25. Aashish Ltd. purchased 5 trucks for ₹ 1,50,000 each on 1st April, 2021. On 1st April, 2022, they sold one truck for ₹ 1,25,000.

Prepare the truck account, provision for depreciation account and truck disposal account if the firm follows straight line method of depreciation @ 10% and the books are closed at the end of 31st March every year.

Ans. Balance of truck account = ₹ 6,00,000
Loss on sale of truck = ₹ 10,000

26. On 1st September, 2020, Kamal bought a plant for ₹ 8,00,000. On 1st July, 2021, another plant was bought for ₹ 6,00,000. The depreciation is written-off at 10% on diminishing balance method and accounts are closed on 31st March, every year. On 1st October, 2022, a part of the second plant costing ₹ 4,00,000 was sold for ₹ 2,10,000 and another plant was bought on the same date for ₹ 2,00,000.

Prepare machine account, machine disposal account and depreciation provision account upto 31st March, 2023.

Competency Based Que

Ans. Balance of plant account = ₹ 12,00,000
Provision for depreciation = ₹ 2,33,000
Loss on sale = ₹ 1,41,500

27. Sabhya Ltd. purchased a machinery for ₹ 18,00,000 on 1st April, 2020. A part of this machinery was sold for ₹ 67,500. On 1st October, 2022, cost of this machine was ₹ 1,20,000 and a new machinery was purchased on the same date for ₹ 2,37,000. The company has adopted the diminishing balance method of calculating depreciation @ 10%.

Show the machinery account, provision for depreciation account and machinery disposal account.

Competency Based Que

Ans. Balance of machinery account = ₹ 19,17,000
Loss on sale = ₹ 24,840

28. In the books of Sahni Ltd. on 1st April, 2022 following balances appear
Machinery account ₹ 5,00,000, provision for depreciation account ₹ 1,16,000.
On 1st October a part of the machinery which was purchased on 1st April, 2019 for ₹ 1,00,000 was sold for ₹ 60,000. Depreciation is charged on machinery @ 20% by written down value method.

Your are required to prepare necessary accounts for the year ended 31st March, 2022.

Ans. Balance of machinery account = ₹ 4,00,000
Gain on sale of machinery = ₹ 2,400

Missing Information

29. Fill up the missing information in the machinery account given below. **Competency Based Que**

You are informed that on 30th June, 2021, the company sold the first machines purchased in 2019 for ₹ 19,250. Depreciation is provided at 20% p.a. on the original cost each year. accounts are closed on 31st March every year.

Dr **Plant Account** Cr

Date	Particulars	Amt (₹)	Date	Particulars	Amt (₹)
2021			2022		
Aug 1	To Bank A/c	60,000	Mar 31	By Depreciation A/c	...
			Mar 31	By Balance c/d	...
		...			...
2022			2023		
Apr 1	To Balance b/d	...	Mar 31	By Depreciation A/c	
Oct 1	To Bank A/c	10,000		A ...	
				B ...	...
			Mar 31	By Balance c/d	
				A ...	
				B ...	....
		...			...

Date	Particulars	Amt (₹)	Date	Particulars	Amt (₹)
2023			2023		
Apr 1	To Balance b/d		Jun 30	By Bank A/c	...
	A ...		Jun 30	By Depreciation A/c	
	B ...	...			...
			2024		
Jun 30	To Gain on Sale of Machine A/c	...	Mar 31	By Depreciation A/c	...
			Mar 31	By Balance c/d	...
		...			...

30. Fill up the missing information in the machinery account given below. **Competency Based Que**

Depreciation is provided at 10% p.a. on the straight line method each year. Accounts are closed on 31st December every year.

This plant was sold on 1st July, 2023 for ₹ 2,40,000.

Dr **Machinery Account** Cr

Date	Particulars	Amt (₹)	Date	Particulars	Amt (₹)
2021			2021		
Jan 1	To Bank A/c	4,00,000	Dec 31	By Depreciation A/c	...
			Dec 31	By Balance c/d	...
		4,00,000			...
2022			2022		
Jan 1	To Balance b/d	...	Dec 31	By Depreciation A/c	...
			Dec 31	By Balance c/d	...
		...			...
2023			2023		
Jan 1	To Balance b/d	...	Jul 31	By Dep. A/c	...
			Jul 31	By Balance c/d	...
			Jul 31	By Profit and Loss A/c (Loss)	...
		...			...

Theoretical Questions

Short Answer Type Questions

1. For which type of assets is the written down value method considered suitable?

Ans. This method is suitable for those assets in relation to which

(i) The amount of repairs and renewals goes on increasing as the asset grows older.

(ii) The possibilities of obsolescence are more.

2. In case of a long-term asset, repair and maintenance expenses are expected to rise in later years than in earlier years.

Which method is suitable for charging depreciation if the management does not want to increase burden on profit and loss account on account of depreciation and repair? NCERT; Competency Based Que

Ans. The company should charge depreciation as per written down value method because under this method depreciation charge declines in later years. Hence, the total of depreciation and repair expense remains similar year after year.

3. State briefly the need for providing depreciation. NCERT

Ans. The need for depreciation arises due to following reasons

(i) **To Ascertain True Net Profit or Net Loss**
Correct profit or loss can be ascertained when all the expenses and losses incurred (for earning revenues) are charged to profit and loss account. Assets are used for earning revenues and their cost is charged in the form of depreciation from profit and loss account.

(ii) **Consideration of Tax**
Depreciation is allowed as an expense in income tax. Hence, it reduces the tax burden on the firm.

(iii) **True and Fair Financial Position**
Balance sheet will not show the correct financial position of the business, if depreciation is not provided on assets as the assests will remain overvalued.

4. What are the causes of depreciation? NCERT

Ans. Various causes of depreciation are as follows

(i) Constant use of asset leads to wear and tear of asset which results in decline in the value of asset.

(ii) Even if the assets are not put to use, their value decreases due to the expiry or passage of time.

(iii) Value of intangible assets like patents, copyrights, trademarks, lease, etc. becomes nil after a pre-determined period. This expiry of legal rights is also referred to as amortisation.

(iv) When old asset becomes outdated/obsolete, then it loses its value.

(v) Decrease/Depletion in the value of natural assets such as mines, oil-wells, etc. due to constant extraction of raw materials from them.

5. What are the effects of depreciation on profit and loss account and balance sheet? NCERT; Competency Based Que

Ans. Depreciation is charged as expenditure in profit and loss account and the depreciation figure is deducted from the value of concerned asset on the assets side of the balance sheet.

In that case on one hand, it reduces the profit of the concern, on the other hand, it reduces the assets side in the balance sheet. Here, it is worth mentioning that depreciation is non-cash expenditure.

6. What are provisions? How are they created? Give accounting treatment in case of provision for doubtful debts. NCERT; Competency Based Que

Ans. The amount set aside for the purpose of providing for any known liability, uncertain loss or expense, the amount of which cannot be ascertained with reasonable accuracy, is referred to as provision.

Provision is a charge against the profits and is created by debiting profit and loss account.

In the balance sheet, the amount of provision may be shown either

(i) on the assets side, by way of deduction from the concerned asset.

(ii) on the liabilities side along with the current liability.

7. Sarojini wants to create a provision for unknown liability, but her accountant refuses to allow it. Is the accountant's decision justified? Explain with features of provision. Competency Based Que

Ans. Accountant's decision is justified because provision can not be created for an unknown liability.

Features of provision are as follows

(i) It is created to meet a known liability.

(ii) Provision is a charge to profit and loss account.

(iii) The liability is known but the amount of such liability cannot be ascertained with reasonable accuracy.

(iv) Creation of provision ensures proper matching of revenue and expenses.

8. Explain the concept of secret reserve. NCERT

Ans. Reserves that are created by overstating liabilities or understanding assets are known as secret reserves. They are not shown in the balance sheet.

It is created by the management to avoid competition by reducing profit. Creation of secret reserve is not allowed by Companies Act which requires full disclosure of all material facts and accounting policies.

9. Distinguish between 'revenue reserve' and 'capital reserve'. NCERT

Ans. Differences between revenue reserve and capital reserve are

Basis	Revenue Reserve	Capital Reserve
Source of Creation	It is created out of revenue profits which arise out of normal operating activities of the business.	It is created primarily out of capital profits which do not arise out of the normal operating activities of the business.
Purpose	It is created for strengthening the financial position of the business.	It is created for the purpose laid down in Companies Act.
Usage	A specific revenue reserve can be utilised only for the earmarked purpose.	It can be utilised for specific purposes as provided in the law in force. e.g. To write-off capital losses or issue of bonus shares.
Dividend	It can be used for dividend.	It cannot be used for dividend.

10. Distinguish between general reserve and specific reserve. NCERT

Ans. The differences between general reserve and specific reserve are

Basis	General Reserve	Specific Reserve
Meaning	The reserves which is not created for a specific purpose is general reserve.	The reserves which are created for a specific purpose are known as specific reserves.
Usage	It can be used for any purpose.	It cannot be used for any purpose other than the specified purpose for which it is created.
Examples	Retained earnings, reserve funds, etc.	Debenture redemption reserve, dividend equalisation reserve, etc.

Long Answer Type Questions

11. Explain the determinants of the amount of depreciation.

Or Explain basic factors affecting the amount of depreciation. NCERT

Ans. (i) **Original** (Historical) **Cost of the Assets**

It includes all the cost incurred on acquisition, installation, freight and transportation, insurance charges, etc. up to the point the asset is ready for use.

In case a second hand asset is purchased, it will include the initial repair cost to put the asset in a workable condition.

(ii) **Estimated Net Residual Value/Scrap Value/Salvage Value**

It is estimated sale value of asset at the end of its useful life.

This residual value is net of expenses for disposal/sale i.e. net residual value is the value arrived at after deducting the expenses necessary for disposal of asset.

e.g. If scrap value of an asset after 10 years is ₹ 10,000 but expenses relating to disposal/sale of asset are ₹ 2,000 then net residual value will be ₹ 8,000.

(iii) **Expected Useful Life**

Useful life of an asset is the estimated economic or commercial life of an asset. Generally, it is expressed in number of years but can also be expressed in other units.

e.g. Number of units of output (in case of mines) or number of working hours.

(iv) **Depreciable Cost**

Depreciable cost of an asset is equal to its cost less net scrap value. It is the depreciable cost which is distributed and charged as depreciation expense over the useful life.

12. Discuss in detail the straight line method and written down value method of depreciation. Distinguish between the two and also give situations where they are useful. NCERT

Ans. (i) **Straight Line Method**

Under this method, a fixed and equal amount in the form of depreciation is charged every year during the life time of the asset.

It is also known as original cost method. As the amount of depreciation remains equal from year to year, it is also called as fixed or equal installment method.

Suitability

This method of depreciation is suitable for assets in which the repair charges are less and the possibility of obsolescence is less and expiration cost depends upon time period involved.

(ii) **Written Down Value Method**

Under this method, depreciation is charged on the book value of the asset rather than original cost. It involves charging a fixed rate on the written down value.

The amount of depreciation goes on reducing, year after year.

As the book value keeps on reducing, it is also known as reducing balance method or diminishing balance method.

Suitability
This method of depreciation is suitable for those assets that have a long life and require more repair with passage of time.

The difference between straight line method and written down value method as given below

Basis	Straight Line Method	Written Down Value Method
Basis of Charging Depreciation	Depreciation is calculated on the original cost.	Depreciation is calculated on the book value.
Annual Depreciation Charge	The amount of depreciation is fixed (constant) for all years.	The amount of depreciation declines year after year.
Recognition by Income Tax Law	It is not recognised by Income Tax Law.	It is recognised by Income Tax Law.
Book Value of the Asset	It becomes zero at the end of its effective life.	It can never be zero.
Effect of Depreciation and Repair on Profit and Loss Account	Unequal effect over the life of the asset, as depreciation remains same over the year but repair cost increase in the later years.	Equal effect over the life of the asset, as depreciation cost is high and repairs are less in the initial years but in the later years the repair cost increase and depreciation cost decreases.

13. Name and explain different type of reserves in details. NCERT

Ans. Reserves are generally classified into

(i) **Revenue Reserves**
The reserves created from revenue profits which arise out of the normal operating activities of the business and are otherwise freely available for distribution as dividend are known as revenue reserves.

Revenue reserves can be classified into

- **General Reserve**
The reserves which are not created for a specific purpose are general reserve.
They strengthen the financial position of the business and are also known as free reserve or contingency reserve.
- **Specific Reserve**
As the name suggest, these are the reserves that are created for some specific purpose and can be utilised only for that purpose.
Examples of specific reserve are given below

(a) **Dividend Equalisation Reserve** This reserve is created to stabilise or maintain dividend rate. In the year of high profit, amount is transferred to dividend equalisation reserve. In the year of low profit, this reserve amount is used to maintain the rate of dividend.

(b) **Workmen Compensation Fund**
It is created to provide for claims of the workers due to accident, etc.

(c) **Investment Fluctuation Fund**
It is created to make for decline in the value of investment due to market fluctuation.

(d) **Debenture Redemption Reserve**
It is created to provide funds for redemption of debentures.

(ii) **Capital Reserve**
The reserves created out of capital profits and not available for distribution as dividend are known as capital reserve.

Capital reserves can be used for writing-off capital losses or issue of bonus shares in case of a company. Examples of capital profits are given below

- Premium on issue of shares or debentures.
- Profit on sale of fixed assets.
- Profit on redemption of debentures.
- Profit on revaluation of fixed assets and liabilities.
- Profits prior to incorporation.
- Profit on re-issue of forfeited shares.
- Capital redemption reserve.
- Profit on forfeiture of shares.

Objective Questions

Multiple Choice Questions (MCQs)

1. Permanent and continuing diminution in the quality, quantity of value of an asset is
(a) obsolescence (b) depreciation
(c) deflation (d) appreciation

2. Which of the following is not considered as a factor affecting depreciation?
(a) Total cost of the assets
(b) Estimated useful life of an asset
(c) Estimates scrap or residual value of an asset
(d) None of the above

3. For a business, depreciation is
(a) liability (b) gain
(c) expense (d) income

4. Which of the following is not the cause of depreciation?
(a) Fall in the market value (b) Wear and tear
(c) Accident (d) Passage of time

5. Which of the following is/are objective(s) of providing depreciation?
(a) To provide funds for replacement
(b) To ascertain the true profit and loss
(c) To ascertain the accurate cost of production
(d) All of the above

6. Discarding the old machinery due to change in technology is referred to as
(a) obsolescence (b) depreciation
(c) depletion (d) appreciation

7. The correct formula for calculating depreciation under original cost method is
(a) (Scrap Value – Cost of Asset)/ Estimated Life of Asset
(b) (Scrap Value × Cost of Asset)/ Estimated Value of Asset
(c) (Cost of Asset – Scrap Value)/ Estimated Life of Asset
(d) Cost of Asset – Scrap Value

8. Under the written down value method, depreciation is computed on
(a) original cost (b) net profit
(c) diminished value (d) cost of assets

9. Which of the following is not the merit of written down value method?
(a) Approved method of depreciation by income tax authorities
(b) The asset can be reduced to zero
(c) Loss due to obsolescence gets reduced
(d) Easy to calculate depreciation under this method

10. Loss on sale of an asset is ...... to ....
(a) debited, profit and loss account
(b) debited, asset account
(c) credited, profit and loss account
(d) debited, depreciation account

11. Which of the following statements is correct about diminishing value method of calculating depreciation?
(a) The rate of depreciation fall year to year
(b) The amount of depreciation fall year to year
(c) The rate of depreciation changes year to year
(d) The amount of depreciation remains same year to year

12. The balance of depreciation account is transferred to ....
(a) manufacturing account (b) trading account
(c) profit and loss account (d) balance sheet

13. The amount of depreciation is ...... to ...... account when the provision for depreciation account is created.
(a) debited, asset (b) credited, asset
(c) debited, provision for depreciation
(d) credited, provision for depreciation

14. Which of the following is not the feature of provision?
(a) An amount set aside out of income or profits
(b) To account for anticipated losses
(c) Charge against profits
(d) None of the above

15. Why a reserve is created in the business?
(a) To ascertain true financial position
(b) To meet the known losses
(c) To meet the unforeseen losses
(d) To ascertain true profit or loss

16. Which of the following is also known as free reserve?
(a) Specific reserve (b) General reserve
(c) Security reserve (d) Capital reserve

17. Workmen compensation reserve is a ...... reserve.
(a) specific (b) general
(c) security (d) capital

18. Which of the following correctly differentiates between general reserve and specific reserves?
Competency Based Que
(a) General reserve is not created for a specific purpose where as specific reserves are created for a specific purpose
(b) General reserve can be used for any purpose where as specific reserves cannot be used for any purpose other than the specified purpose
(c) The example general reserve is retained earnings whereas debenture redemption reserve is an example of specific reserves
(d) All of the above

19. Raghav Ltd. acquired a machine for ₹ 90,000 on 1st October, 2023 and spent ₹ 10,000 for its installation.

The firm writes-off depreciation at the rate of 10% on original cost every year. What is the journal entry for charging depreciation to profit and loss account on 31st March, 2022? **Competency Based Que**

(a) Profit and Loss A/c	Dr	5,000	
To Depreciation A/c			5,000
(b) Profit and Loss A/c	Dr	4,500	
To Depreciation A/c			4,500
(c) Depreciation A/c	Dr	5,000	
To Plant A/c			5,000

(d) None of the above

20. A machine whose book value as on 31st March, 2023 is ₹ 5,83,200 was purchased on 1st April, 2020. Depreciation is charged at 10% on written down value method. What will be the cost of machine?
Competency Based Que
(a) ₹ 2,00,000 (b) ₹ 4,00,000
(c) ₹ 6,00,000 (d) ₹ 8,00,000

21. A machine is purchased for ₹ 1,50,000 and is expected to have a useful life of 10 years. At the end of 10th year, it is expected to have a sale value of ₹ 18,000 but expenses related to its disposal are estimated at ₹ 3,000. Then its depreciable cost will be **Competency Based Que**

(a) ₹ 45,000 (b) ₹ 1,35,000
(c) ₹ 1,50,000 (d) ₹ 1,32,000

22. Sangeeta purchased a machinery for ₹ 1,50,000 by cheque on 1st July, 2022. Another machine was purchased for ₹ 90,000 by cheque on 1st January, 2024. Depreciation is charged at 10% per annum by the straight line method. Accounts are closed each year on 31st December. What will be the journal entry for depreciation on 1st machinery on 31st December, 2024? **Competency Based Que**

(a) Depreciation A/c	Dr	15,000	
To Accumulated Depreciation A/c			15,000
(b) Bank A/c	Dr	15,000	
To Depreciation A/c			15,000
(c) Accumulated Depreciation A/c	Dr	15,000	
To Depreciation A/c			15,000
(d) Depreciation A/c	Dr	15,000	
To Bank A/c			15,000

23. A company bought a machine for ₹ 1,80,000 on credit. Another ₹ 20,000 is spent on its installation. If the estimated useful life is 10 years and scrap value at the end was ₹ 10,000, what will be the amount of depreciation? **Competency Based Que**

(a) ₹ 17,000 (b) ₹ 20,000
(c) ₹ 19,000 (d) ₹ 18,000

24. Original cost of machine is ₹ 12,00,000 with a scrap value of ₹ 75,000 after 4 years. What will be the rate of depreciation as per written down value method? **Competency Based Que**

(a) 100% (b) 25%
(c) 50% (d) 75%

25. A machine was purchased on 1st April, 2021 for ₹ 60,000. It was sold on 30th September, 2022 for ₹ 30,000. Depreciation is charged @ 20% p.a. on 31st March every year on written down value method. What will be the profit and loss on sale of machinery? **Competency Based Que**

(a) ₹ 13,200 (Loss) (b) ₹ 70,000 (Loss)
(c) ₹ 6,800 (Loss) (d) ₹ 13,200 (Profit)

26. A plant costing ₹ 4,00,000 is depreciated @ 20% per annum on written down value method. What will be the value of plant at the end of 2nd year? **Competency Based Que**

(a) ₹ 3,00,000 (b) ₹ 2,88,000
(c) ₹ 2,56,000 (d) ₹ 4,00,000

27. The depreciated value of a machine costing ₹ 20,000 depreciated @ 20% on original cost method after two years is .... and on diminishing value method is .... **Competency Based Que**

(a) ₹ 10,000, ₹ 18,000 (b) ₹ 12,000, ₹ 12,800
(c) ₹ 16,000, ₹ 32,000 (d) ₹ 12,000, ₹ 14,400

28. Cost of a truck is ₹ 1,00,000 and depreciation is charged @ 10% on written down value method. The amount of depreciation for the first year is .... and second year is .... **Competency Based Que**

(a) ₹ 10,000, ₹ 9,000 (b) ₹ 90,000, ₹ 81,000
(c) ₹ 20,000, ₹ 16,400 (d) ₹ 10,000, ₹ 8,100

29. A machine was purchased for ₹ 10,00,000. The deprecation is charged each year @ 20% as per reducing balance method. What is the value of assets at the end of three years? **Competency Based Que**

(a) ₹ 7,00,000 (b) ₹ 2,80,000 (c) ₹ 8,00,000 (d) ₹ 5,12,000

30. If two machines were purchased on the same date with the same amount i.e. ₹ 5,00,000, what will be the amount of difference between the closing balances of two machines after two years. Machine A is depreciated by 20% p.a. on straight line method and Machine B is depreciated by 20% p.a. on diminishing balance method. **Competency Based Que**

(a) Value of machine B is more by ₹ 10,000
(b) Value of machine A is more by ₹ 20,000
(c) Value of machine B is more by ₹ 20,000
(d) Value of machine B is less by ₹ 10,000

31. A machinery was purchased for ₹ 10,00,000. Another ₹ 10,000 were incurred for freight and transportation. Installation expenses amounted to ₹ 40,000 and commission paid on purchases to agent 5% of cost of asset. What is the cost to be recognised in books for the purpose of depreciation? **Competency Based Que**

(a) ₹ 10,00,000 (b) ₹ 11,00,000
(c) ₹ 10,50,000 (d) ₹ 10,10,000

32. Original cost of a machinery ₹ 20,00,000, salvage value ₹ 80,000, expected useful life 10 years. What will be the amount of depreciation for the fourth year according to original cost method? **Competency Based Que**

(a) ₹ 1,92,000 (b) ₹ 1,00,000 (c) ₹ 2,00,000 (d) ₹ 19,20,000

Assertion-Reason

Direction (Q. No. 33 to 42) *Read the following Assertion (A) Reason (R) and choose the correct alternative from the following*

Alternatives

(a) Both Assertion (A) and Reason (R) are true and Reason (R) is the correct explanation of Assertion (A)
(b) Both Assertion (A) and Reason (R) are true, but Reason (R) is not the correct explanation of Assertion (A)
(c) Assertion (A) is true, but Reason (R) is false
(d) Assertion (A) is false, but Reason (R) is true

33. **Assertion** (A) Providing for depreciation also helps in providing for accumulation of funds to facilitate the replacement at the end of its useful life.

Reason (R) Depreciation being non-cash expense reduces the distributable profits and hence facilitates replacement of asset when required.

34. **Assertion** (A) Revenue reserve is created to strengthen the financial position of the organisation so that it is able to meet unforeseen future contingences.

Reason (R) This is an open reserve and can be used to meet any contingency. In companies, it can be used to pay dividends.

35. **Assertion** (A) In straight line method, the amount of depreciation is same every year.

Reason (R) Under this method, a fixed percentage of depreciation is charged on the original cost of the asset every year.

36. **Assertion** (A) Capital reserves may be created out of profit on the sale of land and buildings or other property, plant and equipment.

Reason (R) These reserves are created out of capital profits.

37. **Assertion** (A) Provision for depreciation account is debited at the time of recording the depreciation on an asset.

Reason (R) When provision for depreciation account method is followed, depreciation account is debited at the end of every year.

38. **Assertion** (A) Whenever any depreciable asset is sold during the year, depreciation is charged on it for that entire year.

Reason (R) Whenever any depreciable asset is sold during the year, depreciation is charged on it for the period it has been used in the year of sale.

39. **Assertion** (A) Under diminishing balance method, salvage value is not considered initially.

Reason (R) It assumes that at the end of the asset's life the remaining value shall be its salvage value.

40. **Assertion** (A) Even if adequate maintenance expenditure is incurred with relation to running repairs of an asset, we still need to charge depreciation.

Reason (R) Depreciation is allocation of the cost of an asset over its useful life. Regular repairs required during its life are expensed and depreciation has to be charged anyways.

41. **Assertion** (A) Provision is created by debiting the profit and loss account.

Reason (R) It is created to meet a known liability or a specific contingency, e.g. 'provision for bad and doubtful debts' and 'provision for depreciation', etc.

42. **Assertion** (A) A provision is created irrespective of whether there is profit or loss in the business.

Reason (R) It is available for distribution as dividend among shareholders.

Two Statements Based MCQs

Direction (Q. No. 43 to 50) *Read the following statements carefully and choose the correct alternative*

Alternatives

(a) Both the statements are correct
(b) Both the statements are incorrect
(c) Statement I is correct and Statement II is incorrect
(d) Statement I is incorrect and Statement II is correct

43. **Statement I** Revenue reserve is created out of recurring regular business profits earned from business activities.

Statement II Capital reserve is created out of capital profits which are of non-recurring nature and non-business activities.

44. **Statement I** Depreciation is charged on assets like plant, buildings, etc.

Statement II Depletion is charged in case of intangible assets. It refers to writing-off the value of assets like goodwill, patents and copyrights.

45. **Statement I** In written down value method, the depreciable amount remains same.

Statement II In written down value method, depreciation is charged at a fixed rate on the reducing balance of the asset account.

46. **Statement I** It is not required to provide depreciation on plant and machinery when its market value is higher than its book value.

Statement II Depreciation is provided only on fixed assets except land.

47. **Statement I** Straight line method is very widely used method as it is accepted by the income tax authorities.

Statement II Written down value method is very widely used method as it is accepted by the income tax authorities.

48. **Statement I** Provisions are created by crediting the profit and loss account.

Statement II The amount of provision for expense and loss is a charge against the revenue of the current period.

49. **Statement I** Value of intangible assets like patents, copyrights, trademarks, lease, etc. becomes nil after a pre-determined period. This expiry of legal rights is also referred to as depletion.

Statement II Assets may lose their value due to abnormal reasons like fire, floods or other natural calamities and also due to accidents.

50. **Statement I** An asset can be obsolete while it is not fully depreciated.

Statement II An asset can be obsolete due to the technological innovation or change in market demand for the product.

Matching

51. **Match the following**

Column I	Column II
A. Original cost method	(i) Written down value method
B. Sale of assets	(ii) Accumulated depreciation
C. Reducing balance method	(iii) Straight line method
D. Provision for depreciation	(iv) Disposal of asset

Codes

	A	B	C	D		A	B	C	D
(a)	(i)	(ii)	(iii)	(iv)	(b)	(ii)	(iii)	(iv)	(i)
(c)	(iii)	(iv)	(i)	(ii)	(d)	(i)	(iii)	(ii)	(iv)

52. **Match the following**

Column I	Column II
A. Depletion	(i) Plant and machinery
B. Depreciation	(ii) Oil wells
C. Amortisation	(iii) Patent
D. Residual	(iv) Scrap

Codes

	A	B	C	D		A	B	C	D
(a)	(i)	(ii)	(iii)	(iv)	(b)	(ii)	(i)	(iii)	(iv)
(c)	(iv)	(iii)	(ii)	(i)	(d)	(i)	(iii)	(ii)	(iv)

53. **Match the following**

Column I	Column II
A. Out of date	(i) Depletion
B. Decrease in value of natural asset	(ii) Depreciation
C. Expiry of legal rights	(iii) Amortisation
D. Reduces the tax burden	(iv) Obsolescence

Codes

	A	B	C	D		A	B	C	D
(a)	(i)	(ii)	(iii)	(iv)	(b)	(ii)	(iii)	(iv)	(i)
(c)	(iv)	(i)	(iii)	(ii)	(d)	(i)	(iv)	(ii)	(iii)

54. **Match the following**

Column I	Column II
A. Profit on redemption of debentures	(i) Capital reserve
B. Contingency reserve	(ii) General reserve
C. Debenture redemption reserve	(iii) Specific reserve
D. Supressing the sales	(iv) Secret reserve

Codes

	A	B	C	D		A	B	C	D
(a)	(i)	(ii)	(iii)	(iv)	(b)	(ii)	(iii)	(iv)	(i)
(c)	(iv)	(iii)	(ii)	(i)	(d)	(i)	(iv)	(ii)	(iii)

55. **Match the following**

Column I	Column II
A. Charges against profit	(i) Provisions
B. Appropriation of profit	(ii) Reserves
C. Non-cash expenses	(iii) Asset disposal
D. Discard the asset	(iv) Depreciation

Codes

	A	B	C	D		A	B	C	D
(a)	(i)	(ii)	(iv)	(iii)	(b)	(ii)	(iii)	(iv)	(i)
(c)	(iv)	(iii)	(ii)	(i)	(d)	(i)	(iv)	(ii)	(iii)

Case Based MCQs

Direction *Read the following case study and answer the questions 56 to 58 on the basis of the same*

Sangharsh Ltd. purchased a plant on 1st January, 2021 for ₹ 10,00,000 and ₹ 1,00,000 were spent on its installation. The residual value of the plant after its estimated life of 10 years is ₹ 20,000. The firm is confused about the concept of depreciation. Advise them regarding the same by answering the following questions.

56. **Which among the following factors affecting the amount of depreciation would you suggest the owner to keep in mind?**

(a) Depreciation cost (b) Historical cost
(c) Residual value estimated (d) All of these

57. **Using which statement would you state the importance of straight line method of depreciation?**

(a) Income tax approved
(b) Equality of depreciation
(c) Equal charge against income
(d) No under pressure in later year

58. **Through which statement, would you state the importance of written down value method?**

(a) Income tax approved
(b) Under pressure in later years
(c) Assets can be completely written-off
(d) Simple to calculate

Direction *Read the following case study and answer the questions 59 to 61 on the basis of the same*

Sadhna started a merchandise business. She worked hard and the business started doing well now she is planning to take a step further and wants to expand her business. She decides to maintain proper accounts of her firm as per legal requirements.

When she was working upon it, she realised there are some reserves and provisions to be created, but as she is not an expert, so she approached a Chartered Accountant for suggestions. The Chartered Accountant explained to her various factors with respect to the aforementioned.

59. **Which of the following statements, the Chartered Accountant would have told Sadhna to justify the need to create reserves?**
(a) Reserves strengthen the financial position of the firm
(b) Reserves meet the futher contingencies
(c) Aids in business expansion
(d) All of the above

60. **Why should Sadhna create provisions?**
(a) To store funds
(b) To meet unknown losses and liabilitites
(c) To meet anticipated or known losses and liabilities
(d) None of the above

61. **Which reserve she needs to create if she wants to utilise it freely for any purpose?**
(a) Specific reserve (b) General reserve
(c) Secret reserve (d) Revenue reserve

Direction *Read the following case study and answer the questions 62 and 63 on the basis of the same*

A machinery was purchase by Sam Ltd. for ₹ 18,00,000 on 1st April, 2021.

A part of this machinery costing ₹ 1,20,000 was sold for ₹ 67,500 on 1st October, 2023 and another new machinery was purchased for ₹ 2,37,000.

The depreciation is charged @ 10% p.a. on the written down value method.

62. **What is the accumulated depreciation on the machinery sold for ₹ 67,500 on 1st October, 2021?**
(a) ₹ 27,660 (b) ₹ 30,000 (c) ₹ 4,860 (d) ₹ 10,800

63. **What is the gain or loss on the sale of machinery?**
(a) ₹ 25,890 (b) ₹ 18,440 (c) ₹ 62,500 (d) ₹ 24,840

Direction *Read the following case study and answer the questions 64 and 65 on the basis of the same*

Nand Ltd. purchased a machine for ₹ 54,000 and spent ₹ 6,000 on installation on 1st October, 2021. The effective life estimated at the time of purchase of machinery was 12 years and after the 12 years the residual value will be ₹ 6,000. The machinery needs very low maintenance. The books are closed on 31st March every year.

64. **What is the original cost of machinery on which depreciation is to be charged?**
(a) ₹ 54,000 (b) ₹ 60,000 (c) ₹ 48,000 (d) ₹ 72,000

65. **What is the amount of depreciation charged in the first year?**
(a) ₹ 5,000 (b) ₹ 9,000 (c) ₹ 2,250 (d) ₹ 4,500

Answers

1. (b) depreciation
2. (d) None of the above
3. (c) expense
4. (a) Fall in the market value
5. (d) All of the above
6. (a) obsolescence
7. (c) (Cost of Asset – Scrap Value)/Estimated Life of Asset
8. (c) diminished value
9. (b) The asset can be reduced to zero
10. (a) debited, profit and loss account
11. (b) The amount of depreciation fall year to year
12. (c) profit and loss account
13. (d) credited, provision for depreciation
14. (d) None of the above
15. (c) To meet the unforeseen losses
16. (b) General reserve
17. (a) specific
18. (d) All of the above
19. (a) Depreciation $= 1{,}00{,}000 \times 10/100 \times 6/12 =$ ₹ 5,000
20. (d)

Particulars	Amt (₹)
Let the Cost of Machine on 1st April, 2020	100
(–) Depreciation on 31st March, 2021	(10)
Value of Machinery on 1st April, 2021	90
(–) Depreciation on 31st March, 2022	(9)
Value of Machinery on 1st April, 2022	81
(–) Depreciation on 31st March, 2023	(8.10)
Value of Machinery on 31st March, 2023	72.90

Now, when written down value is 72.9 cost = ₹ 100
When written down value is ₹ 5,83,200, cost is
= 100/72.9 × 5,83,200 = ₹ 8,00,000

21. (b) 1,50,000 – (18,000 – 3,000) = ₹ 1,35,000
22. (a) Depreciation = 1,50,000 × 10% = ₹ 15,000
23. (c) Depreciation = (Cost of Asset – Scrap Value)/ Estimated Life of Asset
= [(1,80,000 + 20,000) – 10,000]/10
= ₹ 19,000
24. (c) Rate of Depreciation $= \left[1 - \sqrt[n]{\frac{S}{C}}\right] \times 100$

Where, n = Expected useful life
S = Scrap value ; C = Cost of an asset

$$\text{Rate of Depreciation} = \left[1 - \sqrt[4]{\frac{75{,}000}{12{,}00{,}000}} \times 100\right] = 50\%$$

25. (a)

Particulars	Amt (₹)
Cost of Machine Purchased on 1st April, 2021	60,000
(–) Depreciation 31st March, 2022 @ 20%	(12,000)
Value of Machinery on 1st April, 2022	48,000
(–) Depreciation on 30th September, 2022 @ 20%	(4,800)
Value of Machinery on 30th September, 2022	43,200
Machinery Sold	(30,000)
Loss on Sale	13,200

26. (c)

Particulars	Amt (₹)
Cost of Machine	4,00,000
(–) Depreciation (Ist Year) @ 20%	(80,000)
Value of Machinery at the End of Ist Year	3,20,000
(–) Depreciation (IInd Year) @ 20%	(64,000)
Value of Machinery at the End of IInd Year	2,56,000

27. (b) **Original Cost Method** = 20,000 – 4,000 (Ist year depreciation) – 4,000 (IInd Year depreciation) = ₹ 12,000

Diminishing Value Method

Particulars	Amt (₹)
Cost of Machine	20,000
(–) Depreciation (Ist Year) @ 20%	(4,000)
Value of Machinery at the End of Ist Year	16,000
(–) Depreciation (IInd Year) @ 20%	(3,200)
Value of Machinery at the End of IInd Year	12,800

28. (a)

Particulars	Amt (₹)
Cost of Machine	1,00,000
(–) Depreciation (Ist Year) @ 10%	(10,000)
Value of Machinery at the End of Ist Year	90,000
(–) Depreciation (IInd Year) @ 10%	(9,000)
	81,000

29. (d)

Particulars	Amt (₹)
Cost of Machine	10,00,000
(–) Depreciation (Ist Year) @ 20%	(2,00,000)
Value of Machinery at the End of Ist Year	8,00,000
(–) Depreciation (IInd Year) @ 20%	(1,60,000)
Value of Machinery at the End of IInd Year	6,40,000
(–) Depreciation (IIIrd Year) @ 20%	(1,28,000)
Value of Machinery at the End of IIIrd Year	5,12,000

30. (c) Value of Machine A = 5,00,000 – 1,00,000 (Ist Year depreciation) – 1,00,000 (IInd Year depreciation) = ₹ 3,00,000

Value of Machine B = 5,00,000 – 1,00,000 (Ist Year depreciation) = ₹ 4,00,000

= 4,00,000 – 80,000 (IInd Year depreciation) = ₹ 3,20,000

31. (b) Cost of Machinery = 10,00,000 + 10,000 + 40,000 + (10,00,000 × 5%) = ₹ 11,00,000

32. (a) Depreciation = ₹ 1,92,000 each year

33. (a) Both Assertion (A) and Reason (R) are true and Reason (R) is the correct explanation of Assertion (A)

34. (a) Both Assertion (A) and Reason (R) are true and Reason (R) is the correct explanation of Assertion (A)

35. (a) Both Assertion (A) and Reason (R) are true and Reason (R) is the correct explanation of Assertion (A)

36. (a) Both Assertion (A) and Reason (R) are true and Reason (R) is the correct explanation of Assertion (A)

37. (d) Provision for depreciation account is credited while charging the depreciation.

38. (d) Assertion (A) is false, but Reason (R) is true

39. (a) Both Assertion (A) and Reason (R) are true and Reason (R) is the correct explanation of Assertion (A)

40. (a) Both Assertion (A) and Reason (R) are true and Reason (R) is the correct explanation of Assertion (A)

41. (b) Both Assertion (A) and Reason (R) are true, but Reason (R) is not the correct explanation of Assertion (A)

42. (c) It is not available for distribution as dividend among shareholders.

43. (a) Both the statements are correct

44. (c) 'Amortisation' is charged in case of intangible assets.

45. (d) In this method, depreciation amount goes on decreasing every year.

46. (d) Statement I is incorrect and Statement II is correct

47. (d) Statement I is incorrect and Statement II is correct

48. (d) Provisions are created by debiting the profit and loss account.

49. (d) Value of intangible assets like patents, copyrights, trademarks, lease etc. becomes nil after a pre-determined period. This expiry of legal rights is also referred to as amortisation.

50. (a) Both the statements are correct

51. (c) (iii) (iv) (i) (ii)

52. (b) (ii) (i) (iii) (iv)

53. (c) (iv) (i) (iii) (ii)

54. (a) (i) (ii) (iii) (iv)

55. (a) (i) (ii) (iv) (iii)

56. (d) All of these

57. (b) Equality of depreciation

58. (a) Income tax approved

59. (d) All of the above

60. (c) To meet anticipated or known losses and liabilities

61. (b) General reserve

62. (a) ₹ 27,660 (12,000 + 10,800 + 4,860)

63. (d) ₹ 24,840 (92,340 – 67,500)

64. (b) ₹ 60,000 (54,000 + 6,000)

65. (c) Depreciation for 1st year $= \left(\frac{60,000 - 6,000}{12}\right) \times \frac{6}{12}$

= ₹ 2,250

09
CHAPTER

Rectification of Errors

Rectification of errors is referred as the procedure of correcting mistakes made in recording the transactions.

▼ YOUR STUDY GOALS

9.1 Errors
- Errors of Omission
- Errors of Commission
- Errors of Principle
- Compensating Errors

9.2 Rectification of Errors

▼ YOUR PRACTICE GOAL

- Topicwise Solved Questions (20 Solved Questions)
- Numerical Questions [32 Questions (Unsolved)]
- Theoretical Questions [10 Questions (with answers)]
- Objective Questions (63 Qs ; MCQs, A-R, Statements, Matching, Case)

9.1 Errors

Accounting errors are the errors committed by persons responsible for recording and maintaining accounts of a business firm in the course of accounting process.

These errors are unintentional mistakes which are commonly committed while recording transactions in the books of accounts. These errors may be committed in the journal, ledger or trial balance or any financial statements.

Classification of Errors

These may be classified as

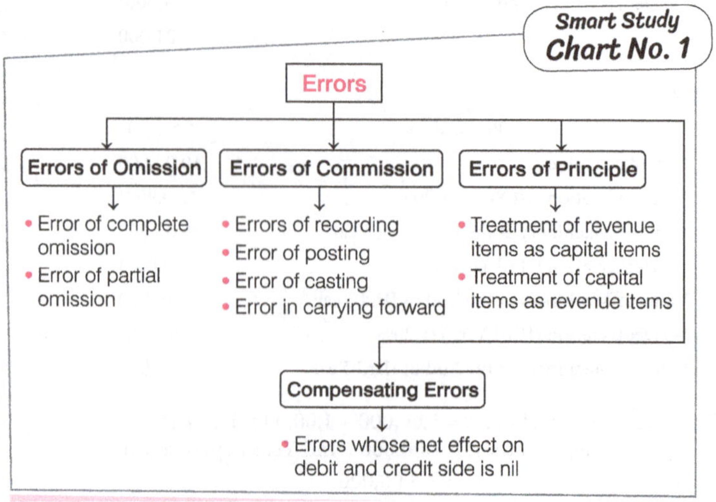

1. Errors of Omission

This error results from a complete or partial omission of recording a transaction in the books of accounts. It includes

Error	Example / Affect
Error of Complete Omission	e.g. Goods return to supplier not recorded. This error does not affect the trial balance.
Error of Partial Omission	e.g. Purchased machinery ₹ 5,000 in cash recorded in cash book but not recorded in machinery account. This error affects the trial balance.

2. Errors of Commission

These errors occur due to any wrong recording committed by the accountant. It includes

Error	Example / Affect
Error of Recording	e.g. Purchase of goods from Nahar on credit is recorded in the sales book and not in the purchases book. This error will not affect the trial balance.
Error of Posting	It can be in the form of • Posting to the wrong side but correct account. e.g. Goods sold to Raghav for ₹ 900 entered to the credit of Raghav's account instead of posting to the debit side of his account. • Posting with wrong amount. e.g. Posting the total of purchase book ₹ 12,000 as ₹ 21,000 in purchase account. • Posting twice in an account. • Errors in posting to the wrong account but correct side. Out of the abovementioned errors, first three errors will affect the trial balance while last one will not affect the total balance.
Error of Casting	e.g. The total of purchases book is written as ₹ 1,800 while actual total is ₹ 8,100. This error affects the trial balance.
Error of Carrying Forward	e.g. The total of purchases book of ₹ 9,000 is carried to next page as ₹ 900. This error affects the trial balance.

3. Errors of Principle

Such errors take place when any of the generally accepted accounting principle is violated or not taken into consideration wherever required (like allocation between capital and revenue items). It includes

Error	Example
Treating Revenue Items as Capital Items	e.g. ₹ 1,000 paid for the repairs of an old machinery but debited to machinery account instead of repairs account.
Treating Capital Items as Revenue Items	e.g. Wages paid for the installation of a new machinery charged to wages account instead of machinery account.

These errors do not affect the trial balance.

4. Compensating Errors

When the net effect of two or more errors on debits and credits of accounts is nil, it is termed as compensating errors. Such errors will not affect the agreement of trial balance.

e.g. Total of purchase book is posted in the ledger as ₹ 10,000 instead of ₹ 1,000 and at the same time Varsha's account is credited in the ledger as ₹ 10,000 instead of ₹ 1,000. As a result, there is an excess credit of ₹ 9,000 in Varsha's account and an excess debit of ₹ 9,000 in purchases account. So, net effect will be nil.

Searching of Errors

Following steps will be useful in treating errors

Step 1 The two columns of the trial balance should be totalled again. If in place of a number of accounts, only one account has been written in the trial balance, then list of such accounts should be checked and totalled again.

Step 2 It should be seen that the cash and bank balances have been written in the trial balance.

Step 3 Exact difference in the trial balance should be determined. Ledger should be properly checked, it is possible that a balance equal to the difference has been omitted from trial balance. The difference should also be halved;
it is possible that balance equal to half the difference has been written in the wrong column.

Step 4 The ledger accounts should be balanced again.

Step 5 The totalling of subsidiary books should be checked again, especially if the difference is ₹ 1, ₹ 100, etc.

Step 6 If the difference is very big, balance in various accounts should be compared with the corresponding accounts in the previous period.
If the figures differ materially, the respective accounts should be checked again.

Step 7 Postings of the amounts equal to the difference or half the difference should be checked. It is possible that an amount has been omitted to be posted or has been posted on the wrong side.

Step 8 If there is still a difference in the trial balance, a complete checking will be necessary. The posting of all the entries including the opening entry should be checked. It may be better to begin with the nominal accounts.

9.2 Rectification of Errors

From the point of view of rectification, the errors may be classified into the following two categories

- Errors which do not affect the trial balance or two-sided errors.
- Errors which affect the trial balance or one-sided errors.

This can be explained as follows

Rectification Process

Step 1 **Wrong Entry** Write the entry which has already been passed in the books, i.e. the wrong entry.

Step 2 **Correct Entry** Write the entry which should have been passed, i.e. the correct entry.

Step 3 **Rectifying Entry** Write the net effect of entries in Step 1 and Step 2 in the following form

Debit of correct entry Credit of wrong entry	} will be debited	Credit of correct entry Debit of wrong entry	} will be credited

I. Errors which do not Affect the Trial Balance or Two-sided Errors

These errors are not disclosed by trial balance, so it tallies even if these errors are made. These errors are made in two or more accounts and can be rectified by recording a journal entry by way of giving the correct debit and credit to the concerned accounts.

These include the following

- Errors of complete omission
- Errors of recording
- Errors of principle
- Compensating errors
- Error of posting to the wrong account but on the correct side

II. Errors which Affect the Agreement of Trial Balance or One-sided Errors

These errors are one-sided errors and are disclosed by the trial balance, so it does not tally if these errors are made. These errors are made only in one account and cannot be rectified by recording a journal entry unless a suspense account is opened. It includes the following

- Error of casting/partial omission/posting twice in A/c
- Error of posting to wrong side, but in correct A/c
- Error in totalling or balancing of an account
- Error in carrying forward/posting with wrong amount

Smart Study Chart No. 2

Rectification Process

Rectification of these errors depends on the stage at which the errors are located.

Stages of Error

Before Preparing Trial Balance

When errors are rectified before the preparation of trial balance, rectification of errors does not require rectification entries but rectification is done by debiting or crediting the respective accounts with the required amount by giving an explanatory note in the particulars column.

After Preparing Trial Balance but before Preparing Final Accounts

At this stage, errors are located and rectified after closing the accounts i.e. after transferring the difference in trial balance to the suspense account but before the preparation of financial statements. The errors here, are rectified by passing a journal entry with the respective account or accounts affected by error and suspense account.

Suspense Account

It is a temporary account which is opened to balance the trial balance.

- If debit side of the trial balance exceeds credit side, the difference is put on the credit side of the trial balance. In this case, 'suspense account' will show a credit balance.
- If credit side of the trial balance exceeds debit side, the difference is put on the debit side of trial balance. In this case, 'suspense account' will show a debit balance.

Disposal of Suspense Account

When all the errors, which affect the equality of trial balance, are located and rectified with the help of the suspense account, the suspense account stands balanced or disposed off.

However, if suspense account shows a balance even after the errors have been rectified, then this means that certain errors are yet to be rectified.

Such balance in suspense account is taken to the balance sheet on assets side, if there is a debit balance or liabilities side, if there is a credit balance.

A Summarised View of Effect of Errors and their Rectification

Effect of Error	Rectification
1. **Before preparation of Trial Balance**	
Excess debit	It is to be made on the credit side by the difference.
Excess credit	It is to be made on the debit side by the difference.
Less debit	It is to be made on the debit side by the difference.
Less credit	It is to be made on the credit side by the difference.
Debit omitted	It is to be made on the debit side by the amount omitted.
Credit omitted	It is to be made on the credit side by the amount omitted.
A debit item wrongly credited in the account	It is to be made on the debit side by the amount to be debited plus amount credited.
A credit item wrongly debited in the account	It is to be made on the credit side by the amount to be credited plus amount debited.
2. **After Preparing Trial Balance** (Using Suspense Account)	
Short debit in one account	Debit that account and credit suspense account
Excess credit in one account	Debit that account and credit suspense account
Short credit in one account	Credit that account and debit suspense account
Excess debit in one account	Credit that account and debit suspense account

Mind Map

RECTIFICATION OF ERRORS

1 Meaning of Errors

- Accounting errors are the errors committed by persons responsible for maintaining accounts of a business
- These errors are unintentional mistakes which are commonly committed while recording transactions
- These errors may be committed in journal, ledger, trial balance or financial statements

2 Errors of Omission

- This error results from a complete or partial omission of recording a transaction in the books of accounts
- It includes error of complete omission and partial omission
- Complete omission does not affect trial balance
- Partial omission affects trial balance

3 Errors of Commission

These errors occur due to any wrong recording of transaction committed by the accountant. It includes

- **Error of Recording** This error does not affect trial balance.
- **Errors of Posting** It can be in the form of following errors
  - Posting to the wrong side but correct account (affect trial balance)
  - Posting with wrong amount (affect trial balance)
  - Posting twice in an account (affect trial balance)
  - Posting to the wrong account but correct side (not affect trial balance)
- **Error of Casting** This error affects trial balance.
- **Error of Carrying Forward** This error affects trial balance.

4 Errors of Principle

- These errors occur due to violation of accounting principles wherever required. It includes treating revenue item as capital and treating capital item as revenue item
- These errors do not affect trial balance

5 Compensating Errors

- When net effect of two or more errors on debit and credit side of accounts is nil, it is known as compensating error
- Such error does not affect trial balance

6 Rectification of Errors

- From the point of view of rectification, the errors may be classified into two categories
- **Two-sided Errors** (Which do not affect trial balance) These errors are rectified by recording a journal entry by way of giving correct debit and credit to the concerned accounts.
- **One-sided Errors** (Which affects trial balance) These errors are ocurred on one side only either on debit or credit side. These errors are rectified by way of suspense account if trial balance is prepared.
  Before preparation of trial balance, these errors are rectified by way of debiting or crediting the respective account with the amount required to remove the effect.

7 Suspense Account

It is a temporary account which is opened to balance a trial balance. If debit side of trial balance exceeds credit side, difference is put on credit side of trial balance. In this case, suspense account shows credit balance. If credit side of trial balance exceeds debit side, difference is put on debit side of trial balance. In this case, suspense account shows debit balance.

Disposal of Suspense Account

- When all the errors are located and rectified with the help of suspense account, the suspense account is balanced or disposed-off.
- If suspense account shows balance even after the errors have been rectified, then this means that certain errors are yet to be rectified.
- Such balance of suspense account is shown on the asset side of balance sheet, if it shows debit balance or on credit side of balance sheet, if it shows credit balance.

Topicwise Solved Questions

Errors which do not Affect Trial Balance (Two-sided Errors)

Solved Question 1 ***(Errors of Recording)*** **Pass the necessary journal entries to rectify the following errors**

(i) A credit purchase of ₹ 810 from Sunita was recorded in the purchase book as ₹ 180.

(ii) A credit purchase of ₹ 900 from Amit was recorded as from Sumit.

(iii) A credit purchase from Manan for ₹ 8,000 was recorded in sales book.

(iv) A credit sale to Ramya for ₹ 527 was recorded in the sales book is ₹ 752.

(v) A credit sale of ₹ 2,100 to Radha was recorded as sales to Adhya.

(vi) A credit sale of machinery to Sadhna was entered in the sales book for ₹ 14,000 as sales.

(vii) A credit sale of ₹ 1,800 to Mani was recorded as a sale to Mona as ₹ 8,100.

(viii) Goods returned by Kanika ₹ 3,100 were recorded in return inwards book as ₹ 310.

(ix) Goods returned to Rama ₹ 2,000 were recorded in return inward book.

(x) Goods returned from Mahi ₹ 2,100 were recorded in return outward book.

Sol. **Rectification Entries in Journal**

Date	Particulars		LF	Amt (Dr)	Amt (Cr)
(i)	Purchases A/c	Dr		630	
	To Sunita				630
	(Being credit purchase of ₹ 810 entered as ₹ 180, now rectified)				
(ii)	Sumit	Dr		900	
	To Amit				900
	(Being credit purchase from Amit wrongly recorded as from Sumit, now rectifed)				
(iii)	Sales A/c	Dr		8,000	
	Purchases A/c	Dr		8,000	
	To Manan				16,000
	(Being credit purchase from Manan wrongly recorded in sales book, now rectified)				
(iv)	Sales A/c	Dr		225	
	To Ramya				225
	(Being credit sales to Ramya for ₹ 527 recoreded as ₹ 752)				
(v)	Radha	Dr		2,100	
	To Adhya				2,100
	(Being credit sales to Radha was recorded as sales to Adhya, now rectified)				
(vi)	Sales A/c	Dr		14,000	
	To Machinery A/c				14,000
	(Being sales of machinery recorded in sales book, now rectified)				
(vii)	Sales A/c	Dr		6,300	
	Mani	Dr		1,800	
	To Mona				8,100
	(Being sales to Mani for ₹ 1,800 recorded as sales to Mona for ₹ 8,100, now rectified)				
(viii)	Return Inward A/c	Dr		2,790	
	To Kanika				2,790
	(Being goods returned from Kanika for ₹ 3,100 wrongly recorded as ₹ 310, now rectified)				

Date	Particulars		LF	Amt (Dr)	Amt (Cr)
(ix)	Rama	Dr		4,000	
	To Return Outward A/c				2,000
	To Return Inward A/c				2,000
	(Being return outward to Rama wrongly recorded as return inward, now rectified)				
(x)	Return Inward A/c	Dr		2,100	
	Return Outward A/c	Dr		2,100	
	To Mahi				4,200
	(Being goods returned from Mahi was recorded in return outward book, now rectified)				

Solved Question 2 *(Errors in Posting to the Wrong Account)* **Pass necessary journal entries to rectify the following errors**

(i) A cash sales of ₹ 1,900 to Nandini was posted to her account instead of sales account.
(ii) A credit sale of ₹ 1,800 to Kamal was posted to Raghav.
(iii) A credit sale of ₹ 1,500 to Meena was posted to the account of Neena.
(iv) A sale of old furniture to Neha for ₹ 3,600 was posted to sales account.
(v) Proprietor withdrew ₹ 9,000 for office use but it was debited to his account.
(vi) Salary of ₹ 19,000 paid to Raj (an employee) was debited to his account.
(vii) An electricity bill of proprietor's residence paid for ₹ 7,900 was debited to electricity expenses account.
(viii) Sarthak, a customer from whom ₹ 2,500 were due, previously written-off as bad debt was recovered and posted to credit of his account.
(ix) A cheque received from Sehgal for ₹ 790 was dishonoured and this amount was posted to the debit to Sayam's account.

Sol.

Rectification Entries in Journal

Date	Particulars		LF	Amt (Dr)	Amt (Cr)
(i)	Nandini	Dr		1,900	
	To Sales A/c				1,900
	(Being credit sales wrongly posted to Nandini's account, now rectified)				
(ii)	Kamal	Dr		1,800	
	To Raghav				1,800
	(Being credit sale to Kamal was wrongly posted to Raghav, now rectified)				
(iii)	Meena	Dr		1,500	
	To Neena				1,500
	(Being credit sale to Meena wrongly posted to Neena's account, now rectified)				
(iv)	Sales A/c	Dr		3,600	
	To Furniture A/c				3,600
	(Being sale of old furniture wrongly posted to sales account, now rectified)				
(v)	Office Expenses A/c	Dr		9,000	
	To Capital A/c				9,000
	(Being amount withdrawn for office use was wrongly posted to proprietor's account, now rectified)				
(vi)	Salary A/c	Dr		19,000	
	To Raj				19,000
	(Being salary paid to Raj was posted to Raj personal account, now rectified)				
(vii)	Drawings A/c	Dr		7,900	
	To Electricity Expenses A/c				7,900
	(Being electricity bill paid to proprietor's residence wrongly debited to electricity expenses account, now rectified)				

Date	Particulars		LF	Amt (Dr)	Amt (Cr)
(viii)	Sarthak	Dr		2,500	
	To Bad Debt Recovered A/c				2,500
	(Being bad debts recovered credited to Sarthak's personal account, now rectified)				
(ix)	Sehgal	Dr		790	
	To Sayam				790
	(Being dishonour of Sehgal's cheque debited to Sayam's account, now rectified)				

Solved Question 3 ***(Errors of Principles)*** **Pass the journal entries to rectify the following errors**

(i) Machinery purchased for ₹ 70,000 from ABC Ltd. were entered in the purchase book.

(ii) Wages of ₹ 9,000 paid for the construction of office building was debited to wages account.

(iii) A second hand computer purchased for ₹ 7,500 was charged to office expenses account.

(iv) Purchases of cement for ₹ 17,000 for construction of building were debited to purchases account.

(v) ₹ 12,500 spent on installation of machinery was debited to wages account.

(vi) Amount of ₹ 6,000 was spent on repairs of furniture was debited to furniture account.

Sol. **Rectification Entries in Journal**

Date	Particulars		LF	Amt (Dr)	Amt (Cr)
(i)	Machinery A/c	Dr		70,000	
	To Purchases A/c				70,000
	(Being machinery purchased was wrongly entered in the purchases book, now rectified)				
(ii)	Building A/c	Dr		9,000	
	To Wages A/c				9,000
	(Being wages paid for constuction of office building was debited to wages account, now rectified)				
(iii)	Office Equipment A/c	Dr		7,500	
	To Office Expenses A/c				7,500
	(Being office computer purchased changed to office expenses account)				
(iv)	Building A/c	Dr		17,000	
	To Purchases A/c				17,000
	(Being cement purchased for building was debited to purchases account, now rectified)				
(v)	Machinery A/c	Dr		12,500	
	To Wages A/c				12,500
	(Being amount paid for installation of machinery debited to wages account, now rectified)				
(vi)	Repairs A/c	Dr		6,000	
	To Furniture A/c				6,000
	(Being repairs of old furniture debited to furniture account wrongly, now rectified)				

Solved Question 4 ***(Errors of Omission)*** **Rectify the following errors**

(i) A credit sale for ₹ 9,500 to Ravi was omitted to be recorded.

(ii) A credit sales of an old furniture for ₹ 3,500 to Rakesh was not recorded at all.

(iii) Return inwards of ₹ 1,400 by Nimmi was not recorded.

(iv) Goods for ₹ 700 were given as free samples were not recorded at all.

(v) ₹ 15,000 paid for rent was omitted to be recorded.

(vi) Outstanding telephone charges of ₹ 7,400 were omitted to be recorded.

Sol. Rectification Entries in Journal

Date	Particulars	LF	Amt (Dr)	Amt (Cr)
(i)	Ravi Dr		9,500	
	To Sales A/c			9,500
	(Being credit sales to Ravi omitted to be recorded, now recorded)			
(ii)	Rakesh Dr		3,500	
	To Furniture A/c			3,500
	(Being credit sale of old furniture to Rakesh omitted to be recorded, now recorded)			
(iii)	Return Inwards A/c Dr		1,400	
	To Nimmi			1,400
	(Being return inwards by Nimmi, now recorded)			
(iv)	Advertisement A/c Dr		700	
	To Purchases A/c			700
	(Being goods given as free samples not recorded, now recorded)			
(v)	Rent A/c Dr		15,000	
	To Cash A/c			15,000
	(Being rent paid not recorded, now recorded)			
(vi)	Telephone Charges A/c Dr		7,400	
	To Outstanding Telephone Charges A/c			7,400
	(Being outstanding telephone charges not recorded, now recorded)			

Solved Question 5 ***(Compensating Errors)*** **Give journal entries to rectify the following**

(i) Mahima's account was short credited by ₹ 900 whereas Sarthak's account was credited in excess of ₹ 900.

(ii) Goods sold to Raja for ₹ 19,000 and to Raj for ₹ 28,000 posted correctly in the sales book but were posted ₹ 28,000 to Raja and ₹ 19,000 to Raj.

(iii) Rohit's account was debited in excess of ₹ 1,500 whereas Mohit's account was short debited by ₹ 1,500.

(iv) Goods purchased from Ramesh for ₹ 9,000 and from Mahesh for ₹ 12,000 were recorded as ₹ 9,000 to Mahesh and ₹ 12,000 to Ramesh. Though it was recorded correctly in the purchases book.

Sol. Rectification Entries in Journal

Date	Particulars	LF	Amt (Dr)	Amt (Cr)
(i)	Sarthak Dr		900	
	To Mahima			900
	(Being short credit of Mahima and excess credit of Sarthak, now rectified)			
(ii)	Raj Dr		9,000	
	To Raja			9,000
	(Being wrong amount credited to Raj and Raja for sales, now rectified)			
(iii)	Mohit Dr		1,500	
	To Rohit			1,500
	(Being short debit to Mohit and excess debit to Rohit, now rectified)			
(iv)	Ramesh Dr		3,000	
	To Mahesh			3,000
	(Being wrong amount recorded to Ramesh and Mahesh account, now rectified)			

Solved Question 6 **Following errors were found in the books of Sanjeev & Sons. Give the necessary entries to correct them.**

(i) A credit sale of ₹ 1,800 to Sama was recorded as sale to Nama as ₹ 8,100.

(ii) Salary paid to Ranjana ₹ 17,000 was debited to her personal account.

(iii) Cartage paid for the newly purchased furniture ₹ 900 posted to cartage account.

(iv) Repairs made for ₹ 750 were debited to the building account.

(v) Rent paid ₹ 11,000 debited to the landlord's account.

(vi) A cheque for ₹ 7,900 received from Sadaf was dishonoured and had been posted to the debit of the sales return account.

Sol. **Rectification Entires in Journal**

Date	Particulars		LF	Amt (Dr)	Amt (Cr)
(i)	Sales A/c	Dr		6,300	
	Sama	Dr		1,800	
	To Nama				8,100
	(Being credit sale of ₹ 1,800 to Sama wrongly recorded as to Nama, now rectified)				
(ii)	Salary	Dr		17,000	
	To Ranjana				17,000
	(Being salary paid to Ranjana debited to her account, now rectified)				
(iii)	Furniture A/c	Dr		900	
	To Cartage A/c				900
	(Being cartage paid for new furniture wrongly posted to cartage account, now rectified)				
(iv)	Repairs A/c	Dr		750	
	To Building A/c				750
	(Being repairs wrongly debited to the building account, now rectified)				
(v)	Rent A/c	Dr		11,000	
	To Landlord's Personal A/c				11,000
	(Being rent paid debited to landlord's account, now rectified)				
(vi)	Sadaf A/c	Dr		7,900	
	To Sales Return A/c				7,900
	(Being dishonour cheque from Sadaf wrongly debited to sales return account, now rectified)				

Solved Question 7 **Rectify the following errors**

(i) Salary paid ₹ 5,000 was debited to employee's personal account.

(ii) Rent paid ₹ 4,000 was posted to landlord's personal account.

(iii) Goods withdrawn by proprietor for personal use ₹ 1,000 were debited to sundry expenses account.

(iv) Cash received from Kohli ₹ 2,000 was posted to Kapur's account.

(v) Cash paid to Babu ₹ 1,500 was posted to Sabu's account.

(vi) Goods sold to Rohan on credit amounting to ₹ 700 were omitted from the accounts although cash received subsequently from him stands posted to his credit.

(vii) On 31st March, goods of the value of ₹ 6,000 were returned by Rohan and were taken into stock on the same date but entry was not passed in the books. **NCERT Modified**

Sol. **Rectification Entries in Journal**

Date	Particulars		LF	Amt (Dr)	Amt (Cr)
(i)	Salaries A/c	Dr		5,000	
	To Employee A/c				5,000
	(Being salary paid to employee ₹ 5,000, wrongly debited to employee's personal account, now rectified)				
(ii)	Rent A/c	Dr		4,000	
	To Landlord's A/c				4,000
	(Being rent paid to landlord ₹ 4,000, wrongly posted to landlord's personal account, now rectified)				
(iii)	Drawings A/c	Dr		1,000	
	To Sundry Expenses A/c				1,000
	(Being goods withdrawn by proprietor for his personal use ₹ 1,000 were wrongly recorded as sundry expenses, now rectified)				
(iv)	Kapur	Dr		2,000	
	To Kohli				2,000
	(Being cash received from Kohli, recorded in Kapur's account, now rectified)				

Date	Particulars		LF	Amt (Dr)	Amt (Cr)
(v)	Babu	Dr		1,500	
	To Sabu				1,500
	(Being cash paid to Babu was posted wrongly to Sabu's account, now rectified)				
(vi)	Rohan	Dr		700	
	To Sales A/c				700
	(Being the rectification of goods sold to Rohan not recorded in the books)				
(vii)	Return Inwards A/c	Dr		6,000	
	To Rohan				6,000
	(Being the entry of goods returned by Rohan and taken into stock omitted from records)				

Solved Question 8 **Rectify the following errors**

(i) Receipt from Ranav for ₹ 780 credited to Manav.

(ii) A credit purchase of ₹ 7,900 from Sanjana was passed in the books as ₹ 9,700.

(iii) Credit sales to Rakesh ₹ 1,000 posted to Mahesh.

(iv) Depreciation provided on machinery of ₹ 5,000 posted as ₹ 500.

(v) Credit purchase from Rohan ₹ 7,000 was not recorded.

(vi) Goods returned to Ramesh ₹ 2,500 were not recorded.

Sol.

Rectification Entries in Journal

Date	Particulars		LF	Amt (Dr)	Amt (Cr)
(i)	Manav	Dr		780	
	To Ranav				780
	(Being receipt from Ranav credited to Manav, now rectified)				
(ii)	Sanjana	Dr		1,800	
	To Purchases A/c				1,800
	(Being wrong amount passed for credit purchase, now rectified)				
(iii)	Rakesh	Dr		1,000	
	To Mahesh				1,000
	(Being credit sales of Rakesh wrongly posted to Mahesh account, now rectified)				
(iv)	Depreciation A/c	Dr		4,500	
	To Machinery A/c				4,500
	(Being depreciation charged on machinery ₹ 5,000 wrongly posted as ₹ 500, now rectified)				
(v)	Purchases A/c	Dr		7,000	
	To Rohan				7,000
	(Being goods purchased from Rohan on credit omitted to be recorded, now recorded)				
(vi)	Ramesh	Dr		2,500	
	To Purchases Return A/c				2,500
	(Being goods returned to Ramesh not recorded, now recorded)				

Errors which Affect Trial Balance (One-sided Errors)

Solved Question 9 **Rectify the following errors which were discovered before preparing the trial balance**

(i) The total of purchases book has been undercast by ₹ 700.

(ii) A payment of wages ₹ 6,000 has been debited to wages account twice.

(iii) A purchase from Sabhya for ₹ 7,500 has been omitted to be posted to her account.

(iv) A credit sale of ₹ 1,500 to Raj was posted to his account as ₹150.

(v) Purchases of ₹ 19,000 from Aman has been posted to the wrong side of his account.

(vi) The total of sales book carried forward ₹ 16,000 less on page 30 and ₹ 26,000 more on page 34.

Sol. (i) Since the amount in purchases book is entered correctly, the creditors's account will be correct. The total of the purchases book is debited to the purchases account. In this case, the total has been undercast by ₹700 i.e. debit side of purchase account has become short by ₹ 700. The rectification will be done by writing the following words on the debit of purchases account.

"To undercasting of purchases book .... ₹ 700" i.e.

Dr **Purchases Account** Cr

Date	Particulars	Amt (₹)	Date	Particulars	Amt (₹)
	To Undercasting of Purchases Book	700			

(ii) In this case the debit side of wages account is debited twice. The rectification here will be done by crediting the wages account by ₹ 6,000.

"To excess amount on the debit side...... ₹ 600" i.e.

Dr **Wages Account** Cr

Date	Particulars	Amt (₹)	Date	Particulars	Amt (₹)
				By Errors in Debiting the Account twice	6,000

(iii) A purchase from Sabhya for ₹ 7,500 has been omitted to be posted to her account. This will affect only Sabhya's account where ₹ 7,500 has not been posted to credit side. The rectification will be done by writing the following words on the credit side of Sabhya's account.

"By omission in posting .... ₹ 7,500" i.e.

Dr **Sabhya's Account** Cr

Date	Particulars	Amt (₹)	Date	Particulars	Amt (₹)
				By Omission in Posting	7,500

(iv) In this case, the mistake is in posting wrong amount in Raj's account only. The rectification will be made by debiting the amount ₹ 1,350 (1,500 – 150) which has been debited by mistake. The following words on debit side of Raj's account will be written.

"To difference in amount on the debit side ...... ₹ 1,350" i.e.

Dr **Raj's Account** Cr

Date	Particulars	Amt (₹)	Date	Particulars	Amt (₹)
	To Difference in Amount	1,350			

(v) In this case, Aman's account has been wrongly debited with ₹19,000 while his account should have been credited with this amount. The rectification will be made by double the amount of entry. i.e. ₹ 38,000 will be written on the credit side of Aman's account.

"By error in posting to the wrong side..... ₹ 38,000" i.e.

Dr **Aman's Account** Cr

Date	Particulars	Amt (₹)	Date	Particulars	Amt (₹)
				By Error in Posting to the Wrong Side	38,000

(vi) In this case, the total of sales book is posted in excess on the credit side of sales account. The rectification will be made by writing the following entry on the debit side of sales account.

Dr **Sales Account** Cr

Date	Particulars	Amt (₹)	Date	Particulars	Amt (₹)
	To Overcasting of Sales Book	10,000			

Solved Question 10 *(Casting Errors)* **Rectify the following errors**

(i) Purchase book was undercast by ₹ 900.
(ii) Sales book was overcast by ₹ 700.
(iii) Purchase return book overcast by ₹ 800.
(iv) Purchase return book was carried forward as ₹ 1,700 instead of ₹ 1,400.
(v) Return inwards book undercast by ₹ 1,100.
(vi) Sales book has been totalled ₹ 750 short.

Sol. **Rectification Entries in Journal**

Date	Particulars		LF	Amt (Dr)	Amt (Cr)
(i)	Purchase A/c	Dr		900	
	To Suspense A/c				900
	(Being purchases book undercast by ₹ 900, now rectified)				
(ii)	Sales A/c	Dr		700	
	To Suspense A/c				700
	(Being sales book overcast, now rectified)				
(iii)	Purchases Return A/c	Dr		800	
	To Suspense A/c				800
	(Being purchase return book overcast, now rectified)				
(iv)	Purchases Return A/c	Dr		300	
	To Suspense A/c				300
	(Being wrong amount carried forward in purchase return book, now rectified)				
(v)	Return Inwards A/c	Dr		1,100	
	To Suspense A/c				1,100
	(Being sales return book undercast by ₹ 1,100, now rectified)				
(vi)	Suspense A/c	Dr		750	
	To Sales A/c				750
	(Being sales book totalled short, now rectified)				

Solved Question 11 *(Error of Posting with Wrong Amount/Posted Twice)* Rectify the following error

(i) A salary of ₹ 16,000 was debited to salaries account twice.

(ii) A credit purchase of ₹ 700 from Samarth was debited to his account as ₹ 70 only.

(iii) Total of returns outwards account ₹ 1,900 has been posted to return outwards account as ₹ 1,200 only.

(iv) Credit sale of ₹ 1,500 made to Sangharsh wrongly posted to the debit of Sangharsh account as ₹ 500.

(v) Nida's account was credited twice with ₹ 900.

(vi) Return inward account was debited twice with ₹ 700.

Sol. **Rectification Entries in Journal**

Date	Particulars		LF	Amt (Dr)	Amt (Cr)
(i)	Suspense A/c	Dr		16,000	
	To Salaries A/c				16,000
	(Being salary posted twice, now rectified)				
(ii)	Suspense A/c	Dr		630	
	To Samarth				630
	(Being Samarth account posted with wrong amount, now rectified)				
(iii)	Suspense A/c	Dr		700	
	To Return Outwards A/c				700
	(Being return outwards account posted with wrong amount, now rectified)				
(iv)	Suspense A/c	Dr		1,000	
	To Sangharsh				1,000
	(Being wrong amount posted in Sangharsh's account, now rectified)				
(v)	Nida	Dr		900	
	To Suspense A/c				900
	(Being Nida's account credited twice, now rectified)				
(vi)	Suspense A/c	Dr		700	
	To Return Inwards A/c				700
	(Being return inward account debited twice, now rectified)				

Solved Question 12 *(Error of Omission in One Account Only)* **Rectify the following errors**

(i) Goods worth ₹ 4,500 returned by Sakhi Ltd. have not been recorded in Sakhi's account.

(ii) Cash received from Chanaya ₹ 6,000 has not been posted to her account.

(iii) Goods withdrawn by proprietor for personal use ₹ 9,000 were not posted to drawings account.

(iv) Bills receivable for ₹ 14,000 received from a debtor was not posted to bills receivable account.

(v) Discount allowed to a debtor ₹ 700 on receiving cash from him was not posted to discount allowed account.

Sol. **Rectification Entries in Journal**

Date	Particulars	LF	Amt (Dr)	Amt (Cr)
(i)	Suspense A/c Dr		4,500	
	To Sakhi			4,500
	(Being Sakhi's account was not credited with return inwards, now rectified)			
(ii)	Suspense A/c Dr		6,000	
	To Chanaya			6,000
	(Being Chanaya's account not recorded with cash received from her, now recorded)			
(iii)	Drawings A/c Dr		9,000	
	To Suspense A/c			9,000
	(Being goods withdraw for personal use, not recorded in drawings account, now rectified)			
(iv)	Bills Receivable A/c Dr		14,000	
	To Suspense A/c			14,000
	(Being bills receivable received from a debtor was not recorded in bills receivable account, now rectified)			
(v)	Discount Allowed A/c Dr		700	
	To Suspense A/c			700
	(Being discount allowed to customer,not posted to discount account, now rectified)			

Solved Question 13 *(Errors of Posting with Wrong Side of the Correct Account)* **Give the journal entries to rectify the following errors using suspense account, where necessary**

(i) Furniture purchased from Alka for ₹ 16,000 was recorded through furniture account correctly but posted to debit of Alka.

(ii) ₹ 7,800 received from Tanya was posted to the debit of her account.

(iii) Credit sales to Heena ₹ 32,000 were recorded in the purchases book as ₹ 20,000 and posted to the debit of Heena as ₹ 2,000.

(iv) Furniture purchased from Neeru ₹ 12,000 was recorded through purchases book as ₹ 10,000 and posted to the debit of Neeru ₹ 4,000.

(v) Goods worth ₹ 1,000 returned to Manya posted to her credit side.

Sol. **Rectification Entries in Journal**

Date	Particulars	LF	Amt (Dr)	Amt (Cr)
(i)	Suspense A/c Dr		32,000	
	To Alka			32,000
	(Being furniture purchased from Alka wrongly debited to her account, now rectified)			
(ii)	Suspense A/c Dr		15,600	
	To Tanya			15,600
	(Being amount wrongly debited, now rectified)			
(iii)	Suspense A/c Dr		22,000	
	Heena Dr		30,000	
	To Purchases A/c			20,000
	To Sales A/c			32,000
	(Being goods sold to Heena ₹ 32,000 wrongly recorded in purchases book as ₹ 20,000 and debited to his account as ₹ 2,000, now rectified)			

Date	Particulars		LF	Amt (Dr)	Amt (Cr)
(iv)	Furniture A/c	Dr		12,000	
	Suspense A/c	Dr		14,000	
	To Neeru				16,000
	To Purchase A/c				10,000
	(Being furniture purchased ₹ 12,000, wrongly recorded in purchases account as ₹ 10,000 and debited to Neeru's account ₹ 4,000, now rectified)				
(v)	Manya A/c	Dr		1,000	
	To Suspense A/c				1,000
	(Being goods returned to Manya were credited to her account)				

Solved Question 14 The trial balance of Shanaya showed a difference of ₹ 160 excess debit were subsequently discovered.

(i) A credit sale of ₹ 2,000 has been credited to the sales and also to the sundry debtors account.
(ii) Purchases book undercast by ₹ 4,500.
(iii) Cash sales to Rana ₹ 6,500 were not posted.
(iv) The purchase of an office table costing ₹ 7,000 has been passed through the purchases day book.
(v) ₹ 1,500 paid for wages to workmen for making showcases had been charged to wages account.
(vi) A purchase of ₹ 660 had been posted to the creditors account as ₹ 500.

Pass necessary journal entries for correcting the above and prepare the 'suspense account' as it would appear in the ledger.

Sol.

Rectification Entries in Journal

Date	Particulars		LF	Amt (Dr)	Amt (Cr)
(i)	Sundry Debtors A/c	Dr		2,000	
	To Suspense A/c				2,000
	(Being the sales wrongly credited to customer's account, now rectified)				
(ii)	Purchases A/c	Dr		4,500	
	To Suspense A/c				4,500
	(Being purchase book undercast by ₹2,000, now rectified)				
(iii)	Suspense A/c	Dr		6,500	
	To Sales A/c				6,500
	(Being cash sales to Rana was not recorded, now rectified)				
(iv)	Furniture A/c	Dr		7,000	
	To Purchases A/c				7,000
	(Being the rectification of mistake by which purchase of furniture was entered in purchases book and hence, debited to purchases account)				
(v)	Furniture A/c	Dr		6,500	
	To Wages A/c				6,500
	(Being the wages paid to workmen for making showcases which should be capitalised and not to be charged to wages account)				
(vi)	Suspense A/c	Dr		160	
	To Creditor's (Personal) A/c				160
	(Being the mistake in crediting the creditor's account less by 60, now rectified)				

Dr **Suspense Account** Cr

Date	Particulars	Amt (₹)	Date	Particulars	Amt (₹)
	To Sales A/c	6,500		By Balance b/d	160
	To Creditors A/c	160		By Sundry Debtors	2,000
				By Purchase A/c	4,500
		6,660			6,660

Suspense account does not show a closing balance. This indicates that errors are rectified and there are no errors left.

Solved Question 15 Trial balance of Kiara Ltd. showed an excess debit of ₹ 300. This was credited to suspense account. The following errors were noticed

(i) One item of purchase of ₹ 125 has been posted from the day book to ledger as ₹ 250.
(ii) The sales return of ₹ 400 from a party has not been posted to that account though the party's account has been credited.
(iii) Depreciation written-off on furniture ₹ 700 was not posted to furniture account.
(iv) Credit sales to Nishant ₹20,000 were recorded as ₹ 14,000.
(v) A cheque for ₹ 750 received from Mahima had been dishonoured and was passed to the debit of 'allowances account.'
(vi) ₹ 15,000 paid for the purchase of a motorcycle for Kiara had been charged to miscellaneous expenses account.

Prepare the suspense account after the rectification of errors.

Sol.

Rectification Entries in Journal

Date	Particulars		LF	Amt (Dr)	Amt (Cr)
(i)	Supplier's/Creditor	Dr		125	
	To Suspense A/c				125
	(Being the mistake in posting from day book to ledger, now rectified)				
(ii)	Sales Return A/c	Dr		400	
	To Suspense A/c				400
	(Being the sales return from a party not posted to 'sale return', now rectified)				
(iii)	Suspense A/c	Dr		700	
	To Furniture A/c				700
	(Being depreciation on furniture was not posted to furniture account, now rectified)				
(iv)	Nishant	Dr		6,000	
	To Sales A/c				6,000
	(Being sales of ₹ 20,000 to Nishant, recorded as ₹ 14,000 now rectified)				
(v)	Mahima	Dr		750	
	To Allowances A/c				750
	(Being the cheque of Mahima dishonoured, previously debited to allowance account)				
(vi)	Drawings A/c	Dr		15,000	
	To Miscellaneous Expenses				15,000
	(Being motorcycle purchased for Kiara debited to her drawings account instead of miscellaneous expenses account as previously done by mistake)				

Dr **Suspense Account** Cr

Date	Particulars	Amt (₹)	Date	Particulars	Amt (₹)
	To Furniture	700		By Balance b/d	300
	To Balance c/d	125		By Suppliers A/c	125
				By Sales Return A/c	400
		825			825

Solved Question 16 While preparing the trial balance, Samar found that the credit side exceeds by ₹ 850 in the trial balance. He opened the suspense account and placed the difference.

(i) Goods worth ₹ 50 returned by Arnav have not been recorded anywhere.
(ii) Goods bought from a merchant for ₹ 110 had been posted to the credit of his account as ₹ 1,100.
(iii) The sales book has been totalled ₹ 300 short.
(iv) Goods purchased ₹ 450 have been posted to the debit of the supplier Rohit.
(v) An item of ₹ 1,000 entered in the sales return book had been posted to the debit of the customer who returned the goods.
(vi) ₹ 200 discount received from a creditor had been duly entered in his account but not posted to discount received account.
(vii) ₹ 160 owing by a customer had been omitted from the schedule of sundry debtors.

(viii) Furniture purchased from Samar ₹ 3,000 has been entered in purchases day book.

(ix) Discount received from H & S Ltd. ₹ 30 has not been entered in the discount column of the cash book.

(x) Discount allowed to Naveen ₹ 80 has not been entered in the discount column of the cash book. The account of Naveen has, however, been correctly posted.

Give journal entries necessary to correct these errors and prepare the suspense account.

Sol.

Rectification Entries in Journal

Date	Particulars		LF	Amt (Dr)	Amt (Cr)
(i)	Return Inward A/c	Dr		250	
	To Arnav				250
	(Being the recording of unrecorded returns)				
(ii)	Merchant A/c	Dr		990	
	To Suspense A/c				990
	(Being excess amount posted to the credit of a merchant account)				
(iii)	Suspense A/c	Dr		300	
	To Sales A/c				300
	(Being the correction arising from undercasting of sales day book)				
(iv)	Suspense A/c	Dr		900	
	To Rohit				900
	(Being the correction of the error by which Rohit was debited instead of being credited by ₹ 450)				
(v)	Suspense A/c	Dr		2,000	
	To Customer A/c				2,000
	(Being amount wrongly debited instead of being credited in the customer account)				
(vi)	Suspense A/c	Dr		200	
	To Discount Received A/c				200
	(Being discount received not posted to the credit of discount received account)				
(vii)	Sundry Debtors A/c	Dr		160	
	To Suspense A/c				160
	(Being customer's account not recorded in the list of sundry debtors)				
(viii)	Furniture A/c	Dr		3,000	
	To Purchases A/c				3,000
	(Being the correction of recording purchase of furniture of ordinary purchases)				
(ix)	H & S Ltd.	Dr		30	
	To Discount A/c				30
	(Being the recording of discount omitted to be recorded)				
(x)	Discount Allowed A/c	Dr		80	
	To Suspense A/c				80
	(Being the correction of omission of the discount allowed from cash book customer's account already posted correctly)				

Dr **Suspense Account** Cr

Date	Particulars	Amt (₹)	Date	Particulars	Amt (₹)
	To Balance b/d	850		By Merchant A/c	990
	To Sales A/c	300		By Sundry Debtors A/c	160
	To Rohit	900		By Discount Allowed	80
	To Customer A/c	2,000		By Balance c/d	3,020
	To Discount Received A/c	200			
		4,250			4,250

Solved Question 17 **Correct the following errors found in the books of Siddharth. The trial balance was out by ₹ 493 excess credit. The difference thus has been posted to a suspense account.**

(i) An amount of ₹ 100 was received from Parth on 31st December, 2023, but has been omitted to enter in the cash book.

(ii) The total of returns inward book for December has been cast ₹ 100 short.

(iii) The purchase of an office table costing ₹ 300 has been passed through the purchases day book.

(iv) ₹ 375 paid for wages to workmen for making showcases had been charged to wages account.

(v) A purchase of ₹ 67 had been posted to the creditors account as ₹ 60.

(vi) A cheque for ₹ 200 received from Kanav had been dishonoured and was passed to the debit of 'allowances account'.

(vii) ₹ 1,000 paid for the purchase of a motor cycle for Siddharth had been charged to 'miscellaneous expenses account'.

(viii) Good amounting to ₹ 100 had been returned by customer and were taken into stock, but no entry in respect thereof, was made into the books.

(ix) A sale of ₹ 200 to Rahul & Co. was wrongly credited to their account.

Sol.

Rectification Entries in Journal

Date	Particulars		LF	Amt (Dr)	Amt (Cr)
(i)	Cash A/c	Dr		100	
	To Parth				100
	(Being the amount received)				
(ii)	Returns Inward A/c	Dr		100	
	To Suspense A/c				100
	(Being the mistake in totalling the returns inward book, now rectified)				
(iii)	Furniture A/c	Dr		300	
	To Purchases A/c				300
	(Being the rectification of mistake by which purchase of furniture was entered in purchases book and hence, debited to purchases account)				
(iv)	Furniture A/c	Dr		375	
	To Wages A/c				375
	(Being the wages paid to workmen for making showcases which should be capitalised and not to be charged to wages account)				
(v)	Suspense A/c	Dr		7	
	To Creditor's (Personal) A/c				7
	(Being the mistake in crediting the creditor's account less by ₹ 7, now rectified)				
(vi)	Kanav	Dr		200	
	To Allowances A/c				200
	(Being the cheque of Kanav dishonoured, previously debited to allowance account)				
(vii)	Drawings A/c	Dr		1,000	
	To Miscellaneous Expenses				1,000
	(Being the motor cycle purchased for Siddharth debited to his drawings account instead of miscellaneous expenses account as previously done by mistake)				
(viii)	Returns Inward A/c	Dr		100	
	To Customer's (Personal) A/c				100
	(Being correction of the omission to record return of goods by customers)				
(ix)	Rahul and Co.	Dr		400	
	To Suspense A/c				400
	(Being the correction of mistake by which the account of Rahul & Co was credited by ₹ 200 instead of being debited)				

Dr **Suspense Account** Cr

Date	Particulars	JF	Amt (₹)	Date	Particulars	JF	Amt (₹)
2011				2011			
Dec 31	To Balance b/d		493	Dec 31	By Returns Inward A/c		100
Dec 31	To Creditor's A/c		7		By Rahul & Co		400
			500				500

Solved Question 18 **On going through the trial balance of Vardhman Ltd., you find that the debit is in excess by ₹ 150. This was credited to suspense account. On a close scrutiny of the books, the following mistakes were noticed.**

(i) The total of debit side of expenses account has been cast in excess by ₹ 50.

(ii) The sales account has been totalled in short by ₹ 100.

(iii) One item of purchase of ₹ 25 has been posted from the day book to ledger as ₹ 250.

(iv) The sales return of ₹ 100 from a party has not been posted to that account though the party's account has been credited.

(v) A credit sale of ₹ 50 has been credited to the sales and also to the sundry debtors' account.

Pass necessary journal entries for correcting the above and prepare the 'suspense account' as it would appear in the ledger.

Sol. **Rectification Entries in Journal**

Date	Particulars	LF	Amt (Dr)	Amt (Cr)
(i)	Suspense A/c Dr		50	
	To Expenses A/c			50
	(Being the mistake in totalling of expenses account, now rectified)			
(ii)	Suspense A/c Dr		100	
	To Sales A/c			100
	(Being the mistake in totalling of sales accounts, now rectified)			
(iii)	Supplier's/Creditor Dr		225	
	To Suspense A/c			225
	(Being the mistake in posting from day book to ledger, now rectified)			
(iv)	Sales Returns A/c Dr		100	
	To Suspense A/c			100
	(Being the sales return from a party not posted to 'sales returns', now rectified)			
(v)	Sundry Debtors Dr		100	
	To Suspense A/c			100
	(Being the sales wrongly credited to customer's account, now rectified)			

Dr **Suspense Account** Cr

Date	Particulars	JF	Amt (₹)	Date	Particulars	JF	Amt (₹)
	To Expenses A/c		50		By Balance b/d		150
	To Sales A/c		100		By Sundry Creditors/Suppliers		225
	To Balance c/d		425		By Sales Returns A/c		100
					By Sundry Debtors		100
			575				575

Note Suspense account exhibits a closing balance. This indicates that there are certain other errors which are not yet rectified.

Missing Information

Solved Question 19 Complete the following rectification entries

Rectification Entries in Journal

Date	Particulars		LF	Amt (Dr)	Amt (Cr)
(i)	......	Dr		4,000	
	To				4,000
	(Being purchase book undercast by ₹ 4,000)				
(ii)	......	Dr		9,000	
	To				9,000
	(Being goods distributed as free samples costing ₹ 9,000 omitted to be recorded, now recorded)				
(iii)	......	Dr		450	
	To				450
	(Being sale of machinery wrongly recorded in sales book, now rectified)				
(iv)	......	Dr		...	
	To				...
	(Being goods purchased for ₹ 2,500 posted to purchase account as ₹ 500, now rectified)				
(v)	......	Dr		...	
	To				...
	(Being bad debts recovered wrongly credited to Soniya ₹ 1,000)				

Sol.

Rectification Entries in Journal

Date	Particulars		LF	Amt (Dr)	Amt (Cr)
(i)	**Purchases A/c**	Dr		4,000	
	To **Suspense A/c**				4,000
	(Being purchase book undercast by ₹ 4,000)				
(ii)	**Advertisement Expenses A/c**	Dr		9,000	
	To **Purchases A/c**				9,000
	(Being goods distributed as free samples costing ₹ 9,000 omitted to be recorded, now recorded)				
(iii)	**Sales A/c**	Dr		450	
	To **Machinery A/c**				450
	(Being sale of machinery wrongly recorded in sales book, now rectified)				
(iv)	**Purchases A/c**	Dr		**2,000**	
	To **Suspense A/c**				**2,000**
	(Being goods purchased for ₹ 2,500 posted to purchase account as ₹ 500, now rectified)				
(v)	Soniya	Dr		**1,000**	
	To Bad Debts Recovered A/c				**1,000**
	(Being bad debts recovered wrongly credited to Soniya ₹ 1,000)				

Solved Question 20 Fill up the missing information in the following rectifying entries

Rectification Entries in Journal

Date	Particulars		LF	Amt (Dr)	Amt (Cr)
(i)	......	Dr		...	
	To				...
	To				...
	(Being credit sales to Saahil for ₹ 8,000 wrongly passed through purchase book, now rectified)				

Date	Particulars	LF	Amt (Dr)	Amt (Cr)
(ii)	…… Dr		…	
	To ……			…
	(Being credit purchase of ₹ 2,300 from Rajesh recorded as ₹ 3,200, now rectified)			
(iii)	…… Dr		…	
	To Suspense A/c			…
	(Being total of sales return book ₹ 7,000 not posted to ledger, now rectified)			
(iv)	…… Dr		29,000	
	To ……			…
	To ……			…
	(Being furniture purchased for ₹ 29,000 from Sanju Ltd. recorded through purchase book as ₹ 20,000)			
(v)	…… Dr		15,000	
	To ……			15,000
	(Being dishonour of cheque for ₹ 15,000 received from Lakshya debited to discount account, now rectified)			

Sol.

Rectification Entries in Journal

Date	Particulars	LF	Amt (Dr)	Amt (Cr)
(i)	**Saahil** Dr		**16,000**	
	To **Purchases A/c**			**8,000**
	To **Sales A/c**			**8,000**
	(Being credit sales to Saahil for ₹ 8,000 wrongly passed through purchase book, now rectified)			
(ii)	**Rajesh** Dr		900	
	To **Purchases A/c**			900
	(Being credit purchase of ₹ 2,300 from Rajesh recorded as ₹ 3,200, now rectified)			
(iii)	**Sales Return A/c** Dr		**7,000**	
	To **Suspense A/c**			**7,000**
	(Being total of sales return book ₹ 7,000 not posted to ledger, now rectified)			
(iv)	**Furniture A/c** Dr		29,000	
	To **Purchases A/c**			**20,000**
	To **Sanju Ltd.**			**9,000**
	(Being furniture purchased for ₹ 29,000 from Sanju Ltd. recorded through purchase book as ₹ 20,000)			
(v)	**Lakshya** Dr		15,000	
	To **Discount A/c**			15,000
	(Being dishonour of cheque for ₹ 15,000 received from Lakshya debited to discount account, now rectified)			

Numerical Questions

Errors which do not Affect the Trial Balance (Two-sided Errors)

1. Rectify the following errors which were detected before preparing the trial balance

(i) Credit sales to Mohan ₹ 7,000 were not recorded.

(ii) A credit sale to Aman for ₹ 3,798 was recorded in the sales book as ₹ 897.

(iii) A credit purchase from Sunder for ₹ 700 was recorded as from Anil.

(iv) A credit sale of ₹ 625 to Mohan was recorded in the sales book as a sale to Madan for ₹ 562.

(v) A credit purchase from Sarthak for ₹ 3,500 was recorded in the sales book for ₹ 5,300.

(vi) Goods returned to Rakesh ₹ 4,000 were recorded as ₹ 4,040.

2. Rectify the following entries giving suitable narrations

(i) A credit sale of machinery to Akash was entered in the sales book for ₹ 7,000.

(ii) Goods return by Kamal ₹ 2,100 were entered in the return inwards book as ₹ 210.

(iii) Goods returned from Mahesh ₹ 1,000 were recorded as ₹ 1,600.

(iv) Credit purchase from Rohan ₹ 9,000 were recorded as ₹ 9,900.

(v) A credit purchase from Dass for ₹ 210 was recorded in the purchases book as for ₹ 120.

(vi) Goods returned by Kesar for ₹ 3,150 were entered in return outwards book.

3. Rectify the following errors

(i) Cash sale of ₹ 3,400 to Samit was posted to the credit of Samit.

(ii) Credit sale of old furniture to X for ₹ 3,400 was credited to the sales account.

(iii) Credit sale of old furniture to Vishal for ₹ 1,700 was posted as ₹ 7,100.

(iv) A cash sale of ₹ 5,100 to Mohan was posted to his account instead of sales account.

(v) A credit purchase of goods from John for ₹ 15,000 was posted to the account of Shan.

(vi) A credit sale of ₹ 8,100 to Sahil was posted to Somil.

4. Pass journal entries to rectify the following errors

Competency Based Que

(i) A sale of an old chair to Nisha for ₹ 4,200 was posted to sales account instead of furniture account.

(ii) A salary of ₹ 800 paid Kailash was debited to his account instead of salaries account.

(iii) A bill of telephone at the proprietor's residence paid for ₹ 1,600 was debited to telephone expenses account.

(iv) The proprietor drew from bank ₹ 500 for office use but the amounts was posted (debited) to his account instead of office expenses account.

(v) A bills of exchange of ₹ 5,000 discounted for ₹ 4,900 has been dishonoured by Nihal. This amount has been debited to bills receivable account instead of Nihal.

(vi) A cheque of ₹ 9,000 received from Roja was dishonoured. The amount was posted to the debit of Rose instead of Roja.

5. Rectify the following errors

(i) A credit sale of an old machine to Sohan for ₹ 6,000 was omitted to be recorded.

(ii) Goods sold for ₹ 16,500 to Sandeep was not recorded at all.

(iii) Salaries outstanding at the end of the month for ₹ 1,20,000 were not recorded.

(iv) Outstanding telephone charges of ₹ 6,000 had been completely omitted.

(v) Material from store ₹ 15,000 and wages ₹ 6,000 had been used in making tools and implements for use in own factory, but no adjustments were made in the books.

(vi) Bad debts written-off ₹ 5,000 were not recorded.

(vii) Discount allowed to a debtor ₹ 100 on receiving cash from him was not recorded.

6. Rectify the following entries giving suitable narrations

Competency Based Que

(i) Goods costing ₹ 400, taken by the proprietor for personal use were not recorded at all.

(ii) Sales return of ₹ 4,800 by Jagat, a customer, were not recorded.

(iii) Goods of the value of ₹ 400 returned to Y, but no entry was made in the books.

(iv) Goods costing ₹ 1,100 were given as charity. But no entry was passed for this transaction.

(v) Goods costing ₹ 500 given as free samples to the customers were not recorded.

(vi) Raw material costing ₹ 2,000 was used in repairing the machine but no entry was passed for the same.

7. Rectify the following errors

(i) Repairs made were debited to building account ₹ 100.
(ii) ₹ 200 paid for rent, debited to landlord's account.
(iii) Wages of ₹ 4,000 paid for construction of building were debited to wages account.
(iv) Machine purchased for ₹ 46,000 from M/s HMT Ltd. were entered in the purchases account.
(v) ₹ 18,000 paid for white-washing the building were debited to building account.
(vi) Installation charges of ₹ 1,500 paid to an engineer for fixing the machine debited to installation charges account.

8. Pass journal entries to rectify the following errors

(i) ₹ 1,400 paid in cash for a typewriter was charged to office expenses account.
(ii) A second hand computer purchased for ₹ 15,000 was charged to office expenses account.
(iii) ₹ 2,500 spent on reconditioning the above computer were charged to repairs account.
(iv) ₹ 8,000 for repairs to the existing furniture were debited to furniture account.
(v) ₹ 5,000 paid for purchase of Bricks for construction of a cycle shed were debited to purchases account.
(vi) Salary ₹ 250 paid to a clerk due to him has been debited to his personal account.

9. Rectify the following errors

(i) Salary account overcast by ₹ 2,000 and electricity charges undercast by ₹ 2,000.
(ii) Purchase book is undercast by ₹ 4,000 and purchases return under cast by ₹ 2,000 and sales return overcast by ₹ 2,000.
(iii) Goods sold to Mr. X amounted ₹ 5,000 was posted to the debit side of X's account with ₹ 500 only. At the same time receipt of ₹ 5,000 from Mr. Y was wrongly credited to Mr. Y's account as 500.

10. Give journal entries to rectify the following errors

(i) Goods purchased from A for ₹ 2,600 were recorded in sales book by mistake.
(ii) Goods for ₹ 4,400 sold to B were passed through purchases book.
(iii) A customer returned goods worth ₹ 1,000. It was recorded in purchases return book.
(iv) A credit sale of ₹ 126 to D was entered in the books as ₹ 162.
(v) Sale of old chairs and table for ₹ 700 was treated as sale of goods.
(vi) Rent of proprietor's residence, ₹ 800 debited to rent account.
(vii) A sale of goods to E for ₹ 2,500 was passed through the purchases book.
(viii) Salary of ₹ 800 paid to F was wrongly debited to his personal account.

11. The following errors were found in the book of Rajan & Sons. Give the necessary entries to correct them. Competency Based Que

(i) Repairs made were debited to building account ₹ 100.
(ii) ₹ 200 paid for rent, debited to landlord's account.
(iii) Salary ₹ 250 paid to a clerk due to him has been debited to his personal account.
(iv) ₹ 200 received from Rina & Co. has been wrongly entered as from Reena & Co.
(v) ₹ 1,400 paid in cash for a typewriter was charged to office expenses account.
(vi) Credit sales to Mohan ₹ 37,000 were posted to Karan.
(vii) Credit purchase from Rohan ₹ 9,000 were posted to Gobind.
(viii) Goods returned to Rakesh ₹ 4,000 were posted to Naresh.
(ix) Goods returned from Mahesh ₹ 1,000 were posted to Manish.
(x) Cash sales ₹ 2,000 were posted to commission account.

12. Give rectifying entries for the following Competency Based Que

(i) A credit sale of goods to Ram ₹ 5,000 has been wrongly passed through the purchases book.
(ii) A credit purchase of goods from Shyam amounting to ₹ 2,000 has been wrongly passed through the sales book.
(iii) A return of goods worth ₹ 2,200 to Mohan was passed through the sales return book.
(iv) A return of goods worth ₹ 1,000 by Ganesh were entered in purchases return book.
(v) Goods for ₹ 11,000 were purchased from Modern Traders on credit, but no entry has yet been passed.
(vi) Purchases return for ₹ 3,000 not recorded in the books.
(vii) Goods for ₹ 1,4,000 sold to Zee Traders on credit were entered in the sales book as ₹ 200 only.
(viii) Goods of the value of ₹ 3,600 returned by Kamal & Co. were included in stock, but no entry was passed in the books.
(ix) Goods purchased for ₹ 1,800 were entered in the purchases book as ₹ 18,000.
(x) An invoice for goods sold to X was overcast by ₹ 200.

13. **Rectify the following errors**

(i) ₹ 2,000 paid to Janak were debited to the account of Janam.

(ii) Furniture purchased on credit for ₹ 12,000 was entered in the purchases account.

(iii) Rent paid ₹ 350 was credited to rent account as ₹ 850.

(iv) Cartage paid for the new furniture ₹ 60 posted to cartage account.

(v) Furniture purchased on credit from Rattan for ₹ 800 posted to his account as ₹ 180.

(vi) Purchases from Amar ₹ 2,100 were omitted from the books.

(vii) Repairs to buildings ₹ 8,500 were debited to buildings account.

(viii) Discount of ₹ 395 received from creditors was not posted to the creditors account from cash book.

(ix) A sale of old machinery for ₹ 600 has been credited to sales account.

(x) Furniture worth ₹ 8,000 purchased on credit omitted to be recorded.

14. **Rectify the following errors** **Competency Based Que**

(i) Sale of old furniture for ₹ 2,000 treated as sale of goods.

(ii) ₹ 15,000 paid of salary to Mr. Rohit, stands debited to his personal account.

(iii) An amount of ₹ 7,000 withdrawn by the proprietor for his personal use has been debited to trade expenses account.

(iv) Cash received from Mr. Sawant ₹ 500 was credited to Mr. Shinde.

(v) Goods sold to Mr. Abhiraj ₹ 350 have been entered in the purchase day book as ₹ 530.

(vi) Repairs to furniture ₹ 300 have been debited to furniture and fixtures account.

(vii) Repairs for building was debited to building account ₹ 500.

(viii) ₹1,500 received as interest was credited to commission account.

(ix) ₹ 5,000 paid for the purchase of computer was charged to office expenses account.

(x) Goods sold to Aryan for ₹ 2,000 on credit were not entered in the sales book.

Errors which Affect the Trial Balance (One-sided Errors)

15. **Rectify the following entries giving suitable narrations**

(i) Purchase book undercast by ₹ 400.

(ii) Return inwards book undercast by ₹ 200.

(iii) The total of sales book has been undercast by ₹ 670.

(iv) The total of purchase book has been overcast by ₹ 530.

(v) The total of the credit side of the cash book was overcast by ₹ 200.

(vi) The total of purchase book was ₹ 2,650. It was carried forward to the next page as ₹ 6,250.

(vii) Return inwards book was short totalled by ₹ 700.

16. **Rectify the following errors**

(i) A payment of ₹ 600 as wages has been debited to wages account twice.

(ii) A purchase on credit from Inder for ₹ 1,500 has been correctly entered in the purchase account. It has been debited to his account as ₹ 150 only.

(iii) Total of return outward account ₹ 2,700 has been posted to return onwards accounts as ₹ 700 only.

(iv) Goods purchased for ₹ 37,500 were posted to purchases account as ₹ 5,700.

(v) Purchases of ₹ 6,800 were posted to purchases as ₹ 680 only.

17. **Pass journal entries to rectify the following errors**

(i) Bad debts of ₹ 700 written-off have not been credited to Mohan's account.

(ii) Depreciation of ₹ 2,100 was charged on machinery. A correct journal entry was made. But it was not posted to depreciation account.

(iii) Total of return inwards book ₹ 1,500 has not been posted to return inwards account.

(iv) A discount of ₹ 16 allowed to Sohan has not been posted to his account.

18. **Rectify the following errors**

(i) Rent received ₹ 1,600 has been correctly entered in cash book. It has been debited to rent account.

(ii) ₹ 3,200 received from Ganesh were debited to his account.

(iii) Credit sales to Mohan ₹ 7,000 were posted to the credit of his account.

(iv) Credit purchase from Rohan ₹ 9,000 were posted to the debit of his account.

(v) Goods returned to Rakesh ₹ 4,000 were posted to the credit of his account.

19. **An accountant failed to balance his trial balance. Later on, some errors were discovered. Give the journal entries to rectify the following errors**

Competency Based Que

(i) A credit balance of ₹ 840 of rent receivable account was shown as ₹ 40.

(ii) Goods worth ₹ 1,620 sold to Tej were correctly entered in the sales book, but were posted to his account as ₹ 162.

(iii) Goods worth ₹ 1,100 purchased from Karan were wrongly entered in the sales book. The account of Karan was correctly credited.
(iv) The total of returns outward book amounting to ₹ 1,200 was not posted to the ledger.
(v) The total of the credit side of Ramesh account was overcast by ₹ 100.
(vi) The sales book was undercast by ₹ 100.

20. Give necessary journal entries to rectify the following errors.
(i) Goods purchased for ₹ 99 had been posted to the credit of the supplier as ₹ 990.
(ii) ₹ 275 received as discount from a creditor was duly entered in his account but it was omitted to be posted to discount account.
(iiii) Sale of furniture for ₹ 1,400 had been entered in sales book.
(iv) ₹ 900 due from a customer were omitted to be taken to the schedule of sundry debtors.
(v) Goods of the value of ₹ 3,000 returned by a customer were taken into the stock but no entry was made in the books.
(vi) ₹ 335 entered in the sales returns book had been posted to the debit of the customer who returned the goods.

21. Pass journal entries to rectify the following errors detected during preparation of trial balance.
(i) Purchases book is undercast by ₹ 2,000.
(ii) Wages paid for construction of office debited to wages account ₹ 40,000.
(iii) A credit sale of goods ₹ 2,400 to Q has been wrongly passed through the purchases book.
(iv) Goods purchased for ₹ 10,000 were posted as ₹ 1,000 to the purchases account.
(v) An amount of ₹ 4,000 due from RP Sharma which had been written-off as a bad debt in a previous year was unexpectedly recovered and has been posted to the personal account of RP Sharma.
(vi) A credit purchase of ₹ 2,080 from Q was passed in the books as ₹ 2,800.
(vii) Goods (cost ₹ 10,000, sales price ₹ 12,000) distributed as free samples among prospective customers was not recorded anywhere.
(viii) Goods worth ₹ 3,000 returned by X & Co. have not been recorded anywhere.

22. Rectify the following errors through suspense account
(i) The total of sales book has been undercast by ₹ 670.
(ii) The total of purchase book has been overcast by ₹ 530.
(iii) Bad debts of ₹ 700 written-off have not been credited to Mohan's account.
(iv) A payment of ₹ 600 as wages has been debited to wages account twice.
(v) Total of return inwards books ₹ 1,500 has not been posted to returns inward account.
(vi) Total of return outwards account ₹ 2,700 has been posted to return inward account as ₹ 270 only.
(vii) A purchase on credit from Inder for ₹ 1,500 has been correctly entered in the purchase book. It has been debited to his account as ₹ 150 only.
(viii) A discount of ₹ 16 allowed to Sohan has not been posted to his account.
(ix) Rent received ₹1,600 has been correctly entered in cash book. It has been debited to rent account.
(x) Depreciation of ₹ 2,100 was charged on machinery. A correct journal entry was made. But it was not posted to depreciation account.

23. A trial balance as on 31st March, 2023 shows a difference which has been carried to suspense account, and the following errors are subsequently discovered

Competency Based Que

(i) Sales return book was overcast by ₹ 4,000 and also the total of a page in the same book ₹ 17,000 was carried forward as ₹ 10,000.
(ii) Bills receivable from Nani for ₹ 400 posted to the credit of bills payable account and credited to Nani.
(iii) Goods worth ₹ 2,130 returned by 'X' were entered in the sales book and were posted therefrom to the credit of his personal account.
(iv) Goods amounting to ₹ 800 sold to Ram were correctly entered in the sales book but posted to Sham's as ₹ 880.
(v) A cash sale of ₹ 250 to 'B', correctly entered in the cash book was posted to the credit of his personal account instead of sales account.

Rectify the entries and prepare suspense account.

Ans. Suspense account (credit) = ₹ 7,980

24. Rectify the following errors and prepare suspense account
(i) Bad debts of ₹ 1,000 were written-off during the year but were not entered anywhere.
(ii) A credit purchase of furniture costing ₹ 2,700 from Heena was entered in the purchase book as ₹ 1,700 and posted therefrom to the debit of her account.
(iii) Goods of the value of ₹ 1,920 returned by Mr. Benji were entered in the purchase book as ₹ 920 and posted therefrom to his credit as ₹ 900.
(iv) Goods of ₹ 840 returned to Zora Supplier were entered in the sales day book as ₹ 480 and posted therefrom to the credit of Mr. Arora as ₹ 450.

(v) ₹ 1,400 for goods purchased from Mr. Arora were entered in sales return book as ₹ 1,440 and posted to his account there from as ₹ 1,040.

(vi) A bill for ₹ 564 for goods purchased from Mr. Akash was entered in the sales book as ₹ 540 and posted therefrom to the account debit of Aman as ₹ 500.

25. **The bookkeeper of a firm, found the difference in the trial balance and raised a suspense account in which he entered the amount of difference. The following errors were discovered. Rectify them and prepare suspense account.** Competency Based Que

(i) A discount of ₹ 120 received from Rohit, had been duly entered in his account, but not posted to the discount account.

(ii) An item of ₹ 280 entered in the sales return book had been posted to the debit of Sohan who returned the goods.

(iii) A dishonoured bills receivable of Kanwar for ₹ 4,800 returned to the firm's bank had been credited to the bank account and debited to bills receivable account.

(iv) Goods bought from Ram amounting to ₹ 9,000 had been posted to the credit of his account as ₹ 1,900.

Ans. Suspense account (debit) = ₹ 7,780

26. **In taking out the trial balance, a bookkeeper finds excess debit of ₹ 3,809. Being desirous of closing his books, he places the difference to a newly opened suspense account which is carried forward. In the next period, he discovered that** Competency Based Que

(i) ₹ 17,715 received from Raj have not been posted to his account.

(ii) A sum of ₹ 9,500 written-off as depreciation on fixtures has not been posted to the depreciation account.

(iii) ₹ 1,50,000 paid for furniture purchased have been charged to ordinary purchases account.

(iv) A discount of ₹ 3,742 allowed to a customer has been credited to him as ₹ 3,648.

(v) The total of the inwards return has been added ₹ 900 short.

(vi) An item of sales for ₹ 5,900 was posted as ₹ 9,500 the sales account.

Give the rectifying entries and prepare the suspense account.

Ans. Total of suspense account = ₹ 17,809

27. **A trial balance shows a difference which has been transferred to suspense account. The following errors are revealed. Rectify them and prepare suspense account.**

(i) Sales returns book was overcast by ₹ 1,000.

(ii) Goods amounting to ₹ 40,000 sold to Ram were correctly entered in the sales book but posted to his account for ₹ 44,000.

(iii) Bills receivable from Anil for ₹ 8,000 posted to the credit of bills payable account and credited to his account.

(iv) A cash sale of ₹ 8,000 to Mohan, correctly entered in the cash book, was posted to the credit of his account in the ledger instead of sales account.

(v) ₹ 4,700 paid in cash for a typewriter was charged to office expenses account.

(vi) Goods amounting to ₹ 700, returned by Neeta were entered in the sales book and posted therefrom to the credit of her account.

Ans. Balance of suspense account (credit) = ₹ 12,400

28. **The trial balance prepared by a bookkeeper showed a difference of ₹ 1,006 which was placed in a newly opened suspense account and carried forward to the next year, when the following errors were discovered** Competency Based Que

(i) Goods purchased for ₹ 99 had been posted to the credit of the supplier as ₹ 990.

(ii) ₹ 275 received as discount from a creditor was duly entered in his account but it was omitted to be posted to discount account.

(iii) Sale of furniture for ₹ 1,400 had been entered in sales book.

(iv) ₹ 900 due from a customer were omitted to be taken to the schedule of sundry debtors.

(v) Goods of the value of ₹ 3,000 returned by a customer were taken into the stock but no entry was made in the books.

(vi) ₹ 335 entered in the sales returns book had been posted to the debit of the customer who returned the goods.

Give necessary journal entries to rectify the above errors and prepare suspense account.

Ans. Opening debit balance of suspense account = ₹ 1,006
Total of suspense account = ₹ 1,791

29. **A bookkeeper prepared a trial balance on 31st March, 2023, which showed a difference of ₹ 2,715.53. The difference was placed to the debit of a suspense account.**
The undermentioned errors were subsequently discovered. Competency Based Que

(i) ₹ 2710, the total of sales return book has been posted to the credit of the purchases return account.

(ii) An item of ₹ 626 written-off as a bad debt from C has not been debited to bad debts account.

(iii) Goods sold to W and X for ₹ 1,600 and ₹ 1,200 respectively, but were recorded in the sales book as to WZ ₹ 1,200 and X as ₹ 1,600.

(iv) Goods of ₹ 850 were returned to B. It was recorded in purchases book as ₹ 580.

(v) An amount of ₹ 675.25 for a credit sale to Govind, although correctly entered in the sales book, has been wrongly posted as ₹ 756.52.

(vi) A sum of ₹ 375.40 owed by Y has been included in the list of sundry creditors.

(vii) An amount of ₹ 750 spent on the repairs of an old machinery has been debited to repairs account.

Pass journal entries to rectify the errors and prepare a suspense account.

Ans. Total of suspense account = ₹ 2,796

30. Rectify the following errors which were discovered after making the trial balance. There was a difference of ₹ 6,700 excess credit in trial balance which was debited to suspense account. **Competency Based Que**

(i) Goods purchased for ₹ 7,500 were posted to purchases account as ₹ 5,700.

(ii) Buildings were written-off by ₹ 3,200 but it was not posted to depreciation account.

(iii) Office chairs were purchased for ₹ 6,200. The amount was debited to purchases account.

(iv) ₹ 7,100 were paid to Prem. The amount was debited to Prerna wrongly.

(v) Purchases of ₹ 6,800 were posted to purchases as ₹ 680 only.

(vi) ₹ 3,200 received from Ganesh were debited to his account.

(vii) Return inwards book was short totalled by ₹ 700.

Ans. Balance in suspense account = ₹ 1,280

Missing Information

31. Fill in the missing information in the following rectifying journal entries **Competency Based Que**

JOURNAL

Date	Particulars	LF	Amt (Dr)	Amt (Cr)
(i)	...... Dr		...	
	To Suspense A/c			...
	(Being salary paid ₹ 13,000 debited in salaries account as ₹ 10,000, now rectified)			
(ii)	...... Dr		1,000	
	To......			1,000
	(Being sales book undercast by ₹ 1,000, now rectified)			
(iii)	Ravanya Dr		...	
	To			...
	(Being goods sold to Ravanya for ₹ 7,000 credited to him as ₹ 5,000, now rectified)			
(iv)	...... Dr		4,000	
	To Reena			4,000
	(Being return inwards of ₹ 2,000 debited to Reena who returned these goods, now rectified)			
(v)	.... Dr		4,000	
	.... Dr		1,000	
	To			5,000
	(Being goods returned to Sita for ₹ 4,000 wrongly credited to Gita as ₹ 1,000, now rectified)			

32. Fill up the missing information in the following rectifying entries **Competency Based Que**

JOURNAL

Date	Particulars	LF	Amt (Dr)	Amt (Cr)
(i)	.... Dr		...	
	To			...
	(Being total of return outwards book ₹ 680 omitted to be posted in the ledger)			
(ii)	.... Dr		...	
	.... Dr		...	
	To			...
	(Being purchases for ₹ 3,000 wrongly entered in the sales book though correctly entered in the personal account)			
(iii)	.... Dr		...	
	To			...
	(Being sale of ₹ 2,200 wrongly credited to X's account as ₹ 2,000)			
(iv)	.... Dr		...	
	.... Dr		...	
	To			...
	(Being sale of furniture for ₹ 5,400 wrongly credited to sales account as ₹ 4,500)			
(v)	.... Dr		...	
	To			...
	(Being rent of proprietors residence ₹ 1,800 debited to rent account)			

Dr **Suspense Account** Cr

Particulars	Amt (₹)	Particulars	Amt (₹)
To Difference in Trial Balance	8,620	By	...
		By	...
To	...	By	...
To	...		
	...		...

Ans. Total of trial balance =₹ 10,200

Theoretical Questions

Short Answer Type Questions

1. Explain the errors of commission and give two examples with measures to rectify them. NCERT

Ans. When a transaction is recorded wrongly in the books of accounts, it is called error of commission.

It includes wrong posting of transactions, wrong totalling or wrong balancing of the accounts, wrong casting of the subsidiary books or wrong recording of amount in the books of original entry.

Example 1 Sales made to X of ₹ 10,000 recorded as ₹ 1,000.

In this case X's account has been debited with ₹ 1,000 instead of ₹ 10,000.

This will be rectified by passing the following entry

X	Dr	9,000	
To Sales A/c			9,000

Example 2 Cash received from Karim ₹ 60,000 posted to Nadim.

In this case cash received from Karim has been wrongly posted to Nadim. Hence Nadim's account has been wrongly credited.

In order to rectify the error, Nadim's account should be debited as it is wrongly credited, and Karim's account should be credited as it is not recorded.

Thus, the rectifying entry will be

Nadim	Dr	60,000	
To Karim			60,000

2. "Error of partial omission does not affect trial balance." Defend or refute with an example. Also, explain error of complete omission. Competency Based Que

Ans. The statement is refuted. Error of partial omission affects the trial balance. When a transaction is partially omitted from recording in the books, it is an error of partial omission.

e.g. Credit sales recorded in the sales book but not posted into debtor's account.

Error of Complete Omission

When a transaction is completely omitted from recording in the books of original record, it is an error of complete omission.

e.g. Credit sales to Shyam for ₹ 3,10,000, omitted to be recorded in books.

3. Explain errors of principle and give two examples with measures to rectify them. NCERT

Ans. When a transaction is recorded in the books of accounts violating the accounting principles, i.e. allocation between capital and revenue items, it is known as error of principle.

Example 1 Wages paid for construction of building are debited to wages account.

In this case, wages paid for the construction of building should be treated as a capital expenditure and accordingly should be debited to the building account. However, the wages account is wrongly debited.

In order to rectify this error, wages account will be credited as it is wrongly debited, and building account will be debited, as it is not recorded.

Thus, the rectifying entry will be

Building A/c	Dr
To Wages A/c	

Example 2 Sale of old machinery recorded as sales.

In this case, the sale of old machinery should not be recorded as sales and the machinery account should have been credited. In order to rectify this error, sales account will be debited, as it is wrongly credited and machinery will be credited, as it is not recorded in the books. Thus, the rectifying entry will be

Sales A/c	Dr
To Machinery A/c	

4. "Such errors are committed in such a way that the effect of one error is neutralised by the effect of other error." Explain the type of error discussed in the statement. Competency Based Que

Ans. The error discussed in the statement is compensating error. These errors involve two errors committed simultaneously. These are committed in such a way that the effect of one error on trial balance is neutralised by the effect of other error. These two errors involve same amount but in the opposite direction. These errors are difficult to detect but both the errors must be detected and rectified.

e.g. The totals of purchases book and sales book are both short by ₹ 1,000. This will reduce the sales and the purchases by ₹ 1,000 and the trial balance will not be affected. Similarly, if rent paid 1,000 has been posted to rent account as ₹ 1,100 and at the wages paid ₹ 3,100 have not been posted to wages account.

5. Name the errors, which do not affect the trial balance.

Ans. Following errors do not affect the agreement of trial balance

(i) Errors of complete omission
(ii) Error of recording
(iii) Errors of principle
(iv) Compensating errors
(v) Error of posting to the wrong account but on the correct side

6. What is a suspense account? Is it necessary that a suspense account will balance off after rectification of the errors detected by the accountant? If not, then what happens to the balance still remaining in suspense account? NCERT; Competency Based Que

Ans. Suspense account is an account which is opened on a temporary basis to balance the trial balance.

No, it is not necessary that a suspense account will balance after rectification of the errors detected by the accountant. Suspense account can remain unbalanced if all the errors are not detected. Balance remaining in the suspense account is transferred to the balance sheet on the assets side, if there is a debit balance, or the liabilities side if there is a credit balance.

Long Answer Type Questions

7. What are different types of errors that are usually committed in recording business transaction? NCERT

Ans. Keeping in view the nature of errors, errors can be classified into the following four categories

(i) **Errors of Commission**
When a transaction is recorded wrongly in the books of accounts, it is called error of commission. Errors of commission can be classified into the following

- **Error of Recording**
This error arises when any transaction is incorrectly recorded in the books of original entry. This error will not affect the trial balance.
- **Error of Casting**
This error arises when a mistake is committed in totalling. This error affects the trial balance.
- **Error of Carrying Forward**
It is an error which arises when a mistake is committed in carrying forward a total of one page on the next page. This error affects the trial balance.
- **Error of Posting**
When the information recorded in the books of original entry are incorrectly entered in the ledger, it is an error of posting.

(ii) **Errors of Omission**
This kind of error arises when a transaction is partially or completely omitted (left out) to be recorded in the books of accounts.
These can be of two types

- **Error of Complete Omission**
When a transaction is completely omitted from recording in the books of original record, it is an error of complete omission. This error does not affect the trial balance.
- **Error of Partial Omission**
When a transaction is partially omitted from recording in the books, it is an error of partial omission. This error affects the trial balance.

(iii) **Errors of Principle**
When a transaction is recorded in the books of accounts violating the accounting principles, i.e. Treating capital items as revenue or *vice-versa* it is known as errors of principle. These errors do not affect the trial balance.

(iv) **Compensating Errors**
When two or more errors are committed in such a way that the net effect of these errors on the debits and credits of accounts is nil, such errors are called compensating errors. These errors do not affect the tallying of trial balance.

8. What kinds of errors would cause difference in the trial balance? Also list examples that would not be revealed by a trial balance. NCERT; Competency Based Que

Ans. The errors that lead to the differences in the trial balance are termed as one-sided errors. These are those errors that affect only one account.

Below are given the errors that cause differences in the trial balance

(i) Wrong casting of any account, this is termed as the error of casting.
(ii) Wrong carrying forward of the balances from previous year's books or from one end of page to another. These types of errors are termed as the errors in carrying forward.
(iii) If entries are posted in the wrong side of accounts.
(iv) Posting of a wrong amount in account, this is termed as the error of posting.
(v) If entries are recorded partially, i.e. The entries are not recorded completely, then due to the error of partial omission, trial balance does not agree.

Examples of errors that would not be revealed in a trial balance is 'sales to Mr. X, omitted to be recorded in the sales day book.'

9. Give the stages of errors and what errors occur at those stages.

Ans. Error may occur at any of the following stages of the accounting process.

At the stage of recording transactions in the journal

(i) Error of principle (ii) Error of omission

(iii) Error of commission

At the stage of posting the entries in the ledger

(i) Error of omission

- Partial omission
- Complete omission

(ii) Error of commission

- Posting to wrong account
- Posting on the wrong side
- Posting of wrong amount

At the stage of the balancing the ledger accounts

(i) Wrong totalling of accounts

(ii) Wrong balancing of accounts

At the stage of preparing the trial balance

(i) Error of omission

(ii) Error of commission

- Recording in the wrong account
- Recording the wrong amount
- Recording in the wrong side

10. What are the steps taken by an accountant to locate the errors in trial balance? NCERT

Ans. The following steps will be useful in locating errors

Step 1 The two columns of the trial balance should be totalled again.

If in place of a number of accounts, only one account has been written in the trial balance, then the list of such accounts should be checked and totalled again.

Step 2 It should be seen that the cash and bank balances have been written in the trial balance.

Step 3 The exact difference in the trial balance should be determined.

The ledger should be properly checked as it is possible that a balance equal to the difference has been omitted from the trial balance. The difference should also be halved; it is possible that balance equal to half the difference has been written in the wrong column.

Step 4 The ledger accounts should be balanced again.

Step 5 The totalling of subsidiary books should be checked again, especially if the difference is ₹ 1, ₹ 100, etc.

Step 6 If the difference is very big, the balance in various accounts should be compared with the corresponding accounts in the previous period. If the figures differ materially, the respective accounts should be checked again.

Step 7 Postings of the amounts equal to the difference or half the difference should be checked.

It is possible that an amount has been omitted to be posted or has been posted on the wrong side.

Step 8 If there is still a difference in the trial balance, a complete checking will be necessary. The posting of all the entries including the opening entry should be checked. It may be better to begin with the nominal accounts.

Objective Questions

Multiple Choice Questions (MCQs)

1. Rectification entries are passed in ....

(a) journal proper

(b) ledger

(c) balance sheet (d) cash book

2. Commission paid for purchase of land is debited to commission account instead of land account. The error committed here is Competency Based Que

(a) error of casting

(b) error in carrying forward

(c) error of compensation

(d) error of principle

3. It is easy to detect .... than ....

(a) frauds, errors (b) mistakes, frauds

(c) errors, frauds (d) errors, mistakes

4. Errors occurred due to wrong posting are called as errors of ....

(a) principle (b) commission

(c) compensating (d) omission

5. Errors not affecting the agreement of trial balance are ....

(a) errors of principle

(b) errors of overcasting

(c) errors of undercasting (d) errors of partial omission

6. Which of the following is not a correct statement?

I. In order to balance the difference of balances in the trial balance, suspense account is opened.

II. When one-sided errors are detected after preparation of trial balance, suspense account is opened. Competency Based Que

Codes

(a) Both are incorrect (b) Only I is incorrect
(c) Only II is incorrect (d) Both are correct

7. Which of the following is not a correct statement?

(a) Trial balance is prepared from the balance of ledger accounts
(b) A trial balance can agree in spite of certain errors
(c) Rectification entries are passed in cash book
(d) There is no need to open a suspense account if the trial balance agrees

8. Which of the following is not an error of principle? NCERT

(a) Purchase of furniture debited to purchases account
(b) Repairs on the overhauling of second hand machinery purchased debited to repairs account
(c) Cash received from Manoj posted to Saroj
(d) Sale of old car credited to sales account

9. If transaction is totally omitted from the books, it is called ....

(a) error of recording (b) error of omission
(c) error of principle (d) error of commission

10. .... usually occurred due to lack of concentration or carelessness of the accountant.

(a) Error of principle (b) Error of omission
(c) Error of posting (d) Error of commission

11. Machinery purchased on credit for ₹ 4,00,000 from Neha Ltd. entered through purchase book, this error is called Competency Based Que

(a) error of principle (b) error of commission
(c) compensation error (d) error of casting

12. An item of ₹ 26,000 has been debited to a personal account as ₹ 62,000. It is an error of Competency Based Que

(a) commission (b) complete error
(c) omission (d) principle

13. Goods of ₹ 9,000 purchased on credit from Mr Amit are recorded in purchases book for ₹ 1,000. Which type of error is this? Competency Based Que

(a) Error of casting (b) Error of recording
(c) Error of carrying forward (d) Error of posting

14. Which of the following is a correct statement?

(a) Suspense account is temporary account which is opened to rectify errors that affect the trial balance
(b) Posting twice in an account, error of partial omission, error in carrying forward, etc. does not affect the agreement of trial balance
(c) Error due to partial omission, error of casting, error in carrying forward and error of principle are one-sided errors
(d) Suspense account is used for rectifying the errors which do not affect trial balance while errors which affect trial balance are not rectified with the help of suspense account

15. Suspense account is opened when ...... does not tally.

(a) balance sheet (b) trading account
(c) profit and loss (d) trial balance

16. Which of the following errors will not affect the trial balance?

(a) Wrong balancing of an account
(b) Posting an amount in the wrong account but on the correct side
(c) Wrong totalling of an account
(d) Carried forward wrong amount in a ledger account

17. Goods returned by Sameer were taken into stock, but no entry was passed in the books. Which of the following accounts should be debited, while rectifying this error? Competency Based Que

(a) Sameer's account
(b) Sales return account
(c) Return outward account
(d) Purchase return account

18. Which of the following errors will be rectified using suspense account? Competency Based Que

(a) Purchases returns book was undercast by ₹ 200
(b) Goods returned by Niharika was not recorded in the books
(c) Goods returned by Avika ₹ 1,000 was recorded in the sales returns book as ₹ 100
(d) A credit sale of goods to Raman was not entered in the sales book

19. If suspense account does not balance-off even after rectification of errors it implies that NCERT

(a) there are some one sided errors only in the books yet to be located.
(b) there are no more errors yet to be located
(c) there are some two-sided errors only yet to be located
(d) there may be both one-sided errors and two-sided errors yet to be located

20. Sold goods to Deepali for ₹ 2,700 but was recorded as ₹ 7,200. Deepali's account will be credited with .... to rectify the error. Competency Based Que

(a) ₹ 4,500 (b) ₹ 9,900
(c) ₹ 2,700 (d) ₹ 7,200

21. **Cash paid to Diya ₹ 11,500 was debited to Dishi's account by ₹ 11,000. What rectification journal entry will be passed?** **Competency Based Que**

(a) Diya Dr 11,500
  To Dishi 11,500
(b) Diya Dr 11,500
  To Suspense A/c 11,500
(c) Suspense A/c Dr 11,500
  To Dishi 11,000
  To Diya 500
(d) Diya Dr 11,500
  To Dishi 11,000
  To Suspense A/c 500

22. **An amount of ₹ 8,460 spent on extension of building was wrongly debited to repairs as ₹ 4,680. In rectification entry, suspense account will be credited by** **Competency Based Que**

(a) ₹ 3,600 (b) ₹ 3,780
(c) ₹ 8,460 (d) ₹ 13,320

23. **Goods sold to Amit for ₹ 640 was recorded in his account as ₹ 460. In rectification entry, his account will be debited with** **Competency Based Que**

(a) ₹ 180 (b) ₹ 460 (c) ₹ 640 (d) ₹ 1,100

24. **An amount of ₹ 18,000 received from Ashok was posted to the debit of Neena. In rectifying entry, ... account will be debited by ....**

(a) suspense, ₹ 36,000 (b) Neena, ₹ 36,000
(c) Ashok, ₹ 18,000 (d) suspense, ₹ 18,000

25. **Which of the following options is correct rectification entry for 'credit sales to Meena ₹ 10,000 were recorded as ₹ 1,000'?** **Competency Based Que**

(a) Meena Dr 10,000
  To Suspense A/c 10,000
(b) Meena Dr 9,000
  To Sales Alc 9,000
(c) Meena Dr 9,000
  To Suspense A/c 9,000
(d) Meena Dr 10,000
  To Sales A/c 10,000

26. **Credit purchase from Mohit ₹ 10,000 was posted to the debit of Rohit as ₹ 11,000. In this case, suspense account will be debited with** **Competency Based Que**

(a) ₹ 29,000 (b) ₹ 10,000
(c) ₹ 21,000 (d) ₹ 19,000

27. **Material ₹ 2,10,000 and wages ₹ 3,000 were used for construction of building. No adjustment entry was made in the books. Rectifying entry will be** **Competency Based Que**

(a) Wages A/c Dr 10,000
  To Building A/c 10,000
(b) Material A/c Dr 10,000
  Building A/c Dr 3,000
  To Cash A/c 13,000
(c) Building A/c Dr 13,000
  To Purchases A/c 10,000
  To Wages A/c 3,000
(d) None of the above

28. **Rashmi was paid cash ₹ 5,600 but Swati was debited by ₹ 4,000. In rectifying entry, suspense account will be** **Competency Based Que**

(a) debited ₹ 5,600
(b) credited ₹ 4,000
(c) credited ₹ 1,600
(d) debited ₹ 1,600

29. **Payment of ₹ 500 to Meeta and ₹ 600 to Seeta was made but Meeta was debited with ₹ 600 and Seeta was debited with ₹ 500. Meeta's account will be credited by**

(a) ₹ 1,100 (b) ₹ 500
(c) ₹ 600 (d) ₹ 100

30. **₹ 350 paid for carriage on sale of goods was credted to carriage inward account when posted from the cash book. Suspense account will be credited by ....**

(a) ₹ 700 (b) ₹ 350
(c) ₹ 200 (d) ₹ 850

31. **Credit purchase from Beena ₹ 9,000 were posted to the debit of his account as ₹ 6,000. Beena's account will be credited by** **Competency Based Que**

(a) ₹ 9,000 (b) ₹ 6,000
(c) ₹ 15,000 (d) ₹ 3,000

32. **Sale of ₹ 200 to Siya was recorded as ₹ 2,000 in the sales book. Sales account will be debited by** **Competency Based Que**

(a) ₹ 2,200 (b) ₹ 2,000
(c) ₹ 1,800 (d) ₹ 200

Assertion-Reason

Direction (Q. No. 33 to 42) *Read the following Assertion (A) and Reason (R) and choose the correct alternative from the following*

Alternatives

(a) Both Assertion (A) and Reason (R) are true and Reason (R) is the correct explanation of Assertion (A)
(b) Both Assertion (A) and Reason (R) are true, but Reason (R) is not the correct explanation of Assertion (A)
(c) Assertion (A) is true, but Reason (R) is false
(d) Assertion (A) is false, but Reason (R) is true

33. **Assertion** (A) On purchase of furniture, the amount spent on repairs should be debited to furniture account.

Reason (R) The amount spent on repairs is a capital expense.

34. **Assertion** (A) If the errors are detected after preparing trial balance, then all the errors are rectified through suspense account.

Reason (R) There may be principal errors, which can be rectified without opening a suspense account.

35. **Assertion** (A) When purchase of an asset is treated as an expense, it is known as error of principle.

Reason (R) Where the accounts being debited is principally incorrect, it is termed as error of principle.

36. **Assertion** (A) Trial balance agrees in case of compensating errors.

Reason (R) Compensating errors cancel out each other, when trial balance is prepared as the mistake pertains to the same amount being credited and later debited on account of two different mistakes.

37. **Assertion** (A) A trial balance is not a conclusive proof of the absolute accuracy of the accounts books.

Reason (R) Even if trial balance agrees, some errors may remain undetected and will not be disclosed by the trial balance.

38. **Assertion** (A) If an entry has not been recorded in the original or subsidiary book at all, then both the aspects of the transaction will be omitted and the trial balance will not be affected.

Reason (R) Errors of omission is when transactions are not recorded in books.

39. **Assertion** (A) When all mistakes are detected and rectified, suspense account will be closed.

Reason (R) Balance of suspense account will be transferred to profit and loss account.

40. **Assertion** (A) The credit balance of suspense account is to be shown on liabilities side of balance sheet.

Reason (R) If the debit total of trial balance is more, then the suspense account shows a credit balance.

41. **Assertion** (A) Machine purchased for ₹ 25,000 wrongly recorded in the purchase book is rectified by opening suspense account.

Reason (R) Two-sided errors cannot be rectified unless a suspense account is opened.

42. **Assertion** (A) When a transaction is recorded in contravention of accounting principles, like treating the purchase of an asset as an expense, it is an error of principle.

Reason (R) In this case, there is no effect on the trial balance since the amounts are placed on the correct side, though in a wrong account.

Two Statements Based MCQs

Direction (Q. No. 43 to 52) *Read the following statements carefully and choose the correct alternative*

Alternatives

(a) Both the statements are correct
(b) Both the statements are incorrect
(c) Statement I is correct and Statement II is incorrect
(d) Statement I is incorrect and Statement II is correct

43. **Statement I** The method of rectification of errors depends on the stage at which the errors are detected.

Statement II There are different stages when the mistakes are identified and then the rectification depends on the stage of identification of errors.

44. **Statement I** In case of error of complete omission, the trial balance does not tally.

Statement II In case of error of partial omission, the trial balance does not tally.

45. **Statement I** When amount is written on wrong side, it is known as an error of principle.

Statement II When amount is written on wrong side, it is known as an error of commission.

46. **Statement I** Rent paid to landlord of the proprietor's house, must be debited to 'drawings account'.

Statement II Rent paid to landlord of the proprietor's house, must be debited to 'rent account'.

47. **Statement I** When one-sided one sided errors are detected after preparation of trial balance, suspense account is opened.

Statement II In order to balance the difference of balances in the trial balance suspense account is opened.

48. **Statement I** All the errors can be rectified only through suspense account.

Statement II Trial balance can never agree inspite of certain errors.

49. **Statement I** If the total of subsidiary books are overcast or undercast, it will affect only one account.

Statement II If the total of purchases book is undercast by 1,000, it will affect only the purchases account because the total is transferred to purchases account.

50. **Statement I** Posting the correct amount on the wrong side of the correct account. This error affects two accounts.

Statement II Cash paid for repairs has been correctly posted to cash book. Thus, only repairs account needs to be rectified.

51. **Statement I** A payment for salaries in cash book posted twice in the salaries account will affect only one account.

Statement II A payment for salaries in cash book posted twice in the salaries account. Here only cash Account needs to be rectified.

52. **Statement I** All such expenses which are incurred from the purchase of an asset to the point when the asset is ready for use, are capital expenses.

Statement II Freight or carriage on bringing the machinery to the factory is a capital expenditure.

Matching

53. **Match the following**

Column I	Column II
A. Unintentional mistake	(i) Suspense account
B. Do not effect the trial balance	(ii) One- sided errors
C. Effect the trial balance	(iii) Errors
D. Imaginery account	(iv) Two-sided errors

Codes

	A	B	C	D		A	B	C	D
(a)	(i)	(ii)	(iii)	(iv)	(b)	(ii)	(iii)	(iv)	(i)
(c)	(iii)	(iv)	(ii)	(i)	(d)	(i)	(iii)	(ii)	(iv)

54. **Match the following**

Column I	Column II
A. Compensatory error	(i) Wrong treatment of capitals and revenue item
B. Error of partial ommisssion	(ii) Do not effect the trial balance
C. Error of complete ommission	(iii) Effect the trial balance
D. Error of principle	(iv) Sales account is credited instead of old machine sold

Codes

	A	B	C	D		A	B	C	D
(a)	(i)	(ii)	(iii)	(iv)	(b)	(ii)	(iii)	(iv)	(i)
(c)	(iv)	(iii)	(ii)	(i)	(d)	(i)	(iii)	(ii)	(iv)

55. **Match the following**

Column I	Column II
A. Compensatory error	(i) Purchase account is debited in case of furniture purchased
B. Error of principle	(ii) One error neutralise other
C. Error of complete ommission	(iii) Transactions completely ommitted in recording

Codes

	A	B	C		A	B	C
(a)	(i)	(ii)	(iii)	(b)	(ii)	(i)	(iii)
(c)	(iv)	(iii)	(ii)	(d)	(i)	(iii)	(ii)

56. **Match the following**

Column I	Column II
A. Goods purchased on credit are not recorded in purchases book	(i) Two-sided error
B. ₹ 5,000 spent on the repairs of building is debited to building account	(ii) One-sided error
C. Sales book is overcast by ₹ 1,000	(iii) Error of principle
D. Purchase of machinery for ₹ 1,000 has been entered in the purchases book	(iv) Error of complete ommission

Codes

	A	B	C	D		A	B	C	D
(a)	(i)	(ii)	(iii)	(iv)	(b)	(ii)	(iii)	(iv)	(i)
(c)	(iv)	(iii)	(ii)	(i)	(d)	(i)	(iv)	(ii)	(iii)

57. **Match the following**

Column I	Column II
A. Purchases return book overcast by ₹ 600	(i) Credit sales account with ₹ 600
B. Purchases book overcast by ₹ 600	(ii) Credit purchases account with ₹ 600
C. Sales book under cast by ₹ 600	(iii) Debit purchases return account with ₹ 600
D. Sales return book undercast by ₹ 600	(iv) Debit sales return account with ₹ 600

Codes

	A	B	C	D		A	B	C	D
(a)	(i)	(ii)	(iii)	(iv)	(b)	(ii)	(iii)	(iv)	(i)
(c)	(iv)	(iii)	(ii)	(i)	(d)	(iii)	(ii)	(i)	(iv)

Case Based MCQs

Direction *Read the following case study and answer the questions 58 and 59 on the basis of the same*

Meena Ltd. is a manufacturing firm that produces electronic gadgets. Recently, during the year end financial close, the accounting team discovered several errors in the company's records. The errors primarily relate to the recording of sales, purchases and expenses. Errors identified were

- A purchase of raw materials worth ₹ 15,000 from a supplier was completely omitted from the purchases journal.
- A sales invoice for ₹ 8,500 was recorded as ₹ 5,800 in the sales account.
- The salary ₹ 12,000 for the month was recorded in the salary account correctly but posted as ₹ 21,000 in cash account.

58. **How will the firm rectify the purchase of raw materials worth ₹ 15,000 from a supplier which was completely omitted from the purchases journal?**

(a) By debiting purchases account and crediting supplier account by ₹ 15,000

(b) By crediting purchases account and debiting supplier by account by ₹ 15,000

(c) By debiting purchases account and crediting suspense account by ₹ 15,000

(d) None of the above

59. How will the firm rectify the error, "salary ₹ 12,000 for the month recorded as ₹ 21,000 in salary account"?

(a) By debiting cash account and crediting salary account by ₹ 21,000

(b) By crediting salary account and debiting cash account by ₹ 21,000

(c) By debiting suspense account and crediting salary account by ₹ 9,000

(d) By debiting saalary account and crediting suspense account by ₹ 9,000

Direction *Read the following case study and answer the questions 60 and 61 on the basis of the same*

Aru Retailers is a chain of retail stores specialising in home appliances. During the annual audit, several errors were identified in the company's accounting records, which need to be rectified before finalising the financial statements.

Errors identified were

- The sales account for the year was overcasted by ₹ 20,000.
- Depreciation account for a delivery truck was undercasted by ₹ 2,500 due to an incorrect calculation.

60. How will the firm rectify overcast of the sales account for the year by ₹ 20,000?

(a) By debiting sales account and crediting supplier account by ₹ 20,000

(b) By crediting sales account and debiting supplier by account ₹ 20,000

(c) By debiting suspense account and crediting sales account by ₹ 20,000

(d) By debiting sales account and crediting suspense account by ₹ 20,000

61. How will the firm rectify the error of undercasting the depreciation account for a delivery truck by ₹ 2,500 due to an incorrect calculation?

(a) By debiting cash account and crediting truck account by ₹ 1,000

(b) By crediting truck account and debiting cash account by ₹ 1,000

(c) By debiting suspense account and crediting depreciation account by ₹ 1,000

(d) By debiting depreciation account and crediting suspense account by ₹ 1,000

Direction *Read the following case study and answer the questions 62 and 63 on the basis of the same*

Sandeepa, a commerce graduate, got job as an accountant at Diya Furniture Enterprises. She is very diligent girl who is working hard to earn her livelihood as she is sole bread earner of her family.

Simba, CEO of Diya Furniture Enterprises asked Sandeepa to make trial balance and then to prepare final accounts. She prepared all the subsidiary books and ledger accounts and then put in place final balances of them in format of trial balance.

Unexpectedly, trial balance total didn't agree. At the same time, Simba came to her cabin and Sandeepa shared her problem with him.

Simba being a benevolent person asked her not to worry and called his brother Cheena, who is a CA in PWC.

Cheena asked Sandeepa to mail him all accounting records. Then, she went home. Next day, Cheena mailed Sandeepa all errors that she has committed while making trial balance. Following errors were identified

- Purchases book undercast by ₹ 9,000.
- Goods withdrawn for personal use by Simba worth ₹ 20,000 were not recorded in books.
- A credit sale of ₹ 16,500 credited to the sales account and also to the sundry debtors account.
- A cheque for ₹ 9,000 received from Ashok was dishonoured and posted to the debit of sales return account.

Sandeepa quickly rectified above errors and prepared a corrected trial balance.

62. Which of the undermentioned options reflect correct rectification entry for 'a credit sale of ₹ 16,500 credited to the sales account and also to the sundry debtors account'?

(a) Sundry Debtors A/c	Dr	33,000	
To Suspense A/c			33,000
(b) Sundry Debtors A/c	Dr	16,500	
To Suspense A/c			16,500
(c) Suspense A/c	Dr	33,000	
To Sundry Debtors A/c			33,000
(d) Suspense A/c	Dr	16,500	
To Sundry Debtors A/c			16,500

63. Which of the following options reflect correct rectification entry for 'purchase book undercast by ₹ 9,000'?

(a) Purchases A/c	Dr	9,000	
To Suspense A/c			9,000
(b) Suspense A/c	Dr	9,000	
To Purchases A/c			9,000
(c) Purchases A/c	Dr	9,000	
To Creditors A/c			9,000
(d) Suspense A/c	Dr	9,000	
Purchase A/c	Dr	9,000	
To Creditors A/c			18,000

Answers

1. (a) journal proper
2. (d) error of principle
3. (c) errors, frauds
4. (b) commission
5. (a) errors of principle
6. (d) Both are correct
7. (c) Rectification entries are passed in cash book
8. (c) Cash received from Manoj posted to Saroj
9. (b) error of omission
10. (d) Error of commission
11. (a) error of principle
12. (a) commission
13. (b) Error of recording
14. (a) Suspense account is temporary account which is opened to rectify errors that affect the trial balance
15. (d) trial balance
16. (b) Posting an amount in the wrong account but on the correct side
17. (b) Sales return account
18. (a) Purchases returns book was undercast by ₹ 200
19. (a) there are some one-sided errors only in the books yet to be located
20. (a) ₹ 4,500 (7,200 – 2,700)
21. (d)

Diya's A/c	Dr	11,500	
To Dishi's A/c			11,000
To Suspense A/c			500

22. (b) ₹ 3,780 (8,460 – 4,680)
23. (a) ₹ 180 (640 – 460)
24. (a) Cash received from Ashok has wrongly been debited to Neena. Thus, Ashok's account will be credited by ₹ 18,000 and Neena's account will also be credited by ₹ 18,000 (to rectify the error made) and suspense account will be debited to balance by ₹ 36,000 (18,000 + 18,000).
25. (b)

Meena	Dr	9,000	
To Sales Alc			9,000

26. (c) ₹ 21,000 (10,000 + 11,000)
27. (c)

Building A/c	Dr	13,000	
To Purchases A/c			10,000
To Wages A/c			3,000

28. (c) credited ₹ 1,600
29. (d) Meeta's account was debited more by ₹ 100 (600 – 500). So, it will be credited by ₹ 100 to rectify the error.
30. (a) Carriage inward account was not debited by ₹ 350, instead carriage on sales account was credited by ₹ 350. Thus to rectify the error, carriage inward account will be debited with ₹ 350 and also carriage on sales account will also be debited with ₹ 350. Thus, suspense account will be credited with ₹ 700 (350 + 350).
31. (c) Beena's account was wrongly debited with ₹ 6,000 instead of crediting with ₹ 9,000. Thus, to rectify the error, Beena's account will be credited with ₹ 9,000 and with ₹ 6,000 for the wrong debit.
32. (c) Siya's account is wrongly credited with ₹ 1,800 more (2,000 – 200). Thus to rectify, her account will be debited with ₹ 1,800.
33. (a) Both Assertion (A) and Reason (R) are true and Reason (R) is the correct explanation of Assertion (A)
34. (d) Assertion (A) is false, but Reason (R) is true
35. (a) Both Assertion (A) and Reason (R) are true and Reason (R) is the correct explanation of Assertion (A)
36. (a) Both Assertion (A) and Reason (R) are true and Reason (R) is the correct explanation of Assertion (A)
37. (a) Both Assertion (A) and Reason (R) are true and Reason (R) is the correct explanation of Assertion (A)
38. (b) Both Assertion (A) and Reason (R) are true, but Reason (R) is not the correct explanation of Assertion (A)
39. (c) Balance of suspense account will be transferred to balance sheet.
40. (b) Both Assertion (A) and Reason (R) are true, but Reason (R) is not the correct explanation of Assertion (A)
41. (c) Two-sided errors can be rectified by recording a journal entry with both affected accounts.
42. (a) Both Assertion (A) and Reason (R) are true and Reason (R) is the correct explanation of Assertion (A)
43. (a) Both the statements are correct
44. (d) Statement I is incorrect and Statement II is correct
45. (d) Statement I is incorrect and Statement II is correct
46. (c) Statement I is correct and Statement II is incorrect
47. (a) Both the statements are correct
48. (b) Both the statements are incorrect
49. (a) Both the statements are correct
50. (d) Statement I is incorrect and Statement II is correct
51. (c) Statement I is correct and Statement II is incorrect
52. (a) Both the statements are correct
53. (c) (iii) (iv) (ii) (i)
54. (c) (iv) (iii) (ii) (i)
55. (b) (ii) (i) (iii)
56. (c) (iv) (iii) (ii) (i)
57. (d) (iii) (ii) (i) (iv)
58. (c) By debiting purchases account and crediting suspense account by ₹ 15,000
59. (c) By debiting suspense account and crediting salary account by ₹ 9,000 (21,000 – 12,000)
60. (d) By debiting sales account and crediting suspense account by ₹ 20,000
61. (d) By debiting depreciation account and crediting suspense account by ₹ 1,000
62. (a)

Sundry Debtors A/c	Dr	33,000	
To Suspense A/c			33,000

63. (a)

Purchases A/c	Dr	9,000	
To Suspense A/c			9,000

PART B
FINANCIAL ACCOUNTING-II

10

CHAPTER

The end product of financial accounting is the preparation of financial statements, i.e. trading and profit and loss account, balance sheet and notes to accounts.

Financial Statements-I

(Without Adjustment)

▼ **YOUR STUDY GOALS**

▼ **YOUR PRACTICE GOAL**

- Topicwise Solved Questions (23 Solved Questions)
- Numerical Questions [33 Questions (Unsolved)]
- Theoretical Questions [12 Questions (with answers)]
- Objective Questions (60 Qs ; MCQs, A-R, Statements, Matching, Case)

10.1 Introduction to Financial Statements

Financial statements are an important source of information for evaluating the performance and prospects of a firm. They show its financial position for the current year. They are also called **final accounts** because they are end of the period statements or the end product of the financial accounting process.

According to **John Myer**, the financial statements provide a summary of the accounts of a business enterprise, the balance sheet reflecting the assets, liabilities and capital as on a certain date and the income statement showing the results of operations during a certain period.

A complete set of financial statements includes

Trading and Profit and Loss Account (or income statement)	It shows the profitability of business operations during an accounting period.
Balance Sheet (or position statement)	It shows the financial position of an enterprise at a particular date.
Schedules and Notes to Accounts	Forms part of balance sheet and profit and loss account, containing detailed information about certain transactions and events.

Objectives of Financial Statements

- To present a true and fair view of the financial performance (profit/loss) of the business.
- To present a true and fair view of the financial position (assets/liabilities) of the business.

Importance of Financial Statements

- Trading account helps in knowing the gross profit earned or gross loss incurred by the business during the accounting period.
- The net profit earned or net loss incurred by the business during the accounting period can be known by preparing profit and loss account.
- Balance sheet provides complete information related to the assets, liabilities and capital of the business at a particular date.
- The profit calculated and various items of balance sheet can be compared with that of previous years. It helps to ascertain whether the business is progressing and whether the financial performance and position of the business has improved or not.
- It helps in the creation of various provisions and reserves to meet future uncertainties and to strengthen the financial position of the firm.

Smart Study Chart No. 1

Users of Accounting Information

Internal Users
- Owners
- Management
- Employees

External Users
- Investors
- Creditors
- Banks and Financial Institutions
- Government
- Other Parties

Preparation of Financial Statements

Financial statements are prepared from trial balance following the accounting concepts and conventions. Preparation of financial statements requires clear understanding of capital and revenue items.

Smart Study Chart No. 2

Capital and Revenue Items

Capital Expenditure
It is an expenditure which is incurred in acquiring or increasing the value of fixed assets or repayment of a long-term liability. It yields benefits which extend to more than one accounting period.
e.g. Purchase of fixed assets, material for construction of building, installation charges of plant and machinery, etc. The effect of capital expenditure is shown in the balance sheet.

Revenue Expenditure
These are the expenditures which are incurred for the day-to-day conduct of the business. Its benefits extend up to one accounting period.
e.g. Purchase of goods, whitewash of building, payment of wages and salaries, etc. Revenue expenditures are shown in trading and profit and loss account.

Capital Receipts
These are those receipts which are received once in a while. It is the amount received by the business on account of capital, loans or sale proceeds of fixed assets.
e.g. Sale of a fixed asset like old machinery, loan taken from a bank, etc. The effect of capital receipts is shown in the balance sheet.

Revenue Receipts
These are those receipts which arise in the normal course of business.
e.g. Interest on investment, sales made by the firm, etc. These receipts are shown in trading account and profit and loss account.

Deferred Revenue Expenditure
It is a revenue expenditure that is incurred during an accounting period but its benefit extends beyond that accounting period. Such expenditure is normally written-off over a period of 3 to 5 years.
e.g. Heavy advertising to launch a new product, etc. The part of deferred revenue expenditure written-off is shown in profit and loss account and the balance part is shown in the balance sheet as fictitious asset.

10.2 Trading Account

Trading account is prepared to find out the gross profit earned or gross loss incurred by the business enterprise as a result of its trading activities during an accounting period.

Features of Trading Account

- It is a nominal account.
- It is based on matching and accrual concept.
- It is prepared on the last day of an accounting year.
- It represents the first stage of final accounts of a trader.
- It contains items of revenue nature only.
- It shows either gross profit or gross loss.

Need and Importance of Trading Account

- It helps to know the gross profit or gross loss.
- It provides information about those expenses which are directly related with purchasing goods. This enables the management to control such expenses.
- It helps to compare closing stock of current year with that of previous years. In case closing stock shows an increasing trend, reasons must be found out, as more the stock, lesser the selling efficiency of the firm.
- The gross profit ratio is compared with the desired ratios or with the ratio of previous years to evaluate the performance. It enables the businessman to take effective measures to safeguard himself against future losses.

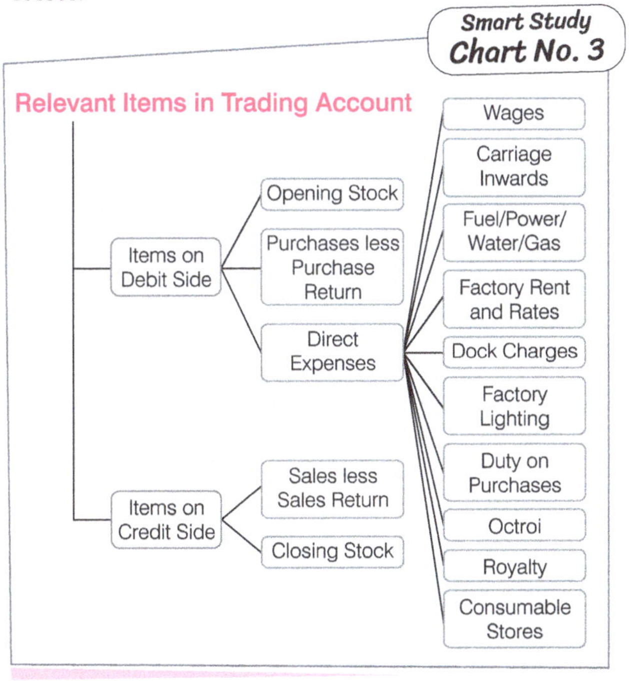

Closing Entries for Trading Account

1. Accounts of various expenses and losses are transferred to the **debit** of the trading account by passing the following entry

Trading A/c Dr
To Opening Stock A/c
To Purchases A/c
To Sales Returns A/c
To Wages A/c
To Carriage Inwards A/c
To Fuel and Gas A/c
To Power and Water A/c
To Carriage and Freight Inwards A/c
To Octroi Duty A/c
To Customs Duty A/c
To Manufacturing Expenses A/c
To Factory Rent and Lighting A/c
To Royalties A/c
To Packaging Expenses A/c
(Being all direct expenses and closing stock transferred to trading account)

2. All gains and incomes will be **credited** to trading account by passing the following entry

Sales A/c Dr
Purchase Returns A/c Dr
Closing Stock A/c Dr
To Trading A/c
(Being the transfer sales, purchase returns and closing stock to trading account)

3. Transfer of gross profit/gross loss

- In case of gross profit

Trading A/c Dr
To Profit and Loss A/c
(Being the gross profit transferred to profit and loss account)

- In case of gross loss

Profit and Loss A/c Dr
To Trading A/c
(Being the gross loss transferred to profit and loss account)

Format of a Trading Account

Trading Account
for the year ended ...

Dr | Cr

Particulars		**Amt (₹)**	**Particulars**		**Amt (₹)**
To Opening Stock		...	By Sales	...	
To Purchases	...		(–) Return Inwards	(...)	...
(–) Return Outwards	(...)	...	By Closing Stock		...
To Direct Expenses		...	By Abnormal Loss of Stock		...
Wages and Salaries			By Gross Loss Transferred to Profit and Loss A/c*		...
Freight Inwards		...			
Carriage Inwards		...			
Gas, Fuel and Power		...			
Freight and Cartage		...			
Manufacturing Expenses or Productive Expenses		...			
To Gross Profit Transferred to Profit and Loss A/c*		...			
		...			...

** Either gross profit or gross loss shall appear.*

10.3 Profit and Loss Account

Trading account takes into account only the direct expenses and direct incomes. There are many other expenses which are incurred by the business.

Profit and loss account considers all such expenses and incomes and gives the net profit made or net loss suffered by a business during a particular period.

It measures net income by matching revenues and expenses according to the accounting principles.

Importance of Profit and Loss Account

- It discloses information about the net profit earned or net loss suffered, during the year.
- If due to higher expenses or abnormal losses during the year, there is net loss, these can be highlighted and actions can be taken to control them.
- The results of the current year can be compared with the results of the previous year.
- The balance sheet can be prepared only after the ascertainment of net profit or net loss for the year.

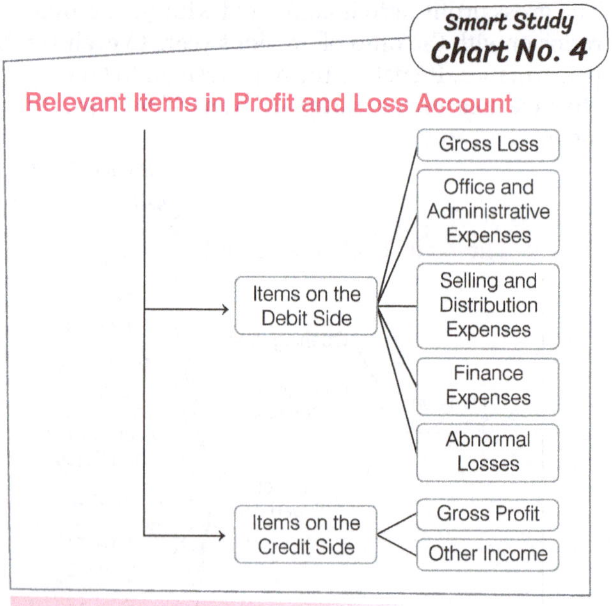

Closing Entries for Profit and Loss Account

1. Accounts of various expenses and losses are transferred to the **debit** of the profit and loss account by passing the following entry

Profit and Loss A/c	Dr
To Salaries A/c	
To Printing and Stationery A/c	
To Interest A/c	
To Rent, Rates and Taxes A/c	
To Postage A/c	
To Insurance A/c	
To Other Expenses and Losses A/c	
(Being the transfer of all expenses to profit and loss account)	

2. All gains and incomes will be **credited** to profit and loss account by passing the following entry

Rent Received A/c	Dr
Commission Received A/c	Dr
Discount Received A/c	Dr
To Profit and Loss A/c	
(Being the transfer of various nominal accounts showing credit balance to profit and loss account)	

3. Transfer of net profit/net loss
   - In case of net profit

Profit and Loss A/c	Dr
To Capital A/c	
(Being the transfer of net profit to capital accounts)	

   - In case of net loss

Capital A/c	Dr
To Profit and Loss A/c	
(Being the transfer of net loss to the capital account)	

Format of Profit and Loss Account

Profit and Loss Account

Dr for the year ended... Cr

Particulars	Amt (₹)	Particulars	Amt (₹)
To Gross Loss b/d (transferred from Trading A/c)	...	By Gross Profit b/d (transferred from Trading A/c)	...
Office Expenses		By Rent from Tenant	...
To Salaries	...	By Rent (Cr)	...
To Salaries and Wages	...	By Discount Received or Discount (Cr)	...
To Rent, Rates and Taxes	...	By Commission Received	...
To Printing and Stationery	...	By Interest on Investments	...
To Postage	...	By Dividend on Shares	...
To Lighting	...	By Bad Debts Recovered	...
To Insurance Premium	...	By Profit on Sale of Assets	...
To Telephone Charges	...	By Income from Other Sources	...
To Legal Charges	...	By Miscellaneous Income	...
To Audit Fees	...	By Net Loss (if any) transferred to Capital A/c	...
To Travelling Expenses	...		
To Establishment Expenses	...		
To Trade Expenses	...		
To General Expenses	...		
Selling and Distribution Expenses			
To Carriage Outwards or Carriage on Sales	...		
To Advertisement	...		
To Commission	...		
To Brokerage	...		
To Bad Debts	...		
To Export Duty	...		

Particulars	Amt (₹)	Particulars	Amt (₹)
To Packing Charges	...		
To Delivery Van Expenses	...		
To Stable Expenses	...		
Miscellaneous Expenses			
To Discount Allowed	...		
To Repairs	...		
To Depreciation	...		
To Interest (Dr)	...		
To Bank Charges	...		
To Entertainment Expenses	...		
To Conveyance Expenses	...		
To Donation and Charity	...		
To Loss on Sale of Assets	...		
To Net Profit transferred to Capital A/c	...		
	...		...

Net Profit and Operating Profit

Net Profit	Operating Profit
It is the profit earned through operating and non-operating activities of the business. Net profit is the excess of gross profit and incidental incomes over the indirect expenses and losses relating to the normal activities of the business. Net Profit = Gross Profit + Other Incomes – Indirect Expenses	It is the profit earned through normal operating activities of the business. It is calculated by deducting the operating expenses from the gross profit. It is also called 'Earning Before Interest and Tax (EBIT). Operating Profit = Gross Profit – Operating Expenses *or* = Net Profit – Non-operating Income + Non-operating Expenses

10.4 Balance Sheet

It is a statement prepared for showing the financial position of business summarising its assets and liabilities at a given date. It is prepared at the end of the accounting period after the trading and profit and loss account have been prepared. It is called a balance sheet because it is a statement of balances of ledger accounts which have not been closed even after the preparation of the trading and profit and loss account.

Characteristics of Balance Sheet

- It is only a statement and not an account.
- It is prepared at a particular point of time and not for a particular period.
- The information provided in it is true only at that particular point of time at which it is prepared.
- It is a summary of balances of those ledger accounts which have not been closed by transferring to trading and profit and loss account.
- It shows the nature and value of assets and liabilities at a given date.
- The total of assets must be equal to the liabilities side.

Importance or Need of a Balance Sheet

- It helps to ascertain the true financial position of the business at a particular point of time.
- It helps in knowing the nature and cost of various assets of the business.
- It provides information about various liabilities of the business.
- It provides information about the exact amount of capital at the end of year.
- It helps in finding out the solvency of the firm (i.e. if assets exceed external liabilities).
- It helps in preparing the opening entries in the beginning of next year since all the balances appearing in the balance sheet are carried forward to the next year.

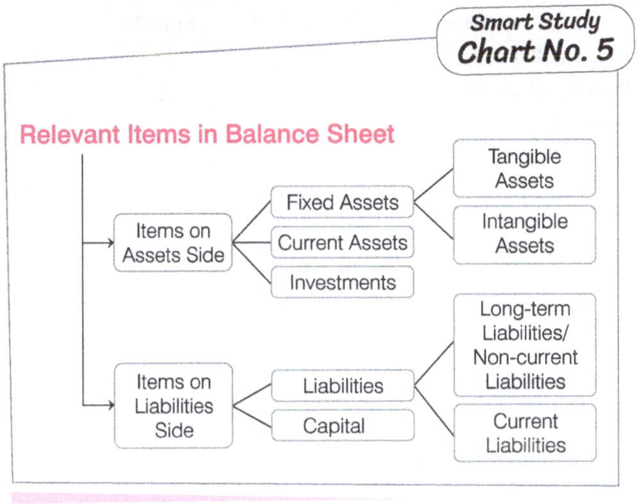

Contingent Liabilities

A contingent liability is one which is not an actual liability. It becomes actual on the happenings of some event which is uncertain. In other word, these may become liabilities in future. There is uncertainty about them. They will become due and payable only on the happening of a certain event, otherwise they will not become payable.

Since such a liability is not actual liability, it is not shown in the balance sheet. Usually, it is mentioned in the form of a footnote below the balance sheet. e.g. Liability in respect of a suit pending in a court of law would become an actual liability if the suit is decided against the firm.

Format of Balance Sheet

There is no prescribed format of balance sheet, for a proprietary and partnership firms. However, Schedule III Part I of the Companies Act, 2013 prescribes the format and the order in which the assets and liabilities of a company should be shown. That format is out of scope of the current syllabus. However, we will study the format of balance sheet derived on the basis of grouping and marshalling of assets and liabilities.

Grouping and Marshalling of Assets and Liabilities

The term grouping means putting together items of similar nature under a common heading, while marshalling refers to the arrangement of assets and liabilities in a particular order. In a balance sheet, the assets and liabilities are arranged either in the order of liquidity or permanence.

Format of Balance Sheet in Order of Liquidity

Balance Sheet
as at...

Liabilities		Amt (₹)	Assets	Amt (₹)
Current Liabilities			**Current Assets**	
Bank Overdraft		...	Cash in Hand	...
Bills Payable		...	Cash at Bank	...
Sundry Creditors		...	Bills Receivable	...
Outstanding Expenses		...	Short-term Investments	...
Unearned Income		...	Sundry Debtors/Book Debts	...
Non-current Liabilities			Closing Stock	...
Long-term Loans		...	Prepaid Expenses	...
Reserves		...	Accrued Income	...
Capital			**Long-term Investments**	...
Opening Balance	...		**Non-current Assets**	
(+) Net Profit	...		Furniture	...
(–) Drawings	(...)		Loose Tools	...
(–) Income Tax	(...)		Motor Vehicle	...
(–) Life Insurance Premium	(...)	...	Plant and Machinery	...

Liabilities	Amt (₹)	Assets	Amt (₹)
		Land and Buildings	...
		Patents and Trademarks	...
		Goodwill	...
	...		...

Format of Balance Sheet in Order of Permanence

Balance Sheet
as at...

Liabilities		Amt (₹)	Assets	Amt (₹)
Capital			**Non-current Assets**	
Opening Balance	...		Goodwill	...
(+) Net Profit	...		Patents and Trademarks	...
(−) Drawings	(...)		Land and Buildings	...
(−) Income Tax	(...)		Plant and Machinery	...
(−) Life Insurance Premium	(...)	...	Motor Vehicle	...
Reserve			Loose Tools	...
Non-current Liabilities			Furniture	...
Long-term Loans		...	**Long-term Investments**	...
Current Liabilities			**Current Assets**	
Unearned Income		...	Accrued Income	...
Outstanding Expenses		...	Prepaid Expenses	...
Sundry Creditors		...	Closing Stock	...
Bills Payable		...	Sundry Debtors	...
Bank Overdraft		...	Short-term Investments	...
			Bills Receivable	...
			Cash at Bank	...
			Cash in Hand	...
		...		...

Opening Journal Entry

The balances of various accounts in balance sheet are carried forward from one accounting period to another accounting period. In fact, the balance sheet of an accounting period becomes the opening trial balance of the next accounting period. Next year, an opening entry is made which opens the accounts contained in the balance sheet. While passing an opening entry, all assets account are debited and all liabilities accounts are credited.

Mind Map

1 Introduction to Financial Statements

The end product of financial accounting is the preparation of financial statements, i.e. trading account, profit and loss account, balance sheet and notes to accounts.

2 Capital and Revenue Items

- **Capital Expenditure** It is an expenditure which is inncurred in acquiring or increasing the value of fixed assets or repayment of long-term liability. It yields benefits for more than one accounting period.
- **Revenue Expenditure** These are the expenditures which are incurred for day-to-day conduct of the business. It extends benefits upto one accounting period.
- **Capital Receipts** These are the receipts which are received once in a while. It is the amount received by the business on account of capital, loans or sale proceeds of the fixed assets.
- **Revenue Receipts** These are those receipts which arise in the normal course of business.
- **Deferred Revenue Expenditure** It is a revenue expenditure that is incurred in an accounting period but its benefit extends beyond that accounting period. Such expenditure is normally written-off over 3 to 5 years.

FINANCIAL STATEMENTS-I (WITHOUT ADJUSTMENT)

3 Trading Account

This account is prepared to find out the gross profit earned or gross loss incurred by the business enterprise as a result of its trading activities during an accounting period.

Format

Trading Account
for the year ended...

Dr | | | Cr

Particulars	Amt (₹)	Particulars	Amt (₹)
To Opening Stock	—	By Sales —	
To Purchases —		(–) Return Inwards —	—
(–) Return Outwards —	—	By Closing Stock	—
To Direct Expenses	—	By Abnormal Loss of Stock	—
To Wages and Salaries	—	By Gross Loss*	—
To Gross Profit*	—		
Total	—		—

*Either gross profit or gross loss will appear

4 Profit and Loss Account

This account considers all such expenses and incomes (which are not covered by trading account) and gives the net profit made or net loss suffered by a business during a particular period.

Format

Profit and Loss Account
for the year ended...

Dr | | | Cr

Particulars	Amt (₹)	Particulars	Amt (₹)
To Gross Loss b/d	—	By Gross Profit b/d	—
(All relevant items to be appeared here)		(All relevant items to be appeared here)	
To Net Profit*	—	By Net Loss*	—
	—		—

*Either net profit or net loss will appear

Relevant Items in Profit and Loss Account
Items on Debit Side
- Gross loss
- Office and administrative expenses
- Selling and distribution expenses
- Finance expenses
- Abnormal losses

Items on Credit Side
- Gross profit
- Other income

5 Balance Sheet

It is a statement prepared for showing the financial position of business summarising its assets and liabilites at a given date. It is prepared at the end of accounting period.

Format

Balance Sheet
as at...

Liabilities	Amt (₹)	Assets	Amt (₹)
All relevant items to be appeared here	—	All relevant items to be appeared here	—
	—		—

Relevant Items in Balance Sheet
Items on Asset Side
- Fixed assets: Tangible and intangible assets
- Current assets
- Investments

Items on Liabilities Side
- Liabilities: Non-current liabilities and current liabilities
- Capital

Topicwise Solved Questions

Capital and Revenue Items

Solved Question 1 State with reasons whether the following are capital expenditure, revenue expenditure or deferred revenue expenditure

(i) An amount of ₹ 5,000 spent for the incorporation of a company to start business.

(ii) A sum of ₹ 5,000 spent on the overhauling of a second hand delivery van.

(iii) Repairs costing ₹ 600 carried out on a boiler.

(iv) ₹ 2,500 paid as legal expenses for raising a loan and ₹ 2,500 spent for issue of capital.

(v) ₹ 2,00,000 spent on advertisement and is estimated to benefit for next 4 years.

Sol. (i) It is a capital expenditure because it was paid to acquire a right to carry on business.

(ii) It is a capital expenditure as it was spent to make a capital asset fit for use.

(iii) It is a revenue expenditure because it does not add to the profit earning capacity of the business.

(iv) It is a capital expenditure because it is incurred for raising funds for the business.

(v) It is a deferred revenue expenditure because the money spent on advertisement will not be exhausted within the accounting period.

Solved Question 2 State with reasons whether the following are capital expenditure, revenue expenditure or deferred revenue expenditure

(i) ₹ 3,500 paid for repairs of a second hand van purchased recently before using it.

(ii) ₹ 6,700 spent on conversion of a hand-driven machine into a power-driven machine.

(iii) ₹ 5,400 spent on repairing various machines.

(iv) 300 paid as wages for the erection of a new machine.

(v) Advertisement of the shop in a local cinema theatre.

Sol. (i) It is a capital expenditure because the amount has been spent before the van is put to use.

(ii) It is a capital expenditure because the money was paid to add to the earning capacity of the machine.

(iii) It is a revenue expenditure because the sum was spent to maintain the existing machines.

(iv) It is a capital expenditure because the money was spent to make the asset ready for use.

(v) Deferred revenue expenditure as its benefit will be available beyond the current year.

Solved Question 3 State with reason whether the following receipts are capital or revenue in nature

(i) Received ₹ 10,00,000 grant from government for the construction of quarters for the staff.

(ii) Compensation received from improvement trust for compulsory shifting of business to another place.

(iii) ₹ 9,500 received from a customer whose account was previously written-off as bad.

(iv) Received ₹ 18,000 as interest on investment.

(v) Received ₹ 2,20,000 as subsidy from State Government.

Sol. (i) ₹ 10,00,000 grant from the government is capital receipt, since it is received for construction of quarters.

(ii) It is a revenue receipt since it will reduce the cost of shifting the business from one place to another.

(iii) It is a revenue receipt because it is received in the normal course of business.

(iv) It is a revenue receipt because it is received in the normal course of business.

(v) It is a revenue receipt because it is received in the normal course of business and reduces the cost of production of the goods produced by the firm.

Solved Question 4 State, giving reasons, which of the following would be treated as capital receipts and revenue receipts

(i) A grant of ₹ 3,00,000 received from the State Government for constructing a library for the welfare of employees.

(ii) A compensation of ₹ 90,000 received from a customer who cancelled a contract prematurely.

(iii) Sale of investments worth ₹ 2,00,000.

(iv) ₹ 70,000 received from a customer whose account was previously written-off as bad debts.

(v) A grant of ₹ 10,00,000 received from the issue of shares.

Sol. (i) It is a capital receipt because the amount is received for construction of an asset.

(ii) It is a revenue receipt because the amount received is in substitution of future income.

(iii) It is a capital receipt because it is received from sale of an asset.

(iv) It is a revenue receipt because the debt was written-off as a revenue loss.

(v) It is a capital receipt because capital is raised.

Trading Account

Solved Question 5 Prepare a trading account as on 31st March, 2023 from the following balances

Particulars	Amt (₹)	Particulars	Amt (₹)
Stock on 1st April, 2022	1,00,000	Factory Rent	1,10,000
Purchases	5,00,000	Office Rent	18,750
Sales	12,50,000	Purchases Return	30,000
Freight	16,250	Sales Return	50,000
Coal, Gas and Water	5,500	Wages	75,000
Carriage on Purchases	20,000	Factory Lighting	27,000
Carriage on Sales	25,000		

Closing stock as on 31st March, 2023 was ₹1,50,000.

Sol.

Trading Account
for the year ended 31st March, 2023

Dr Cr

Particulars		Amt (₹)	Particulars		Amt (₹)
To Opening Stock		1,00,000	By Sales	12,50,000	
To Purchases	5,00,000		(–) Sales Return	(50,000)	12,00,000
(–) Purchases Return	(30,000)	4,70,000	By Closing Stock		1,50,000
To Freight		16,250			
To Wages		75,000			
To Coal, Gas and Water		5,500			
To Factory Rent		1,10,000			
To Factory Lighting		27,000			
To Carriage on Purchases		20,000			
To Gross Profit transferred to Profit and Loss A/c		5,26,250			
		13,50,000			13,50,000

Solved Question 6 Prepare trading account for the year ended 31st March, 2023 from the following information

Adjusted purchases	₹ 27,50,000	Wages	₹ 35,000
Sales	₹ 31,25,000	Freight outwards	₹ 5,000
Freight inwards	₹ 6,000	Carriage outwards	₹ 7,500
Carriage inwards	₹ 9,000	Closing stock	₹ 2,50,000

Sol.

Trading Account
for the year ended 31st March, 2023

Dr Cr

Particulars	Amt (₹)	Particulars	Amt (₹)
To Adjusted Purchases	27,50,000	By Sales	31,25,000
To Freight Inwards	6,000		
To Carriage Inwards	9,000		
To Wages	35,000		
To Gross Profit transferred to Profit and Loss A/c	3,25,000		
	31,25,000		31,25,000

Important Problem Solving Points

- Adjusted Purchases = Net Purchases + Opening Stock – Closing Stock
- Closing stock has not been shown on the credit side of trading account since it has already been adjusted while computing the adjusted purchases.
- Freight outwards and carriage outwards are not entered in the trading account because they are indirect expenses and will appear in the profit and loss account.

Solved Question 7 **Prepare the trading account of the firm for the year ended 31st March, 2023 from the following information**

Opening Stock : Raw Material ₹ 1,20,000; Finished Goods ₹ 2,10,000

Closing Stock : Raw Material ₹ 1,05,000; Work-in-progress ₹ 30,000; Finished Goods ₹ 1,65,000

Purchases ₹ 5,40,000, Purchase Return ₹ 15,000, Sales ₹10,50,000, Sales Return ₹ 9,000, Wages ₹ 1,95,000, Factory Lighting ₹ 1,35,000, Carriage Inwards ₹ 30,000, Carriage Outwards ₹ 45,000.

Sol.

Trading Account
for the year ended 31st March, 2023

Dr | Cr

Particulars		Amt (₹)	Particulars		Amt (₹)
To Opening Stock			By Sales	10,50,000	
Raw Material	1,20,000		(−) Sales Return	(9,000)	10,41,000
Finished Goods	2,10,000	3,30,000	By Closing Stock		
To Purchases	5,40,000		Raw Material	1,05,000	
(−) Purchases Return	(15,000)	5,25,000	Work-in-progress	30,000	
To Wages		1,95,000	Finished Goods	1,65,000	3,00,000
To Factory Lighting		1,35,000			
To Carriage Inwards		30,000			
To Gross Profit c/d		1,26,000			
		13,41,000			13,41,000

Solved Question 8 **Calculate closing stock and cost of goods sold from the following information**

Opening stock	**₹ 37,500**	**Purchases return**	**₹ 6,750**
Sales	**₹ 1,20,000**	**Carriage inwards**	**₹ 7,500**
Sales return	**₹ 7,500**	**Gross profit**	**₹ 45,000**
Net purchases	**₹ 68,250**		

Sol. Net Sales = Sales − Sales Return = 1,20,000 − 7,500 = ₹ 1,12,500

Cost of Goods Sold = Net Sales − Gross Profit

= 1,12,500 − 45,000 = ₹ 67,500

Now, Closing Stock = Opening Stock + Net Purchases + Carriage Inwards − Cost of Goods Sold

= 37,500 + 68,250 + 7,500 − 67,500 = ₹ 45,750

Important Point to be Noted

Since net purchases are already mentioned implies that the amount is taken after the deduction of return outwards.

Solved Question 9 **Compute cost of goods sold for the year 2024 with the help of the following information**

Sales	**₹ 20,00,000**	**Purchases**	**₹ 15,00,000**
Wages	**₹ 1,00,000**	**Stock (1st April, 2023)**	**₹ 3,00,000**
Stock (31st March, 2024)	**₹ 4,00,000**	**Freight inwards**	**₹ 1,00,000**

Sol. Cost of Goods Sold = Opening Inventory + Direct Expenses + Net Purchases − Closing Inventory

= 3,00,000 + (1,00,000 + 1,00,000) + 15,00,000 − 4,00,000 = ₹ 16,00,000

Solved Question 10 **Net sales for the year ended 31st March, 2024 is ₹ 7,12,500. Find out gross profit and cost of goods sold when**

(i) Gross profit is 20% on sales. **(ii) Gross profit is 20% on cost.**

Sol. (i) Gross Profit $= 7{,}12{,}500 \times \frac{20}{100} =$ ₹ 1,42,500

Cost of Goods Sold = Sales − Gross Profit = 7,12,500 − 1,42,500 = ₹ 5,70,000

(ii) Gross profit is 20% on cost

Let cost be ₹ 100 ; Gross profit will be 20% of 100 = 20

Sales = Cost + Gross Profit = 100 + 20 = ₹ 120

Now, If sales are ₹ 120 and gross profit = ₹ 20

If sales ₹ 7,12,500, then gross profit $= 7{,}12{,}500 \times \frac{20}{120} =$ ₹ 1,18,750

Also, Cost of goods sold = 7,12,500 – 1,18,750 = ₹ 5,93,750

Solved Question 11 **Calculate gross profit from the following information**

Opening stock ₹ 5,000, Net purchases ₹ 9,100, Carriage inwards ₹ 1,000 and closing stock ₹ 6,100. Gross profit on sales is 40%.

Sol. Cost of Goods Sold = Opening Stock + Net Purchases + Carriage Inwards – Closing Stock

= 5,000 – 9,100 + 1,000 – 6,100 = ₹ 9,000

Now,

Let sales be ₹ 100 ; Gross profit will be ₹ 40

Cost of goods sold will be 100 – 40 = ₹ 60

If cost of goods sold is ₹ 60 then gross profit is ₹ 40

If cost of goods sold is ₹ 9,000 then gross profit will be $9{,}000 \times \frac{40}{60} =$ ₹ 6,000

Solved Question 12 **In a burglary at the godown of Bharat Goel on the night of 14th July, 2020 part of the stock was stolen. From the following particulars, find out the estimated value of loss of stock by theft.**

Stock on 1st April, 2020	**₹ 1,20,000**
Purchases from 1st April to 14th July, 2020	**₹ 8,20,000**
Sales from 1st April to 14th July, 2020	**₹ 12,00,000**
Stock remaining after burglary	**₹ 24,000**

The normal rate of gross profit for his business is 30% of selling price.

Sol.

Trading Account

Dr for the period 1st April to 14th July, 2020 Cr

Particulars	Amt (₹)	Particulars	Amt (₹)
To Opening Stock	1,20,000	By Sales	12,00,000
To Purchases	8,20,000	By Closing Stock (Balancing figure)	1,00,000
To Gross Profit @ 30% on Sales	3,60,000		
	13,00,000		13,00,000

	Amt (₹)
Stock on 14th July, 2020 as calculated above	1,00,000
(–) Stock remaining after burglary	(24,000)
Value of stock stolen	76,000

Solved Question 13 **From the following information, pass necessary closing entries in the journal proper of M/s Sam Traders**

Particulars	Amt (₹)
Opening Inventory	2,00,000
Purchases	13,44,000
Carriage Inwards	60,000
Wages	1,00,000
Sales	22,00,000
Return Inwards	2,00,000
Return Outwards	1,44,000
Closing Inventory	4,00,000

Sol.

JOURNAL

Date	Particulars		LF	Amt (Dr)	Amt (Cr)
	Return Outwards A/c	Dr		1,44,000	
	To Purchases A/c				1,44,000
	(Being the transfer of returns to purchases account)				
	Sales A/c	Dr		2,00,000	
	To Return Inward A/c				2,00,000
	(Being the transfer of returns to sales account)				
	Sales A/c	Dr		20,00,000	
	To Trading A/c				20,00,000
	(Being the transfer of balance of sales account to trading account)				
	Trading A/c	Dr		15,60,000	
	To Opening Inventory A/c				2,00,000
	To Purchases A/c (13,44,000 – 1,44,000)				12,00,000
	To Wages A/c				1,00,000
	To Carriage Inwards A/c				60,000
	(Being the transfer of balances of opening inventory, purchases and wages accounts)				
	Closing Inventory A/c	Dr		4,00,000	
	To Trading A/c				4,00,000
	(Being the incorporation of value of closing inventory)				
	Trading A/c	Dr		8,40,000	
	To Gross Profit				8,40,000
	(Being the amount of gross profit)				
	Gross Profit	Dr		8,40,000	
	To Profit and Loss A/c				8,40,000
	(Being the transfer of gross profit to profit and loss account)				

Profit and Loss Account

Solved Question 14 **From the following information, prepare profit and loss account of a trader for the year ended 31st March, 2024.**

Particulars	Amt (₹)
Gross Profit	4,00,000
Salaries and Wages	20,000
Commission Allowed	10,000
Commission Received	5,000
Interest Paid	7,000
Postage and Telephones	8,000
Discount Allowed	500
Discount Received	2,500
Interest Received	4,000
Carriage Outwards	2,500
Freight Outwards	1,500
Dividend Received	3,800
Rent Paid	6,000
Rent Received	16,000
Apprenticeship Fee Received	12,000
Brokerage Paid	3,000
General Expenses Paid	18,000
Miscellaneous Incomes	14,000
Depreciation on Furniture	12,000

Sol.

Profit and Loss Account
for the year ended 31st March, 2024

Dr | Cr

Particulars	Amt (₹)	Particulars	Amt (₹)
To Salaries and Wages	20,000	By Gross Profit b/d	4,00,000
To Commission Allowed	10,000	By Commission Received	5,000
To Interest Paid	7,000	By Interest Received	4,000
To Carriage Outwards	2,500	By Discount Received	2,500
To Freight Outwards	1,500	By Dividend Received	3,800
To Discount Allowed	500	By Rent Received	16,000
To Rent Paid	6,000	By Apprenticeship Fees Received	12,000
To Brokerage Paid	3,000	By Miscellaneous Incomes	14,000
To General Expenses	18,000		
To Depreciation on Machines	12,000		
To Postage and Telephones	8,000		
To Net Profit (transferred to Capital Account)	3,68,800		
	4,57,300		4,57,300

Solved Question 15 **From the following balances, prepare trading and profit and loss account of Nanda Ltd. for the year ending 31st March, 2024.**

Particulars	Amt (₹)
Stock as on 1st April, 2023	1,50,000
Sales	12,89,600
Sales Return	9,600
Purchases	12,43,000
Purchases Returns	3,000
Freight Inwards	4,000
Carriage Outwards	6,000
Salaries	30,000
Bank Interest	2,000
Printing and Stationery	7,000
Discount Received	900
Discount Allowed	1,600
Audit Fees	3,000
Insurance Premium	2,600
Trade Expenses	2,500

Stock on 31st March, 2024 was ₹ 1,70,000.

Sol.

Trading and Profit and Loss Account
for the year ended 31st March, 2024

Dr | Cr

Particulars		Amt (₹)	Particulars		Amt (₹)
To Opening Stock		1,50,000	By Sales	12,89,600	
To Purchases	12,43,000		(–) Sales Return	(9,600)	12,80,000
(–) Purchases Return	(3,000)	12,40,000	By Closing Stock		1,70,000
To Freight Inwards		4,000			
To Gross Profit (transferred to profit and loss account)		56,000			
		14,50,000			14,50,000
To Carriage Outwards		6,000	By Gross Profit (transferred from profit and loss account)		56,000
To Salaries		30,000	By Discount Received		900

Particulars	Amt (₹)	Particulars	Amt (₹)
To Bank Interest	2,000		
To Printing and Stationery	7,000		
To Insurance Premium	2,600		
To Discount Allowed	1,600		
To Audit Fees	3,000		
To Trade Expenses	2,500		
To Net Profit (transferred to capital account)	2,200		
	56,900		56,900

Solved Question 16 **Calculate operating profit from the following balances.**

Net profit ₹ 3,00,000, profit on sale of furniture ₹ 45,000, interest on loans ₹ 60,000, rent received ₹ 30,000, donation ₹ 6,000, salary 15,000.

Sol. Operating Profit = Net Profit − Non-operating Income + Non-operating Expenses
= 3,00,000 − 75,000 + 66,000 = ₹ 2,91,000

where, Non-operating Income = Profit on Sale of Furniture + Rent Received = 45,000 + 30,000 = ₹ 75,000
Non-operating Expenses = Donation + Interest on Loan = 6,000 + 60,000 = ₹ 66,000

Solved Question 17 **Calculate the gross profit, operating profit and net profit from the following balances extracted from the books of M/s Pawan and Sons.**

Opening stock ₹ 1,50,000, Net purchases ₹ 18,00,000, Net sales ₹ 33,00,000, Direct expenses ₹ 1,80,000, Administration expenses ₹ 1,35,000, Selling and distribution expenses ₹ 1,95,000, Loss due to fire ₹ 60,000, Closing stock ₹ 2,10,000.

Sol. Gross Profit = Sales − Cost of Good Sold
= 33,00,000 − 19,20,000 = ₹ 13,80,000

where, Cost of Goods Sold = Opening Stock + Purchases + Direct Expenses − Closing Stock
= 1,50,000 + 18,00,000 + 1,80,000 − 2,10,000 = ₹ 19,20,000

Net Profit = Gross Profit − Indirect Expenses = 13,80,000 − 3,90,000 = ₹ 9,90,000

where, Indirect Expenses = Administration Expenses + Selling and Distribution Expenses + Loss Due to Fire
= 1,35,000 + 1,95,000 + 60,000 = ₹ 3,90,000

Operating Profit = Net Profit + Non-operating Expenses (Loss due to fire)
= 9,90,000 + 60,000 = ₹ 10,50,000

Final Accounts

Solved Question 18 **Write up a balance sheet of Sangat for the year ended 31st March, 2024 with the following information supplied**

Capital account ₹ 36,000, Drawings ₹ 9,000, Cash ₹ 1,350, Debtors ₹ 40,100, Bills receivable ₹ 7,500, Bills payable ₹ 6,000, Fixtures and furniture ₹ 6,750, Bank ₹ 18,750, Loan from Shylock ₹ 9,000, Sundry creditors ₹ 64,500, Land and Building ₹ 21,000, Closing stock ₹ 18,200, Net profit ₹ 7,150.

Sol.

Balance Sheet
as at 31st March, 2024

Liabilities		Amt (₹)	Assets	Amt (₹)
Bills Payable		6,000	Cash	1,350
Loan from Shylock		9,000	Bills Receivable	7,500
Sundry Creditors		64,500	Bank	18,750
Sangat's Capital	36,000		Sundry Debtors	40,100
(+) Net Profit	7,150		Stock	18,200
(−) Drawings	(9,000)	34,150	Land and Building	21,000
			Fixtures and Furniture	6,750
		1,13,650		1,13,650

Solved Question 19 **Prepare trading and profit and loss account and a balance sheet from the following balances of Kanika Ltd. on 31st March, 2023**

Particulars	Amt (₹)	Particulars	Amt (₹)
Stock on 1st April, 2022	500	Commission (Cr)	200
Bills Receivable	2,250	Return Outwards	250
Purchases	19,500	Trade Expenses	100
Wages	1,400	Office Fixtures	500
Insurance	550	Cash in Hand	250
Sundry Debtors	15,000	Cash at Bank	2,375
Carriage Inwards	400	Rent and Taxes	550
Commission (Dr)	400	Carriage Outwards	725
Interest on Capital	350	Sales	25,000
Stationary	225	Bills Payable	1,500
Return Inwards	650	Creditors	9,825
Capital	8,950		

The closing stock was valued at ₹ 12,500.

Sol.

Trading and Profit and Loss Account
for the year ended 31st March, 2023

Dr | Cr

Particulars		Amt (₹)	Particulars		Amt (₹)
To Opening Stock		500	By Sales	25,000	
To Purchases	19,500		(–) Return Inwards	(650)	24,350
(–) Return Outwards	(250)	19,250	By Closing Stock		12,500
To Wages		1,400			
To Carriage Inwards		400			
To Gross Profit c/d		15,300			
		36,850			36,850
To Commission (Dr)		400	By Gross Profit b/d		15,300
To Interest on Capital		350	By Commission (Cr)		200
To Stationary		225			
To Insurance		550			
To Trade Expenses		100			
To Rent and Taxes		550			
To Carriage Outwards		725			
To Net Profit transferred to Capital A/c		12,600			
		15,500			15,500

Balance Sheet of Kanika
as at 31st March, 2023

Liabilities		Amt (₹)	Assets	Amt (₹)
Creditors		9,825	Cash in Hand	250
Bills Payable		1,500	Cash at Bank	2,375
Capital	8,950		Bill Receivable	2,250
(+) Net Profit	12,600	21,550	Office Fixtures	500
			Stock	12,500
			Sundry Debtors	15,000
		32,875		32,875

Solved Question 20 **Prepare trading and profit and loss account and a balance sheet from the following balances of Kartik Ltd. on 31st March, 2023**

Particulars	Amt (₹)	Particulars	Amt (₹)
Opening Stock	25,000	Sales	3,70,000
Purchases	1,06,000	Capital	5,00,000
Factory Rent	25,000	Loans	3,00,000
Wages and Salaries	60,000	Creditors	1,70,000
Productive Expenses	28,000	Bad Debts Recovered	25,000
Discount	10,000		
Carriage Inwards	18,000		
Bad Debts	5,000		
Depreciation	16,000		
Stationery	15,000		
Packing	10,000		
Bank Charges	6,000		
Establishment Expenses	18,000		
Interest on Loan	30,000		
Cash in Hand	90,000		
Bank	70,000		
Debtors	1,80,000		
Plant	2,00,000		
Buildings	4,00,000		
Trademarks	15,000		
Patents	25,000		
Charity	13,000		
	13,65,000		13,65,000

Closing stock was valued at ₹ 6,000.

Sol.

Trading Profit and Loss Account
for the year ending 31st March, 2023

Dr | Cr

Particulars	Amt (₹)	Particulars	Amt (₹)
To Opening Stock	25,000	By Sales	3,70,000
To Purchases	1,06,000	By Closing Stock	6,000
To Factory Rent	25,000		
To Wages and Salaries	60,000		
To Productive Expenses	28,000		
To Carriage Inwards	18,000		
To Gross Profit c/d	1,14,000		
	3,76,000		3,76,000
To Charity	13,000	By Gross Profit b/d	1,14,000
To Depreciation	16,000	By Bad Debts Recovered	25,000
To Bad Debts	5,000		
To Stationery	15,000		
To Bank Charges	6,000		
To Packing	10,000		
To Establishment Expenses	18,000		
To Interest on Loan	30,000		

Particulars	Amt (₹)	Particulars	Amt (₹)
To Discount	10,000		
To Net Profit (transferred to capital account)	16,000		
	1,39,000		1,39,000

Balance Sheet
as at 31st March, 2023

Liabilities		Amt (₹)	Assets	Amt (₹)
Creditors		1,70,000	Cash in Hand	90,000
Loans		3,00,000	Bank	70,000
Capital	5,00,000		Debtors	1,80,000
(+) Net Profit	16,000	5,16,000	Closing Stock	6,000
			Plant	2,00,000
			Buildings	4,00,000
			Patents	25,000
			Trademarks	15,000
		9,86,000		9,86,000

Point to Remember

If amount is given combinedly for 'wages and salaries', it is shown in trading account and if 'salaries and wages' is given, it is shown in profit and loss account.

Solved Question 21 **From the following balances of M/s Nilu Sarees as on 31st March, 2022, prepare trading and profit and loss account and balance sheet as on date.** **NCERT Modified**

Particulars	Amt (₹)	Particulars	Amt (₹)
Opening Stock	10,000	Sales	2,28,000
Purchases	78,000	Capital	70,000
Carriage Inwards	2,500	Interest	7,000
Salaries	30,000	Commission	8,000
Commission	10,000	Creditors	28,000
Wages	11,000	Bills Payable	2,370
Rent and Taxes	2,800		
Repair	5,000		
Telephone Expenses	1,400		
Legal Charges	1,500		
Sundry Expenses	2,500		
Cash in Hand	12,000		
Debtors	30,000		
Machinery	60,000		
Investments	90,000		
Drawings	18,000		

Closing stock as on 31st March, 2022 ₹ 22,000.

Sol.

Trading and Profit and Loss Account
for the year ended 31st March, 2022

Dr | | | Cr

Particulars	Amt (₹)	Particulars	Amt (₹)
To Opening Stock	10,000	By Sales	2,28,000
To Purchases	78,000	By Closing Stock	22,000
To Carriage Inwards	2,500		
To Wages	11,000		
To Gross Profit transferred to Profit and Loss A/c	1,48,500		
	2,50,000		2,50,000
To Salaries	30,000	By Gross Profit transferred from Trading A/c	1,48,500
To Commission	10,000	By Interest	7,000
To Rent and Taxes	2,800	By Commission	8,000
To Repair	5,000		
To Telephone Expenses	1,400		
To Legal Charges	1,500		
To Sundry Expenses	2,500		
To Net Profit transferred to Capital A/c	1,10,300		
	1,63,500		1,63,500

Balance Sheet
as at 31st March, 2022

Liabilities		Amt (₹)	Assets	Amt (₹)
Capital	70,000		Machinery	60,000
(+) Net Profit	1,10,300		Investment	90,000
	1,80,300		Debtors	30,000
(−) Drawings	(18,000)	1,62,300	Cash in Hand	12,000
Creditors		28,000	Closing Stock	22,000
Bills Payable		2,370		
Suspense Account		21,330		
		2,14,000		2,14,000

Note • Total of debit side of trial balance is ₹ 3,64,700 and total of credit side of trial balance is ₹ 3,43,370. The difference in credit side is ₹ 21,330.
- Difference in credit side of trial balance ₹ 21,330 will be treated as liabilities and posted in liabilities side of balance sheet.

Missing Information

Solved Question 22 **With the help of trial balance given below of Saahil Ltd. on 31st March, 2022, complete the missing information.**

Name of Account	Debit Balance (₹)	Credit Balance (₹)
Opening Stock	12,400	—
Sales	—	91,400
Purchases	38,100	—
Purchases Return	—	1,350
Sales Return	2,400	—
Carriage Inwards	1,750	—

Closing stock on 31st March, 2022 is valued at ₹ 15,250.

Trading Account
for the year ended 31st March, 2022

Dr | | Cr

Particulars		Amt (₹)	Particulars		Amt (₹)
To		...	By Sales	91,400	...
To Purchases	38,100	...	(–) Sales Returns	(...)	...
(–) Purchases Return	(...)	...	By		
To Carriage Inwards		...			
To Gross Profit c/d		...			
		...			...

Sol.

Trading Account
for the year ended 31st March, 2022

Dr | | Cr

Particulars		Amt (₹)	Particulars		Amt (₹)
To **Opening Stock**		**12,400**	By Sales	91,400	
To Purchases	38,100		(–) Sales Return	**(2,400)**	**89,000**
(–) Purchases Return	**(1,350)**	**36,750**	By **Closing Stock**		**15,250**
To Carriage Inwards		**1,750**			
To Gross Profit c/d		**53,350**			
		1,04,250			**1,04,250**

Solved Question 23 **With the help of the following balances, fill the missing information of the profit and loss account given below**

Particulars	Amt (₹)
Gross Profit	8,00,000
Salaries and Wages	40,000
Commission Received	10,000
Interest Received	14,000
Carriage Outwards	8,000
Freight Outwards	5,000
Discount Received	3,000
Dividend Received	7,600
Rent Paid	12,000
Rent Received	32,000
Apprenticeship Fee Received	24,000
Brokerage Paid	6,000
General Expenses Paid	36,000
Miscellaneous Income	28,000
Depreciation on Machines	24,000
Postage and Telephones	16,000

Profit and Loss Account
for the year ended 31st March, 2023

Dr | | Cr

Particulars	Amt (₹)	Particulars	Amt (₹)
To Salaries and Wages	40,000	By	...
To	...	By Commission Received	10,000
To Interest Paid	14,000	By Interest Received	8,000
To	...	By	...
To	...	By Dividend Received	7,600
To Discount Allowed	1,000	By Rent Received	32,000
To Rent Paid	12,000	By	...
To Brokerage Paid	6,000	By Miscellaneous Income	28,000

Particulars	Amt (₹)	Particulars	Amt (₹)
To General Expenses	36,000		
To	...		
To Postage and Telephones	16,000		
To ...... (transferred to capital account)	...		
	...		...

Sol.

Profit and Loss Account
for the year ended 31st March, 2023

Dr | Cr

Particulars	Amt (₹)	Particulars	Amt (₹)
To Salaries and Wages	40,000	By **Gross Profit**	**8,00,000**
To **Commission Allowed**	**20,000**	By Commission Received	10,000
To Interest Paid	14,000	By Interest Received	8,000
To **Carriage Outwards**	**5,000**	By **Discount Received**	**5,000**
To **Freight Outwards**	**3,000**	By Dividend Received	7,600
To Discount Allowed	1,000	By Rent Received	32,000
To Rent Paid	12,000	By **Apprenticeship Fees Received**	**24,000**
To Brokerage Paid	6,000	By Miscellaneous Incomes	28,000
To General Expenses	36,000		
To **Depreciation on Machines**	**24,000**		
To Postage and Telephones	16,000		
To **Net Profit** (transferred to capital account)	**7,37,600**		
	9,14,600		**9,14,600**

Numerical Questions

Capital and Revenue Items

1. **State whether the following are capital, revenue and deferred revenue expenditures** **Competency Based Que**

(i) ₹ 10,000 spent on dismantling, removing and reinstalling plant and machinery.

(ii) Legal expenses ₹ 20,000 on defending a suit for breach of contract to supply goods.

(iii) Premium ₹ 10,000 given for a lease.

(iv) ₹ 15,000 paid as commission on the issue of debentures.

(v) Replacement of old machine by a new one.

2. **State whether the following are capital, revenue and deferred expenditure stating reasons in each case** **Competency Based Que**

(i) ₹ 750 carriage paid on goods purchased.

(ii) Damages ₹ 1,500 paid on account of breach of contract to supply certain goods.

(iii) ₹ 20,000 spent on cleaning and levelling the land purchased for business.

(iv) ₹ 12,000 spent on petrol for delivery van.

(v) Advertising expenses ₹ 26,000 incurred for launching a new product in the market.

3. **State with reason whether the following receipts are capital or revenue in nature** **Competency Based Que**

(i) Investments which were purchased in 2020 for ₹ 12,00,000 sold in 2024 for ₹ 15,00,000.

(ii) For the welfare of employees, a recreation centre was constructed at a cost of ₹ 14,00,000, ₹ 8,00,000 was received from the State Government as grant for its construction.

(iii) Received ₹ 4,00,000 from the issue of shares.

(iv) ₹ 9,00,000 is contributed by a partner as capital.

(v) ₹ 12,000 received from sale of old machine.

4. **State with reason whether the following receipts are capital or revenue in nature** **Competency Based Que**

(i) Received ₹ 15,000 as interest on investment.

(ii) Received ₹ 1,20,000 as subsidy from State Government.

(iii) ₹ 22,000 received from sale of an old machine.

(iv) Fees of ₹ 3,500 received from apprentices.

(v) A compensation of ₹ 2,75,000 received from Improvement Trust for compulsory removal of the factory.

Trading Account

5. **From the following information of Rahul for the year ended 31st March, 2024. Prepare trading account**

Particulars	Amt (₹)
Purchases	30,00,000
Sales	36,00,000
Return Inwards	24,000
Return Outwards	30,000
Carriage on Purchases	36,000
Wages	60,000
Power Expenses	48,000
Stock on 1st April, 2023	72,000
Stock on 31st March, 2024	90,000

Ans. Gross profit transferred to profit and loss account =₹ 4,80,000

6. **From the following information, prepare trading account for the year ended 31st March, 2024**

Particulars	Amt (₹)	Particulars	Amt (₹)
Opening Stock	1,60,000	Sales	20,00,000
Purchases	8,00,000	Return Outwards	48,000
Return Inwards	80,000	Carriage on Purchases	32,000
Freight Inwards	26,000	Factory Rent	48,000
Wages and Salaries	1,20,000	Office Rent	30,000
Coal, Gas and Water	8,800	Factory Lighting	43,200
Carriage on Sales	40,000	Manufacturing Expenses	1,28,000

Closing stock is valued at ₹ 1,20,000.

Ans. Gross profit transferred to profit and loss account = ₹ 7,22,000

7. **From the following balances of accounts for the year ended 31st March, 2024, prepare trading account** **Competency Based Que**

Particulars	Amt (₹)
Opening Stock -Raw Material	20,000
-Finished Goods	10,000
Purchases	3,12,000
Sales	5,20,000
Freight	18,000
Coal	22,000
Wages	10,000
Gas and Water	11,000
Factory Lighting	5,000
Sales Return	20,000
Purchases Return	8,000
Carriage on Sales	15,000

Particulars	Amt (₹)
Carriage Inwards	10,000
Office Rent	14,000
Factory Rent	15,000
Dock Charges	16,000
Import Duty	4,000
Packaging Expenses	2,000
Closing Stock - Raw Material	26,000
- Finished Goods	15,000

Ans. Gross profit transferred to profit and loss account =₹ 89,000

8. **Prepare trading account for the year ended 31st March, 2024 for a trader from the following information**

Sales ₹ 16,06,000; Purchases (Adjusted with closing stock) ₹ 13,84,000; Wages ₹ 60,000; Sales return ₹ 6,000; Purchases return ₹ 4,000; Opening stock ₹ 36,000; Closing stock ₹ 16,000.

Ans. Gross profit transferred to profit and loss account = ₹ 1,24,000

9. **From the following information, prepare the trading account for the year ended 31st March, 2023.**

Competency Based Que

Adjusted purchases ₹ 30,00,000; Sales ₹ 42,80,000; Return inwards ₹ 80,000; Freight and packing ₹ 30,000; Packing expenses on sales ₹ 40,000; Depreciation ₹ 72,000; Factory expenses ₹ 1,20,000; Closing stock ₹ 2,40,000.

Ans. Gross profit transferred to profit and loss account =₹ 10,50,000

10. Purchases during the year are ₹ 14,00,000; Opening stock ₹ 9,00,000; Return outwards ₹ 1,10,000; Direct expenses ₹ 1,30,000 ; Closing stock ₹ 10,00,000 and Sales ₹ 20,00,000.

What is the gross profit?

Ans. Gross profit =₹ 5,50,000

11. **Find out the value of closing stock from the following information.**

Opening stock ₹ 55,000; Purchases during the year ₹ 3,20,000; Freight and carriage on purchases ₹ 10,000; Sales ₹ 4,20,000; Goods are sold at a profit of 20% on cost.

Ans. Closing stock =₹ 35,000

12. If total purchases during the year are ₹ 16,00,000; Return outwards ₹ 40,000; Direct expenses ₹ 1,20,000 and 2/3rd of the goods are sold for ₹ 12,20,000.

Calculate gross profit.

Ans. Gross profit =₹ 1,00,000

13. **From the following balances extracted from the books of M/s Ahuja and Nanda. Calculate the amount of**

NCERT

(i) Cost of goods available for sale
(ii) Cost of goods sold during the year
(iii) Gross profit

Opening stock ₹ 25,000 ; Credit purchases ₹ 7,50,000
Cash purchases ₹ 3,00,000 ; Credit sales ₹ 12,00,000
Cash sales ₹ 4,00,000 ; Wages ₹ 1,00,000
Salaries ₹ 1,40,000 ; Closing stock ₹ 30,000
Sales return ₹ 50,000 ; Purchases return ₹ 10,000

Ans. (i) ₹ 11,65,000 (ii) ₹ 11,35,000 (iii) ₹ 4,15,000

14. **In a burglary at the godown of Seth Brothers' on the night 27th September, 2023, part of the stock was stolen. From the following particulars, find out the estimated value of loss of stock by theft.**

Competency Based Que

Stock on 1st April, 2023 ₹ 80,000

Purchase from 1st April to 27th September, 2023 ₹ 6,40,000

Sales from 1st April to 27th September, 2023 ₹ 9,00,000

Stock remaining after burglary ₹ 42,000

The normal rate of gross profit for his business is 30% of the selling price.

Ans. Value of stock stolen = Closing stock on 27th September, 2023 – Stock remaining after burglary
= (90,000 – 42,000)
= ₹ 48,000

15. **Net sales during the year 2023 is ₹ 4,25,000. Find out gross profit and cost of good sold, if**

(i) gross profit is 25% on sales.
(ii) gross profit is 25% on cost.

Ans. (i) Gross profit = ₹ 1,06,250
Cost of goods sold =₹ 3,18,750
(ii) Gross profit = ₹ 85,000
Cost of goods sold = ₹ 3,40,000

16. **Pass the necessary journal entries on the basis of the following trading account.**

Trading Account
Dr for the year ended 31st March, 2024 Cr

Particulars	Amt (₹)	Particulars	Amt (₹)
To Opening Stock	7,00,000	By Net Sales	25,00,000
To Net Purchases	10,00,000	By Closing Stock	5,00,000
To Wages and Salaries	2,00,000		
To Freight Inwards	80,000		
To Other Direct Expenses	1,20,000		
To Gross Profit transferred to Profit and Loss A/c	9,00,000		
	30,00,000		30,00,000

Profit and Loss Account

17. From the following information, prepare a profit and loss account for the year ending 31st March, 2017 **NCERT**

Particulars	Amt (₹)
Gross Profit	60,000
Rent	5,000
Salary	15,000
Commission Paid	7,000
Interest Paid on Loan	5,000
Advertising	4,000
Discount Received	3,000
Printing and Stationery	2,000
Legal Charges	5,000
Bad Debts	1,000
Depreciation	2,000
Interest Received	4,000
Loss by Fire	3,000

Ans. Net profit = ₹ 18,000

18. From the following balances of the books of M/s Neerav & Co., prepare a profit and loss account **Competency Based Que**

Particulars	Amt (₹)	Particulars	Amt (₹)
Gross Profit	10,50,000	Salaries and Wages	48,000
Discount Received	68,000	Discount Allowed	12,000
Interest Paid	20,000	Interest Received	8,000
Com. Paid to Salesman	56,000	Commission Received	28,000
Fire Insurance Paid	24,000	Freight Outwards	60,000
Printing and Stationery	30,000	Rent Received	50,000
Rent Paid	56,000	Entertainment Expenses	32,000
Postage and Telegrams	22,000	Sales Promotion Exp.	17,000
Bad Debts	13,000	Audit Fees	38,000
Depreciation on Machines	20,000	Miscellaneous Income	51,600
Carriage Outwards	16,400	Repairs & Maintenance	13,600
Travelling Expenses	26,000	Water and Electricity for Office	12,000
Packing Expenses	42,000		
Bank Charges	7,600	Telephone Expenses	24,000
Loss by Fire	14,000	Gain on Sale of a Machine	2,400
Loss on Sale Furniture	16,000	Income from Investments	46,000
Dividend Rec. on Shares	24,000	Loss by Theft	4,000
Advertising and Publicity Expenses	36,000	Legal Expenses	45,000

Ans. Net profit = ₹ 6,24,400

19. From the following balances of the books of M/s Neerav & Co., prepare a trading and profit and loss account

Particulars	Amt (₹)	Particulars	Amt (₹)
Opening Stock	1,250	Plant and Machinery	6,230
Sales	11,800	Return Outwards	1,380
Depreciation	667	Cash in Hand	895
Commission (Cr)	211	Salaries	750
Insurance	380	Debtors	1,905
Carriage Inwards	300	Discount (Dr)	328
Furniture	670	Bills Receivable	2,730
Printing Charges	481	Wages	1,589
Carriage Outwards	200	Return Inwards	1,659
Capital	9,228	Bank Overdraft	4,000
Creditors	1,780	Purchases	8,679
Bills Payable	541	Cash in Hand	47
Bad Debts	180		

The value of stock on 31st March,2024 was ₹ 3,700.

Ans. Gross profit = ₹ 3,403 ; Net profit = ₹ 628

20. From the following balances of M/s Naveen and Sons for the year ended 31st March, 2023, calculate the amount of gross profit, operating profit and net profit.

Opening stock ₹ 2,00,000, Net sales ₹ 44,00,000, Net purchases ₹ 24,00,000, Direct expenses ₹ 24,00,000, Administration expenses ₹ 1,80,000, Selling and distribution expenses ₹ 2,60,000, Loss due to fire ₹ 80,000, Closing stock ₹ 2,80,000.

Ans. Gross profit =18,40,000; Operating profit = 14,00,000 Net profit = 13,20,000

21. From the following balances, calculate gross profit, operating profit and net profit. **Competency Based Que**

Particulars	Amt (₹)	Particulars	Amt (₹)
Opening Stock	1,00,000	Commission Paid	1,200
Purchases	9,50,000	Commission Received	3,000
Sales	12,50,000	Travelling Expenses	2,400
Purchases Return	35,000	Office Expenses	1,750
Sales Return	50,000	Interest on Long-term Loans	11,000
Wages & Salaries	40,000	Dividend on Investments	1,400
Advertising	6,000	Printing and Stationery	1,800
Salaries	89,000	Loss on Sale of Machinery	17,500
Rent and Taxes	31,000	Carriage Outwards	700
Lighting	7,500	Loss by Theft	12,550
		Gain on Sale of Building	25,000

Closing stock was valued at ₹ 1,25,000

Ans. Gross profit = ₹ 2,70,000; Operating profit = ₹ 1,31,650 Net profit = ₹ 1,17,000

22. The following balances were extracted from the books of Garima Aggarwal on 31st March, 2023

Particulars	Amt (₹)	Particulars	Amt (₹)
Capital	98,000	Loan	31,520
Drawings	8,000	Sales	2,61,440
General Expenses	10,000	Purchases	1,88,000
Building	44,000	Motor Car	8,000

Particulars	Amt (₹)	Particulars	Amt (₹)
Machinery	37,360	Reserve Fund	3,600
Stock	64,800	Commission (Credit)	5,280
Power	8,960	Car Expenses	7,200
Taxes and Insurance	5,260	Bills Payable	15,400
Wages	28,800	Cash	320
Debtors	25,120	Bank Overdraft	13,200
Creditors	10,000	Charity	420
Bad Debts	2,200		

Stock on 31st March, 2023 was valued at ₹ 23,500. Prepare the trading and profit and loss accounts for the year ended 31st March, 2023.

Ans. Gross profit = ₹ 64,880; Net profit = ₹ 45,080

23. Prepare trading and profit and loss accounts of Ramya for the year ended 31st March, 2023 from the following balances Competency Based Que

Name of Account	Debit Balance (₹)	Credit Balance (₹)
Capital	—	3,00,000
Stock on 1st April, 2022	60,000	—
Cash at Bank	20,000	—
Cash in Hand	10,000	—
Machinery	2,00,000	—
Furniture	26,000	—
Purchases	4,00,000	—
Wages	1,00,000	—
Carriage Inwards	66,000	—
Salaries	1,40,000	—
Discount Allowed	8,000	—
Discount Received	—	10,000
Advertising	1,00,000	—
Office Expenses	80,000	—
Sales	—	10,00,000
Sundry Debtors	1,80,000	—
Sundry Creditors	—	80,000
	13,90,000	13,90,000

Value of closing stock as on 31st March, 2023 was ₹ 1,00,000.

Ans. Gross profit = ₹ 4,74,000; Net proft = ₹ 1,56,000

24. The following are the balances as at 31st December, 2023 taken from the books of Shanaya Lal

Particulars	Amt (₹)	Particulars	Amt (₹)
Sales	2,92,000	Postage and Telegram	620
Purchases	2,68,300	Miscellaneous Expenses	900
Return Inwards	1,300	Bad Debts	400
Return Outwards	2,200	Debtors	22,000
Stock	17,600	Office Furniture	1,500
Carriage Inwards	2,400	Machinery	59,000
Rent, Rates and Taxes	2,200	Drawings	1,910
Discount Allowed	3,750	Capital	72,500
Printing	720	Loan	5,000
Insurance	500	Creditors	12,800
Travelling Expenses	1,400		

The stock on 31st December, 2023 was ₹ 25,000. Prepare the trading account, profit and loss account for the year ended 31st December, 2023.

Ans. Gross profit = ₹ 29,600; Net profit = ₹ 19,110

Final Accounts

25. Prepare final accounts from the following information of M/s Rajesh as on 31st March, 2024

Particulars	Amt (₹)	Particulars	Amt (₹)
Debit Balances		Bank Deposit	80,000
Stock (1st April, 2023)	10,000	Drawings	18,000
Salaries	40,000	Machinery	70,000
Purchases	80,000	**Credit Balances**	
Return Inwards	2,000	Sales	2,30,000
Carriage	1,500	Capital	80,000
Wages	12,000	Interest	10,000
Repairs	6,000	Commission	5,000
Trade Expenses	4,000	Return Outwards	2,000
Rent and Taxes	3,200	Creditors	21,700
Cash in Hand	28,000	Bills Payable	20,000
Debtors	14,000		

Closing stock as on 31st March, 2024 was ₹ 2,30,000.

Ans. Gross profit = ₹ 1,56,500; Net profit = ₹ 1,18,300
Balance sheet = ₹ 2,22,000

26. Prepare final accounts from the following information of M/s Rajesh as on 31st March, 2023.

Dr **Trial Balance** Cr

Particulars	Debit Balance (₹)	Particulars	Credit Balance (₹)
Purchases	2,30,000	Capital	3,00,000
Opening Stock (1st April, 2022)	10,000	Sales	3,10,000
		Sundry Creditors	20,000
Salaries and Wages	30,000	Return Outwards	2,000
Returns Inwards	1,000	Loan from Bank	36,500
Carriage Inwards	2,000	Discount Received	2,500
Carriage Outwards	1,500	Commission	4,500
Furniture and Fittings	30,000		
Sundry Debtors	45,000		
Dock Charges	15,000		
Electric Power	10,000		
Fuel, Gas and Water	5,000		
Bad Debts	1,500		
Advertisement	6,000		
Cash in Hand	30,000		
Cash at Bank	80,200		
Motor Cars	80,000		
Repairs	1,800		
Interest on Loan	4,500		
Household Expenses (Drawings)	24,000		
Business Premises	60,000		
Insurance	8,000		
	6,75,500		6,75,500

Closing as on 31st March, 2023 was ₹ 2,31,000.

Ans. Gross profit = ₹ 70,000; Net profit = ₹ 23,700
Balance sheet = ₹ 3,56,200

27. **From the following trial balance of Mr. A Lal, prepare trading and profit and loss account and balance sheet as on 31st March, 2017** **NCERT**

Name of Account	Debit Balance (₹)	Credit Balance (₹)
Stock as on 1st April, 2016	16,000	—
Purchases and Sales	67,600	1,12,000
Return Inwards and Outwards	4,600	3,200
Carriage Inwards	1,400	—
General Expenses	2,400	—
Bad Debts	600	—
Discount Received	—	1,400
Bank Overdraft	—	10,000
Interest on Bank Overdraft	600	—
Commission Received	—	1,800
Insurance and Taxes	4,000	—
Scooter Expenses	200	—
Salaries	8,800	—
Cash in Hand	4,000	—
Scooter	8,000	—
Furniture	5,200	—
Building	65,000	—
Debtors and Creditors	6,000	16,000
Capital	—	50,000

Closing stock ₹ 15,000.

Ans. Gross profit = ₹ 40,600; Net profit = ₹ 27,200
Balance sheet = ₹ 1,03,200

28. **The trial balance of Manya shows the following balances as at 31st December, 2023**

Particulars	Debit Balance (₹)	Particulars	Credit Balance (₹)
Purchases	1,20,000	Capital	2,26,150
Sales Return	3,000	Sales	2,54,000
Plant and Machinery	1,80,000	Purchases Return	2,550
Opening Stock	80,000	Discount Received	1,600
Discount Allowed	700	Sundry Creditors	40,000
Bank Charges	200	Bills Payable	10,000
Sundry Debtors	90,000		
Salaries	14,000		
Wages	20,000		
Freight : In	2,000		
Freight : Out	2,400		
Rent, Rates and Taxes	4,000		
Advertisements	4,000		
Cash at Bank	14,000		
	2,67,150		2,67,150

Closing stock was valued at ₹ 70,000. Prepare final accounts for the year ending 31st December, 2023.

Ans. Gross profit = ₹ 10,1550; Net profit = ₹ 77,850
Balance sheet = ₹ 3,54,000

29. **The trial balance of a trader shows the following balances as on 31st March, 2023.**
Prepare trading and profit and loss account for the year ended 31st March, 2023 and balance sheet as on the date.

Particulars	Debit Balance (₹)	Particulars	Credit Balance (₹)
Purchases	80,000	Bills Payable	5,000
Cash at Bank	57,000	Sundry Creditors	20,000
Advertisement	2,000	Discount Received	800
Rent, Rates and Taxes	2,000	Purchases Return	1,200
Freight : In	1,000	Sales	1,47,000
Freight : Out	1,200	Capital	1,63,150
Sales Return	1,500		
Plant and Machinery	90,000		
Opening Stock	40,000		
Discount Allowed	350		
Bank Charges	100		
Sundry Debtors	45,000		
Salaries and Wages	7,000		
Wages	10,000		
	3,37,150		3,37,150

Closing stock was valued at ₹ 2,25,000.

Ans. Gross profit = ₹ 2,40,700; Net profit = ₹ 228,850
Balance sheet = ₹ 22,17,000

30. **Prepare a trading and profit and loss account for the year ended on 31st March, 2023 and the balance sheet as at that date. The stock on 31st March, 2023 was ₹ 2,16,000.** **Competency Based Que**

Particulars	Amt (₹)	Particulars	Amt (₹)
Drawings	6,000	Commissions (Cr)	1,200
Interest on X Loans	1,500	Loan from X	10,000
Sundry Debtors	25,400	Capital	40,000
Commissions	1,800	Creditors for Rent	500
Bills Receivables	3,500	Sundry Creditors	5,600
Scooter Repairs	850	Bills Payable	3,000
Scooter	6,600	Sales	1,98,650
Land and Building	20,000	Return Outwards	2,600
Discount Allowed	640	Discount Received	750
Bad Debts	600		
Stock (1st April, 2022)	10,000		
Purchases	1,58,000		
Wages	2,000		
Return Inwards	3,520		
Carriage on Purchase	2,360		
Carriage on Sales	710		
Office Salaries	4,800		
Duty on Imported Goods	2,700		
Rent and Taxes	2,400		
Bank Balance	7,820		
	2,62,300		2,62,300

Ans. Gross profit = ₹ 2,38,670; Net profit = ₹ 2,27,320
Balance sheet = ₹ 2,80,420

31. From the following balances of Dynaya jain, prepare final accounts as on 31st March, 2024

Competency Based Que

Particulars	Amt (₹)	Particulars	Amt (₹)
Life Insurance Premium Paid	6,000	Interest on Loan	2,400
Capital	1,37,450	Freight Inwards	1,100
Leasehold Land	60,000	Freight Outwards	3,000
Motor Vehicles	50,000	Rent (Fac. 1/3, Off. 2/3)	7,500
Cash in Hand	1,300	Legal Expenses	800
Fixed Deposit with Punjab & Sindh Bank	10,000	Miscellaneous Receipts	500
Salaries	9,600	Sundry Debtors	30,000
Discount (Cr)	2,100	Sundry Creditors	14,400
Trademarks	5,000	Donation Received	600
Loose Tools	7,200	Bad Debts	4,750
Return Outwards	2,800	Bad Debts Recovered	4,000
Return Inwards	6,600	Sales Tax Collected	3,900
Trade Expenses	1,200	Bank Charges	2,800
Unproductive Expenses	5,800	Loan on Mortgages	20,000
Productive Expenses	27,000	Interest Received	2,400
Sales	2,30,000	Bills Receivables	5,800
Purchases	1,46,800		
Stock (1st April, 2023)	23,500		

Value of closing stock was ₹ 35,000 on 31st March, 2024.

Ans. Gross profit = ₹ 60,300; Net profit = ₹ 34,550
Balance sheet = ₹ 2,04,300

32. From the following balance of the ledger of Shri Gajendra Singh, prepare trading and profit and loss account and balance sheet

Particulars	Debit (₹)	Credit (₹)
Stock on 1st April, 2021	90,000	—
Stock on 31st March, 2022	1,38,600	—
Purchases and Sales	6,90,000	10,37,400
Returns	37,500	45,600
Commission on Purchases	3,600	—
Freight, Octroi and Carriage	78,000	—
Wages and Salary	32,400	—
Fire Insurance Premium	2,460	—
Business Premises	1,20,000	—
Sundry Debtors	78,300	—
Sundry Creditors		80,100
Goodwill	24,000	—
Patents	25,200	—
Coal, Gas and Power	22,800	—
Printing and Stationery	6,300	—
Postage and Telegram	2,130	—
Travelling Expenses	12,750	—
Drawings	21,600	—
Depreciation	3,000	—
General Expenses	25,050	—
Capital	—	2,69,280
Investments	24,000	
Interest on Investments	—	2,400
Custom Duty on Imported Goods	13,500	—
Cash in Hand	7,710	—
Banker's Account	—	15,600
Commission	13,800	13,200
Loan on Mortgage	—	90,000
Interest on Loan	9,000	—
Bills Payable	—	6,840
Bills Receivable	13,620	—
Income Tax	9,000	—
Horses and Carts	60,900	—
Discount on Purchases	—	4,800
	15,65,220	15,65,220

Ans. Gross profit = ₹ 1,15,200 ; Net profit = ₹ 61,110
Balance sheet = ₹ 4,92,330

Hint (i) Closing stock appears inside the balance sheet, therefore it will be shown only on the assets side.
(ii) Commission on purchase will be shown on the debit side of trading account.
(iii) 'Investments' will be shown on assets side and 'interest on investments' on the credit side of profit and loss account.
(iv) 'Loan on mortagage' will be shown on the liabilities side and 'interest on loan' on the debit side of profit and loss account.
(v) Income tax will be treated as drawings.

Missing Information

33. Complete the following balance sheet with the help of the given trial balance

Competency Based Que

Trial Balance

Particulars	Amt (₹)	Particulars	Amt (₹)
Debit Balance			
Cash in Hand	11,600	Rent and Rates	1,600
Cash at Bank	14,000	Salaries	21,000
Debtors	15,000	Drawings	6,000
Stock (1st April, 2023)	10,000	Purchases	15,000
Buildings	80,000	Office Expense	3,000
Wages	8,000	**Credit Balance**	
Bills Receivables	12,000	Sales	60,000
Interest	500	Capital	1,00,000
Bad Debts	1,500	Creditors	20,000
Repairs	800	Bill Payables	23,000
Depreciation	1,200	Interest Received	4,200
Furniture	6,000		

Stock as on 31st March, 2024 was valued at ₹ 12,000.

Balance Sheet
as at 31st March, 2024

Particulars		Amt (₹)	Particulars	Amt (₹)
......		...	......	...
Bills Payables		23,000	Cash in Bank	14,000
Capital Account			......	...
......	...		Debtors	15,000
(+) Net Profit	13,600		......	...
	1,13,600		Furniture	6,000
(–)	...	...	Buildings	80,000
		...		...

Theoretical Questions

Short Answer Type Questions

1. What are financial statements and what information is provided by them? NCERT

Ans. Financial statements are the final/end products of an accounting process, which begins with the identification of accounting information and recording it in the books of primary entry. Financial statements are prepared following the accounting concepts and conventions. These statements are prepared at the end of accounting period and give information about the financial position and performance of an enterprise.

Trading and profit and loss account present a true and fair view of the financial performance of the business in the form of profit and loss during the year. Balance sheet presents a true and fair view of the financial position of the business.

2. What are the objectives of preparing financial statements? NCERT

Ans. The basic objectives of preparing financial statements are

(i) To present a true and fair view of the working of the business.
(ii) To help to judge the effectiveness of the management.
(iii) To provide sufficient and reliable information to various persons interested in financial statements.
(iv) To facilitate efficient allocation of resources.
(v) To disclose various accounting policies.
(vi) To provide information about the cash flows.
(vii) To provide information about the earning capacity.
(viii) To provide financial data on assets (economic resources) and liabilities (obligations) of an enterprise.

3. "Ramaiya & Bros. purchased goodwill from Sohail & Bros." Identify the type of expenditure in given statement. Also, give four examples of the type identified. Competency Based Que

Ans. The expenditure incurred for purchase of goodwill is a capital expenditure.

The examples of capital expenditure are

(i) Payment of wages for construction or extension of building.
(ii) Payment of wages for addition of rooms or erection of sheds in the building.
(iii) Carriage, cartage and freight paid on acquiring assets such as plant and machinery, furniture, etc.
(iv) Repairs of assets, purchased second hand.

4. What are the features of a trading account?

Ans. Features of trading account are

(i) Trading account is the first stage in the preparation of final accounts.
(ii) It provides information about gross profit and gross loss.
(iii) Balance of trading account is transferred to profit and loss account.
(iv) Trading account is a nominal account.
(v) Trading account relates to a particular accounting period and is prepared at the end of that period.
(vi) Trading account records only revenue items and not capital items.

5. What are the features of profit and loss account?

Ans. Features of profit and loss account are

(i) It is prepared after preparing the trading account.
(ii) While preparing profit and loss account, accrual basis of accounting is followed.
(iii) Profit and loss account relates to a particular accounting period and is prepared at the end of that period.
(iv) It provides information about the net profit or net loss.

6. Discuss the need of preparing a balance sheet.

NCERT; Competency Based Que

Ans. The need of preparing a balance sheet is stated in the following points

(i) It helps to ascertain the true financial position of the business at a particular point of time.

(ii) It helps in ascertaining the nature and cost of various assets of the business such as the amount of closing stock, amount owing from debtors, amount of fictitious assets, etc.

(iii) It helps in determining the nature and amount of various liabilities of the business.

(iv) It gives information about the exact amount of capital at the end of the year and the addition or deduction made into it in the current year.

(v) It helps in finding out whether the firm is solvent or not. The firm is solvent if the assets exceed the external liabilities. It would be insolvent if opposite is the case.

7. Distinguish between capital receipts and revenue receipts.

Ans. The differences between capital receipts and revenue receipts are

Basis	Capital Receipts	Revenue Receipts
Meaning	The amount received in form of capital introduced, loans taken and sale proceeds of the fixed assets is known as capital receipts.	The amount received mainly by selling of goods and serivces is known as revenue receipts.
Nature	Capital receipts are capital in nature.	Revenue receipts are revenue (i.e. day-to-day activities) in nature.
Treatment	Capital receipts are shown on the liabilities side of balance sheet.	Revenue receipts are shown at the credit of either trading account or profit and loss account.
Examples	Sale of fixed assets, capital contribution and loans taken, etc. are some example of capital receipts.	Profit on sale of assets, sale of goods, interest received on loans (advanced), royalty, etc. are some examples of revenue receipts.

8. Give four points of difference between trading and profit and loss account.

Ans. The differences between trading account and profit and loss account

Basis	Trading Account	Profit and Loss Account
Relation	Trading account is a part of profit and loss account.	Profit and loss account is the main account.
Purpose	The gross profit or gross loss is ascertained from the trading account.	The profit and loss account is prepared to ascertain the net profit or net loss of the business.
Transfer of Balance	The balance of the trading account is transferred to the profit and loss account.	The balance of the profit and loss account is transferred to the capital account of the proprietor.
Items	Items shown in the trading account are purchases, sales, stock, direct expenses, etc.	Items like indirect expenses related to sales, distribution, administration, finance, etc. are shown in the profit and loss account.

9. State any four differences between trial balance and balance sheet.

Ans. Differences between trial balance and balance sheet are as follows

Basis	Trial Balance	Balance Sheet
Objective	It is prepared to check the arithmetical accuracy of recording.	It is prepared to reveal the financial position of the business.
Necessity	It is not necessary to prepare trial balance.	It is necessary to prepare balance sheet to complete accounting process.
Listed Accounts	In trial balance, all types of accounts are listed.	In balance sheet, balance of real and personal accounts are listed.
Net Profit or Loss	It does not contain information about net profit/loss of the business.	Details of capital account in balance sheet provides information about net profit or loss.

10. Differentiate between tangible and intangible assets.

Ans. Following are the differences between tangible and intangible assets

Basis	Tangible Assets	Intangible Sheet
Meaning	Tangible assets are those assets which can be seen and touched.	Intangible assets are those assets which can not be seen and touched.
Examples	Examples of tangible assets are land, building, machinery, etc.	Examples of intangible assets are goodwill, patent, trademark, etc.
Security	These assets can be used as security for loan purpose.	These assets can't be used as security for loan purpose due to non-physical existence.
Depreciation	These assets are depreciated by time. Thus, depreciation is charged on fixed assets.	These assets are amortised.

Long Answer Type Questions

11. What is a balance sheet? What are its characteristics?

NCERT

Ans. The balance sheet is a statement prepared for showing the financial position of the business summarising its assets and liabilities at a given date. It is prepared at the end of the accounting period after the trading and profit and loss account have been prepared.

The assets reflect debit balances and liabilities (including capital) reflect credit balances.

It is called a balance sheet because it is a statement of balances of ledger accounts which have not been closed till the preparation of the trading and profit and loss account.

Features/Characteristics of balance sheet are as follows

(i) Balance sheet is prepared at a particular point of time and not for a particular period.
(ii) It is only a statement and not an account.
(iii) It is prepared after the preparation of trading and profit and loss account.
(iv) It shows the financial position of the business.
(v) It is a summary of balances of those ledger accounts which have not been closed by transferring to the trading and profit and loss account.
(vi) It shows the nature and value of assets.
(vii) It shows the nature and amount of liabilities.
(viii) The total of assets side must be equal to the liabilities side.

12. Distinguish between profit and loss account and balance sheet.

Ans. The differences between profit and loss account and balance sheet are

Basis	Profit and Loss Account	Balance Sheet
Types of Account	Only nominal accounts are entered in profit and loss account.	It records personal and real accounts.
Objective	The objective of preparing profit and loss account is to ascertain the net profit or loss of the business.	The purpose of preparing balance sheet is to understand the financial position of the firm.
Sides	The left hand side of the profit and loss account is the debit and the right hand side is credit.	It has liabilities at its left hand side and assets at right hand side.
Nature	Profit and loss account is an account. We use the word 'To' before accounts at the debit side and 'By' at the credit side.	Balance sheet is not an account, it is a statement. We do not use 'To' or 'By' in it.
Specific Date/Period	Profit and loss account shows the performance of the accounting period, generally a year.	Balance sheet shows the position of assets and liabilities on a particular date.
Types of Expenditure	Revenue expenditure are recorded in the profit and loss account.	Capital expenditure are entered at the assets side of the balance sheet.

Objective Questions

Multiple Choice Questions (MCQs)

1. The term financial statements comprises of
(a) profit and loss account (b) trading account
(c) balance sheet (d) All of these

2. What kind of expenses are shown in the trading account?
(a) Direct expenses (b) Indirect expenses
(c) Operating expenses (d) None of these

3. Final accounts are prepared to ascertain
(a) operating profit
(b) value of liabilities
(c) value of assets
(d) financial position and profit or loss

4. Gross profit or loss is transferred from
(a) trading account
(b) profit and loss account
(c) balance sheet
(d) None of the above

5. An account prepared to ascertain net profit or loss is
(a) trading account (b) profit and loss account
(c) balance sheet (d) None of these

6. Wages and salaries are recorded on the
(a) debit of trading account
(b) credit of trading account
(c) debit of profit and loss account
(d) credit of profit and loss account

7. Salaries and wages are recorded on the
(a) debit of trading account
(b) credit of trading account
(c) debit of profit and loss account
(d) credit of profit and loss account

8. Is is not an account but only a statement of assets and liabilities.
(a) Trading account
(b) Profit and loss account
(c) Balance sheet
(d) None of the above

9. **Carriage for ₹ 10,000 paid on purchase of a second hand machinery is treated as**
(a) revenue expenditure (b) capital expenditure
(c) revenue receipt (d) capital receipt

10. **Received ₹ 1,00,000 as subsidy from State Government is treated as**
(a) revenue expenditure (b) capital expenditure
(c) revenue receipt (d) capital receipt

11. **₹ 10,000 spent on repainting the factory building is treated as**
(a) revenue expenditure (b) capital expenditure
(c) revenue receipt (d) capital receipt

12. **Receipt of ₹ 20,00,000 grant from government for the construction of quarter for the staff is treated as**
(a) revenue expenditure (b) capital expenditure
(c) revenue receipt (d) capital receipt

13. **Carriage inward and wages are recorded on the .... side of the ....**
(a) debit, trading account (b) credit, trading account
(c) debit, profit and loss account
(d) credit, profit and loss account

14. **Choose the correct chronological order of ascertainment of the following profits from the profit and loss.** NCERT; Competency Based Que
(a) Operating Profit, Net Profit, Gross Profit
(b) Operating Profit, Gross Profit, Net Profit
(c) Gross Profit, Operating Profit, Net Profit
(d) Gross Profit, Net Profit, Operating Profit

15. **Which of the following is correct?** NCERT; Competency Based Que
(a) Operating Profit = Operating Profit − Non-operating Expenses − Non-operating Incomes
(b) Operating Profit = Net Profit + Non-operating Expenses + Non-operating incomes
(c) Operating Profit = Net Profit + Non-operating Expenses − Non-operating Incomes
(d) Operating Profit = Net Profit − Non-operating Expenses + Non-operating Incomes

16. **Outstanding salaries is shown in balance sheet on**
(a) assets side (b) liabilities side
(c) Can be on both sides (d) None of these

17. **The excess of asets over liabilities represents the .... of the owner.**
(a) net profit (b) capital
(c) drawings (d) gross profit

18. **If the total of debit side of profit and loss account is greater than the total of credit side, the difference is ....**
(a) gross profit (b) net profit
(c) gross loss (d) net loss

19. **Under .... assumption, the expenditure is classified as revenue and capital expenditure.**
(a) consistency (b) money measurement
(c) going concern (d) prudence

20. **Which of the following statement(s) is/are correct?**
(a) Revenue expenditure gives benefit within the accounting period
(b) Revenue expenditure are recurring in nature
(c) Revenue expenses is treated is an expense of the current year
(d) Revenue expenditures are non-recurring in nature

21. **Which of the following is/are incorrect?** Competency Based Que
(a) Net Sales = Cash Sales + Credit Sales − Sales Return
(b) Net Purchases = Cash Purchases + Credit Purchases − Purchases Return
(c) Gross Profit = Net Sales + Cost of Goods Sold
(d) Cost of Goods Sold = Cost of Production − Closing Stock

22. **While calculating operating profit, the following are not taken into account.** NCERT
(a) Normal transactions
(b) Abnormal items
(c) Expenses of a purely financial nature
(d) Both (b) and (c)

23. **Opening stock ₹ 60,000, purchases ₹ 1,09,200, expenses on purchases ₹ 12,000, sales ₹ 1,80,000, expenses on sales ₹ 6,000, closing stock ₹ 73,200. Calculate the cost of goods sold.** Competency Based Que
(a) ₹ 96,000 (b) ₹ 1,28,000
(c) ₹ 1,08,000 (d) ₹ 1,54,000

24. **BHET Electronics has the following financial information for the year ending 31st December, 2024**
Opening inventory ₹ 10,000; Purchases ₹ 25,000; Closing Inventory ₹ 12,000; Sales revenue ₹ 50,000; Operating expenses ₹ 15,000. What is the gross profit for BHET Electronics? Competency Based Que
(a) ₹ 15,000 (b) ₹ 27,000
(c) ₹ 25,000 (d) ₹ 30,000

25. **Net sales during the year 2023 is ₹ 6,50,000. Gross profit is 25% on sales. Find out cost of goods sold.** Competency Based Que
(a) ₹ 4,90,000 (b) ₹ 4,87,500
(c) ₹ 1,42,500 (d) 0

26. **Calculate the gross profit and choose the correct option, if rate of gross profit is 25% on sales and cost of goods sold is ₹ 90,000.** Competency Based Que
(a) ₹ 30,000 (b) ₹ 18,000
(c) ₹ 22,500 (d) ₹ 15,000

27. **Calculate the value of closing stock from the following, if the rate of gross profit is 40% on sales.**
Opening stock ₹ 1,20,000 ; Purchases ₹ 9,30,000; Sales ₹ 15,60,000 Competency Based Que
(a) ₹ 5,10,000 (b) ₹ 2,66,000
(c) ₹ 1,14,000 (d) ₹ 3,27,000

28. **Rahul Ltd. reported the following for the year ending 31st December, 2024**
Opening stock ₹ 15,000; Purchases ₹ 40,000 ; Closing stock ₹ 20,000 ; Sales ₹ 70,000; Operating expenses ₹ 10,000. What is the net profit for Rahul Ltd.? Competency Based Que
(a) ₹ 20,000 (b) ₹ 30,000 (c) ₹ 25,000 (d) ₹ 15,000

29. **Sangharsh Ltd. reported the following information for the year ending 30th June, 2024**
Sales revenue ₹ 2,50,000 ; Cost of goods sold ₹ 1,50,000 ; Operating expenses ₹ 50,000; Depreciation ₹ 20,000. What is the operating profit for Gourmet Dine? Competency Based Que
(a) ₹ 80,000 (b) ₹ 70,000
(c) ₹ 90,000 (d) ₹ 60,000

30. **Fabric World Textile Mill has the following balances for the year ending 31st March, 2024**
Cash ₹ 25,000; Accounts receivable ₹ 10,000
Inventory ₹ 30,000 ; Current liabilities ₹ 20,000
Long-term liabilities ₹ 15,000
What is the capital of Fabric World Textile Mill? Competency Based Que
(a) ₹ 30,000 (b) ₹ 40,000
(c) ₹ 50,000 (d) ₹ 55,000

31. **Which of the following is correct entry to record closing stock of ₹ 1,12,000, its market value is ₹ 1,20,000 in the book?** Competency Based Que
(a) Debit Trading A/c by ₹ 1,12,000; Profit and Loss A/c by ₹ 8,000 and Credit Closing Stock by ₹ 1,20,000
(b) Debit Closing Stock by ₹ 1,20,000.and Credit Trading A/c by ₹ 1,12,000 and Profit and Loss A/c by ₹ 8,000
(c) Debit Closing Stock by ₹ 1,12,000 and Credit Trading A/c by ₹ 1,12,000
(d) Debit Closing Stock by ₹ 1,20,000.and Credit Trading A/c by ₹ 1,20,000

32. **Operating profit earned by Vaishali in 2023-24 was ₹ 17,00,000. Her non-operating incomes were ₹ 1,50,000 and non-operating expenses were ₹ 3,75,000. Calculate the profit earned during the year.** Competency Based Que
(a) ₹ 14,75,000 (b) ₹ 9,62,500
(c) ₹ 25,87,500 (d) ₹ 11,12,500

Assertion-Reason

Direction (Q. No. 33 to 42) *Read the following Assertion (A) and Reason (R) and choose the correct alternative from the following*

Alternatives
(a) Both Assertion (A) and Reason (R) are true and Reason (R) is the correct explanation of Assertion (A)
(b) Both Assertion (A) and Reason (R) are true, but Reason (R) is not the correct explanation of Assertion (A)
(c) Assertion (A) is true, but Reason (R) is false
(d) Assertion (A) is false, but Reason (R) is true

33. **Assertion** (A) The purpose of the trading account is to calculate the gross profit of a business.
Reason (R) The trading account includes all the revenues and expenses related to the core operations of buying and selling goods.

34. **Assertion** (A) In the profit and loss account, the net profit is calculated by subtracting operating expenses from gross profit.
Reason (R) Operating expenses represent the costs incurred in the day-to-day operations of a business.

35. **Assertion** (A) Closing stock is deducted from purchases to calculate the cost of goods sold in the trading account.
Reason (R) Closing stock represents the value of unsold goods at the end of the accounting period.

36. **Assertion** (A) The profit and loss account shows the financial position of a business at a specific point in time.
Reason (R) The profit and loss account summarises the revenues, expenses and net profit or loss generated by a business during a specific period.

37. **Assertion** (A) The purpose of preparing the final accounts is to provide information about the financial performance and position of a business.
Reason (R) Final accounts include the trading account, profit and loss account, and balance sheet, which collectively present a comprehensive view of a company's financial activities.

38. **Assertion** (A) The trading account includes only direct expenses.
Reason (R) The trading account is primarily concerned with determining the gross profit of a business.

39. **Assertion** (A) The balance sheet provides information about the financial position of a company at a specific point in time.

Reason (R) The balance sheet includes assets, liabilities and owner's equity, which represent the company's resources, obligations and ownership interests, respectively.

40. **Assertion** (A) Personal income tax and life insurance premium paid by the firm on behalf of the proprietor are not shown in profit and loss account if appearing in trial balance.

Reason (R) The amount withdrawn by the proprietor for his/her personal use is debited to profit and loss account.

41. **Assertion** (A) In income statement, the expenses incurred during the year are matched with the revenue earned during the year on accrual basis.

Reason (R) Profit is the excess of revenue over expenses and the loss is the opposite of profit when expenses are more than revenue.

42. **Assertion** (A) Expenditure incurred on the improvement of fixed assets to increase their production capacity such as increasing the seating capacity in a cinema hall is a capital expenditure.

Reason (R) Any expenditure which increases the value of a fixed asset is a capital expenditure. It is incurred on the acquisition of fixed assets.

Two Statements Based MCQs

Direction (Q. No. 43 to 50) *Read the following statements carefully and choose the correct alternatives*

Alternatives

(a) Both the statements are correct
(b) Both the statements are incorrect
(c) Statement I is correct and Statement II is incorrect
(d) Statement I is incorrect and Statement II is correct

43. **Statement I** Current assets consist of either cash or all those assets which can be converted into cash at a later date.

Statement II These assets are generally used to pay the current (short-term) liabilities.

44. **Statement I** Revenue expenditure is a recurring expenditure incurred everyday on running and managing the busines.

Statement II It includes all expenses incurred on repairs, replacements and maintenance of existing assets.

45. **Statement I** Capital expenditure is shown in the trading and profit and loss account.

Statement II Revenue expenses are shown in balance sheet.

46. **Statement I** Warehousing expenses, export duties, royalty, etc are shown to debit side of trading account.

Statement II Direct expenses are shown to debit side of trading account.

47. **Statement I** Trading account records the purchases of goods alongwith the expenses incurred in bringing those goods and putting them in a saleable condition.

Statement II Purchases are shown as a deduction out of sales on the debit side of trading account.

48. **Statement I** Contingent liabilities are not shown in the main body of the balance sheet.

Statement II These are shown below the balance sheet by way of a footnote.

49. **Statement I** Profit and loss account discloses information about the net profit earned during the year or net loss suffered during the year.

Statement II If due to higher expenses or abnormal losses during the year there is net loss, these can be highlighted and actions can be taken to control them.

50. **Statement I** The percentage of gross profits on the amount of sales will show the success of the trading concern.

Statement II With the help of the ratio of gross profit to sales, a trader can compare his performance year after year.

Matching

51. Match the following

Column I	Column II
A. Trading account	(i) Depreciation is debited
B. Balance sheet	(ii) Closing stock is shown in credit side
C. Profit and loss account	(iii) Closing stock is never included (if not adjusted)
D. Trial balance	(iv) Financial position is determined

Codes

	A	B	C	D		A	B	C	D
(a)	(ii)	(iv)	(i)	(iii)	(b)	(i)	(ii)	(iii)	(iv)
(c)	(ii)	(i)	(iii)	(iv)	(d)	(iv)	(ii)	(iii)	(i)

52. Match the following

Column I	Column II
A. Capital expenditure	(i) Repairs of assets purchase second hand
B. Revenue expenditure	(ii) Amount received from sale of old machine
C. Capital receipts	(iii) Repairs of assets purchased after one year
D. Revenue recceipts	(iv) Amount received as interest on investment

Codes

	A	B	C	D
(a)	(i)	(ii)	(iii)	(iv)
(b)	(i)	(iii)	(ii)	(iv)
(c)	(iv)	(iii)	(ii)	(i)
(d)	(iv)	(ii)	(i)	(iii)

53. **Match the following**

Column I	Column II
A. Interest received	(i) Capital expenditure
B. Loan received for business	(ii) Revenue receipts
C. Advertisement expenses	(iii) Capital receipts
D. Purchase of machine	(iv) Deferred revenue expenditure

Codes

	A	B	C	D		A	B	C	D
(a)	(i)	(ii)	(iii)	(iv)	(b)	(iii)	(i)	(iv)	(ii)
(c)	(ii)	(iii)	(iv)	(i)	(d)	(iv)	(iii)	(ii)	(i)

54. **Match the following**

Column I	Column II
A. Profit and loss account	(i) Closing stock
B. Trading account	(ii) Capital
C. Balance sheet (liabilities)	(iii) Net profit
D. Balance sheet (assets)	(iv) Gross profit

Codes

	A	B	C	D
(a)	(i)	(ii)	(iii)	(iv)
(b)	(iv)	(iii)	(ii)	(i)
(c)	(iv)	(i)	(iii)	(ii)
(d)	(iii)	(iv)	(ii)	(i)

55. **Match the following**

Column I	Column II
A. Wages and salaries	(i) Income side of trading account
B. Salaries	(ii) Income side of profit and loss account
C. Closing stock	(iii) Expense side of trading account
D. Interest received on investments	(iv) Expense side of profit and loss account

Codes

	A	B	C	D		A	B	C	D
(a)	(iii)	(iv)	(i)	(ii)	(b)	(i)	(ii)	(iii)	(iv)
(c)	(iv)	(iii)	(ii)	(i)	(d)	(ii)	(iii)	(iv)	(i)

Case Based MCQs

Direction *Read the following case study and answer the questions 56 to 58 on the basis of the same*

Simple Apparels is ready to close its books for the financial year ending 31st December, 2024. Here are the details

Cash ₹ 18,000; accounts receivable ₹ 9,000 ; Inventory (Opening) ₹ 10,000 ; Inventory (Closing) ₹ 15,000 ; Purchases ₹ 40,000; Sales revenue ₹ 1,20,000 ; Operating expenses ₹ 20,000; Loan payable ₹ 10,000 ; Capital ₹ 30,000.

56. **Calculate the Cost of Goods Sold (CoGS) for Simple Apparels.**
(a) ₹ 35,000 (b) ₹ 40,000 (c) ₹ 45,000 (d) ₹ 50,000

57. **What is the gross profit for Simple Apparels?**
(a) ₹ 70,000 (b) ₹ 60,000
(c) ₹ 50,000 (d) ₹ 85,000

58. **Determine the net profit for Simple Apparels.**
(a) ₹ 25,000 (b) ₹ 30,000
(c) ₹ 65,000 (d) ₹ 40,000

Direction *Read the following case study and answer the questions 59 and 60 on the basis of the same*

Raj and Jagadish engage in a manufacturing business. They have lack of knowledge of bookkeeping therefore, they appointed Jai as their accountant. He prepares their financial statements. Following balances are extracted from the trial balance of M/s Raj and Jagadish shows the balance as follows

Cash ₹ 20,000 ; Accounts receivable ₹ 12,000; Inventory ₹ 15,000; Equipment ₹ 50,000 ; Accounts payable ₹ 10,000 ; Long-term loans ₹ 25,000 ; Sales revenue ₹ 150,000 ; Cost of goods sold ₹ 80,000 ; Operating expense ₹ 40,000 ; Depreciation ₹ 5,000.

59. **Determine the net profit.**
(a) ₹ 15,000 (b) ₹ 10,000
(c) ₹ 12,000 (d) ₹ 25,000

60. **What will be the capital balance?**
(a) ₹ 25,000 (b) ₹ 30,000 (c) ₹ 62,000 (d) ₹ 15,000

Answers

1. (d) All of these
2. (a) Direct expenses
3. (d) financial position and profit or loss
4. (a) trading account
5. (b) profit and loss account
6. (a) debit of trading account
7. (c) debit of profit and loss account
8. (c) Balance sheet
9. (b) capital expenditure
10. (d) capital receipt
11. (a) revenue expenditure
12. (d) capital receipt
13. (a) debit, trading account
14. (c) Gross Profit, Operating Profit, Net Profit
15. (c) Operating Profit = Net Profit + Non-operating Expenses – Non-operating Incomes
16. (b) liabilities side
17. (b) capital
18. (d) net loss
19. (c) going concern
20. (c) Revenue expenses is treated is an expense of the current year
21. (c) Gross Profit = Net Sales + Cost of Goods Sold
22. (d) Both (b) and (c)
23. (c) Cost of Goods Sold = Opening Stock + Purchases + Expenses on Purchases – Closing Stock
    = 60,000 + 1,09,200 + 12,000 – 73,200
    = ₹ 1,08,000
24. (b) Gross Profit = Sales – Cost of Goods Sold
    = 50,000 – (10,000 + 25,000 – 12,000)
    = ₹ 27,000
25. (b) Cost of Goods Sold = Net Sales – Gross Profit
    = 6,50,000 – 1,62,500 (6,50,000 × 25%) = ₹ 4,87,500
26. (a) Gross profit will be 25% on sales. So, profit % on cost
    $= \frac{25}{75}$ or $\frac{1}{3}$ cost
27. (c) Closing Stock = Cost of Goods Sold – (Opening Stock + Purchases)
28. (c) CoGS = Opening Stock + Purchases – Closing Stock
    = 15,000 + 40,000 – 20,000 = ₹ 35,000
    Gross Profit = Sales – CoGS = 70,000 – 35,000 = ₹ 35,000
    Net Profit = Gross Profit – Operating Expenses
    = 35,000 – 10,000 = ₹ 25,000
29. (b) Operating Profit = Sales – CoGS – Operating Expenses + Depreciation
    = 2,50,000 – 1,50,000 – 50,000 + 20,000 = ₹ 70,000
30. (a) Total Assets = Cash + Accounts Receivable + Inventory
    = 25,000 + 10,000 + 30,000 = ₹ 65,000
    Total Liabilities = Current Liabilities + Long-term Liabilities
    = 20,000 + 15,000 = ₹ 35,000;
    Capital = Total Assets – Total Liabilities = 65,000 – 35,000
    = ₹ 30,000
31. (c) According to the convention of conservatism, stock is valued at cost or net realisable value whichever is lower.
32. (a) Net Profit = Operating Profit – Non-operating Expenses + Non-operating Income
33. (a) Both Assertion (A) and Reason (R) are true and Reason (R) is the correct explanation of Assertion (A)
34. (a) Both Assertion (A) and Reason (R) are true and Reason (R) is the correct explanation of Assertion (A)
35. (a) Both Assertion (A) and Reason (R) are true and Reason (R) is the correct explanation of Assertion (A)
36. (d) Assertion (A) is false, but Reason (R) is true
37. (a) Both Assertion (A) and Reason (R) are true and Reason (R) is the correct explanation of Assertion (A)
38. (b) Both Assertion (A) and Reason (R) are true, but Reason (R) is not the correct explanation of Assertion (A)
39. (a) Both Assertion (A) and Reason (R) are true and Reason (R) is the correct explanation of Assertion (A)
40. (c) The amount withdrawn by the proprietor for his/her personal use is not a business expense. It should therefore not be debited to profit and loss account.
41. (b) Both Assertion (A) and Reason (R) are true, but Reason (R) is not the correct explanation of Assertion (A)
42. (a) Both Assertion (A) and Reason (R) are true and Reason (R) is the correct explanation of Assertion (A)
43. (a) Both the statements are correct
44. (a) Both the statements are correct
45. (b) Capital expenditure is shown in the balance sheet and revenue expenses are shown in trading and profit and loss account.
46. (d) Warehousing expenses, export duties are indirect expenses and are shown in profit and loss account.
47. (c) Purchases returns are shown as a deduction out of purchases on the debit side of trading account.
48. (a) Both the statements are correct
49. (a) Both the statements are correct
50. (a) Both the statements are correct
51. (a) (ii) (iv) (i) (iii)
52. (b) (i) (iii) (ii) (iv)
53. (c) (ii) (iii) (iv) (i)
54. (d) (iii) (iv) (ii) (i)
55. (a) (iii) (iv) (i) (ii)
56. (a) CoGS = Opening Inventory + Purchases – Closing Inventory
    = 10,000 + 40,000 – 15,000 = ₹ 35,000
57. (d) Sales Revenue – CoGS = 1,20,000 – 35,000 = ₹ 85,000
58. (c) Net Profit = Gross Profit – Operating Expenses
    = 85,000 – 20,000 = ₹ 65,000
59. (d) Net Profit = Gross Profit – Operating Expenses – Depreciation Expense
    = (1,50,000 – 80,000) – 40,000 – 5,000 = ₹ 25,000
60. (c) Capital Balance = Total Assets – Total Liabilities
    = (20,000 + 12,000 + 15,000+ 50,000) – (10,000 + 25,000) = ₹ 62,000

11 CHAPTER

Financial Statements-II (with Adjustments)

The financial accounts are prepared on 'accrual concept' basis. Thus, revenues earned during the year (whether received or not) and expenses incurred during the year (whether paid or not) are accounted or adjusted.

YOUR STUDY GOALS

YOUR PRACTICE GOAL

- Topicwise Solved Questions (19 Solved Questions)
- Numerical Questions [30 Questions (Unsolved)]
- Theoretical Questions [6 Questions (with answers)]
- Objective Questions (62 Qs ; MCQs, A-R, Statements, Matching, Case)

11.1 Introduction

In order to ascertain true profit or loss of a business for a particular year, all expenses and incomes related to that period should be taken into consideration.

Sometimes it is noticed that after preparation of trial balance, but before final accounts are prepared, some business transactions have been completely or partially omitted or are wrongly recorded.

Besides this, there are some incomes or expenses, which relate to the next year, but have been received or paid in the current year. Therefore, it is necessary to incorporate these adjustments while preparing final accounts.

Need for Adjustments in Preparing the Final Accounts

- To ascertain the true profit or loss of the business.
- To determine the true financial position of the business.
- To make a record of the transactions earlier omitted in the books.
- To rectify the errors committed in the books.
- To make adjustment for prepaid expenses.
- To make adjustment for unearned income.
- To make a record of accrued income.
- To make a record of outstanding expenses.
- To provide for other reserves and provisions, depreciation, etc.

11.2 Adjustments in Preparation of Financial Statements

All such items which need to be brought into books of accounts at the time of preparing the final accounts are referred to as 'adjustments'.

Some common adjustments relate to

- Closing stock
- Outstanding expenses
- Prepaid/Unexpired expenses
- Depreciation
- Accrued income
- Income received in advance
- Bad debts
- Provision for bad and doubtful debts
- Provision for discount on debtors
- Manager's commission
- Interest on capital
- Interest on drawings
- Interest on loan
- Abnormal or accidental losses
- Goods taken for personal use
- Goods distributed as free samples

Journal entries which are recorded to give effect to these adjustments are known as **adjusting entries.**

1. Closing Stock

It is the stock/inventories which remained unsold at the end of the accounting period. It is valued at cost or net realisable value, whichever is lower.

(i) **When it is given in the Trial Balance**
The closing stock is shown only in the balance sheet on the assets side as a current asset.

(ii) **When it is given outside the Trial Balance** (In adjustment)
This means that the stock was valued only after the end of the year.
Treatment in Final Accounts
- Shown on the credit side in trading account.
- Shown as current asset on the assets side.

2. Outstanding Expenses (Expenses Due but not Paid or Expenses Unpaid or Due)

The expenses which have become due during the current accounting period but are actually paid in the next accounting period, are termed as outstanding expenses. e.g. Outstanding wages, salary, etc.

(i) **When it is given in the Trial Balance**
It will be shown on the liabilities side as a current liability.

(ii) **When it is given outside the Trial Balance** (In adjustment)
Treatment in Final Accounts
- Added to that particular expense in trading account (if direct expense) or the profit and loss account (if indirect expense) on the debit side, as the case may be.
- Recorded as a current liability on the liabilities side in balance sheet.

3. Prepaid Expenses (Expenses Paid in Advance or Unexpired Expenses)

The expenses which have been paid in advance i.e. whose payment has been made in current accounting year but they relate to next accounting year, are called prepaid expenses. e.g. Unexpired insurance, interest paid in advance, etc.

(i) **When it is given in the Trial Balance**
It will be shown on the assets side as a current asset.

(ii) **When it is given outside the Trial Balance** (In adjustment)
Treatment in Final Accounts
- Deducted from the particular expense on the debit side in trading account (if direct expense) or profit and loss account (if indirect expense), as the case may be.
- Shown as a current asset on the asset side in balance sheet.

4. Accrued Income (Outstanding Income or Income Receivable)

Income which has been earned during the current accounting period and has become due but not received during the current accounting period, is termed as accrued income, e.g. Commission receivable, rent receivable, etc.

(i) **When it is given in the Trial Balance**
It will be shown on the assets side as a current asset.

(ii) **When it is given outside the Trial Balance** (in adjustment)
Treatment in Final Accounts
- Added to the particular income on the credit side in the profit and loss account.
- Shown as a current asset on the assets side in the balance sheet.

5. Income Received in Advance (Unearned or Unaccrued Income)

Income received but not earned during the current accounting year is termed as income received in advance.

(i) **When it is given in the Trial Balance**
It will be shown on the liabilities side in balance sheet.

(ii) **When it is given outside the Trial Balance** (In adjustment)
Treatment in Final Accounts
- Deducted from the concerned income on the credit side in profit and loss account.
- Shown as a current liability on the liabilities side in balance sheet.

6. Depreciation

Depreciation is the reduction in the value of fixed asset due to its use, wear and tear or obsolescence.

(i) **When it is given in the Trial Balance**
It will be shown on the debit side in profit and loss account.

(ii) **When it is given outside the Trial Balance** (In adjustment)
Treatment in Final Accounts
- Written on the debit side as depreciation in profit and loss account.
- Deducted out of that particular asset on the assets side in the balance sheet.

7. Bad Debts

Debts which cannot be recovered or become irrecoverable from debtors are called bad debts.

(i) **When it is given in the Trial Balance**
It will be shown on the debit side of profit and loss account.

(ii) **When it is given outside the Trial Balance** (In adjustment)
Treatment in Final Accounts
- Shown as a separate item on the debit side in profit and loss account or will be added to the bad debts which appeared in the trial balance.
- Deducted from the amount due from debtors on the assets side in balance sheet.

Key Point
It is to be noted that both type of bad debts appearing in trial balance and outside the trial balance are charged to profit and loss account, but only those bad debts which are given outside the trial balance are deducted from debtors.

8. Provisions for Bad and Doubtful Debts

Debtors may include such debtors who are not likely to pay due to any reason. A provision for such bad or doubtful debts is created to cover any possible loss on account of bad debts likely to occur in future. This provision is generally created at a fixed rate on the debtors.

(i) **When it is given in the Trial Balance**
It will be shown as a deduction from total of bad debts and new provision.

(ii) **When it is given outside the Trial Balance** (In adjustment)
Treatment in Final Accounts
- Written on debit side as a separate item in profit and loss account or added to the bad debts on its debit side.
- Deducted from the amount of sundry debtors on the asset side in balance sheet.

9. Provision for Discount on Debtors

Cash discount is generally allowed to those debtors who pay before the due date or within a fixed period. Therefore, a provision for such discount is made in the current year, for those debtors who will make early payment in the next accounting period.

(i) **When it is given in the Trial Balance**
It will be shown on the debit side in profit and loss account.

(ii) **When it is given outside the Trial Balance** (In adjustment)
Treatment in Final Accounts
- Recorded on the debit side as a separate item in profit and loss account.
- Deducted from the debtors on the assets side in balance sheet.

10. Interest on Capital

The amount invested by the proprietor or owner in his business is termed as capital. Interest on capital is the cost of using the capital invested in the business.

(i) **When it is given in the Trial Balance**
It will be shown on the debit side of profit and loss account.

(ii) **When it is given outside the Trial Balance** (in Adjustment)
Treatment in Final Accounts
- Written on the debit side in profit and loss account as it is an expense of the business.
- Added to the capital account on the liabilities side in balance sheet.

11. Interest on Drawings

Drawings are the amount that the proprietor or owner has taken from the business for his personal use. Interest on drawings is charged from the proprietor, as drawings reduce capital.

(i) **When it is given in the Trial Balance**
It will be shown on the credit side of profit and loss account.

(ii) **When it is given outside the Trial Balance** (In adjustment)
Treatment in Final Accounts
- Shown on the credit side of profit and loss account as it is a gain for the business.
- Deducted from the proprietor's capital on the liabilities side in balance sheet.

12. Manager's Commission

Managers, also sometimes, are entitled to commission on net profits in addition to their salaries. It is always calculated at the end of the accounting period. It is always given as an adjustment.

Treatment in Final Accounts
- Shown on debit side of profit and loss account.
- Recorded on the liabilities in balance sheet side as commission payable.

Smart Study **Chart No. 1**

Calculation of Commission Payable

Fixed Percentage of Net Profits before Charging such Commission

In this case, commission will be calculated as
Commission = Net Profit before Commission × Rate of Commission

Fixed Percentage on Net Profits after Charging such Commission

In this case, commission is calculated as

$$\text{Commission} = \text{Net Profit before such Commission} \times \frac{\text{Rate of Commission}}{100 + \text{Rate of Commission}}$$

13. Interest on Loan

If the business has taken a loan, then interest on such loan will be an expense for the firm. If up-to-date interest has not been paid on the loan, the unpaid interest will have to be calculated and will be treated just like outstanding expenses.

(i) **When it is given in the Trial Balance**
It will be shown on the debit side as a separate item.

(ii) **When it is given outside the Trial Balance** (In adjustment)
Treatment in Final Accounts
- Written on the debit side in profit and loss account as it is an expense of the business.
- Outstanding amount of interest will be added to the loan account on the liabilities side in balance sheet.

14. Interest on Loan Given

When loan appears on the debit side of trial balance, it means the amount has been lent to outsiders. It is an asset for the firm and interest on such loan will be an income for the firm.

(i) **When it is given in the Trial Balance**
It will be shown on the credit side as a separate item.

(ii) **When it is given outside the Trial Balance** (In adjustment)
Treatment in Final Accounts
- Written on the credit side in profit and loss account.
- Accrued interest on such loan will be added to loan account on the assets side.

Goods and Services Tax (GST)

It is a comprehensive indirect tax under which all indirect taxes like excise duty, sales tax, VAT, service tax have been merged. GST is paid at the time of purchase and GST is collected from the customers at the time of sale, i.e.

1. **GST Paid** GST paid on purchase is set-off against GST collected (i.e. Output GST) hence, till it is set-off, it is treated as an asset. GST paid within the state is bifurcated into two parts
   - Input Central GST (Input CGST)
   - Input State GST (Input SGST)
2. **GST Collected** GST collected from customers on sale is payable to government after setting it off against GST paid (Input GST). Hence, till it is set-off, it is treated as a liability. GST collected within the state is bifurcated into two parts
   - Output Central GST (Output CGST)
   - Output State GST (Output SGST)

Adjustment of GST

- If Input CGST/SGST is more than Output CGST/SGST, the balance is shown on the assets side like a advance payment.
- If Output CGST/SGST is more than Input CGST/SGST, the balance is shown on the liabilities side like the amount payable to the government.

GST related to Adjustment Items

1. **GST Applicable on Outstanding Expenses** GST is levied on outstanding expenses. e.g. Rent amounting to ₹ 25,000 is outstanding and CGST and SGST @ 8% are levied, the adjustment entry will be

Rent A/c	Dr	25,000	
Input CGST A/c	Dr	2,000	
Input SGST A/c	Dr	2,000	
To Outstanding Rent A/c			29,000

Note

- If outstanding expenses are shown inside the trial balance, then GST will not be levied on such expenses as it implies that adjusting entry has already been passed including GST.
- Wages and salaries are exempted from GST.

2. **GST for Prepaid Expenses** GST is not required to be calculated on prepaid expenses.

   e.g. Rent paid is ₹ 10,000 out of which ₹ 2,500 is paid for the next year. CGST and SGST are @ 5% each, the journal entry will be

Rent A/c	Dr	10,000	
Input CGST A/c	Dr	375	
Input SGST A/c	Dr	375	
To Bank A/c			10,750

On passing adjustment entry for prepaid rent

Prepaid Rent A/c	Dr	2,500	
To Rent A/c			2,500

3. **GST Applicable on Income Earned but Not Received/Accrued Income** GST is also levied on accrued income. e.g. Commission earned but not received amounting to ₹ 30,000 is given in adjustment and CGST and SGST are @ 8% each, the journal entry will be

Accrued Commission A/c	Dr	34,800	
To Commission Received A/c			30,000
To Output CGST A/c			2,400
To Output SGST A/c			2,400

4. **GST for Income Received in Advance** If income received in advance is given in adjustments, then GST is not required to be calculated on such income as GST has already been credited at the time of receipt of income.

Integrated Goods and Services Tax (IGST)

IGST is levied on inter-state supply (i.e. supply outside the State) of goods and/or services, import of goods and/or services into India and export of goods and/or services from India.

- GST paid on purchase from outside the State is called input integrated GST (Input IGST).
- GST collected from sales outside the State is called output integrated GST (Output IGST).

Input IGST is adjusted against Output IGST and the balance is shown in the balance sheet.

15. Abnormal Loss of Goods (By Fire or Theft)

Sometimes losses occur due to some abnormal circumstances such as fire, theft, earthquake, accidents, abnormal spoilage/leakage/breakages/pilferage, etc. such losses are called abnormal losses.

(i) **When it is given in the Trial Balance**
It will be shown on the debit side of profit and loss account.

(ii) **When it is given outside the Trial Balance** (In adjustment)
Treatment in Final Accounts
- Trading account will either be credited with cost of the goods destroyed or loss of goods can be deducted from purchases on the debit side.
- The value of irrecoverable loss of stock is shown on the debit side as a separate item in profit and loss account.
- Any amount, which is due from the insurance company is shown on the asset side.

Loss of Fixed Assets If any fixed asset of the firm is destroyed due to some accident like fire, earthquake, etc. the loss will be shown on the debit side of profit and loss account and also deducted from the value of assets on the asset side of the balance sheet.

16. Goods Taken for Personal Use

When the goods are taken by the proprietor for his personal use from the business, it is treated as drawings.

(i) **When it is given in the Trial Balance**
It will be deducted from the capital on the liabilities side of the balance sheet.

(ii) **When it is given outside the Trial Balance** (In adjustment)
Treatment in Final Accounts
- Deducted from purchases on the debit side of trading account.
- Deducted from the capital on the liabilities side of the balance sheet.

17. Goods Distributed as Free Samples/Charity

To promote sales or welfare of society, goods are distributed as free samples or given away as charity. When goods are distributed as free samples or given away as charity, the stock gets reduced.

(i) **When it is given in the Trial Balance**
It will be shown on the debit side of the profit and loss account as advertisement/charity expense.

(ii) **When it is given outside the Trial Balance** (In adjustment)
Treatment in Final Accounts
- Deducted from purchases on the debit side of trading account.
- Shown on the debit side of the profit and loss account as advertisement/charity expense.

A Summarised View of Treatment of Adjustments in Final Accounts

S. No.	Adjustment	Adjustment Entry	Treatment in Trading Account	Treatment in Profit and Loss Account	Treatment in Balance Sheet
1.	Closing stock	Closing Stock A/c Dr To Trading A/c	Show on the credit side	No effect	Show on the assets side
2.	Outstanding expenses	Expenses A/c Dr Input CGST A/c Dr Input SGST A/c Dr To Outstanding Expense A/c	Show on the debit side (Add to respective direct expenses)	Show on the debit side (Add to respective direct expense)	Show on the liability side
3.	Prepaid or unexpired expenses	Prepaid Expenses A/c Dr To Expenses A/c	Show on the debit side (Subtract from respective direct expenses)	Show on the debit side (Substract from respective direct expenses)	Show on the assets side
4.	Accrued or outstanding income	Accrued Income A/c Dr To Income A/c To Output CGST A/c To Output SGST A/c	No effect	Show on the credit side (Add to respective income)	Show on the assets side
5.	Unearned or income received in advance	Income A/c Dr To Income Received in Advance A/c To Output CGST A/c To Output SGST A/c	No effect	Show on the credit side	Show on the liability side

S. No.	Adjustment	Adjustment Entry	Treatment in Trading Account	Treatment in Profit and Loss Account	Treatment in Balance Sheet
6.	Depreciation (When no provision is maintained)	Depreciation A/c Dr To Assets A/c Profit and Loss A/c Dr To Depreciation A/c	No effect	Show on the debit side	Show on the assets side (Subtract from respective fixed assets)
7.	Depreciation (When provision is maintained)	Depreciation A/c Dr To Provision for Depreciation A/c Profit and Loss A/c Dr To Depreciation A/c	No effect	Show on debit side % of depreciation × (Fixed assets – Provision for fixed asset)	Show on the assets side (Subtract total accumulated depreciation from fixed asset)
8.	Bad debts	Bad Debts A/c Dr To Debtors A/c Profit and Loss A/c Dr To Bad Debts A/c	No effect	Show on the debit side	Show on the assets side (Subtract from debtors)
9.	Provision for doubtful debts	Profit and Loss A/c Dr To Provision for Doubtful Debts A/c	No effect	Show on the debit side	Show on the assets side (Subtract from debtors)
10.	Provision for discount on debtors	Profit and Loss A/c Dr To Provision for Discount on Debtors	No effect	Show on the debit side (Calculate on good debtors after adjusting bad debts and provision for doubtful debts)	Show on the assets side (Subtract from debtors)
11.	Manager's commission	Profit and Loss A/c Dr To Manager's Commission A/c	No effect	Show on the debit side	Show on the liability side
12.	Interest on capital	Interest on Capital A/c Dr To Capital A/c Profit and Loss A/c Dr To Interest on Capital A/c	No effect	Show on the debit side	Show on the liability side (Add to owner's capital)
13.	Interest on drawings	Drawing A/c Dr To Interest on Drawings A/c	No effect	Shown on the credit side	Add to the drawings and then deduct from capital
14.	Interest on loan	Interest on Loan A/c Dr To Loan A/c	No effect	Show on the debit side	Show in the liability side (Add to loan)
15.	Goods distributed among staff/charity/free sample	Staff Welfare Expense A/c Dr *or* Charity A/c Dr *or* Free Sample A/c Dr To Purchases A/c To Input CGST A/c To Input SGST A/c	Show on credit side *or* Subtract from purchase, shown in debit side	Show on the debit side	No effect
16.	Drawings of goods for personal use	Drawings A/c Dr To Purchases A/c To Input CGST A/c To Input SGST A/c	Show in debit side (Subtract from purchase)	No effect	Show on the liability side (Subtract from owner's capital)
17.	Abnormal or Accidental loss	**If Goods are Insured** (i) Loss by Accident/Fire A/c Dr To Trading A/c To Input CGST A/c To Input SGST A/c (ii) Insurance Co. A/c Dr Profit and Loss A/c Dr To Loss by Accident/Fire A/c	Show on the credit side (With the cost of goods destroyed)	Show on the debit side (Amount recoverable from insurance company)	Shown on the asset side (Amount accepted by insurance company)
		If Goods are Not Insured Profit and Loss A/c Dr To Trading A/c To Input CGST A/c To Input SGST A/c	Show on the credit side (With the cost of goods destroyed)	Show on the debit side (With the cost of goods destroyed)	No effect

Mind Map

FINANCIAL STATEMENTS-II (WITH ADJUSTMENTS)

1 Need for Adjustments in Final Accounts

- To ascertain true profit or loss
- To determine true financial position
- To rectify the errors committed in the books
- To make a record of the transactions earlier omitted in the books
- To make adjustment of prepaid expenses, outstanding expenses, accrued income, unaccrued income, depreciation, provisions, etc

2 Adjustments in Preparation of Financial Statements

Some common adjustments relate to

- Closing stock
- Outstanding expenses
- Prepaid expenses
- Depreciation
- Accrued income
- Unaccrued income
- Bad debts
- Provision for bad debts
- Provision for discount on debtors
- Manager's commission
- Interest on capital
- Interest on drawings
- Interest on loan
- Abnormal losses
- Goods taken for personal use
- Goods distributed as free samples

Some of them are elaborated here

3 Adjustment of Unaccrued Income

When it is given in Trial Balance
- Shown on liabilities side of balance sheet

When it is given outside of Trial Balance
- Shown in profit and loss account on credit side by way of deduction from respective income
- Shown on liabilities side of balance sheet

4 Adjustment of Depreciation

When it is given in Trial Balance
- Shown on debit side of profit and loss account

When it is given outside of Trial Balance
- Shown on debit side of profit and loss account
- Shown as deduction from respective asset on asset side of balance sheet

5 Adjustment of Bad Debts

When it is given in Trial Balance
- Shown on the debit side of profit and loss account

When it is given outside of Trial Balance
- Shown on debit side separately in profit and loss account or by adding to existing bad debts given in trial balance
- Shown by deducting from debtors in balance sheet on asset side

6 Adjustment of Provision for Discount on Debtors

When it is given in Trial Balance
- Shown on debit side of profit and loss account

When it is given outside of Trial Balance
- Shown on debit side of profit and loss account
- Shown on asset side of balance sheet by way of deduction from debtors

7 Adjustment of Interest on Capital

When it is given in Trial Balance
- Shown on debit side of profit and loss account

When it is given outside of Trial Balance
- Shown on debit side of profit and loss account
- Shown on liability side of balance sheet by adding it to capital

8 Adjustment of Manager's Commission

- Shown on debit side of profit and loss account
- Shown on the liabilities side of balance sheet

Calculated as
- Before Charging Commission = Net Profit × Rate/100
- After Charging Commission

$$= \text{Net Profit} \times \frac{\text{Rate}}{100 + \text{Rate of Commission}}$$

9 Adjustment of Interest on Loan

When it is given in Trial Balance
- Shown on debit side of profit and loss account

When it is given outside of Trial Balance
- Shown on debit side of profit and loss account
- Shown on liabilities side of balance sheet

10 Adjustment of GST

- If Input CGST/SGST exceeds Output CGST/SGST, the balance is shown as an asset, like an advance payment
- If Output CGST/SGST exceeds Input CGST/SGST, the balance is shown as a liability, representing the amount payable to the government

11 Integrated Goods and Services Tax (IGST)

- GST paid on purchases from outside the state is called Input IGST
- GST collected on sales outside the state is called Output IGST
- Input IGST is adjusted against Output IGST and the balance is shown in the balance sheet

Topicwise Solved Questions

Adjustments 1 to 6

Solved Question 1 **From the following trial balance of a Naresh as on 31st March, 2024, prepare his final accounts and give the closing entries.**

Particulars	Amt (Dr)	Particulars	Amt (Cr)
Furniture	12,000	Sales	2,50,000
Cash in Hand	8,000	Returns Outwards	1,000
Cash at Bank	16,000	Capital	50,000
Purchases (Adjusted)*	80,000	Creditors	7,000
Returns Inwards	2,000	Bills Payables	10,000
Wages	11,000	Commission	2,000
Power and Fuel	9,000		
Carriage Inwards	3,000		
Insurance	4,000		
Buildings	50,000		
Plant	40,000		
Patents	15,000		
Salaries	14,000		
Closing Stock (31st March, 2024)*	6,000		
Drawings	10,000		
Debtors	40,000		
	3,20,000		3,20,000

Adjustments

(i) Wages are outstanding for ₹ 3,000.

(ii) Salaries for the month of March are outstanding for ₹ 6,000.

(iii) Insurance paid in advance ₹ 700.

(iv) Commission is accrued for ₹ 1,200.

Sol.

Trading and Profit and Loss Account

for the year ended 31st March, 2024

Dr | Cr

Particulars		Amt (₹)	Particulars		Amt (₹)
To Purchases (Adjusted)	80,000		By Sales	2,50,000	
(–) Returns Outwards	(1,000)	79,000	(–) Returns Inwards	(2,000)	2,48,000
To Wages	11,000				
(+) Outstanding	3,000	14,000			
To Power and Fuel		9,000			
To Carriage Inwards		3,000			
To Gross Profit c/d		1,43,000			
		2,48,000			2,48,000
To Salaries	14,000		By Gross Profit b/d		1,43,000
(+) Outstanding	6,000	20,000	By Commission	2,000	
To Insurance	4,000		(+) Accrued Commission	1,200	3,200
(–) Prepaid	(700)	3,300			
To Net Profit transferred to Capital A/c		1,22,900			
		1,46,200			1,46,200

JOURNAL (Closing Entries)

Date	Particulars		LF	Amt (Dr)	Amt (Cr)
2024					
Mar 31	Trading A/c	Dr		1,05,000	
	To Purchases A/c				80,000
	To Wages A/c				11,000
	To Power and Fuel A/c				9,000
	To Carriage Inwards A/c				3,000
	To Returns Inwards A/c				2,000
	(Being the transfer of balances to trading account)				
Mar 31	Sales A/c	Dr		2,50,000	
	Returns Outwards A/c	Dr		1,000	
	To Trading A/c				2,51,000
	(Being the transfer of balances trading account)				
Mar 31	Profit and Loss A/c	Dr		18,000	
	To Insurance A/c				4,000
	To Salaries A/c				14,000
	(Being the transfer of balances to profit and loss account)				
Mar 31	Commission A/c	Dr		2,000	
	To Profit and Loss A/c				2,000
	(Being the transfer of the balance to profit and loss account)				
Mar 31	Profit and Loss A/c	Dr		1,22,900	
	To Capital A/c				1,22,900
	(Being the transfer of net profit to capital account)				
Mar 31	Capital A/c	Dr		10,000	
	To Drawings A/c				10,000
	(Being drawing transferred to capital account)				

Balance Sheet
as at 31st March, 2024

Liabilities		Amt (₹)	Assets	Amt (₹)
Capital	50,000		Buildings	50,000
(+) Net Profit	1,22,900		Furniture	12,000
	1,72,900		Plant	40,000
(−) Drawings	(10,000)	1,62,900	Patents	15,000
Creditors		7,000	Closing Stock (31st March, 2024)	6,000
Bills Payables		10,000	Debtors	40,000
Outstanding Expenses			Cash at Bank	16,000
Salaries	6,000		Cash in Hand	8,000
Wages	3,000	9,000	Insurance Prepaid	700
			Commission Accrued	1,200
		1,88,900		1,88,900

Solved Question 2 **From the following trial balance of a Vyom for the year ended 31st March, 2024 prepare his trading account, profit and loss account and balance sheet as on that date.**

Trial Balance

Particulars	Amt (Dr)	Particulars	Amt (Cr)
Debtors	24,500	Capital	70,000
Drawings	5,200	Creditors	52,900
Insurance	600	Sales	98,000
General Expenses	3,000	Rental Income	15,000
Salaries	15,000	Interest on Investments	20,000
Patents	7,500	Loan	10,000

Particulars	Amt (Dr)	Particulars	Amt (Cr)
Machinery	20,000	Returns Outwards	2,000
Cash in Hand	500		
Cash at Bank	2,700		
Purchases	40,700		
Returns Inwards	600		
Wages	10,000		
Investments	80,000		
Fuel and Power	4,000		
Carriage Outwards	3,200		
Carriage Inwards	2,400		
Opening Stock	8,000		
Buildings and Land	40,000		
	2,67,900		2,67,900

Adjustments

(i) Closing stock on 31st March, 2024 ₹ 18,000.

(ii) Depreciate buildings and land at 10%, machinery at 15% and patents 20%.

(iii) Salaries for ₹ 5,000 are outstanding.

(iv) Rent has been received in advance for ₹ 3,000.

(v) Interest on investment has accrued for ₹ 6,000.

(vi) Insurance is prepaid for ₹ 100.

Sol.

Trading and Profit and Loss Account
for the year ended 31st March, 2024

Dr | Cr

Particulars		Amt (₹)	Particulars		Amt (₹)
To Opening Stock		8,000	By Sales	98,000	
To Purchases	40,700		(−) Returns Inwards	(600)	97,400
(−) Returns Outwards	(2,000)	38,700	By Closing Stock		18,000
To Wages		10,000			
To Fuel and Power		4,000			
To Carriage Inwards		2,400			
To Gross Profit c/d		52,300			
		1,15,400			1,15,400
To Insurance	600		By Gross Profit b/d		52,300
(−) Prepaid	(100)	500	By Rental Income	15,000	
To General Expenses		3,000	(−) Received in Advance	(3,000)	12,000
To Salaries	15,000		By Interest on Investments	20,000	
(+) Outstanding	5,000	20,000	(+) Accrued Interest	6,000	26,000
To Carriage Outwards		3,200			
To Depreciation					
Buildings	4,000				
Machines	3,000				
Patents	1,500	8,500			
To Net Profit transferred to Capital A/c		55,100			
		90,300			90,300

Balance Sheet
as at 31st March, 2024

Liabilities		Amt (₹)	Assets		Amt (₹)
Creditors		52,900	Cash in Hand		500
Loan		10,000	Cash at Bank		2,700
Outstanding Salaries		5,000	Debtors		24,500
Rent Received in Advance		3,000	Closing Stock		18,000
Capital	70,000		Interest Accrued		6,000
(+) Net Profit	55,100		Insurance Prepaid		100
	1,25,100		Buildings and Land	40,000	
(−) Drawings	(5,200)	1,19,900	(−) Depreciation	(4,000)	36,000
			Machinery	20,000	
			(−) Depreciation	(3,000)	17,000
			Patents	7,500	
			(−) Depreciation	(1,500)	6,000
			Investments		80,000
		1,90,800			1,90,800

Adjustments 7 to 9

Solved Question 3 **The following is the trial balance of Mr. Ramhan for the year ended 31st March, 2023. Prepare his final accounts.**

Trial Balance

Particulars	Amt (Dr)	Particulars	Amt (Cr)
Drawings	5,000	Capital	40,000
Machinery	50,000	Creditors	16,700
Furniture	2,000	Sales	4,30,000
Opening Stock (1st April, 2022)	60,000	Provisions for Discount on Debtors	5,000
Trucks	30,000	Returns Outwards	8,000
Debtors	40,000	Provision for Doubtful Debts	3,500
Cash in Hand	6,000	Discount Received	1,500
Cash at Bank	11,000	Commission	2,000
Wages — Factory	3,000		
Office	4,000		
Purchases	2,50,000		
Bills Receivables	7,000		
Returns Inwards	9,000		
Rent	10,000		
Lighting	2,000		
Telephone	3,500		
Advertisement	6,500		
Bad Debts	2,100		
Discount Allowed	5,600		
	5,06,700		5,06,700

The following adjustments are required to be made

(i) Closing stock on 31st March, 2023 was ₹ 51,000.

(ii) Write-off further bad debts ₹ 2,000.

(iii) Provide for doubtful debts @ 5% on debtors.

(iv) Make a provision for 2% discount on debtors.

(v) Rent for March 2023 is due but has not been paid ₹ 3,500.

Sol.

In the Books of Mr. Rahman
Trading and Profit and Loss Account
for the year ended 31st March, 2023

Dr | Cr

Particulars		Amt (₹)	Particulars		Amt (₹)
To Opening Stock		60,000	By Sales	4,30,000	
To Purchases	2,50,000		(–) Returns Inwards	(9,000)	4,21,000
(–) Returns Outwards	(8,000)	2,42,000	By Closing Stock		51,000
To Wages (Factory)		3,000			
To Gross Profit c/d		1,67,000			
		4,72,000			4,72,000
To Wages (Office)		4,000	By Gross Profit b/d		1,67,000
To Rent	10,000		By Discount Received		1,500
(+) Outstanding	3,500	13,500	By Commission		2,000
To Lighting		2,000			
To Telephones		3,500			
To Advertisement		6,500			
To Discount Allowed	5,600				
(+) New Provision for Discount on Debtors	722				
	6,322				
(–) Old Provison for Discount on Debtors	(5,000)	1,322			
To Bad Debts	2,100				
(+) Further Bad Debts	2,000				
(+) New Provision for Doubtful Debts	1,900				
	6,000				
(–) Old Provision for Doubtful Debts	(3,500)	2,500			
To Net Profit transferred to Capital A/c		1,37,178			
		1,70,500			1,70,500

Balance Sheet
as at 31st March, 2023

Liabilities		Amt (₹)	Assets		Amt (₹)
Capital	40,000		Machinery		50,000
(+) Net Profit	1,37,178		Furniture		2,000
	1,77,178		Trucks		30,000
(–) Drawings	(5,000)	1,72,178	Debtors	40,000	
Creditors		16,700	(–) Further Bad Debts	(2,000)	
Rent Outstanding		3,500		38,000	
			(–) New Provision for Doubtful Debts @ 5%	(1,900)	
				36,100	
			(–) Provision for Discount on Debtors @ 2%	(722)	35,378
			Closing Stock		51,000
			Bills Receivables		7,000
			Cash in Hand		6,000
			Cash at Bank		11,000
		1,92,378			1,92,378

Solved Question 4 **From the following trial balance of Shikha Enterprises prepare final accounts.**

Trial Balance
as on 31st March, 2023

Particulars	Debit Balance (₹)	Credit Balance (₹)
Capital	—	55,000
Drawings	3,000	—
Opening Stock	16,400	—
Purchases	31,100	—
Factory Rent	2,500	—
Sales	—	50,000
Returns	1,980	—
Rent and Taxes	6,000	—
Bad Debts	400	—
Reserve for Bad Debts	—	1,500
Discount	2,375	—
Commission Received	—	255
Debtors and Creditors	20,250	18,500
Furniture	6,000	—
Machinery	12,000	—
Goodwill	7,500	—
Wages and Salaries	7,000	—
Salaries (for 10 months)	5,000	—
Advertisement	9,000	—
Investment in Debentures	8,500	—
Loans and Advances	—	13,750
	1,39,005	1,39,005

Adjustments

(i) Closing stock ₹ 17,250. **(ii) Rent of ₹ 4,000 has been prepaid.**

(iii) Provide 2% reserve for bad debts on debtors. It was realised that our debtor worth ₹ 1,000 proved to be bad and has to be written-off.

(iv) Write-off depreciation @ 7.5% on machinery and 15% on furniture.

(v) Create discount on creditors @ 3%.

Sol.

In the Books of Shikha Enterprises
Trading and Profit and Loss Account
for the year ended 31st March, 2023

Dr Cr

Particulars		Amt (₹)	Particulars		Amt (₹)
To Opening Stock		16,400	By Sales	50,000	
To Purchases		31,100	(–) Sales Return	(1,980)	48,020
To Factory Rent		2,500	By Closing Stock		17,250
To Wages and Salaries		7,000			
To Gross Profit c/d		8,270			
		65,270			65,270
To Salaries	5,000		By Gross Profit b/d		8,270
(+) Outstanding Salaries (WN1)	1,000	6,000	By Discount on Creditors (WN3)		555
To Rent and Taxes	6,000		By Commission Received		255
(–) Prepaid Rent	(4,000)	2,000	By Net Loss (Transferred to Capital Account)		12,380
To Depreciation on					
Machinery	900				
Furniture	900	1,800			
To Discount		2,375			
To Advertisement		9,000			

Particulars		Amt (₹)	Particulars	Amt (₹)
To Bad Debts (Old)	400			
(+) Bad Debts (New)	1,000			
(+) Provision for Doubtful Debts (New)	385			
(WN2)	1,785			
(−) Provision for Doubtful Debts (Old)	(1,500)	285		
		21,460		21,460

Balance Sheet
as at 31st March, 2023

Liabilities		Amt (₹)	Assets		Amt (₹)
Capital	55,000		Machinery	12,000	
(−) Net Loss	(12,380)		(−) Depreciation 7.5%	(900)	11,100
	42,620		Furniture	6,000	
(−) Drawings	(3,000)	39,620	(−) Depreciation 15%	(900)	5,100
Outstanding Salaries		1,000	Debtors	20,250	
Loans and Advances		13,750	(−) Bad Debts	(1,000)	
Creditors	18,500			19,250	
(−) Discount on Creditors	(555)	17,945	(−) Provision for Doubtful Debts 2%	(385)	18,865
			Closing Stock		17,250
			Prepaid Rent		4,000
			Goodwill		7,500
			Investment in Debentures		8,500
		72,315			72,315

Working Notes

1. In trial balance, salaries are given ₹ 5,000 for 10 months and 2 months are outstanding.
   ∴ 2 months outstanding amount will be ₹ 1,000
2. Reserve for doubtful debt 2% on 19,250 = ₹ 385
3. Discount on creditors 3% on 18,500 = ₹ 555

Adjustments 10 to 14

Solved Question 5 **From the following trial balance of Mr. Garg as on 31st March, 2018, prepare trading account and profit and loss account and balance sheet.**

Trial Balance

Particulars	Amt (Dr)	Particulars	Amt (Cr)
Stock on 1st April, 2017	500	Capital	2,000
Purchases	1,500	Sales	3,500
Land and Building	2,000	Sundry Creditors	750
Bills Receivable	300	Commission	50
Wages	300	Bills Payable	300
Machinery	800	Loan	600
Carriage Inward	100		
Carriage Outward	100		
Power	150		
Salaries	200		
Discount Allowed	30		
Drawings	100		
Insurance Premium	20		
Cash at Bank	500		
Cash in Hand	100		
Investments	500		
	7,200		7,200

Adjustments

(i) Stock as on 31st March, 2018 is valued at ₹ 200.
(ii) Provide depreciation @ 10% on machinery and @ 5% on land and building.
(iii) Outstanding salaries amounted to ₹ 50.
(iv) Insurance premium is paid in advance to the extent of ₹ 10.
(v) Allow interest on capital @ 6% per annum.
(vi) Interest on loan @ 12% per annum is due for one year.

Sol.

Trading and Profit and Loss Account
for the year ended 31st March, 2018

Dr Particulars		Amt (₹)	Particulars	Cr Amt (₹)
To Opening Stock		500	By Sales	3,500
To Purchases		1,500	By Closing Stock	200
To Wages		300		
To Carriage Inward		100		
To Power		150		
To Gross Profit c/d		1,150		
		3,700		3,700
To Salaries	200		By Gross Profit b/d	1,150
(+) Outstanding Salaries	50	250	By Commission	50
To Carriage Outward		100		
To Insurance Premium	20			
(−) Prepaid Insurance	(10)	10		
To Discount Allowed		30		
To Depreciation on				
Machinery	80			
Land and Building	100	180		
To Interest on Loan		72		
To Interest on Capital		120		
To Net Profit (Transferred to capital account)		438		
		1,200		1,200

Balance Sheet
as on 31st March, 2018

Liabilities		Amt (₹)	Assets		Amt (₹)
Capital	2,000		Land and Building	2,000	
(+) Interest on Capital	120		(−) Depreciation	(100)	1,900
(+) Net Profit	438		Machinery	800	
	2,558		(−) Depreciation	(80)	720
(−) Drawings	(100)	2,458	Investments		500
Loan	600		Closing Stock		200
(+) Interest Outstanding	72	672	Bills Receivable		300
Sundry Creditors		750	Cash at Bank		500
Bills Payable		300	Cash in Hand		100
Outstanding Salaries		50	Prepaid Insurance		10
		4,230			4,230

Solved Question 6 Prepare trading account, profit and loss account and balance sheet from the following particulars for the year ended 31st December, 2022.

Name of Accounts	Debit Balance (₹)	Credit Balance (₹)
Cash in Hand	7,600	—
Cash at Bank	16,218	—
Purchases and Sales	3,16,000	6,50,000
Return Inwards	5,000	—

Name of Accounts	Debit Balance (₹)	Credit Balance (₹)
Return Outwards	—	3,600
Carriage on Purchases	2,000	—
Carriage on Sales	600	—
Fuel and Power	7,800	—
Stock (1st January, 2022)	56,420	—
Building	1,64,000	—
Machinery	2,25,000	—
Debtors and Creditors	1,44,000	44,000
Investments	1,00,000	—
Interest on Investments	—	2,000
Loan from Narayan on 1st July, 2022 @ 10% per annum	—	40,000
Repairs	8,562	—
General Expenses	40,800	—
Provision for Bad Debts	—	4,200
Wages and Salaries	39,440	—
Miscellaneous Receipts	—	9,040
Interest on Mr. Narayan's Loan	1,400	—
Capital	—	4,00,000
Drawings	18,000	—
	11,52,840	11,52,840

Adjustments

(i) Bad debts ₹ 2,000.

(ii) Provision for doubtful debts is to be maintained at 5% on sundry debtors.

(iii) Provision for 2% discount on debtors and creditors.

(iv) Manager is entitled to get the commission at 10% on net profit after charging such commission.

(v) Closing stock was valued at ₹ 60,000.

(vi) Allow interest on capital @ 10%.

(vii) Charge ₹ 1,000 as interest on drawings.

Sol.

Trading and Profit and Loss Account

Dr — for the year ended 31st December, 2022 — Cr

Particulars		Amt (₹)	Particulars		Amt (₹)
To Opening Stock		56,420	By Sales	6,50,000	
To Purchases	3,16,000		(−) Return Inwards	(5,000)	6,45,000
(−) Return Outwards	(3,600)	3,12,400	By Closing Stock		60,000
To Carriage on Purchases		2,000			
To Fuel and Power		7,800			
To Wages and Salaries		39,440			
To Gross Profit c/d		2,86,940			
		7,05,000			7,05,000
To Carriage on Sales		600	By Gross Profit b/d		2,86,940
To Repairs		8,562	By Interest on Investments		2,000
To General Expenses		40,800	By Miscellaneous Receipts		9,040
To Further Bad Debts	2,000		By Provision for Discount on Creditors		880
(+) New Provision	7,100		By Interest on Drawings		1,000
	9,100				
(−) Old Provision	(4,200)	4,900			
To Interest on Narayan's Loan	1,400				
(+) Outstanding Interest	600	2,000			

Particulars	Amt (₹)	Particulars	Amt (₹)
To Provision for Discount on Debtors	2,698		
To Interest on Capital (4,00,000 × 10%)	40,000		
To Manager's Commission (Outstanding)	18,209		
To Net Profit transferred to Capital A/c	1,82,091		
	2,99,860		2,99,860

Balance Sheet
as at 31st December, 2022

Liabilities		Amt (₹)	Assets		Amt (₹)
Sundry Creditors	44,000		Cash in Hand		7,600
(−) Provision for Discount			Cash at Bank		16,218
on Creditors @ 2%	(880)	43,120	Sundry Debtors	1,44,000	
Narayan's Loan	40,000		(−) Bad Debts	(2,000)	
(+) Outstanding Interest	600	40,600		1,42,000	
Manager's Commission		18,209	(−) Provision for Bad Debts @ 5%	(7,100)	
Capital	4,00,000			1,34,900	
(+) Interest on Capital	40,000		(−) Provision for Discount on Debtors @ 2%	(2,698)	1,32,202
	4,40,000		Closing Stock		60,000
(+) Net Profit	1,82,091		Investments		1,00,000
	6,22,091		Machinery		2,25,000
(−) Drawings	(18,000)		Building		1,64,000
	6,04,091				
(−) Interest on Drawings	(1,000)	6,03,091			
		7,05,020			7,05,020

Working Notes

1. Manager's commission = (2,99,860 − 99,560) = 2,00,300 × $\frac{10}{110}$ = ₹ 18,209

2. Interest on loan = 40,000 × $\frac{10}{100} \times \frac{6}{12}$ = ₹ 2,000

   (−) Already paid = ₹ (1,400)

   Outstanding = ₹ 600

Adjustments 15 to 17 (Including GST)

Solved Question 7 **From the following trial balance, prepare final accounts as on 31st March, 2023**

Trial Balance

Particulars	Debit Balance (₹)	Credit Balance (₹)
Capital	—	15,000
Provision for Doubtful Debts	—	500
Creditors	—	4,700
Sales	—	20,000
Bank Overdraft	—	3,000
Commission	—	400
Furniture	700	—
Machine	8,000	—
Buildings	10,000	—
Bad Debts	200	—
Debtors	4,000	—
Opening Stock	4,500	—
Purchases	7,000	—

Particulars	Debit Balance (₹)	Credit Balance (₹)
Advertising	500	—
Interest on Bank Overdraft	200	—
Insurance Premium	800	—
General Expenses	1,500	—
Salaries	5,200	—
Cash in Hand	1,000	—
	43,600	43,600

Adjustments

(i) Closing stock is valued at ₹ 3,600.

(ii) Stock costing ₹ 2,000 was destroyed by fire. The insurance company accepted a claim of ₹ 800.

(iii) Provision for doubtful debts is to be maintained at 5% of debtors.

(iv) Depreciate furniture by 10% and machines and buildings by 5%.

Sol.

In the Books of the Firm
Trading and Profit and Loss Account
for the year ended 31st March, 2023

Dr | Cr

Particulars		Amt (₹)	Particulars		Amt (₹)
To Opening Stock		4,500	By Sales		20,000
To Purchases	7,000		By Closing Stock		3,600
(−) Stock Lost by Fire	(2,000)	5,000			
To Gross Profit c/d		14,100			
		23,600			23,600
To Bad Debts		200	By Gross Profit		14,100
To Depreciation			By Commission		400
Furniture	70		By Provision for Doubtful Debts (Old)	500	
Machines	400		(−) New Provision for Doubtful Debts		
Buildings	500	970	@ 5% on ₹ 24,000	(200)	300
To Advertising		500			
To Interest on Bank Overdraft		200			
To Insurance Premium		800			
To General Expenses		1,500			
To Salaries		5,200			
To Loss by fire (not covered by insurance claim)		1,200			
To Net Profit transferred to Capital A/c		4,230			
		14,800			14,800

Balance Sheet
as at 31st March, 2023

Liabilities		Amt (₹)	Assets		Amt (₹)
Capital	15,000		Furniture	700	
(+) Net Profit	4,230	19,230	(−) Depreciation	(70)	630
Creditors		4,700	Machines	8,000	
Bank Overdraft		3,000	(−) Depreciation	(400)	7,600
			Buildings	10,000	
			(−) Depreciation	(500)	9,500
			Closing Stock		3,600
			Debtors	4,000	
			(−) Provision for Doubtful Debts @ 5%	(200)	3,800
			Cash in Hand		1,000
			Insurance Company (Claim)		800
		26,930			26,930

Solved Question 8 From the following trial balance of a trader, prepare his final accounts as on 31st March, 2023

Particulars	Debit Balance (₹)	Credit Balance (₹)
Drawings	2,240	—
Capital	—	16,000
Debtors and Creditors	8,000	2,960
Bank Loan at 5%	—	3,200
Purchases and Sales	19,200	24,000
Cash in Hand	2,400	—
Returns	1,600	3,200
Establishment Expenses	4,000	—
Insurance	800	—
Bad Debts	800	—
Commission	—	800
Provision for Doubtful Debts	—	1,000
Investments	6,400	—
Opening Stock	4,800	—
Furniture and Fixtures	960	—
Sales Tax Collected	—	840
Bills Receivables	4,800	—
Bills Payables	—	4,000
	56,000	56,000

Adjustment required

(i) The proprietor used the goods for the following purposes

(a) For personal use ₹ 500. (b) For charity ₹ 100. (c) For staff welfare ₹ 300.

(ii) Stock worth ₹ 2,000 was destroyed by fire during the year. The insurance company paid full claim.

(iii) Closing stock is ₹ 5,000. (iv) Depreciate furniture by ₹ 10%.

(v) Make a provision for doubtful debts at 5% on debtors.

(vi) No interest has been paid on bank loan.

(vii) Salaries of ₹ 200 are outstanding and insurance of ₹ 500 is prepaid.

Sol.

In the Books of the Firm
Trading and Profit and Loss Account
for the year ended 31st March, 2023

Dr | Cr

Particulars			Amt (₹)	Particulars		Amt (₹)
To Opening Stock			4,800	By Sales	24,000	
To Purchases		19,200		(–) Returns	(1,600)	22,400
(–) Returns		(3,200)		By Closing Stock		5,000
(–) Goods Drawn for various Uses						
(–) For Personal Use	(500)					
(–) For Staff Welfare	(300)					
(–) For Charity	(100)	(900)				
(–) Stock Lost by Fire		(2,000)	13,100			
To Gross Profit c/d			9,500			
			27,400			27,400
To Establishment Expenses			4,000	By Gross Profit b/d		9,500
To Salaries Outstanding Expenses			200	By Commission		800
To Insurance		800				
(–) Prepaid		(500)	300			
To Interest on Bank Loan @ 5%			160			

Particulars		Amt (₹)	Particulars	Amt (₹)
To Bad Debts	800			
(+) New Provision for Doubtful Debts	400			
	1,200			
(−) Old Provision for Doubtful Debts	(1,000)	200		
(Given in trial balance)				
To Depreciation on Furniture @ 10%		96		
To Staff Welfare Expenses (Goods used)		300		
To Charity (Goods used)		100		
To Net Profit transferred to Capital A/c		4,944		
		10,300		10,300

Balance Sheet
as at 31st March, 2023

Liabilities			Amt (₹)	Assets		Amt (₹)
Bills Payables			4,000	Cash in Hand		2,400
Creditors			2,960	Bills Receivable		4,800
Sales Tax Payable (Collected)			840	Insurance Company		2,000
Outstanding Expenses				Investments		6,400
Salaries		200		Prepaid Insurance		500
Interest on Bank Loan		160	360	Closing Stock		5,000
Bank Loan			3,200	Debtors	8,000	
Capital		16,000		(−) Provision for 5% Doubtful Debts	(400)	7,600
(+) Net Profit		4,944		Furniture	960	
		20,944		(−) Depreciation	(96)	864
(−) Drawings	(2,240)					
(−) Goods used	(500)	(2,740)	18,204			
			29,564			29,564

Solved Question 9 **From the following trial balance prepare trading account, profit and loss account and balance sheet for the year ended 31st December, 2022.**

Particulars	Amt (₹)	Particulars	Amt (₹)
Capital	10,00,000	Sundry Creditors	97,000
Life Insurance Premium	8,000	Sales	12,00,000
Plant and Machinery	2,50,000	Returns Outwards	10,000
Stock in the Beginning	1,50,000	Discount (Dr)	8,000
Purchases	8,72,000	Discount (Cr)	12,000
Return Inwards	20,000	Rent for Premises Sublet	10,000
Sundry Debtors	2,10,000	Lighting	5,000
Furniture	92,000	Salaries	2,13,000
Freehold Property	4,00,000	Cash	1,58,000
Freight and Duty	20,000	Loan from Bank at 10% per annum on 1st January, 2022	1,00,000
Carriage Inwards	8,000		
Carriage Outwards	2,000	Bank Interest (Dr)	9,000
Trade Expenses	4,000		

Adjustments

(i) Stock on 31st December, 2022 was valued at ₹ 3,00,000.

(ii) Stock for ₹ 50,000 was burnt by fire on 25th December, 2022 and the insurance company admitted the claim of ₹ 30,000.

(iii) Good worth ₹ 15,000 were distributed as free samples, goods worth ₹ 12,000 were used for personal purposes by the proprietor and goods worth ₹ 8,000 were given away as charity.

(iv) Use of goods in business worth ₹ 20,000.

(v) Machine worth ₹ 50,000 burnt by fire on 30th December, 2022 which was not insured.

Sol.

Trading and Profit and Loss Account
for the year ended 31st December, 2022

Dr Particulars		Amt (₹)	Particulars		Cr Amt (₹)
To Opening Stock		1,50,000	By Sales	12,00,000	
To Purchases	8,72,000		(−) Return Inwards	(20,000)	11,80,000
(−) Return Outwards	(10,000)		By Closing Stock		3,00,000
	8,62,000				
(−) Loss by Fire	(50,000)				
	8,12,000				
(−) Free Samples	(15,000)				
	7,97,000				
(−) Drawings in Goods	(12,000)				
	7,85,000				
(−) Charity in Goods	(8,000)				
	7,77,000				
(−) Use in Business	(20,000)	7,57,000			
To Freight and Duty		20,000			
To Carriage Inwards		8,000			
To Gross Profit c/d		5,45,000			
		14,80,000			14,80,000
To Carriage Outwards		2,000	By Gross Profit b/d		5,45,000
To Trade Expenses		4,000	By Discount Received		12,000
To Discount Allowed		8,000	By Rent		10,000
To Lighting		5,000			
To Salaries		2,13,000			
To Bank Interest	9,000				
(+) Interest Outstanding	1,000	10,000			
To Loss by Fire		20,000			
To Free Samples		15,000			
To Charity		8,000			
To Loss of Machine by Fire		50,000			
To Net Profit transferred to Capital A/c		2,32,000			
		5,67,000			5,67,000

Balance Sheet
as at 31st December, 2022

Liabilities		Amt (₹)	Assets		Amt (₹)
Bank Loan	1,00,000		Cash		1,58,000
(+) Outstanding Interest	1,000	1,01,000	Sundry Debtors		2,10,000
Sundry Creditors		97,000	Closing Stock		3,00,000
Capital	10,00,000		Insurance Company		30,000
(+) Net Profit	2,32,000		Furniture		92,000
	12,32,000		Plant and Machinery	2,50,000	
(−) Life Insurance			(−) Loss by Fire	(50,000)	2,00,000
Premium (Drawings)	(8,000)		Freehold Property		4,00,000
	12,24,000		Use of Goods in Business		20,000
(−) Drawing in Goods	(12,000)	12,12,000			
		14,10,000			14,10,000

Working Note

Interest on loan = 1,00,000 × 10/100 = ₹ 10,000

Already paid = ₹ (9,000)

Outstanding = ₹ 1,000

Solved Question 10 **From the following trial balance of Jain Brothers, prepare trading and profit and loss account, and a balance sheet as at 31st March, 2022.**

Name of Accounts	Amt (Dr)	Name of Accounts	Amt (Cr)
Purchases	18,00,000	Sales	35,56,000
Return Inwards	45,000	Return Outwards	62,000
Carriage on Purchases	26,000	Creditors	2,80,000
Carriage on Sales	15,000	Interest on Investments	36,000
Stock as on 1st April, 2021	3,22,000	Provision for Bad Debts	29,000
Cash	30,000	Commission Received	75,000
Building	15,00,000	Capital	22,60,000
Machinery	7,20,000	Output CGST	2,50,000
Fuel, Power and Gas	85,000	Output SGST	2,50,000
Debtors	8,15,000		
Investments	1,60,000		
Rent	4,00,000		
General Expenses (Including insurance Premium of ₹ 20,000 paid for one year ending 30th September, 2022)	1,50,000		
Wages and Salaries	2,10,000		
Drawings	2,20,000		
Input CGST	1,50,000		
Input SGST	1,50,000		
	67,98,000		67,98,000

Adjustments

(i) Depreciation to be charged on building @ 5% and on machinery @ 10%.

(ii) Stock on 31st March, 2022 was valued at ₹ 5,67,000.

(iii) Bad debts write-off ₹ 15,000 and create a provision 5% on debtors.

(iv) Create a provision for discount on sundry debtors at 2%.

(v) 1/3 of the commission received is in respect of work to be done next year.

(vi) Charge ₹ 11,000 as interest on drawings.

(vii) Rent is payable at the rate of ₹ 40,000 per month. Outstanding rent is subjected to levy of CGST and SGST @ 9% each.

Sol.

Trading and Profit and Loss Account
for the year ended 31st March, 2022

Dr | Cr

Particulars		Amt (₹)	Particulars		Amt (₹)
To Stock (1st April, 2021)		3,22,000	By Sales	35,56,000	
To Purchases	18,00,000		(–) Return Inwards	(45,000)	35,11,000
(–) Return Outwards	(62,000)	17,38,000	By Closing Stock		5,67,000
To Carriage on Purchases		26,000			
To Fuel, Power and Gas		85,000			
To Wages and Salaries		2,10,000			
To Gross Profit c/d		16,97,000			
		40,78,000			40,78,000
To Carriage on Sales		15,000	By Gross Profit b/d		16,97,000
To Depreciation			By Interest on Investments		36,000
Building	75,000		By Commission Received	75,000	
Machinery	72,000	1,47,000	(–) 1/3 Received in Advance	(25,000)	50,000
To Rent	4,00,000		By Interest on Drawings		11,000
(+) Outstanding (WN1)	80,000	4,80,000			
To General Expenses	1,50,000				
(–) Prepaid Insurance	(10,000)	1,40,000			

Particulars		Amt (₹)	Particulars	Amt (₹)
To Bad Debts	15,000			
(+) New Provision	40,000			
	55,000			
(–) Old Provision	(29,000)	26,000		
To Provision for Discount on Debtors		15,200		
To Net Profit transferred to Capital Account		9,70,800		
		17,94,000		17,94,000

Balance Sheet
as at 31st March, 2022

Liabilities		Amt (₹)	Assets		Amt (₹)
Creditors		2,80,000	Cash		30,000
Outstanding Rent		94,400	Sundry Debtors	8,15,000	
Commission Received in Advance		25,000	(–) Bad Debts	(15,000)	
Capital	22,60,000			8,00,000	
(+) Net Profit	9,70,800		(–) Provision for Doubtful Debts	(40,000)	
(–) Drawings and Interest on Drawings	(2,31,000)	29,99,800		7,60,000	
Output CGST	2,50,000		(–) Provision for Discount on Debtors	(15,200)	7,44,800
(–) Input CGST (1,50,000 + 7,200)	(1,57,200)	92,800	Closing Stock		5,67,000
Output SGST	2,50,000		Prepaid Insurance		10,000
(–) Input SGST (1,50,000 + 7,200)	(1,57,200)	92,800	Investments		1,60,000
			Machinery	7,20,000	
			(–) Depreciation	(72,000)	6,48,000
			Building	15,00,000	
			(–) Depreciation	(75,000)	14,25,000
		35,84,800			35,84,800

Working Notes

	Amt (₹)
1. Total Rent for the Year (40,000 × 12)	= 4,80,000
(–) Rent Paid during the Year	= (4,00,000)
Outstanding Rent	= 80,000

2. Adjustment Entry for Outstanding Rent

Rent A/c	Dr	80,000	
Input CGST A/c	Dr	7,200	
Input SGST A/c	Dr	7,200	
To Outstanding Rent A/c			94,400

Solved Question 11 Trial balance of Pratap & Sons as at 31st March, 2022 was as follows

Name of Accounts	Amt (Dr)	Name of Accounts	Amt (Cr)
Drawings	5,000	Capital	1,00,000
Purchases	68,000	Sales	1,50,000
Sundry Debtors	40,000	Bank Overdraft	12,000
Stock	30,000	Commission	2,000
Return Inward	3,000	Provision for Bad Debts	4,000
Salary	17,000	Creditors	20,000
Office Expenses	2,000	Loan	15,000
Leasehold Property	80,000		
Bad Debts	3,000		
Stationery	1,000		
Furniture	9,000		

Name of Accounts	Amt (Dr)	Name of Accounts	Amt (Cr)
Wages	10,000		
Input IGST	35,000		
	3,03,000		3,03,000

Prepare trading and profit and loss account for the year ended 31st March, 2022 and balance sheet as at that date after taking into consideration the following information

(i) Stock on 31st March, 2022 was ₹ 20,000.

(ii) Provision for doubtful debts is to be maintained @ 5%.

(iii) A fire occured in the godown and stock of the value of ₹ 5,000 was destroyed. It was insured and the insurance company admitted the claim of ₹ 4,000. The stock was purchased paying IGST @ 18%.

(iv) Commission received in advance ₹ 500.

Sol.

Trading and Profit and Loss Account

for the year ended 31st March, 2022

Dr | Cr

Particulars		Amt (₹)	Particulars		Amt (₹)
To Opening Stock		30,000	By Sales A/c	1,50,000	
To Purchases	68,000		(−) Sales Return	(3,000)	1,47,000
(−) Loss by Fire	(5,000)	63,000	By Closing Stock		20,000
To Wages		10,000			
To Gross Profit c/d		64,000			
		1,67,000			1,67,000
To Salary		17,000	By Gross Profit b/d		64,000
To Office Expenses		2,000	By Commission A/c	2,000	
To Bad Debts	3,000		(−) Unearned Commission A/c	(500)	1,500
(+) New Provision	2,000				
	5,000				
(−) Old Provision	(4,000)	1,000			
To Stationery		1,000			
To Loss by Fire A/c		1,900			
To Net Profit		42,600			
		65,500			65,500

Balance Sheet

as at 31st March, 2022

Liabilities		Amt (₹)	Assets		Amt (₹)
Capital	1,00,000		Furniture		9,000
(+) Net Profit	42,600		Leasehold Property		80,000
(−) Drawings	(5,000)	1,37,600	Debtors	40,000	
Creditors		20,000	(−) New Provision	(2,000)	38,000
Loan		15,000	Stock		20,000
Advance Commission		500	Insurance Company		4,000
Bank Overdraft		12,000	Input IGST	35,000	
			(−) Loss by Fire	(900)	34,100
		1,85,100			1,85,100

Working Notes

Adjustment Entry for Loss by Fire

		Dr	Cr
1. Loss by Fire A/c	Dr	5,900	
To Purchases A/c			5,000
To Input IGST A/c (5,000 × 18%)			900
2. Insurance Company A/c	Dr	4,000	
Profit and Loss A/c	Dr	1,900	
To Loss by Fire A/c			5,900

Comprehensive

Solved Question 12 **Prepare trading and profit and loss account of a trader for the year ending 31st March, 2023 and his balance sheet as on that date from the following trial balance.**

Particulars	Amt (Dr)	Particulars	Amt (Cr)
Purchases	2,50,000	Loan from Raman @ 10%	20,000
Cash in Hand	3,000	Sales	4,10,000
Cash at Bank	15,000	Returns Outwards	5,000
Returns Inwards	6,000	Provision for Doubtful Debts	11,000
Carriage on Purchases	12,000	Creditors	1,00,000
Bad Debts	6,000	Interest on Investments	2,000
Carriage on Sales	11,000	Miscellaneous Receipts	38,000
Power and Fuel	22,000	Capital	2,00,000
Stock on 1st April, 2022	40,000		
Plant	80,000		
Investments	30,000		
Repairs	12,000		
General Expenses	21,000		
Land and Buildings	2,15,000		
Stationery	12,000		
Interest on Loan	1,000		
Debtors	50,000		
	7,86,000		7,86,000

Adjustments

(i) General expenses include insurance premium of ₹ 1,600 paid for one year up to 30th June, 2023.
(ii) Write-off ₹ 3,000 as bad debts and create a provision of 5% on debtors.
(iii) The loan from Raman was taken on 1st July, 2022.
(iv) Closing stock is valued at ₹ 36,000 (market value ₹ 40,000).
(v) Depreciate land and buildings at 10%.

Sol.

In the Book of the Firm
Trading and Profit and Loss Account
for the year ended 31st March, 2023

Dr | Cr

Particulars		Amt (₹)	Particulars		Amt (₹)
To Opening Stock		40,000	By Sales	4,10,000	
To Purchases	2,50,000		(−) Returns Inwards	(6,000)	4,04,000
(−) Returns Outwards	(5,000)	2,45,000	By Closing Stock		36,000
To Carriage on Purchases		12,000			
To Power and Fuel		22,000			
To Gross Profit c/d		1,21,000			
		4,40,000			4,40,000
To Stationery		12,000	By Gross Profit b/d		1,21,000
To Bad Debts (Trial balance)	6,000		By Interest on Investments		2,000
(+) Bad Debts (Adjustment)	3,000		By Miscellaneous Receipts		38,000
New Provision for Doubtful Debts (Adjustment)	2,350				
	11,350				
(−) Old Provision for Doubtful Debts (Trail balance)	(11,000)	350			
To Carriage on Sales		11,000			
To Repairs		12,000			
To General Expenses	21,000				
(−) Prepaid Insurance	(400)	20,600			
To Interest on Loan	1,000				
(+) Outstanding Interest	500	1,500			

Particulars	Amt (₹)	Particulars	Amt (₹)
To Depreciation on Land and Buildings	21,500		
To Net Profit transferred to Capital A/c	82,050		
	1,61,000		1,61,000

Balance Sheet
as at 31st March, 2023

Liabilities		Amt (₹)	Assets		Amt (₹)
Creditors		1,00,000	Cash in Hand		3,000
Loan for Raman		20,000	Cash at Bank		15,000
Interest Outstanding		500	Debtors	50,000	
Capital	2,00,000		(−) Bad Debts (Adjustment)	(3,000)	
(+) Net Profit	82,050	2,82,050		47,000	
			(−) Now Provision for Doubtful Debts @ 5%	(2,350)	44,650
			Closing Stock		36,000
			Prepaid Insurance		400
			Investments		30,000
			Land and Buildings	2,15,000	
			(−) Depreciation	(21,500)	1,93,500
			Plant		80,000
		4,02,550			4,02,550

Working Note

Interest on Loan

Interest @ 10% on ₹ 20,000 for 9 months from 1st July, 2022 to 31st March, 2023

$$= 2,000 \times \frac{9}{12} = ₹\ 1,500$$

(−) Already Paid = (1,000)

Interest Outstanding = 500

Solved Question 13 From the following trial balance of Mr. Sarthak Chand Sen, prepare trading and profit and loss account for the year ended 31st March, 2023 and his balance sheet as on that date.

Trial Balance

Particulars	Amt (Dr)	Particulars	Amt (Cr)
Bad Debts	2,000	Capital	2,10,000
Carriage Inwards	4,000	Creditors	65,400
Purchases	5,60,000	Sales	6,80,000
Returns Inwards	15,000	Loan	60,000
Furniture	18,000	Discount	600
Wages	55,000	Purchase Returns	21,000
Debtors	70,000	Bills Payables	32,000
Rent	25,000		
Drawings	15,000		
Interest on Loan	2,000		
General Expenses	4,000		
Salaries	5,000		
Cash in Hand	10,000		
Land and Buildings	2,40,000		
Advertising	12,000		
Salesman's Commission	7,000		
Opening Stock	25,000		
	10,69,000		10,69,000

Adjustments

(i) There were further bad debts of ₹ 3,200 which could not be recorded earlier.

(ii) Rent is paid at the rate of ₹ 2,000 per months.

(iii) Create a provision for doubtful debts at 5% of net debtors.

(iv) Closing stock as on 31st March, 2023 is valued at ₹ 36,000.

(v) A purchase of furniture for ₹ 12,000 was included in purchases by mistake.

Sol.

In the Books of the Firm
Trading and Profit and Loss Account
for the year ended 31st March, 2023

Dr | Cr

Particulars		Amt (₹)	Particulars		Amt (₹)
To Opening Stock		25,000	By Sales	6,80,000	
To Purchases	5,60,000		(−) Sales Returns	(15,000)	6,65,000
(−) Purchase Returns	(21,000)		By Closing Stock		36,000
	5,39,000				
(−) Furniture Purchased	(12,000)	5,27,000			
To Carriage Inwards		4,000			
To Wages		55,000			
To Gross Profit c/d		90,000			
		7,01,000			7,01,000
To Bad Debt (Trial balance)	2,000		By Gross Profit b/d		90,000
(+) Bad Debts (Additional)	3,200	5,200	By Discount		600
To Provision for Doubtful Debts (@ 5% on ₹ 66,800)		3,340			
To Rent	25,000				
(−) Prepaid Rent	(1,000)	24,000			
To General Expense		4,000			
To Salesman's Commission		7,000			
To Salaries		5,000			
To Advertising		12,000			
To Interest on Loan		2,000			
To Net Profit transferred to Capital A/c		28,060			
		90,600			90,600

Balance Sheet
as at 31st March, 2023

Liabilities		Amt (₹)	Assets		Amt (₹)
Loan		60,000	Cash in Hand		10,000
Creditors		65,400	Debtors	70,000	
Bills Payables		32,000	(−) New Bad Debts	(3,200)	
Capital	2,10,000			66,800	
(+) Net Profit	28,060		(−) 5% Provision for Doubtful Debtors	(3,340)	63,460
	2,38,060		Closing Stock		36,000
(−) Drawings	(15,000)	2,23,060	Prepaid Rent		1,000
			Furniture	18,000	
			(+) Purchases	12,000	30,000
			Land and Buildings		2,40,000
		3,80,460			3,80,460

Solved Question 14 **From the following trial balance of Monika Textiles as at 31st March, 2022, prepare, trading and profit and loss account and balance sheet. Also pass the necessary adjustment entries.**

Name of Accounts	Debit Balance (₹)	Credit Balance (₹)
Stock at Commencement	15,00,000	—
Purchases and Sales	1,09,00,000	1,80,00,000
Manufacturing Wages	8,00,000	—
Fuel, Power and Lighting	12,00,000	—
Salaries	11,00,000	—
Income Tax	5,50,000	—
Loan to X @ (10% per annum)	5,00,000	—
Interest on X's Loan	—	30,000
Apprentice Premium	—	4,50,000
Rent	4,00,000	—
Rent Owing	—	60,000
Furniture (Includes furniture of ₹ 1,00,000 purchased on 1st October, 2021)	5,00,000	—
Bills Receivable and Bills Payable	6,00,000	1,60,000
Plant	72,00,000	—
Debtors and Creditors	28,00,000	13,00,000
Capital	—	1,00,00,000
Cash	19,50,000	—
	3,00,00,000	3,00,00,000

Additional Information

(i) **Closing stock was valued at ₹ 30,00,000.**
(ii) **Goods worth ₹ 5,00,000 were sold and dispatched on 28th March, 2022 but no entry was passed to this effect.**
(iii) **Goods costing ₹ 7,00,000 were purchased and included into stock but no entry was passed to record the purchases.**
(iv) **Create a provision of 2% for discount on debtors.**
(v) **Apprentice premium received on 1st April, 2021 was for 3 years.**
(vi) **Depreciate furniture by 10% per annum.**
(vii) **Salaries for the month of March, 2022 are still outstanding.**

Sol.

JOURNAL

Date	Particulars		LF	Amt (Dr)	Amt (Cr)
(i)	Closing Stock A/c	Dr		30,00,000	
	To Trading A/c				30,00,000
	(Being closing stock transferred to trading account)				
(ii)	Debtors A/c	Dr		5,00,000	
	To Sales A/c				5,00,000
	(Being goods sold but omitted to be recorded)				
(iii)	Purchase A/c	Dr		7,00,000	
	To Creditors A/c				7,00,000
	(Being goods purchased but omitted to be recorded)				
(iv)	Profit and Loss A/c	Dr		66,000	
	To Provision for Discount on Debtors A/c				66,000
	(Being provision for discount charged from profit and loss account)				
(v)	Apprentice Premium A/c	Dr		3,00,000	
	To Apprentice Premium Received in Advance A/c				3,00,000
	(Being apprentice premium received in advance)				
(vi)	Depreciation A/c	Dr		45,000	
	To Furniture A/c				45,000
	(Being depreciation charged on furniture)				

Date	Particulars		LF	Amt (Dr)	Amt (Cr)
(vii)	Salary A/c	Dr		1,00,000	
	To Salary Outstanding A/c				1,00,000
	(Being salary outstanding)				

Trading and Profit and Loss Account
for the year ending 31st March, 2022

Dr | Cr

Particulars		Amt (₹)	Particulars		Amt (₹)
To Opening Stock		15,00,000	By Sales	1,80,00,000	
To Purchases	1,09,00,000		(+) Sales (Adjustment)	5,00,000	1,85,00,000
(+) Creditors	7,00,000	1,16,00,000	By Closing Stock		30,00,000
To Manufacturing Wages		8,00,000			
To Fuel, Power and Lighting		12,00,000			
To Gross Profit c/d		64,00,000			
		2,15,00,000			2,15,00,000
To Rent		4,00,000	By Gross Profit b/d		64,00,000
To Provision for Discount on Debtors		66,000	By Interest on X's Loan	30,000	
To Depreciation on Furniture (WN)		45,000	(+) Accrued Interest	20,000	50,000
To Salaries	11,00,000		By Apprentice Premium	4,50,000	
(+) Outstanding Salaries	1,00,000	12,00,000	(−) Received in Advance	(3,00,000)	1,50,000
To Net Profit transferred to Capital A/c		48,89,000			
		66,00,000			66,00,000

Balance Sheet
as at 31st March, 2022

Liabilities		Amt (₹)	Assets		Amt (₹)
Bills Payable		1,60,000	Cash		19,50,000
Creditors	13,00,000		Bills Receivable		6,00,000
(+) Purchases	7,00,000	20,00,000	Debtors	28,00,000	
Rent Owing		60,000	(+) Sales	5,00,000	
Apprentice Premium Received in Advance		3,00,000		33,00,000	
Salary Outstanding		1,00,000	(−) Provision for Discount	(66,000)	32,34,000
Capital	1,00,00,000		Closing Stock		30,00,000
(+) Net Profit	48,89,000		Loan to X		5,00,000
	1,48,89,000		Accrued Interest on X's Loan		20,000
(−) Drawings (Income Tax)	(5,50,000)	1,43,39,000	Furniture	5,00,000	
			(−) Depreciation	(45,000)	4,55,000
			Plant		72,00,000
		1,69,59,000			1,69,59,000

Working Notes

1. Calculation of depreciation on furniture is as follows **Amt (₹)**

Depreciation on ₹ 4,00,000 for 1 year	=	40,000
Depreciation on ₹ 1,00,000 for 6 months	=	5,000
	=	45,000

2. Income tax will be treated as drawings.
3. Salaries ₹ 11,00,000 given in trial balance for 11 months. Therefore, 1 month salary ₹ 1,00,000 is outstanding.
4. Interest on loan $\left(5,00,000 \times \frac{10}{100}\right)$ = 50,000

= (30,000)

Accrued Interest = 20,000

Solved Question 15 **Following is the trial balance of Mr. Nand Kishore as at 31st March, 2024, you are required to prepare a trading and profit and loss account for the year ended 31st March, 2024 and a balance sheet as at the date, after making necessary adjustments.**

Trial Balance

Particulars	Debit Balance (₹)	Credit Balance (₹)
Mr. Nand Kishore's Capital Account	—	80,000
Mr. Nand Kishore's Drawings Account	6,000	—
Plant and Machinery (Balance on 1st April, 2023)	20,000	—
Plant and Machinery (Additions on 1st October, 2023)	5,000	—
Stock on 1st April, 2023	15,000	—
Purchases	82,000	—
Returns Inwards	2,000	—
Sundry Debtors	20,600	—
Furniture and Fixtures	5,000	—
Freight and Duty	2,000	—
Carriage Outwards	500	—
Rent, Rates and Taxes	4,600	—
Printing and Stationery	800	—
Trade Expenses	400	—
Sundry Creditors	—	10,000
Sales	—	1,20,000
Returns Outwards	—	1,000
Postage and Telegrams	800	—
Provision for Doubtful Debts	—	400
Discounts	—	800
Rent of Premises sub-let for Year to 30th October, 2024	—	1,200
Insurance Charges	700	—
Salaries and Wages	21,300	—
Cash in Hand	6,200	—
Cash at Bank	20,500	—
	2,13,400	2,13,400

Adjustments

(i) **Stock on 31st March, 2024 was valued at ₹ 14,600.**

(ii) **Write-off ₹ 600 as bad debts.**

(iii) **The provision for doubtful debts is to be maintained at 5% on sundry debtors.**

(iv) **Create a provision for discounts on debtors and on creditors at 2%.**

(v) **Provide for depreciation on furniture and fixture at 5% p.a and on plant and machinery at 20% p.a.**

(vi) **Insurance prepaid was ₹ 100.**

(vii) **A fire occurred on 25th March, 2024 in the godown and stock of the value of ₹ 5,000 was destroyed. It was fully insured and the insurance company admitted the claim in full.**

Sol.

In the Books of Nand Kishore
Trading and Profit and Loss Account
for the year ended 31st March, 2024

Dr | Cr

Particulars		Amt (₹)	Particulars		Amt (₹)
To Stock		15,000	By Sales	1,20,000	
To Purchases	82,000		(–) Returns	(2,000)	1,18,000
(–) Returns	(1,000)	81,000	By Closing Stock		14,600
To Freight and Duty		2,000	By Insurance Company (Good destroyed)		5,000
To Gross Profit transferred to Profit and Loss A/c		39,600			
		1,37,600			1,37,600

Particulars		Amt (₹)	Particulars		Amt (₹)
To Salaries and Wages		21,300	By Gross Profit Transferred from Trading A/c		39,600
To Rent, Rates and Taxes		4,600	By Discounts		800
To Postage and Telegrams		800	By Reserve for Discounts on Creditors		200
To Trade Expenses		400	By Rent Received	1,200	
To Printing and Stationery		800	(−) Received in Advance	(600)	600
To Carriage Outwards		500			
To Insurance Charges	700				
(−) Prepaid Insurance	(100)	600			
To Depreciation					
Plant and Machinery (WN)	4,500				
Furniture and Fixtures (5% of ₹ 5,000)	250	4,750			
To Provision for Doubtful Debts Required	1,000				
(+) Bad Debts	600				
	1,600				
(−) Existing Provisions	(400)	1,200			
To Provision for Discount on Debtors		380			
To Net Profit		5,870			
		41,200			41,200

Balance Sheet
as at 31st March, 2024

Liabilities		Amt (₹)	Assets		Amt (₹)
Rent Received in Advance		600	Cash at Bank		20,500
Sundry Creditors	10,000		Cash in Hand		6,200
(−) Reserve for Discounts	(200)	9,800	Sundry Debtors	20,000	
Capital on 1st April, 2023	80,000		(−) Provisions for Doubtful Debts	(1,000)	
(+) Net Profit	5,870			19,000	
	85,870		(−) Provision of Discounts	(380)	18,620
(−) Drawings	(6,000)	79,870	Stock		14,600
			Insurance Prepaid		100
			Insurance Company's		5,000
			Plant and Machinery on 1st April, 2023	20,000	
			(+) Addition	5,000	
				25,000	
			(−) Depreciation	(4,500)	20,500
			Furniture and Fixture	5,000	
			(−) Depreciation	(250)	4,750
		90,270			90,270

Working Note

Depreciation on plant and machinery = 20% of 20,000 + 20% of 2,500 (for 6 months) = 4,000 + 500 = ₹ 4,500

Solved Question 16 **From the following ledger balances of Surya Traders, prepare trading and profit and loss account for the year ended 31st March, 2022 and balance sheet as at that date after making the necessary adjustments.**

Name of Accounts	Amt (Dr)	Name of Accounts	Amt (Cr)
Stock	20,000	Sales	2,45,000
Cash	5,000	Creditors	30,000
Bank	10,000	Bills Payable	4,000
Carriage on Purchases	1,500	Capital	2,00,000
Purchases	1,90,000	Output CGST	10,000
Drawings	9,000	Output SGST	10,000
Wages	55,000		
Machinery	1,00,000		

Name of Accounts	Amt (Dr)	Name of Accounts	Amt (Cr)
Debtors	27,000		
Postage	300		
Sundry Expenses	1,700		
Rent	4,500		
Furniture	35,000		
Input CGST	20,000		
Input SGST	20,000		
	4,99,000		4,99,000

Additional Information

(i) **Stock on 31st March, 2022 valued at ₹ 40,000.**

(ii) **Goods worth ₹ 3,000 were distributed as free sample and goods worth ₹ 1,500 were used for personal purposes by the proprietor. These goods were purchased paying CGST and SGST @ 6% each.**

(iii) **Depreciate furniture by 10%.**

Sol.

Trading and Profit and Loss Account
for the year ending 31st March, 2022

Dr | Cr

Particulars		Amt (₹)	Particulars	Amt (₹)
To Opening Stock		20,000	By Sales	2,45,000
To Purchases	1,90,000		By Closing Stock	40,000
(−) Drawings	(5,000)			
(−) Free Sample	(3,000)	1,82,000		
To Carriage		1,500		
To Wages		55,000		
To Gross Profit c/d		26,500		
		2,85,000		2,85,000
To Postage		300	By Gross Profit	26,500
To Sundry Expenses		1,700		
To Rent		4,500		
To Advertisement		3,360		
To Depreciation on Furniture		3,500		
To Net Profit		13,140		
		26,500		26,500

Balance Sheet
as at 31st March, 2022

Liabilities		Amt (₹)	Assets		Amt (₹)
Capital	2,00,000		Machine		1,00,000
(+) Net Profit	13,140		Furniture	35,000	
(−) Drawings (9,000 + 5,600)	(14,600)	1,98,540	(−) Depreciation	(3,500)	31,500
Creditors		30,000	Debtors		27,000
Bills Payable		4,000	Closing Stock		40,000
			Cash		5,000
			Bank		10,000
			Input CGST	19,520	
			(−) Output CGST	(10,000)	9,520
			Input SGST	19,520	
			(−) Output SGST	(10,000)	9,520
		2,32,540			2,32,540

Working Notes

1. Adjustment Entry for Free Sample of Goods

Advertisement A/c	Dr	3,360	
To Purchase A/c			3,000
To Input CGST A/c			180
To Input SGST A/c			180

2. Adjustment Entry for Goods taken for Personal Use

Drawings A/c	Dr	5,600	
To Purchase A/c			5,000
To Input CGST A/c			300
To Input SGST A/c			300

Solved Question 17 **Prepare trading, profit and loss account and balance sheet from the following particulars as on 31st March, 2022.**

Name of Accounts	Debit Balance (₹)	Credit Balance (₹)
Cash in Hand	20,000	—
Cash at Bank	1,80,000	—
Purchase and Sales	22,00,000	35,00,000
Return Inwards	60,000	—
Return Outwards	—	75,000
Carriage on Purchases	44,000	—
Carriage on Sales	21,000	—
Fuel and Power	1,55,000	—
Stock (1st April, 2021)	3,60,000	—
Bad Debts	62,000	—
Bad Debts Provision	—	25,000
Debtors and Creditors	8,20,000	3,00,000
Capital	—	21,70,000
Investments	2,00,000	—
Interest on Investments	—	20,000
Loan from X (@ 18% per annum)	—	1,00,000
Repairs	15,200	—
General Expenses	1,06,000	—
Land and Buildings	18,00,000	—
Wages and Salaries	1,80,000	—
Miscellaneous Receipts	—	1,200
Bills Payable	—	52,000
Stationery	20,000	—
	62,43,200	62,43,200

Additional Information

(i) Written-off ₹ 20,000 as bad debts and provision for doubtful debts is to be maintained at 5% on debtors.
(ii) Loan from X was taken on 1st August, 2021. No interest has been paid so far.
(iii) Included in general expenses is insurance premium ₹ 12,000, paid for one year ending 30th June, 2022.
(iv) 1/3 of wages and salaries is to be charged to trading account and the balance to profit and loss account.
(v) Entire stationery was used by the proprietor for his personal own purpose.
(vi) Closing stock was valued at ₹ 5,00,000.

Sol.

Trading and Profit and Loss Account
for the year ended 31st March, 2022

Dr | Cr

Particulars		Amt (₹)	Particulars		Amt (₹)
To Stock 1st April, 2021		3,60,000	By Sales	35,00,000	
To Purchases	22,00,000		(−) Return Inwards	(60,000)	34,40,000
(−) Return Outwards	(75,000)	21,25,000	By Closing Stock		5,00,000
To Carriage on Purchases		44,000			
To Fuel and Power		1,55,000			

Particulars		Amt (₹)	Particulars	Amt (₹)
To Wages and Salaries		60,000		
To Gross Profit c/d		11,96,000		
		39,40,000		39,40,000
To Carriage on Sales		21,000	By Gross Profit b/d	11,96,000
To Wages and Salaries		1,20,000	By Interest on Investments	20,000
To Repairs		15,200	By Miscellaneous Receipts	1,200
To General Expenses	1,06,000			
(–) Prepaid Insurance	(3,000)	1,03,000		
To Bad Debts	62,000			
(+) Further Bad Debts	20,000			
(+) New Provision for Doubtful Debts	40,000			
	1,22,000			
(–) Old Provision	(25,000)	97,000		
To Outstanding Interest		12,000		
To Net Profit Transferred to Capital A/c		8,49,000		
		12,17,200		12,17,200

Balance Sheet
as at 31st March, 2022

Liabilities		Amt (₹)	Assets		Amt (₹)
Bills Payable		52,000	Cash in Hand		20,000
Creditors		3,00,000	Cash at Bank		1,80,000
Loan from X	1,00,000		Debtors	8,20,000	
(+) Outstanding Interest	12,000	1,12,000	(–) Further Bad Debts	(20,000)	
Capital	21,70,000			8,00,000	
(+) Net Profit	8,49,000		(–) Provision for Doubtful Debts	(40,000)	7,60,000
	30,19,000		Closing Stock		5,00,000
(–) Drawings (Stationery used)	(20,000)	29,99,000	Prepaid Insurance		3,000
			Investments		2,00,000
			Land and Buildings		18,00,000
		34,63,000			34,63,000

Working Notes

1. Provision for Doubtful Debts $= (8,20,000 - 20,000) \times \frac{5}{100} =$ ₹ 40,000
2. Interest on Loan (from August, 2021 to March, 2022) $= 1,00,000 \times \frac{18}{100} \times \frac{8}{12} =$ ₹ 12,000
3. Prepaid Insurance Premium $= 12,000 \times \frac{3}{12} =$ ₹ 3,000
4. Wages and salaries to be debited
   (i) in trading account $= 1,80,000 \times \frac{1}{3} =$ ₹ 60,000
   (ii) in profit and loss account $= 1,80,000 \times \frac{2}{3} =$ ₹ 1,20,000

Missing Information

Solved Question 18 **From the following trial balance of Sarnath and Sons, complete the trading account and profit and loss account for the year ending 31st December, 2022 and a balance sheet as on that date.**

Particulars	Amt (Dr)	Particulars	Amt (Cr)
Opening Stock	10,400	Capital	32,000
Purchases	31,000	Creditors	4,000
Sales Returns	600	Sales	40,000
Debtors	8,000	Commission	5,480
Building	10,000	Rent	4,000
Machinery	7,200		
Furniture	3,200		
Bills Receivable	4,000		
Salaries	3,200		
Tax	400		
Insurance	600		
Carriage on Purchases	1,800		
Trade Expenses	600		
Travelling Expenses	880		
Wages	2,000		
Cash	1,600		
	85,480		85,480

Adjustments

(i) Closing stock ₹ 24,000.

(ii) Rent due but not received ₹ 200.

(iii) Commission to the extent of ₹ 280 received in advance.

Trading and Profit and Loss Account
for the year ended 31st December, 2022

Dr | Cr

Particulars	Amt (₹)	Particulars		Amt (₹)
To Opening Stock	10,400	By Sales	40,000	
To Purchases	31,000	(–) Sales Returns	(600)	...
To Carriage on Purchases	1,800	By ...		...
To Wages	2,000			
To Gross Profit c/d	...			
				...
To Salaries	3,200	By Gross Profit b/d		...
To Tax	400	By Commission	5,480	
To Insurance	600	......	...	...
To Trade Expenses	600	By Rent	4,000	
To Travelling Expenses	880	......	...	...
To Net Profit transferred to Capital A/c	...			
	...			...

Sol.

Trading and Profit and Loss Account
for the year ended 31st December, 2022

Dr | Cr

Particulars	Amt (₹)	Particulars		Amt (₹)
To Opening Stock	10,400	By Sales	40,000	
To Purchases	31,000	(–) Sales Returns	(600)	**39,400**
To Carriage on Purchases	1,800	By **Closing Stock**		**24,000**
To Wages	2,000			
To Gross Profit c/d	**18,200**			
	63,400			**63,400**

Particulars	Amt (₹)	Particulars		Amt (₹)
To Salaries	3,200	By Gross Profit b/d		**18,200**
To Tax	400	By Commission	5,480	
To Insurance	600	(–) **Unearned Commission**	**(280)**	**5,200**
To Trade Expenses	600	By Rent	4,000	
To Travelling Expenses	880	(+) **Accrued Rent**	**200**	**4,200**
To Net Profit transferred to Capital A/c	**21,920**			
	27,600			**27,600**

Solved Question 19 **Prepare final accounts of a trader from the following trial balance as on 31st March, 2023**

Particulars	Amt (Dr)	Particulars	Amt (Cr)
Wages	15,000	Sales	4,80,000
Salaries	25,000	Capital	2,10,000
Carriage Inward	5,000	Sundry Creditors	30,000
Carriage Outward	4,000	Bills Payables	25,000
Returns Inwards	3,000	Discount Received	10,000
Purchases	3,60,000	Returns Outwards	5,000
Opening Stock	12,000		
Printing and Stationery	4,600		
Trade Expenses	2,400		
Rent, Rates and Taxes	8,000		
Discount Allowed	6,000		
Cash in Hand	15,000		
Cash at Bank	80,000		
Sundry Debtors	70,000		
Bad Debts	10,000		
Bills Receivables	30,000		
Investments	50,000		
Plant	60,000		
	7,60,000		7,60,000

The following adjustments are required to be made

(i) Closing stock is value at ₹ 18,000.

(ii) Stock costing ₹ 20,000 was stolen and it was not insured.

(iii) Depreciate on plant by 10%.

(iv) Create a provision of 5% on debtors and 2% for discount on debtors.

(v) A plant costing ₹ 60,000 was purchased on 31st August, 2022 but it was by mistake recorded in purchases book.

In the Books of the Firm
Trading and Profit and Loss Account
for the year ended 31st March, 2023

Dr | Cr

Particulars		Amt (₹)	Particulars		Amt (₹)
To Opening Stock		12,000	By Sales	4,80,000	
To Purchases	3,60,000		(–) Returns Inward	(3,000)	4,77,000
(–) Returns Outward	(5,000)		By …		…
…	…				
	2,95,000				
(–)…	(…)	…			
To Carriage Inward		5,000			
To Wages		15,000			
To Gross Profit c/d		1,88,000			
		…			…

Particulars		Amt (₹)	Particulars		Amt (₹)
To ...		...	By Gross Profit b/d		1,88,000
To Bad Debts		10,000	By Discount Received		10,000
To ...		...			
To ...		...			
To Salaries		25,000			
To Carriage Outwards		4,000			
To Depreciation					
(i) ...	...				
(ii) ...	...	...			
To Printing and Stationery		4,600			
To Trade Expenses		2,400			
To Rent, Rates and Taxes		8,000			
To Discount Allowed		6,000			
To Net Profit transferred to Capital A/c		...			
		...			...

Balance Sheet
as at 31st March, 2023

Liabilities		Amt (₹)	Assets		Amt (₹)
Share Capital	2,10,000		Plant	60,000	
(+) Net Profit	...	...	(+)...	...	
Creditors		30,000		1,20,000	
Bills Payables		25,000	(−)...	(...)	...
			Investments		50,000
			......		...
			Debtors	70,000	
			... Provision for Doubtful @ 5%	...	
		...	... Provision for Discount	...	...
			Bills Receivables		30,000
			Cash at Bank		80,000
			Cash in Hand		15,000
		3,68,670			3,68,670

Sol.

In the Books of the Firm
Trading and Profit and Loss Account
for the year ended 31st March, 2023

Dr | Cr

Particulars		Amt (₹)	Particulars		Amt (₹)
To Opening Stock		12,000	By Sales	4,80,000	
To Purchases	3,60,000		(−) Returns Inward	(3,000)	4,77,000
(−) Returns Outward	(5,000)		By **Closing Stock**		**18,000**
Plant	**(60,000)**				
	2,95,000				
(−) Stock Lost by Theft	**(20,000)**	**2,75,000**			
To Carriage Inward		5,000			
To Wages		15,000			
To Gross Profit c/d		1,88,000			
		4,95,000			**4,95,000**
To **Loss by Theft**		**20,000**	By Gross Profit b/d		1,88,000
To Bad Debts		10,000	By Discount Received		10,000
To New Provision for Doubtful Debts		**3,500**			
To Provision for Discount on Debtors (See balance sheet)		**1,330**			
To Salaries		25,000			

Particulars		Amt (₹)	Particulars	Amt (₹)
To Carriage Outwards		4,000		
To Depreciation				
(i) Old Plant	**6,000**			
(ii) New Plant for 7 Months	**3,500**	**9,500**		
To Printing and Stationery		4,600		
To Trade Expenses		2,400		
To Rent, Rates and Taxes		8,000		
To Discount Allowed		6,000		
To Net Profit transferred to Capital A/c		**1,03,670**		
		1,98,000		**1,98,000**

Balance Sheet
as at 31st March, 2023

Liabilities		Amt (₹)	Assets		Amt (₹)
Share Capital	2,10,000		Plant	60,000	
(+) Net Profit	**1,03,670**	**3,13,670**	(+) **New Plant (Purchases)**	**60,000**	
Creditors		30,000		1,20,000	
Bills Payables		25,000	(–) **Depreciation**	**(9,500)**	**1,10,500**
			Investments		50,000
			Closing Stock		**18,000**
			Debtors	70,000	
			(–) Provision for Doubtful Debts @ 5%	**(3,500)**	
			(–) Provision for Discount	**(1,330)**	**65,170**
			Bills Receivables		30,000
			Cash at Bank		80,000
			Cash in Hand		15,000
		3,68,670			3,68,670

Numerical Questions

Adjustments 1 to 6

1. From the following trial balance of Sambhav and Sons, prepare trading and profit and loss account for the year ended and balance sheet as on 31st March, 2023.

Trial Balance
as on 31st March, 2023

Particulars	Debit Balance (₹)	Particulars	Credit Balance (₹)
Royalties	4,000	Sundry Creditors	56,000
Drawings	10,000	Sales	81,000
Wages	6,000	Purchase Returns	3,000
Purchases	71,000	Capital	2,50,000
Cash	10,000	Bills Payable	20,000
Sales Returns	5,000	Bank Overdraft	40,000
Bank	40,000		
Insurance	1,000		
Furniture	34,000		
Buildings	1,20,000		
Sundry Debtors	1,00,000		
Bad Debts	1,000		
Sundry Expenses	3,000		
Travelling Expenses	2,000		
Opening Stock	24,000		
Carriage Outwards	1,600		
Rent	1,000		
Carriage Inward	400		
Salaries	16,000		
	4,50,000		4,50,000

Additional Information

Closing stock was valued ₹ 54,000.

Ans. Gross profit = ₹ 27,600 ; Net profit = ₹ 2,000 ; Balance sheet = ₹ 3,58,000

2. From the following trial balance of a trader, prepare his profit and loss account and balance sheet in the vertical form as on 31st March, 2023

Particulars	Amt (Dr)	Particulars	Amt (Cr)
Debtors	14,500	Capital	71,000
Drawings	5,250	Return Outwards	200
General Expenses	3,000	Sales	99,080
Insurance	600	Creditors	6,300
Salaries	15,000	Commission Earned	2,000
Investments	10,000	Long-term Loan	10,000
Goodwill	7,500		
Plant	20,000		
Land and Buildings	40,000		
Opening Stock (1st April, 2022)	5,760		
Carriage Inwards	2,040		
Carriage on Sales	3,200		
Fuel and Power	4,730		
Wages	10,480		
Return Inwards	680		
Purchases	40,670		
Cash at Bank	2,600		
Cash in Hand	1,000		
Discount Allowed	500		
Interest	1,000		
Bad Debts	70		
	1,88,580		1,88,580

Adjustments

(i) Closing stock was valued at ₹ 3,480.

(ii) Depreciation on plant and buildings at 10%.

Ans. Gross profit = ₹ 38,400 ; Net profit = ₹ 11,030 ; Balance sheet = ₹ 93,080

3. Prepare trading and profit and loss account for the year ended 31st March, 2023 and a balance sheet as at that date, from the following trial balance extracted from the books of Kanishka Garg.

Name of Accounts	Amt (Dr)	Name of Accounts	Amt (Cr)
Opening Stock	2,000	Sales	27,000
Purchases	8,000	Purchases Return	400
Sales Return	600	Discount	520
Carriage Inwards	360	Creditors	2,500
Carriage Outwards	80	Bills Payable	180
Wages	4,200	Capital	7,500
Salaries	2,750		
Plant and Machinery	9,000		
Furniture and Fixtures	800		
Debtors	5,200		
Bills Receivable	250		
Cash	630		
Trade Expenses	370		
Lighting (Factory)	140		
Rent and Taxes	720		
Selling Expenses	1,050		
Insurance	150		
Drawings	1,800		
	38,100		38,100

Adjustments

(i) Stock on 31st March, 2023 was valued at ₹ 2,400 (realisable value ₹ 3,000).

(ii) Wages outstanding for March, 2022 amounted to ₹ 300.

(iii) Salaries outstanding for March, 2022 amounted to ₹ 250.

(iv) Prepaid insurance amounted to ₹ 30.

(v) Provide depreciation on plant and machinery at 5% and on furniture at 20%.

Ans. Gross profit = ₹ 14,200; Net profit = ₹ 8,770; Balance sheet = ₹ 17,700

4. From the following trial balance of Neeraj Lal, prepare trading and profit and loss account for the year ended 31st March, 2023 and a balance sheet as on that date.

Competency Based Que

Trial Balance
as on 31st March, 2023

Particulars	Debit Balance (₹)	Particulars	Credit Balance (₹)
Opening Stock	80,000	Sales	10,80,000
Purchases	3,20,000	Purchase Return	16,000
Sales Return	24,000	Discount	20,800
Carriage Inwards	14,400	Sundry Creditors	1,00,000
Carriage Outwards	3,200	Bills Payable	7,200
Wages	1,68,000	Capital	3,00,000
Salaries	1,10,000		
Plant and Machinery	3,60,000		
Furniture	32,000		
Sundry Debtors	2,08,000		
Bills Receivable	10,000		
Cash in Hand	25,200		
Travelling Expenses	14,800		
Lighting (Factory)	5,600		
Rent and Taxes	28,800		
General Expenses	42,000		
Insurance	6,000		
Drawings	72,000		
	15,24,000		15,24,000

Adjustments

(i) Stock on 31st March, 2023 was valued at ₹ 96,000 (market value ₹ 1,20,000).

(ii) Wages outstanding for March, 2023 amounted to ₹ 12,000.

(iii) Salaries outstanding for March, 2023 amounted to ₹ 10,000.

(iv) Prepaid insurance amounted to ₹ 1,200.

(v) Provide depreciation on plant and machinery at 5% and on furniture at 20%.

Ans. Gross profit = ₹ 5,68,000 ; Net profit = ₹ 3,50,800 ; Balance sheet = ₹ 7,08,000

Adjustments 7 to 9

5. The following balances were taken from the books of Ashish for the year ended 31st March, 2016. Prepare his final accounts as on that date.

Particulars	Amt (₹)	Particulars	Amt (₹)
Plant and Machinery	42,000	Reserve Fund	5,000
Capital	90,000	Creditors	41,400
Drawings	15,000	Sales	1,80,000
Accumulated Dep.	1,000	Postage	800
Opening Stock	4,000	Bad Debts	500
Purchases	85,000	Prov. for Doub. Debts	900
Debtors	60,000	Discount Received	400
Carriage Inwards	3,000	Rent Received	2,400
Furniture	14,000	Insurance	800
Carriage Outwards	600	Salaries	40,000
Rent and Taxes	4,200	Wages	10,200
Cash in Hand	6,000		
Cash at Bank	35,000		

Adjustments

(i) Provide depreciation on plant and machinery at 10% and furniture 5%.

(ii) Prepaid insurance is ₹ 200.

(iii) Outstanding wages are ₹ 800 and rent ₹ 1,800.

(iv) Create a provision for doubtful debts at 5% on debtors and for discount on debtors at 2% of debtors.

Ans. Gross profit = ₹ 77,000; Net profit = ₹ 23,160; Balance sheet = ₹ 1,53,060

6. From the following trial balance of Seerat Enterprise, you are required to prepare trading account, profit and loss account for the year ending on 31st March, 2023 and balance sheet as on that date.

Trial Balance
as on 31st March, 2023

Particulars	Debit Balance (₹)	Credit Balance (₹)
Opening Stock	45,200	—
Capital	—	3,00,000
Drawings	20,000	—
Furniture	60,000	—
Prepaid Insurance	1,770	—
Debtors and Creditors	70,000	1,29,250
Purchase and Sales	57,000	1,20,000
Plant and Machinery	50,000	—
Investment	68,000	—
Factory Insurance	26,000	—
Audit Fees	21,000	—
Carriage Inwards	1,800	—
Land and Buildings	1,40,000	—
Rent	7,120	—
Reserve for Bad Debts	—	6,000
Carriage Outwards	8,360	—
Returns	2,000	9,000
Discount	1,000	7,000
Commission Received	—	8,000
	5,79,250	5,79,250

Adjustments

(i) Write-off bad debts ₹ 2,000 and provide 2.5% reserve for bad debts on debtors.
(ii) Closing stock valued at cost price ₹ 46,000 and market price ₹ 40,000.
(iii) Provide depreciation @ 5% on building and 10% on machinery.
(iv) Rent prepaid ₹ 3,560.
(v) Outstanding carriage inward is ₹ 1,200.

Ans. Gross profit = ₹ 35,800 ; Net profit = ₹ 7,180 ; Balance sheet = ₹ 4,17,630

7. From the following trial balance of Samay for the year ended 31st March, 2023, prepare his trading and profit and loss account and balance sheet.

Particulars	Amt (Dr)	Particulars	Amt (Cr)
Debtors	25,000	Capital	90,000
Bills Receivable	15,000	Sales	2,00,000
Buildings	1,10,000	Discount	2,000
Plant	90,000	Commission	4,500
Opening Stock	10,000	Creditors	92,000
Purchases (Adjusted)	80,000	Bills Payables	25,500
Closing Stock	5,000		
Insurance Prepaid	6,000		
Factory Lighting	2,000		
Factory Rent	3,000		
Trade Expenses	4,000		
Manufacturing Expenses	1,200		
Wages	4,800		
Carriage Inwards	1,200		
Insurance Account	14,000		
Freight	800		
Packing Expenses	3,000		
Discount Allowed	1,000		
Bad Debts	2,000		
Cash in Hand	500		
Cash at Bank	15,500		
Investments	20,000		
	4,14,000		4,14,000

Adjustments

(i) Charge depreciation @ 10% on buildings and 5% on plant.
(ii) There are further bad debts of ₹ 500.
(iii) Create provision for doubtful debts at 5% on debtors.
(iv) A commission of ₹ 1,500 has accrued but not yet received.

Ans. Gross profit = ₹ 97,000; Net profit = ₹ 63,775; Balance sheet = ₹ 2,71,275

8. Following is the trial balance of Kamana Enterprises. You are required to prepare trading and profit and loss account for the year ended 31st March, 2023 and balance sheet as on that date after taking into account the additional information provided to you.

Competency Based Que

Trial Balance
as on 31st March, 2023

Particulars	Debit Balance (₹)	Credit Balance (₹)
Capital Account	—	50,000
Drawings	1,750	—
Opening Stock	8,000	—
Purchase and Sales	16,500	22,500
Returns	625	750
Carriage Outwards	425	—
Wages – Productive	1,000	—
– Unproductive	600	—
Salaries	1,000	—
Travelling Expenses	1,125	—
Trade Expenses	325	—
Fuel and Coal	250	—
Discount	460	550
Sundry Expenses	225	—
Bad Debts	200	—
Plant and Machinery	20,000	—
Furniture	5,500	—
Packing Expenses	175	—
Sundry Debtors and Creditors	10,090	6,750
Cash in Hand	2,200	—
Investments	10,250	—
Reserve for Doubtful Debts	—	150
	80,700	80,700

Additional Information

(i) Closing stock of goods on 31st March, 2023 valued at ₹ 7,100 at cost price and ₹ 7,500 as market price.
(ii) Travelling expenses include ₹ 125 spent on personal travelling.
(iii) ₹ 175 are to be written-off as bad debts which were due from Mr. Aniket, a debtor and 5% provision for doubtful debts is to be maintained on debtors.
(iv) Reserve for discount on debtors as well as on creditors is to be maintained at 2% and 3% respectively.
(v) Provide 10% depreciation on plant and machinery and furniture.

Ans. Gross profit = ₹ 3,650 ; Net profit = ₹ 2,942 ; Balance sheet = ₹ 51,730

9. **From the following trial balance, prepare trading account, profit and loss account and balance sheet for the year ended 31st December, 2022.**

Particulars	Amt (₹)	Particulars	Amt (₹)
Opening Stock	10,000	Sales	5,20,000
Purchases	3,00,000	Purchases Returns	10,000
Debtors	1,40,000	Creditors	1,00,000
Drawings	20,000	Provision for Bad Debts	4,000
Sales Returns	16,000	Bills Payable	30,000
Wages	24,000	Bank Overdraft	20,000
Salaries	40,000	Capital	7,20,000
Repairs	12,000		
Bad Debts	8,000		
Carriage	4,000		
Discount	6,000		
Land and Building	4,00,000		
Plant and Machinery	3,00,000		
Furniture and Fixtures	80,000		
Cash	4,000		
Goodwill	40,000		
	14,04,000		14,04,000

Adjustments

(i) Closing stock ₹ 40,000.
(ii) Further bad debts ₹ 6,000.
(iii) Create a reserve for doubtful debts @ 5%.
(iv) Create a provision for discount on debtors and creditors @ 2%.
(v) Charge depreciation on plant and machinery, and furniture and fixtures @ 10% per annum.

Ans. Gross profit = ₹ 2,16,000; Net profit = ₹ 1,02,754; Balance sheet = ₹ 9,50,754

Adjustments 10 to 14

10. **Prepare final accounts for the year ended 31st March, 2023 from the following trial balance of Nandini Sharma.**

Trial Balance

Particulars	Amt (Dr)	Particulars	Amt (Cr)
Purchases	2,50,000	Sales	5,00,000
Returns Inwards	12,000	Returns Outwards	10,000
Carriage	8,000	Creditors	1,00,000
Wages	60,000	Bills Payables	2,000
Trade Expenses	2,000	Commission	1,000
Insurance	1,200	Loan from Bank @ 12%	30,000
Repairs	8,000	Capital	2,40,000
Debtors	1,15,000	Rent Received	5,000
Printing and Stationery	6,000		
Advertising	15,000		
Bills Receivables	4,000		
Opening Stock	30,000		
Cash in Hand	12,000		
Cash at Bank	28,000		
Interest on Bank Loan	2,800		
Machines	2,80,000		
Furniture	34,000		
Drawings	20,000		
	8,88,000		8,88,000

Adjustments

(i) Closing stock on 31st March, 2023 was ₹ 21,000.
(ii) Rent of ₹ 1,200 has been received in advance.
(iii) Allow 5% interest on capital and charges ₹ 900 as interest on drawings.
(iv) Commission earned during the year but not received was ₹ 2,100.

Ans. Gross profit = ₹ 1,71,000 ; Net profit = ₹ 1,31,000 ; Balance sheet = ₹ 4,96,100

11. **From the following trial balance of Nandini & Co. as on 31st March, 2019. Prepare final accounts after considering the adjustments given below.**

Competency Based Que

Particulars	Debit Balance (₹)	Credit Balance (₹)
Loose Tools	1,10,000	—
Furniture and Fixtures	81,000	—
Bad Debts	1,400	—
Sundry Debtors	81,600	—
Stock (31st March, 2022)	52,000	—
Purchases	77,000	—
Sales Cash	—	21,000
Sales Credit	—	81,000
Returns	400	600
Advertisements	4,800	—
Rate, Taxes and Insurances	6,000	—
Repairs and Maintenance	1,200	—
Salaries (2/3rd for Factory)	18,000	—
Rent (Paid for 11 Months)	2,200	—
Machinery (Includes ₹ 24,000 purchased on 1st October, 2022)	84,000	—
Capital	—	3,60,000
Provision for Doubtful Debts	—	8,000
Sundry Creditors	—	70,000
Drawings	14,000	—
Interest	—	1,200
Dividend	—	2,800
Bank Balance	40,000	—
Royalty	6,000	—
9% Bank Loan (30th September, 2022)	—	40,000
Carriage Outwards	4,000	—
Discount	1,000	—
	5,84,600	5,84,600

Adjustments

(i) Closing stock valued at ₹ 1,00,000.
(ii) Write-off ₹ 2,000 as bad debts and create a provision for doubtful debts @ 5% on sundry debtors.

(iii) Depreciate machinery by 10% p.a. and loose tools is valued at ₹ 1,00,000.

(iv) Charge interest on capital @ 2% p.a.

Ans. Gross profit = ₹ 55,200; Net profit = ₹ 8,220; Balance sheet = ₹ 4,73,420

12. From the following figures prepare the trading and profit and loss account for the year ended 31st March, 2022 and the balance sheet as at that date.

Name of Accounts	Amt (Dr)	Name of Accounts	Amt (Cr)
Stock (1st April, 2021)	1,50,000	Sundry Debtors	1,64,000
Purchases	16,00,000	Loan from Vishal	20,000
Sales	24,00,000	Interest on Vishal's Loan	3,000
Motor Car	3,00,000	Furniture	40,000
Car Expenses	84,000	Land and Building	4,00,000
Rent	11,000	Capital	5,00,000
Salaries	70,400	Sundry Creditors	1,82,600
Bad Debts	3,000	Returns Inward	15,000
Provision for Bad Debts	16,200	Returns Outward	12,000
Commission (Cr)	9,200	Cash in Hand	32,800
Wages	2,50,000		
Insurance	16,800		

Additional Information Competency Based Que

(i) Commission include ₹ 3,200 being commission received in advance.

(ii) Write-off ₹ 4,000 as further bad debts and maintain bad debts provision at 5% on debtors.

(iii) Expenses paid in advance are : Wages ₹ 10,000 and insurance ₹ 2,400.

(iv) Rent and salaries have been paid for 11 months.

(v) Loan from Vishal has been taken at 18% per annum interest.

(vi) Depreciate furniture by 15% per annum and motor car by 20% per annum.

(vii) Closing stock was valued at ₹ 1,20,000.

Ans. Gross profit = ₹ 5,27,000 ; Net profit = ₹ 2,77,400 ; Balance sheet = ₹ 9,91,200

13. Prepare trading account, profit and loss account for the year ended on 31st March, 2023 and balance sheet as on that date.

Trial Balance
as on 31st March, 2023

Particulars	Debit Bal. (₹)	Particulars	Credit Bal. (₹)
Opening Stock	14,400	Creditors	19,300
Debtors	30,000	Returns Outwards	750
Return Inwards	1,650	Sales	20,000
Rent, Rates and Insurance	2,250	Discount	365
Productive Wages	2,525	Capital	75,000
Discount	390	Outstanding Interest	650
Interest	475	Loan	7,500
Loss by Fire	1,650		
Salaries	1,850		
Purchases	24,350		
Drawings	2,500		
Carriage Outwards	1,275		
Loose Tools	17,500		
Plant and Machinery	14,000		
Cash in Hand	1,250		
Cash at Bank	7,500		
	1,23,565		1,23,565

Adjustments

(i) Stock as on 31st March, 2018, amounted to ₹ 48,500.

(ii) Charge depreciation on loose tools @ 10% and on plant and machinery @ 15%.

(iii) Prepaid insurance amounted to ₹ 500 and outstanding rent ₹ 400.

(iv) Charge interest on capital @ 5% and on drawings 7%.

(v) Outstanding salary ₹ 650.

Ans. Gross profit = ₹ 26,325 ; Net profit = ₹ 10,738; Balance Sheet = ₹ 1,15,400

Hint Amount of drawing given in trial balance is ₹ 2,500. So, 7% on ₹ 2,500 = ₹ 175

Interest on drawings is charged for 6 months only. Therefore 175/2 = 88.

It means, drawings 2,500 + 88 = ₹ 2,588

14. From the following information prepare financial statements of M/S Rajan and Bros. for the year ending 31st March, 2022.

Name of Accounts	Amt (Dr)	Name of Accounts	Amt (Cr)
Stock (1st April, 2021)	33,600	Capital	1,56,000
Sales Returns	16,000	Sales	6,18,000
Purchases	4,86,000	Return Outward	11,400
Freight Inwards	17,200	Trade Creditors	9,600
Rent and Taxes	11,400	10% Bank Loan (1st July, 2021)	48,000
Salaries	18,600		
Trade Debtors	48,000	Income from Investment	7,200
Bank Interest	2,000	Discount Received	4,500
Printing and Advertising	29,200		
Cash at Bank	36,600		
Discount Allowed	2,680		
Investment	50,000		
Furniture	7,600		
General Expenses	7,220		
Audit Fees	1,000		
Insurance	1,600		
Travelling Expenses	6,000		
Plant and Machinery	60,000		
Drawings	20,000		
	8,54,700		8,54,700

Additional Information

(i) Depreciation on plant and machinery @ 10% per annum, a machine has been purchased on 1st July, 2021 for ₹ 24,000.

(ii) The manager is entitled to a commission of 10% of the net profit before charging such commission.

(iii) Closing stock-in-trade is valued at ₹ 12,000 (Cost), ₹ 12,400 (Market price).

(iv) Rent outstanding ₹ 10,000.

Ans. Gross profit = ₹ 88,600 ; Net profit = ₹ 3,240 ; Balance sheet = ₹ 2,08,800

15. **The following is the trial balance of Ram Krishan Vyas on 31st March, 2022. Prepare trading and profit and loss account, and balance sheet after making the following adjustments.** **Competency Based Que**

(i) Value of closing stock ₹ 29,638.

(ii) Depreciate plant and machinery @ 10%, furniture @ 5% and horses and carts by ₹ 1,000. Also write-off goodwill by ₹ 3,000.

(iii) Provide 5% for doubtful debts on debtors.

(iv) Prepaid expenses insurance ₹ 300 and taxes ₹ 190.

(v) 3/5th of insurance and taxes, rent and general expenses to be charged to factory and the balance to the office.

(vi) Advertising is to be written-off over 3 years.

(vii) Commission to manager @ 10% on net profit after charging such commission.

Name of Accounts	Amt (Dr)	Name of Accounts	Amt (Cr)
Plant and Machinery	19,720	Capital	80,000
Manufacturing Wages	34,965	Creditors	50,160
Salaries	10,135	Bank Loan	10,000
Furniture	9,480	Purchases Return	1,140
Freight on Purchases	1,980	Sales	2,46,850
Freight on Sales	2,150	Provision for Bad Debts	6,000
Building	25,000		
Manufacturing Expenses	9,455		
Fuel and Power	1,276		
Electricity (Factory)	986		
Insurance and Taxes	4,175		
Goodwill	30,000		
Rent	2,400		
Debtors	78,140		
Stable Expenses	2,473		
Opening Stock	34,170		
Horses and Carts	5,165		
Purchases	97,165		
Sales Returns	3,170		
General Expenses	8,000		
Bad Debts	1,485		
Interest and Bank Charges	475		
Advertising	4,500		
Bank Balance	7,540		
Cash	145		
	3,94,150		3,94,150

Ans. Gross profit = ₹ 86,010 ; Net profit = ₹ 52,550 ; Balance sheet = ₹ 1,97,965

Hints (i) Advertising to be debited to profit and loss account

$$= 4{,}500 \times \frac{1}{3}$$

$$= ₹\ 1{,}500$$

(ii) **Calculation of Provision for Doubtful Debts**

	Amt (₹)
To Bad Debts	1,485
(+) New Provision	3,907
	5,392
(–) Old Provision	(6,000)
	(608)

When the resultant figure is negative, it will be shown on the credit side of profit and loss account.

Adjustments 15 to 17 (Including GST)

16. **From the following trial balance of Namita, you are required to prepare trading account and profit and loss account for the year ended 31st March, 2019 and balance sheet as on that date.**

Particulars	Debit Balance (₹)	Particulars	Credit Balance (₹)
Drawings	2,000	Capital	80,000
Motor Car	30,000	Sundry Creditors	25,000
Cash in Hand	1,000	Dividend	4,800
Bills Receivable	20,000	Commission	2,535
Wages	1,000	8% Loan (taken on 1st July, 2018)	13,700
Discount	235		
Rent	300	Purchases Return	400
Advertisement	2,500	Sales	38,680
Bad Debts	500		
Travelling Expenses	1,000		
Purchases	27,400		
Machinery	30,000		
Office Expenses	500		
Sales Returns	680		
Opening Stock	10,000		
Sundry Debtors	35,500		
Carriage Outward	500		
Cash at Bank	2,000		
	1,65,115		1,65,115

Adjustments

(i) Stock on 31st March, 2019 was valued at ₹ 28,000.

(ii) Create a provision for doubtful debts on sundry debtors @ 5%.

(iii) Depreciate motor car by 5% p.a. and machinery by 7% p.a.

(iv) Outstanding expenses rent ₹ 800 and wages ₹ 1,000

(v) Charge interest on capital @ 3% p.a.

(vi) Goods of ₹ 4,000 withdrawn by proprietor for personal use.

Ans. Gross profit = ₹ 31,000; Net profit ₹ 23,403; Balance sheet = ₹ 1,41,125

17. **Prepare trading account, profit and loss account for the year ending 31st March, 2019 and balance sheet as on that date from the following trial balance and additional information.** **Competency Based Que**

Trial Balance
as on 31st March, 2019

Particulars	Debit Balance (₹)	Particulars	Credit Balance (₹)
Machinery	1,00,000	Discount	2,000
Sundry Debtors	1,20,800	Sales	77,500
Furniture	36,000	Purchases Return	4,800
Stock (1st April, 2018)	20,000	Creditors	52,000
Wages	1,800	10% Bank Loan (taken on 1st Oct, 2018)	76,000
Electricity Charges	4,600		
Insurance	5,000	Provision for Doubtful Debts	1,600
Factory Rent	4,600		
Travelling Expenses	3,600	Bank Overdraft	53,300
Advertisement	2,500	Capital	1,00,000
Office Rent	3,000		
Purchases	49,300		
Sales Return	2,800		
Bad Debts	1,200		
Drawings	12,000		
	3,67,200		3,67,200

Adjustments

(i) Stock as on 31st March, 2019 amounted to ₹ 57,000.

(ii) Depreciate machinery and furniture @ 5%.

(iii) Unexpired insurance ₹ 1,000.

(iv) ₹ 800 are written-off as bad debts and create a provision for reserve for doubtful debts @ 5% on sundry debtors and reserve for discount on debtors @ 2% and discount on creditors @ 3%.

(v) Outstanding expenses i.e. wages ₹ 2,200 and office rent ₹ 1,400.

(vi) Goods withdrawn worth ₹ 2,000 by owner for personal use.

Ans. Gross profit = ₹ 60,600; Net profit = ₹ 25,780; Balance sheet = ₹ 2,98,920

18. **From the following trial balance of Nidan Enterprise, prepare the trading account and profit and loss account for the year ended 31st March, 2023 and balance sheet as on that date.** **Competency Based Que**

Trial Balance
as on 31st March, 2023

Particulars	Debit Balance (₹)	Particulars	Credit Balance (₹)
Cash in Hand	5,200	Capital	50,000
Opening Stock	10,370	Bank Loan	15,000
Goodwill	10,000	Bills Payable	8,500
Patents	4,000	Creditors	38,260
Cash at Bank	4,400	General Reserve	1,500
Freight	2,500	Dividend	2,000
Power and Fuel	1,500	Interest on Fixed	3,440
Furniture	12,000	Deposits	40,000
Purchases	35,260	Sales	
Mobile Charges	3,200		
Factory Salaries	2,400		
Repairs	800		
Lighting	1,000		
Carriage Outwards	360		
Professional Charges	1,240		
Debtors	40,000		
Plant and Machinery	13,700		
Office Equipments	10,000		
Carriage Inwards	770		
	1,58,700		1,58,700

Adjustments

(i) Closing stock was ₹ 32,000.

(ii) Write-off 50% of patents, depreciate plant and machinery by 10% p.a. and office equipments by 20%.

(iii) Reserve for bad debts is to be created @ 5% and discount on debtors @ 2%.

(iv) Outstanding expenses i.e. mobile charges ₹ 300 and freight ₹ 500.

(v) Charge interest on capital @ 5%.

(vi) Goods of ₹ 2,000 distributed on free sample.

Ans. Gross profit = ₹ 20,700; Net profit ₹ 6,610; Balance sheet = ₹ 1,23,170

19. **From the following balances, prepare trading, profit and loss account, and a balance sheet as at 31st March, 2022.**

Name of Accounts	Amt (Dr)	Name of Accounts	Amt (Cr)
Stock (1st April, 2021)	40,000	Goodwill	32,000
Purchases	5,84,000	Furniture and Fittings	1,16,000
Duty and Clearing Charges	68,000	Repair Charges	5,800
		Bank	48,000
Capital	3,20,000	Salaries	2,20,000
Sales	11,80,000	General Expenses	36,000

Name of Accounts	Amt (Dr)	Name of Accounts	Amt (Cr)
Rent	20,000	Debtors	4,60,000
Returns Inwards	32,000	Creditors	2,70,000
Cash Discount Allowed	30,000		
Cash Discount Received	38,000		
Drawings	1,16,200		

Take the following adjustments into account

(i) General expenses include ₹ 10,000 chargeable to furniture purchased on 1st October, 2021.
(ii) Create a reserve of 5% on debtors for bad and doubtful debts after treating ₹ 60,000 as a bad debt.
(iii) Rent for two months is outstanding.
(iv) Depreciation on furniture and fittings for the year is to be at the rate of 10% per annum.
(v) Closing stock was ₹ 80,000, but there was a loss by fire on 20th March to the extent of ₹ 16,000. Insurance company admitted the claim in full.
(vi) Goods costing ₹ 5,000 were used by the proprietor.
(vii) Goods costing ₹ 3,000 were distributed as free samples.

Ans. Gross profit = ₹ 5,60,000 ; Net profit = ₹ 1,97,100 ; Balance sheet = 6,69,000

20. **From the following trial balance extracted from the books of Jagdish, prepare trading and profit and loss account for the year ended 31st March, 2022 and balance sheet as at that date.** **Competency Based Que**

Name of Accounts	Amt (Dr)	Name of Accounts	Amt (Cr)
Opening Stock	15,500	Sales	2,07,300
Purchases	1,06,000	Purchases Return	2,100
Sales Return	5,100	Loan from Mrs. Jagdish @ 9% p.a.	30,000
Wages	26,000		
Salaries	10,000	Discount	1,200
Rent and Taxes	2,200	Sundry Creditors	9,600
Repairs	4,900	Capital	60,000
Telephone Expenses	1,800	Output IGST	10,000
Miscellaneous Expenses	2,800		
Stationery	1,000		
Postage Expenses	1,000		
Land and Buildings	35,000		
Plant and Machinery	50,000		
Furniture	5,000		
Sundry Debtors	30,000		
Bad Debts	600		
Freight on Purchases	2,800		
Carriage on Sales	4,000		
Cash in Hand	5,000		
Cash at Bank	5,500		
Input CGST	2,000		
Input SGST	2,000		
Input IGST	2,000		
	3,20,200		3,20,200

Adjustments

(i) Provide depreciation on land and building @ 2%, plant and machinery @ 10% and furniture @ 15%.
(ii) Stock on 31st March, 2022 was ₹ 14,900.
(iii) General manager is entitled to a commission of 10% of the net profit after charging such commission.
(iv) Miscellaneous expenses included an insurance premium of ₹ 600 paid in advance for the next year.
(v) Loan from Mrs. Jagdish was taken on 1st October, 2021. Interest has not yet been paid.
(vi) Create provision for doubtful debts @ 5% on sundry debtors.
(vii) Wages for March, 2022 amounting to ₹ 2,100 have not yet been paid.

Ans. Gross profit = ₹ 66,800 ; Net profit = ₹ 28,182; Balance sheet = ₹ 1,38,050

21. **From the following trial balance of M/S Rajat and Sons as at 31st March, 2022, prepare trading and profit loss account, and balance sheet.**

Name of Accounts	Amt (Dr)	Name of Accounts	Amt (Cr)
Purchases	1,62,505	Sales	2,52,400
Stock (1st April, 2021)	26,725	Capital	12,000
Wages	22,137	Creditors	30,526
Salaries	5,555	Prov. for Doubt Debts	5,200
Power and Fuel	2,350	Bills Payable	3,950
Postage and Telegraph	4,246	Outstanding Wages	2,000
General Expenses	4,431	Outstanding Gen. Exp.	700
Stationery	1,400	Output CGST	4,000
Machinery	7,250	Output SGST	4,000
Bad Debts	525		
Loan to Raghav @ 10% p.a. (1st December, 2021)	3,000		
Drawings	4,452		
Debtors	50,200		
Cash in Hand	2,500		
Cash at Bank	7,500		
Input CGST	5,000		
Input SGST	5,000		
	3,14,776		3,14,776

Adjustments

(i) Stock on 31st March, 2022 was valued at ₹ 12,550.
(ii) Debtors include ₹ 500 due from a customer who has become insolvent.
(iii) Provision for doubtful debts is to be maintained at 5% on debtors.
(iv) Depreciate machinery by 10%.

(v) Goods costing ₹ 1,500, purchased paying CGST and SGST @ 9% each, were destroyed by fire and insurance company admitted a claim for ₹ 1,000.

Ans. Gross profit = ₹ 52,733 ; Net profit = ₹ 37,396; Balance sheet = ₹ 82,120

22. From the following trial balance of M/S Pratap and Sons as at 31st March, 2022, prepare trading and profit and loss account, and balance sheet.

Competency Based Que

Name of Accounts	Debit Balance (₹)	Credit Balance (₹)
Opening Stock	62,500	—
Purchases and Sales	5,00,000	8,75,000
Debtors and Creditors	75,000	43,750
Bills Receivable and Bills Payable	37,500	33,750
Wages and Salaries	31,250	—
Drawings and Capital	62,500	4,66,000
Carriage	10,000	—
Commission	—	16,750
Leasehold Property	5,00,000	—
10% Bank Loan	—	50,000
Interest on Bank Loan	3,000	—
Furniture and Fixture	25,000	—
Plant and Machinery	1,38,750	—
Insurance	21,250	—
Bad Debts Recovered	—	8,000
Input CGST	15,000	—
Input SGST	15,000	—
Input IGST	10,000	—
Output CGST	—	19,000
Output SGST	—	19,000
Cash in Hand	14,500	—
Cash at Bank	10,000	—
	15,31,250	15,31,250

Adjustments

(i) Stock on 31st March, 2022 was valued at ₹ 50,000.

(ii) Goods costing ₹ 10,000 were taken by the proprietor for his personal use but not entry has been made in the books of account. These goods were purchased paying IGST @ 18%.

(iii) Depreciate furniture and fixture by 10% and plant and machinery by 15% p.a. Machinery included a machine which was purchased for ₹ 38,500 on 30th September, 2021.

(iv) Outstanding wages and salaries are ₹ 12,500 and prepaid insurance is ₹ 5,000.

Ans. Gross profit = ₹ 3,18,750 ; Net profit = ₹ 3,06,550 ; Balance sheet = ₹ 8,40,250

Comprehensive

23. From the following balances extracted from the books of Sharma, prepare the trading and profit and loss account for the year ended 31st March, 2022 and balance sheet as at that date after taking into consideration the adjustments given below.

Competency Based Que

Trial Balance
as at 31st March, 2022

Name of Accounts	Debit Balance (₹)	Credit Balance (₹)
Drawing and Capital	15,000	1,00,000
Purchases and Sales	1,44,200	1,90,000
Returns	2,600	5,400
Sundry Debtors and Creditors	36,400	71,500
Stock (1st April, 2021)	39,600	—
Bad Debts	6,000	—
Bill Receivable and Payable	24,000	46,000
Cash in Hand	600	—
Office Expenses	12,420	—
Sales Van	30,000	—
Sales Van Expenses	2,800	—
Discount	—	5,820
Rent and Taxes	21,400	—
Telephone Charges	2,100	—
Postage and Telegram	1,900	—
Furniture	10,000	—
Printing and Stationery	5,500	—
Commission	16,800	—
Carriage Inwards	6,400	—
Salaries and Wages	41,000	—
	4,18,720	4,18,720

Additional Information

(i) Closing stock was valued at ₹ 1,23,400.

(ii) Depreciate furniture and machinery @ 10% per annum and sales van @ 20% per annum.

(iii) Outstanding rent amounted to ₹ 1,800.

(iv) Bad debts ₹ 400.

(v) Make a provision for doubtful debts @ 5% on debtors.

(vi) Charge one-fourth of salaries and wages to the trading account.

(vii) A new machinery was purchased on credit and installed on 31st December, 2021 costing ₹ 30,000. No entry for the same has yet been passed in the books.

Ans. Gross profit = ₹ 1,26,000, Net profit = ₹ 10,150 ; Balance sheet = 2,44,450

24. The following trial balance has been taken from the books of Nandini as on 31st December, 2023. You are required to prepare the trading and the profit and loss account for the year ended 31st December, 2023 and the balance sheet as at that date. **Competency Based Que**

Particulars	Debit Balance (₹)	Credit Balance (₹)
Capital Account	—	80,000
Drawings	4,800	—
Stock (31st December, 2023)	40,000	—
Office Furniture	13,000	—
Printing and Stationery	1,200	—
Coal, Gas and Water	600	—
Freight and Clearing Charges	3,500	—
Purchases Adjusted	65,000	—
Sundry Creditors	—	15,000
Bank Loan (at 16% taken on 1st Jan, 2023)	—	20,000
Discount	950	—
Repairs to Plant	1,000	—
Sales	—	2,05,350
Factory Rent	2,500	—
Salaries	2,800	—
Manufacturing Wages	24,000	—
Advertising	19,000	—
Plant and Machinery	70,000	—
Office Rent	3,600	—
Miscellaneous Expenses	1,000	—
Bad Debts Provision	—	1,000
Bills Receivable	22,000	—
Bills Payable	—	1,500
Carriage Outwards	1,500	—
Insurance	600	—
Interest on Bank Loan	1,000	—
Cash at Bank	7,500	—
Cash in Hand	3,500	—
Sundry Debtors	33,800	—
	3,22,850	3,22,850

The following adjustments are required

(i) Depreciate plant and machinery @ 10%, office furniture @ 7½%.

(ii) Provision for bad debts to be raised to 5% and reserve for discount on creditors to 1%.

(iii) Insurance premium was paid for six months upto 31st March, 2025.

(iv) Sales include ₹ 350 worth of goods which were taken by the proprietor.

(v) Half of the advertising account is to be carried to a suspense account and to be written-off in the subsequent 2 years.

(vi) ₹ 100 were paid in advance for factory rent.

(vii) An outstanding bill for repairs amounting to ₹ 250 remains to be paid.

Ans. Gross profit = ₹ 1,09,850; Net profit = ₹ 76,035; Balance sheet = ₹ 1,90,035

25. The following were the balances extracted from the books of Yogita as on 31st March, 2022.

Competency Based Que

Particulars	Amt (₹)	Particulars	Amt (₹)
Cash in Hand	540	Sales	98,780
Cash at Bank	2,630	Return Outwards	500
Purchases	40,675	Capital Account	62,000
Return Inwards	680	Sundry Creditors	6,300
Wages	8,480	Rent	9,000
Fuel and Power	4,730		
Carriage on Sales	3,200		
Carriage on Purchases	2,040		
Opening Stock	5,760		
Building	32,000		
Freehold Land	10,000		
Machinery	20,000		
Salaries	15,000		
Patents	7,500		
General Expenses	3,000		
Insurance	600		
Drawings	5,245		
Sundry Debtors	14,500		

Taking into account the following adjustments, prepare the trading and profit and loss account and balance sheet as at 31st March, 2022.

(i) Stock in hand on 31st March, 2022 was ₹ 6,800.

(ii) Machinery is to be depreciated @ 10% and patents @ 20%.

(iii) Salaries for the month of March, 2022 amounting to ₹ 1,500 were outstanding.

(iv) Insurance includes an annual premium of ₹ 170 on a policy expiring on 30th September, 2022.

(v) Further bad debts are ₹ 725. Create a provision of 5% on debtors.

(vi) Rent receivable ₹ 1,000.

Ans. Gross profit = 43,715; Net profit = 25,586; Balance sheet = ₹ 90,141

Hint (i) Prepaid insurance = 170 × 6/12 = 85 (from April to September, 2022)

(ii) Provision for doubtful debts = $(14,500 - 725) \times \frac{5}{100}$ = ₹ 689

26. The following trial balance was taken from the books of Mr. Babban. Prepare trading and profit and loss account and balance sheet for the year ended 31st March, 2023.

Competency Based Que

Particulars	Amt (Dr)	Particulars	Amt (Cr)
Salaries	90,970	Rent Received	2,500
Carriage Inwards	29,290	Bills Payable	26,000
Carriage Outwards	24,040	Discounts	5,860
Purchases	6,00,000	Purchases Return	13,000
Sales Return	64,580	Sales	11,00,430
Bad Debts	5,250	Bad Debts Provision	7,000

Particulars	Amt (Dr)	Particulars	Amt (Cr)
Land and Buildings	1,20,000	Loan on Mortgage	90,000
Cash at Bank	1,13,760	Sundry Creditors	1,06,250
Motor Vehicles	1,00,000	Capital	2,85,000
Stock on 1st April	68,390		
Cash in Hand	20,500		
Interest paid on Loan	3,000		
Sundry Debtors	2,01,000		
Drawings	30,000		
Bills Receivables	68,820		
General Expenses	34,890		
Advertising	32,600		
Rates, Taxes and Insurance	28,950		
	16,36,040		16,36,040

Adjustments

(i) Depreciate land and buildings at 10%.
(ii) Interest on loan at 12% p.a. is unpaid for six months.
(iii) Goods costing ₹ 5,000 were sent to a customer on sale or return basis for ₹ 6,000 on 30th March, 2023 and has been recorded in the books as actual sale.
(iv) Prepaid insurance amounted to ₹ 1,000.
(v) Salaries and rates outstanding amounted to ₹ 8,000 and ₹ 4,000.
(vi) The provision for doubtful debts to be maintained at 5% on sundry debtors.
(vii) Stock in hand on 31st March, 2023 was valued at ₹ 54,000.

Ans. Gross profit = ₹ 4,04,170; Net profit = ₹ 1,61,680; Balance sheet = ₹ 6,56,330

27. Following balances have been taken from the books of Neena at the end of the trading period ending 31st March, 2023.

Pass the adjustment entires and prepare trading account, profit and loss account and balance sheet as on that date. **Competency Based Que**

Particulars	Amt (₹)	Particulars	Amt (₹)
Sales	1,00,000	Printing and Stationery	400
Purchases	30,000	Rates and Taxes	500
Opening Stock	10,000	Trade Expenses	600
Capital	70,000	Business Premises	60,000
Salaries	6,000	Furniture	6,000
Wages	4,000	Bills Receivables	4,000
Carriage Outwards	3,000	Bills Payables	3,000
Carriage Inwards	2,000	Sundry Debtors	25,000
Return Inward	1,500	Sundry Creditors	43,400
Returns Outwards	2,500	Machinery	18,000
Rent	1,200	Investments at 12%	5,000
Freight & Dock Charges	2,400	Loan to Reema (Dr)	6,000
Insurance	1,000	Drawings	3,000
Bad Debts	2,200	Cash in Hand	6,500
Discount (Dr)	600	Cash at Bank	20,000

Adjustments

(i) Stock in hand on 31st March, 2023 ₹ 15,000.
(ii) Rent for March is outstanding ₹ 200.
(iii) Wages are unpaid ₹ 500, salaries are outstanding ₹ 1,200.
(iv) Insurance has been paid upto 30th June, 2023.
(v) A stationery bill has been outstanding for ₹ 200.
(vi) Depreciate machinery by 10%, furniture by 5% and business premises by 8%.
(vii) Interest on loan to Reema has accrued for one year at 6%.
(viii) Interest on investment is due for one year.
(ix) Interest on capital is allowed at 12%.
(x) Goods costing ₹ 300 are used for staff welfare.
(xi) Goods costing ₹ 1,000 are taken for personal use by Neena. Provide 5% on debtors for doubtful debts.

Ans. Gross profit = ₹ 68,400; Net profit = ₹ 35,660; Balance sheet = ₹ 1,58,560; Trial balance = ₹ 2,18,900

28. Following balances were extracted from the books of M/s Shri Shyam Apparel on 31st March, 2022 **Competency Based Que**

Name of Accounts	Amt (Dr)	Name of Accounts	Amt (Cr)
Stock on 1st April, 2021	1,50,000	Drawings	50,000
Purchases	8,20,000	Capital	8,50,000
Sales	12,00,000	Plant and Machinery	4,00,000
Postage and Telegram	8,000	Accumulated Depre.	90,000
Bad Debts	4,000	Sundry Debtors	2,06,000
Prov. for Doubt. Debts	8,000	Furniture	50,000
Discount Received	4,000	Freight Inwards	20,000
Rent Revenue	12,000	Carriage Outwards	5,000
Insurance	7,000	Rent, Rates and Taxes	46,000
Salaries	2,00,000	Printing and Stationery	8,000
Wages	13,000	Creditors	1,95,000
Cash in Hand	62,000	Input CGST	15,000
Cash at Bank	2,55,000	Input SGST	15,000

Prepare trading and profit and loss account, and balance sheet as on 31st March, 2022, giving effect to the following

(i) Closing stock was ₹ 1,50,000.
(ii) Wages were outstanding ₹ 5,000.
(iii) Provision for doubtful debts is to be maintained by 5% of sundry debtors.
(iv) Depreciate plant and machinery by 10% and furniture by 5%.
(v) Sundry creditors include ₹ 10,000 due to Ramesh who is also included in sundry debtors at ₹ 15,000.

(vi) New furniture for ₹ 12,000 was purchased on 1st April, 2021. Old furniture valued at ₹ 2,000 was exchanged and balance was paid by cheque. Purchase of furniture was recorded at the net value of furniture, i.e. ₹ 10,000. The firm had purchased this furniture by paying IGST @ 18%.

(vii) A fire occured on 27th March, 2022 destroying stock costing ₹ 10,000, which were purchased paying CGST and SGST @ 9% each. Insurance company conveyed acceptance of claim of ₹ 7,500 on 10th April, 2022. Final accounts were prepared on 1st July, 2022.

Ans. Gross profit = ₹ 3,52,000; Net profit = ₹ 41,400 ; Balance sheet = ₹ 9,81,400

Hint (i) Loss by fire in profit and loss account = 2,500 + 1,800 = ₹ 4,300

(ii) Sundry creditors will be decreased by ₹ 10,000

Missing Information

29. From the following trial balance of a trader for the year ended 31st March, 2023, complete his balance sheet as on that date. **Competency Based Que**

Trial Balance

Particulars	Amt (Dr)	Particulars	Amt (Cr)
Debtors	24,500	Capital	70,000
Drawings	5,200	Creditors	52,900
Insurance	600	Sales	98,000
General Expenses	3,000	Rental Income	15,000
Salaries	15,000	Interest on Investments	20,000
Patents	7,500	Loan	10,000
Machinery	20,000	Returns Outwards	2,000
Cash in Hand	500		
Cash at Bank	2,700		
Purchases	40,700		
Return Inwards	600		
Wages	10,000		
Investments	80,000		
Fuel and Power	4,000		
Carriage Outwards	3,200		
Carriage Inwards	2,400		
Opening Stock	8,000		
Land and Buildings	40,000		
	2,67,900		2,67,900

Adjustments

(i) Closing stock on 31st March, 2023 ₹ 18,000.

(ii) Depreciate buildings and land at 10%, machines at 15% and patents 20%.

(iii) Salaries for ₹ 5,000 are outstanding.

(iv) Rent has been received in advance for ₹ 3,000.

(v) Interest on investment has accrued for ₹ 6,000.

(vi) Insurance is prepaid for ₹ 100.

Balance Sheet
as at 31st March, 2023

Liabilities		Amt (₹)	Assets		Amt (₹)
Creditors		52,900	Cash in Hand		500
Loans		10,000	Cash at Bank		2,700
......		...	Debtors		24,500
Rent Received in Advance		...	......		...
Capital	70,000		......		...
... Net Profit	55,100		......		100
... Drawings	...	...	Land and Buildings	40,000	
			(–) Depreciation	(...)	...
			Machinery	20,000	
			(–) Depreciation	(...)	...
			Patents	7,500	
			(–) Depreciation	(...)	...
			Investments		80,000
		...			...

30. Complete the final accounts of a trader from the following trial balance as on 31st March, 2023. **Competency Based Que**

Trial Balance

Particulars	Amt (Dr)	Particulars	Amt (Cr)
Wages	45,000	Sales	2,33,000
Salaries	24,500	8% Loan	40,000
Plant	1,00,000	Creditors	18,900

Particulars	Amt (Dr)	Particulars	Amt (Cr)
Furniture	18,000	Bills Payable	2,000
Debtors	32,000	Capital	80,000
Bills Receivables	12,500	Discount	3,000
Cash in Hand	6,300	Purchases Return	5,000
Repair Expenses	3,700	Interest received on Investments	2,000
Factory Lighting	1,400		
Opening Stock	10,000		
Rent and Rates	7,000		
Travelling Expenses	10,500		
Drawings	18,000		
Investments in 12% Bonds	20,000		
Insurance	2,000		
Sales Return	6,000		
Purchases	60,000		
Carriage Inwards	3,000		
Carriage on Sales	1,000		
Interest paid on Loan	3,000		
	3,83,900		3,83,900

Adjustments

(i) Closing stock on 31st March, 2023 was ₹ 15,000.
(ii) Wages include ₹ 6,000 paid for the errection of plant during the year.
(iii) Repairs to furniture of ₹ 2,000 were debited to furniture during the year.
(iv) Salaries for ₹ 5,500 are outstanding for the month of March.
(v) Insurance is paid for full one year upto 30th June, 2023.

In the Books of the Firm
Trading and Profit and Loss Account
for the year ended 31st March, 2023

Dr | Cr

Particulars		Amt (₹)	Particulars		Amt (₹)
To Opening Stock		10,000	By Sales	2,33,000	
To Purchases	60,000		... Returns	(6,000)	...
(−) Purchases Return	(5,000)	55,000	By ...		...
To Carriage Inwards		3,000			
To Wages	45,000				
...	...	39,000			
To Factory Lighting		1,400			
To Gross Profit c/d		...			
		...			...
To Salaries	24,500		By Gross Profit b/d		...
(+) Outstanding Salaries	5,500	30,000	By Interest on Investments	2,000	
To Carriage on Sales		1,000	... Interest Accrued	400	...
To Travelling Expenses		10,500	By Discount		3,000
To Rent and Rates		7,000			
To Repairs Expenses	3,700				
...	...	...			
To Insurance	2,000				
...	...	...			
To Interest on Loan	3,000				
...	...	...			
To Net Profit transferred to Capital A/c		...			
		...			...

Balance Sheet
as at 31st March, 2023

Liabilities		Amt (₹)	Assets		Amt (₹)
Creditors		18,900	Cash in Hand		6,300
Bills Payable		2,000	Bills Receivable		12,500
......		...	Debtors		32,000
......		...	......		...
18% Loan		40,000	Prepaid Insurance		...
Capital	80,000		Interest on Investments Accrued		...
(+) Net Profit	...		Furniture	18,000	
	1,60,100		...	...	...
(−) Drawings	(18,000)	...	Plant	1,00,000	
			Erection Wages	6,000	...
			Investments – 12% Bonds		20,000
		2,08,700			2,08,700

Theoretical Questions

Short Answer Type Questions

1. What are the adjusting entries? Why are they necessary for preparing final accounts?

Or **Why is it necessary to record the adjusting entries in the preparation of final accounts?**

NCERT; Competency Based Que

Ans. It is the entry passed to record expenses and incomes that relate to the accounting period but are yet to be paid or received.

The need of making various adjustments are stated below

(i) To ascertain the true profit or loss of the business.
(ii) To determine the true financial position of the business.
(iii) To make a record of the transactions earlier omitted in the books.
(iv) To rectify the errors committed in the books.
(v) To complete the incomplete transactions.

2. What is meant by closing stock? Show its treatment in final accounts. **NCERT**

Ans. Closing stock implies the value of unsold goods at the end of an accounting period. Closing stock is valued at cost or net realisable value, whichever is lower.

If closing stock is given in adjustment it will be shown on the credit side of trading account and will also be shown on the assets side of balance sheet under current assets. If closing stock is given in trial balance, it will only be shown on the assets side of balance sheet under current assets.

3. State the meaning of **NCERT**

(i) Outstanding expenses
(ii) Prepaid expenses
(iii) Income received in advance
(iv) Accrued income

Ans. (i) **Outstanding Expenses**
Those expenses whose benefit have been derived during the current year but payment is not made at the end of the year are known as outstanding expenses.

(ii) **Prepaid Expenses**
Those expenses which have been paid in current year but the benefit of which will be available in the next accounting year are known as prepaid expenses.

(iii) **Income Received in Advance**
The income or portion of income which is received during the current accounting year but has not been earned is called unearned income.

(iv) **Accrued Income**
It refers to the income which has been earned but not received during the current accounting period.

4. What is meant by provision for doubtful debts? What relevant accounts are prepared and what journal entries are recorded in final accounts? How is the amount for provision for doubtful debts calculated? **NCERT**

Ans. The provision for doubtful debts is the estimated amount of bad debts that will arise from amount receivable from debtors.

A provision is created to cover possible loss on account of bad debts likely to occur in future. The relevant account prepared is 'provision for doubtful debts account'.

Following journal entry is recorded in books of account

Profit and Loss A/c Dr

To Provision for Doubtful Debts A/c

(Being adjustment for provision for doubtful debts)

The amount of provision for doubtful debts is calculated in the following manner

$$(\text{Debtors} - \text{Further Bad Debts}) \times \frac{\text{Percentage of Provision}}{100}$$

5. Show the treatment of prepaid expenses and depreciation, at the time of preparation of final accounts?

(i) When given inside the trial balance.

(ii) When given outside the trial balance. NCERT; Competency Based Que

Ans. (i) **Prepaid Expenses**

If Given Outside the Trial Balance If the given expense is a direct expense it will be deducted from the related expense on the debit side of trading account.

If the given expense is a indirect expense it will be deducted from the related expense on the debit side of profit and loss account and it will be shown on the asset side of balance sheet under current assets.

If Given in Trial Balance In case prepaid expense is given outside the trial balance it will only be shown on the assets side as current asset.

(ii) **Depreciation**

If Given Outside the Trial Balance Depreciation is shown as a separate item on the debit side of profit and loss account and is shown on the assets side of balance sheet by way of deduction from the value of concerned fixed assets.

If Given in Trial Balance If depreciation appears in the trial balance, it will only be shown on the debit side of profit and loss account.

6. What adjusting entries would you record for the following? NCERT; Competency Based Que

(i) Depreciation

(ii) Discount on debtors

(iii) Interest on capital

(iv) Manager's commission

Ans. (i) **Depreciation – Adjusting Entry**

Depreciation A/c Dr

To Concerned Asset A/c

or To Provision for Depreciation A/c

(Being depreciation charged)

(ii) **Discount on Debtors – Adjusting Entry**

Profit and Loss A/c Dr

To Provision for Discount on Debtors A/c

(Being adjustment of discount on debtors adjusted)

(iii) **Interest on Capital – Adjusting Entry**

Interest on Capital A/c Dr

To Capital A/c

(Being interest on capital adjusted)

(iv) **Manager's Commission – Adjusting Entry**

Manager's Commission A/c Dr

To Commission Payable/Outstanding Commission A/c

(Being manager commission adjusted)

Objective Questions

Multiple Choice Questions (MCQs)

1. Closing stock is valued at cost price or market price whichever is ....

(a) more (b) less

(c) zero (d) equal

2. At the time of preparing final accounts, the entries that need to be accounted for in the books of accounts are

(a) opening entries

(b) closing entries

(c) adjustment entries (d) final account entry

3. If the rent of one month is still to be paid the adjustment entry will be NCERT

(a) Debit outstanding rent account and Credit rent account

(b) Debit profit and loss account and Credit rent account

(c) Debit rent account and Credit profit and loss account

(d) Debit rent account and Credit outstanding rent account

4. What will be the journal entry for writing-off further bad debts in the book of accounts?

(a) Debit Debtors A/c and Credit Provision for Bad Debts A/c

(b) Debit Provision for Bad Debts A/c and Credit Debtors A/c

(c) Debit Bad Debts A/c and Credit Debtors A/c

(d) Debit Debtors A/c and Credit Bad Debts A/c

5. What will be the journal entry for goods distributed among staff?
(a) Debit Staff Welfare Expense A/c and Credit Purchases A/c
(b) Debit Free Sample A/c and Credit Staff Welfare Expense A/c
(c) Debit Staff Welfare Expense A/c and Credit Debtors A/c
(d) Debit Free Samples A/c and Credit Purchases A/c

6. Which of the following is not the need or objective for adjustments in preparation of final accounts?
(a) To ascertain the true profit or loss of the business
(b) To determine the true financial position of the business
(c) To make a record of the transactions earlier omitted in the books
(d) None of the above

7. Expenses due but not paid are accounted due to
(a) accrual concept (b) prudence concept
(c) matching concept
(d) revenue recognition concept

8. Debtors previously written-off as bad, are recovered. These will be credited to which account?
(a) Trading (b) Profit and loss
(c) Balance sheet (d) None of these

9. If the income received in advance is given outside the trial balance, it will be shown in Competency Based Que
(a) trading account, as deduction from the respective income
(b) profit and loss account, as deduction from the respective income and in the asset side of the balance sheet
(c) profit and loss account, as deduction from the respective income and in the liabilites side of the balance sheet
(d) balance sheet in the liabilities side

10. If the indirect expense due but not paid is given outside the trial balance, it will be shown in Competency Based Que
(a) trading account, as deduction from the respective income
(b) profit and loss account, as deduction from the respective income and in the liabilities side of the balance sheet
(c) profit and loss account, as addition to the respective expense and in the liabilities side of the balance sheet
(d) balance sheet in the liabilities side

11. Payment made to a creditor, subject to cash discount, will
(a) reduce a liability, reduce an asset and add to expenses
(b) reduce a liability, add to an asset and add to revenue
(c) reduce an asset, reduce a liability and add to revenue
(d) reduce a liability, reduce an asset and decrease expenses

12. Goods distributed as charity. The effect of this entry will be
(a) it is the proprietor drawings
(b) it is deducted from purchases in the trading account
(c) it will be shown on the debit side of the profit and loss account
(d) Both (b) and (c)

13. Which of the following statements is correct?
(a) Outstanding wages given in the trial balance are transferred to trading account
(b) If nothing is mentioned, the manager's commission should be allowed as a percentage of net profit after charging such commission
(c) If depreciation is not provided, both fixed asset and profit will be shown at inflated amount
(d) Closing stock implies the value of unsold goods at the beginning of an accounting period

14. In case of sole proprietor business, income tax is considered as
(a) business expense
(b) proprietor's expense
(c) capital expense
(d) All of the above

15. Pre-payment of insurance premium will appear in the balance sheet and insurance account as
(a) a liability and a debit balance
(b) an asset and a debit balance
(c) an asset and a credit balance
(d) a liability and a credit balance

16. If the closing stock is understated, what will be the effect on the net profit?
(a) Overstated (b) Understated
(c) No effect (d) Cannot be determined

17. Income received in advance is deducted from the income because of
(a) accrual concept
(b) prudence concept
(c) matching concept
(d) revenue recognition concept

18. If the insurance premium paid ₹ 1,000 and prepaid insurance ₹ 300. The amount of insurance premium shown in profit and loss account will be NCERT
(a) ₹ 1,300 (b) ₹ 1,000
(c) ₹ 300 (d) ₹ 700

19. Following information is taken from the trial balance of a Raj enterprise.
Sales ₹ 2,00,000; purchase ₹ 1,20,000, wages ₹ 14,000.
Closing stock was ₹ 6,000 more than opening stock. What will be the gross profit? Competency Based Que
(a) ₹ 72,000 (b) ₹ 36,000
(c) ₹ 80,000 (d) ₹ 92,000

20. **If the opening capital is ₹ 1,50,000 as on 1st April, 2023 and additional capital introduced ₹ 30,000 on 1st January, 2024. Interest charge on capital 10% p.a. The amount of interest on capital shown in profit and loss account as on 31st March, 2024 will be** Competency Based Que

(a) ₹ 9,000 (b) ₹ 12,000
(c) ₹ 15,750 (d) ₹ 18,000

21. **If goods lost by fire costing ₹ 30,000 (market value ₹ 40,000) and claim accepted by an insurance company is 15% of the value of goods lost, then what amount will be debited to profit and loss account?**

(a) ₹ 22,500 (b) ₹ 7,500
(c) ₹ 30,000 (d) ₹ 40,000

22. **What amount will be shown in profit and loss account for the insurance premium, if the insurance premium paid ₹ 3,000 and prepaid insurance ₹ 900?**

(a) ₹ 9,000 (b) ₹ 2,100
(c) ₹ 1,400 (d) ₹ 3,200

23. **An enterprise has received rent for the office accommodation for one year amounting to ₹ 36,000 on 1st August, 2023. The year ends on 31st March, 2024. How much amount is pre-received?** Competency Based Que

(a) ₹ 24,000 (b) ₹ 12,000
(c) ₹ 6,000 (d) ₹ 3,000

24. **Which of the undermentioned options reflect correct treatment for following adjustment? Debtors appearing in the books for ₹ 1,13,400. Make provision of 5% on debtors for doubtful debts.** Competency Based Que

(a) ₹ 5,670 debited to profit and loss account and deducted from sundry debtors in balance sheet
(b) ₹ 13,080 debited to profit and loss account and deducted from sundry debtors in balance sheet
(c) ₹ 5,670 debited to trading account and deducted from sundry debtors in balance sheet
(d) ₹ 13,080 debited to trading account and deducted from sundry debtors in balance sheet

25. **What will be the provision for doubtful debts credited to profit and loss account, if the balance of provision for doubtful debts (as on 1st April, 2023) ₹ 2,500, bad debts during the year were ₹ 600. Provision for doubtful debts is required @ 5% on debtors of ₹ 20,000?** Competency Based Que

(a) ₹ 1,000 (b) ₹ 900
(c) ₹ 800 (d) ₹ 1,200

26. **What will be the amount shown on liabilities side of balance sheet, if the loan from bank @ 12% per annum is ₹ 16,00,000 and the interest on loan is due for the whole year?**

(a) ₹ 16,00,000 (b) ₹ 16,24,000
(c) ₹ 17,80,000 (d) ₹ 17,92,000

27. **What will be the net capital to be shown in the balance sheet, if capital of a firm ₹ 10,00,000, rate of interest @ 10% and drawings ₹ 60,000?**

(a) ₹ 10,00,000 (b) ₹ 9,50,000
(c) ₹ 10,40,000 (d) ₹ 11,60,000

28. **During the year ended 31st March, 2023, salaries have been paid for only 11 months upto February for ₹ 44,000, salary for the month of March has not been paid. What amount will appear in profit and loss account?** Competency Based Que

(a) ₹ 48,000 (b) ₹ 24,000
(c) ₹ 42,000 (d) ₹ 32,000

29. **What will be the correct journal entry of the interest on loan @ 6% p.a. is due for the whole year for a loan of ₹ 1,50,000?** Competency Based Que

(a) Outstanding Interest A/c	Dr	9,000	
To Interest on Loan A/c			9,000
(b) Interest on Loan A/c	Dr	9,000	
To Outstanding Interest A/c			9,000
(c) Accrued Interest A/c	Dr	9,000	
To Interest on Loan A/c			9,000
(d) Interest on Loan A/c	Dr	9,000	
To Accrued Interest A/c			9,000

30. **Find the amount to be shown in the balance sheet for the machinery on 31st December, 2023 if the cost of new machine purchased on 1st January, 2023 is ₹ 4,50,000; estimated life of machine 5 years, residual value after 5 years is ₹ 75,000.** Competency Based Que

(a) ₹ 18,750 (b) ₹ 4,31,250
(c) ₹ 3,75,000 (d) ₹ 2,50,000

31. **What will be the adjusting closing entry necessary as on 31st March, 2023, if the rent paid ₹ 18,000 (including rent paid ₹ 15,000 per annum paid upto 30th June, 2023)?** Competency Based Que

(a) Debit Rent Prepaid A/c with ₹ 3,750 and Credit Cash A/c with ₹ 3,750
(b) Debit Rent Prepaid A/c with ₹ 1,350 and Credit Cash A/c with ₹ 1,350
(c) Debit Rent Prepaid A/c with ₹ 3,750 and Credit Rent A/c with ₹ 3,750
(d) Debit Rent Prepaid A/c with ₹ 1,350 and Credit Cash A/c with ₹ 1,350

32. **The trial balance of a trader as on 31st March, 2023 shows debtors at ₹ 80,000 and bad debts at ₹ 1,500. However, it has been further known that a debtor from whom ₹ 300 was to be received, nothing is recoverable. How much amount will appear in the balance sheet under the debtors?** Competency Based Que

(a) ₹ 79,700 (b) ₹ 80,300
(c) ₹ 78,200 (d) ₹ 81,800

33. The trial balance as on 31st March, 2023 shows sundry debtors at ₹ 2,00,000, bad debts at 12,600 and old provision for doubtful debts as ₹ 25,000. It is required to have a new provision for doubtful debts at 5% of debtors. The amount that will be shown in the profit and loss account for the provision for doubtful debt will be Competency Based Que

(a) ₹ 4,800 (b) ₹ 2,400 (c) ₹ 10,000 (d) ₹ 15,000

Assertion-Reason

Direction (Q. No. 34 to 43) *Read the following Assertion (A) and Reason (R) and choose the correct alternative from the following*

Alternatives

(a) Both Assertion (A) and Reason (R) are true and Reason (R) is the correct explanation of Assertion (A)
(b) Both Assertion (A) and Reason (R) are true, but Reason (R) is not the correct explanation of Assertion (A)
(c) Assertion (A) is true, but Reason (R) is false
(d) Assertion (A) is false, but Reason (R) is true

34. Assertion (A) Outstanding expenses are recorded as liabilities in the final accounts.

Reason (R) Outstanding expenses represent amounts that have been incurred but not yet paid.

35. Assertion (A) Closing stock is always valued at cost price.

Reason (R) The lower of cost or market price rule is applied to closing stock valuation.

36. Assertion (A) An increase in prepaid expenses results in a decrease in current liabilities.

Reason (R) Prepaid expenses are expenses paid in advance and are considered assets until consumed.

37. Assertion (A) Adjustments for accrued income increase the total income reported in the profit and loss account.

Reason (R) Accrued income represents income that has been earned but not yet received.

38. Assertion (A) Unearned revenue is recorded as a liability in the balance sheet.

Reason (R) Unearned revenue represents money received for services that have not yet been delivered.

39. Assertion (A) If closing stock is given in adjustment it will be shown on the credit side of trading account and will also be shown on the assets side of balance sheet under current assets.

Reason (R) If closing stock is given in trial balance, it will only be shown on the assets side of balance sheet under current assets.

40. Assertion (A) The provision for doubtful debts is the estimated amount of bad debts that will arise from amount receivable from debtors.

Reason (R) A provision is created to cover possible loss on account of bad debts likely to occur in future. The relevant account prepared is 'provision for doubtful debts account'.

41. Assertion (A) Those expenses whose benefit have been derived during the current year but payment is not made at the end of the year are known as outstanding expenses.

Reason (R) If the given expense is a direct expense it will be deducted from the related expense on the debit side of trading account.

42. Assertion (A) The salary paid in advance is not an expense because it neither reduces assets or nor increase liabilities.

Reason (R) The salary paid in advance is an asset it is not an expense because it neither reduces assets or nor increase liabilities.

43. Assertion (A) Goods worth 1,800 taken by the proprietor for personal use should be credited to capital account.

Reason (R) Goods taken by the proprietor for personal use should be credited to purchase account as less goods are left in the business for sale.

Two Statements Based MCQs

Direction (Q. No. 44 to 51) *Read the following statements carefully and choose the correct alternative*

Alternatives

(a) Both the statements are correct
(b) Both the statements are incorrect
(c) Statement I is correct and Statement II is incorrect
(d) Statement I is incorrect and Statement II is correct

44. Statement I In every adjustment, atleast there are three effects.

Statement II Every item of trial balance has only one effect.

45. Statement I Depreciation if not shown in the trial balance, it will be shown on the debit side of the profit and loss account and subtracted from the respective asset in balance sheet.

Statement II Depreciation if not shown in the trial balance, it will be shown on the credit side of the profit and loss account and subtracted from the respective asset in balance sheet.

46. **Statement I** If closing stock is given outside the trial balance, it is shown on the debit side of the trading account only.

Statement II If closing stock is given outside the trial balance, it is shown on the assets side of the balance only.

47. **Statement I** If the rent of one month is still to be paid, then the adjustment entry will be debit rent account and credit outstanding rent account.

Statement II If the rent received in advance ₹ 2,000, then the adjustment entry will be debit profit and loss account and credit rent account.

48. **Statement I** Accrued income is credited to the profit and loss account and shown in the balance sheet as current asset.

Statement II According to accrual concept of accounting, income is recognised when goods or services have been sold, whether the amount has been received or not.

49. **Statement I** The income which is received during the current accounting year, but it has not been earned, is termed as accrued income.

Statement II The expenses which become due during the current accounting period, but are actually paid in the next accounting period, are termed as outstanding expenses.

50. **Statement I** The closing stock is valued before the end of the year and is recorded in the books.

Statement II The closing stock appears in the debit side of the trial balance.

51. **Statement I** The financial accounts are prepared on 'accrual concept' basis.

Statement II According to this concept, expenses are incurred in the period when benefit in terms of goods and services is received and not when payment is made.

Matching

52. Match the following

Column I	Column II
A. Gross profit	(i) Expenses not yet paid
B. Net profit	(ii) Revenue from sales minus Cost of goods sold
C. Depreciation	(iii) Profit remaining after all expenses are deducted
D. Outstanding expenses	(iv) Allocation of cost of an asset over its useful life

Codes

	A	B	C	D		A	B	C	D
(a)	(i)	(ii)	(iii)	(iv)	(b)	(ii)	(iii)	(iv)	(i)
(c)	(iv)	(ii)	(i)	(iii)	(d)	(i)	(iii)	(ii)	(iv)

53. Match the following

Column I	Column II
A. Trading account	(i) Final statement showing assets and liabilities
B. Balance sheet	(ii) Total revenue minus total expenses
C. Profit and loss account	(iii) Amount withdrawn by the owner from the business
D. Drawings	(iv) Summary of gross profit or loss from trading activities

Codes

	A	B	C	D		A	B	C	D
(a)	(i)	(ii)	(iii)	(iv)	(b)	(ii)	(iii)	(iv)	(i)
(c)	(iv)	(i)	(ii)	(iii)	(d)	(i)	(iii)	(ii)	(iv)

54. Match the following

Column I	Column II
A. Manager commission payable	(i) Allocation of cost
B. Closing inventory	(ii) Current liability
C. Depreciation	(iii) Valued at cost or market price, whichever is low

Codes

	A	B	C		A	B	C
(a)	(ii)	(i)	(iii)	(b)	(ii)	(iii)	(iv)
(c)	(iv)	(i)	(ii)	(d)	(i)	(iii)	(ii)

55. Match the following

Column I	Column II
A. Outstanding	(i) Income received in advance
B. Prepaid	(ii) Income due but not received
C. Accrued	(iii) Expenses due but not paid
D. Unearned	(iv) Expenses paid in advance

Codes

	A	B	C	D		A	B	C	D
(a)	(i)	(ii)	(iii)	(iv)	(b)	(ii)	(iii)	(iv)	(i)
(c)	(iv)	(iii)	(ii)	(i)	(d)	(i)	(iii)	(ii)	(iv)

Case Based MCQs

Direction *Read the following case study and answer the questions 56 and 57 on the basis of the same*

Niharika Das is working for the past 8 years as a Chartered Accountant at Anu Apparels in Dhule, Maharashtra. Anu Apparels deals in ethenic clothes and dresses. Niharika Das on 31st March, 2023, prepared trial balance after preparation of accounts and subsidiary books.

Her trial balance total also agreed. But Niharika Das, being a diligent CA checked all the books of accounts again and discovered some of the information which were not taken into consideration. She immediately incorporated the adjustments while preparing final accounts of Anu Apparels.

Following trial balance was prepared by Niharika Das and additional information found by her

Trial Balance
as of 31st March, 2024

Particulars	Debit Balance (₹)	Credit Balance (₹)
Cash	30,000	—
Bank	1,00,000	—
Debtors	2,00,000	—
Equipment	2,50,000	—
Capital	—	4,00,000
Creditors	—	55,000
Sales	—	3,00,000
Salaries	1,00,000	—
Rent	50,000	—
Depreciation	25,000	—
Total	7,55,000	7,55,000

Adjustments

(i) Closing stock (unsold services) is valued at ₹ 1,50,000.

(ii) Outstanding salaries of ₹ 10,000 need to be accounted for.

(iii) Prepaid rent of ₹ 5,000 included in the rent expense.

(iv) Bad debts of ₹ 2,000 need to be written-off.

(v) Depreciation on equipment needs to be calculated at 10%.

56. At what amount, equipment will be shown in balance sheet?

(a) ₹ 2,50,000
(b) ₹ 2,20,000
(c) ₹ 2,25,000
(d) ₹ 2,75,000

57. At what amount, rent will be shown in profit and loss account?

(a) ₹ 45,000 (b) ₹ 50,000
(c) ₹ 40,000 (d) ₹ 55,000

Direction *Read the following case study and answer the questions 58 to 60 on the basis of the same*

DEF Traders is a wholesale trading company that deals in electronic goods. For the financial year ending 31st March, 2024, the company has provided the following financial information and adjustments

Particulars	Debit Balance (₹)	Credit Balance (₹)
Capital		2,70,000
Drawings	19,440	—
Land and Building	75,000	—
Plant and Machinery	42,810	—
Furniture and Fixtures	3,750	—
Carriage Inwards	13,110	—
Wages	64,410	—
Salaries	14,010	—
Provision for Bad Debts	—	7,410
Sales	—	2,73,690
Sales Return	5,280	—
Bank Charges	420	—
Gas and Water	2,160	—
Rates and Taxes	2,520	—
Discount	—	360
Purchases	1,26,480	—
Purchases Return	—	25,380
Bills Receivable	3,810	—
Trade Expenses	5,970	—
Sundry Debtors	1,13,400	—
Sundry Creditors	—	36,510
Stock (1st April, 2022)	79,260	—
Apprentice Premium	—	1,500
Fire Insurance	1,470	—
Cash at Bank	39,000	—
Cash in Hand	2,550	—
	6,14,850	6,14,850

Adjustments

(i) Charge depreciation on land and building at 2.5% on plant and machinery at 10% and on furniture and fixtures at 10%. Make provision of 5% on debtors for doubtful debts.

(ii) Carry forward the following unexpired amounts
(a) Fire insurance ₹ 375
(b) Rates and taxes ₹ 720
(c) Apprentice premium ₹ 1,200
(d) Closing stock ₹ 88,170

58. Which of the undermentioned amount is correct answer for apprentice premium to be shown in profit and loss account?

(a) ₹ 300 (b) ₹ 1,500
(c) ₹ 1,200 (d) ₹ 1,800

59. Which of the following will be the amount of rates and taxes shown in profit and loss account?

(a) ₹ 3,240 (b) ₹ 2,520
(c) ₹ 1,800 (d) ₹ 720

60. At what amount, land and building will be shown balance sheet?

(a) ₹ 75,000 (b) ₹ 76,800
(c) ₹ 76,875 (d) ₹ 73,125

Direction *Read the following case study and answer the questions 61 and 62 on the basis of the same*

Santoshi Garg recently cleared her final CA exam in her 1st attempt. She is now appointed as a CA in Samratha Textiles, Surat. On 31st March, 2023, she prepared trial balance whose total also agreed. But later she discovered some additional information which has to be taken into account while preparing final accounts. After taking into account few adjustments, he prepared final accounts of Samratha Textiles.

Following trial balance was prepared by CA Santoshi Garg and undermentioned adjustments were discovered by her

Trial Balance
as of 31st March, 2023

Particulars	Debit Balance (₹)	Credit Balance (₹)
Cash	1,00,000	—
Bank	50,000	—
Debtors	1,50,000	—
Opening Stock	1,00,000	—
Machinery	2,00,000	—
Capital	—	4,90,000
Creditors	—	80,000
Sales	—	5,00,000
Purchases	3,00,000	—
Rent	60,000	—
Salaries	1,20,000	—
Provision for Bad Debts	—	10,000
	10,80,000	10,80,000

Adjustments

(i) Closing stock is to be valued at ₹ 1,20,000.

(ii) Outstanding salaries of ₹ 20,000 need to be accounted for.

(iii) Prepaid rent amounting to ₹ 10,000 is included in the rent expense.

(iv) Bad debts amounting to ₹ 5,000 are identified and will be written-off.

(v) Depreciation on fixed assets is to be calculated at 15%.

61. **The amount of gross profit will be**

(a) ₹ 2,20,000 (b) ₹ 4,00,000
(c) ₹ 6,20,000 (d) ₹ 3,40,000

62. **The amount of machinery to be shown in the balance sheet.**

(a) ₹ 3,70,000 (b) ₹ 1,70,000
(c) ₹ 2,70,000 (d) ₹ 2,30,000

Answers

1. (b) less
2. (c) adjustment entries
3. (d) Debit rent account and Credit outstanding rent account
4. (c) Debit Bad Debts A/c and Credit Debtors A/c
5. (a) Debit Staff Welfare Expense A/c and Credit Purchases A/c
6. (d) None of the above
7. (a) accrual concept
8. (b) Profit and loss
9. (c) profit and loss account, as deduction from the respective income and in the liabilites side of the balance sheet
10. (c) profit and loss account, as addition to the respective expense and in the liabilities side of the balance sheet
11. (c) reduce an asset, reduce a liability and add to revenue
12. (d) Both (b) and (c)
13. (c) If depreciation is not provided, both fixed asset and profit will be shown at inflated amount
14. (b) proprietor's expense
15. (c) an asset and a credit balance
16. (b) Understated
17. (a) accrual concept
18. (d) ₹ 700 (1,000 – 300)
19. (a) Gross Profit = Sales + Difference in Stock – Purchases – Wages
 = 2,00,000 + 6,000 – 1,20,000 – 14,000 = ₹ 72,000
20. (c) Interest on capital = 1,50,000 × 10% = ₹ 15,000
 (+) Interest on additional capital = 30,000 × 10% × 3/12 = ₹ 750
 Total interest on capital = ₹ 15,750
21. (b) [30,000 – (30,000 × 75%)] = ₹ 7,500
22. (b) Amount of insurance premium = 3,000 – 900 = ₹ 2,100
23. (b) Rent income only for eight months has been earned and the remaining rent for four months will be earned only in the next year i.e. 36,000 × 4/12 = ₹ 12,000.
24. (a) Provision of 5% on debtors for doubtful debts
 = 1,13,400 × 5/100 = ₹ 5,670
25. (b) Provision already existing = 2,500
 (–) Bad debts = (600)
 (–) Provision (New) @ 5% on debtors of ₹ 20,000 = (1,000)
 Provision for doubtful debts credited to profit and loss account = 900

26. (d) Interest $= 16{,}00{,}000 \times 12\% =$ ₹ 1,92,000
The amount shown on liabilities side of balance sheet
$16{,}00{,}000 + 1{,}92{,}000 =$ ₹ 17,92,000

27. (c) Interest on capital $= 10{,}00{,}000 \times 10\% =$ ₹ 1,00,000
Net Capital = Capital + Interest on Capital − Drawings
$= 10{,}00{,}000 + 1{,}00{,}000 - 60{,}000 =$ ₹ 10,40,000

28. (a) To Salaries = ₹ 44,000
(+) Salaries Outstanding = ₹ 4,000
= ₹ 48,000

29. (b) Interest on Loan A/c Dr 9,000
To Outstanding Interest A/c 9,000

30. (c) Depreciation on machinery
$= \dfrac{(4{,}50{,}000 - 75{,}000)}{5} =$ ₹ 75,000
Amount to be shown in the balance sheet for the machinery on 31st December, 2023
$= 4{,}50{,}000 - 75{,}000 =$ ₹ 3,75,000

31. (c) Prepaid rent $= 15{,}000 \times \dfrac{3}{12} =$ ₹ 3,750

32. (a)

Debtors	=	₹ 80,000
(–) Additional Bad Debts	=	₹ (300)
	=	₹ 79,700

33. (b)

		Amt (₹)
By Old Provision for Doubtful Debts	=	25,000
(–) Bad Debts	=	(12,600)
	=	12,400
(–) New Provision for Doubtful Debts required @ 5% on Debtors	=	(10,000)
	=	2,400

34. (a) Both Assertion (A) and Reason (R) are true and Reason (R) is the correct explanation of Assertion (A)
35. (d) Assertion (A) is false, but Reason (R) is true
36. (a) Both Assertion (A) and Reason (R) are true and Reason (R) is the correct explanation of Assertion (A)
37. (a) Both Assertion (A) and Reason (R) are true and Reason (R) is the correct explanation of Assertion (A)
38. (a) Both Assertion (A) and Reason (R) are true and Reason (R) is the correct explanation of Assertion (A)
39. (b) Both Assertion (A) and Reason (R) are true, but Reason (R) is not the correct explanation of Assertion (A)
40. (a) Both Assertion (A) and Reason (R) are true and Reason (R) is the correct explanation of Assertion (A)
41. (c) If the given expense is a direct expense it will be added to the related expense on the debit side of trading account.
42. (a) Both Assertion (A) and Reason (R) are true and Reason (R) is the correct explanation of Assertion (A)
43. (d) Assertion (A) is false, but Reason (R) is true
44. (d) In every adjustment, atleast there are two effects.
45. (d) Statement I is incorrect and Statement II is correct
46. (b) Closing stock given outside the trial balance is shown on the credit side of the trading account and also shown on the assets side of the balance sheet.
47. (c) If the rent received in advance ₹ 2,000, then the adjustment entry will be debit rent account and credit rent received in advance account.
48. (a) Both the statements are correct
49. (d) The income which become due during the current accounting period but are actually received in the next accounting period are termed as accrued income.
50. (a) Both the statements are correct
51. (a) Both the statements are correct
52. (b) (ii) (iii) (iv) (i)
53. (c) (iv) (i) (ii) (iii)
54. (a) (ii) (i) (iii)
55. (c) (iv) (iii) (ii) (i)
56. (c) Value of Equipment − Depreciation value
$2{,}50{,}000 - 2{,}50{,}000 \times 10\% =$ ₹ 2,25,000
57. (a) $50{,}000 - 5{,}000 =$ ₹ 45,000
58. (a) Apprenticeship Premium - Unexpired
$= 1{,}500 - 1{,}200 =$ ₹ 300
59. (c) Rent and Taxes − Unexpired $= 2{,}520 - 720 =$ ₹ 1,800
60. (d) Land and Building - Depreciation
$= 75{,}000 - 1{,}875 =$ ₹ 73,125
61. (a) Gross Profit = Sales − (Opening Stock + Purchases) − Closing Stock)
$= 5{,}00{,}000 - (1{,}00{,}000 + 3{,}00{,}000 - 1{,}20{,}000)$
= ₹ 2,20,000
62. (b) Value of Machinery − Depreciation Value
$= 2{,}00{,}000 - 2{,}00{,}000 \times 15\%$
= ₹ 1,70,000

12

CHAPTER

"Single entry system is a system of bookkeeping in which, as a rule, only records of cash and of personal accounts are maintained, it is always incomplete double entry varying with the circumstances." — *Kohler*

YOUR STUDY GOALS

12.1 Meaning of Incomplete Records

12.2 Ascertainment of Profit or Loss under the Incomplete Records

YOUR PRACTICE GOAL

- Solved Questions (12 Solved Questions)
- Numerical Questions [20 Questions (Unsolved)]
- Theoretical Questions [7 Questions (with answers)]
- Objective Questions (50 Qs ; MCQs, A-R, Statements, Matching, Case)

Accounts from Incomplete Records

12.1 Meaning of Incomplete Records

Accounting records which are not maintained in accordance with the principles of double entry system are known as accounts from incomplete records or single entry system of accounting.

Under this system, both the aspects are recorded for certain transactions only, while for others only one aspect is recorded. Some transactions are ignored and not recorded at all.

Features of Incomplete Records

- It is an inaccurate, unscientific and unsystematic method of recording business transactions.
- Cash book is usually maintained but business and personal transactions of the proprietor are usually mixed-up.
- Only cash accounts and personal accounts are maintained. Thus, real and nominal accounts are not taken into consideration.
- This system is suitable for small size business where the number of transactions are less.
- It lacks uniformity as it is a mere adjustment of double entry system.
- It is difficult to prepare final accounts due to absence of all nominal and real accounts in the ledger.
- Profit under this system is only an estimate based on available information and therefore true and correct profits cannot be determined.

Reasons/Uses of Incomplete Records

- Single entry system can be adopted even by people who do not have the proper knowledge of accounting principles.
- As specialised accountants are not required, it is an inexpensive mode of maintaining records.
- As only a few books are maintained, time consumed in maintaining records is also less.
- It is a convenient mode of maintaining records as the owner may record only important transactions according to the need of a business.

Limitations of Incomplete Records

- This is incomplete method of maintaining accounting records as both the aspects (debit and credit) of every transaction are not recorded.
- As the accounts are incomplete in nature, there are strong chances of fraud.
- Arithmetical accuracy of accounts cannot be checked, as trial balance cannot be prepared.
- Correct ascertainment and evaluation of financial results of business operations cannot be made.
- Accounts of different organisations are not comparable due to lack of uniformity.
- Profit or loss for the year cannot be ascertained with accuracy.
- Any information obtained under this system is unreliable and doubtful.
- In absence of proper balance sheet, firm may not be able to avail itself of various financial facilities from banks.

12.2 Ascertainment of Profit or Loss under the Incomplete Records

In case of organisations maintaining incomplete records, the amount of profit or loss can be ascertained using any of the following methods

Smart Study **Chart No. 1**

Methods

Statement of Affairs or Net Worth Method
By preparing the statement of affairs as at the beginning and as at the end of the accounting period.

Conversion Method
By preparing trading and profit and loss account and the balance sheet by putting the accounting records in proper order.

Note Conversion method is not in syllabus. Therefore, it has not been discussed.

Statement of Affairs Method

Statement of affairs is a statement of all assets and liabilities. In this method, assets are shown on one side and the liabilities on the other, just as in case of a balance sheet.

It is also based on accounting equation, *viz*.

Capital = Assets − Liabilities

Format of Statement of Affairs

Statement of Affairs
as at.........

Liabilities	Amt (₹)	Assets	Amt (₹)
Bank Overdraft	...	Cash in Hand	...
Bills Payable	...	Cash at Bank	...
Sundry Creditors	...	Bills Receivable	...
Outstanding Expenses	...	Sundry Debtors	...
Incomes Received in Advance	...	Stock	...
Capital (Balancing Figure)	...	Prepaid Expenses	...
		Accrued Income	...
		Furniture	...
		Plant and Machinery, etc.	...
	...		...

Calculation of Profit or Loss by Statement of Affairs or Net Worth Method

Step 1 Prepare the statement of affairs at the beginning of the year to find out opening capital.

↓

Step 2 Prepare the statement of affairs at the end of the year to find out closing capital.

↓

Step 3 Adjust the capital at the end of the year by adding the amount of drawings made by the proprietor during the year and deduct any fresh capital introduced during the year.

↓

Step 4 Now, compare the adjusted closing capital with the opening capital.
If the adjusted closing capital is more than the opening capital, it is **profit**. If the adjusted closing capital is less than opening capital, then it is the **loss** suffered during the year.

Format of Statement of Profit and Loss

Statement Showing Profit or Loss
for the year ended ...

Particulars	Amt (₹)
Capital at the End of the Year (Computed from statement of affairs as at the end of year)	...
(+) Drawings During the Year	...
(–) Additional Capital Introduced During the Year	(...)
Adjusted Capital at the End of Year	...
(–) Capital in the Beginning of Year (Computed from statement of affairs as at the beginning of year)	(...)
Profit or Loss Made During the Year	...

The same can be computed using following equation

> Profit or Loss = Capital at the End – Capital in the Beginning + Drawings during the Year – Capital Introduced during the Year

Revised Statement of Affairs

Generally, profit and loss in this system is calculated by comparing the opening and closing capital.

That profit is not the actual net profit as there are certain adjustments (like depreciation, bad debts, provisions, etc.) which are required to be made. In order to ascertain the net profit, a revised statements of affairs is prepared.

For this, following steps are followed

Step 1 Prepare the statement of affairs at the beginning of the year and at the end, to calculate the opening and closing capital.

Step 2 Statement of profit/loss is prepared where all the additional information of adjustments is taken into account.

Step 3 Adjustments that result in increase in expenses or losses are deducted from profit. e.g. Depreciation, bad debts, provision for doubtful debts, interest on capital, outstanding expenses, etc.

Step 4 Adjustments that result in increase in income and gains are added to profit. e.g. Prepaid expenses, etc.

Step 5 A revised statement of affairs is prepared, where all adjustments are recorded again to make the accounts more clear and correct as per double entry system. In this manner, adjustments are recorded at two places.

Mind Map

ACCOUNTS FROM INCOMPLETE RECORDS

1 Meaning of Incomplete Records

- Accounting records which are not maintained according to the principle of double entry system are known as accounts from incomplete records or single entry system of accounting
- Under this system, both the aspects of debit and credit are recorded for certain transactions only, while for others only one aspect is recorded. Some transactions are ignored and not recorded at all

2 Uses of Incomplete Records

- This system can be adopted even by people who do not have proper knowledge of accounting principles
- It is an inexpensive mode of maintaining records
- Time consumed is also very less
- It is a convenient mode of maintaining records

3 Ascertainment of Profit or Loss under Incomplete Records

In case of organisations maintaining incomplete records, the amount of profit or loss can be ascertained using any of the following methods

- **Statement of Affairs or Net Worth Method** By preparing the statement of affairs as at the beginning and as at the end of the accounting period.
- **Conversion Method** By preparing trading and profit and loss account and the balance sheet by putting the accounting records in proper order. This method not in the syllabus.

4 Statement of Affairs Method

- It is a statement of all assets and liabilities. In this method, assets are shown on one side and liabilities on the other, just as in the case of a balance sheet.
- It is also based on the accounting equation, i.e. Capital = Assets – Liabilities

Format

Statement of Affairs

Liabilities	Amt (₹)	Assets	Amt (₹)
Bank Overdraft	—	Cash in Hand	—
Bills Payable	—	Cash at Bank	—
Sundry Creditors	—	Bills Recievables	—
Outstanding Expenses	—	Sundry Debtors	—
Income recieved in Advance		Stock	—
Capital (Balancing Figure)	—	Prepaid Expenses	—
		Accrued Income	—
		Furniture	—
		Plant and Machinery	—
	—		—

5 Calculation of Profit or Loss by Statement of Affairs Method

Step 1 Prepare the statement of affairs at the beginning of the year to find out opening capital.

Step 2 Prepare the statement of affairs at the end of the year to find out closing capital.

Step 3 Adjust the capital at the end of the year by adding the amount of drawings made by the proprietor during the year and deduct any fresh capital introduced during the year.

Step 4 Now, compare the adjusted closing capital with the opening capital.
- If the adjusted closing capital is more than the opening capital, it is profit.
- If the adjusted closing capital is less than the opening capital, then it is the loss suffered during the year.

Format

Statement Showing Profit or Loss
for the year ended...

Particulars	Amt (₹)
Capital at the End of the Year	—
(+) Drawings during the Year	—
(–) Additional Capital introduced during the Year	—
Adjusted Capital at the End of the Year	—
(–) Capital at the Beginning of the Year	—
Profit or Loss Made during the Year	—

6 Revised Statement of Affairs

Generally, profit and loss in this system is calculated by comparing the opening and closing capital. That profit is not the actual net profit as there are certain adjustments which are required to be made. In order to ascertain the net profit, a revised statement of affairs is prepared.

For this, the following steps are followed

Step 1 Prepare the statement of affairs at the beginning of year and at end, to calculate the opening and closing capital.

Step 2 Statement of profit/loss is prepared where all the additional information of adjustments is taken into account.

Step 3 Adjustments that result in an increase in expenses or losses are deducted from profit.

Step 4 Adjustments that result in an increase in income and gains are added to profit.

Step 5 A revised statement of affairs is prepared, where all adjustments are recorded again to make the accounts more clear and correct as per the double entry system.

Solved Questions

Solved Question 1 **Shubh maintains records as per single entry system. The following information is available from his book.**

Particulars	Amt (₹)
(i) Capital in the Beginning	5,00,000
(ii) Capital at the End	9,40,000
(iii) Drawings during the Year	1,44,000
(iv) Fresh Capital Introduced during the Year	2,40,000

Calculate his profit/loss during the year.

Sol. Profit/Loss = Capital at the End – Capital in the Beginning + Drawings during the Year – Capital Introduced during the Year

= 9,40,000 – 5,00,000 + 1,44,000 – 2,40,000

Profit = ₹ 3,44,000

Alternatively

Statement of Profit or Loss
for the year ended...

Particulars	Amt (₹)
Capital at the End	9,40,000
(+) Drawings	1,44,000
	10,84,000
(–) Additional Capital	(2,40,000)
Adjusted Capital at the End	8,44,000
(–) Capital in the Beginning	(5,00,000)
Profit during the Year	3,44,000

Solved Question 2 **Salil is keeping his accounts according to single entry system. From the following information, calculate his capital at the beginning.**

Particulars	Amt (₹)
Capital at the End of the Year	1,35,200
Drawings made during the Year	38,400
Fresh Capital Introduced during the Year	16,000
Profit of the Current Year	36,000

Sol. **Statement of Profit or Loss**
for the year ended

Particulars	Amt (₹)
Capital at the End of the Year	1,35,200
(+) Drawings during the Year	38,400
	1,73,600
(–) Capital Introduced during the Year	(16,000)
	1,57,600
(–) Profit during the Year	(36,000)
Capital at the Beginning of the Year	1,21,600

Solved Question 3 **Kanwar commenced business on 1st January, 2023 with a capital of ₹ 10,000, which he deposited into bank account opened for the purpose. He kept his books on single entry system.**

(i) On the same date, he brought furniture, which cost ₹ 2,000.

(ii) He made purchases of goods worth ₹ 6,500.

(iii) On 31st December, 2023 stock was valued at ₹ 8,300.

(iv) There were book debts amounting to ₹ 3,400 of which ₹ 200 represented debts which were irrecoverable.

(v) Amount due to suppliers amounted to ₹ 3,600.

(vi) Bank passbook showed a balance of ₹ 1,450.

(vii) Kanwar withdrew three times from business for his private expenses, each time he withdrew ₹ 600 and in addition he used ₹ 500 worth of goods from his shop.

(viii) He took ₹ 1,000 as loan from his wife during the year.

(ix) He gave ₹ 200 to his son from business, which he omitted to enter.

You are required to prepare a statement showing profit or loss in the business for the year ending 31st December, 2023 from the above information.

Sol. **Statement of Affairs**
as at 31st December, 2023

Liabilities	Amt (₹)	Assets		Amt (₹)
Creditors	3,600	Bank		1,450
Loan from Wife	1,000	Stock		8,300
Capital (Bal. figure)	10,350	Debtors	3,400	
		(–) Bad Debts	(200)	3,200
		Furniture		2,000
	14,950			14,950

Statement Showing Profit or Loss
for the year ending 31st December, 2023

Particulars		Amt (₹)
Closing Capital as on 31st December, 2023		10,350
(+) Drawings During the Year		
Drawings in Cash (600 × 3)	1,800	
Drawings in Goods	500	
Drawings in Cash (To Son)	200	2,500
Adjusted Capital at the End		12,850
(–) Opening Capital		(10,000)
Profit for the Year		2,850

Solved Question 4 **Sambhal started his business on 1st January, 2023 with a capital of ₹ 2,25,000. On 31st December, 2023 his position was as under**

Particulars	Amt (₹)
Cash	49,500
Bills Receivable	37,500
Plant	24,000
Land and Building	90,000
Furniture	25,000

He owned ₹ 22,500 from Mr. Nath. He also withdrew ₹ 4,000 per month for personal use. Ascertain his profit or loss for the year ended 31st December, 2023.

Sol.

Statement of Affairs
as at 31st December, 2023

Liabilities	Amt (₹)	Assets	Amt (₹)
Mr. Nath's Loan	22,500	Cash	49,500
Capital (Bal. fig.)	2,03,500	Bills Receivable	37,500
		Plant	24,000
		Land and Building	90,000
		Furniture	25,000
	2,26,000		2,26,000

Statement of Profit or Loss
for the year ended 31st December, 2023

Particulars	Amt (₹)
Capital at the End	2,03,500
(+) Drawings (4,000 × 12)	48,000
	2,51,500
(−) Capital in the Beginning	(2,25,000)
Profit for the Year	26,500

Solved Question 5 **Nandini keeps her book under single entry system. Here assets and liabilities were as under**

Particulars	31st December, 2022 (₹)	31st December, 2023 (₹)
Sundry Debtors	68,000	64,000
Stock	78,000	90,000
Cash	2,000	1,800
Plant and Machinery	1,20,000	1,60,000
Sundry Creditors	30,000	39,800

During the year, she withdrew ₹ 6,000 every month for her personal use and introduced ₹ 20,000 as additional capital. Calculate the profit/loss for the year ending 31st December, 2023.

Sol.

Statement of Affairs
as at 31st December, 2022

Liabilities	Amt (₹)	Assets	Amt (₹)
Sundry Creditors	30,000	Cash	2,000
Capital (Bal. fig.)	2,38,000	Debtors	68,000
		Stock	78,000
		Plant and Machinery	1,20,000
	2,68,000		2,68,000

Statement of Affairs
at as 31st December, 2023

Liabilities	Amt (₹)	Assets	Amt (₹)
Sundry Creditors	39,800	Cash	1,800
Capital (Bal. fig.)	2,76,000	Debtors	64,000
		Stock	90,000
		Plant and Machinery	1,60,000
	3,15,800		3,15,800

Statement of Profit or Loss
for the year ended 31st December, 2023

Particulars	Amt (₹)
Capital at the End of the Year	2,76,000
(+) Drawings during the Year (6,000 × 12)	72,000
	3,48,000
(−) Additional Capital during the Year	(20,000)
	3,28,000
(−) Capital in the Beginning	(2,38,000)
Profit during the Year	90,000

Solved Question 6 **Sameer started a firm on 1st January, 2023 with a capital of ₹ 60,000. He borrowed a sum of ₹ 24,000 from his wife @ 10% p.a. (interest not yet paid) for business on 1st April, 2023 and also introduced ₹ 9,000 as further capital.**
On 31st December, his position was

Particulars	Amt (₹)
Cash	3,600
Debtors	42,000
Creditors	36,000
Stock	56,400

He also withdrew ₹ 12,000 during the year. Calculate his profit or loss during the year.

Sol.

Statement of Affairs
as at 31st December, 2023

Liabilities		Amt (₹)	Assets	Amt (₹)
Creditors		36,000	Cash	3,600
Mrs. Kartik's Loan	24,000		Stock	56,400
(+) Interest on Loan $\left(24{,}000 \times \frac{10}{100} \times \frac{9}{12}\right)$	1,800	25,800	Debtors	42,000
Capital (Balancing figure)		40,200		
		1,02,000		1,02,000

Statement Showing Profit or Loss
for year ended 31st December, 2023

Particulars	Amt (₹)
Capital at the End	40,200
(+) Drawings	12,000
	52,200

Particulars	Amt (₹)
(–) Capital Introduced During the Year	(9,000)
Adjusted Capital at the End	43,200
(–) Capital in the Beginning	(60,000)
Net Loss for the Year	16,800

Solved Question 7 **Shivakshi started a business with capital of ₹ 6,00,000 on 1st October, 2022. She borrowed from her friend Sunil, a sum of ₹ 1,50,000 @ 10% p.a. (interest paid) for business and brought an additional amount of capital ₹ 1,12,500. On 31st March, 2023, her position was**

Particulars	Amt (₹)
Cash	45,000
Creditors	4,50,000
Debtors	5,25,000
Stock	7,05,000

She also withdrew ₹ 12,000 p.m. for the year.

Calculate profit or loss for the year.

Sol. **Statement of Affairs**
as at 31st March, 2023

Liabilities	Amt (₹)	Assets	Amt (₹)
Creditors	4,50,000	Cash	45,000
Loan from Friends	1,50,000	Stock	7,05,000
Capital (Balancing Figure)	6,75,000	Debtors	5,25,000
	12,75,000		12,75,000

Statement Showing Profit or Loss
for the year ended 31st March, 2023

Particulars	Amt (₹)
Capital at the End of the Year i.e. 31st March, 2023	6,75,000
(+) Drawings Made During in the Year (12,000 × 6)	72,000
	7,47,000
(–) Additional Capital Introduced	(1,12,500)
Adjusted Capital at the End	6,34,500
(–) Capital in the Beginning of the Year i.e. 1st October, 2022	(6,00,000)
Profit Made During the Year 2023	34,500

Note Interest is already been paid thus, no treatment for the same is being done here.

Solved Question 8 **From the following information of Janaki Prasad, find out his profit/loss for the year ended 31st December, 2023.**

Particulars	31st December, 2022	31st December, 2023
Cash	30,000	92,000
Creditors	25,000	22,000
Receivables	30,000	2,20,000
Stock	36,000	75,000
Vehicle	—	1,80,000
Furniture	12,000	15,000

He introduced additional capital by selling his investment ₹ 1,00,000 @ 2% premium. His drawings during the year were ₹ 8,000 p.m.

Sol. **Statement of Affairs**
as at 31st December, 2022

Liabilities	Amt (₹)	Assets	Amt (₹)
Creditors	25,000	Cash	30,000
Capital (Bal. fig.)	83,000	Receivables	30,000
		Stock	36,000
		Furniture	12,000
	1,08,000		1,08,000

Statement of Affairs
as at 31st December, 2023

Liabilities	Amt (₹)	Assets	Amt (₹)
Creditors	22,000	Cash	92,000
Capital (Bal. fig.)	5,60,000	Receivables	2,20,000
		Stock	75,000
		Vehicle	1,80,000
		Furniture	15,000
	5,82,000		5,82,000

Statement of Profit or Loss
for the year ended 31st December, 2023

Particulars	Amt (₹)
Capital at the End of the Year	5,60,000
(+) Drawings (8,000 × 12)	96,000
	6,56,000
(–) Additional Capital (1,00,000 + 2% of ₹ 1,00,000)	(1,02,000)
	5,54,000
(–) Opening Capital in the Beginning	(83,000)
Profit during the Year	4,71,000

Solved Question 9 **Neelam keeps her records on the single entry system. The following information is available from her books.**

Particulars	2022 (₹)	2023 (₹)
Cash	55,000	88,000
Stock	20,000	35,000
Creditors	7,000	14,000
Debtors	10,000	40,000
Furniture	4,000	24,000
Office Equipments	20,000	35,000
Bills Receivable	10,000	12,000
Motor Van	—	60,000

During the year, she withdrew ₹ 5,000 p.m. as drawings and also introduced ₹ 20,000 as fresh capital. Write-off depreciation @ 10% on motor van and @ 5% on furniture. There is an outstanding rent of ₹ 3,600.
Ascertion her profit or loss during the year ending 2023.

Sol.

Statement of Affairs
for the year ending 2022

Liabilities	Amt (₹)	Assets	Amt (₹)
Creditors	7,000	Cash	55,000
Capital (Bal. fig.)	1,12,000	Stock	20,000
		Debtors	10,000
		Bills Receivables	10,000
		Furniture	4,000
		Office Equipment	20,000
	1,19,000		1,19,000

Statement of Affairs
for the year ending 2023

Liabilities	Amt (₹)	Assets	Amt (₹)
Creditors	14,000	Cash	88,000
Capital (Bal. fig.)	2,80,000	Stock	35,000
		Debtors	40,000
		Bills Receivable	12,000
		Furniture	24,000
		Office Equipment	35,000
		Motor Van	60,000
	2,94,000		2,94,000

Statement of Profit or Loss
for the year ending 2023

Particulars		Amt (₹)
Closing Capital at the End of the Year 2023		2,80,000
(+) Drawings during the Year 2023 (5,000 × 12)		60,000
		3,40,000
(−) Additional Capital		(20,000)
		3,20,000
(−) Opening Capital in the Beginning of the Year 2023		(1,12,000)
Profit for the Year 2023 before Adjustments		2,08,000
(−) Depreciation Furniture @ 5%	1,200	
Motor Van @ 10%	6,000	(7,200)
		2,00,800
(−) Rent Outstanding		(3,600)
Net Profit after Adjustments		1,97,200

Statement of Affairs (After Adjustments)
for the year ending 2023

Liabilities		Amt (₹)	Assets		Amt (₹)
Creditors		14,000	Cash		88,000
Outstanding Rent		3,600	Stock		35,000
Opening Capital	1,12,000		Debtors		48,000
(+) Capital	20,000		Bills Receivables		12,000
(−) Drawings	(60,000)		Furniture	24,000	
(+) Net Profit	1,97,200	2,69,200	(−) Depreciation	(1,200)	22,800
			Motor Van	60,000	
			(−) Depreciation	(6,000)	54,000
			Office Equipments		35,000
		2,86,800			2,86,800

Solved Question 10 **Rahul Aggarwal, a trader does not keep proper books of accounts. However, he furnishes you the following information for the years ending 31st December, 2022 and 2023.**

Statement of Affairs
as at 31st December, 2022

Liabilities	Amt (₹)	Assets	Amt (₹)
Sundry Creditors	3,00,000	Cash in Hand	45,000
Capital	3,58,000	Cash at Bank	3,000
		Stock-in-trade	4,00,000
		Debtors	1,20,000
		Office Equipment	50,000
		Furnitures	40,000
	6,58,000		6,58,000

His position on 31st December, 2023 was as follows

Cash in hand ₹ 30,000, cash at bank ₹ 40,000, stock-in-trade ₹ 4,50,000, debtors ₹ 1,80,000, bills receivable ₹ 20,000, office equipment ₹ 50,000, sundry creditors ₹ 2,00,000, furniture ₹ 40,000.

Calculate his net profit for the year and prepare a final statement of affairs after adjustments.

(i) During the year, he introduced ₹ 60,000 as further capital.

(ii) He also withdrew ₹ 40,000 as drawings.

(iii) Depreciation should be written-off on furniture @ 10% and on office equipment @ 5%.

(iv) A provision of 5% is to be made on bills receivables.

(v) 5% debtors are doubtful and ₹ 1,000 are bad.

Sol. **Statement of Affairs** (Before Adjustments)
as at 31st December, 2023

Liabilities	Amt (₹)	Assets	Amt (₹)
Sundry Creditors	2,00,000	Cash in Hand	30,000
Capital (Balancing figure)	6,10,000	Cash at Bank	40,000
		Stock-in-trade	4,50,000
		Debtors	1,80,000
		Bills Receivable	20,000
		Office Equipment	50,000
		Furniture	40,000
	8,10,000		8,10,000

Statement of Profit or Loss
for the year ended 31st December, 2023

Particulars	Amt (₹)
Capital as on 31st December, 2023 Before Adjustment of Depreciation	6,10,000
(+) Drawings	40,000
	6,50,000
(−) Capital Introduced During the Year	(60,000)
Profit Before Adjustment	5,90,000
(−) Opening Capital	(3,58,000)
	2,32,000

Particulars		Amt (₹)
(–) Depreciation on Furniture	(4,000)	
Depreciation on Office Equipment	(2,500)	
Bad Debts	(1,000)	
Provision for Doubtful Debt @ 5% (1,80,000 – 1,000)	(8,950)	
Provision on Bills Receivable	(1,000)	17,450
Net Profit		2,14,550

Statement of Affairs (After Adjustment)
as at 31st December, 2023

Liabilities		Amt (₹)	Assets		Amt (₹)
Sundry Creditors		2,00,000	Cash in Hand		30,000
Capital (Opening)	3,58,000		Cash at Bank		40,000
(+) Capital Introduction	60,000		Stock-in-trade		4,50,000
Profit	2,14,550		Bills Receivable	20,000	
	6,32,550		(–) Provision for B/R	(1,000)	19,000
(–) Drawings	(40,000)	5,92,550	Debtors	1,80,000	
			(–) Bad Debts	(1,000)	
			(–) Provision for Doubtful Debt	(8,950)	1,70,050
			Office Equipment	50,000	
			(–) Depreciation	(2,500)	47,500
			Furniture	40,000	
			(–) Depreciation	(4,000)	36,000
		7,92,550			7,92,550

Missing Information

Solved Question 11 **From the following information, find the missing value.**

Statement of Profit or Loss
for the year ended 31st December, 2023

Particulars	Amt (₹)
Capital at the End of the Year as on 31st December, 2023	39,550
...... Drawings	4,500
Adjusted Capital at the End	...
...... Opening Capital	40,000
Net Profit	...

Sol.

Statement of Profit or Loss
for the year ended 31st December, 2023

Particulars	Amt (₹)
Capital at the End of the Year as on 31st December, 2023	39,550
(+) Drawings	4,500
Adjusted Capital at the End	**44,050**
(–) Opening Capital	40,000
Net Profit	**4,050**

Solved Question 12 **From the following information, find the missing value.**

Statement of Profit or Loss
for the year ended 31st March, 2023

Particulars		Amt (₹)
Capital as on 31st March, 2023 before Adjustment of Depreciation		61,000
(+) Drawings		4,000
		65,000
(–) Capital Introduced during the Year		(6,000)
Profit before Adjustment		59,000
... Opening Capital		....
		...
... Depreciation on Furniture	400	
Depreciation on Office Equipment	250	650
Net Profit		22,550

Sol.

Statement of Profit or Loss
for the year ended 31st March, 2023

Particulars		Amt (₹)
Capital as on 31st March, 2023 before Adjustment of Depreciation		61,000
(+) Drawings		4,000
		65,000
(–) Capital Introduced during the Year		(6,000)
Profit before Adjustment		59,000
(–) Opening Capital		**(35,800)**
		23,200
(–) Depreciation on Furniture	(400)	
Depreciation on Office Equipment	(250)	(650)
		22,550

Numerical Questions

1. Traya keeps his books on single entry system. Her capital on 1st April, 2023 was ₹ 15,00,000 and her capital after one year on 31st March, 2024 was ₹ 25,50,000.

He withdrew ₹ 7,500 per month for his domestic expenses and introduced fresh capital of ₹ 24,000 during the year.

Find out his profit and prepare a statement of profit.

Ans. Profit = ₹ 11,16,000

2. Calculate capital at the beginning from the following information.

Particulars	Amt (₹)
Profit of the Current Year	54,000
Capital at the End of the Year	2,02,800
Drawings made during the Year	57,600
Fresh Capital Introduced during the Year	24,000

Ans. Capital at the beginning = ₹ 1,82,400

3. Sandhya keeps her accounts according to single entry system.

The following information is drawn from her books for the year ended 31st December, 2023.

Particulars	Amt (₹)
Capital as on 1st January, 2023	2,10,000
Capital as on 31st December, 2023	6,25,000
Drawings during the Year for Personal Use	1,20,000
He Sold his Personal Investments during the Year and Introduced the Money into his Business	50,000

Find out her profit from business.

Ans. Profit earned during the year = ₹ 4,85,000

4. From the following information of Siya, find out her profit for the year ended 31st March, 2023.

Particulars	31st March, 2022	31st March, 2023
Cash in Hand	10,000	24,000
Cash at Bank	50,000	1,60,000
Debtors	60,000	4,40,000
Creditors	30,000	20,000
Bills Payable	20,000	24,000
Stock in Hand	72,000	1,50,000
Car	—	3,60,000
Furniture	24,000	30,000

She introduced fresh capital of ₹ 2,00,000 during the year and drew for her personal expense ₹ 16,000 per month.

Ans. Profit for the year ended 31st March, 2023 = ₹ 9,46,000

5. The capital of Sagar on 1st April, 2023 was ₹ 10,00,000 and on 31st March, 2024 was ₹ 9,60,000. He withdrew from the business ₹ 16,000 per month for private use. He also paid ₹ 40,000 for his personal income tax and the instalment of the loan of his personal house at the rate of ₹ 30,000 per month from the business.

He also sold his shares of Tata Finance costing ₹ 2,00,000 at a profit of 20% and invested half of this amount in the business.

Calculate the profit or loss of Sagar's business.

Competency Based Que

Ans. Profit during the year = ₹ 4,32,000

6. Yogesh keeps his books on single entry system, the following figures were available on 31st March, 2024.

Debtors 45,000; cash in hand ₹ 1,872; stock in trade ₹ 24,000; furniture ₹ 7,200; trade creditors ₹ 9,000; bank overdraft ₹ 1,800. He had started business on 1st April, 2023 with ₹ 33,000. During the year, his drawings were ₹ 18,000.

Prepare a statement showing a profit for the year, after writing-off 10% for depreciation on furniture.

Ans. Profit during the year = ₹ 51,552

7. Sambhav started a business with a capital of ₹ 1,80,000 on 1st April, 2023. On 1st July, 2023, he borrowed a sum of ₹ 72,000 @ 9% per annum (for business purpose) from his brother on which interest is not yet paid. He introduced a further capital of ₹ 27,000 into business. On 31st March, 2024, his position was as cash ₹ 10,800, stock ₹ 1,69,200, debtors ₹ 1,26,000 and creditors ₹ 1,08,000. He withdrew ₹ 36,000 as drawings during the year.

Find out the profit or loss for the year 2023-2024.

Competency Based Que

Ans. Loss = ₹ 49,860

8. Nilesh does not keep records as per double entry system. His balances as on 1st January, 2023 were

Liabilities	Amt (₹)	Assets	Amt (₹)
Bills Payable	40,000	Cash	40,000
Creditors	3,60,000	Stock	3,60,000
Capital	8,00,000	Debtors	4,40,000
		Furniture	3,20,000
		Machinery	40,000
	12,00,000		12,00,000

At the end of the year, his position was as follows

Particulars	Amt (₹)
Cash	60,000
Stock	5,40,000
Debtors	7,00,000
Furniture	3,60,000
Machinery	40,000
Creditors	6,00,000

He withdrew ₹ 10,000 per month out of which he spent ₹ 14,000 for business purpose.

Prepare the statement of profit or loss.

Ans. Profit = ₹ 3,96,000

9. Mr. Mahesh maintains his books of accounts from incomplete records. His books provide the following information

Particulars	1st April, 2021 (₹)	31st March, 2022 (₹)
Cash	1,200	1,600
Bills Receivable	—	2,400
Debtors	16,800	27,200
Stock	22,400	24,400
Investments	—	8,000
Furniture	7,500	8,000
Creditors	14,000	15,200

He withdrew ₹ 300 per month for personal expenses. He sold his investment of ₹ 16,000 at 2% premium and introduced that amount into business.

Prepare the statement of affairs and ascertain the profit or loss of the year.

Ans. Profit = ₹ 9,780

Hint Sale price of investment = 16,000 + 2% of 16,000 = ₹ 16,320

10. Mr. A tells that his capital on 31st December, 2022 is ₹ 3,74,000 and his capital on 1st January, 2022 was ₹ 3,84,000. He further informs you that during the year, he gave a loan to his sister that amounts to ₹ 70,000 on private account. He withdrew ₹ 6,000 per month as drawings. He used a flat for his personal purpose on which ₹ 2,000 per month as rent was paid from business account.

He paid electricity charges at an average rate of ₹ 200 per month of that flat from business account. During the year, he sold his bonds of ₹ 40,000 @ 2% premium and used that money as an additional capital for business.

You are required to prepare a statement of profit or loss for the year 2022. Competency Based Que

Ans. Profit = ₹ 1,17,600

Hint Selling Price of Bond $= 40{,}000 + \frac{2}{100} \times 40{,}000 =$ ₹ 40,800

11. Miss Priyanka does not keep her books properly. Following information is available from her books

Particulars	1st April, 2022 (₹)	31st March, 2023 (₹)
Creditors (Suppliers)	...	17,500
Outstanding Electricity Bill	1,100	2,250
Stock as Raw Material	10,000	2,000
Stock as Finished Products	2,000	2,500
Fixed Assets	30,000	34,000
Debtors (Customers)	35,000	...
Cash at Bank	25,000	21,000
Cash in Hand	15,000	1,800
Capital	78,000	83,550

During the year, Miss Priyanka sold her private scooty for ₹ 7,000 and invested this amount into business. She has withdrawn ₹ 2,500 p.m. for meeting her personal expenses.

You are required to prepare statement of profit or loss and statement of affairs.

Ans. Profit for the year = ₹ 28,550

12. A trader is not keeping proper books of accounts. Find his profit and loss for the year ending 31st March, 2023 and prepare his final statement of affairs from the following information Competency Based Que

Particulars	31st March, 2022	31st March, 2023
Cash in Hand	13,600	9,600
Cash at Bank	16,000 (Dr)	12,000 (Cr)
Stock in Hand	48,000	60,000
Debtors	36,000	68,000
Creditors	24,000	12,000
Bills Receivables	2,000	—
Loan from Sarthak @ 12% p.a.	—	16,000
Furniture	1,20,000	1,20,000

He withdrew ₹ 5,000 per month and ₹ 20,000 to give a personal loan to his brother. The rent of his house at the rate of ₹ 600 per month and electricity charges 300 per month were also paid from the business accounts.

He had hit a jackpot prize of ₹ 80,000 out of which he invested half the amount in the business.

Two months salaries @ ₹ 5,000 per month are due and insurance premium @ ₹ 2,000 per annum was paid on 1st July, 2022 for one year.

Loan from Sarthak was taken on 1st April, 2022 and interest was not paid. Fixed assets are to be depreciated @ 5% p.a.

Ans. Profit = ₹ 40,360

13. Mr. Ramlal Sharma commenced business on 1st January, 2022 with a capital of ₹ 1,00,000 which he deposited into his business account. On the same date, he brought furniture of ₹ 20,000 and goods of ₹ 65,000. On 31st December, 2022 his position was as under

(i) Stock was valued at ₹ 83,000.
(ii) Book debts amounted to ₹ 34,000 of which ₹ 2,000 represented debts are irrecoverable.
(iii) Creditors amounted to ₹ 36,000.
(iv) Bank passbook showed a balance of ₹ 14,500.
(v) He withdrew three times from business for his private expenses, each time he withdrew ₹ 6,000. Besides he used ₹ 5,000 worth of goods from his shop.
(vi) He took ₹ 10,000 as loan from his wife.
(vii) He gave ₹ 2,000 to his brother from business which he forgot to enter.

You are required to prepare a statement showing profit/loss for the year ending 31st December, 2022.

Competency Based Que

Ans. Profit = ₹ 28,500

Hint Drawings = [(6,000 × 3) + 5,000 + 2,000]

14. Sandeep Sharma started business on 1st January, 2023 with a capital of ₹ 2,00,000, which he deposited into his business account. On the same date, he bought furniture of ₹ 40,000 and goods of ₹ 1,30,000.

On 31st December, 2023 his position was as under

(i) Stock was valued at ₹ 1,66,000.
(ii) Creditors amounted to ₹ 72,000.
(iii) He took ₹ 20,000 as loan from his wife.
(iv) He gave ₹ 4,000 to his brother from business which he forgot to enter.
(v) Bank passbook showed a balance of ₹ 29,000.
(vi) Bad debts amounted to ₹ 1,28,000 of which ₹ 4,000 represented debts are irrecoverable.
(vii) He withdrew three times from business for his private expenses, each time he withdrew ₹ 12,000.

Besides, he used ₹ 10,000 worth of goods from his shop.

You are required to prepare a statement showing profit or loss for the year ending 31st December, 2023.

Ans. Profit = ₹ 47,000

15. On 1st April, 2021 X started a business with ₹ 40,000 as his capital. On 31st March, 2022, his position was as follows

Particulars	Amt (₹)
Creditors	30,000
Bills Payable	10,000
Bank	10,000
Debtors	50,000
Stock	40,000
Plant	68,000
Furniture	12,000

During the year 2021-2022, X drew ₹ 24,000. On 1st October, 2021, he introduced further capital amounting to ₹ 30,000.

You are required to ascertain profit or loss made by him during the year, 2021-2022 after considering the following objectives.

Adjustments

(i) Plant is to be depreciated @ 10%.
(ii) A provision @ 5% is to be made against debtors.

Also prepare the statement of affairs as at 31st March, 2022.

Ans. Profit = ₹ 84,700 ; Adjusted Capital (31st March, 2022) = ₹ 1,30,700 ; Total of Statement of Affairs (as at 31st March, 2022) = ₹ 1,70,700

16. Narendra keeps his accounts a single entry system. His position at beginning of 2023 was as follow

Cash in hand ₹ 2,800, cash at bank ₹ 7,800, stock in hand ₹ 32,000, sundry debtors ₹ 20,000; furniture ₹ 8,000, sundry creditors ₹ 14,000.

His position at the end of 2023 was as follows

Cash in hand ₹ 4,000; cash at bank ₹ 12,600, stock in hand ₹ 28,000, sundry debtors ₹ 25,000, TV set ₹ 10,000, Furniture ₹ 12,000 and sundry creditors ₹ 16,300.

During the year he withdrew from the business ₹ 3,24,000 of which ₹ 10,000 were spent in purchasing a TV set for the business.

(i) Depreciate furniture and TV set by 10% for 2023 only.
(ii) Write-off ₹ 200 as bad debts.
(iii) Provide 5% on debtors for doubtful debts.

Calculate profit or loss for the year ended 31st December, 2023 and also prepare a final statement of affairs.

Competency Based Que

Ans. Profit = ₹ 29,060; Statement of affairs = ₹ 87,960

17. Mr. Sanjeev Saxena runs a small shop and does not keep proper books of accounts. He furnishes following information **Competency Based Que**

Statement of Affairs
as at 31st March, 2023

Liabilities	Amt (₹)	Assets	Amt (₹)
Wages Outstanding	2,500	Cash at Bank	32,800
Creditors	37,670	Cash in Hand	3,990
Capital	3,81,795	Stock	25,000
		Debtors	10,175
		Machinery	2,50,000
		Building	1,00,000
	4,21,965		4,21,965

His position on 31st March, 2023 was as follows
Machinery ₹ 2,50,000, building ₹ 1,00,000, stock ₹ 40,000, debtors ₹ 8,605, cash in hand ₹ 7,670, cash at bank ₹ 20,190 and creditors ₹ 32,840.

During the year, he introduced ₹ 7,500 as further capital and withdrew ₹ 48,000 as drawings. Depreciation should be written-off @ 10% on machinery.

Calculate the net profit for the year and prepare a revised statement of affairs.

Ans. Net profit = ₹ 27,330

18. Manvendra who keeps incomplete records, gives you the following information

Particulars	1st April, 2022 (₹)	31st March, 2023 (₹)
Stock in Hand	37,400	40,800
Debtors	24,000	28,000
Creditors	18,000	3,000
Bills Receivable	8,000	10,000
Bills Payable	2,000	400
Furniture	1,200	1,200
Building	24,000	24,000
Bank Balance	8,700	6,700 (Overdraft)

You are also given the following information

(i) A provision of ₹ 2,900 is required for bad and doubtful debts.
(ii) Depreciation @ 5% is to be written-off on building and furniture.
(iii) Wages outstanding ₹ 6,000; Salaries outstanding ₹ 2,400.
(iv) Insurance has been prepaid to the extent of ₹ 500.
(v) Legal expenses outstanding ₹ 1,400.
(vi) Drawings of Manvendra during the year were ₹ 15,040.

Prepare a statement of profit as on 31st March, 2023 and a final statement of affairs as at that date.

Ans. Opening capital = ₹ 83,300 ; Closing capital = ₹ 93,900 ; Net profit = ₹ 12,180 ; Total of final statement of affairs = ₹ 1,00,340

Missing Information

19. From the following information, find the missing value. Competency Based Que

Statement of Profit or Loss
for the year ended 31st December, 2023

Particulars	Amt (₹)
Capital at the End of the Year as on 31st December	20,190
..... Drawings	6,000
	...
.....Capital Introduced during the Year	4,500
Adjusted Capital at the End	...
.....Opening Capital	30,000
Net	...

20. From the following information, find the missing value. Competency Based Que

Statement of Profit and Loss
for the year ended 31st March, 2023

Particulars	Amt (₹)
Capital as on 31st March, 2023 before Adjustment of Depreciation	1,22,000
..... Drawings	8,000
	...
..... Capital Introduced during the Year	12,000
Profit before Adjustment	...
..... Opening Capital	71,600
	...
..... Depreciation on Furniture	(1,300)
Net	...

Theoretical Questions

Short Answer Type Questions

1. "From the incomplete records, amount of profit or loss cannot be ascertained." Do you agree with the statement? Give valid explanation. Competency Based Que

Ans. No, the statement is not correct.
From the incomplete records, the amount of profit or loss can be ascertained by following two methods

(i) **By Statement of Affairs or Net Worth Method**
In this method, statement of affairs is prepared at the beginning and at the end of accounting period.

(ii) **By Conversion Method**
In this method, trading and profit and loss account and the balance sheet is prepared.

2. What is statement of affairs?

Ans. A statement of affairs is a statement of all assets and liabilities. In this method, assets are shown on one side and the liabilities on the other, just as in case of a balance sheet. It is also based on accounting equation, *viz.* Capital = Assets – Liabilities

3. Enumerate the steps to be followed to calculate profit/loss by statement of affairs method. Competency Based Que

Ans. For the calculation of profit or loss, given below steps should be followed

(i) Firstly, prepare the statement of affairs at the beginning of the year for calculating opening capital.

(ii) Then, prepare the statement of affairs at the end, to calculate the closing capital.

(iii) Prepare statement of profit or loss to find profit earned or loss incurred during the year.

4. Enumerate the steps to be followed to calculate net profit/loss after adjustments by net worth method.

Ans. Following steps are followed to calculate net profit/loss after adjustments by net worth method

(i) Prepare the statement of affairs at the beginning of the year and at the end, to calculate the opening and closing capital.

(ii) Statement of profit/loss is prepared where all the additional informations of adjustments are taken into account.

(iii) Adjustments that result in increase in expenses or losses are deducted from profit e.g. Depreciation, bad debts, provision for doubtful debts, interest on capital, outstanding expenses, etc.

(iv) Adjustments that result in increase in income and gains are added to profit e.g. Prepaid expenses, etc.

(v) After that, a revised statement of affairs is prepared, where all adjustments are recorded again to make the accounts more clear and correct as per double entry system.

Long Answer Type Questions

5. What is meant by statement of affairs? How can the profit or loss of a trader be ascertained with the help of a statement of affairs?

Ans. A statement of affairs is a statement of all assets and liabilities. It is a statement in which assets are shown on one side and the liabilities on the other, just as in case of a balance sheet. Under this method, profits or losses of the business are ascertained by comparing capital at the end, and capital at the beginning of the accounting period.

Capital in the beginning is calculated by preparing 'opening statement of affairs' and capital at the end is calculated by preparing 'closing statement of affairs'. After calculating opening and closing capital, a statement showing profit and loss is prepared to ascertain the profit or loss of the period.

Statement Showing Profit or Loss

for the year ended ......

Particulars	Amt (₹)
Capital at the End of the Year (Computed from statement of affairs as at the end of year)	...
(+) Drawings During the Year	...
(–) Additional Capital Introduced During the Year	(...)
Adjusted Capital at the End of Year	...
(–) Capital in the Beginning of Year (Computed from statement of affairs as at the beginning of year)	(...)
Profit or Loss Made During the Year	...

6. Differentiate between statement of affairs and balance sheet.

Ans. The differences between statement of affairs and balance sheet are

Basis	Statement of Affairs	Balance Sheet
Objective	The objective of preparing statement of affairs is to estimate the capital on a particular date.	The objective of preparing balance sheet is to show the true financial position of an entity on a particular date.
Accounting Method	When accounts are prepared under single entry system of accounting, statement of affairs is prepared.	When accounts are prepared under double entry system of accounting, balance sheet is prepared.
Reliability	It is less reliable as it is prepared from incomplete records.	It is more reliable as it is prepared from double entry records.
Omission	Omission of assets or liabilities cannot be discovered easily.	Omission of assets or liabilities can be discovered easily and can be traced from accounting records.
Trial Balance	Statement of affairs is not based on trial balance.	Balance sheet is based on the trial balance.

7. Differentiate between double entry system and single entry system.

Ans. The differences between double entry system and single entry system are

Basis	Double Entry System	Single Entry System
Recording of Aspects	This system records both the aspects of a transaction.	This system does not record both the aspects of a transaction, for some transactions two aspects, for some other one aspect and yet for others no aspect at all are recorded.
Type of Accounts	Under double entry system, all accounts i.e., personal, real and nominal are maintained.	Under single entry system, only personal accounts and cash book are maintained.
Arithmetical Accuracy	Under this system, arithmetical accuracy of books of accounts can be checked by preparing a trial balance.	Under this system, arithmetical accuracy of books of accounts cannot be checked, as a trial balance cannot be prepared.
Authenticity	This system is considered authentic by the court.	The court does not consider this system as authentic.
Use	Double entry system is used by almost all business.	Single entry system is used by only small business and institutions.
Adjustments	Under this system, adjustments are made at the time of preparing final accounts.	Due to incompleteness of accounts, there is no provision to make adjustments.

Objective Questions

Multiple Choice Questions (MCQs)

1. Which of the following account is maintained under single entry system?

(a) Real account (b) Nominal account
(c) Personal account (d) None of these

2. Incomplete records are usually maintained by

(a) government (b) small traders
(c) society (d) company

3. Single entry system of accounting is ....

(a) unscientific (b) inaccurate
(c) unsystematic (d) All of these

4. In case of accounting from incomplete records, opening capital is calculated by preparing

(a) cash account
(b) closing statement of affairs
(c) opening statement of affairs
(d) None of the above

5. What are the reasons for preparing accounts under single entry system?

(a) It is less expensive
(b) It is suitable for small concerns
(c) It is very simple
(d) All of the above

6. For calculating opening capital, which of the following should be added in closing capital?

(a) Profit and drawings (b) Loss
(c) Profit
(d) Loss and drawings

7. Single entry system can only provide .... degree of .... as no proper method of accounting is followed in preparation of profit and loss.

(a) low, accuracy
(b) low, record
(c) high, accuracy (d) high, record

8. Which among the following is the limitation of accounting for incomplete records?

(a) Unscientific
(b) Difficulty in preparation of final accounts
(c) Preparation of trial balance is not possible
(d) All of the above

9. If closing capital is more than opening capital, than difference will be

(a) profit
(b) loss
(c) profit, if no additional capital is introduced
(d) No profit no loss

10. If closing capital is less than opening capital, than difference will be a

(a) profit (b) loss
(c) loss, if there is no drawings
(d) No profit no loss

11. In the single entry system .... is not possible, hence there are always the chances of errors and frauds.

(a) internal check (b) internal control
(c) cash credit (d) None of these

12. Which of the following principle(s) is/are not followed by the single entry system?

(a) Revenue recognition (b) Matching concept
(c) Dual aspect (d) All of these

13. Under single entry system, the main account book kept is ....

(a) cash book (b) purchases book
(c) sales book (d) purchases return book

14. What are the common objectives between the double entry system and single entry system? Competency Based Que

(a) To determine profit/loss during the year
(b) To ascertain amount due from the debtors
(c) To know the financial position of the business
(d) Both (a) and (c)

15. Profit under net worth method, where there are no drawings and no additional capital, is the difference between Competency Based Que

(a) closing capital and opening capital
(b) assets and liabilities
(c) capital and liabilities (d) assets and capital

16. Profit = Capital at the End + ... − Capital in the Beginning − Capital Introduced.

(a) Sales (b) Purchases
(c) Drawings (d) Loss

17. Which of the following is not the reason for the single entry system being defective? Competency Based Que

(a) Only one account is maintained
(b) The trial balance cannot be prepared
(c) The net profit cannot be accurately calculated
(d) The possibility of fraud and misappropriation is great

18. If closing owner's equity is ₹ 1,000, opening owner's equity is ₹ 500, profit is ₹ 700, then there must be a .... of ₹ 200 during the year.

(a) drawings (b) stock
(c) loss (d) None of these

19. **Liabilities are ₹ 30,000 and the assets amounts to ₹ 47,000. What will be the amount of capital?** **Competency Based Que**

(a) ₹ 77,000 (b) ₹ 30,000 (c) ₹ 17,000 (d) ₹ 47,000

20. **If opening capital is ₹ 15,000, drawings ₹ 1,250, capital introduced during the period ₹ 2,500 and closing capital ₹ 22,500, the value of profit earned during the period will be** **Competency Based Que**

(a) ₹ 5,000 (b) ₹ 6,250 (c) ₹ 7,500 (d) ₹ 10,000

21. **Opening capital is ₹ 40,000 and the closing capital is ₹ 45,000. What will be the profit/loss?** **Competency Based Que**

(a) Profit of ₹ 5,000 (b) Loss of ₹ 5,000
(c) Profit of ₹ 2,000 (d) Loss of ₹ 2,000

22. **If capital in the beginning is ₹ 21,000, fresh capital introduced during the year is ₹ 7,000, amount withdrawn during the year is ₹ 13,000 and the profit during the year is ₹ 12,000, then the closing capital will be** **Competency Based Que**

(a) ₹ 27,000 (b) ₹ 15,000 (c) ₹ 41,000 (d) ₹ 1,000

23. **If the capital at the end of the year is ₹ 80,000, the additional capital during the year is ₹ 60,000, the year's drawings are ₹ 40,000 and the loss in the year is ₹ 1,20,000, what will be the opening capital?** **Competency Based Que**

(a) ₹ 20,000 (b) ₹ 80,000
(c) ₹ 1,40,000 (d) ₹ 1,80,000

24. **Calculate closing capital from the information Opening capital ₹ 1,40,000, profit for the year ₹ 40,000, drawings ₹ 14,000. During the year proprietor sold ornaments of his wife for ₹ 40,000 and invested the same in business.** **Competency Based Que**

(a) ₹ 2,34,000 (b) ₹ 2,06,000
(c) ₹ 1,66,000 (d) ₹ 1,74,000

25. **Opening and closing capital are ₹ 90,000 and ₹ 1,10,000 respectively. Total profit earned is ₹ 70,000. The amount of the drawings will be** **Competency Based Que**

(a) ₹ 60,000 (b) ₹ 30,000 (c) ₹ 10,000 (d) ₹ 50,000

Assertion-Reason

Direction (Q. No. 26 to 35) *Read the following Assertion (A) and Reason (R) and choose the correct alternative from the following*

Alternatives

(a) Both Assertion (A) and Reason (R) are true and Reason (R) is the correct explanation of Assertion (A)
(b) Both Assertion (A) and Reason (R) are true, but Reason (R) is not the correct explanation of Assertion (A)
(c) Assertion (A) is true, but Reason (R) is false
(d) Assertion (A) is false, but Reason (R) is true

26. **Assertion** (A) Single entry system accounting is more prone to errors and fraud as compared to double entry system of accounting.

Reason (R) Single entry system accounting have built-in checks and balances that are present in double entry system of accounting, making it easier for errors and for fraudulent activities to be detected.

27. **Assertion** (A) Single entry system accounting may not provide a complete picture of the financial position of a business.

Reason (R) Single entry system accounting typically records only cash transactions and does not capture non-cash transactions such as credit sales or purchases.

28. **Assertion** (A) Preparing a cash book summary is required to assess the closing cash balance.

Reason (R) All receipts from debit and all payments made within that time are also included in the cash book summary and the balancing figure shows the balance.

29. **Assertion** (A) Single entry system accounting involves recording only cash transactions, whereas double entry accounting requires recording both debit and credit entries for every transaction.

Reason (R) Single entry system accounting is simpler to implement compared to double entry accounting.

30. **Assertion** (A) A statement of affairs differs from a balance sheet because the statement of affairs is prepared based on improper source documents.

Reason (R) Statement of affairs is similar to a balance sheet, it is the statement of assets and liabilities of the business enterprise.

31. **Assertion** (A) The accuracy of the accounts cannot be evaluated because a trial balance cannot be prepared in single entry system.

Reason (R) In case of incomplete records, it is challenging to convince tax authorities that the computation on the record is accurate.

32. **Assertion** (A) Transactions are recorded unsystematically, as there are no specific rules of bookkeeping under this system of incomplete records.

Reason (R) Incomplete records generally give details of only one aspect of all the financial transactions of a business.

33. **Assertion** (A) In the incomplete records, the arithmetical accuracy of accounts cannot be determined.

Reason (R) Incomplete records are based on a single entry system due to which trial balance cannot be prepared.

34. **Assertion** (A) Incomplete records fail to provide details of assets, liabilities, incomes and expenses of the firm.

Reason (R) Hence the profitability, liquidity and solvency position of the firm cannot be judged. Thus, the owner finds it difficult to raise funds from the banks and outsiders.

35. **Assertion** (A) Profits can be easily and quickly calculated if the books are kept on single entry system.

Reason (R) Sole traders prefer to keep their books on single entry system.

Two Statements Based MCQs

Direction (Q. No. 36 to 43) *Read the following statements carefully and choose the correct alternative*

Alternatives

(a) Both the statements are correct
(b) Both the statements are incorrect
(c) Statement I is correct and Statement II is incorrect
(d) Statement I is incorrect and Statement II is correct

36. **Statement I** Single entry system accounting does not provide a systematic method for tracking assets, liabilities and equity.

Statement II Single entry system accounting does not focuses on recording cash transactions.

37. **Statement I** In complete records refers to a situation in which an organisation is not using double entry system of accounting.

Statement II Incomplete records refers to a situation in which an organisation is using more informal accounting system, such as a single entry system.

38. **Statement I** Single entry system accounting may lead to inaccuracies in financial reporting due to the absence of a standardised method for recording transactions.

Statement II Single entry system accounting relies on informal record keeping methods, which may result in inconsistencies and errors in financial records.

39. **Statement I** The value of opening capital can be calculated by creating an opening statement of affairs at the beginning of the accounting period.

Statement II The value of closing capital can be calculated by creating an opening statement of affairs at the beginning of the accounting period.

40. **Statement I** Single entry system accounting is suitable for small businesses with simple financial transactions.

Statement II Single entry system accounting requires less time and resources to maintain compared to double entry accounting.

41. **Statement I** In incomplete records, both the aspects of every transaction are recorded in it.

Statement II This method is suitable only for small size business where the number of transactions are less.

42. **Statement I** Partnership firms of professionals can keep their books of accounts on single entry system.

Statement II Profits cannot be easily and quickly calculated if the books are kept on single entry system.

43. **Statement I** Statement of affairs method is the statement of all assests and liabilities.

Statement II Statement of affairs method is also known as conversion method.

Matching

44. Match the following

Column I	Column II
A. Double entry system	(i) Systematic method
B. Statement of affairs	(ii) Conversion method
C. Single entry system	(iii) Incomplete method
D. Trading , profit and loss	(iv) Net worth method

Codes

	A	B	C	D
(a)	(i)	(ii)	(iii)	(iv)
(b)	(ii)	(iii)	(iv)	(i)
(c)	(i)	(iv)	(iii)	(ii)
(d)	(i)	(iii)	(ii)	(iv)

45. Match the following

Column I	Column II
A. Incomplete records	(i) Method used to calculate profit or loss by adjusting the net worth over a period.
B. Profit and loss statement (in incomplete records)	(ii) The process of determining profit/loss by comparing the opening and closing capital.
C. Conversion method	(iii) The accounts where records are not maintained for all transactions.
D. Net worth	(iv) The statement prepared to calculate profit or loss in the absence of detailed accounting records.

Codes

	A	B	C	D
(a)	(i)	(ii)	(iii)	(iv)
(b)	(ii)	(iii)	(iv)	(i)
(c)	(iii)	(iv)	(i)	(ii)
(d)	(i)	(iii)	(ii)	(iv)

Case Based MCQs

Direction *Read the following case study and answer the questions 46 and 47 on the basis of the same*

Saanchi Grocery Store operates using a single entry system of accounting. The owner, Saanchi Gupta, maintains basic records of cash transactions but does not record non-cash transactions or keep detailed accounts for assets, liabilities, and equity. In recent times, Ms. Gupta realised that she needs to prepare financial statements for the bank to apply for a loan. However, she is concerned about the accuracy and completeness of her records.

46. Which of the following challenges, Ms. Gupta might face in preparing financial statements using the single entry system of accounting with incomplete records?

(a) Incomplete financial records
(b) Lack of detailed accounts
(c) Compliance concerns
(d) All of the above

47. What would you recommend her to get the bank loan approved?

(a) She should consider transitioning to double-entry accounting
(b) She should use accounting software designed for small businesses to streamline record-keeping processes and improve the accuracy of financial data
(c) She should regularly reconcile her cash records with bank statements and other financial documents to identify discrepancies
(d) All of the above

Direction *Read the following case study and answer the questions 48 to 50 on the basis of the same*

Mr. Ram Krishna Murthy runs his firm M/S Shri Shyam Apparels on single entry system. The amounts of opening assets and closing assets of the firm are ₹ 80,000 and ₹ 1,30,000 respectively and the amounts of opening and closing external liabilities are ₹ 50,000 and ₹ 80,000 respectively.

48. What will be the profit if there is no drawings made and no additional capital brought in by the proprietor Mr. Ram Krishna Murthy?

(a) ₹ 28,000 (b) ₹ 18,000 (c) ₹ 20,000 (d) ₹ 10,000

49. What is the amount of profit if there are no drawings but ₹ 10,000 was introduced as additional capital?

(a) No profit (b) ₹ 10,000
(c) ₹ 18,000 (d) ₹ 20,000

50. What is the amount of profit if drawings of Ram Krishna Murthy amounted to ₹ 8,000 but no additional capital was introduced?

(a) ₹ 10,000 (b) ₹ 8,000
(c) ₹ 18,000 (d) ₹ 28,000

Answers

1. (c) Personal account
2. (b) small traders
3. (d) All of these
4. (c) opening statement of affairs
5. (d) All of the above
6. (d) Loss and drawings
7. (a) low, accuracy
8. (d) All of the above
9. (c) profit, if no additional capital is introduced
10. (c) loss, if there is no drawings
11. (a) internal check
12. (d) All of these
13. (a) cash book
14. (d) Both (a) and (c)
15. (a) closing capital and opening capital
16. (c) Drawings
17. (a) Only one account is maintained
18. (a) drawings
19. (c) Capital = Assets − Liabilities = 47,000 − 30,000
    = ₹ 17,000
20. (b) Profit = Closing Capital + Drawings − Opening Capital − Additional Capital
    = 22,500 + 1,250 − 15,000 − 2,500 = ₹ 6,250
21. (a) Profit = Closing Capital − Opening Capital
    = 45,000 − 40,000 = ₹ 5,000
22. (a) Closing Capital = Opening Capital − Drawings + Additional Capital + Profit
    = 21,000 − 13,000 + 7,000 + 12,000 = ₹ 27,000
23. (d) Opening Capital = Closing Capital + Drawings − Additional Capital − Profit
    = 80,000 + 40,000 − 60,000 − (− 1,20,000) = ₹ 1,80,000
24. (b) Closing Capital = Opening Capital − Drawings + Additional Capital + Profit
    = 1,40,000 − 14,000 + 40,000 + 40,000 = ₹ 2,06,000
25. (d) Drawings = Opening Capital − Closing Capital + Additional Capital + Profit
    = 90,000 − 1,10,000 + 70,000 = ₹ 50,000
26. (c) Single entry system accounting lacks built-in checks and balances that are present in double entry accounting, making it easier for errors to go undetected and for fraudulent activities to occur.

27. (a) Both Assertion (A) and Reason (R) are true and Reason (R) is the correct explanation of Assertion (A)
28. (a) Both Assertion (A) and Reason (R) are true and Reason (R) is the correct explanation of Assertion (A)
29. (a) Both Assertion (A) and Reason (R) are true and Reason (R) is the correct explanation of Assertion (A)
30. (b) Both Assertion (A) and Reason (R) are true, but Reason (R) is not the correct explanation of Assertion (A)
31. (b) Both Assertion (A) and Reason (R) are true, but Reason (R) is not the correct explanation of Assertion (A)
32. (a) Both Assertion (A) and Reason (R) are true and Reason (R) is the correct explanation of Assertion (A)
33. (a) Both Assertion (A) and Reason (R) are true and Reason (R) is the correct explanation of Assertion (A)
34. (b) Both Assertion (A) and Reason (R) are true, but Reason (R) is not the correct explanation of Assertion (A)
35. (d) Assertion (A) is false, but Reason (R) is true
36. (c) Single entry system accounting primarily focuses on recording cash transactions and does not maintain detailed accounts for assets, liabilities and equity.
37. (a) Both the statements are correct
38. (a) Both the statements are correct
39. (c) The value of closing capital can be calculated by making a closing statement of affairs.
40. (a) Both the statements are correct
41. (d) In incomplete records, only one aspect of every transaction is recorded in it.
42. (a) Both the statements are correct
43. (c) Statement of affairs method is also known as net worth method.
44. (c) (i) (iv) (iii) (ii)
45. (c) (iii) (iv) (i) (ii)
46. (d) All of the above
47. (d) All of the above
48. (c) Capital at Beginning = Opening Assets – Opening Liabilities
    = 80,000 – 50,000 = ₹ 30,000

    Closing Capital = Closing Assets – Closing Liabilities
    = 1,30,000 – 80,000 = ₹ 50,000

    Profit = Cosing Capital – Opening Capital
    = 50,000 – 30,000 = ₹ 20,000
49. (b) Profit = Closing Capital – Opening Capital – Additional Capital
    = 50,000 – 30,000 – 10,000 = ₹ 10,000
50. (d) Profit = Closing Capital + Drawings – Opening Capital
    = 50,000 + 8,000 – 30,000 = ₹ 28,000

PROJECT WORK

Project Report

A project report is a written statement of what the analyser analyses in his/her evaluation. The project report needs to be prepared with great care and consideration.

A project report should

- be handwritten
- be concise
- be clear
- have diagrammatic presentation
- have topics with suitable headings
- end up with conclusion

Elements

Try to ensure that your report contains the following elements

Title Page

This should include the project title, name of the company on which you are conducting your research and name of the student. You can also list the name of your school, class and subject teacher.

Acknowledgement

It is usual to thank those individuals, who have particularly provided useful assistance, technical or otherwise, during your project. In this, you praise your supervisor as he/she will have invested quite a lot of time in overseeing your progress. You can also give a note of thank to the department of the company, which provides you a relevant data.

Content Page

This should list the main sections and sub-sections of your report. Choose self-explanatory titles with their respective pages and use double spacing for clarity. Content should be impressive and explanatory so that the reader would clearly understand the motto of the project.

Try to avoid too many levels of sub-heading.

Introduction

This is one of the most important component of the project report. It should begin with a clear statement of what the project is about, so that the nature and scope of the project can be understood by a reader. It should summarise everything which you set out to achieve and provide a clear summary of the project's background, relevance and main contributions. The introduction should set the context for the project and should provide the reader with a summary of the key things to look out for in, the remainder of the report. It is useful in stating the main objectives of the project as part of the introduction.

Background

The background section of the report should set the project into action, it specifies the problem of the company, what remedial actions were taken by the company, what are its effects. It gives the layout of the whole project.

Body of Report

The central part of the report usually consists of three or four sections detailing the technical work undertaken during the project. The structure of these sections is highly project dependent. They can reflect the chronological development of the project. It includes the detailed description regarding the matter of the project.

Evaluation

This might involve quantitative and qualitative evaluation such as expressibility, functionality, ease-of-use, etc of a product. At some point, you should also evaluate the strengths and weaknesses of what you have done. It includes certain questionnaires, sampling test which help in evaluating the result on the basis of truths and facts.

Conclusion

The conclusion should list the things, which have been learnt as a result of the work you have done. It shows the ultimate response of the project undertaken by a student. It should be expressive and impressive so that a reader would clearly evaluate the result and rate you on the basis of your presentation.

Project Work

Title of the Project	:	....
		....
Company Chosen for the Project	:	....
		....
		....
Name	:	....
School	:	....
Year	:	....
Class	:	XI
Submitted To	:	....

Acknowledgement

I would like to extend my sincere and heartfelt gratitude to my Accounts Teacher Mr/Ms........................... who have helped me in this endeavor and has always been very cooperative and without his/her help, cooperation, guidance and encouragement the project couldn't have been what it evolved to be.

I extend my heartfelt thanks to my faculty for their guidance and constant supervision as well as for providing me the necessary information regarding the project.

I am also thankful to my parents for their cooperation and encouragement.

Last but not the least, gratitute to all my friends who helped me (directly or indirectly) to complete this project within a limited time frame.

Thanks again to all who helped me.

Name of the Student ....

Roll No. ....

Certificate

This is to Certify that the project work ....

is the bonafide work of .... (Name of the student) who

carried out the work under my supervision ....

____

(Name and Signature of
Teacher/Supervisor)

INDEX

S.No.	Title of Project Work	Page No.	Remarks	Teacher's Signature
1.	Collection of Source Documents and Preparation of Vouchers			
2.	Preparation of Bank Reconciliation Statement			
3.	**Comprehensive** Case Study of a Sole Proprietor, willing to Start a Driving School and also to sell car accessories			

Project I Collection of Source Documents, Preparation of Vouchers, Recording of Transactions with the Help of Vouchers

Situation

Mr Kartik Makkar, M.Com, started his own business under the name of Kartik Makkar & Sons, at Abulane, Meerut on 1st January, 2024, to deal in a variety of electronic goods.

He introduced ₹ 6,00,000 as capital out of which ₹ 1,00,000 was in cash and balance by cheque. Enclosed herewith are the original papers relating to his business transactions for the month of January 2024. You are required to prepare voucher for each finanacial transaction and record the transactions with the help of vouchers.

Transaction 1

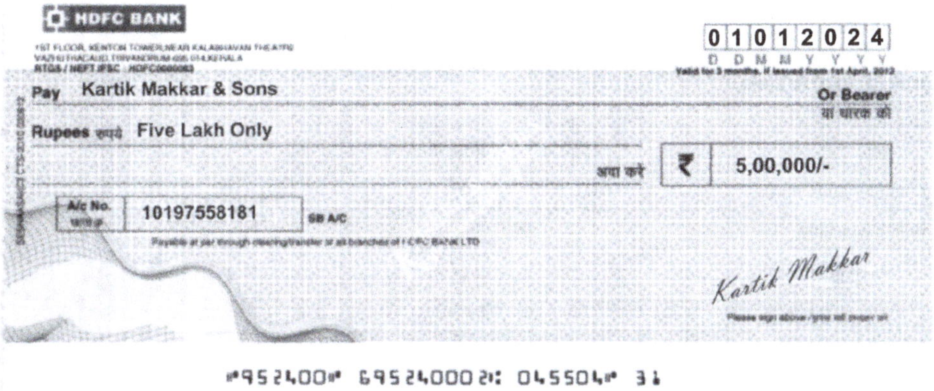

Transaction 2

Ram & Co				
Furnishers and Decorators				
Begum Bridge, Meerut				
M/s Kartik Makkar & Sons, Abulane, Meerut				
Bill No. 426				2nd Jan, 2024
S. No.	Particulars	Quantity	Rate (₹)	Amount (₹)
1.	Shelves	20	2,200	44,000
2.	Chairs	18	400	7,200
3.	Tables	9	600	5,400
4.	Cabinets	8	3,800	30,400
5.	Show Case	3	11,000	33,000
				1,20,000
		Less 5%		6,000
				1,14,000
	Rupees One Lakh Fourteen Thousand Only			
E & O E				For Ram & Co.

Project Work

Transaction 3

Ordeal Store Greater Kailash, Delhi	
M/s Kartik Makkar & Sons Meerut	3rd Jan, 2024
Particulars	Amount (₹)
15 Ceiling Fans @ 6,000 each	90,000
28 Electric Irons @ 2,000 each	56,000
Rupees One Lakh Forty Six Thousand Only	1,46,000
Received by Cheque No. 13551 on AXIS Bank Ltd.	
	For Ordeal Stores

Transaction 4

RAJ & BROS. Shastri Nagar, Meerut **Cash Memo** (Original)		
M/s Kartik Makkar & Sons Meerut		4th Jan, 2024
S.No.	Particulars	Amount (₹)
1. One Compuer and Printer		74,000
2. One Billing Machine		16,000
Rupees Ninty Thousand Only		90,000
Received in full vide Cheque No. 13552 on AXIS Bank Ltd., Meerut		
		For Raj & Bros.

Transaction 5

Vishal Electronics & Co. 14, Nehru Place, Delhi	Invoice No. 536
M/s Kartik Makkar and Sons Abulane, Meerut Order No. 6	5th Jan, 2024
Particulars	Amount (₹)
4 Water Heaters @ 8,000 each	32,000
1 Air Conditioner @ 40,000 each	40,000
	72,000
Less : 10% Discount	7,200
	64,800
Rupees Sixty Four Thousand Eight Hundred Only R/R enclosed	
E. & O.E	For Vishal Electronics & Co.

Transaction 6

Kartik Makkar & Sons Abulane, Meerut Cash Memo	6th Jan, 2024
Particulars	Amount (₹)
5 Ceiling Fans @ 6,000 each	30,000
Less : Cash Discount	2,000
	28,000
Rupees Twenty Eight Thousand Only Received-Vide cheque No. 43525 on Punjab National Bank	
For Kartik Makkar & Sons	

Transaction 7 : On 8th Jan, 2024

Cash paid ₹ 5,000 for advertisement in newspaper

Transaction 8

Kartik Makkar & Sons Abulane, Meerut **M/s Gaur & Sons,** Meerut Order No. 48	Invoice No. 1 9th Jan, 2024
Particulars	Amount (₹)
4 Water Heaters @ 15,000 each	60,000
5 Ceiling Fans @ 8,000 each	40,000
28 Electric Irons @ 5,000 each	1,40,000
2 Air Conditioner @ 47,000 each	94,000
	3,34,000
Rupees Three Lakhs Thirty Four Thousand Only	
E. & O.E. For Kartik Makkar & Sons	

Transaction 9

Raj & Co.
No. 1234 Begum Bridge, Meerut 10th Jan, 2024
Receipt (Original)
Received with thanks form M/s Kartik Makkar & Sons, Meerut sum of Rupees Fifty Thousand Only, as part payment of Bill No. 426 dated 2nd January, 2024 through cheque No. 13553 on AXIS Bank Ltd., Meerut
₹ 50,000/-
For Raj & Co.

Transaction 10

Kartik Makkar & Sons Abulane, Meerut M/s Veenu Bros, Haryana Series No. 72	Invoice No. 2 11th Jan, 2024
Particulars	Amount (₹)
5 Ceiling Fans 10,000 each	50,000
Less : Trade Discount	6,000
	44,000
Rupeese Forty Four Thousand Only Goods Sent by Transport	
For Kartik Makkar & Sons	

Transaction 11 : On 12 Jan, 2024

Received ₹ 2,00,000 as part payment against Bill No. 1, dated 9th January, 2024 vide cheque no. 43557 on the Union Bank, Meerut

Transaction 12

Vishal Electronics 14, Nehru Place, Delhi	Invoice No. 247 13th Jan, 2024
M/s Kartik Makkar and Sons Abulane, Meerut Order No. 21	
Particulars	Amount (₹)
3 Mini TVS @ 5,000 each	15,000
	15,000
Rupees Fifteen Thousand Only	
E. & O. E.	For Vishal Electronics

Transaction 13

Manohar & Sons Valley Bazar, Meerut Cash Memo (Duplicate)	15th Jan, 2024
Particulars	Amount (₹)
1 Air Conditioner @ 30,000 each	30,000
	30,000
Rupees Thirty Thousand Only Received Cash	
	For Manohar & Sons

Transaction 14

Bill of Exchange

Meerut — 16th Jan, 2024

Stamp

One month after date pay M/s Kartik Makkar & Sons or order the sum of Rupees Twenty Two Thousand Only, value received

For Kartik Makkar & Sons
Kartik Makkar

₹ 22,000
To
M/s Veenu Bros, Haryana

In addition to the above allowed M/s Veenu Brothers a discount of ₹ 2,000.

Transaction 15 : Only 24 Jan, 2024

Mr Kartik Makkar withdrew ₹ 6,000 from bank account for personal use vide cheque no. 13554.

Transaction 16 : On 25 Jan, 2024

Premium paid ₹ 7,000/- for fire and burglary insurance for the year by cheque no. 13555.

Transaction 17

Promissory Note		
₹ 15,000	Meerut	25th Jan, 2024
Two months after date, I/We promise to pay Ms Vishal Electronics or order sum of Rupees Fifteen Thousand Only for the value received.		
		For Kartik Makkar & Sons
		Kartik Makkar

Transaction 18 : On 30 Jan, 2024

Amount paid by cheque numbered 13556, ₹ 3,000 for printing of receipt books, cash memos and letter-heads.

Transaction 19 : On 30 Jan, 2024

Salary of ₹ 12,000 paid to salesman for the month of January, by cheque numbered 13557.

Event as on 30 Jan, 2024

Inventory was counted and valued ₹ 1,61,800.

Solution. Project is to prepare vouchers with the help of source documents and record transactions with the help of vouchers.

Voucher for Transaction 1

Kartik Makkar & Sons, Abulane, Meerut No. : 1 **Receipt Voucher**	Date 1st Jan, 2024
Particulars	Amount (₹)
Bank Account	5,00,000 (Dr)
Capital Account	5,00,000 (Cr)
Amounts (in words) Rupees Five Lakhs Only	
(Being capital introduced through cheque)	
	Authorised Signatory

Kartik Makkar & Sons, Abulane, Meerut No. : 2 **Receipt Voucher**	Date 1st Jan, 2024
Particulars	Amount (₹)
Cash Account	1,00,000 (Dr)
Capital Account	1,00,000 (Cr)
Amounts (in words) Rupees One Lakh Only	
(Being business started with cash)	
	Authorised Signatory

Voucher for Transaction 2

Kartik Makkar & Sons, Abulane, Meerut No. : 1 **Journal Voucher**	Date 2nd Jan, 2024
Particulars	Amount (₹)
Furniture and Fixtures Account	1,14,000 (Dr)
Ram & Co.	1,14,000 (Cr)
Amounts (in words) Rupees One Lakh Fourteen Thousand Only	
(Being furniture purchased from Ram Co. Bill No. 426)	
	Authorised Signatory

Note ₹ 6,000 being trade discount has not been recorded.

Voucher for Transaction 3

No. 1	**Kartik Makkar & Sons**, Abulane, Meerut **Payment Voucher**	Date 3rd Jan, 2024
	Particulars	Amount (₹)
	Purchases Account	1,46,000 (Dr)
	Bank Account	1,46,000 (Cr)
	Amount (in words) Rupees One Lakh Forty Six Thousand Only	
	Received with thanks Rupees One Lakh Forty Six Thousand vide Cheque No. 13551	
Receiver's Signature		**Authorised Signatory**

Voucher for Transaction 4

No. : 2	**Kartik Makkar & Sons**, Abulane, Meerut **Payment Voucher**	Date 4th Jan, 2024
	Particulars	Amount (₹)
	Office Equipments	
	Computer and Printer	74,000 (Dr)
	Billing Machine	16,000 (Dr)
	Bank Account	90,000 (Cr)
	Amount (in words) Rupees Ninty Thousand Only	
	Received with thanks Rupees Ninty Thousand Only vide Cheque No. 13552.	
Receiver's Signature		**Authorised Signatory**

Voucher for Transaction 5

No. : 1	**Kartik Makkar & Sons**, Abulane, Meerut **Purchase Voucher**	Date 5th Jan, 2024
	Particulars	Amount (₹)
	Purchases Account	64,800 (Dr)
	Vishal Electronics	64,800 (Cr)
	Amounts (in words) Rupees Sixty Four Thousand Eight Hundred Only	
	Being water heaters and air conditioner purchased vide Invoice No. 536	
		Authorised Signatory

Voucher for Transaction 6

No. : 3	**Kartik Makkar & Sons**, Abulane Meerut **Receipt Voucher**	Date 6th Jan, 2024
	Particulars	Amount (₹)
	Bank Account	28,000 (Dr)
	Discount Allowed	2,000 (Cr)
	Sales	30,000 (Cr)
	Amounts (in words) Rupees Thirty Thousand Only	
	Being ceiling fans sold vide Cheque No. 43525 on PNB	
		Authorised Signatory

Voucher for Transaction 7

Kartik Makkar & Sons, Abulane, Meerut No. : 3 Payment Voucher	Date 8th Jan, 2024
Particulars	Amount (₹)
Advertisement Expense	5,000 (Dr)
Cash Account	5,000 (Cr)
Amount (in words) Rupees Five Thousand Only	
Received with thanks Rupees Five Thousand in Cash.	
Receiver's Signature	**Authorised Signatory**

Voucher for Transaction 8

Kartik Makkar & Sons, Abulane, Meerut No. : 1 Sales Voucher	Date 9th Jan, 2024
Particulars	Amount (₹)
Gaur & Sons	3,34,000 (Dr)
Sales Account	3,34,000 (Cr)
Amounts (in words) Rupees Three Lakhs Thirty Four Thousand Only	
(Being water heaters, etc., sold vide Bill No. 1)	
	Authorised Signatory

Voucher for Transaction 9

Kartik Makkar & Sons, Abulane, Meerut No. : 4 Payment Voucher	Date 10th Jan, 2024
Particulars	Amount (₹)
Ram & Co.	50,000 (Dr)
Bank Account	50,000 (Cr)
Amounts (in words) Rupees Fifty Thousand Only	
Received Rupees Fifty Thousand Only against Bill No. 426 dated 2nd January, 2024 through Cheque No. 13553.	
Receiver's Signature	**Authorised Signatory**

Voucher for Transaction 10

Kartik Makkar & Sons, Abulane, Meerut No. : 2 Sales Voucher	Date 11th Jan, 2024
Particulars	Amount (₹)
M/s Veenu Bros.	44,000 (Dr)
Sales Account	44,000 (Cr)
Amounts (in words) Rupees Forty Four Thousand Only	
(Being ceiling fans sold vide Bill No. 2)	
	Authorised Signatory

Voucher for Transaction 11

Kartik Makkar & Sons, Abulane Meerut No. : 4 **Receipt Voucher**	Date 12th Jan, 2024
Particulars	Amount (₹)
Bank Account	2,00,000 (Dr)
Gaur & Sons	2,00,000 (Cr)
Amounts (in words) Rupees Two Lakhs Only	
(Being part payment received against Bill No. 1 dated 9th January, 2024 vide Cheque. No. 43557 drawn on Union Bank, Meerut) **Authorised Signatory**	

Voucher for Transaction 12

Kartik Makkar & Sons, Abulane, Meerut No. : 2 **Purchase Voucher**	Date 13th Jan, 2024
Particulars	Amount (₹)
Purchases Account	15,000 (Dr)
Vishal Electronics	15,000 (Cr)
Amounts (in words) Rupees Fifteen Thousand Only	
(Being mini TVs purchased vide Bill No. 247 dated 13th January, 2024) **Authorised Signatory**	

Voucher for Transaction 13

Kartik Makkar & Sons, Abulane, Meerut No. : 5 **Payment Voucher**	Date 15th Jan, 2024
Particulars	Amount (₹)
Purchases Account	30,000 (Dr)
Cash Account	30,000 (Cr)
Amounts (in words) Rupees Thirty Thousand Only	
Received with thanks Rupees Thirty Thousand in Cash against vide Bill No. 213 Dated 15th January, 2024 **Receiver's Signature** **Authorised Signatory**	

Voucher for Transaction 14

Kartik Makkar & Sons, Abulane, Meerut No. : 2 **Journal Voucher**	Date 16th Jan, 2024
Particulars	Amount (₹)
Bills Receivable Account	22,000 (Dr)
Discount Allowed	2,000 (Dr)
M/s Veenu Bros.	24,000 (Cr)
Amounts (in words) Rupees Twenty Two Thousand Only	
(Being bills receivable received and discount allowed against Bill No. 2 dated 11th January, 2024) **Authorised Signatory**	

Voucher for Transaction 15

Kartik Makkar & Sons, Abulane, Meerut No. : 6 **Payment Voucher**	Date 24th Jan, 2024
Particulars	Amount (₹)
Drawings Account	6,000 (Dr)
Bank	6,000 (Cr)
Amounts (in words) Rupees Six Thousand Only	
Received with thanks Rupees Six Thousand Only vide Cheque No. 13554. **Receiver's Signature**	**Authorised Signatory**

Voucher for Transaction 16

Kartik Makkar & Sons, Abulane, Meerut No. : 7 **Payment Voucher**	Date 25th Jan, 2024
Particulars	Amount (₹)
Insurance Account	7,000 (Dr)
Bank Account	7,000 (Cr)
Amounts (in words) Rupees Seven Thousand Only	
Received with thanks Rupees Seven Thousand Only Cheque No. 13555. **Receiver's Signature**	**Authorised Signatory**

Voucher for Transaction 17

Kartik Makkar & Sons, Abulane, Meerut No. : 3 **Journal Voucher**	Date 25th Jan, 2024
Particulars	Amount (₹)
M/s Vishal Electronics	15,000 (Dr)
Promissory Note Two Months after Date	15,000 (Cr)
Amounts (in words) Rupees Fifteen Thousand Only	
Being promissory note issued, two months after date.	**Authorised Signatory**

Voucher for Transaction 18

Kartik Makkar & Sons, Abulane, Meerut No. : 8 **Payment Voucher**	Date 30th Jan, 2024
Particulars	Amount (₹)
Printing and Stationery Account	3,000 (Dr)
Bank Account	3,000 (Cr)
Amounts (in words) Rupees Three Thousand Only	
Received with thanks Rupees Three Thousand Only vide Cheque No. 13556. **Receiver's Signature**	**Authorised Signatory**

Voucher for Transaction 19

No. : 9	**Kartik Makkar & Sons**, Abulane, Meerut **Payment Voucher**	Date 30th Jan, 2024
	Particulars	Amount (₹)
	Salary Account	12,000 (Dr)
	Bank Account	12,000 (Cr)
	Amounts (in words) Rupees Twelve Thousand Only	
	Received with thanks Rupees Twelve Thousand Only vide Cheque No. 13557.	
	Receiver's Signature	**Authorised Signatory**

Memorandum for event on 30th January, 2024.

Kartik Makkar & Sons

Memorandum

Enclosed is a list of unsold goods in stock on 30th January, 2024. Worth ₹ 1,61,800/- only.

Dated : 30th January, 2024 **Signature of Valuer**

JOURNAL

(In the Books of Kartik Makkar & Sons)

Date	Particulars		LF	Amt (Dr)	Amt (Cr)
2024					
Jan 2	Furniture and Fixtures A/c	Dr		1,14,000	
	To Ram & Co				1,14,000
	(Being furniture and fixtures purchased on credit vide bill no. 426)				
Jan 6	Discount Allowed A/c	Dr		2,000	
	To Sales A/c				2,000
	(Being goods sold and cheque no. 43525 on PNB is received, allowed discount)				
Jan 16	Discount Allowed A/c	Dr		2,000	
	To Veenu Bros				2,000
	(Being bill of exchange written on received and allowed them discount for ₹ 2,000)				

(In the Books of Kartik Makkar & Sons)

Dr **Cash Book** Cr

Date	Particulars	LF	Cash (₹)	Bank (₹)	Date	Particulars	LF	Cash (₹)	Bank (₹)
2024					2024				
Jan 1	To Capital A/c		1,00,000	5,00,000	Jan 3	By Purchases A/c			1,46,000
Jan 6	To Sales A/c			28,000	Jan 4	By Office Equip. A/c			90,000
Jan 12	To Gaur & Sons			2,00,000	Jan 8	By Advertisement A/c		5,000	
					Jan 10	By Ram & Co			50,000
					Jan 15	By Purchases A/c		30,000	
					Jan 24	By Drawings A/c			6,000
					Jan 25	By Insurance A/c			7,000
					Jan 30	By Printing & Stationery A/c			3,000
					Jan 30	By Salary A/c			12,000
					Jan 30	By Balance c/d		65,000	4,14,000
			1,00,000	7,28,000				1,00,000	7,28,000
2024									
Feb 1	To Balance b/d		65,000	4,14,000					

Purchase Book

Date	Particulars	Invoice No.	LF	Details	Total Amt (₹)
2024					
Jan 5	**Vishal Electronics**	536			
	4 Water Heaters @ 8,000 each			32,000	
	1 Air Conditioners @ 40,000 each			40,000	
				72,000	
	(–) Trade Discount (10%)			7,200	64,800
Jan 15	**Vishal Electronics**	247			
	3 Mini TVs @ 5,000 each			15,000	15,000
Jan 31	**Purchase A/c** **Dr**				79,800

Sales Book

Date	Particulars	LF	Details	Total Amt (₹)
2024				
Jan 9	**M/s Gaur & Sons**			
	4 Water Heaters @ 15,000 each		60,000	
	5 Ceiling Fans @ 8,000 each		40,000	
	28 Electric Irons @ 5,000 each		1,40,000	
	2 Air Conditioners @ 47,000 each		94,000	3,34,000
Jan 11	**M/s Veenu Bros**			
	5 Ceiling Fans @ 10,000 each		50,000	
	(–) Trade Discount		6,000	44,000
2024				
Jan 3	**Sales A/c** **Cr**			3,78,000

Bills Receivable Book

S.No.	From whom Received	Acceptor	Date of	Term Bill	Date of Maturity	Amount (₹)	How Disposed
1	Veenu Bros	Veenu Bros	16th Jan, 2024	1 Month	19th Feb, 2024	22,000	

Bills Payable Book

S.No.	Date of Bill	Name of Drawer	Payee	Term	Date of Maturity	Amount (₹)	Remarks
1	25th Jan, 2024	Kartik Makkar & Sons	Kartik Makkar & Sons	2 Months	28th March, 2024	15,000	

Project 2 Preparation of Bank Reconciliation Statement with the given Cash Book and the Pass Book

Vardhman & Co Bank Reconciliation Statement

Situation

Ankit Jain works as a cashier for Vardhman & Co, his responsibilities include entering and maintaining the firm's cash book and preparing a bank reconciliation statement at the end of the month.

The firm's cash book for March 2024 which Ankit has just finished entering and balancing for the month end is shown below. A copy of the firm's bank statement from the ICICI Bank Ltd. dated 31st March, 2024 has just been received and is also illustrated.

You are to make the entries necessary to update the cash book and reconcile the cash book with Bank Statement.

Vardhman & Co.

Cash Book

Receipts			Payments		
Date	Details	Bank	Date	Details	Bank
2024			2024		
1 Mar	Balance b/d	✓ 12,60,500	1 Mar	Munjal & Co Rent	✓ 2,00,000
4 Mar	Raja Ltd	✓ 3,10,000	4 Mar	S.Subbu 210725	✓ 1,83,500
8 Mar	Vishal Bros	✓ 13,500	5 Mar	RK & Co 210726	✓ 5,54,000
11 Mar	Neha Limited	24,000	8 Mar	Bata & Son 210727	✓ 1,60,000
11 Mar	Nayyar & Sons	53,000	13 Mar	K.Mohan 210728	16,000
12 Mar	V.Parikh	✓ 1,50,500	14 Mar	N.Laxmi 210729	14,000
13 Mar	Vipul Shah	1,000	15 Mar	Ravish & Co 210730	500
14 Mar	Rajesh Ltd	1,000	16 Mar	Oprah Instruments 210731	1,000
15 Mar	Sky Automation Pvt Ltd	11,000	17 Mar	Fashion Stores 210732	10,000
16 Mar	City Ventures	4,200	18 Mar	Swaroop Garage 210733	5,000
17 Mar	Spencer Partners	4,550	19 Mar	Jason Ltd 210734	2,000
18 Mar	Reliance Communication	4,000	20 Mar	Sharda Gandhi 210735	1,250
19 Mar	Bindals Store	1,500	21 Mar	Maruti Ltd 210736	7,500
20 Mar	Mona & Co	29,000	22 Mar	Max Insurance (DD)	✓ 69,500
25 Mar	A.Varmani	1,04,500	25 Mar	Vijay Computers 210737	✓ 9,00,000
31 Mar	Balance c/d	3,02,000	30 Mar	Rates (DD)	✓ 1,50,000
		22,74,250			22,74,250
			1 Apr	Balance b/d	3,02,000

Vardhman & Co
Pass Book

ICICI Bank				STATEMENT
3F, Sector 3, Shastri Nagar, Meerut				
Account	Vardhman & Co		**Account No.**	24569810
Date	31st March, 2024			

Date	Details	Debit	Credit	Balance
2024				
1 Mar	Balance			✓ 12,60,500 Cr
1 Mar	Munjal & Co	✓ 2,00,000		10,60,500 Cr
4 Mar	Raja Ltd		✓ 3,10,000	13,70,500 Cr
7 Mar	210725	✓ 1,83,500		11,87,000 Cr
11 Mar	Ronak Ltd		77,000	12,64,000 Cr
13 Mar	V.Parikh		✓ 1,50,500	14,14,500 Cr
15 Mar	Cheques		✓ 13,500	14,28,000 Cr
18 Mar	210727	✓ 1,60,000		12,68,000 Cr
18 Mar	210726	✓ 5,54,000		7,14,000 Cr
22 Mar	Max Insurance (DD)	✓ 69,500		6,44,500 Cr
27 Mar	210720	✓ 9,00,000		2,55,500 Dr
28 Mar	Mahonar's		57,000	1,98,500 Dr
29 Mar	Rates	✓ 1,50,000		3,48,500 Dr
29 Mar	Bank Interest	26,500		3,75,000 Dr
29 Mar	Bank Charges	22,500		3,97,500 Dr

The numerical difference between the pass book and cash book is ₹ 3,97,500 (–) ₹ 3,02,000 = ₹ 95,500. This is the difference which Ankit will have to reconcile.

Solution

To reconcile the cash book with the bank pass book following five steps are taken in practical.

Step 1. *Tick off the items which are found both in cash book and bank statement. Put (3) sign before such items.* Items ticked (3) will neither be recorded in amended cash book nor in bank reconciliation statement.

Step 2. *Update the cash book from the bank statement.*

The unticked items on the bank statement indicate items that have gone through the bank account but have not yet been entered in Vardhman & Co's cash book. *These are*

			Amt (₹)
Receipt	11 Mar	Ronak	77,000
Receipt	28 Mar	Manohar	57,000
Payment	29 Mar	Bank Interest	26,500
Payment	29 Mar	Bank Charges	22,500

These items now need to be entered in the cash book to update it.

Step 3. *Balance the cash book bank columns to produce an updated balance*

Amended Cash Book

Dr	Receipts			Payments	Cr
Date	Details	Bank (₹)	Date	Details	Bank (₹)
2024			2024		
	To Ronak Ltd	77,000	31 Mar	By balance b/d	3,02,000
	To Manohar's	57,000		By Bank Interest	26,500
	To balance c/d	2,17,000		By Bank Charges	22,500
		3,51,000			3,51,000
				By balance b/d	2,17,000

The balance of bank column of cash book stands at ₹ 2,17,000 (overdraft) but the bank statement shows a balance of ₹ 3,97,500 (overdraft). Thus, a difference of ₹ 1,80,500 (*i.e.,* 3,97,500 – 2,17,000) still exist.

The remaining difference is dealt with in the Bank Reconciliation Statement.

Step 4. *Identify the remaining unticked items from the cash book. These are*

		Amt (₹)
Receipt	11 Mar	24,000
Receipt	11 Mar	53,000
Receipt	13 Mar	1,000
Receipt	14 Mar	1,000
Receipt	15 Mar	11,000
Receipt	16 Mar	4,200
Receipt	17 Mar	4,550
Receipt	18 Mar	4,000
Receipt	19 Mar	1,500
Receipt	20 Mar	29,000
Receipt	25 Mar	1,04,500
Payments	13 Mar	16,000
Payments	14 Mar	14,000
Payments	15 Mar	500
Payments	16 Mar	1,000
Payments	17 Mar	10,000
Payments	18 Mar	5,000
Payments	19 Mar	2,000
Payments	20 Mar	1,250
Payments	21 Mar	7,500

These items should appear on next month's bank statement and are timing differences. These are the items which will be required in the preparation of the bank reconciliation statement.

Step 5. *Preparation of Bank Reconciliation Statement.*

(*i*) Enter the Cash book Balance - The balance figure to use, as 'per the cash book' is the revised cash book balance after entering the items that appeared on the bank statement which had not previously been entered.

(*ii*) Add cheques issued but not presented for payment *i.e.,* unpresented cheques. *They are*

		Amt (₹)
K. Mohan	(Cheque No. 210728)	16,000
N. Mohan	(Cheque No. 210729)	14,000
Ravish & Co	(Cheque No 210730)	500
Oprah Instruments	(Cheque No 210731)	1,000
Fashion Stores	(Cheque No 210732)	10,000
Swaroop Garage	(Cheque No 210733)	5,000
Jason Ltd	(Cheque No 210734)	2,000
Sharda Ltd	(Cheque No 210735)	1,250
Maruti Ltd	(Cheque No 210736)	7,500
		57,250

(*iii*) Deduct cheques paid into the bank for collection but not yet collected. *They are*

	Amt (₹)
Neha Ltd	24,000
Nayyar & Sons	53,000
Vipul Shah	1,000
Rajesh Ltd	1,000
Sky Automation Pvt Ltd	11,000
City Ventures	4,200
Spencer Partners	4,550
Reliance Communication	4,000
Bindals Store	1,500
Mona & Co	29,000
A. Varmani	1,04,500
	2,37,750

(*iv*) Completing the Reconciliation - Now that all the outstanding items have been added or deducted, the recalculated balance on the bank reconciliation statement should be the same as the final bank statement balance.

Bank Reconciliation Statement

as on 31st March, 2024

Particulars			Plus Items (₹)	Minus Items (₹)
Overdraft (Cr. Balance) as per Cash Book				2,17,000
Add	Cheques issued but not presented for payment			
	K.Mohan (Ch. No. 210728)	16,000		
	N.Laxmi (Ch. No. 210729)	14,000		
	Ravish & Co (Ch. No. 210730)	500		
	Oprah Instruments (Ch. No. 210731)	1,000		
	Fashion Stores (Ch. No. 210732)	10,000		
	Swaroop Garage (Ch. No. 210733)	5,000		
	Jason Ltd (Ch. No. 210734)	2,000		
	Sharda Ltd (Ch. No. 210735)	1,250		
	Maruti Ltd (Ch. No. 210736)	7,500	57,250	
Less	Cheques paid into bank for collection but not yet collected			
	Neha Ltd.	24,000		
	Nayyar & Sons	53,000		
	Vipul Shah	1,000		
	Rajesh Ltd	1,000		
	Sky Automation Pvt Ltd	11,000		
	City Ventures	4,200		
	Sencer Partners	4,550		
	Reliance Communication	4,000		
	Bindals Store	1,500		
	Mona & Co.	29,000		
	A Varmani	1,04,500		2,37,750
	Overdraft (Dr. Balance) as per Pass Book		3,97,500	
			4,54,750	4,54,750

Project 3 Comprehensive

Case Study of a Sole Proprietor, willing to Start a Driving School and also to Sell Car Accessories

Situation

On 1st January, 2024 Mr Veer Das decided to start a driving school and also to sell car accessories through same place. For this purpose he bought a workshop at a cost of ₹ 20,00,000 and decided to invest ₹ 7,50,000 as a further capital in the proposed business. He employed assistants and training staff for this purpose. He wants to start with 5 second hand cars. For further funds he approached Punjab National Bank and secured a loan of 18,00,000 @ 10% per annum. The loan was payable in 4 instalments along with interest due.

	Amt (₹)
Purchased cars	13,00,000
Security depsoited for electricity connection with electricity board	60,000
Security deposited with BSNL for telephone and Internet connection	1,50,000
Purchased furniture	1,20,000
Fees received from students	19,50,000
Bought car accessories	3,30,000
Sale of car accessories	4,80,000
Wages paid	2,70,000
Salaries paid	3,75,000
Electricity charges	1,42,500
Advertisement	66,000
Postage and call	28,500
General expenses	18,000
Insurance premium	13,800
Bought laptop and printer	90,000

He withdrew ₹ 36,000 per month as drawings and repaid the annual instalment of bank loan along with interest due to 31st December, 2024. Assume all transactions took place through Punjab National Bank.

You are required to

(1) Journalise these transactions after considering the following information
   (i) Depreciate building by 5% and cars and furniture @ 10% per annum
   (ii) Stationery unpaid ₹ 27,000
   (iii) Advertisement include unissued material worth ₹ 12,000.
   (iv) Insurance prepaid ₹ 4,500
   (v) Stock of car accessories ₹ 58,500.
(2) Post them into ledger and prepare trial balance.
(3) Prepare financial statements for the year ended 31st December, 2024.

Solution

Project is to record the transactions in journal book, post them into ledger accounts, draw a trial balance and to prepare the trading and profit and loss account and balance sheet.

(1)

JOURNAL

Date	Particulars		LF	Amt (Dr)	Amt (Cr)
2024					
Jan 01	Building A/c	Dr		20,00,000	
	Bank A/c	Dr		7,50,000	
	To Capital A/c				27,50,000
	(Being capital invested in business)				
Jan 01	Bank A/c	Dr		18,00,000	
	To Bank Loan A/c				18,00,000
	(Being loan taken from PNB *i.e.,* 80% of ₹ 22,50,000)				
	Cars A/c	Dr		13,00,000	
	To Bank A/c				13,00,000
	(Being cars purchased)				
Jan 01	Electricity Board A/c	Dr		60,000	
	BSNL A/c	Dr		1,50,000	
	To Bank A/c				2,10,000
	(Being security deposited)				
	Furniture A/c	Dr		1,20,000	
	To Bank A/c				1,20,000
	(Being furniture purchased)				
	Bank A/c	Dr		19,50,000	
	To Fees from Students A/c				19,50,000
	(Being fees received from driving school during year)				
	Purchases A/c	Dr		3,30,000	
	To Bank A/c				3,30,000
	(Being accessories purchased for cars)				
	Bank A/c	Dr		4,80,000	
	To Sales A/c				4,80,000
	(Being cars accessories sold)				
	Wages A/c	Dr		2,70,000	
	Salaries A/c	Dr		3,75,000	
	Electricity Charges A/c	Dr		1,42,500	
	Advertisement A/c	Dr		66,000	
	Stationery A/c	Dr		28,500	
	General Expenses A/c	Dr		18,000	
	Insurance A/c	Dr		13,800	
	To Bank A/c				9,13,800
	(Being expenses paid)				
	Laptop and Printer A/c	Dr		90,000	
	To Bank A/c				90,000
	(Being printer purchased)				
	Drawings A/c (36,000 × 12)	Dr		4,32,000	
	To Bank A/c				4,32,000
	(Being drawings made during year)				
	Interest on Bank Loan A/c	Dr		1,80,000	
	To Bank Loan A/c				1,80,000
	(Being interest due as bank loan *i.e.,* 10% ₹ 18,00,000)				
	Bank Loan A/c	Dr		6,30,000	
	To Bank A/c				6,30,000
	(Being first instalment on loan paid along with interest @ 10% on loan *i.e.,* ₹ 4,50,000 + ₹ 1,80,000)				

Date	Particulars	LF	Amt (Dr)	Amt (Cr)
2024 Dec. 31	Depreciation A/c Dr To Building A/c To Cars A/c To Furniture A/c (Being depreciation provided on tangible fixed assets)		2,42,000	 1,00,000 1,30,000 12,000
	Stationery A/c Dr To Stationery Outstanding A/c (Being stationery due but not paid)		27,000	 27,000
	Stock of Advertisement A/c Dr To Advertisement A/c (Being stock of advertisement material)		12,000	 12,000
	Prepaid Insurance A/c Dr To Insurance A/c (Being insurance prepaid)		4,500	 4,500
	Closing Stock A/c Dr To Purchases A/c (Being stock of accessories purchased for cars left)		58,500	 58,500
	Total		1,15,29,800	1,15,29,800

(2)

Ledger Accounts

Building Account

Dr | Cr

Date	Particulars	JF	Amt (₹)	Date	Particulars	JF	Amt (₹)
2024 Jan 01	To Capital A/c		20,00,000	2024 Dec 31 Dec 31	By Depreciation A/c By Balance c/d		1,00,000 19,00,000
			20,00,000				20,00,000
2025 Jan 01	To Balance b/d		19,00,000				

Bank Account

Dr | Cr

Date	Particulars	JF	Amt (₹)	Date	Particulars	JF	Amt (₹)
2024 Jan 01	To Capital A/c To Bank Loan A/c To Fees from Students A/c To Sales A/c		7,50,000 18,00,000 19,50,000 4,80,000	2024 Dec 31	By Cars A/c By Electricity Board (Security) By BSNL (Security) By Furniture A/c By Purchases A/c By Wages A/c By Salaries A/c By Electricity Charges A/c By Advertisement A/c By Stationery A/c By General Expenses A/c By Insurance A/c By Laptop and Printer A/c By Drawings A/c By Bank Loan A/c By Balance c/d		13,00,000 60,000 1,50,000 1,20,000 3,30,000 2,70,000 3,75,000 1,42,500 66,000 28,500 18,000 13,800 90,000 4,32,000 6,30,000 9,54,200
			49,80,000				49,80,000
2025 Jan 01	To Balance b/d		9,54,200				

Capital Account

Dr | Cr

Date	Particulars	JF	Amt (₹)	Date	Particulars	JF	Amt (₹)
2024				2024			
Dec 31	By Balance c/d		27,50,000	Jan 01	By Building A/c		20,00,000
					By Bank A/c		7,50,000
			27,50,000				27,50,000
				2025			
				Jan 01	By Balance b/d		27,50,000

Bank Loan Account

Dr | Cr

Date	Particulars	JF	Amt (₹)	Date	Particulars	JF	Amt (₹)
2024				2024			
Dec 31	To Bank A/c		6,30,000	Jan 01	By Bank A/c		18,00,000
Dec 31	To Balance c/d		13,50,000	Dec 31	By Interest A/c		1,80,000
			19,80,000				19,80,000
				2025			
				Jan 01	By Balance b/d		13,50,000

Cars Account

Dr | Cr

Date	Particulars	JF	Amt (₹)	Date	Particulars	JF	Amt (₹)
2024				2024			
Jan 01	To Bank A/c		13,00,000	Dec 31	By Depreciation A/c		1,30,000
				Dec 31	By Balance c/d		11,70,000
			13,00,000				13,00,000
2025							
Jan 01	To Balance b/d		11,70,000				

Electricity Board Account

Dr | Cr

Date	Particulars	JF	Amt (₹)	Date	Particulars	JF	Amt (₹)
2024				2024			
Jan 01	To Bank A/c		60,000	Dec 31	By Balance c/d		60,000
			60,000				60,000
2025							
Jan 01	To Balance b/d		60,000				

BSNL Account

Dr | Cr

Date	Particulars	JF	Amt (₹)	Date	Particulars	JF	Amt (₹)
2024				2024			
Jan 01	To Bank A/c		1,50,000	Dec 31	By Balance c/d		1,50,000
			1,50,000				1,50,000
2025							
Jan 01	To Balance b/d		1,50,000				

Furniture Account

Dr | Cr

Date	Particulars	JF	Amt (₹)	Date	Particulars	JF	Amt (₹)
2024				2024			
Jan 01	To Bank A/c		1,20,000	Dec 31	By Depreciation A/c		12,000
				Dec 31	By Balance c/d		1,08,000
			1,20,000				1,20,000
2025							
Jan 01	To Balance b/d		1,08,000				

Dr **Fees from Students Account** Cr

Date	Particulars	JF	Amt (₹)	Date	Particulars	JF	Amt (₹)
2024 Dec. 31	To Trading A/c		19,50,000	2024	By Bank A/c		19,50,000
			19,50,000				19,50,000

Dr **Purchases Account** Cr

Date	Particulars	JF	Amt (₹)	Date	Particulars	JF	Amt (₹)
2024	To Bank A/c		3,30,000	2024 Dec 31 Dec 31	By Closing Stock A/c By Trading A/c		58,500 2,71,500
			3,30,000				3,30,000

Dr **Sales Account** Cr

Date	Particulars	JF	Amt (₹)	Date	Particulars	JF	Amt (₹)
2024 Dec 31	To Trading A/c		4,80,000	2024	By Bank A/c		4,80,000
			4,80,000				4,80,000

Dr **Wages Account** Cr

Date	Particulars	JF	Amt (₹)	Date	Particulars	JF	Amt (₹)
2024 Dec 31	To Bank A/c		2,70,000	2024 Dec 31	By Trading A/c		2,70,000
			2,70,000				2,70,000

Dr **Salaries Account** Cr

Date	Particulars	JF	Amt (₹)	Date	Particulars	JF	Amt (₹)
2024	To Bank A/c		3,75,000	2024 Dec 31	By Profit and Loss A/c		3,75,000
			3,75,000				3,75,000

Dr **Electricity Charges Account** Cr

Date	Particulars	JF	Amt (₹)	Date	Particulars	JF	Amt (₹)
2024	To Bank A/c		1,42,500	2024 Dec 31	By Profit and Loss A/c		1,42,500
			1,42,500				1,42,500

Dr **Advertisement Account** Cr

Date	Particulars	JF	Amt (₹)	Date	Particulars	JF	Amt (₹)
2024	To Bank A/c		66,000	2024 Dec 31 Dec 31	By Stock of Advertisement A/c By Profit and Loss A/c		12,000 54,000
			66,000				66,000

Dr **Stationery Account** Cr

Date	Particulars	JF	Amt (₹)	Date	Particulars	JF	Amt (₹)
2024	To Bank A/c To Stationery Outstanding A/c		28,500 27,000	2024 Dec 31	By Profit and Loss A/c		55,500
			55,500				55,500

Dr **General Expenses Account** Cr

Date	Particulars	JF	Amt (₹)	Date	Particulars	JF	Amt (₹)
2024				2024			
	To Bank A/c		18,000	Dec 31	By Profit and Loss A/c		18,000
			18,000				18,000

Dr **Insurance Account** Cr

Date	Particulars	JF	Amt (₹)	Date	Particulars	JF	Amt (₹)
2024				2024			
	To Bank A/c		13,800	Dec 31	By Prepaid Insurance A/c		4,500
				Dec 31	By Profit and Loss A/c		9,300
			13,800				13,800

Dr **Laptop and Printer Account** Cr

Date	Particulars	JF	Amt (₹)	Date	Particulars	JF	Amt (₹)
2024				2024			
Jan 01	To Bank A/c		90,000	Dec 31	By Balance c/d		90,000
			90,000				90,000
2025							
Jan 01	To Balance b/d		90,000				

Dr **Drawings Account** Cr

Date	Particulars	JF	Amt (₹)	Date	Particulars	JF	Amt (₹)
2024				2024			
	To Bank A/c		4,32,000	Dec 31	By Balance c/d		4,32,000
			4,32,000				4,32,000
2025							
Jan 01	To Balance b/d		4,32,000				

Dr **Interest on Bank Loan Account** Cr

Date	Particulars	JF	Amt (₹)	Date	Particulars	JF	Amt (₹)
2024				2024			
Dec 31	To Bank Loan A/c		1,80,000	Dec 31	By Profit and Loss A/c		1,80,000
			1,80,000				1,80,000

Dr **Stationery Outstanding Account** Cr

Date	Particulars	JF	Amt (₹)	Date	Particulars	JF	Amt (₹)
2024				2024			
Dec 31	To Balance c/d		27,000	Dec 31	By Stationery A/c		27,000
			27,000				27,000
				2025			
				Jan 01	By Balance b/d		27,000

Dr **Stock of Advertisement Account** Cr

Date	Particulars	JF	Amt (₹)	Date	Particulars	JF	Amt (₹)
2024				2024			
Dec 31	To Advertisement A/c		12,000	Dec 31	By Balance c/d		12,000
			12,000				12,000
2025							
Jan 01	To Balance b/d		12,000				

Dr **Prepaid Insurance Account** Cr

Date	Particulars	JF	Amt (₹)	Date	Particulars	JF	Amt (₹)
2024 Dec 31	To Insurance A/c		4,500	2024 Dec 31	By Balance c/d		4,500
			4,500				4,500
2025 Jan 01	To Balance b/d		4,500				

Dr **Closing Stock Account** Cr

Date	Particulars	JF	Amt (₹)	Date	Particulars	JF	Amt (₹)
2024 Dec 31	To Purchases A/c		58,500	2024 Dec 31	By Balance c/d		58,500
			58,500				58,500
2025 Jan 01	To Balance b/d		58,500				

Dr **Depreciation Account** Cr

Date	Particulars	JF	Amt (₹)	Date	Particulars	JF	Amt (₹)
2024 Dec 31	To Building A/c		1,00,000	2024 Dec 31	By Profit and Loss A/c		2,42,000
Dec 31	To Cars A/c		1,30,000				
Dec 31	To Furniture A/c		12,000				
			2,42,000				2,42,000

Trial Balance

as on 31st December, 2024

S. No.	Name of Accounts	Debit Balance (₹)	Credit Balance (₹)
1.	Building	19,00,000	—
2.	Bank	9,54,200	—
3.	Capital	—	27,50,000
4.	Bank Loan	—	13,50,000
5.	Cars	11,70,000	—
6.	Electricity Board	60,000	—
7.	BSNL	1,50,000	—
8.	Furniture	1,08,000	—
9.	Fees from Students	—	19,50,000
10.	Purchases	2,71,500	—
11.	Sales	—	4,80,000
12.	Wages	2,70,000	—
13.	Salaries	3,75,000	—
14.	Electricity Charges	1,42,500	—
15.	Advertisement	54,000	—
16.	Postage and Call	55,500	—
17.	General Expenses	18,000	—
18.	Insurance	9,300	—
19.	Laptop and Printer	90,000	—
20.	Drawings	4,32,000	—
21.	Interest on Bank Loan	1,80,000	—
22.	Depreciation	2,42,000	—
23.	Salaries Outstanding	—	27,000
24.	Stock of Advertisement	12,000	—
25.	Prepaid Insurance	4,500	—
26.	Closing Stock of Goods (31st December, 2024)	58,500	—
	Total	65,57,000	65,57,000

(3) Financial Statements

Trading and Profit and Loss A/c

Dr — for the year ending 31st December, 2024 — Cr

Particulars		Amt (₹)	Particulars	Amt (₹)
To Purchases		2,71,500	By Sales A/c	4,80,000
To Wages		2,70,000	By Fees from Students	19,50,000
To Gross Profit c/d		18,88,500		
		24,30,000		24,30,000
To Salaries		3,75,000	By Gross Profit b/d	18,88,500
To Electricity Charges		1,42,500		
To Advertisement		54,000		
To Stationery		55,500		
To General Expenses		18,000		
To Insurance		9,300		
To Interest on Bank Loan		1,80,000		
To Depreciation				
Building	1,00,000			
Cars	1,30,000			
Furniture	12,000	2,42,000		
To Net Profit Transferred to Capital A/c		8,12,200		
		18,88,500		18,88,500

Balance Sheet

as at 31st December, 2024

Liabilities		Amt (₹)	Assets		Amt (₹)
Stationery Outstanding		27,000	Bank		9,54,200
Bank Loan		13,50,000	Prepaid Insurance		4,500
Capital	27,50,000		Closing Sock		58,500
(+) Net Profit	8,12,200		Stock of Advertisement		12,000
	35,62,200		Building	20,00,000	
(–) Drawings	4,32,000	31,30,200	(–) Depreciation	1,00,000	19,00,000
			Cars	13,00,000	
			(–) Depreciation	1,30,000	11,70,000
			Furniture	1,20,000	
			(–) Depreciation	12,000	1,08,000
			Laptop and Printer		90,000
			Electricity Board (Security Deposit)		60,000
			BSNL (Security Deposit)		1,50,000
		45,07,200			45,07,200

Bar Diagrams and Pie Charts for Expenses

Bar Diagram of Indirect Expenses

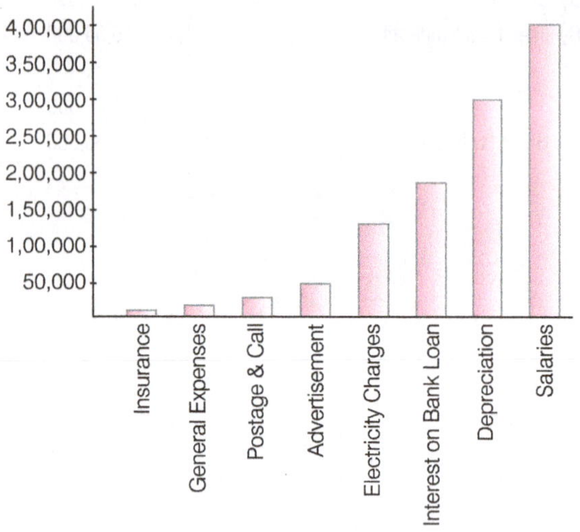

Pie Chart of Indirect Expenses

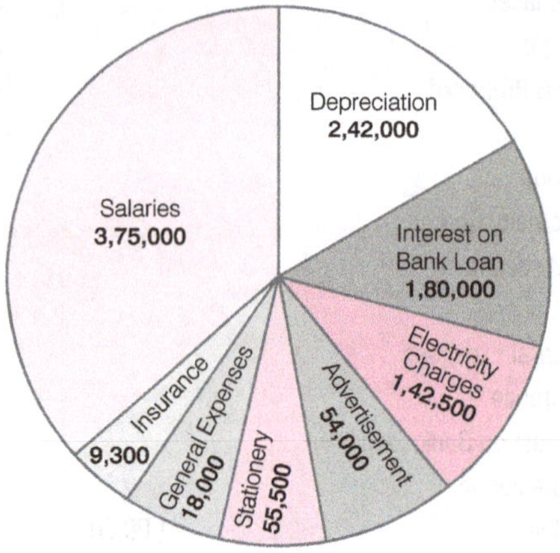

Bar Diagram of Direct and Indirect Expenses

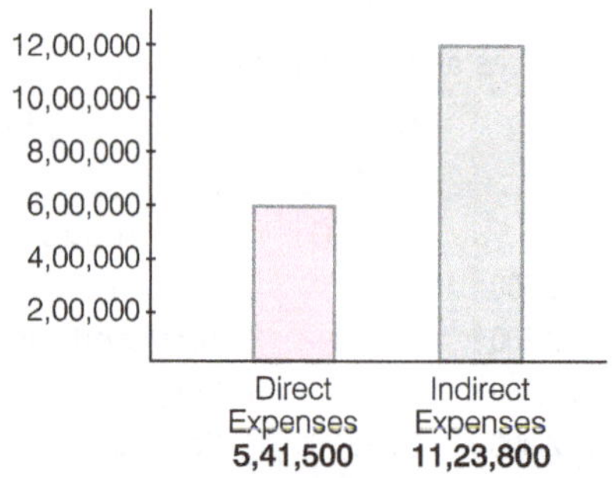

Pie Chart of Direct and Indirect Expenses

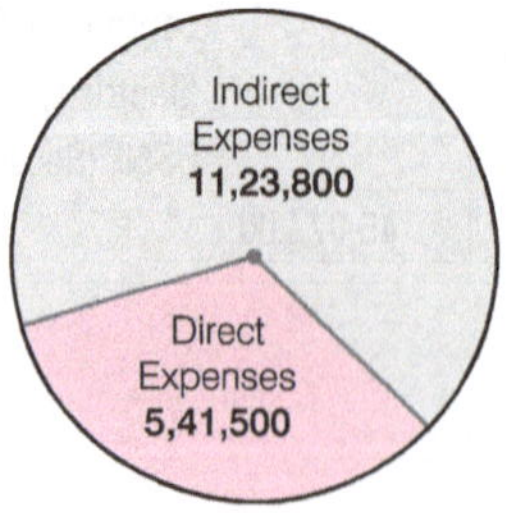

Project Work

Bar Diagrams and Pie Charts for Liabilities

Bar Diagram of Liabilities

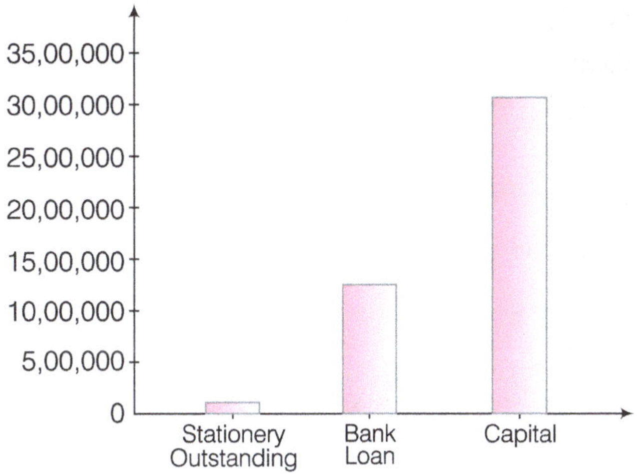

Pie Chart of Liabilities

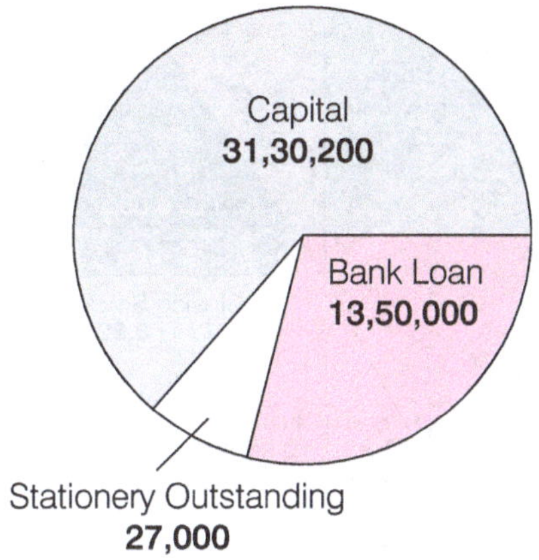

Bar Diagrams and Pie Charts for Assets

Bar Diagram of Assets

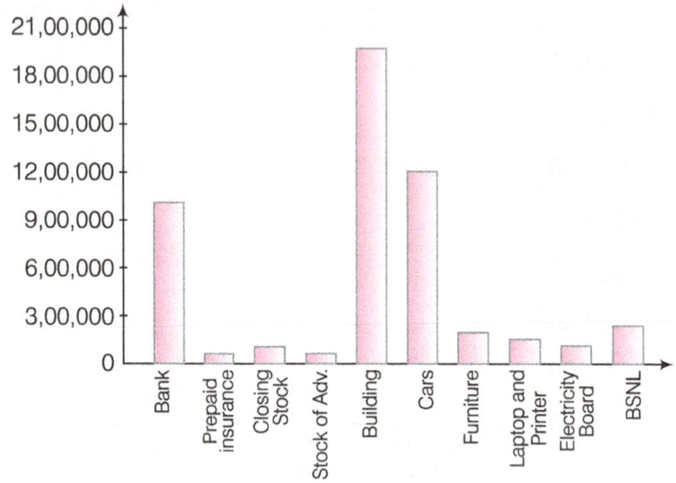

Pie Chart of Assets

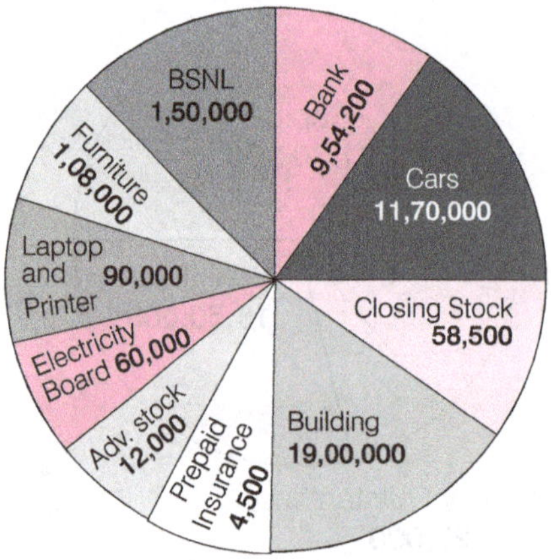

SAMPLE
QUESTION PAPERS (1-3)

SAMPLE QUESTION PAPER 1

A Highly Simulated Sample Question Paper for CBSE Class XI Examination

ACCOUNTANCY

Time : 3 Hours **Max. Marks : 80**

General Instructions

1. This question paper contains 34 questions divided in two parts A and B.
2. Alll questions in both the parts are compulsory.
3. All parts of questions should be attempted at one place.
4. Marks for questions are indicated against each questions.
5. There is no overall choice. However, an integral choice has been provided in **7** questions of **one** mark, **2** questions of **three** marks, **1** question of **four** marks and **2** questions of **six** marks.

Part-A

1. The last step of accounting process is (1)

(a) communicating (b) indentifying
(c) summarising (d) interpreting result

2. Which of these is not a business transaction? (1)

(a) Bought furniture of ₹ 10,000 for business
(b) Paid for salaries of employees ₹ 5,000
(c) Paid son's fees from her personal bank account ₹ 20,000
(d) Paid son's fees from business ₹ 2,000

Or Which of the following must be a characteristic of a standard voucher?

(a) It should be printed on good quality paper
(b) Debit or credit amount should be written in figures against the amount
(c) Description of transaction should be given account wise
(d) All of the above

3. Identify the incorrect statement. (1)

(a) India has followed dual GST model, i.e. Central (GST) and State (GST)
(b) Goods and services tax is a value added tax
(c) An integrated tax (GST) would be levied and collected by the centre on interstate supply of goods and services
(d) The list of exempted goods and services are different for the Centre and the State

Or According to ...., the entire life of business should be divided into time intervals for the measurement of the profits of business.

(a) going concern concept (b) accounting period principle
(c) consistency concept (d) principle of prudence

4. Which source document is prepared by the seller for goods sold against cash? (1)

(a) Pay-in-slip (b) Receipt (c) Cash memo (d) Invoice

5. Which of the following accounts are related to expenses, losses, revenue, gain, etc like salary account? (1)

(a) Real (b) Nominal (c) Assets (d) Liabilities

Or By what amount will be bank account debited with, if goods are sold to Sid at the list price of ₹ 4,00,000 less 20% trade discount and 2% cash discount and paid 50% by cheque?

(a) ₹ 3,20,000 (b) ₹ 1,60,000 (c) ₹ 1,56,800 (d) None of these

6. During the year, *Z* had cash sales of ₹ 1,95,000 and credit sales of ₹ 80,000. His expenses for the year were ₹ 1,35,000 out of which ₹ 40,000 are still to be paid. Find out *Z*'s income following accrual basis of accounting. (1)

(a) ₹ 1,00,000 (b) ₹ 1,80,000 (c) ₹ 1,40,000 (d) ₹ 1,30,000

7. When there is return of goods in a journal, then a debit note is prepared and sent to supplier, what type of journal is used for this purpose? (1)

(a) Sales return journal (b) Purchase return journal
(c) Cash sale journal (d) Cash purchase journal

8. A cheque of ₹ 2,345 issued by Z was recorded in deposit column as ₹ 2,435. To ascertain the balance as cash book of Z (1)

(a) ₹ 2,345 should be added to the balance as per passbook
(b) ₹ 2,435 should be subtracted from the balance as per passbook
(c) ₹ 4,780 should be subtracted from the balance as per passbook
(d) ₹ 10 should be added to the balance as per passbook

Or The debit balance in Naman's cash book is ₹ 40,960. A bill for ₹ 9,900 discounted with the bank is entered in the cash book without recording the discount charges of ₹ 900. What will be the amount in passbook?

(a) ₹ 40,960 (b) ₹ 40,060 (c) ₹ 41,860 (d) None of these

9. An asset was purchased ₹ 5,00,000, ₹ 5,000 were incurred for freight and transportation, ₹ 20,000 spent on installation expenses and commission paid on purchase to agent 5% of cost of asset. Pass the necessary journal entry. (1)

(a) Cash A/c	Dr	5,50,000	
To Asset A/c			5,50,000
(b) Asset A/c	Dr	5,50,000	
To Purchases A/c			5,50,000
(c) Asset A/c	Dr	5,50,000	
To Cash A/c			5,50,000
(d) Purchases A/c	Dr	5,50,000	
To Asset A/c			5,50,000

10. What will be the journal entry to record transfer of asset sold to a asset disposal account? (1)

(a) Asset A/c Dr
To Asset Disposal A/c

(b) Asset Disposal A/c Dr
To Cash A/c

(c) Cash A/c Dr
To Asset Disposal A/c

(d) Asset Disposal A/c Dr
To Asset A/c

Or ……… is an example of source documents which is used by the purchaser for returning the purchased goods.

(a) Debit note (b) Credit note (c) Invoice (d) Pay-in-slip

11. The objectives of accounting are varied. Which of the following are the objectives of accounting? (1)

(i) Maintain systematic and complete record of business transactions.
(ii) Ascertain financial position of business.
(iii) Provide useful information to various interested parties.

Codes

(a) Only (i) (b) Only (iii) (c) (i) and (ii) (d) All of these

12. **Assertion** (A) NOP Ltd. purchased a machinery of ₹ 20,000 which is supposed to last for 20 years. The accountant decides to spread the cost of machinery for next 20 years for calculation of profit and loss.

Reason (R) According to consistency concept, accounting principles and methods should remain consistent from one year to another. (1)

Alternatives

(a) Both Assertion (A) and Reason (R) are true and Reason (R) is the correct explanation of Assertion (A)
(b) Both Assertion (A) and Reason (R) are true, but Reason (R) is not the correct explanation of Assertion (A)
(c) Assertion (A) is false, but Reason (R) is true
(d) Assertion (A) is true, but Reason (R) is false

13. On 1st April, 2024, balance of cash column of cash book was ₹ 10,000. After receiving ₹ 2,000 from Raj, giving a cheque of ₹ 3,200 to Sham and making payment of wages ₹ 500, balance of cash will be (1)

(a) ₹ 11,500 (b) ₹ 8,300 (c) ₹ 8,800 (d) ₹ 6,300

14. Overdraft as per cash book is ₹ 10,000. Cheque deposited but not credited ₹ 2,500. Cheques issued but not enashed ₹ 35,000. What is the balance as per passbook? (1)

(a) Balance ₹ 9,000 (b) Overdraft ₹ 9,000 (c) Overdraft ₹ 11,000 (d) Balance ₹ 11,000

15. Bank charges ₹ 5,000 debited twice in passbook. What should be done in BRS if overdraft as per cash book is starting point? (1)

(a) ₹ 5,000 must be deducted (b) ₹ 5,000 must be added
(c) ₹ 10,000 must be deducted (d) ₹ 10,000 must be added

16. State the advantages offered by accrual basis of accounting. (3)

Or Give any three points of difference between bookkeeping and accounting.

17. Record the following transactions during the week ending 30th December, 2022 with a weekly imprest of ₹ 500. (3)

Date	Particulars	Amt (₹)
Dec 24	Stationery	100
Dec 25	Bus Fare	12
Dec 25	Cartage	40
Dec 26	Taxi Fare	80
Dec 27	Wages to Casual Labour	90
Dec 29	Postage	80

18. From the following information, complete the missing information using a suspense account. (3)

Date	Particulars	LF	Amt (Dr)	Amt (Cr)
(i)	.... Dr		...	
	Sales A/c Dr		...	
	To Suspense A/c			...
	(Being purchase of ₹ 4,000 from Bheem was entered in sales book but Bheem's personal account was rightly credited, now rectified)			
(ii)	Nakul Dr		...	
	To Suspense A/c			...
	(Being sales to Nakul of ₹ 4,300 credited to his account as ₹ 3,400, now rectified)			
(iii)	Sales A/c Dr		...	
	.... Dr		...	
	To Furniture A/c			...
	(Being sale of old furniture of ₹ 5,400 was credited to sales account as ₹ 4,500 now rectified)			

19. Prepare bank reconciliation statement of Shri Subhash Bhalla as on 31st December, 2022. (4)

(i) The payment of a cheque for ₹ 550 was recorded twice in the passbook.
(ii) Withdrawal column of the passbook was undercast by ₹ 200.
(iii) A cheque of ₹ 200 has been debited in the bank column of the cash book but it was not sent to bank at all.
(iv) Interest on bank overdraft ₹ 300 charged by the bank.
(v) ₹ 500 in respect of dishonoured bill were entered in the passbook but not in the cash book.
(vi) Overdraft as per passbook is ₹ 20,000.

20. Balaji & Co. has been charging depreciation @ 15% per annum on straight line method. It now wants to change the method to diminishing balance method, the rate of depreciation being 30% per annum. Can the company do so? **(4)**

Or When should revenue be recognised as per revenue recognition principle? Are there exceptions to the general rule?

21. In taking out a trial balance, a bookkeeper finds that debit total exceeds the credit total by ₹ 7,040. The amount is placed to the credit of a newly opened suspense account. Subsequently, the following mistakes were discovered. You are required to pass the necessary entries for rectifying the mistakes and show the suspense account. **(6)**

(i) Sales day book was overcast by ₹ 2,000.
(ii) A sale of ₹ 1,000 to Gokul Prasad was wrongly debited to Kanti Prasad.
(iii) General expenses ₹ 360 was posted as ₹ 1,600.
(iv) Cash received from Shanti Prasad was debited to his account ₹ 3,000.
(v) While carrying forward the total of one page of the purchase book to the next, the amount of ₹ 24,700 was entered as ₹ 26,500.

22. Pass the journal entries for the following transactions **(6)**

(i) Purchased goods from Sangeet of ₹ 80,000; plus SGST 6% and CGST 6%.
(ii) Hemant who owed to Manu ₹ 10,000 is declared insolvent and 55 paise in a rupee is received from his estate.
(iii) Sold goods to Amitoj at the list price of ₹ 75,000 less 20% trade discount; plus SGST 6% and CGST 6%.
(iv) Purchased machinery from Atul for ₹ 40,000 and paid him by means of bank draft purchased from bank for ₹ 40,040.

23. WHERE Ltd. is a manufacturing firm and has a machinery worth ₹ 50,00,000. As on 1st April, 2018 the provision for depreciation stood at ₹ 50,00,000. WHERE Ltd. charges depreciation on machinery at 20% p.a. by the diminishing balance method. A piece of machinery purchased on 1st April, 2016 for ₹ 10,00,000 was sold on 1st October, 2018 for ₹ 6,00,000. **(6)**

(i) Under written down value method, a fixed and equal amount in the form of depreciation is charged every year during the lifetime of the asset.
(a) True (b) False (c) Can't say (d) Partially true

(ii) Which of the following is the probable reason for WHERE Ltd's adoption of written down value method for charging depreciation?
(a) The machinery is such that its repair charges are low
(b) The possibility of obsolescence of machinery is low
(c) The machinery is such that it is affected by technological changes and require more repair expenses with passage of time
(d) None of the above

(iii) What is the total depreciation charged on the machinery sold?
(a) ₹ 4,24,000 (b) ₹ 3,60,000 (c) ₹ 4,40,000 (d) None of these

(iv) What is the written down value of the machinery sold?
(a) ₹ 5,76,000 (b) ₹ 10,00,000 (c) ₹ 6,40,000 (d) None of these

(v) What is the balance carried down in the machinery account?
(a) ₹ 50,00,000 (b) ₹ 40,00,000 (c) ₹ 44,24,000 (d) None of these

(vi) Profit/Loss on machine sold is
(a) ₹ 24,000 (loss) (b) ₹ 40,000 (loss) (c) ₹ 24,000 (profit) (d) ₹ 40,000 (profit)

Or MJ Ltd. purchased a second hand plant for ₹ 1,80,000 and spent ₹ 20,000 on its installation and freight on 1st July, 2018. Depreciation was provided @ 10% p.a. on reducing balance method. On 31st December, 2020, 1/5th of the plant was damaged due to fire and scrap was sold for ₹ 10,000. It was decided to buy a new plant for ₹ 60,000 on 1st January, 2021. Prepare plant account for 3 years assuming that books were closed on 31st March every year.

24. Write a two-column cash book with cash and bank columns from the following transactions and post them into ledger. Also pass necessary journal entries related to discount allowed and discount received. **(6)**

2022	
Mar 1	Cash in hand ₹ 30,000.
Mar 3	Purchased goods for cash ₹ 12,000.
Mar 5	Deposited in bank ₹ 10,000.
Mar 8	Cash sales ₹ 20,000.
Mar 10	Cash withdrew from bank for office use ₹ 4,000.

Mar 12 Received cash from Daksh ₹ 6,000 and allowed him discount of ₹ 200.
Mar 15 Received cheque from Kanika ₹ 4,000 and deposited in the bank on the same day, allowed her discount ₹ 150.
Mar 18 Received cheque from Sakshi for ₹ 10,000 (not banked).
Mar 19 Cheque received from Sakshi deposited in the bank.
Mar 24 Paid to Simran by cheque ₹ 5,000, she allowed discount ₹ 250.
Mar 27 Withdrew from bank for personal use ₹ 3,000.
Mar 28 Sold goods on credit to Deeksha ₹ 8,000.
Mar 30 Purchased goods on credit from Simran ₹ 10,000.
Mar 31 Received cheque from Deeksha ₹ 4,000 and deposited in the bank.
Mar 31 Bank charges for the month ₹ 200.

Or Following is the trial balance of Raj Nayak as on 31st March, 2023.

Name of Accounts	LF	Debit Balance (₹)	Credit Balance (₹)
Capital		—	6,40,000
Fixed Assets		3,60,000	—
Drawings		1,20,000	—
Debtors		4,80,000	—
Creditors			3,60,000
Purchases		14,20,000	—
Sales		—	21,00,000
Bank Balance		90,000	—
Cash in Hand		60,000	—
Salaries		3,30,000	—
Rent		2,40,000	—
Total		31,00,000	31,00,000

Having prepared the trial balance, it was discovered that following transactions remained unrecorded

(i) Goods were sold on credit amounting to ₹ 80,000.
(ii) Paid to creditors ₹ 44,000 by cheque.
(iii) Goods worth ₹ 14,000 were returned to a supplier.
(iv) Paid salary ₹ 30,000 by cheque.

Required

(a) Pass journal entries for the above mentioned transactions and post them into ledger.
(b) Redraft the trial balance.

Part-B

25. Which of the following is correct? (1)

(a) Net Sales = Cash Sales + Credit Sales – Sales Return (b) Net Sales = Cash Sales + Credit Sales + Sales Return
(c) Net Sales = Total Sales – Credit Sales (d) Net Sales = Sales + Credit Sales

26. In which of the following cases, closing stock will not be shown in the trading account? (1)

(a) When valuation of closing stock is on FIFO method
(b) When closing stock is not ascertained accurately
(c) When closing stock is adjusted in the purchases
(d) When it is appearing outside the trial balance

27. **Statement I** Outstanding wages given in the trial balance are transferred to trading account.

Statement II Assets side of balance sheet is always equal to capital. (1)

Alternatives

(a) Both the statements are correct (b) Both the statements are incorrect
(c) Statement I is correct and Statement II is incorrect (d) Statement I is incorrect and Statement II is correct

Or Find out the closing stock from the following

Opening stock = ₹ 20,000, Sales = ₹ 1,00,000, Purchases = ₹ 70,000, Rate of gross profit on cost = $33\frac{1}{3}\%$

(a) ₹ 20,000 (b) ₹ 35,000 (c) ₹ 15,000 (d) ₹ 45,000

28. Type of accounts shown in the balance sheet are (1)

(i) Nominal (ii) Personal (iii) Real

Codes

(a) Only (i) (b) (ii) and (iii) (c) (i) and (iii) (d) Only (ii)

Or Liability which is payable on the happening of an event is ....

(a) fixed liability (b) contingent liability (c) non-current liability (d) None of these

29. Opening capital = ₹ 60,000; Drawings = ₹ 5,000; Capital added during the year = ₹ 10,000; Closing capital = ₹ 90,000. Find profit/loss for the year. (1)

(a) ₹ 15,000 (b) ₹ 25,000 (c) ₹ 18,000 (d) ₹ 10,000

30. Calculate closing stock from the following details (3)

Opening stock	₹ 20,000
Cash sales	₹ 60,000
Purchases	₹ 70,000
Credit sales	₹ 40,000
Rate of gross profit on cost $33\frac{1}{3}\%$	

Or Calculate opening stock from the following details

Closing stock	₹ 20,000
Cash sales	₹ 60,000
Net purchases	₹ 70,000
Net credit sales	₹ 40,000
Return outward	₹ 5,000
Return inward	₹ 7,000
Rate of gross profit on cost $33\frac{1}{3}\%$	

31. State the objectives of preparing financial statements. (3)

32. Differentiate between a balance sheet and trial balance. (3)

33. Kartik started a firm on 1st April, 2019 with a capital of ₹ 30,000. On 1st July, 2019, he borrowed from his wife a sum of ₹ 12,000 @ 9% per annum (interest not yet paid) for business and introduces a further capital of his own amounted to ₹ 4,500. On 31st March, 2020 his position was, cash ₹ 1,800, stock ₹ 28,200, debtors ₹ 21,000 and creditors ₹ 18,000. Ascertain his profit or loss taking into account ₹ 6,000 for his drawings during the year. (4)

34. The following balances have been extracted from the trial balance of M/s Runway Shine Ltd. Prepare a trading and profit and loss account and a balance sheet as on 31st December, 2022.

Name of Accounts	Amt (₹)	Name of Accounts	Amt (₹)
Purchases	1,50,000	Sales	2,50,000
Opening Stock	50,000	Return Outwards	4,500
Return Inwards	2,000	Interest Received	3,500
Carriage Inwards	4,500	Discount Received	400
Cash in Hand	77,800	Creditors	1,25,000
Cash at Bank	60,800	Bills Payable	6,040

Name of Accounts	Amt (₹)	Name of Accounts	Amt (₹)
Wages	2,400	Capital	1,00,000
Printing and Stationery	4,500		
Discount	400		
Bad Debts	1,500		
Insurance	2,500		
Investment	32,000		
Debtors	53,000		
Bills Receivable	20,000		
Postage and Telegraph	400		
Commission	200		
Interest	1,000		
Repair	440		
Lighting Charges	500		
Telephone Charges	100		
Carriage Outwards	400		
Motor Car	25,000		
	4,89,440		4,89,440

Additional Information

(i) Further bad debts ₹ 1,000, discount on debtors ₹ 500 and make a provision on debtors @ 5%.
(ii) Interest received on investment @ 5%.
(iii) Wages and interest outstanding ₹ 100 and ₹ 200 respectively.
(iv) Depreciation charged on motor car @ 5% p.a.
(v) Closing stock ₹ 32,500. (6)

Answers

1. (a) 2. (c) *Or* (d) 3. (d) *Or* (b) 4. (c) 5. (b) *Or* (c) 6. (c) 7. (b)
8. (b) *Or* (b) 9. (c) 10. (d) *Or* (a) 11. (d) 12. (b) 13. (a) 14. (b)
15. (b) 17. Balance of petty cash book = ₹ 98
19. Credit balance as per cash book = ₹ 18,650
23. (i) (b) (ii) (c) (iii) (a) (iv) (a) (v) (b) (vi) (c)

Or

Balance of plant account
2018-19 = ₹ 1,85,000; 2019-20 = ₹ 1,66,500
Loss on sale of plant = ₹ 20,802 ; 2020-21 = ₹ 1,78,380

24. Cash balance = ₹ 38,000; Bank balance = ₹ 15,800
Or Total of trial balance = ₹ 31,36,000
25. (a) 26. (c) 27. (b) *Or* (c) 28. (b) *Or* (b) 29. (b)
30. Closing stock = ₹ 15,000 *Or* Opening stock = ₹ 25,000 33. Loss = ₹ 8,310
34. Net profit = ₹ 66,010; Total of balance sheet = ₹ 2,97,350

SAMPLE QUESTION PAPER 2

A Highly Simulated Sample Question Paper for CBSE Class XI Examination

ACCOUNTANCY

Time : 3 Hours **Max. Marks : 80**

General Instructions

1. This question paper contains 34 questions divided in two parts A and B.
2. Alll questions in both the parts are compulsory.
3. All parts of questions should be attempted at one place.
4. Marks for questions are indicated against each questions.
5. There is no overall choice. However, an integral choice has been provided in **7** questions of **one** mark, **2** questions of **three** marks, **1** question of **four** marks and **2** questions of **six** marks.

Part-A

1. Which of the following is not the qualitative characteristic of accounting information? **(1)**

(a) Reliability (b) Relevance
(c) Comparability (d) Simple

2. Credit purchase from Rohan ₹ 9,000 was posted to the debit of Gobind as ₹ 10,000. In this case, suspense account will be debited with **(1)**

(a) ₹ 9,000 (b) ₹ 10,000
(c) ₹ 19,000 (d) None of these

Or Interest received worth ₹ 1,000 and sales worth ₹ 5,00,000 are shown

(a) in debit column and credit column respectively of trial balance
(b) in credit column and debit column respectively of trial balance
(c) in credit column of trial balance
(d) in debit column of trial balance

3. Which of the following is/are the limitation(s) of accounting? **(1)**

(a) It relates to the past transactions (b) It is quantitative and financial in nature
(c) Both (a) and (b) (d) It does not act as an evidence

4. Financial transactions in the books of accounts are recorded on the basis of **(1)**

(a) voucher (b) cash memo
(c) debit note (d) None of these

Or Which of the following will be recorded in cash book?

(a) Trade discount of ₹ 5,000 (b) Bad debts of ₹ 3,000
(c) Credit purchases of ₹ 25,000 (d) None of these

5. What adjustment entry is passed at the end of the year for outstanding expenses? **(1)**

(a) Expenses A/c Dr
To Outstanding Expenses A/c

(b) Outstanding Expenses A/c Dr
To Expenses A/c

(c) Outstanding Expenses A/c Dr
To Cash A/c

(d) Expenses A/c Dr
To Cash A/c

6. While doing balancing of accounts, personal and real accounts are balanced and nominal accounts are (1)

(a) taken to profit and loss account
(b) closed by transferring to trading and profit and loss account
(c) left with balancing figure
(d) two-sided entry is passed

Or Neeraj Ltd. is engaged in a laptop trading business the total assets of business are ₹ 10,40,000 and outside liabilities are ₹ 1,80,000. What will be the owner's equity?

(a) ₹ 12,20,000 (b) ₹ 9,60,000 (c) ₹ 8,60,000 (d) Can't be determined

7. Written down value of an asset after 3 years of depreciation on reducing balance method @ 15% p.a. is ₹ 49,130. What was its original value? (1)

(a) ₹ 40,000 (b) ₹ 80,000 (c) ₹ 45,000 (d) ₹ 70,200

8. The credit balance as per cash book is ₹ 1,500. Cheques for ₹ 400 were deposited but were not collected. The cheques issued but not presented were ₹ 100, ₹ 125, ₹ 50. Balance as per passbook will be (1)

(a) ₹ 1,625 (b) ₹ 2,175 (c) ₹ 1,375 (d) ₹ 825

Or Paid to Z ₹ 11,500 in full settlement of ₹ 12,000. Posting will be made in Z's account as

(a) ₹ 12,000 on debit side (b) ₹ 12,000 on credit side
(c) ₹ 11,500 on debit side (d) ₹ 11,500 on credit side

9. What will be the journal entry for 'wages paid ₹ 5,000' for installation of machinery? (1)

(a) Machinery A/c	Dr	5,000	
To Cash A/c			5,000
(b) Machinery A/c	Dr	5,000	
To Wages A/c			5,000
(c) Cash A/c	Dr	5,000	
To Machinery A/c			5,000
(d) Wages A/c	Dr	5,000	
To Machinery A/c			5,000

Or Undercasting of sales book is corrected by .... sales account.

(a) debiting (b) crediting
(c) No treatment required (d) Can't say

10. Each and every branch has its separate set of objectives. Which of these branches of accounting directly or indirectly helps in management decisions? (1)

(i) Cost accounting (ii) Management accounting
(iii) Financial accounting

Codes

(a) Only (ii) (b) (i) and (ii) (c) (i) and (iii) (d) All of these

11. Which of the following about cash book is not true? (1)

(a) It serves the purpose of both journal as well as the ledger (cash) account
(b) It is also called the book of original entry
(c) When a cash book is maintained, transactions of cash are not recorded in the journal and no separate account for cash or bank is required in the ledger
(d) It records both cash and credit transactions

12. Received ₹ 38,000 from Kartik in full settlement of his account for ₹ 40,000. What will be the effect on Kartik's account? (1)

(a) Kartik account will be debited with ₹ 38,000
(b) Kartik account will be debited with ₹ 40,000
(c) Kartik account will be credited with ₹ 40,000
(d) Kartik account will be credited with ₹ 38,000

13. On 1st April, 2023, a plants was purchased by XYZ Ltd. for ₹ 2,00,000. The rate of depreciation was charged at 40%. Under dimishing balance method, calculate the depreciation amount for 31st March, 2024. (1)

(a) ₹ 40,000 (b) ₹ 80,000 (c) ₹ 1,20,000 (d) ₹ 48,000

14. A company bought a machine for ₹ 90,000 on credit. Another ₹ 10,000 is spent on its installation. If the estimated useful life is 5 years and scrap value of the end was ₹ 5,000, what will be the rate of depreciation? (1)

(a) 17% (b) 18% (c) 19% (d) 20%

15. Assertion (A) When the cheques are not presented for payment, favourable balance as per the cash book is less than that of the passbook.

Reason (R) If an entry of payment has been recorded in the passbook but not in the cash book, then the balance of passbook will be less than of cash book. (1)

Alternatives

(a) Both Assertion (A) and Reason (R) are true and Reason (R) is the correct explanation of Assertion (A)
(b) Both Assertion (A) and Reason (R) are true, but Reason (R) is not the correct explanation of Assertion (A)
(c) Assertion (A) is true, but Reason (R) is false
(d) Assertion (A) is false, but Reason (R) is true

16. Define briefly management accounting, social responsibility accounting and human resource accounting. (3)

Or Goods and Services Tax (GST) can be classified under these given categories.

(i) CGST (ii) SGST (iii) UTGST (iv) IGST

Explain any two.

17. Prepare a bank reconciliation statement from the following particulars. (3)

On the 31st December, 2022, I had an overdraft of ₹ 7,500 as shown by my passbook.

(i) I have issued cheques amounting to ₹ 2,500 of which cheques worth ₹ 2,000 only seem to have been presented for payment.
(ii) Cheques amounting to ₹ 1,000 have been paid in by me on 30th December but out of those, only ₹ 750 were credited in the passbook.
(iii) I also find that a cheque for ₹ 100 which I had debited to bank account in my books has been omitted to be banked.
(iv) There is debit in my passbook of ₹ 250 for interest.
(v) An entry of ₹ 300 of a payment by a customer directly into the bank appears in the passbook.
(vi) My passbook also shows a credit of ₹ 600 to my account being interest on my investments collected directly by my bankers.

18. Prepare accounting equation from the following information (3)

(i) Rama started business with cash ₹ 1,00,000; machinery ₹ 50,000 and goods ₹ 50,000.
(ii) Sold $\frac{1}{2}$ of above stock (goods) at 10% profit for cash.
(iii) Rent paid ₹ 500, outstanding salary ₹ 1,500.

19. From the following information, draw up a trial balance in the books of Shri Manmohan as on 31st March, 2023
Capital ₹ 1,12,000; purchases ₹ 28,800; discount allowed ₹ 960; carriage inwards ₹ 6,960; carriage outwards ₹ 1,840; sales ₹ 48,000; return inwards ₹ 240; return outwards ₹ 560; rent and taxes ₹ 960; plant and machinery ₹ 64,560; stock on 1st April, 2022 ₹ 12,400; sundry debtors ₹ 16,160; sundry creditors ₹ 9,600; investments ₹ 2,880; commission received ₹ 1,440; cash in hand ₹ 80; cash at bank ₹ 8,080; motor cycle ₹ 27,680 and stock on 31st March, 2023 (not adjusted) ₹ 16,400. (4)

20. Enter the following transactions in a simple cash book for December 2022. (4)

Date	Particulars	Amt (₹)
Dec 1	Cash in Hand	48,000
Dec 4	Cash Received from Ram	16,000
Dec 8	Rent Paid	8,000
Dec 11	Purchased Goods for Cash	24,000

Date	Particulars	Amt (₹)
Dec 17	Cash Sales	36,000
Dec 20	Stationery Purchased	1,200
Dec 23	Cash Paid to Ramesh	8,000
Dec 27	Paid Salary	4,000
Dec 29	Paid Wages	2,000

Or Trial balance of Anita did not agree and she put the difference to suspense account. She discovered the following errors

(i) Sales return book overcast by ₹ 8,175.

(ii) Purchase return to Arpit ₹ 3,125 was not posted to his account.

(iii) Installation charges on new machinery purchased ₹ 1,750 were debited to sundry expenses account as ₹ 175.

(iv) Rent paid for residential accommodation of Anita (the proprietor) ₹ 5,200 was debited to rent account as ₹ 5,000.

Rectify the errors and prepare suspense account to ascertain the difference in trial balance.

21. Explain full disclosure principle. (6)

22. From the following information, complete the following journal entries (6)

Date	Particulars		LF	Amt (Dr)	Amt (Cr)
(i)	Purchases A/c	Dr		1,60,000	
	Input CGST A/c (6%)	Dr		...	
	Input SGST A/c (6%)	Dr		...	
	To Ramesh				...
	(Being goods purchased from Ramesh worth ₹ 1,60,000 on credit, plus CGST and SGST of 6% each)				
(ii)	Cash A/c	Dr		...	
	Bad Debts A/c	Dr		...	
	To Ramdas				20,000
	(Being Ramdas as who received ₹ 20,000 was declared insolvent and final payment of 60 paisa received from Ramdas)				
(iii)	Sita	Dr		1,12,000	
	To Sales A/c				...
	To Output CGST A/c (6%)				...
	To Output SGST A/c (6%)				...
	(Being goods sold to Sita for ₹ 1,00,000 on credit, plus CGST and SGST of 6% each)				
(iv)	Interest on Capital A/c	Dr		...	
	To Capital A/c				...
	(Being 10% interest due on capital ₹ 10,00,000 for 6 months)				
(v)	....	Dr		10,000	
	To				10,000
	(Being salary ₹ 10,000 due but not paid)				
(vi)	Cash A/c	Dr		...	
	Discount Allowed A/c	Dr		...	
	To Sanjeev				30,000
	(Being cash received ₹ 29,800 from Sanjeev in full settlement ₹ 30,000)				

23. On 1st January, 2019, Satkar Transport Ltd. purchased 3 buses for ₹ 10,00,000 each. On 1st July, 2021, one bus was involved in an accident and was completely destroyed and ₹ 7,00,000 were received from the insurance company in full settlement. Depreciation is written-off @ 15% p.a. on diminishing balance method. Prepare bus account from 2019 to 2022. Books are closed on 31st December, every year. (6)

Or A company purchased on 1st July, 2014 machinery costing ₹ 30,000. It further purchased machinery on 1st January, 2015 costing ₹ 20,000 and on 1st October, 2015 costing ₹ 10,000. On 1st April, 2016 one-third of the machinery installed on 1st July, 2014 became obsolete and was sold for ₹ 3,000.

The company follows financial year as the accounting year.

Show how the machinery account would appear in the books of company if depreciation is charged @ 10% per annum on written down value method.

24. Enter the following transactions in proper subsidiary books of Balram. **(6)**

2023			**Amt (₹)**
Jan	1	Sold goods to Ramesh	21,000
		Bought from Hari Ram	31,200
Jan	2	Ramesh returned goods	3,000
		Sold to Dina Nath	22,000
Jan	2	Purchased goods from Mangal	28,000
Jan	4	Returned goods to Mangal	4,000
Jan	4	Bought from Devi Dayal	13,000
Jan	4	Sold to Zakir Hussain	14,000
Jan	5	Zakir Hussain returned goods	1,800
Jan	6	Sold to Ram Saran	20,000
Jan	6	Sold to Ghanshyam	12,000
Jan	7	Ram Saran returned goods	2,000
Jan	7	Bought from Devi Dayal	28,000
Jan	8	Returned goods to Devi Dayal	3,000
Jan	9	Purchased goods from Raghu Nath subject to a trade discount of 10%	40,000
Jan	10	Sold to Raja Ram goods subject to trade discount of 5%	20,000

Or Give rectifying entries for the following

(i) A credit sale of goods to Ram ₹ 5,000 has been wrongly passed through the purchases book.

(ii) A credit purchase of goods from Shyam amounting to ₹ 2,000 has been wrongly passed through the sales book.

(iii) A return of goods worth ₹ 2,200 to Mohan was passed through the sales return book.

(iv) A return of goods worth ₹ 1,000 by Ganesh were entered in purchases return book.

(v) Goods for ₹ 11,000 were purchased from Modern Traders on credit, but no entry has yet been passed.

(vi) Purchases return for ₹ 3,000 not recorded in the books.

(vii) Goods for ₹ 14,000 sold to Zee Traders on credit were entered in the sales book as ₹ 200 only.

(viii) Goods of the value of ₹ 3,600 returned by Kamal Co. were included in stock, but no entry was passed in the books.

(ix) Goods purchased for ₹ 1,800 were entered in the purchases book as ₹ 18,000.

(x) An invoice for goods sold to X was overcast by ₹ 200.

Part-B

25. What is prepared in sole proprietorship business with the objective of calculating gross profit or gross loss of the business?

(i) Trading account (ii) Profit and loss account (iii) Balance sheet **(1)**

Codes

(a) Only (i) (b) (i) and (ii)

(c) Only (ii) (d) (ii) and (iii)

26. Choose the correct chronological order of ascertainment of the following profits from the profit and loss. **(1)**

(a) Operating Profit, Net Profit, Gross Profit (b) Operating Profit, Gross Profit, Net Profit

(c) Gross Profit, Net Profit, Operating Profit (d) Gross Profit, Net Profit, Operating Profit

Or In case of sole proprietor business, income tax is considered as

(a) business expense (b) proprietor's expense (c) capital expense (d) All of these

27. Calculate net sales from the following information (1)

Cost of Goods Sold = ₹ 1,00,000; Gross profit 20% on sales

(a) ₹ 1,00,000 (b) ₹ 1,25,000 (c) ₹ 25,000 (d) ₹ 75,000

28. Which of the following statement is correct? (1)

(a) Balance sheet is prepared with the balance of personal account
(b) Fixed assets are kept for conversion into cash as quickly as possible
(c) Excess of debit in profit and loss account is called net loss
(d) Balance sheet is prepared for a particular period

Or Manager's commission is always treated as .... expenses.

(a) prepaid (b) outstanding (c) Either (a) or (b) (d) None of these

29. Statement I Balance sheet contains only the balances of personal and real accounts.

Statement II Drawings are not shown in the balance sheet as it is a personal expense of the owner. (1)

Alternatives

(a) Both the statements are correct
(b) Both the statements are incorrect
(c) Statement I is correct and Statement II is incorrect
(d) Statement I is incorrect and Statement II is correct

30. Calculate operating profit from the following.

Net profit ₹ 10,00,000, dividend received ₹ 12,000, loss on sale of furniture ₹ 24,000, loss by fire ₹ 1,00,000, salaries ₹ 2,40,000, interest on loan from bank ₹ 20,000, rent received ₹ 48,000, donation ₹ 10,200. (3)

Or Calculate the amount of gross profit, operating profit and net profit on the basis of the following balances extracted from the books of M/s Vishal and Sons for the year ended 31st March, 2023.

Opening stock ₹ 1,00,000, net sales ₹ 22,00,000, net purchases ₹ 12,00,000, direct expenses ₹ 1,20,000, administration expenses ₹ 90,000, selling and distribution expenses ₹ 1,30,000, loss due to fire ₹ 40,000, closing stock ₹ 1,40,000.

31. Why is it necessary to record the adjusting entries in the preparation of final accounts? (3)

32. Why is it necessary to create a provision for doubtful debts at the time of preparation of final accounts? (3)

33. Mr Girdhari Lal does not keep full double entry records. His balance as on 1st January, 2021 is as

Liabilities	Amt (₹)	Assets	Amt (₹)
Sundry Creditors	35,000	Cash in Hand	5,000
Bills Payable	15,000	Cash at Bank	20,000
Capital	40,000	Sundry Debtors	18,000
		Stock	22,000
		Furniture	8,000
		Plant	17,000
	90,000		90,000

His position at the end of the year is

Particulars	Amt (₹)
Cash in Hand	7,000
Stock	8,600
Debtors	23,800
Furniture	15,000
Plant	20,350
Bills Payable	20,200
Creditors	15,000

He withdrew ₹ 500 per month out of which he spent ₹ 1,500 for business purpose. Prepare the statement of profit or loss. (4)

34. Aman Mathur recently cleared his final CA exam in his 1st attempt. He is now appointed as a CA in Gopal Das Textiles, Chandni Chowk. On 31st March, 2020, he prepared trial balance whose total also agreed. But later he discovered some additional information which has to be taken into account while preparing final accounts. After taking into account few adjustments, he prepared final accounts of Gopal Das Textiles. Following trial balance was prepared by CA Aman Mathur and undermentioned adjustments were discovered by him.

Name of Accounts	Debit Balance (₹)	Credit Balance (₹)
Cash in Hand	20,000	—
Cash at Bank	1,80,000	—
Purchase and Sales	22,00,000	35,00,000
Return Inwards	60,000	—
Return Outwards	—	75,000
Carriage on Purchases	44,000	—
Carriage on Sales	21,000	—
Fuel and Power	1,55,000	—
Stock (1st April, 2019)	3,60,000	—
Bad Debts	62,000	—
Bad Debts Provision	—	25,000
Debtors and Creditors	8,20,000	3,00,000
Capital	—	21,70,000
Investments	2,00,000	—
Interest on Investments	—	20,000
Loan from X (@ 18% per annum)	—	1,00,000
Repairs	15,200	—
General Expenses	1,06,000	—
Land and Buildings	18,00,000	—
Wages and Salaries	1,80,000	—
Miscellaneous Receipts	—	1,200
Bills Payable	—	52,000
Stationery	20,000	—
Total	62,43,200	62,43,200

Additional Information

(a) Written-off ₹ 20,000 as bad debts and provision for doubtful debts is to be maintained at 5% on debtors.

(b) Loan from X was taken on 1st August, 2018. No interest has been paid so far.

(c) Included in general expenses is insurance premium ₹ 12,000, paid for one year ending 30th June, 2020.

(d) $\frac{1}{3}$ of wages and salaries is to be charged to trading account and the balance to profit and loss account.

(e) Entire stationery was used by the proprietor for his personal purpose.

(f) Closing stock was valued at ₹ 5,00,000. **(6)**

(i) Which of the following amount of loan will be shown in balance sheet?
(a) ₹ 1,12,000 (b) ₹ 88,000 (c) ₹ 1,00,000 (d) ₹ 1,24,000

(ii) Calculate the amount of wages and salaries to be debited to profit and loss account?
(a) ₹ 60,000 (b) ₹ 1,80,000 (c) ₹ 1,20,000 (d) ₹ 3,00,000

(iii) Which of the following will be the correct treatment for entire stationery used by proprietor for his personal purpose?
(a) Only shown in balance sheet as drawings
(b) Shown as expense in profit and loss account and drawings in balance sheet
(c) Shown as expense in trading account and drawings in balance sheet
(d) None of the above

(iv) Which of the following amount of prepaid insurance premium will be shown in balance sheet?
(a) ₹ 6,000 (b) ₹ 5,000 (c) ₹ 4,000 (d) ₹ 3,000

(v) Which of the following amount of debtors will be shown in the balance sheet?
(a) ₹ 82,000 (b) ₹ 76,000 (c) ₹ 80,000 (d) ₹ 73,910

(vi) Which of the following amount of general expense is shown in profit and loss account?
(a) ₹ 97,000 (b) ₹ 94,000 (c) ₹ 1,03,000 (d) ₹ 1,09,000

Answers

1. (d) **2.** (c) *Or* (c) **3.** (c) **4.** (a) *Or* (d) **5.** (a) **6.** (b) *Or* (c)
7. (b) **8.** (a) *Or* (a) **9.** (a) *Or* (b) **10.** (d) **11.** (d) **12.** (c)
13. (b) **14.** (c) **15.** (b) **17.** Overdraft as per cash book = ₹ 8,300

18. Assets = Liabilities + Capital
2,02,000 = 1,500 + 2,00,500

19. Total of trial balance = ₹ 1,71,600

20. Cash balance = ₹ 52,800 *Or* Total of suspense account = ₹ 8,175

22. Input CGST, SGST = ₹ 9,600; Output CGST, SGST = ₹ 6,000; Cash = ₹ 29,800; Discount allowed = ₹ 200

23. Balance of bus account = ₹ 10,44,013; Profit on accidental bus = ₹ 31,688; Depreciation on accidental bus = ₹ 54,188

Or

Balance of machinery account = ₹ 39,330 (Mach. I = ₹ 14,985; Mach. II = ₹ 15,795; Mach. III = ₹ 8,550)
Loss on sale of machine (Mach. I) (1/3) = ₹ 5,325

24. Total of purchases book = ₹ 1,36,200; Total of sales book = ₹ 1,08,000; Total of purchases return book = ₹ 7,000 ; Total of sales return book = ₹ 6,800

25. (a) **26.** (c) *Or* (b) **27.** (b) **28.** (c) *Or* (b) **29.** (c)

30. Operating profit = ₹ 10,94,200 *Or* Gross profit = ₹ 9,20,000; Operating profit = ₹ 7,00,000; Net profit = ₹ 6,60,000

33. Profit = ₹ 4,050

34. (i) (a) (ii) (c) (iii) (a) (iv) (d) (v) (b) (vi) (c)

SAMPLE QUESTION PAPER 3

A Highly Simulated Sample Question Paper for CBSE Class XI Examination

ACCOUNTANCY

Time : 3 Hours **Max. Marks : 80**

General Instructions

1. This question paper contains 34 questions divided in two parts A and B.
2. Alll questions in both the parts are compulsory.
3. All parts of questions should be attempted at one place.
4. Marks for questions are indicated against each questions.
5. There is no overall choice. However, an integral choice has been provided in **7** questions of **one** mark, **2** questions of **three** marks, **1** question of **four** marks and **2** questions of **six** marks.

Part-A

1. If total assets of the business are ₹ 4,50,000 and outside liabilities are ₹ 2,00,000, calculate owner's equity. (1)
(a) ₹ 6,50,000 (b) ₹ 2,50,000 (c) ₹ 4,50,000 (d) ₹ 2,00,000

2. Which of the following are two-sided errors? (1)
(a) Machinery purchased recorded in purchase book (b) Old furniture sold recorded as sale of goods
(c) Both (a) and (b) (d) None of these

Or Given-Imprest amount =₹ 10,000. What will be the amount of reimbursement, if following expenses were incurred by the petty cashier during the month?
Wages =₹ 1,900, Tiffin =₹ 1,200, Small repairs =₹ 900, General expenses =₹ 450.
(a) ₹ 1,900 (b) ₹ 2,100 (c) ₹ 4,000 (d) ₹ 4,450

3. Purchase of office furniture of ₹ 10,000 has been debited to general expense account. Which type of error is it? (1)
(a) Error of omission (b) Error of commission
(c) Error of principle (d) Compensating error

Or If bank balance as per cash book is ₹ 50,000, cheques issued but not presented for payment of ₹ 6,000 and bank charges of ₹ 400 were not entered in the cash book, then balance as per passbook will be
(a) ₹ 50,000 (b) ₹ 56,000 (c) ₹ 55,600 (d) ₹ 56,400

4. Debtors are included under (1)
(a) bills receivable (b) fixed assets (c) trade receivables (d) trading account

5. Sales return is also called (1)
(a) return outward (b) return inward (c) bills payable (d) goods return

6. How many categories are there in GST for accounting purpose? (1)
(a) 5 (b) 6 (c) 7 (d) 4

Or According to .... principle, there should be reporting of all the significant information relating to the economic affairs of the business.
(a) full disclosure (b) accounting period (c) materiality (d) prudence

7. Which of the following is/are business transaction(s)? (1)

(i) Goods worth ₹ 10,000 purchased on credit.
(ii) Purchasing air conditioner ₹ 15,000 for cash for personal use.
(iii) Owner not keeping good health.
(iv) Owner purchased a car of ₹ 5,00,000 for his son.

Codes

(a) Only (i) (b) (ii) and (iii) (c) (iii) and (iv) (d) Only (iv)

Or What will be the journal entry for adjustment of advanced commission if commission of ₹ 2,500 is received, half of which is in advance?

(a) Commission A/c	Dr	2,500	
To Commission Received in Advance A/c			2,500
(b) Commission A/c	Dr	1,250	
To Commission Received in Advance A/c			1,250
(c) Cash A/c	Dr	2,500	
To Commission A/c			2,500

(d) None of the above

8. Date of purchase 1st January, 2021, purchase price ₹ 1,00,000. On 30th September, 2022, this machine was sold for ₹ 50,000. Depreciation is provided on straight line method basis. The loss on sale will be (1)

(a) ₹ 10,000 (b) ₹ 15,000 (c) ₹ 0 (d) ₹ 20,000

9. The amount due from customers which could not be recovered and requires to be written-off is booked into (1)

(a) bad debt recovered account
(b) cash withdrawal
(c) goods withdrawn
(d) bad debts account

10. Goods costing ₹ 50,000 (selling price ₹ 60,000) were destroyed by fire. What will be the journal entry? (1)

(a) Loss by Fire A/c	Dr	50,000	
To Purchases A/c			50,000
(b) Purchases A/c	Dr	50,000	
To Loss by Fire A/c			50,000
(c) Cash A/c	Dr	50,000	
To Loss by Fire A/c			50,000
(d) Loss by Fire A/c	Dr	50,000	
To Cash A/c			50,000

Or While preparing BRS, a cheque of ₹ 1,000 received from a debtor recorded in cash book but omitted to be banked. When balance as per cash book is the starting point, it will be ....

(a) added
(b) subtracted
(c) no treatment required
(d) can't say

11. A firm earns a revenue of ₹ 20,000 and the expenses to earn this revenue are ₹ 12,000. Calculate its income. (1)

(a) ₹ 20,000
(b) ₹ 12,000
(c) ₹ 8,000
(d) Zero

12. Deepti wants to buy a building for her business on 1st May, 2020. Which of the following is relevant data her decision? (1)

(a) Similar business acquired the required building in 2020 for ₹ 10,00,000
(b) Building cost details of 2015
(c) Building cost details of 2018
(d) Similar building cost in August, 2019 for ₹ 25,00,000

13. As per principle of conservatism, which of the following is incorrect? **(1)**

(a) Provision for doubtful debts is created in anticipation of actual bad debts
(b) Closing stock is always valued at the realisable value
(c) Joint life insurance policy is shown at the surrender value
(d) None of the above

14. Assertion (A) If goods worth ₹ 4,000 are sold for ₹ 3,500 at credit, then assets will decrease, liabilities will be unchanged and capital will decrease.

Reason (R) In case, goods are sold on credit, goods (assets) are decreased and debtors (assets) are increased. Also if goods are sold at a loss, the capital is reduced. **(1)**

Alternatives

(a) Both Assertion (A) and Reason (R) are true and Reason (R) is the correct explanation of Assertion (A)
(b) Both Assertion (A) and Reason (R) are true, but Reason (R) is not the correct explanation of Assertion (A)
(c) Assertion (A) is true, but Reason (R) is false
(d) Assertion (A) is false, but Reason (R) is true

15. Goods bought for cash at list price of ₹ 50,000 at 20% trade discount and 5% cash discount. Following entry will be passed

Purchases A/c Dr X
    To Cash A/c Y
    To Discount Received A/c Z

Here X, Y, Z are **(1)**

(a) ₹ 12,000, ₹ 10,000, ₹ 2,000
(b) ₹ 50,000, ₹ 32,500, ₹ 12,500
(c) ₹ 40,000, ₹ 38,000, ₹ 2,000
(d) ₹ 5,000, ₹ 3,250, ₹ 1,250

16. Briefly define the following terms **(3)**

(i) Liabilities (ii) Purchases (iii) Sales

Or Write any three points of difference between cash basis of accounting and accrual basis of accounting.

17. Complete the missing journal entries. **(3)**

JOURNAL

Date	Particulars		LF	Amt (Dr)	Amt (Cr)
2022					
Jul 1	Richa	Dr		1,00,000	
	To Cash A/c				...
	To Discount Received A/c				...
	(Being ₹ 95,000 paid to Richa in full settlement of her account of ₹ 1,00,000)				
Jul 5	....	Dr		2,00,000	
	....				80,000
	....				1,20,000
	(Being goods purchased for cash ₹ 80,000 and on credit from Hritik Roshan for ₹ 1,20,000)				
Jul 18	Furniture A/c	Dr		1,00,000	
	To				1,00,000
	(Being furniture worth ₹ 1,00,000 bought and paid by cheque)				

18. Enter the following transactions in a two column cash book. **(3)**

Date	Particulars	Amt (₹)
2019		
Jul 1	Cash in Hand	3,50,000
Jul 3	Cash Deposited into Bank	40,000
Jul 5	Paid to Mahima	30,000

Date	Particulars	Amt (₹)
Jul 8	Goods Purchased	40,000
Jul 10	Received from Sohan Lal	98,000
Jul 16	Goods Sold	40,000
Jul 21	Paid to Sawant	29,500
Jul 28	Paid Wages for the Month	50,000
	Paid in Full Settlement of ₹ 40,000 to Sushil	39,000
Jul 29	Cash Withdrawn from Bank for Office Use	4,000
Jul 30	Salary Paid through Cheque	15,000

19. Rectify the following errors and use suspense account where necessary. (4)

(i) ₹ 2,500 paid for office furniture was debited to office expenses account.

(ii) A cash sale of ₹ 7,500 to Saksham was correctly entered in the cash book but was posted to the credit of Saksham's account.

(iii) Goods amounting to ₹ 1,800, returned by Aryan, were entered in the sales book and posted therefrom to the credit of Aryan's account.

(iv) Bills receivable received from Sangeet for ₹ 5,000 was posted to the credit of bills payable account and credited to Sangeet's account.

Or From the following information, draw up a trial balance in the books of Ramesh Kumar as on 31st March, 2022.

Capital ₹ 2,80,000; purchases ₹ 72,000; discount allowed ₹ 2,400; carriage inwards ₹ 17,400; carriage outwards ₹ 4,600; sales ₹ 1,20,000; return inward ₹ 600; return outward ₹ 1,400; rent and taxes ₹ 2,400; plant and machinery ₹ 1,61,400; stock on 1st April, 2021 ₹ 31,000; sundry debtors ₹ 40,400; sundry creditors ₹ 24,000; investments ₹ 7,200; commission received ₹ 3,600; cash in hand ₹ 200; cash at bank ₹ 20,200; motor cycle ₹ 69,200 and stock on 31st March, 2022 (not adjusted) ₹ 41,000.

20. Briefly explain the historical cost concept. (4)

21. Khandelwal & Sons is a manufacturing firm. Following information about it is available

Assets Cash in hand ₹ 1,00,000; Cash at bank ₹ 1,10,000; Debtors (Karun ₹ 90,000; Geeta ₹ 50,000); Stock ₹ 3,20,000 and Machinery ₹ 4,00,000.

Liabilities Creditors: Avinash & Co. ₹ 70,000.

The following transactions took place during the month of January, 2021. (6)

Jan 2	Deposited into bank ₹ 30,000.
Jan 4	Purchased from Raghav goods of the list price of ₹ 70,000 at 10% trade discount.
Jan 5	Returned to Raghav goods worth ₹ 8,000.
Jan 7	Issued a cheque to Raghav in full settlement of their account after deducting cash discount @ 5%
Jan 10	Sold to Dishant goods worth ₹ 80,000.
Jan 12	Received cash ₹ 60,000 and cheque ₹ 8,000 from Dishant. The cheque was sent to bank on the same day. Discount allowed ₹ 1,000.
Jan 14	Purchased machinery from Ronak & Co. on credit for ₹ 50,000.
Jan 16	Khandelwal withdrew goods for his personal use ₹ 20,000.
Jan 18	Sold to Anuj goods valued ₹ 32,000.
Jan 19	Issued cheque to Ronak & Co. ₹ 50,000.
Jan 20	Returned by Anuj goods worth ₹ 4,000.
Jan 21	Purchased goods from Gaurav for ₹ 80,000. Trade discount 10%.
Jan 22	Accepted a bill drawn by Gaurav for ₹ 72,000 at 1 month.
Jan 27	Received from Anuj ₹ 20,000. Discount allowed ₹ 100.
Jan 27	Goods purchased for cash ₹ 60,000.
Jan 28	Withdrew from bank ₹ 40,000.
Jan 29	Paid salaries by cheque ₹ 10,000.
Jan 30	Paid rent ₹ 5,600.
Jan 31	Received commission in cash ₹ 3,200.

(i) Purchase of goods from Raghav on 4th January will be recorded on that date in
(a) cash book (b) purchase book
(c) journal proper (d) None of these

(ii) What amount is finally paid to Raghav on 7th January?
(a) ₹ 62,000 (b) ₹ 63,000
(c) ₹ 55,000 (d) ₹ 52,250

(iii) What will be the balance in sales book as on 31st January?
(a) ₹ 80,000 (b) ₹ 32,000
(c) ₹ 1,12,000 (d) ₹ 1,08,000

(iv) What will be the balance in sales return book and purchase return book respectively on 31st January?
(a) ₹ 4,000; ₹ 8,000 (b) ₹ 8,000; ₹ 4,000
(c) ₹ 8,000; ₹ 16,000 (d) None of these

(v) Which of the following entry represents contra entry?
(a) Purchases from Raghav on 4th January (b) Goods sold to Anuj on 18th January
(c) Amount withdrawn from bank on 28th January (d) None of these

(vi) Credit balance of bank account in cash book shows
(a) cash withdrawn from bank (b) cash deposited in bank
(c) overdraft (d) None of these

22. From the following particulars, prepare a bank reconciliation statement as on 31st March, 2023. (6)

(i) Bank balance as per cash book is ₹ 1,00,000.
(ii) A cheque for ₹ 10,000 deposited but not recorded in the cash book. Bank has collected and credited this cheque.
(iii) A bank deposit of ₹ 2,000 was recorded in the cash book as if there is no bank column therein.
(iv) A cheque issued for ₹ 2,500 was recorded as ₹ 2,050 in the cash column. Bank has made the payment of this cheque.
(v) The debit balance of ₹ 15,000 as on the previous day was brought forward as a credit balance.
(vi) The payment side of the cash book (bank column) was undercast by ₹ 1,000.
(vii) A cash discount allowed of ₹ 1,120 was recorded as ₹ 1,210 in the bank column.
(viii) A cheque of ₹ 5,000 received from a debtor was recorded in the cash book but not deposited in the bank for collection.
(ix) One outgoing cheque of ₹ 3,000 was recorded twice in the cash book.

23. A firm purchased on 1st January, 2020 a second hand plant for ₹ 72,000 and spent ₹ 8,000 on its installation.

On 1st July in the same year, another plant costing ₹ 40,000 was purchased. On 1st July, 2022 plant brought on 1st January, 2020 was sold for ₹ 24,000 and a new plant purchased for ₹ 1,28,000 on the same date. Depreciation is provided annually on 31st December @ 10% p.a. on the written down value method. Show the plant account from 2020 to 2022. (6)

Or Following balances appear in the books of Mukesh Sharma, as on 1st April, 2022

Machinery Account	₹ 80,000
Provision for Depreciation Account	₹ 31,000

On 1st July, 2022, a machinery which was purchased on 1st April, 2019 for ₹ 12,000 was sold for ₹ 5,000 plus CGST and SGST @ 6% each and on the same date another machinery was purchased for ₹ 3,200 plus CGST and SGST @ 6% each. The firm charges depreciation @ 15% p.a. by fixed installment method and followed financial year.

Prepare machinery account and provision for depreciation account for the year 2022-23. Also, pass journal entry for the sale of machinery.

24. Analyse the effect of each transaction and prove that the accounting equation (A = L + C) always remains balanced. (6)

(i) Introduced ₹ 4,00,000 as cash and ₹ 25,000 by stock.
(ii) Purchased plant for ₹ 1,50,000 by paying ₹ 7,500 in cash and balance at a later date.
(iii) Deposited ₹ 3,00,000 into the bank.
(iv) Purchased office furniture for ₹ 50,000 and made payment by cheque.
(v) Purchased goods worth ₹ 40,000 for cash and for ₹ 17,500 on credit.
(vi) Goods amounting to ₹ 22,500 was sold for ₹ 30,000 on cash basis.
(vii) Goods costing to ₹ 40,000 was sold for ₹ 62,500 on credit basis.
(viii) Cheque issued to the supplier of goods worth ₹ 17,500.